MW00354751

Decolonization, Self-Determination, and the Rise of Global Human Rights Politics

This volume presents the first global history of human rights politics in the age of decolonization. The conflict between independence movements and colonial powers shaped the global human rights order that emerged after World War II. It was also critical to the genesis of contemporary human rights organizations and humanitarian movements. Anti-colonial forces mobilized human rights and other rights language in their campaigns for self-determination. In response, European empires harnessed the new international politics of human rights for their own ends, claiming that their rule, with its promise of "development," was the authentic vehicle for realizing them. Ranging from the postwar partitions and the wars of independence to indigenous rights activism and postcolonial memory, this volume offers new insights into the history and legacies of human rights, self-determination, and empire to the present day.

A. DIRK MOSES is Frank Porter Graham Distinguished Professor in Global Human Rights History at the University of North Carolina at Chapel Hill. He is the author of *The Problems of Genocide* (2021).

MARCO DURANTI is Senior Lecturer in Modern European and International History at the University of Sydney. He is the author of *The Conservative Human Rights Revolution* (2017).

ROLAND BURKE is Senior Lecturer in World History at La Trobe University, Victoria. He is the author of *Decolonization and the Evolution of International Human Rights* (2010).

Human Rights in History

Edited by

Stefan-Ludwig Hoffmann, University of California, Berkeley

Samuel Moyn, Yale University, Connecticut

This series showcases new scholarship exploring the backgrounds of human rights today. With an open-ended chronology and international perspective, the series seeks works attentive to the surprises and contingencies in the historical origins and legacies of human rights ideals and interventions. Books in the series will focus not only on the intellectual antecedents and foundations of human rights, but also on the incorporation of the concept by movements, nation-states, international governance, and transnational law.

A full list of titles in the series can be found at:
www.cambridge.org/human-rights-history

Decolonization, Self-Determination, and the Rise of Global Human Rights Politics

Edited by

A. Dirk Moses
University of North Carolina

Marco Duranti
University of Sydney

Roland Burke
La Trobe University, Victoria

To Lisa,
with scholarly greetings
Dirk   July 19, 2020

CAMBRIDGE
UNIVERSITY PRESS

CAMBRIDGE
UNIVERSITY PRESS

University Printing House, Cambridge CB2 8BS, United Kingdom

One Liberty Plaza, 20th Floor, New York, NY 10006, USA

477 Williamstown Road, Port Melbourne, VIC 3207, Australia

314–321, 3rd Floor, Plot 3, Splendor Forum, Jasola District Centre, New Delhi – 110025, India

79 Anson Road, #06–04/06, Singapore 079906

Cambridge University Press is part of the University of Cambridge.

It furthers the University's mission by disseminating knowledge in the pursuit of education, learning, and research at the highest international levels of excellence.

www.cambridge.org
Information on this title: www.cambridge.org/9781108479356
DOI: 10.1017/9781108783170

First published 2020

A catalogue record for this publication is available from the British Library.

Library of Congress Cataloging-in-Publication Data
Names: Moses, A. Dirk, editor. | Duranti, Marco, editor. | Burke, Roland, author.
Title: Decolonization, self-determination, and the rise of global human rights / edited by A. Dirk Moses, Marco Duranti, Roland Burke.
Description: Cambridge ; New York, NY : Cambridge University Press, 2020. | Series: Human rights in history | Includes bibliographical references and index.
Identifiers: LCCN 2019042605 (print) | LCCN 2019042606 (ebook) | ISBN 9781108479356 (hardback) | ISBN 9781108749701 (paperback) | ISBN 9781108783170 (epub)
Subjects: LCSH: Human rights–History–20th century. | Decolonization–History–20th century. | Self-determination, National–History–20th century.
Classification: LCC JC571 .D3515 2020 (print) | LCC JC571 (ebook) | DDC 323.09/045–dc23
LC record available at https://lccn.loc.gov/2019042605
LC ebook record available at https://lccn.loc.gov/2019042606

ISBN 978-1-108-47935-6 Hardback

Contents

Notes on Contributors

ROLAND BURKE is author of *Decolonization and the Evolution of International Human Rights* (2010), and Senior Lecturer in World History at La Trobe University. His research examines the history of human rights, and in particular, the shifts in meaning that attached to the Universal Declaration of Human Rights (*Journal of Global History, International History Review, History & Memory*), the place of social rights (*Humanity*), and evolving relationship between decolonization and human rights (*Journal of World History* and *Human Rights Quarterly*).

ELEANOR DAVEY writes about the histories of aid, activism, and anti-colonialism. She is the author of *Idealism beyond Borders: The French Revolutionary Left and the Rise of Humanitarianism, 1954–1988* (2015), which was jointly awarded the International Studies Association Ethics Section Book Prize (2017).

MARCO DURANTI is Senior Lecturer in Modern European and International History at the University of Sydney. His research investigates the genesis of international law and organizations, above all in relation to the history of human rights, European integration, and right-wing movements. He has been a visiting fellow at the European University Institute, Sciences Po Paris, the University of Konstanz, and most recently the Lauterpacht Centre for International Law and Wolfson College at the University of Cambridge. He is author of *The Conservative Human Rights Revolution: European Identity, Transnational Politics, and the Origins of the European Convention* (2017).

CINDY EWING is the Assistant Professor of Contemporary International History at the University of Toronto. She is currently working on her first monograph, which examines how postcolonial internationalism in South and Southeast Asia shaped the making of international human rights.

MARY ANN HEISS is an associate professor of history at Kent State University, where she teaches courses in the history of US foreign relations, the Cold War, and the twentieth-century world. Her current research addresses the UN's role in decolonization; among her published work on that subject is *Fulfilling the Sacred Trust: The UN Campaign for International Accountability* for Dependent Territories in the Era of Decolonization (forthcoming).

MICHAEL HUMPHREY is Professor Emeritus at the Department of Sociology and Social Policy at the University of Sydney. He works in comparative sociology and has published widely on Islam in the West; the Lebanese diaspora; social relations of globalization; war, political violence, and terrorism; human rights, reconciliation, and transitional justice; violence, displacement, and urban securitization; neoliberal urbanization, corruption, and the corporate state. His main books in the field are *The Politics of Atrocity and Reconciliation: From Terror to Trauma* (2002) and, with Estela Valverde, *Amnesty and Transitional Justice: the Judicialisation of Politics* (2020).

BONNY IBHAWOH is the Messecar Professor in History and Global Human Rights at McMaster University, Ontario. He is also the Director of the Centre for Peace Studies at McMaster University. He has taught in universities in Africa, Europe, and North America. Previously, he was a Human Rights Fellow at the Carnegie Council for Ethics and International Affairs, New York, and Research Fellow at the Danish Institute for Human Rights, Copenhagen. He has held visiting professorships at the Bernard and Audre Rapoport Center for Human Rights and Justice and the University of Texas at Austin. He has served as a research consultant for several human rights organizations including the Canadian Museum of Human Rights. Dr. Ibhawoh's publications include *Imperial Justice* (2013), *Imperialism and Human Rights* (2007), *and Human Rights in Africa.* (2018).

STEVEN L. B. JENSEN is senior researcher at the Danish Institute for Human Rights. He holds a PhD in history from the University of Copenhagen. He is the author of *The Making of International Human Rights: The 1960s, Decolonization and the Reconstruction of Global Values* (2016), which won in 2017 the prizes for Best Book on Human Rights and Best Book on International Organization from the International Studies Association. Before joining the Danish Institute, he held positions with the Danish Ministry of Foreign Affairs and with the United Nations in Geneva. Among his most recent publications is a coedited volume *Histories of Global Inequality: New Perspectives* (2019). He is currently working on a project on the history of social and economic rights.

MIGUEL BANDEIRA JERÓNIMO is Senior Research Fellow at the Centre for Social Studies at the University of Coimbra, Portugal. Among other publications, he authored The *"Civilizing Mission" of Portuguese Colonialism (c.1870–1930)* (2015), and coedited *Internationalism, Imperialism and the Formation of the Contemporary World* (2017). He coordinates the international research project "The Worlds of (Under) Development: Processes and Legacies of the Portuguese Colonial Empire in a Comparative Perspective (1945–1975)."

JENNIFER JOHNSON is Associate Professor of History at Brown University. Her first book, *The Battle for Algeria: Sovereignty, Health Care and Humanitarianism* (2016) analyzed the Algerian War and demonstrated the centrality of health and humanitarianism to the nationalists' efforts. She is currently working on a second book project about family planning, state building, and international organizations in postcolonial North Africa.

MIRANDA JOHNSON is a Senior Lecturer in the Department of History and Art History at the University of Otago. A historian of the modern Pacific world, focusing on indigenous, cross-cultural, and colonial histories, she is the author of the prize-winning book *The Land Is Our History: Indigeneity, Law, and the Settler State* (2016) and coeditor with Warwick Anderson and Barbara Brookes of *Pacific Futures: Past and Present* (2018).

BARBARA KEYS is Professor of US and International History at the University of Durham, and author of *Reclaiming American Virtue: The Human Rights Revolution of the 1970s* (2014). She is currently finishing a manuscript on anti-torture campaigns since 1945.

RAPHAËLLE KHAN is Research Fellow at the Institute for Strategic Research (IRSEM, Paris) and teaches at Sciences Po Paris. She is also affiliated to the Center for the Advanced Study of India at the University of Pennsylvania. She received a PhD in history and international relations from King's College London. Among her recent publications, Raphaëlle coedited a volume titled *Theorizing Indian Foreign Policy* (2017). She is currently working on a book manuscript on India's role in the transformation of the international order and global and imperial conceptions of sovereignty between World War I and the 1960s.

JOSÉ PEDRO MONTEIRO is currently a junior researcher at the Centre for Social Studies, University of Coimbra, Portugal, where he is working on a research project on the history of citizenship politics in Portuguese late colonialism. He obtained his PhD from the Institute of Social Sciences (2017) on the international history of Portuguese "native" labor politics. Among other publications, he recently coedited *Internationalism, Imperialism and the Formation of the Contemporary World* (2017), and published the book *Portugal e a Questão do Trabalho Forçado: um império sob escrutínio (1944–1962)* (2018).

A. DIRK MOSES is Frank Porter Graham Distinguished Professor in Global Human Rights History at the University of North Carolina at Chapel Hill. He is the author and editor of publications on intellectual history, genocide, and memory, most recently, *The Problems of Genocide* (2021), and, as coeditor, of *The Holocaust in Greece* (2018), and *Postcolonial Conflict and the Question of Genocide: The Nigeria–Biafra War, 1967–1970* (2018), and *Genocide: Key Themes* (2021).

JESSICA WHYTE is Scientia Fellow (Philosophy and Law) and Associate Professor of Philosophy at the University of New South Wales. Her work integrates political philosophy, intellectual history, and political economy to analyze contemporary forms of sovereignty, human rights, humanitarianism, and militarism. She is author of *Catastrophe and Redemption: The Political Thought of Giorgio Agamben* (2013) and *The Morals of the Market: Human Rights and the Rise of Neoliberalism* (2019). She is currently working on a project on the moral economy of warfare.

JAY WINTER is Charles J. Stille Professor of History emeritus at Yale University. He is an authority on World War I, and the author, with Antoine Prost, of *René Cassin and the Rights of Man: From the Great War to the Universal Declaration* (2013).

Acknowledgments

The editors would like to acknowledge Nikolas Kompridis, Samuel Moyn, and Glenda Sluga for the critical role they played in the launching of this project and its conceptualization. We extend our thanks to Steven L. B. Jensen, Meredith Terretta, Eric D. Weitz, and Jess Whyte for critical comments on drafts of the introduction to this volume, as well as to other colleagues for suggesting references and revisions. We are also appreciative of the anonymous reviewers' constructive suggestions for improvements to the original typescript.

The transnational research networks and intellectual collaborations that gave rise to the present volume would not have been possible without funding provided by the University of Sydney, Western Sydney University, and New York University. These included grants from the University of Sydney's China Studies Centre, International Program Development Fund, 'International Society' Faculty of Arts Research Cluster, the School of Philosophical and Historical Inquiry, and the Sydney Intellectual History Network. We are grateful for their generosity and support. Aspects of the final preparation of the manuscript were supported by funding from the Australian Research Council (DP170100291).

Introduction
Human Rights, Empire, and After

Roland Burke, Marco Duranti, and A. Dirk Moses

In the space of a decade, the history of human rights has been transformed by a wave of scholarship revisiting its origins, evolution, and conceptual bounds. In the place of optimistic and well-settled narratives of human rights, characterized by a deep chronology, inclusive definition, and evolutionary progress, a new human rights history has posited the collapse of empire and the place of anti-colonial nationalism as one of the premier issues.[1] The contention has centered on the relationship between international and national ideas of rights. On the one hand, a global human rights discourse proclaimed individual rights above and beyond the state. On the other, an older rights language from the French Revolution bestowed, or promised, rights inhering primarily in national citizenship.[2]

---

[1] Samuel Moyn has published the most influential of these "revisionist" accounts. See Moyn, *The Last Utopia: Human Rights in History* (Cambridge MA: Belknap/Harvard University Press, 2010). The principal revisionist target is Paul Gordon Lauren's survey work, *The Evolution of International Human Rights: Visions Seen* (Philadelphia: University Pennsylvania Press, 1998), which develops its narrative in this gradual and incremental mode, where anti-colonialism is positioned primarily as an era for the extension of rights, and the amplification of norms, as opposed to a radical discontinuity.

[2] For an illustrative set of these debates, which are now voluminous and intricate, see Eric D. Weitz, "Samuel Moyn and the New History of Human Rights," *European Journal of Political Theory* 12, no. 1 (2013): 89–91; Seyla Benhabib; "Moving Beyond False Binarisms: On Samuel Moyn's *The Last Utopia*," *Qui Parle* 22, no. 1 (2013): 81–93; Philip Alston, "Does the Past Matter? On the Origins of Human Rights," *Harvard Law Review* 126, no. 7 (2013): 2043–81; Jenny Martinez, "Human Rights and History," *Harvard Law Review Forum* 126 (2013): 221–40; Christopher McCrudden, "Human Rights Histories," *Oxford Journal of Legal Studies* 35, no. 1 (2015): 179–212; Sarita Cargas, "Questioning Samuel Moyn's Revisionist History of Human Rights," *Human Rights Quarterly* 38, no. 2 (2016): 411–25; Stefan-Ludwig Hoffmann, "Human Rights and History," *Past & Present*, no. 232 (2016): 279–310; Samuel Moyn, "The End of Human Rights History," *Past & Present*, no. 233 (2016): 307–22; Lynn Hunt, "The Long and the Short of the History of Human Rights," *Past & Present*, no. 233 (2016): 323–31. Addressing the relationship between these phenomena across a slightly different axis of the historiography, see the appraisal from Robert Brier, "Beyond the Quest for a 'Breakthrough': Reflections on the Recent Historiography on Human Rights," *European History Yearbook* (2015): 155–74; Roland Burke, "'How Time Flies': Celebrating the Universal Declaration of Human Rights in the 1960s," *International History Review* 38, no. 2 (2016): 394–420.

New histories of human rights have argued that the newly independent nation-states of the 1950s and 1960s momentarily combined the aspirations of citizenship and the "rights of man" with the more maximal universalism exemplified by the 1948 Universal Declaration of Human Rights (UDHR). Postcolonial constitutions, generally in the form of uneasily agreed compromises between nationalist and imperial elites, often invoked the UDHR or other universal human rights concepts directly, conferring on their citizenries the political, economic, and social freedoms enumerated therein.[3] The provenance of these rights was typically described by nationalist elites as both the promised fruit of sovereignty and the birthright of universal humanity.[4] These interlaced rights traditions exposed tensions within postwar human rights languages and practices, which aspired to transcendent, suprastate standards while relying on the state to protect and deliver rights.[5] By the 1970s, however, the revolutionary vehicle of citizenship rights via national emancipation receded, seemingly discredited by the failures of new states to live up to their promises and their faltering parallel project for global economic redistribution.[6] In their place, an influential new human rights vision, advanced mostly by politicians in the United States and a cresting wave of nongovernmental organizations (NGOs), emerged as an internationally situated discourse. This version of human rights, born in pessimism, was

[3] On the evolution of these constitutional provisions in British colonial settings, see Charles Parkinson, *Bills of Rights and Decolonization* (Oxford: Oxford University Press, 2007), and the initial study from Stanley de Smith, *The New Commonwealth and Its Constitutions* (London: Stevens & Sons, 1964); on the wider question of international human rights cited within postcolonial constitutions, see Hurst Hannum, "The Status of the Universal Declaration of Human Rights in National and International Law," *Georgia Journal of International and International Comparative Law* 25, no. 1 (1996): 355–77.

[4] On the genealogy and boundaries of the category of humanity, see Paul Betts, "Universalism and Its Discontents: Humanity as a Twentieth-Century Concept," in *Humanity: A History of European Concepts in Practice from the Sixteenth Century to the Present*, ed. Fabian Klose and Mirjam Thulin (Göttingen: Vandenhoeck & Ruprecht, 2016), 51–70; Ilana Feldman and Miriam Ticktin, "Introduction: Government and Humanity," in *In the Name of Humanity: The Government of Threat and Care*, ed. Feldman and Ticktin (Durham, NC: Duke University Press, 2010), 1–26; Thomas Laqueur, "Mourning, Pity, and the Work of Narrative in the Making of 'Humanity,'" in *Humanitarianism and Suffering: The Mobilization of Empathy*, ed. Richard Ashby Wilson and Richard D. Brown (Cambridge: Cambridge University Press, 2009), 31–57. On the lasting ambiguities of the categories of citizen and human, see Frederick Cooper, *Citizenship, Inequality, and Difference: Historical Perspectives* (Princeton, NJ: Princeton University Press, 2018), 1–14.

[5] Roland Burke, "Human Rights Internationalism," in *Internationalisms: A Twentieth-Century History*, ed. Patricia Clavin, Sunil Amrith, and Glenda Sluga (Cambridge: Cambridge University Press, 2017), 287–314.

[6] The atrophy of social and economic equality as a meaningful feature within human rights, and its implications, serves as prime subject for Samuel Moyn, *Not Enough: Human Rights in an Unequal World* (Cambridge, MA: Harvard University Press, 2018).

less inclined to regard the state as a repository for hopes. While at least as universalistic as the early postwar in its terrain of concern, and more energetic in proselytizing global norms, the balance of these norms was shifted and repartitioned. Human rights began to operate, in vernacular terms, without the expansive vision of social and economic rights that it had held when wielded by nationalists and postwar social democrats.[7]

As the revisionist historiography has observed, human rights "broke through" in the 1970s, particularly in the West. The precondition of this transformation for North American and European publics was a degree of narrowing of human rights: the excision of utopian optimism and disruptive, transformative promise. The admirable NGO activism of, say, Amnesty International, was predicated on a conception of *international* human rights as civil and political rights claims against authoritarian and totalitarian states. For the many NGOs, this was mostly an artifact of pragmatic and tactical choices and dynamics: the feasibility of mass mobilization in those places where there was some prospect of success, and where there existed sufficient knowledge to document abuses with precision.[8] For others, particularly in the emerging neoconservative movement, the campaign to capture and define the term was more openly ideological, notably in US NGO Freedom House, and in a cohort of US Congressional leaders that exalted the right to emigrate (from the Soviet Union) as the most foundational freedom of all.[9]

Likewise, anti-colonialism lost its place in the Western minimalist redefinition of human rights that occurred across the 1970s, when so many of its priorities were written out of the sparing agenda of Amnesty International, though anti-communists continued to launch broadsides against the Soviet Union for violations of the right to self-determination. But human rights triumphed over anti-imperialism less by the exhaustion of the latter than by the former's appeal to a new cohort of Western middle-class supporters attracted by the rhetoric of exerting righteous pressure abroad rather than effecting reform at home. NGO successes were dramatic, but they were enabled by an equally dramatic focus away from transformative and optimistic horizons.

---

[7] Moyn, *Last Utopia*, 84, 87–9, 98; cf. Roland Burke, *Decolonization and the Evolution of International Human Rights* (Philadelphia: University of Pennsylvania Press, 2010), and extended substantially by Steven Jensen, *The Making of International Human Rights: The 1960s, Decolonization, and the Reconstruction of Global Values* (Cambridge: Cambridge University Press, 2016).

[8] Roberta Cohen, "People's Republic of China: The Human Rights Exception," *Human Rights Quarterly* 9, no. 4 (1987): 447–549.

[9] Carl Bon Tempo, "From the Center-Right: Freedom House and Human Rights in the 1970s and 1980s," in *The Human Rights Revolution: An International History*, ed. Petra Goedde and William Hitchcock (New York: Oxford University Press, 2012), 223–43.

This revisionist historiography has raised two further lines of inquiry that our authors undertake in this volume. First, while the broadest arc of anti-colonialism and human rights has been traced, contested, and recontested, the question of the relationship between actor categories and postcolonial policies that, in retrospect, have been classified as human rights measures is of signal importance.[10] Postcolonial actors engaged in policies and endeavors that certainly conformed to the substance of securing human rights for their citizenries. Embryonic efforts to establish welfare state provisions were widely attempted in South Asia. Systems for government accountability and citizen remedy were devised, notably in the Tanzanian Ombudsman experiment. Land redistribution plans, and women's economic and social advancement, were variously outlined across every continent, typically sponsored from above, but often enacted with community initiative. Whether, and how, these kinds of measures constituted human rights activity is an intricate question, reflecting as much about the definitional vernacular of "human rights" as it does the national projects involved. These were major reforms, typically with some emancipatory effects, while not necessarily being emphatic in their invocation of language itself, or wholly animated by a philosophy that expressed faith in the inherent agency and equality of individuals. As the chapters in this book demonstrate, their subjects commonly invoked other rights traditions and languages – national rights, indigenous rights, treaty rights, civil and political rights, and so on – in justifying political reform.[11] Rather than assume a stable meaning of human rights and "discover" these phenomena decades later, we ask: How did various rights languages intersect and morph through social and political contests and transitions? When, and how, did human rights language find form in the substance of policy, advocacy, or political transformation?

[10] On the potential delta between grand and less grand scales as an optic for human rights history, see Meredith Terretta, "From Below and to the Left? Human Rights and Liberation Politics in Africa's Postcolonial Age," *Journal of World History*, 24, no. 2 (2013): 389–416; "'We Had Been Fooled into Thinking that the UN Watches over the Entire World': Human Rights, UN Trust Territories, and Africa's Decolonisation," *Human Rights Quarterly* 34, no. 2 (2012): 329–60; Samuel Moyn, "The Recent Historiography of Human Rights," *Annual Review of Law and Social Science* 8 (2012): 123–40; and the essays from Mark Bradley, "Writing Human Rights History," *Il Mestiere di storico* 3, no. 2 (2011): 13–30; William Hitchcock, "The Rise and Fall of Human Rights? Searching for a Narrative from the Cold War to the 9/11 Era," *Human Rights Quarterly* 37, no. 1 (2015): 80–106.

[11] Additional exploration of renovated approaches in this field of history is elaborated in Steven L. B. Jensen and Roland Burke, "From the Normative to the Transnational Methods in the Study of Human Rights History," in *Research Methods in Human Rights: A Handbook*, ed. Bård A. Andreassen, Hans-Otto Sano, and Siobhán McInerney-Lankford (Cheltenham: Edward Elgar, 2017), 117–40.

Second, recent research has been largely confined to the Atlantic world with diffusionist assumptions of non-Europeans learning human rights from their colonial administrators or the UN; this book is a contribution to globalizing the history of human rights in the age of decolonization. The pressing need, then, is for granular case studies written by specialists based on a careful examination of primary sources extending beyond the orthodox complement of Western government and NGO archives. Accordingly, the contributors to this collection draw on overlooked historical materials as well as more conventional archival sources to reconstruct the rights politics of an array of figures with divergent aims and worldviews: colonized and colonizers, activists and diplomats, policymakers in postcolonial states and the leadership of Western NGOs involved in both rights and humanitarianism. Accounting for such variegated perspectives affords a greater comprehension of the alternative rights languages available to, say, colonized peoples whose leaders looked to political independence while contending with the late colonial state. What did they mean by human rights if and when they invoked them, and how was this language adapted to local circumstances? Our authors' investigations draw out the implications for the relationship between rights and empire as it changed over the course of the closing half of the twentieth century by reconstructing how it was enacted and reshaped by a diverse collection of actors. Their subjects articulated and deployed the discourses of anti-colonialism and rights, including human rights, as they were encountered in the field, the street, and from within sites of institutional power.

The new research showcased in this volume does not bear out the thesis that the anti-colonial mobilization of self-determination and other emancipatory claims marginalized human rights.[12] It demonstrates the difficulty of identifying any singular moment of "breakthrough" as

---

[12] These arguments are most advanced most notably by Reza Afshari, Jan Eckel, and Samuel Moyn. See Afshari, "On Historiography of Human Rights Reflections on Paul Gordon Lauren's *The Evolution of International Human Rights: Visions Seen*," *Human Rights Quarterly* 29, no. 1 (2007): 1–67; Eckel, "Human Rights and Decolonization," *Humanity* 1, no. 1 (2010): 111–35; Eckel, *The Ambivalence of Good: Human Rights in International Politics since the 1940s*, trans. Rachel Ward (Oxford: Oxford University Press, 2019), ch. 5; Moyn, "Imperialism, Self-Determination, and the Rise of Human Rights," in Goedde and Hitchcock, *Human Rights Revolution*, 159–78; Moyn, *Last Utopia*, ch. 3. For counterpoints, see Stephen L. B. Jensen, "Decolonization: The Black Box of Human Rights?" *Human Rights Quarterly* 41, no. 1 (2019): 200–3; Brad Simpson, "Self-determination and Decolonization," in *The Oxford Handbook of the Ends of Empire*, ed. Martin Thomas and Andrew Thompson (Oxford: Oxford University Press, 2018), ch. 19; Meredith Terretta, "Anti-Colonial Lawyering, Postwar Human Rights, and Decolonization across Imperial Boundaries in Africa," *Canadian Journal of History* 52, no. 3 (2017): 448–52; Andrew Thompson, "Unravelling the Relationships

definitive of human rights and its ascent as the premier moralism in the postcolonial world. Rather than a sequential relationship of human rights breaking through after the waning legitimacy of revolutionary self-determination as a creed in the West, the chapters here show the persistence of diversity among and within human rights rhetorics into and after the 1970s. National liberation, notionally supplanted and replaced in the "breakthrough," often remained a central lodestar in these rights constellations.[13] From the outset across the anti- and postcolonial worlds, political demands coalesced around human rights as a language of preference because they were more capacious than competing utopianisms of classical political liberalism, doctrinaire socialism, and essentialist nationalism, and more capable of accommodating the specific configuration of myriad struggles, ambitions, and grievances. Anti-colonial campaigns could deploy them to dissent and to indict abuses, or to inspire when framing the aspirations of new societies, or mapping out major realignments in the international system. Human rights became a perennial aspect of anti-imperial and postcolonial phraseology not for its conceptual clarity, but for its versatility as a language with all-purpose emancipatory potential.

In other words, human rights were appealing as a maximal utopia across imperial and postcolonial worlds. Among "Third World" peoples, rights were often connected to local struggle, and operated in a key defined by expansiveness, optimism, and radical potential. There was no finer example than the rapid inscription of the right to self-determination as a foundational human right in the early 1950s, an early Third World project, and one that implied a much more radical vision of rights than the otherwise impressive catalogue produced a handful of years earlier by the General Assembly. Later initiatives on the "permanent sovereignty over natural resources" and a right to economic self-determination, were more revolutionary still, with sequelae that would define much of the North–South human rights fracture across the 1960s.[14] The cumulative

between Humanitarianism, Human Rights, and Decolonization: Time for a Radical Rethink?," in Thomas and Thompson, *Oxford Handbook of the Ends of Empire*, ch. 20; Eric D. Weitz, "Self-determination: How a German Enlightenment Idea Became the Slogan of National Liberation and a Human Right," *American Historical Review* 120, no. 2 (2015): 462–96.

[13] A. Dirk Moses, "Human Rights and Genocide: A Global Historical Perspective," Gerald Stourzh Lecture on the history of human rights and democracy, University of Vienna, May 21, 2014, www.univie.ac.at/gerald-stourzh-lectures/2014.pdf

[14] On earlier contestations within the field of international law over imperial claims to property rights and sovereignty over colonized territories, see Andrew Fitzmaurice, *Sovereignty, Property and Empire, 1500–2000* (Cambridge: Cambridge University Press, 2014).

effect of the book's chapters, then, question the proposition that human rights were marginal to decolonization.

From the Rights of Nations to Human Rights

More than half a century after the peak era of decolonization, the incompatibility of formal empire and human rights may seem axiomatic. Since the catastrophic failure of the Iraq and Afghanistan wars in the 2000s, the flirtation between empire and human rights, manifested in muscular interventionist idealism advocated by liberal hawks and neoconservative crusaders, has fallen into disrepute. Those liberal imperialists who envisioned colonialism as a vehicle for the advancement of the liberties and welfare of colonized peoples have mostly passed from the scene, or migrated to other discourses. In the seemingly endless catalogue of abuses practiced by colonial administrations, the appeal of nationalism as the emancipation of first resort has been well established.[15] Since Wilsonian and Soviet ideas of collective rights captivated anti-colonial politicians in the early 1920s, the rights of nations or, as a salvage position, nominated ethnic minorities within them, seemed the avenue of greatest promise for national liberation.[16] Before 1945, those occasional international human rights declarations issued by American and European notables mostly ignored nations.[17] The 1929 Declaration of the International Rights of Man, led by the Russian émigré jurist André Mandelstam, exemplified a briefly renascent cosmopolitan tradition and spoke of "sovereign individuals."[18] Even Lord Sankey's Declaration of the Rights of Man in 1940, endorsed by Indian independence leader

[15] See notably, "Declaration of the Rights and Duties of Nations," adopted by the American Institute of International Law, Washington, DC, January 6, 1916, reproduced in Elihu Root, *American Journal of International Law* 10, no. 2 (1916): 211–21.

[16] Mark Mazower, "The Strange Triumph of Human Rights," *Historical Journal* 47, no. 2 (2004): 379–98; Mazower, "Minorities and the League of Nations in Interwar Europe," *Daedalus* 126, no. 2 (1997): 47–64; Erez Manela, *The Wilsonian Moment: Self-Determination and the International Origins of Anticolonial Nationalism* (Princeton, NJ: Princeton University Press, 2007).

[17] For a treatment of the developments of the interwar, see Jan Herman Burgers, "The Road to San Francisco: The Revival of the Human Rights Idea in the Twentieth Century," *Human Rights Quarterly* 14, no. 4 (1992): 447–77; Jarna Petman, "Human Rights, Democracy and the Left," *Unbound* 2 (2006): 63–90.

[18] Philip Marshall Brown, "The New York Session of the Institut de Droit International," *American Journal of International Law* 24, no. 1 (1930): 126–8. For discussion of the 1929 Declaration and its context, see Lauren, *Visions Seen*, 114; Charles R. Beitz, *The Idea of Human Rights* (New York: Oxford University Press, 2009), 15–16; Daniel J. Whelan, *Indivisible Human Rights: A History* (Philadelphia: University of Pennsylvania Press, 2010), 47–52.

Jawaharlal Nehru, was silent on any requirement for colonial self-deter-mination.[19] The Cambridge law professor Hersch Lauterpacht, perhaps the most prolific writer on international human rights law in the early 1940s, was preoccupied with the difficulties that accompanied sovereignty as opposed to a benefit that accrued to individuals in securing it.[20] Although the 1941 Atlantic Charter famously affirmed "the right of all peoples to choose the form of government under which they live," this aim was not explicitly coupled to any particular individual rights, nor was there agreement between its British and US signatories as to whether its application extended beyond Axis-occupied Europe.[21]

As World War II drew to its close, human rights arrived as perhaps the principal innovation of the postwar blueprint, at least rhetorically – and one that initially seemed distant in its potential disruptions to the older global architecture of empire.[22] The ambiguity of the phrasing of the relevant passages of the UN Charter, and their exhortatory inflexion, attenuated the perceived bite of undertaking to "promote" human rights. Despite professions of enthusiasm for self-government in the Charter, efforts to establish self-determination during the drafting process for the UDHR, predictably, went nowhere, even with the cynical sponsorship of the Soviet bloc, and, more persuasively and passionately, Asian and Arab legations.

More than anything else, the belief in race as an ordering system of the world cut through the universalist claims regarding human rights. White civilizational confidence, shaken somewhat, but seeking to reconsolidate its moral and material supremacy, was willing to embrace the idea as part of its global patrimony, and bestow it accordingly.[23] Ardent enthusiasts for imperialism thus proclaimed support for human rights with little appreciation of risk, most famously the South African Field Marshall,

---

[19] Burke, *Decolonization and the Evolution of International Human Rights*, 15–16.

[20] Hersch Lauterpacht, "The Law of Nations, the Law of Nature and the Rights of Man Author," *Transactions of the Grotius Society* 29 (1943): 1–33. The tension between popular sovereignty, implied in democratic nation-states, and individual right seemed a central issue in this period, presumably after the rise of totalitarianisms supposedly underwritten by the people, Hermann Friedmann, "The Rights of Man," *Transactions of the Grotius Society* 24 (1938): 133–45.

[21] Cf. Elizabeth Borgwardt, *A New Deal for the World: America's Vision for Human Rights* (Cambridge, MA: Harvard University Press, 2005), 14–86.

[22] On the contours of the new postwar order in American thought, see Mark Bradley, *The World Reimagined* (Cambridge: Cambridge University Press, 2016); and, on its formulation, see Glenn Mitoma, *Human Rights and the Negotiation of American Power* (Philadelphia: University of Pennsylvania Press, 2013).

[23] Marilyn Lake and Henry Reynolds, *Drawing the Global Colour Line: White Men's Countries and the International Challenge of Racial Equality* (Cambridge: Cambridge University Press, 2008).

Jan Smuts, who included the phrase as coauthor of the UN Charter's preamble.[24] And Smuts was far from alone; in the terminal period of imperial rule, when the language of trusteeship was in favor, human rights was readily included in the imperial vocabulary.[25] For European empires defending their rule of overseas territories at the nascent UN, the principle of equal agency for all humans was perhaps begrudgingly acceptable – just not yet.[26] When a more vigorous nationalist wind emerged, this easy formula ceased to be effective. A strategy of formalistic and rhetorical acceptance of norm in the abstract, and immediate dissembling and deferral of policy action to deliver it, rapidly lost credibility in the UN, and across Asia, Africa, and the Middle East.[27]

Imperial embrace of human rights speaks not merely to expediency, but to the sheer capaciousness of the term and the tensions within it. For at least some liberal imperialists, and even a handful of francophone African nationalists, human rights may well have been understood as integral to the purpose of empire, interlaced as they were with the discourses of humanitarianism and notions of imperial citizenship.[28] In the late 1940s and into the 1950s, human rights drew

---

[24] Christof Heyns and Willem Gravett, "'To Save Succeeding Generations from the Scourge of War': Jan Smuts and the Ideological Foundations of the United Nations," *Human Rights Quarterly* 39, no. 3 (2017): 574–605; Saul Dubow, "Smuts, the United Nations and the Rhetoric of Race and Rights," *Journal of Contemporary History* 43, no. 1 (2008): 45–74; Bill Schwarz, *The White Man's World* (New York: Oxford University Press, 2011), 305–8; and the wider discussion of South Africa's negotiation of a reconfigured world in Ryan Irwin, *The Gordian Knot: Apartheid and the Unmaking of the Liberal World Order* (New York: Oxford University Press, 2012).

[25] Kevin Grant, *A Civilised Savagery: Britain and the New Slaveries in Africa, 1884–1926* (New York: Routledge, 2005), 167–72.

[26] For a compelling discussion of the emancipatory and utopian dimension of assimilation and "civilizational" ideas, see Saliha Belmessous, *Assimilation and Empire: Uniformity in French and British Colonies, 1541–1954* (Oxford: Oxford University Press, 2014).

[27] Timothy Parsons, *The Second British Empire: In the Crucible of the Twentieth Century* (London: Rowman, 2014), 8–12, 128–53, 237–41; for the later period, see Stephen Howe, "Crosswinds and Countercurrents: Macmillan's Africa in the 'Long View' of Decolonisation," in *The Wind of Change: Harold Macmillan and British Decolonization*, ed. Larry Butler and Sue Stockwell (London: Palgrave Macmillan, 2013), 252–6.

[28] There is abundant and compelling scholarship on humanitarianism and empire, see generally, Michael Barnett, *Empire of Humanity: A History of Humanitarianism* (Ithaca, NY: Cornell University Press, 2011); Abigail Green, "Humanitarianism in Nineteenth-Century Context," *Historical Journal* 57, no. 4 (2014): 1157–75; Rob Skinner and Alan Lester, "Humanitarianism and Empire: New Research Agendas," *Journal of Imperial and Commonwealth History* 40, no. 5 (2012): 729–47. See also the earlier work from Andrew Porter, "Trusteeship, Anti-Slavery, and Humanitarianism," in *The Oxford History of the British Empire*, vol. III: *The Nineteenth Century*, ed. Andrew Porter and Wm Roger Louis (Oxford: Oxford University Press, 1999), 198–221; and, in the American context, Kenton Clymer, "Humanitarian Imperialism: David Prescott Barrows and the White Man's Burden in the Philippines," *Pacific Historical Review* 45, no. 4 (1976): 495–517.

on nineteenth-century traditions of humanitarian and civilizational rhetoric, ideas that were well established in imperial understandings of their own enterprise.[29]

Humanitarian and imperial projects were very frequently interlocking and symbiotic. The moral capital of the former exchanged for the material resources of the latter, a transaction that at least in part animated the nineteenth-century British imperial campaign against the slave trade, which licensed the massive extension of the Royal Navy's writ to squeeze rival empires' slave-based economies.[30] Pretensions of humanitarian concern underwrote grotesque human rights abuses, most strikingly in Belgian King Leopold II's company state the Congo from the 1890s. Critics of Leopold did not oppose empire; they entreated a humanitarian European rule over predatory exploitation, believing that humanitarian work and imperial administration was happily synchronous.[31] Those features of Christianized paternalism that so often infused humanitarian movements of the early nineteenth-century were the showpiece of imperial legitimacy, and the substance of civilizational tutelage.[32]

Much as human rights would become in Western Europe and the USA in the 1970s, nineteenth-century humanitarianism was a doctrine oriented toward export.[33] Demands for overseas intervention, often against another malign empire, almost always drew on the language of a humanitarian duty and compassion, principally within Britain, which insistently cast its empire as uniquely humane.[34] These demands

---

[29] For further discussion, see Fabian Klose, "Human Rights for and against Empire: Legal and Public Discourses in the Age of Decolonisation," *Journal of the History of International Law* 18 (2016): 317–38.

[30] The literature on abolitionism and empire is vast, see notably Amalia Ribi Forclaz, *Humanitarian Imperialism: The Politics of Anti-Slavery Activism, 1880–1940* (Oxford: Oxford University Press, 2015); Derek R. Peterson, ed., *Abolitionism and Imperialism in Britain, Africa, and the Atlantic* (Athens: Ohio University Press, 2010); Seymour Drescher, *Abolition: A History of Slavery and Antislavery* (Cambridge: Cambridge University Press, 2009); Drescher, "The Shocking Birth of British Abolitionism," *Slavery & Abolition* 33, no 4 (2012): 571–93; Robyn Blackburn, *The American Crucible: Slavery, Emancipation and Human Rights* (London: Verso, 2011).

[31] Anthony Webster, *The Debate on the Rise of British Imperialism* (Manchester: Manchester University Press, 2006); Alice L. Conklin, "Colonialism and Human Rights: A Contradiction in Terms? The Case of French West Africa, 1895–1914," *American Historical Review* 103, no. 2 (1998), 419–42.

[32] Andrea Major, *Slavery, Abolitionism and Empire in India, 1772–1843* (Liverpool: Liverpool University Press, 2012), 244–78.

[33] The affinities between old and new humanitarian interventionist mobilizations, particularly those of the 2000s, are discussed extensively in Jean Bricmont, *Humanitarian Imperialism: Using Human Rights to Sell War* (New York: New York University Press, 2006).

[34] The durability of this self-mythologization, and its manifest inaccuracy, has been well demonstrated, see the recent work from Aidan Forth, *Barbed-Wire Imperialism: Britain's*

diminished sharply, though not entirely, when the new imperial administration demonstrated its own abusive hand to the victim territory.[35]
Campaigns to eradicate "traditional" abuses of customary law, an effort
that frequently held a kernel of emancipatory value, typically replaced
traditional abusive structures with much the same systems, but with an
imperial suzerain grafted upon them.[36]

Humanitarianism was thus an intellectual configuration that not only
could coexist with empire, it seemed almost to require it, in ways that
were mostly inconsistent with its overlapping discursive formation, individual rights; the term "human rights" hardly featured in the nineteenth
century. Humanitarian movements were not typically convinced of the
equality and agency of all peoples – features that were almost constitutive
of human rights as it emerged after WWII.[37] Humanitarian politics, with
rare exceptions, were deeply imbricated in white racial paternalism. As
pioneers of the rhetoric of "anti-politics," humanitarians professed only
the concern of conscience, moved by the most elemental and corporeal
needs of humanity.[38]

Empire of Camps, 1876–1903 (Berkeley: University of California Press, 2017); Kim
Wagner, "Savage Warfare: Violence and the Rule of Colonial Difference in Early
British Counterinsurgency," *History Workshop Journal* 85, no. 1 (2018): 217–37.

[35] The primary mode of dissent proposed reformism within empire, and did not pose a
question of its legitimacy, see Bernard Porter, *Critics of Empire: British Radical Attitudes to
Colonialism in Africa 1895–1914* (London, 1968).

[36] Mamdani, *Citizen and Subject: Contemporary Africa and the Legacy of Late Colonialism*
(Princeton, NJ: Princeton University Press, 1996). On the gendered aspect of this
colonial humanitarian discourse, see Charlotte Walker-Said, "The Trafficking and
Slavery of Women and Girls: The Criminalization of Marriage, Tradition, and Gender
Norms in French Colonial Cameroon, 1914–1945," in *Sex Trafficking, Human Rights,
and Social Justice*, ed. Tiantian Zheng (New York: Routledge, 2010), 150–69; Walker-
Said, "Christian Social Movements in Cameroon at the End of Empire: Transnational
Solidarities and the Communion of the World Church" in *Relocating World Christianity:
Interdisciplinary Studies in Universal and Local Expressions of Christianity*, ed. Joel Cabrita,
Emma Wild-Wood, and David Maxwell (Leiden: Brill, 2017), 189–212.

[37] Michael Geyer, "Humanitarianism and Human Rights: A Troubled Rapport," in *The
Emergence of Humanitarian Intervention: Ideas and Practice from the Nineteenth Century to
the Present*, ed. Fabian Klose (Cambridge: Cambridge University Press, 2016), 31–55.

[38] There was doubtlessly affective power behind much of the humanitarian impulse, and its
often florid expression. See notably the work on affect and humanitarianism, notably the
outstanding Margaret Abruzzo, *Polemical Pain: Slavery, Cruelty, and the Rise of
Humanitarianism* (Baltimore: Johns Hopkins University Press, 2011); and "The
Cruelty of Slavery, The Cruelty of Freedom: Colonization and the Politics of
Humaneness in the Early Republic," in *Affect and Abolition in the Anglo-Atlantic,
1770–1830*, ed. Stephen Ahern (Aldershot: Ashgate, 2013), 189–209. See also, on
more recent affective mechanism of sight, and its implied moralism, as discussed in
Heidi Fehrenbach and Davide Rodogno, eds., *Humanitarian Photography: A History*
(New York: Cambridge University Press, 2015), 1–21.

Nevertheless, the logic of humanitarianism, even as it was advanced in the late Victorian and Edwardian empire, did provide the foundations for a serious critique of colonial rule. Roger Casement, perhaps the most iconic figure in the early twentieth-century British humanitarian movement, commenced his crusade against the abuses of foreign imperialisms. An Irish nationalist – the British would hang him in 1916 for his part in the Easter Uprising that year – he concluded with absolute confidence that empire itself was inherently disposed to abuse; and self-determination the most essential humanitarian intervention.[39] He counterpoised national liberation, rather than international human rights, to empire. The rights of man would be realized in independent nation-states.

While the maritime imperial order survived World War I, the breakup of the continental land empires, Russia, Ottoman, and Germany, and US President Wilson's ban on annexing their territories, led to a renewal of civilizational and humanitarian missions. The Paris Peace Conference in 1919 and new League of Nations ignored the claims of colonial peoples to independence, and assigned the territories of the defeated powers to the victorious Entente Powers, mainly Britain and France, in the form of trusteeships called mandates. The rhetoric, and to some extent, the logistical connections between humanitarianism and empire were thereby revitalized during the interwar years in the form of a humane mission for imperial control in the League of Nations mandate system.[40] Humanitarianism's putative place outside politics barely survived a second total war, and the wars of decolonization that followed it, however. Who resided within humanity, and who disbursed compassion, were promptly and inevitably engaged as part of a contest for the symbolic high ground of morality.[41] Humanitarianism and human rights remained lexical wildcards that could be played by imperialist and nationalist alike, for radically different aims, a dynamic evident across several of the chapters in this collection.[42]

---

[39] Dean Pavlakis, *British Humanitarianism and the Congo Reform Movement, 1896–1913* (Aldershot: Ashgate, 2015); Grant, *Civilised Savagery*; Andrew Porter, "Sir Roger Casement and the International Humanitarian Movement," *Journal of Imperial and Commonwealth History* 29, no. 2 (2010): 59–74.

[40] There was at least some recognition of the tension between empire and humanitarian categories, see notably J. P Daughton, "Behind the Imperial Curtain: International Humanitarian Efforts and the Critique of French Colonialism in the Interwar Years," *French Historical Studies* 34, no. 3 (2011): 503–28.

[41] Susan Pedersen, *The Guardians: The League of Nation and the Crisis of Empire* (Oxford: Oxford University Press, 2015).

[42] On the informal logics of contemporary humanitarian practices, see Didier Fassin, *Humanitarian Reason: A Moral History of the Present* (Berkeley: University of California Press, 2011); Michal Givoni, *The Care of the Witness: A Contemporary History of Testimony in Crises* (New York: Cambridge University Press, 2016). For a survey of recent

The gulf between empire's grand ideology and its practice was more readily discerned by those closest to colonial administration.[43] The contradictions were a constant source of anxiety for colonial ministries in the early 1950s, and a still more intense source of resentment and frustration from local colonial administrators. While some European officials embraced the new international human rights systems as consistent with their values, as well as a potent instrument for containing communism at home and abroad, their colonial colleagues wrote dismayed memoranda. The European Convention on Human Rights (1950), the first formal treaty arrangement to have the words "human rights" in its title, permitted state parties to exclude and restrict application in colonial territories. Proponents of the European Convention, among them avid imperialists such as Winston Churchill, believed its guarantees of civil and political rights reflected the Christian and humanist values that had once unified European civilization and its imperial extensions.[44]

Ultimately, the imperialist effort to manage the new human rights language, and to isolate it from anti-colonialism, proved terminal.[45] No UN human rights treaties would follow the European Convention's example, despite a sustained effort to preserve the territorial application provision from both France and Britain. Only a handful of years after the adoption of the UDHR, which implicitly prohibited discrimination on the basis of colonial status, the ideal global order was reconfigured: a world of nation-states, each securing those agreed universal human rights

anthropological literature on humanitarianism, see Peter Redfield and Erica Bornstein, "An Introduction to the Anthropology of Humanitarianism," in *Forces of Compassion: Humanitarianism Between Ethics and Politics*, ed. Bornstein and Redfield (Santa Fe, NM: School for Advanced Research, 2011), 3–30; Redfield, "Humanitarianism," in *A Companion to Moral Anthropology*, ed. Didier Fassin (Malden, MA: Blackwell, 2012), 451–67.

[43] Fabian Klose, *Human Rights in the Shadow of Colonial Violence: The Wars of Independence in Kenya and Algeria* (Philadelphia: University of Pennsylvania Press, 2013).

[44] Marco Duranti, *The Conservative Human Rights Revolution: European Identity, Transnational Politics, and the Origins of the European Convention* (New York: Oxford University Press, 2017); A. W. Brian Simpson, *Human Rights and the End of Empire: Britain and the Genesis of the European Convention* (Oxford: Oxford University Press, 2001); Christopher Roberts, *The Contentious History of the International Bill of Human Rights* (Cambridge, Cambridge University Press, 2015), 129, 136–8.

[45] See, for elaboration, Emma Stone MacKinnon, "Declaration as Disavowal: The Politics of Race and Empire in the Universal Declaration of Human Rights," *Political Theory* 47, no. 1 (2019): 57–81; Jessica Pearson, "Defending Empire at the United Nations: The Politics of International Colonial Oversight in the Era of Decolonisation," *Journal of Imperial and Commonwealth History* 45, no. 3 (2017): 525–49; and on the related question of humanity and refugees, see Lucy Mayblin, "Colonialism, Decolonisation, and the Right to be Human: Britain and the 1951 Geneva Convention on the Status of Refugees," *Journal of Historical Sociology* 27, no. 3 (2014): 423–41.

for their citizens.[46] This was the moment in which universal human rights, popular sovereignty, and liberal anti-colonial nationalism appeared to fly in formation.[47] It was a perishable arrangement.

Optimistic visions of national freedom and human rights for the freed citizenries of postcolonial states began to wane in the late 1950s. The year 1958 alone witnessed several authoritarian transitions, including the concentration of executive power in a symbolically potent beacon, Kwame Nkrumah's Ghana. Pakistan's dysfunctional democracy suffered its first successful coup, led by Mohammed Ayub Khan. His political program replaced the unrealized promise of universal human rights with a patronizing scheme of "Basic Rights," which Khan argued were best suited to his underdeveloped nation.[48] A generation of grave disappointments, punctuated by catastrophic violence in Biafra, Bangladesh, and, later, Cambodia, produced a steady migration to less hopeful and less revolutionary horizons.[49] Among a new generation of Western human rights movements, and those who cast anti-colonialism as the vanguard of a global revolution, hopes for the transformative and humane rebirth of nations and peoples dimmed.[50]

In Britain, Amnesty International was born in 1961, as the disappointments of the Third World were becoming manifest, and the increasingly visual nature of global media began transmitting horrors with greater

---

[46] Cf. Christian Reus-Smit, *Individual Rights and the Making of the International System* (Cambridge: Cambridge University Press, 2011); Reus-Smit, "Struggles for Individual Rights and the Expansion of the International System," *International Organization* 65, no. 2 (2011): 207–42.

[47] Burke, *Decolonization and the Evolution of International Human Rights.* See also the work of Bonny Ibhawoh. Ibhawoh, *Human Rights in Africa* (Cambridge: Cambridge University Press, 2018); Ibhawoh, "Testing the Atlantic Charter: Linking Anticolonialism, Self-determination and Universal Human Rights," *International Journal of Human Rights* 18, nos. 7–8 (2014): 842–60; Ibhawoh, "Human Rights and National Liberation: The Anticolonial Politics of Nnamdi Azikiwe," in *Leadership in Colonial Africa: Disruption of Traditional Frameworks and Patterns,* ed. Baba G. Jallow (New York: Palgrave Macmillan, 2014), 55–68.

[48] Mohammed Ayub Kahn, *Friends Not Masters: A Political Autobiography* (Oxford: Oxford University Press, 1967), ix, 90–2, 204–7.

[49] On the impact of the Biafran case in particular, see Lasse Heerten, "The Dystopia of Postcolonial Catastrophe: Self-determination, the Biafran War of Secession, and the 1970s Human Rights Moment," in *The Breakthrough: Human Rights in the 1970s,* ed. Jan Eckel and Samuel Moyn (Philadelphia: University of Pennsylvania Press, 2014), 15–32; Bradley Simpson, "The Biafran Secession and the Limits of Self-determination," *Journal of Genocide Research* 16, nos. 2–3 (2014): 337–54; and the chapters in A. Dirk Moses and Lasse Heerten, eds., *Postcolonial Conflict and the Question of Genocide: The Nigeria–Biafra War, 1967–1970* (Abingdon: Routledge, 2018).

[50] For a more complex account of the interrelationship between the *tiers-mondiste* cohort, and the milieu which generated a new humanitarian politics, see Eleanor Davey, *Idealism Beyond Borders: The French Revolutionary Left and the Rise of Humanitarianism, 1954–1988* (Cambridge: Cambridge University Press, 2015).

fidelity. Amnesty International rapidly sought, with decidedly mixed success, to cultivate nodes and local sections all over the world, though its membership kept an overwhelming center of gravity in the Western middle-class. Global in its advocacy, and its professed authority, Amnesty International's disposition was primarily to assist the oppressed outside national borders, rather than to mobilize the oppressed within them. Its tools were self-consciously modest and moderate, sending out an armada of letters of concern on behalf of a particular persecuted individual, or "prisoner of conscience."[51] Amnesty International's emergence across the 1960s, and the explosive growth in sibling organizations in the 1970s, foremost Helsinki Watch (later Human Rights Watch), elevated the place of international human rights norms in daily discourse. These human rights causes were, predominantly, overseas; defined as individualized injustice.[52] Western publics had soured on the claims of nation-building., whether on Western, Sino, Soviet, or endogenous socialist models.[53] Transformative hope would instead start at the less abstract and grandiose level of ending grotesque ills. It was an approach that, arguably, over succeeded in canalizing human rights energy into the areas of greatest affective power and urgency.[54]

Amnesty International's mass letter campaigns, relentlessly documentarian approach, and studiously produced visual campaigns harnessed political moralism in a new manner.[55] Human rights could become the crusade of the concerned citizen, as opposed to the language of the directly repressed or elite foreign policy actors. Lighting a candle was a more resonant channel for solidarity than the dry juridical approach of earlier NGOs, like the International Commission of Jurists.[56] It afforded a more universalistic engagement with the plight of the persecuted than

---

[51] Sarah Snyder, "Exporting Amnesty International to the United States: Transatlantic Human Rights Activism in the 1960s," *Human Rights Quarterly* 34, no. 3 (2012): 779–99; Ann Marie Clark, *Diplomacy of Conscience: Amnesty International and Changing Human Rights Norms* (Princeton, NJ: Princeton University Press, 2007).

[52] On the pessimism of human rights politics emerging around this period, see Wendy Brown, "'The Most We Can Hope For ...': Human Rights and the Politics of Fatalism," *South Atlantic Quarterly* 103, nos. 2–3 (2004): 453–61.

[53] The temporal coincidence is observed, briefly, in Thomas Borstelmann, *The 1970s: A New Global History from Civil Rights to Economic Inequality* (Princeton, NJ: Princeton University Press, 2013), 187–8.

[54] Roland Burke, "'They Think Such Things Don't Matter': Emotional Diplomacy and Human Rights," *Human Rights Quarterly* 39, no. 2 (2017): 273–95.

[55] Jonathan Power, *Like Water on Stone: The Story of Amnesty International* (Boston: Northeastern University Press, 2001); cf. Stephen Hopgood, *Keepers of the Flame: Understanding Amnesty International* (Ithaca, NY: Cornell University Press, 2006).

[56] Howard Tolley, *The International Commission of Jurists: Global Advocates for Human Rights* (Philadelphia: University of Pennsylvania Press, 1994).

the patchwork jurisdiction of the European Court of Human Rights, the Inter-American Court, or the barely functional UN bodies. While moderate in its methods, its was, for practical purposes, adamantine in its principles; namely, to channel public pressure against abusive regimes of every ideological flavor. By the end of the 1970s, the "Forgotten Prisoners" who had catalyzed Amnesty International's birth were no longer forgotten; nor was the freedom Amnesty's campaigns had secured for so many of them.[57] For those countless it assisted, Amnesty literally saved lives, winning quiet concessions for individual cases, from governments irritated and exhausted by the power of perpetual embarrassment. For the regimes against which railed in public broadsides and private complaints, Amnesty's efficacy was frustratingly real.[58] Animated by a strong focus on individual cases and integrity of person abuses, Amnesty secured human rights on the least normatively contested terrain.

This triaged moralism did have its problems insofar as it drew the crusade into narrower ambitions, but was also elemental to Amnesty's spectacular success. Its vision was palliation of the worst, and for the disappeared, the victims of SAVAK, BOSS, the DINA, and an alphabet of other acronymically obscured death squads, that was far from a small development. Its capacity to leverage Western public pressure against allies added a new factor to foreign policymaking; even if that factor was never especially consistent. For diplomats practiced at evasions in the UN and regional forums, the organization, and its nascent siblings, certainly seemed to have more teeth than any preceding human rights mechanism.[59]

Postcolonial abuses, abundant and appalling, met with righteous venom: even, or perhaps especially, from those once sympathetic to decolonization.[60] In much of the advocacy of these new human rights NGOs (HRNGOs), the nation-state, so central to the securing of rights in the Western domestic realm, was excised from the Western human

---

[57] Mümtaz Soysal, Nobel Lecture, December 11, 1977, available at www.nobelprize.org/prizes/peace/1977/amnesty/lecture, accessed October 2, 2018.

[58] See, for example, the private irritation of the Shah of Iran at AI activism in Parviz Radji, *In the Service of the Peacock Throne* (London: Hamilton, 1983), 107–13; and the collected governmental denunciations in *AI in Quotes* (London: Amnesty International, 1976).

[59] Iain Guest, *Behind the Disappearances Argentina's Dirty War against Human Rights and the United Nations* (Philadelphia: University of Pennsylvania Press, 1990).

[60] Rupert Emerson, "The Fate of Human Rights in the Third World," *World Politics* 27, no. 2 (1975): 201–26; cf. the markedly more generous, Emerson, *From Empire to Nation: The Rise of Self-Assertion of Asian and African Peoples* (Boston: Beacon Press, 1962). Arthur Schlesinger Jr. was perhaps the bluntest critic of the limits of self-determination, and exemplified the 1970s shift in attitude as to how rights related to collective national sovereignty, see the discussion in Moyn, *Last Utopia*, 118–19.

rights architecture as irrelevant or irretrievable.[61] By the late 1960s, having been compelled to release their overseas territories, and the grave political liability that attached to maintaining colonial rule, the almost former imperial powers now began to embrace an activist advocacy of human rights with more enthusiasm. After almost two decades spent fending away communist and Third World criticism, they could pursue the diplomacy and politics of virtue abroad with less encumbrance, most especially against the Soviet empire, in solidarity with its nascent dissident movement.[62] They were joined in the early 1970s by a US government, led first by Congress, and then by President Jimmy Carter, as well as a portion of the public seeking to reclaim "American virtue," in Barbara Keys's felicitous phrase.[63] This was a crusade distasteful of grand ambitions for statehood and sovereignty.[64] The emergent wave of HRNGOs joined older humanitarian organizations in their century-long effort to find the minimum possible altitude for ambition, well below the "common standard of achievement" of 1948, or the world-shaking nationalist promises of the 1955 Asian–African Conference in Bandung.[65]

As human rights, among the Western audience, shifted to this parsimonious utopia, Latin American, Asian, and African states transmuted human rights into another project – that of global economic redistribution,

---

[61] The "minimalist" quality, which was acutely apparent in the Latin American context, is observed in the insightful conclusion from Patrick William Kelly, *Sovereign Emergencies: Latin America and the Making of Global Human Rights Politics* (Cambridge: Cambridge University Press, 2018), 272–303.

[62] Barbara Keys, *Reclaiming American Virtue: The Human Rights Revolution of the 1970s* (Cambridge, MA: Harvard University Press, 2014); cf. the genealogy of the 1960s proposed in the pioneering study from Jensen, *Making of International Human Rights*. Jensen's account, which orbits a collection of postcolonial voices, demonstrates that the Western "breakthrough" was merely one aspect of a wider constellation of developments.

[63] Sarah Snyder, *From Selma to Moscow: How Human Rights Activists Transformed U.S. Foreign Policy* (New York: Columbia University Press, 2018); Snyder, "'A Call for U.S. Leadership': Congressional Activism on Human Rights," *Diplomatic History* 37, no. 2 (2013): 372–97; Keys, *Reclaiming American Virtue*.

[64] Cf. Brad Simpson, "Self-Determination, Human Rights, and the End of Empire in the 1970s," *Humanity: An International Journal of Human Rights, Humanitarianism and Development* 4, no. 2 (2013): 239–60.

[65] Eckel and Moyn, *Breakthrough*. On the ambitions of Bandung, and their ultimate disappointments, see Umut Ozsu, "'Let Us First of All Have Unity among Us': Bandung, International Law, and the Empty Politics of Solidarity," in *Bandung, Global History, and International Law: Critical Pasts and Pending Futures*, ed. Luis Eslava, Michael Fakhri, and Vasuki Nesiah (Cambridge: Cambridge University Press, 2017), 293–307; Robert Vitalis, "The Midnight Ride of Kwame Nkrumah and Other Fables of Bandung," *Humanity: An International Journal of Human Rights, Humanitarianism and Development* 4, no. 2 (2013): 261–88.

exemplified by the campaign for a New International Economic Order (NIEO), which gained force across 1974 and 1975. Railing, with considerable reason, against the "existing, unjust economic order," their hopes were – if anything – more transformative and revolutionary than anything proposed in the 1940s and 1950s, at least in terms of the global balance of wealth. For the most voluble governmental proponents of the NIEO, human rights, in the prevailing Western variant, were neocolonial intrusion masquerading as moralism, a critique rendered more subtly by scholars from the Global South. Humanitarian aid, with its attached technocrats and conditionality, was the paternalism of the missionary. Humanitarianism itself, most especially in the laws of armed conflict, was found in need of decolonization. Although the fictions of impartial compassion that attended humanitarianism, a discourse with a much longer and well-furnished history within imperial projects, were already recognized, explicit association of "human rights" as imperialist was a new phenomenon.[66] "Western human rights," as they had begun to be wielded by Amnesty International and more energetic Western foreign services, emerged as a new front in the interstate clash between North and South.[67] For two decades, state elites clashed on the purportedly imperial quality of universality as enshrined in human rights norms, a debate which much of the activist community – particularly in the Global South – simply maneuvered around, consumed with the problems of immediate abuses, as opposed to abstractions.[68]

Human rights movements could never manage fully equilateral attention to every dialect of a language that covered so many disparate, and often contradictory, priorities. Variations in emphasis are hardly remarkable: they are a constituent virtue of the discourse. The ability for so many emancipatory claims to invoke variants of human rights language,

---

[66] Humanitarianism, and in particular, rhetorics of humanitarian action to subtend imperial intervention, have been revivified as a source of historical interest. See notably, Klose, *Emergence of Humanitarian Intervention*, and Davide Rodogno, *Against Massacre: Humanitarian Interventions in the Ottoman Empire, 1815–1914* (Princeton, NJ: Princeton University Press, 2012); cf. the more generous account of humanitarian interventions from Gary Bass, *Freedom's Battle: The Origins of Humanitarian Intervention* (New York: Vintage, 2008).

[67] Burke, "Human Rights Day after the 'Breakthrough': Celebrating the Universal Declaration of Human Rights at the United Nations in 1978 and 1988," *Journal of Global History* 10, no. 1 (2015): 147–70.

[68] For the most extensive and provocative argument on the continuities of imperialism and human rights, see Makau Mutua, *Human Rights: A Political and Cultural Critique* (Philadelphia: University of Pennsylvania Press, 2000). Gregory Mann observes a more complex process set of continuities and interactions between empire and HRNGOs, see *From Empires to NGOs in the West African Sahel: The Road to Nongovernmentality* (New York: Cambridge University Press, 2015).

and to do so with evident sincerity, was apparent at least as early as the early postwar, when the framers of the UDHR tried to stich these strands into a mostly coherent set of articles.[69] The challenge of decolonization, and particularly, the 1970s, was not so much the proliferation of different species in the human rights ecosystem, than the growing inclination toward exclusivism and definitional monopoly. NGOs arrived at a particular balance of concerns; typically the most immediate and appalling. For state elites from the Global South, the exclusivism was in a different key – with human rights redefined as global economic redistribution. For those more candidly illiberal national liberation movements, human rights were more or less material and logistical support for armed insurrection; with the remainder of the UDHR merely platitudinous humanitarian posturing.[70] All attempted to define the category, and none succeeded. Greater appreciation of the contended space of human rights in the era of decolonization requires analytical deference to the diversity, and the coalescing of various rights claims around "human rights," even when they communed with older and different rights philosophies and political programs.[71]

The Histories of Human Rights and Empire

The chapters in this volume show that these engagements between human rights and empire did not operate as separate and autonomous abstractions. For those involved, there was no clean distinction between the rights invoked by national liberation movements and human rights. The Indian nationalist and feminist Hansa Mehta, in a 1949 conversation with the British Labour politician Marguerite Bowie, discussed a "blueprint for heaven," one that was being enacted at once domestically in national reform movements and internationally in the UDHR.[72] As Indonesian nationalist leader, Mohammed Hatta, reflected in 1956, there was an affinity between how anti-colonialists perceived their cause and the language of universal human rights. When Indonesian

---

[69] Mary Ann Glendon, *A World Made New* (New York: Random House, 2001).
[70] *Proceedings of the UN–OAU Conference on Southern Africa, Oslo, 9–14 April, 1973* (Oslo: United Nations, 1973).
[71] See now the global analysis of Eric D. Weitz, *A World Divided: The Global Struggle for Human Rights in the Age of Nation-States* (Princeton, NJ: Princeton University Press, 2019).
[72] CBS Television, *"Vanity Fair:* Extemporaneous Discussion with Mrs. Roosevelt, Mrs. Mehta, and Miss Bowie of the Work of the Human Rights Commission," 12:30 p.m., June 21, 1949, New York City, transcript, 3. Subject File No. 15, Reports on CHR, Hansa Mehta Papers, Nehru Memorial Library and Museum (NMLM), New Delhi, India.

nationalists were read the content of the UDHR, Hatta wrote, "it was as if they heard themselves speaking."[73] Human rights and anti-colonial emancipation were a commingled freedom struggle in the 1940s and 1950s. While tensions would emerge, these did not correspond to any single geopolitical development, nor the total obsolescence of one by the other. The shift was linguistic and conceptual, as the meaning of the term human rights, at least in Western vernacular, began to narrow in ways that foreclosed the bolder economic and social revolutionary potential they had held in Third World imagination. Human rights were not born from the death of anti-colonialism. Human rights in the West died as a viable means for expressing any optimistic anti-colonial vision.

This refashioning of human rights in the 1970s cast aside much of the most vital content and appeal of human rights for postcolonial peoples.[74] For many in the Third World, transnational capitalism, rising antipathy to resource transfers and state building from the wealthy states, and all of the disappointed hopes of a meaningful sovereignty – the signature ambition of the original campaign against empire – were excised from this new human rights agenda. The World Bank's "basic needs"-oriented approach to development, adopted in 1972, set the stage for "Structural Adjustment Programs," eviscerating ambition and replacing it with sur-vival.[75] A "human rights" discourse that had refounded itself in absolute minimalism, or in the word of one US ambassador, the hope of making "an awful situation slightly less awful" was the promise of the barest palliation, not the promise of liberation.[76] Given the prevalence of appal-ling – and rising – global repression, particularly in Latin America and South Asia, and abundant misery, this was hardly unreasonable, but it did shift the human rights agenda away from the grand to the immediate and desperate.

After a decade of definitional contraction in human rights language across the political West, the early 1990s did begin to regenerate a more generous and inclusive appreciation of how wide and ambidextrous rights were, and the rediscovery of global activisms which had empha-sized quite different concerns. Foremost of these was women's rights,

---

[73] Mohammad Hatta, "Colonial Society and the Ideals of Social Democracy," in *Indonesian Political Thinking, 1945–1965*, ed. Herbert Feith and Lance Castles (Ithaca, NY: Cornell University Press, 1970), 35.
[74] Moyn, *Last Utopia*, 148, 218.
[75] Gilbert Rist, *The History of Development: From Western Origins to Global Faith* (London: Zed, 2002), 162.
[76] Hearings Before the Subcommittees on Asian and Pacific Affairs and on Human Rights and International Organizations of the Committee on Foreign Affairs, House of Representatives. August–September, December 1982 (Washington, DC: US Congress, 1983), 238.

which had organized in transnational networks well before the HRNGOs, and had successfully built out an impressive system of trans-local solidarities, and a much more ambitious vision of reform and advocacy.[77] So, too, Indigenous peoples, who found common cause not merely with other first nations, but with Amnesty International, with women's rights NGOs, and often with environmental activism.[78] The variegated texture of this more developed global human rights movement was unmistakable by June 1993, at the opening of the World Conference on Human Rights in Vienna. In the basement of the Austria Centre, the NGO universe advocated not merely for the now classical priorities of torture and arbitrary detention and execution, but for the Declaration on the Rights of Indigenous Peoples, and recognition that women's rights constituted human rights. Survival International, Amnesty International, and the Women's International League for Peace and Freedom were all part of an overlapping human rights movement; sometimes intersecting, sometimes not, but all conversing in a comprehensible language.[79] Although Western activism still hewed closer to the narrower ambitions of the 1970s, more citizenries had begun to recover human rights for their own aspirations.

For some historians, the anti-colonial embrace of human rights as a language against empire was illusory, explained away as instrumentalist, serving as a sharp rhetorical adornment to a profoundly different cause, that of nationalism.[80] Given that instrumental deployment of human rights has been the companion of countless modern political movements, the accurate observation that self-determination struggles drew on rights language offers little insight into how, why, and by whom human rights were used, or the implications and purposes of fusing local projects with

---

[77] Arvonne Fraser, "The Feminization of Human Rights," *Foreign Service Journal* 70, no. 12 (1993): 31–7; Wendy Parker and Pauline Comeau, "Women Succeed in Vienna Where Others Fail," *Tribune des Droits Humains* (1993): 22–4; Charlotte Bunch, "The Global Campaign for Women's Human Rights," *The Review: International Commission of Jurists* 50 (1993): 105–9.

[78] Jeff Corntassel, "Partnership in Action? Indigenous Political Mobilization and Co-optation during the First UN Indigenous Decade (1995–2004)," *Human Rights Quarterly* 29, no. 1 (2007): 137–66; Pamela Martin and Franke Wilmer, "Transnational Normative Struggles and Globalization: The Case of Indigenous Peoples in Bolivia and Ecuador," *Globalizations* 5, no. 4 (2008): 583–98; Ronald Niezen, "Recognizing Indigenism: Canadian Unity and the International Movement of Indigenous Peoples," *Society for Comparative Study of Society and History* 42, no. 1 (2000): 119–48; Tracey Ulltveit-Moe, "Amnesty International and Indigenous Rights: Congruence or Conflict?", *American Indian Law Review* 31, no. 2 (2006/7): 717–42.

[79] *Terra Viva: The Independent Daily of the World Conference on Human Rights* (Vienna: IPS-Inter Press Service in technical cooperation with *Der Standard* (1993)), vols. 1–13.

[80] Simpson, *Human Rights and the End of Empire*, 512–13; Afshari, "Historiography of Human Rights Reflections," 50.

universalist significance. In their conspicuous even-handedness, exemplified by the nomination of abused figures from Western, communist, and Third Worlds, Amnesty International worked assiduously to position its organization, and human rights, outside ideological conflicts. This sort of studious disavowal was an explicit means for Amnesty and other emergent HRNGOs to set themselves apart from other social movements, and to ascend as the foremost Western "anti-politics."[81] South Asian constitutionalists and Caribbean advocates of welfare planning rendered their projects as human rights, not for narrow tactical gain, but as a means of connecting local freedom projects with a wider global enterprise.

This volume shows that these connections often represented an effort to define and realize the substance of human rights in particular national settings. Those phenomena dismissed as instrumentalist were vehicles for moving beyond an ethereal, universal claim and toward a specific emancipatory goal. As for the apologists and representatives of colonial forces, they believed that the use of repressive measures against those who would challenge colonial rule could be justified in the name of a higher call to better the lot of the colonized, or defended as necessary prophylaxis against the presumed catastrophe of communist influence. Overlooking the appeal this perverse moral logic held among European and American audiences, working in both colonial and Cold War technocratic registers, is to underestimate the ideational power of liberal imperialism and its neocolonial successors.

Contributors across the volume, many of them pioneers of the new human rights history, traverse the geography of empire and its remnants. They pursue the interactions between human rights and decolonization across the twentieth century. Empire and rights are historicized through a network of overlapping sites, as opposed to marshalled into a catalogue of emancipatory triumph or utopian disappointment. Instead of any unitary heuristic, the cases suggest the pluripotent capacity of human rights claims, wielded by nationalists, imperialists, activists, and internationalists alike, for profoundly different purposes. The ecumenism with which these groups migrated contests of legitimacy into the language of human rights was integral to the steady ascent of the discourse and the eclipse of its rivals.

The historical investigations in this volume are organized into three thematic groupings, beginning with the struggle of colonized peoples to

---

[81] Samuel Moyn, "The Continuing Perplexities of Human Rights," *Qui Parle* 22, no. 1 (2013): 103–4; Moyn, "Human Rights: Moral or Political?," in *Human Rights: Moral or Political?*, ed. Adam Etinson (Oxford: Oxford University Press, 2018), 69–87.

assert their individual and collective human rights, above all the right to self-determination, before moving on to the place of human rights in the construction of postcolonial states. It concludes with colonial and neo-colonial efforts to mold human rights norms so as to undermine the emancipatory potential of anti-colonial conceptions of human rights. The editors are cognizant of critiques of histories of empire that privilege colonial sources and perspectives, which rightly challenge imperial historians to decolonize the history of decolonization, as well as the editors' own positionality as white male scholars educated and employed in Western educational institutions.[82] Attempting to strike a balance between diverse methodological approaches to the history of decolonization, the empirical research underpinning the various contributions to this volume straddles the divide between, on the one hand, the archives of imperial powers and Western NGOs, and, on the other, material that reflects African, Asian, and indigenous perspectives, including documents produced by the colonized themselves.

Part I of this volume investigates how the language of human rights and self-determination became embedded in anti-colonialist struggles. Human rights offered a language more responsive and comprehensive than conventional nationalism and an avenue for advancing these ideals in a global forum. Challenging the recent tendency to cleave anti-colonialism from the human rights story, Bonny Ibhawoh (Chapter 1) contends that this division, central to the "new histories," rests on an ahistorical assumption that the language was already settled by the 1940s. In British Africa, anti-colonialism offered an alternate vision of human rights that sought in part to challenge a hegemonic colonial rights agenda which emphasized the individual insistently. In this setting, the relationship between self-determination in anti-colonialism and nation-state-oriented, individual-centered "human rights" was not simply one of succession or displacement but also one of tension and contestation.

Marco Duranti (Chapter 2) investigates the relationship between decolonization in the French empire and the nascent UN human rights system after World War II. French officials, faced with pressure to implement UN human rights standards in their African colonies, found themselves unable to reconcile their own constitutional doctrine of assimilationism, premised on a universalist conception of "the rights of man," with the existence of unequal colonial rights regimes based on cultural difference. Private petitions sent to the United Nations from individuals and NGOs around the world drew attention to the French

---

[82] See Chapter 1 in this volume.

state's abuse of colonial subjects, above all in the Maghreb. These anti-colonial activists, whether residing within French colonial territories or abroad, conceived of the defense of civil liberties as inseparable from the struggle for independence. While citations of UN human rights standards declined over the course of the 1950s, petitioners left no doubt that guarantees of individual freedoms and trade union rights were a prerequisite for national self-determination.

Jennifer Johnson (Chapter 3), in her study of humanitarian law in the Algerian War of Independence, demonstrates the ways in which the terrain of global moralism became a battleground for imperial authorities and the liberation movement. As the Algerian National Liberation Front fought kinetic battles, its political wing waged a campaign for the conceptual plane of international humanitarian law. Both bloodshed and its palliation became a means for advancing nationalist primacy, and, contrarily, the basis for French assertions of civilizational superiority. The radically egalitarian premise of humanitarianism, that all suffering beings are equally entitled to compassion and protection, clashed with the nationalist and imperialist ideologies that in practice had long structured the French Red Cross's activities, revealing the tenacity of old civilizational hierarchies in postwar French humanitarian discourse.

Miranda Johnson (Chapter 4) charts indigenous encounters with human rights in Australia, Canada, and New Zealand, which gathered momentum in the early 1960s. Competing interstate rights presumed international recognition as a nation-state, a recognition denied to, and not always sought by, Indigenous peoples in settler societies. Scarcely more promising was the state of human rights law as it existed in the 1960s, when the language was almost silent on Indigenous peoples. Human rights, with their inherent emphasis on universal individuals, mapped poorly to particular indigenous collectivities and broken colonial agreements, and limited the potential gains to narrow areas of labor and legal equality. Navigation of a path forward required the generation of a new rights tradition, hewn from elements of human rights, more specific moralistic narratives in settler societies, and long dormant imperial-era legal obligations. This newly synthesized tradition, eventually and reluctantly accepted by settler colonies in the 2007 Declaration on the Rights of Indigenous Peoples, was both more and less than the UDHR.[83]

---

[83] Megan Davis, "Indigenous Struggles in Standard-Setting: The United Nations Declaration on the Rights of Indigenous Peoples," *Melbourne Journal of International Law* 9, no. 2 (2013): 439–71; GA Res. 61/295. United Nations Declaration on the Rights of Indigenous Peoples, September 13, 2007, available at www.un.org/esa/socdev/unpfii/documents/DRIPS_en.pdf, accessed April 10, 2018.

The long and late codification of the rights of the indigenous of rights indicated both substantial ellipses in the human rights discourse and its capacity for renovation.

Mary Ann Heiss (Chapter 5) charts the inevitable incoherence that accompanied human rights instrumentalization, primarily in the realm of self-determination. For US policymakers in the Eisenhower administration, human rights, inclusive of the nationalist *cri de cœur*, the right to self-determination, were powerful indictments upon the Soviet regime. More challenging was their equivalent potency against America's European allies. Finding a defensible median between these interests, which collided dramatically in late 1960, in the UN Declaration Against Colonialism, was an exhibition in the perils of crafting a moralistic weapon with broadband effects.[84] Bold demands for the universal application of self-determination and human rights, passionate invocations of 1776, and timorous reference to British, French, and Portuguese repression, was a partial solution, and only partially convincing.

Part II of the volume traces the transformation of the still plastic notion of human rights in the emergence of postcolonial statehood. As the place of the individual was opened up in the process of empire's end, the status of imperial subject shifted to postcolonial citizen. This transition was often framed in terms of human rights, yet the relationship between the categories of citizen and human remained perilously ill-defined. A. Dirk Moses (Chapter 6) finds another gulf between the emergent human rights ideals and the coercive mass movement of peoples. As Eleanor Roosevelt dreamt of "A World Made New," and delegations pondered the linguistic elegance of their draft UDHR, the partitions of the later 1940s – India, Palestine, and Germany – remade the worlds of whole communities, and almost invariably, remade them in misery.[85] Postwar partitions represented humanitarian catastrophes of enormous proportions: official and unofficial population expulsions of many millions of

---

[84] For a wide survey of the paradoxical quality of self-determination in the US diplomatic armamentarium, and its national life, see Bradley Simpson, "The United States and the Curious History of Self-determination," *Diplomatic History* 36, no. 4 (2012): 675–94; Simpson, "Denying the 'First Right': The United States, Indonesia, and the Ranking of Human Rights by the Carter Administration, 1976–1980," *International History Review* 31, no. 4 (2009): 798–826.

[85] For the European context of partitions and coerced transfers, see G. Daniel Cohen, 'The "Human Rights Revolution" at Work: Displace Persons in Postwar Europe," and Lora Wildenthal, "Rudolf Laun and the Human Rights of Germans in Occupied and Early West Germany," in *Human Rights in the Twentieth Century* ed. Stefan-Ludwig Hoffmann (Cambridge: Cambridge University Press, 2011), 45–61, 125–46; Matthew Frank, *Making Minorities History: Population Transfer in Twentieth-Century Europe* (Oxford: Oxford University Press, 2017), 356–78.

people, occasioning over a million deaths and lasting bitterness. Older languages on the "standard of civilization" continued to shape international human rights law, including the newly enunciated standards of the 1946 UN General Assembly declaration on genocide.[86] Bringing these partitions into the frame allows the limits and contradictions of these postwar deliberations to be seen in a new light. Through meticulous historicization, Moses recasts the orthodoxy on key inter- and postwar historical actors, most notably Edvard Beneš in Czechoslovakia and Zionist icons Chaim Weizmann and Norman Bentwich.

Cindy Ewing's research (Chapter 7) connects the national rights debates of South Asia to the international project of human rights, placing early independence constitutions within the frame of an emerging global human rights vision. Constitutions were the site where the grand ambitions of the UDHR encountered the reality of national politics in Burma, Ceylon, and India, in the form of perennial tensions on minorities, family and personal status law, and in the formalization of limits on previously ambiguous state power. More proximate to the practical challenges of codifying a human rights system into a national reality, South Asian polities in the late 1940s prefigured some of the defining debates that the UN would encounter in its second decade, when it was seized with the difficulty of an equilibrium between individual and collective, and universal and particular.

Raphaélle Khan (Chapter 8) takes up the Indian perspective and its place in the international realm, primarily at the UN. Debates carried out domestically interacted in productive ways with the foundering global efforts of the 1950s and early 1960s. India, which had been compelled to face the tensions within human rights in its own nation-building process, was among the few states that had sustained and practical experience of placing self-determination, the welfare state, and collective minority protections in a human rights document.[87] As Khan demonstrates, the complexity of Indian interventions contradict any easy assumption that rights were no more than an instrumental weapon for securing sovereignty. Sovereignty itself was always insufficient, given that the rights of the large Indian transnational community were a common a target for discrimination, most visibly in South Africa. India's positions were not without contradiction, rendered acute in the inconsistent

---

[86] See brief discussion in Lydia H. Liu, "Shadows of Universalism: The Untold Story of Human Rights around 1948," *Critical Inquiry* 40, no. 4 (2014): 385–417.

[87] The general disposition of Indian internationalism, in the independence era, is further addressed in Manu Bhagavan, *The Peacemakers: India and the Quest for One World* (New Delhi: HarperCollins, 2012).

application of self-determination.[88] The orientation of Indian nationalist representatives, foremost the feminist and anti-colonial activist, Hansa Mehta, reflected neither unshackled utopian ambition nor narrow instrumentalism.

Steven Jensen (Chapter 9) draws Jamaica, and the Caribbean world, to the center of human rights developments in the 1960s. Much as South Asian nationalists had pursued a decade earlier, the newly independent state embarked on a conjoined project that embraced a national human rights agenda with international rights activism under the leadership of its energetic First Minister, Norman Manley. While its fruits would become evident across the late 1960s, Jamaica's period of greatest vitality occurred in the liminal period between full imperial control and full independence. In this protracted moment, when the shape of the prospective state, was being determined, Jamaica built a foundation which led it to a foremost place in the UN human rights system. Jamaica's influence here, which was decoupled from its strategic weight, revealed the limits of those human rights narratives which finds origins in the major Western democracies.

Michael Humphrey (Chapter 10) approaches the violence of empire over half-a-century later, in the nascent legal mechanisms to find accountability for historical human rights abuses in the terminal years of colonial rule.[89] Two colonial atrocities serve as an avenue to examine the long-deferred project of holding empire to account for abuses that were, like many, not remedied by the eventual achievement of sovereignty. In 2011, the Hague Civil Court awarded individual monetary compensation – and legal recognition – to the victims of the 1947 Rawagede massacre by Dutch authorities. In 2012, the British High Court found Mau Mau veterans could seek redress for the systematic policy of torture and mass arbitrary detention by the British across the 1950s. While there was scope for legal remedy for torture, the political

---

[88] On the contradictions rights, and in particular, self-determination, posed within anti-colonialism, see Lydia Walker, "Decolonization in the 1960s: On Legitimate and Illegitimate Nationalist Claims-making," *Past & Present* 242, no. 1 (2019): 227–64; Talbot Imlay, "International Socialism and Decolonisation during the 1950s: Competing Rights and the Postcolonial Order," *American Historical Review* 118, no. 4 (2013): 1105–32.

[89] Although there would be no serious legal remedy for decades, the acute tension between the rising professions of human rights as Western idealism, and escalating repression as contemporary reality, is well shown in studies of British campaigns in the Middle East and Africa, see Brian Drohan, *Brutality in an Age of Human Rights: Activism and Counterinsurgency at the End of the British Empire* (Ithaca, NY: Cornell University Press, 2017); Caroline Elkins, *Britain's Gulag: The Brutal End of Empire in Kenya* (London: Cape, 2005); David Anderson, *Histories of the Hanged: Britain's Dirty War in Kenya and the End of Empire* (London: Hachette, 2011).

sequelae of British repression were not so easily addressed – the Mau Mau were actively written out of the postcolonial polity in the effort to ensure a stable transition from colonial to national. Collective national narratives of anti-colonial struggle, defined as a singular people, elided these particular injustices experienced by individuals, and the persistence of harm well after self-determination had been secured.

Part III of the volume explores how colonial and neocolonial forces mobilized human rights in response to decolonization. Liberal imperialists and their successors played a critical role in mapping the boundaries, spatial and conceptual, of the universality that was being inscribed into the texts which supposedly set out the principles of the new postwar world. As imperialist and anti-imperialist, government and NGO, national citizen and transnational activist progressively discovered in the postcolonial era, custodianship of human rights, and the inscription of their priorities into that phrase, was the essence of the struggle. Radically dissimilar projects were transformed into advocacy within human rights discourse. Although France's well-upholstered mythologization as universalist liberator was an established fixture in international diplomacy, Miguel Bandeira Jerónimo and José Pedro Monteiro (Chapter 11) find another defensive custodianship of human rights in the efforts of Portuguese colonial and governmental ideologues, who sought to wield human rights as a reputational asset. Even as human rights crystallized in the 1950s as the foremost weapon against continued imperial rule, Portugal's diplomatic corps embraced the language as the licensing discourse for lusophone Africa with remarkable enthusiasm. The confidence with which the Salazar regime boasted of its imperial human rights credentials, despite fascist politics at home, reveals the ambidextrous quality rights language retained into the 1970s.

There was no shared movement toward a unified meaning of human rights, and the effort to refashion these older imperial claims into the ascendant language of human rights not unique to Salazar's Portugal, as Roland Burke (Chapter 12) demonstrates in the case of South Africa, which sought to recast the racial dictatorship of *apartheid* into a form compatible with the lexicon of human rights, self-determination, and multiculturalism. Beginning in the early 1960s, *apartheid*, rebadged "Separate Development'" and later "Plural Relations" paid linguistic deference to the new idealisms of rights, self-determination, and development. Acutely aware of the potency of human rights critique, the regime sought not so much to contest human rights norms, but to place its project as consistent with the post-1945 world. The continual metamorphosis of apartheid's global sale sits as powerful example of how discourses of freedom hold ample capacity for subversion.

Jay Winter (Chapter 13) distinguishes between the two forms of rights discourse in the writings and practice of the 1968 Nobel Laureate, René Cassin. These two variants of rights were evident in his capacity both as vice-president of the Conseil d'Etat from 1944 to 1960, and in his role as a French delegate to the United Nations from 1945, and as international human rights advocate in a number of organizations thereafter. The first position he adopted was advocacy of humanitarian rights, understood as falling within the laws of war. Victims of war, in or out of uniform, could properly demand reparation as a right and not as charity.[90] Overlaid upon these humanitarian rights were human rights, as articulated in the UDHR he helped to draft. Cassin's human rights set down a supra-national standard for state conduct in both peace and war, as compared to his category of a humanitarian right. The contradictions in where, and to whom, he applied these two categories, be it to Jewish refugees in Palestine as compared to Palestinian peoples, or to Algerians in the French empire, were inescapable, and sometimes paralyzing. Cassin's universalism fissioned into two when it came to violent conflicts between Europeans and non-Europeans.

Barbara Keys (Chapter 14) illustrates how, after anxiety on the American right over self-determination had receded, the managerial challenge of the country's own imperial legacies persisted. The logic of intervention was all but discredited by the course of the Vietnam War, but new mechanisms to pursue human rights proved problematic. Fueled by a decade of cumulative guilt over the war, and the grotesque abuses carried out by its South Vietnamese client, Congress sought redemption by linking aid to human rights conditions. As the USA removed itself from direct combat in the early 1970s, it also sought to cleanse itself of the conflict, and the decade of moral compromise that had shattered its self-image. Withdrawing the supply of assistance that underwrote an abusive regime abroad served as a symbolic means for reinfusing a sense of virtue at home.

Eleanor Davey (Chapter 15), surveying events a decade later, finds the implications of a contested humanitarianism still dawning upon the International Committee of the Red Cross (ICRC).[91] Wars of national liberation, which had only deepened in the years after Algeria, presented

---

[90] Equality of veterans benefits was a touchstone for debates in the interwar period, Michael Goebel, *Anti-Imperial Metropolis: Interwar Paris and the Seeds of Third World Nationalism* (Cambridge: Cambridge University Press, 2015), 107–8, 188–90, 236.

[91] Further background is given in Fabian Klose, "The Colonial Testing Ground: The ICRC and the Violent End of Empire," *Humanity* 2, no. 1 (2011): 107–26; Helen Kinsella, "Superfluous Injury and Unnecessary Suffering: National Liberation Movements and the Laws of War," *Political Power and Social Theory* 32 (2017): 205–31.

a fundamental threat to the precepts of humanitarianism, not simply a competition for ownership. When the ICRC's specialists gazed uneasily at Portuguese Africa, whether the claims of liberation could be set within the architecture of international humanitarian law involved more than philosophical disquisition. Informed by empirical inquiry among the liberation movements, the ICRC sought to reconcile the practice of the liberation movements in the 1970s and the spirit of Solferino. Their efforts were lent urgency by the context of a rising effort to "decolonize" the laws of war, which posed a looming threat to the ICRC's monopoly as arbiter of humanitarian norms. Whatever was resolved in Guinea would also have to be set alongside a growing chorus within the UN and the Organization of African Unity for a specially privileged class of struggle – that against racial dictatorship and colonialism.

Jessica Whyte (Chapter 16) further reveals the ambiguities of human rights discourse as an emancipatory instrument in her examination of the hyper-individualistic Liberté sans Frontières (LSF), the less luminous counterpart to humanitarian organization Médecins sans Frontières. During the first flourishing moment of neoliberalism in the 1980s, LSF promulgated a vision of the narrowest individual liberty – notionally against developmental dictatorships, which were myriad and egregious in their abuses – but with implications that undercut any credible nation building project. LSF's evangelism found purpose in market purity, as opposed to human well-being. The intense antipathy of LSF's members not merely to totalitarian state formation, but any serious attempt at securing economic sovereignty and material security for peoples of the Third World, was the mirror image of the pathological statism of failed postcolonial authoritarians.[92]

In recent interventions on the history of rights, the era of decolonization and its legacies has been one of the defining exhibits, one which recasts the trajectory of all of which came before and after. Yet the content of human rights and their operation emerge as so contested and versatile that a discrete transitional moment, where anti-colonialism was superseded by human rights, ceases to hold as an effective schema for analysis.[93] Human rights ascended as a language for moral claims, and the epochal ideological conflicts of the twentieth century were reset within it. Sovereignty, nationhood, economic justice, humanity, and

---

[92] Cf. the statist project of global economic redistribution, to bolster Third World sovereignty, Roland Burke, discussed in "Competing for the Last Utopia? The NIEO, Human Rights, and the World Conference for the International Women's Year, Mexico City, June 1975," *Humanity* 6, no. 1 (2015): 47–61.

[93] Frederick Cooper, "Afterword: Social Rights and Human Rights in the Time of Decolonisation," *Humanity* 3, no. 3 (2012): 477–8.

individual freedom were not abandoned for human rights, but repartitioned. These became tensions inside human rights, not rivals to it.

Throughout the 2010s, much scholarly energy has been devoted to
abstract questions about the philosophical content and implications of
human rights histories or, more profoundly still, the exhaustion of its
utility as an approach.[94] This volume demonstrates that even supremely
erudite grand generalization understates the richness of human rights
history, particularly addressing an intrinsically diverse subject: empire,
anti-colonialism, and rights. These scholars trace so many variegated
cases of human rights, shaped by different contexts, and deployed with
a distinct set of attached meanings – often overlapping, but driven by
their own logic. In so doing, their contributions show the power of
particular histories of a universalistic discourse, rather than seeking to
subordinate particular discourses to a universalizing historical scheme.

Human rights were embedded in anti-colonial freedom movements
and at least in part, constitutive of its hopes. In turn, the contours of the
human rights concept were defined and sharpened by a global, distributed
endeavor to grant meaning to the term. As jurists in newly independent
nations drafted their plans for freedom, they conceived of their work as
part of more than a national effort. Indigenous organizers discovered
human rights as a bridge to a larger cohort of activism and also discovered
its deficiencies for the cause of Indigenous peoples. The transnational
indigenous rights movement would eventually expand the concept of
human rights and work to remedy its silences. When approached at close
range, the projects – and conflicts – charted across this volume were the
translation of the universalistic promise into universally meaningful claim.
Even the UDHR, for all of its cross-cultural sources and earnest, if often
hesitant, commitment to inclusion, could only provide the outlines of a
globally relevant universalism. In wielding the language of human rights,
and finding its application, these campaigns against empire began to
populate that vision with a more universal collection of experiences and
perspectives.

---

[94] The connection between a context of a deep political crisis, and one of historiography, is
at least implied in these discussions. In her defense of human rights, written in a context
of renascent authoritarianism, appalling inequality, and florid racial nationalism,
Kathyrn Sikkink invokes "the longer history of human rights" for "a more positive
message that could help sustain" activism, see Sikkink, *Evidence for Hope: Making
Human Rights Work in the 21st Century* (Princeton, NJ: Princeton University Press,
2017), 7.

Part I

Anti-Colonial Struggles and the Right to Self-Determination

1   Seeking the Political Kingdom
Universal Human Rights and the Anti-colonial Movement in Africa

Bonny Ibhawoh

Amidst the anti-colonial movement of the 1950s, Kwame Nkrumah, the nationalist politician who became the first prime minister of independent Ghana, outlined the key principle of his anti-colonial campaign. Rejecting the idea of gradual decolonization contingent on his country's preparedness for self-rule, Nkrumah demanded immediate political independence from British rule. He urged his countrymen and women: "Seek ye first the political kingdom, and all other things shall be added unto you."[1] His reference was the biblical injunction in Matthew 6:33, "Seek ye first the Kingdom of God and his righteousness; and all things shall be added to you." Nkrumah went on to stress the primacy of the struggle for national liberation, stating, "we prefer independence with danger and uncertainties to servitude in tranquility."[2] For Nkrumah and many African nationalist leaders of this era, the political struggle for self-determination took precedence over all other matters confronting colonized peoples. Nkrumah's quest for the "political kingdom" symbolized a tendency to view self-rule as the paramount rights question in the colonial state. In his words, "self-determination is a means of further realization of our social, economic and cultural potentialities. It is political freedom that dictates the pace of economic and social progress."[3] For Nkrumah, the collective right to self-government was a prerequisite to fulfilling other rights aspirations.

The primacy accorded national self-determination by those living under colonial domination shaped their interpretations of human rights. Self-determination alluded not only to political independence but also to the capacity of people to choose their own paths to economic and social development. For African nationalist leaders of the era, collective

[1] Kwame Nkrumah, *The Autobiography of Kwame Nkrumah* (Nelson: London, 1957), 146.
[2] George M. Houser, *No One Can Stop the Rain: Glimpses of Africa's Liberation Struggle* (London: Pilgrim Press, 1989), 69.
[3] *Gold Coast Weekly Review*, July 20, 1955. Quoted in Martin L. Kilson, "Nationalism and Social Classes in British West Africa," *Journal of Politics* 20 (1958): 380.

political freedom was the most fundamental right. "What do we mean when we talk of freedom?" Julius Nyerere of Tanzania asked in one of his many political treatises. His answer expressed a hierarchy of rights in which "national freedom" and collective economic and social well-being took precedence over individual civil liberties. He stated

> First, there is national freedom; that is, the ability of the citizens of Tanzania to determine their own future, and to govern themselves without interference from non-Tanzanians. Second, there is freedom from hunger, disease, and poverty. And third, there is personal freedom for the individual; that is, his right to live in dignity and equality with all others, his right to freedom of speech, freedom to participate in the making of all decisions which affect his life.[4]

This ordering of freedoms that prioritized the collective right to self-determination over individual liberties stood in sharp contrast to the ordering of universal human rights at its mid-twentieth-century moment of inception at the United Nations. Within this dominant "generations of rights" framework, first generation of individual-centered civil and political rights come before second-generation economic and social rights and third-generation collective solidarity rights. Shaped by Enlightenment notions of liberal individualism, the twentieth-century crises of nationalism in Europe, and postwar Great Powers politics, universal human rights came to mean primarily, individual-centered entitlements. To be sure, this ordering of rights was always contested – by socialist arguments for the primacy of economic and social rights, and by anti-colonial activists who prioritized the collective right to self-determination over other rights.

In this chapter, I examine the politics of rights prioritization in the age of empire and decolonization. While Western statesmen or stateswomen negotiating an international human rights order at the UN privileged individual civil liberties as the primary human rights, African nationalists campaigning against colonial domination prioritized the collective right to self-determination as the first human rights. African political leaders were skeptical of discussions of individual state-centered rights at the UN orchestrated by the same European imperial powers that were actively denying Africans the right to self-determination. They rejected imperial defensives at the UN and the attempts to delink national liberation struggles in the colonies from the emergent universal human rights movement. Instead, they framed self-determination in terms of the collective rights of peoples and as a fundamental human right. Their

---

[4] Julius Nyerere, *Man and Development: Binadamu Na Maendeleó* (Oxford: Oxford University Press, 1974), 25.

collective rights agenda would be progressively incorporated into the international human rights system with the emergence of a postcolonial UN. Rather than simply marking the *succession* or *displacement* of paradigmatic individual-centered state-centric human rights, I read anti-colonial prioritization of collective rights as deliberative assertions of an alternative human rights order, a counter-ordering of rights that emerged from anti-colonial struggles and the misgivings of colonized peoples about "universal" human rights in the age of empire. This is evident in the writings of African nationalist leaders such as Jomo Kenyatta who decried Britain's denial of "elementary human rights" to Kenyans and Nnamdi Azikiwe who called on Africans not to "accept as their destiny, the denial of human rights."[5]

Turning Points and Breakthrough Moments

Human rights scholarship has been critiqued for being obsessed with the notion of breakthroughs moments and paying less attention to historical processes and trends over time.[6] Indeed, recent scholarship seems to converge around identifying seminal moments and turning points in the development of human rights. Key debates have tuned on human rights genealogy and the intellectual and political provenance of rights as idea, discourse, and movement.[7] Interest has also centered on how to interpret the historical development of human rights, whether in terms of progress, continuities, or ruptures. New transnational human rights histories have challenged earlier grand "textbook narratives" of human rights whose status as uncontested truths rested on endless repetition.[8] These mostly teleological grand narratives trace a history of human rights running

---

[5] Jomo Kenyatta, *Facing Mount Kenya: The Tribal Life of the Gikuyu* (New York: Vintage, 1965), 189–90; Nnamdi Azikiwe, *Zik: A Selection from the Speeches of Nnamdi Azikiwe* (Cambridge: Cambridge University Press, 1961), 50.

[6] Steven L. B. Jensen and Roland Burke, "From the Normative to the Transnational: Methods in the Study of Human Rights History," in *Research Methods in Human Rights: A Handbook*, ed. Bård-Anders Andreassen, Hans-Otto Sano, and Siobhán McInerney-Lankford (Northampton: Edward Elgar, 2017), 124.

[7] For some exemplary works, see Louis Henkin, *The Rights of Man Today* (Boulder, CO: Westview Press, 1978); Paul Gordon Lauren, *The Evolution of International Human Rights: Visions Seen* (Philadelphia, University of Pennsylvania Press 2003); John M. Headley, *The Europeanization of the World: On the Origins of Human Rights and Democracy* (Princeton, NJ: Princeton University Press, 2007); Lynn Hunt, *Inventing Human Rights: A History* (New York: Norton, 2008); Elizabeth Borgwardt, *A New Deal for the World: America's Vision for Human Rights* (Cambridge, MA: Belknap Press of Harvard University Press, 2005).

[8] Miia Halme-Tuomisaari and Pamela Slotte, "Revisiting the Origins of Human Rights: Introduction," in *Revisiting the Origins of Human Rights*, ed. Miia Halme-Tuomisaari and Pamela Slotte (Cambridge: Cambridge University Press, 2015), 11.

seamlessly through defining events such as the Magna Carta, the British Revolution and Bill of Rights, the US Revolution, the French Revolution and the Declaration of the Rights of Man, the Holocaust, and post–World War II internationalism. A key critique of these narratives is that they are based almost exclusively on events that occurred within the boundaries of the European world. There is little or no attention to the non-European world in these narratives, which also tends to marginalize the histories of imperial violence and colonization.[9] Another critique is that these grand narratives represent an instrumental view of human rights history, imposing coherence, continuity, and closure on the *longue durée* history of human rights. The methodological tools of legal positivism and textual formalism in legal disciplines, where most of these early narratives emerged, inevitably produced representative and interpretative "blind spots" in human rights history. Global political developments, including the mid-twentieth-century anti-colonial movements and decolonization that were transformative historical developments with worldwide ramifications, were deemed to have had no autonomous impact on the chronology, substance, and precedents in the evolution of human rights.[10]

More recent transnational histories have sought to remedy these flaws. Historians now recognize that we can do much to further our understanding of global political discourse by not taking the term "human rights" or its genealogy for granted.[11] We can produce more representative histories by carefully attending to different rights claims and by locating those claims in local political and social contexts. Insights from recent scholarship have transitioned from a singular narrative of human rights history toward a constellation of human rights histories with complementarity of global, regional, and thematic accounts. As human rights historiography become finer in its granularity, it has also become more attentive to the varied meanings with the term "human rights," the diverse expressions of the idea in local vernacular, the shifts in those meanings over time, and the problematic nature of the claim to universality. Human rights histories are becoming less triumphalist and more inclined to differentiate between various emancipatory campaigns across time and space.[12]

---

[9] José-Manuel Barreto, "Imperialism and Decolonization as Scenarios of Human Rights History," in *Human Rights from a Third World Perspective: Critique*, ed. José-Manuel Barreto (Newcastle upon Tyne: Cambridge Scholars, 2013), 20.

[10] Jensen and Burke, "From the Normative to the Transnational," 119, 123.

[11] Kenneth Cmiel, "The Recent History of Human Rights," *American Historical Review* 109, no. 1 (February 2004): 126.

[12] Jensen and Burke, "From the Normative to the Transnational," 120.

Transnational human rights histories have shown that rights discourses and movements have facilitated progressive change; but they have also operated historically to insulate power and sustain structures of ideological, cultural, economic, and political hegemony. The language of international human rights has been used to institutionalize, legitimize, normalize, and reproduce existing relations of domination.[13] It is essential, therefore, that we pay attention not only to the emancipatory outcomes of rights talk but also to the ways in which rights have been used to make claims and counterclaims in defense of particular interests, and against others, at different moments. By expanding the defining locus of human rights history to the imperial and postimperial eras, transnational histories draw attention to the role of non-Western actors, ideas, and struggles in the development of international human rights. Where earlier grand narratives tended to be drawn along European frontiers, new histories show how developments in the Global South shaped the human rights movement. It is now well established that the international politics of decolonization had significant repercussions creating international and regional human rights standards. What remains uncertain, however, is the more specific place of local anti-colonial struggles in the broader human rights story.

Placing Anti-colonial Struggles

African history, long treated as a footnote in the global human rights story, is gaining more attention in the bourgeoning historiography.[14] However, assessing the place of anti-colonialism in the global human rights story continues to be complicated by two factors. The first has to do with the dominance of a "hegemonic Eurocentric understanding of human rights" that undergirds much of human rights historiography.[15] The second relates to the sources and methods preferred by historians in constructing human rights histories. Human rights embody a set of values; the most important are historically the notions of human dignity, freedom, and equality. International human rights, as we understand

---

[13] Nicola Perugini and Neve Gordon, *The Human Right to Dominate* (Oxford: Oxford University Press, 2015).

[14] Fabian Klose, *Human Rights in the Shadow of Colonial Violence: The Wars of Independence in Kenya and Algeria* (Philadelphia: University of Pennsylvania Press, 2013); Saul Dubow, *South Africa's Struggle for Human Rights* (Athens: Ohio University Press, 2012); Bonny Ibhawoh, *Human Rights in Africa* (Cambridge: Cambridge University Press, 2018).

[15] José-Manuel Barreto, "Introduction: Decolonial Strategies and Dialogue in the Human Rights Field," in Barreto, *Human Rights from a Third World Perspective*, 24.

them today, are not only individual claims against authorial power but also extend to a broad spectrum of collective rights claims anchored on moral obligations that people have toward each other. The international human rights regime spans the gamut of individual civil liberties outlined in the Universal Declaration of Human Rights (UDHR) and the UN Covenant on Civil and Political Rights to the collective rights of peoples to self-determination in the 1960 UN Declaration on Decolonization and the communal rights entitlements affirmed in the 1966 Covenant on Economic, Social and Cultural Rights. Narratives of individual-centered rights, which inform much of human rights scholarship and orients activism, privilege certain interpretations of human rights, and overlook historic tensions in the meanings and ordering of rights.

In human rights historiography, the vocabulary of "human rights" remains inextricably linked with possessive individualism, operating as the ideological groundwork for the rise of capitalism and mass democracy.[16] This interpretation of "universal human rights," is framed as paradigmatic. However, in the age of empire, interpretations of human rights centered primarily on the collective rights of peoples appealed more to those living under colonial domination than a notion of human rights premised on narrow possessive individualism. In Africa, nationalists and anti-colonial activists articulated an alternate vision of human rights that prioritized the collective rights of people to self-determination over atomized individual liberties. The relationship between self-determination within anti-colonialism and individual-centered "human rights" was not simply one of succession or displacement; it was also one of contestation and repudiation.

The second complication of placing anti-colonialism within human rights history arises from the tendency of historians to over-rely on more easily accessible Western records and metropolitan archives. Despite the recognition that international human rights history cannot be written credibly from sources that are exclusively and narrowly limited to Western thought and thinkers, the human rights story has been constructed as a markedly more Western story than the full historical record merits.[17] There are limits to what UN records and Western archives can tell us about the place of anti-colonialism and decolonization in the human rights story. Debates on the colonial question occurred occasionally at

---

[16] Martti Koskenniemi, "Foreword: History of Human Rights as Political Intervention in the Present," in Halme-Tuomisaari and Slotte, *Revisiting the Origins of Human Rights*, xiv.

[17] Jensen and Burke, "From the Normative to the Transnational," 125; Jean Quataert, "Review of *The International Human Rights Movement: A History*," *Journal of Human Rights* 13, no. 4 (2013): 537.

the UN, but it was in the colonies that the decolonization process played out. For the first two decades of the UN, most African countries were under colonial domination and unrepresented at the organization. African political leaders were largely excluded from early debates about fashioning "universal" human rights. The limitations of UN records and textual formalism in constructing transnational human rights histories of this period are obvious. To gain the perspectives of the colonized, we must shift attention to the informal spaces to which they were marginalized in the age of empire.

Among anti-colonial activists, big power politics and imperial defensiveness at the UN engendered deep skepticism of the postwar international human rights agenda. African political leaders were not persuaded by discussions of individual state-centered rights at the UN orchestrated by the same European imperial powers that were actively denying Africans the right to self-determination. African insistence on prioritizing collective solidarity rights over individual liberties cannot simply be considered as attempts to displace paradigmatic human rights. It is also simplistic if not disingenuous, to explain their counter-ordering of rights in terms of a new postcolonial UN majority emptying human rights of its original meaning or hijacking it for authoritarian political agenda.[18] African political leaders confronting colonial repression at home and imperial defensiveness aboard, framed collective rights as the most fundamental human rights mainly because this ordering of rights was more relevant to their lived political and social realities.

Anti-colonial activists were not alone in challenging the assumed primacy of individual-centered civil and political rights. The position that economic rights constituted the "primary rights for survival" – instead of belonging to the second generation of rights, as has become the prevailing view – was a view also forcefully forwarded by late nineteenth-century socialist activists in the United Kingdom. Rather than being a momentary challenge to paradigmatic "first-generation" civil and political rights, socialist insistence on the primacy of economic rights was a central tension characterizing the making of rights claims over a much longer period.[19]

---

[18] Dore Gold, *Tower of Babble: How the United Nations Has Fueled Global Chaos* (New York: Crown Forum, 2013), 33.

[19] Gregory Claeys, "Socialism and the Language of Rights: The Origins and Implications of Economic Rights," in Halme-Tuomisaari and Slotte, *Revisiting the Origins of Human Rights*, 228. Claeys argues that UK socialists "prioritized rights claims based upon actual labour and its produce rather than abstract claims rooted in need."

The Colonial Limits of "Universal" Human Rights

Several studies have drawn attention to the role of power and interest at the UN in general and the erection of the postwar human rights regime in particular.[20] They show that far from a pure quest to establish a normatively objective universal morality, the position taken by states in the early debates about human rights were influenced by propagandistic and strategic geopolitical motives aimed at projecting domestic values into the international arena. This allowed the United States and victorious European states "to occupy the moral high ground by day and sleep the sleep of the just by night."[21] The UN was an arena where all initiatives, even on human rights questions, followed a decidedly political logic and sprang from complex state interests.

The main concern of European statesmen and stateswomen in early discussions about human rights at the UN was postwar international peace and security, and the balance of power in Europe. The "colonial question" sometimes complicated this agenda, but it was not a primary concern. At the first general assembly in 1946, the UN passed a resolution on "non-self-governing peoples" which expressed awareness of the problems and political aspirations of colonized people and recognition that the colonial question was a "vital concern to the peace and general welfare of the world community."[22] In general, however, before the 1960s, the UN Security Council shied away from racial or colonial matters. Nationalist liberation movements especially by nonwhites in European-controlled areas were treated as the domestic affairs of controlling European power and not subject to UN intervention. The work of the UN Human Rights Commission in its early days consisted of underlying struggles over what rights to include and which ones to leave out.[23]

Discussions about colonies occasionally became a source of embarrassment for imperial powers, but that did not deter resolute rejection of human rights proposals that were considered political interference in

---

[20] Mark Mazower, "The Strange Triumph of Human Rights, 1933–1950," *Historical Journal* 47 (2004): 379–99; Mark Mazower, *No Enchanted Palace: The End of Empire and the Ideological Origins of the United Nations* (Princeton, NJ: Princeton University Press, 2009); Kirsten Sellars, *The Rise and Rise of Human Rights* (Stroud: Sutton, 2002).

[21] Sellars, *Rise and Rise of Human Rights*, 65.

[22] United Nations, General Assembly Resolutions on Non-self-governing peoples. A/RES/9 (I) of February 9, 1946, accessed January 12, 2018, http://research.un.org/en/docs/decolonization/keydocs

[23] Johannes Morsink, *The Universal Declaration of Human Rights: Origins. Drafting and Intent* (Philadelphia: University of Pennsylvania Press, 1999), 12–14.

colonial affairs. For example, a 1953 proposal by Arab and Asian states for Tunisian independence on the basis of the UN principle of the right to self-determination, was rejected as an interference into France's domestic affairs.[24] There could also be no serious debate on political issues such as the liberation war in Algeria. Despite compelling evidence of atrocities and gross human rights violations, Western powers at the UN supported the French position that the North African conflict fell under France's domestic jurisdiction. South Africa's racism would be debated mainly in terms of the treatment of people of Indian origin because apartheid was viewed as an internal problem.

Anti-colonial activists were keenly aware of the politics of imperial self-interest in discussions about human rights at the UN. They highlighted the contradictions in the discourse of human rights by imperial countries and the realities of state repression and violence in the colonies.[25] They noted, for example, that neither the emergent doctrine of universal human rights nor the more established Geneva Conventions on the Conduct of War had any significant impact on British military campaigns against the Mau Mau in Kenya or the French war against the Algerian National Liberation Front (FLN) in Algeria. Although the European Convention came into effect in Kenya in 1953, just over a year into the Mau Mau insurgency, it had little impact on the conflict.[26] The atrocities perpetrated in these campaigns marked some of the most egregious human rights violations of the twentieth century.[27] Yet, both conflicts came up only marginally in discussions about human rights and the colonial question at the UN. Even less impactful on colonial conditions was the European Convention on Human Rights which the UK ratified in 1951 and Belgium in 1955. The European Christian conservatives who authored the Convention saw human rights as emerging from a shared regional culture nominally Christian. Despite the rhetoric of inalienable "rights and freedoms," such rights were not considered appropriate for all persons everywhere. In particular, they were deemed

---

[24] United States Department of State, *The Department of State Bulletin*, Office of Public Communication Bureau of Public Affairs, 28 (1953): 396.

[25] Klose, *Human Rights in the Shadow of Colonial Violence*, 6.

[26] Huw Bennett, *Fighting the Mau: The British Army and Counter-Insurgency in the Kenya Emergency* (Cambridge: Cambridge University Press, 2013), 80.

[27] For Kenya, see Caroline Elkins, *Imperial Reckoning: The Untold Story of Britain's Gulag in Kenya* (New York: Henry Holt, 2005); David Anderson, *Histories of the Hanged: The Dirty War in Kenya and the End of Empire* (New York: Norton, 2005); Wunyabari Maloba, *Mau and Kenya: An Analysis of a Peasant Revolt* (Bloomington: Indiana University Press, 1998). For Algeria, see Alistair Horne, *A Savage War of Peace: Algeria 1954–1962* (London: Macmillan, 1977); Martin Evans, *Algeria: France's Undeclared War* (Oxford: Oxford University Press, 2012).

inapplicable to nonwhite European colonies, not least those Winston Churchill as British Under-Secretary of State described as the "African aboriginal, for whom civilization has no charms."[28]

Although anti-colonial activists drew on an emergent lexicon of universal human rights in their struggles for self-determination, they doubted its transformative potential. They were not alone in their skepticism of the new international human rights agenda. The UN's creators envisioned a world organization that would address rights violations but also protect the interests of empire. The acceptance of human rights at this moment was conditioned by pessimism among the great powers such that it would have little practical effect.[29] The South African statesman Jan Smuts, who introduced the concept of "human rights" into the UN Charter, remained a firm believer in white supremacy and could not countenance extending the human rights principles he so vigorously championed at the UN to the nonwhite populations of his own country. Delegates of the white minority South African government at the UN strongly opposed discussions about racial discrimination in their country, seeing it an undue interference in their internal affairs and a violation of sovereignty.

The adoption of the UDHR in 1948 did not elicit much excitement in the colonies. Doubt and cynicism arose partly from the sense that it took the suffering of "whites" during World War II to jolt world powers into action, whereas colonial atrocities had left the world indifferent. It did not escape African independence activists that colonial massacres and atrocities against Indigenous people in the Congo and in South West Africa (Namibia) described as the "first genocide of the twentieth century"[30] did not garner enough outrage and indignation to trigger a rights revolution.[31] When Japan, fresh from its victories in the Pacific, pressed for including a language promoting racial equality in the Covenant of the League, it received a cold response from the United States and other key European powers. This was in spite of a majority vote for the proposal from delegates at the Paris Peace Conference and calls for the inclusion of a statement on *human rights* in the Covenant.[32]

---

[28] Quoted in Marco Duranti, *The Conservative Human Rights Revolution: European Identity, Transnational Politics, and the Origins of the European Convention* (Oxford: Oxford University Press, 2017), 126.

[29] Mazower, *No Enchanted Palace*, 30–5.

[30] Jeremy Sarkin-Hughes, *Colonial Genocide and Reparations Claims in the 21st Century: The Socio-Legal Context of Claims under International Law by the Herero against Germany for Genocide in Namibia, 1904–1908* (Westport, CN: Praeger, 2009), 5.

[31] *West African Pilot*, March 13, 1945, 8.

[32] Paul Gordon Lauren, *Power and Prejudice: The Politics and Diplomacy of Radical Discrimination* (Boulder, CO: Westview Press, 1988), 98.

Responding to Japanese proposals for a racial equality clause at the 1919 Versailles Conference, British statesman Arthur Balfour stated that it was "true that all men of a particular nation are created equal, but not that a man in Central Africa was created equal to a European."[33] Japan was eventually convinced to omit the word "race" from its proposal altogether. The United States also demanded that "equality" be stricken and that any mention of justice be placed in the preamble rather than an article, which might imply enforcement.[34] Wilsonian rhetoric of self-determination and the promising human rights impulses of post–World War I internationalism did not coalesce into a global rights movement. That would wait until Europe encountered its own era of tyranny and atrocities. As historian Mark Mazower put it "such was the shock of being subjected to a regime of unprecedented and unremitting violence that in the space of eight years following the war, a sea-change took place in European's political attitudes, and they rediscovered the virtues of democracy."[35]

The sudden rediscovery of human rights and democracy by European imperial powers was met with skepticism in the colonies. British hurried efforts to enact a constitutional bill of rights fashioned after the European Convention in the colonies in the late 1950s did not gain wide support. Some African leaders saw this late rhetorical embrace of human rights as an imperial strategy to douse the fervor of nationalist anti-colonial movements and a means of achieving decolonization on terms favorable to European colonists and settlers. Swazi politicians thought that pre-independence British insistence on enacting a bill of rights was disingenuous and showed lack of confidence in Africans. Why, they asked, had no one heard of a bill of rights while the British were firmly in command? "But now that they are withdrawing, we hear a great deal about them."[36] To these Swazi politicians, the imperial instrumentality of human rights was manifest.

A Lexicon for Liberation

In the age of empire, African political leaders were also skeptical of the UN's peace and security agenda. They were less interested in the

---

[33] A. J. Balfour, quoted in Adom Getachew, *Worldmaking after Empire: The Rise and Fall of Self-Determination* (Princeton, NJ: Princeton University Press, 2019), 22.

[34] Vernon D. Johnson, "The Structural Causes of Anticolonial Revolutions in Africa," *Alternatives: Global, Local, Political*, 18, no. 2 (1993), 206. For a detailed account of how the race issue was handled at the peace talks and the League of Nations, see Lauren, *Power and Prejudice.*

[35] *Dark Continent: Europe's Twentieth Century* (New York: Vintage, 2000), 140.

[36] Quoted in Denis Cowen, "Human Rights in Contemporary Africa," *Natural Law Forum* 9, no. 1 (1964): 11.

specific procedures for assuring world peace than in the reaffirmation of faith in fundamental human rights, in the dignity and worth of the human person, in the equal rights of men and women and of all nations.[37] They noted with disapproval that the framers of the UN Charter in 1945 first declared their determination to "save succeeding generations from the scourge of war" and then only secondly to "reaffirm faith in fundamental human rights, in the dignity and worth of the human person, in the equal rights of men and women and of nations large and small."[38] Judging by their policies, attitudes, and stands, nationalist leaders in Africa and Asia would have reversed the order of affirmation. They would have affirmed, first, "faith in fundamental human rights [and] in the dignity and worth of the human person" and only secondly their determination "to save succeeding generations from the scourge of war."[39]

As the politics of imperial defensiveness became evident in UN debates, the engagement of African leaders with international human rights discourse served two purposes. The first was to highlight the hypocrisy and contradictions of European imperial positions on human rights questions. "Those who call themselves protectors of civilized standards," Julius Nyerere wrote in 1958 "can ignore this at their own cost, that under the Declaration of Human Rights, Africans are people too, all of them, not just the most advanced ones."[40] The second purpose of nationalist engagement with human rights discourse was to reinforce longstanding struggles for independence with the new legitimatizing lexicon of human rights. In the changed international geopolitical landscape of the post–World War II world, European imperial powers favored gradual decolonization – what British officials described as the "progressive evolution of self-government" in the colonies.[41] A new crop of African nationalists countered with demands for immediate unconditional independence based on the fundamental collective human right to self-determination.

The Guinean nationalist Sekou Touré expressed his political credo of dignity and equality for Africans and campaign against French colonial rule both in terms of the French Declaration of the Rights of Man and the

---

[37] Ali A. Mazrui, "The United Nations and Some African Political Attitudes," *International Organization* 18, no. 3 (Summer, 1964), 501.

[38] United Nations, Charter of the United Nations, www.un.org/en/charter-united-nations, accessed May 7, 2017.

[39] Mazrui, "United Nations and Some African Political Attitudes," 509.

[40] "The Entrenchment of Privilege," *Africa South* 2, no. 2 (1958): 85–90.

[41] John Hargreaves, *The End of Colonial Rule in West Africa: Essays in Contemporary History* (London: Macmillan, 1979), 51.

UDHR.[42] In Algeria, Ferhat Abbas the FLN leader drew on the wartime discourse of the right to self-determination to articulate political demands for independence. In his manifesto in 1943, *Manifeste du Peuple Algérien*, Abbas referenced the right of people to choose their own government affirmed in the Atlantic Charter. After France's defeat in World War II, he asked the Vichy government to implement comprehensive reforms in Algeria in line with new global norms that warranted the redefining of the relationship between France and its colonies. In response to pressure by French authorities on Muslim Algerians to actively participate in the fight against Hitler for the liberation of their "Arabian brothers" in Tunisia, Abbas stated that if the war was being fought for the liberation of people of all races and religions as proclaimed by the Allied leaders, Muslim Algerians would be willing to commit themselves wholeheartedly to this endeavor. However, he linked participation in the war to specific political demands, one of which was the convening of a conference where elected Muslim representatives would negotiate political, economic, and social equality for the Muslim population. Abbas also demanded the abolition of colonial repression, the right of self-determination for all peoples, and an Algerian constitution anchored in human rights.[43]

In the Gold Coast (Ghana), a vigorous anti-colonial campaign led by the charismatic Kwame Nkrumah rejected British wartime reforms and demanded complete independence from British rule. A central theme in Nkrumah's anti-colonialism was social equality and political self-determination. "The peoples of the colonies," he wrote, "know precisely what they want. They wish to be free and independent, to be able to feel themselves . . . equal with all other peoples, and to work out their own destiny without interference."[44] It was in this context that Nkrumah urged his countrymen and women to prioritize the cause of national liberation – to seek first the political kingdom before all other things. Because the "political kingdom" could only be achieved through collective struggle, solidarity rights had to be prioritized over individual rights. In this phase of state building, the collective right to self-government was considered a prerequisite to fulfilling other rights aspirations. Nkrumah also highlighted the contradictions in British rhetorical support for human rights and its policies in the colonies. He questioned why Britain considered an election based on universal franchise and constitutional

[42] John Marcum, "Sékou Touré & Guinea," *Africa Today* 6, no. 5 (1959): 6.
[43] Klose, *Human Rights in the Shadow of Colonial Violence*, 24–5.
[44] Kwame Nkrumah, *Revolutionary Path* (London: Panaf, 1980), 40.

rights a prerequisite for independence in the Gold Coast but ruled it out for white-minority-ruled Southern Rhodesia.[45]

In Nigeria, the nationalist politician Nnamdi Azikiwe used the platform for his wide-circulating newspaper *West African Pilot* to highlight the contradictions and illogicalities of imperial human rights discourse. His positions on these questions were shaped by his experiences of colonial oppression at home and racial discrimination in the United States where he studied at black universities in the 1930s. Encounters with African-American intellectuals at Howard University and Lincoln University shaped his anti-colonial politics and views of rights questions. Azikiwe linked the struggles for self-determination in the colonies with US President Roosevelt's four freedoms, the Atlantic Charter, and, later, the debates about universal human rights at the UN. He decried British colonial rule as a "benevolent despotism" that committed the African to political servitude and economic serfdom. He deplored the hypocrisy of European imperialists who espoused political freedoms and social equality in Europe and at the UN, but were ambivalent about extending these rights to Africans.[46] Following Prime Minister Churchill's statement that the principles of self-determination outlined in the Atlantic Charter applied only to Europe and not to British colonies, Azikiwe wrote that it was imperative for Africans to prepare their own political blueprint rather than rely on "those who are too busy preparing their own."[47] In 1943 he published his *Political Blueprint of Nigeria* in which he outlined a rights-based vision for Nigeria's independence which referenced the Atlantic Charter and Woodrow Wilson's Fourteen Points, using both to support his uniquely anti-colonial rights agenda.

At a time when European colonial powers sought to drive a wedge between self-determination struggles in the colonies and discussions about universal human rights at the UN, Azikiwe insisted on the fundamental interrelatedness of both ideas. He countered British attempts to delink national liberation struggles in the colonies from the emergent universal human rights movement. "The people of Nigeria," he insisted, "cannot continue to accept as their destiny the denial of human rights. We, too, have a right to live, to enjoy freedom, and to pursue happiness like other human beings."[48] Azikiwe also led the drafting of the Freedom

---

[45] Geoffrey Bing, *Reap the Whirlwind: An Account of Kwame Nkrumah's Ghana from 1950 to 1966* (London: MacGibbon & Kee, 1968), 167.

[46] Azikiwe, *Zik*, 82, 159.

[47] Nnamdi Azikiwe, *Political Blueprint of Nigeria* (Lagos: African Book Company, 1945), 72.

[48] Azikiwe, *Zik*, 50.

Charter, which served as a manifesto for his pro-independence political platform.[49] The Charter affirmed the right of all peoples to choose the form of government under which they may live. It also condemned slavery, servitude, and imperialism; affirmed the equality of all persons; the right to basic education and healthcare and even the right to recreation and leisure. He urged representatives from Liberia, one of only three African member countries of the UN at its founding, to be the voices of people of color and the "degraded and oppressed races in the world."[50]

In Tanganyika, Julius Nyerere referenced frequently the repression and injustices of colonial rule as derogations from basic human dignity and fundamental human rights. He stated that the anti-colonial struggle was a movement for fundamental human rights, based on the belief in the equality of human beings, in their rights and duties as citizens.[51] Similarly, the Kenyan nationalist leader Jomo Kenyatta framed oppressive British policies in terms of collective human rights violations. Kenyatta was particularly critical of Britain's 1930 "Kenya White Paper" which declared that the mission of Britain was to "work continuously for the training and education of the Africans toward higher intellectual, moral, and economic level."[52] "It is beyond our comprehension," Kenyatta argued

to see how a people can reach so-called "higher level" while they are denied the most elementary *human rights* to self-expression, freedom of speech, the right to form social organizations to improve their condition and, above all, the rights to move freely in their own country. These are the rights that the Gikuyu people had enjoyed from time immemorial until the arrival of the "mission of Great Britain."[53]

Instead of advancing "toward a higher intellectual, moral, and economic level," Kenyatta claimed that the African had been reduced to a state of serfdom, his initiative in social, economic, and political structure had been denied, and he had been subjected to the most inferior position in society.[54] Even though the voices of these indigenous political leaders

---

[49] National Council for Nigeria and the Cameroons "Freedom Charter," reprinted in *West African Pilot*, January 4, 1949.
[50] Azikiwe, *Zik*, 60.
[51] Julius Nyerere, *Freedom and Unity: Uhuru na umoja; A Selection from Writings and Speeches, 1952–65* (London: Oxford University Press, 1967), 76.
[52] L. C. A. Knowles, *Charles Matthew Knowles, The Economic Development of the British Overseas Empire* (London: Routledge, 2005), vol. 1, 195.
[53] Jomo Kenyatta, *Facing Mount Kenya: The Tribal Life of the Gikuyu* (New York: Vintage Books, 1965), 189–90. My emphasis.
[54] Kenyatta, *Facing Mount Kenya*, 190.

and activists in the colonies were not always heard or considered in the early debates about human rights at the UN and other international forums, their positions show critical engagement with these debates.

Human rights discourses within anti-colonial movements were certainly not limited to vocal political elites or prolific intellectuals. Anti-colonial human rights ideology also found expression in grassroots networks and activities. Local activists mobilized human rights language to protest the everyday violence and injustices of colonial rule. The global political upheavals unleashed by the World Wars provided ordinary Africans with opportunities to express discontent and opposition to colonial rule in international arenas such as the League of Nations Mandate Commission and later the UN Trusteeship Council which was specifically mandated to promote "respect for human rights and fundamental freedoms and recognition of the interdependence of peoples of the world."[55] Anti-colonial activists and their metropolitan allies viewed UN trust territories as the most politically and legally viable channel through which to address the human rights abuses particular to colonial rule.[56] Africa's UN trust territories were therefore pivotal sites for the conception of human rights and a "birthplace of the postwar international human rights project."[57]

The majority of these petitions to UN bodies were from ordinary people – market traders and farmers, civil servants, taxi drivers, market traders, and farmers, women and youth groups, and rural peasants. The issues they raised concerned both collective and individual rights. In French Cameroon, petitioners appealed to *droits de l' homme* not only in the call for self-determination but also to demand protection of individual rights codified in international law. They sent a list with the names of people that French and British administrators had deported, arrested, and killed, appealing to the international community to protect specific individuals. In Tanganyika, Africans petitioned the UN Trusteeship Council to demand protection from the violence and injustice by British officials and European settlers.[58] In Zanzibar,

---

[55] United Nations, "The United Nations and Decolonization: International Trusteeship System," accessed September 23, 2016, www.un.org/en/decolonization/its.shtml

[56] Roger S. Clark, "The International League for Human Rights and South West Africa 1947–1957: The Human Rights NGO as Catalyst in the International Legal Process," *Human Rights Quarterly* 3, no. 4 (1981): 101.

[57] Meredith Terretta, "We Had Been Fooled into Thinking that the UN Watches over the Entire World: Human Rights, UN Trust Territories, and Africa's Decolonization," *Human Rights Quarterly*, 34 no. 2 (2012): 345.

[58] Tanzania National Archives, Foreign Affairs 37681/5/3. Petition of the African Government Employees Association, Mwanza to the Visiting United Nations Trusteeship Council Mission to Tanganyika, August 10, 1951.

anti-colonial activists formed the Human Rights League, an organization whose primary objective was to advocate for national self-government and whose leaders drew on the language of international human rights to justify their cause.[59]

To construct a fully representative history of human rights and decolonization, it is essential that we pay as much attention to the margins and outposts of empires as we have to imperial centers and metropoles. This requires attending to anti-colonial ideas and movements at the grassroots and interpretations of human rights in local vernaculars. Given the objective of human rights ideology to give voice to the marginalized, it is crucial that histories of human rights be written not only from the top-down perspectives of dominant actors in mainstream political processes, but also from the bottom-up perspectives of local everyday struggles. Histories of human rights centered predominantly on influential political actors and institutions risk becoming hegemonic narratives that reinforce the epistemic power of some while marginalizing others.

Conclusion

Despite their misgivings about the imperial rights discourse, nationalists and anti-colonial activists drew on the human rights lexicon in struggles for civil liberties and self-determination. As the voices of formerly colonized Afro-Asian countries gained recognition at the UN following the wave of independence of the 1950s and 1960s, the tenor of international human rights debates changed significantly. Newly independent African and Asian countries became the driving force behind the salience given to the right to self-determination as a fundamental collective human right – a theme obscured in earlier discussions. The votes of newly independent Afro-Asian states were crucial in bringing about the adoption of two crucial documents that expanded the meaning of human rights – the Declaration on the Granting of Independence to Colonial Countries and Peoples in 1960 and the Convention on the Elimination of Racial Discrimination in 1965. The former reaffirmed the fundamental human rights, the dignity, and worth of all humans but went further to explicitly affirm the equal right of peoples of all nations to self-determination. Significantly, it also recognized that individual rights could only be fully achieved when the collective rights of nationhood and self-determination

---

[59] National Archives of the United Kingdom, CO 822/2193, "The Human Rights League, Zanzibar," confidential memorandum, November 8, 1961.

were attained – an argument that African nationalists had long made in the cause of national liberation. The 1966 Covenant on Civil and Political Rights which explicitly articulates the right to self-determination also reflects the influence that self-determination and anti-colonialism had on the development of the human rights idea.

What can the politics of anti-colonial rights prioritization tell us about the development of international human rights? For one, it shows that decisions about what claims qualify as "human rights," the ordering of these rights, and even the presentation of right histories are deeply political and ideological. Most rights histories produced in the West tend to concentrate on civil and political rights framed mainly in terms of the development of the relations between authorial power and individual freedoms. These rights histories celebrate the restraint on state power over the individual as the model for institutional developments everywhere.[60] This decidedly state-centric approach anchored on possessive individualism contrasts with postcolonial human rights discourse whose dominant theme is the history of Western domination over non-European territories and the tension between individual liberties and the collective rights of peoples.[61] This postcolonial theme is evident in contemporary debates on regional human rights regimes – the African Charter on Human and People's Rights adopted by the Organization of African Unity in 1981 and the American Convention on Human Rights (Pact of San José) adopted by many Latin American and Caribbean countries in 1969. Both regional documents affirm the collective rights of peoples and outline the relationship between human rights and human duties.[62]

In the age of decolonization, African nationalists and anti-colonial activists interpreted human rights first and foremost as the collective right of peoples to self-determination. They understood human rights not simply in terms of claims that individuals hold against the state but also as collective entitlements that subjugated groups hold against dominating states. Emancipation meant that not only the liberties of individuals but also the collective freedom of peoples to determine their own

[60] Koskenniemi, "Foreword," xvii.
[61] For example, Barreto, *Human Rights from a Third World Perspective*; William Twining, ed., *Human Rights, Southern Voices: Francis Deng, Abdullahi An-Na'im, Yash Ghai and Upendra Baxi* (Cambridge: Cambridge University Press, 2009); Francis Deng and Abdullahi Ahmed Na'im, *Human Rights in Africa: Cross-cultural Perspectives* (Washington, DC: Brookings Institution, 1990).
[62] Makau Mutua, "The Banjul Charter: The Case for the African Cultural Fingerprint," in *Cultural Transformation and Human Rights in Africa*, ed. Abdullahi An-Na'im (New York: Zed Books, 2002), 65–70. See American Convention on Human Rights, Art. 32.

fate. The question of human rights was therefore inextricably linked with the question of national liberation. The undergirding premise was that only the emancipated sovereignty of peoples could guarantee other rights. The linkages between the individual rights of the individual and the collective rights of people would find resonance in international human rights through the struggles of those deprived en masse of human rights in the age of empire.

2 Decolonizing the United Nations
Anti-colonialism and Human Rights in the French Empire

Marco Duranti

The Rights of Man and the French Colonial State

The relationship between anti-colonialism and global human rights norms after World War II poses a conundrum for historians of the French empire.[1] The principle of self-determination, while proclaimed in the UN Charter, was not included in the Universal Declaration of Human Rights, nor was there agreement that self-determination required outright independence. On occasion, delegates to international forums like the UN General Assembly referred to the Universal Declaration to critique colonial rule, but this finding alone says little about whether anti-colonial activists elsewhere conceived of the struggle for independence in these terms.[2] There are, moreover, linguistic ambiguities particular to the French case. Among English speakers, "human rights" had a marked internationalist character, being rarely uttered before its appearance in the UN Charter. French speakers preferred to use the "rights of man" (*droits de l'homme*) in the place of "human rights" (*droits humains*), as did official French-language versions of UN documents.

In the francophone world, the defense of the rights of man was a longstanding republican trope with no obvious relation to the United Nations. Nor did *droits de l'homme* necessarily have anti-colonial connotations.[3] Imperial apologists often justified colonial rule in the name of

---

[1] For an overview of the principal lines of contestation in the historiography on human rights and decolonization, see the Introduction to this volume.

[2] On the place of decolonization in the construction of the UN human rights system, see Roland Burke, *Decolonization and the Evolution of International Human Rights* (Philadelphia: University of Pennsylvania Press, 2010); Steven Jensen, *The Making of International Human Rights: The 1960s, Decolonization, and the Reconstruction of Global Values* (Cambridge: Cambridge University Press, 2016); A. W. Brian Simpson, *Human Rights and the End of Empire: Britain and the Genesis of the European Convention* (Oxford: Oxford University Press, 2001).

[3] On the deeper French origins of the rights of man and Universal Declaration, see Dan Edelstein, *On the Spirit of Rights* (Chicago: University of Chicago Press, 2018); Lynn Hunt, *Inventing Human Rights: A History* (New York: Knopf, 2007); Samuel Moyn, "On the Genealogy of Morals," *The Nation* 284 (April 16, 2007): 25–31.

the rights of man and civilizational uplift because they insisted that France was the vessel and vehicle of those rights: they were universal but not international, instantiated in progressive states like theirs. The French colonial state's violence in suppressing uprisings was thus defended as historically necessary and morally defensible.[4]

This chapter investigates the interplay of imperialism, anti-colonialism, and the UN human rights system against the backdrop of decolonization in the French empire. Its findings complicate this relationship in three respects. First, in contestations over human rights in the French empire, there was no rigid distinction between conceptions of the rights of man in the national, imperial, and international spheres. This was true as much of the colonizer as the colonized, which in the latter case included both colonial subjects championing independence and those arguing for reforms within a French constitutional framework. Second, French colonialists made concerted efforts to ensure that anti-colonialism would not be viewed as a human rights movement by suppressing public awareness of those sources that could establish a link between anti-colonialism and human rights. They did so not only in response to the rise of anti-colonial agitation at the UN General Assembly but also in response to hundreds of private petitions sent to the UN Secretariat and their own internal assessment that French colonial practices were incompatible with UN human rights standards. Finally, many anti-colonialist actors made no clear delineation between the defense of civil liberties and self-determination, viewing the two as interdependent. Guarantees of individual rights were an essential condition for national emancipation as much self-determination was a prerequisite for the enjoyment of individual rights.

The present chapter plumbs two sets of sources: on the one hand, correspondence among French officials bringing to light their efforts to disqualify anti-colonialism as a human rights movement and, on the

---

[4] On the relationship between French republican discourses of colonialism, citizenship, and rights, see Alice L. Conklin, *A Mission to Civilize: The Republican Idea of Empire in France and West Africa, 1895–1930* (Stanford, CA: Stanford University Press, 1997); Fred Cooper, *Citizenship between Empire and Nation: Remaking France and French Africa, 1945–1960* (Princeton, NJ: Princeton University Press, 2014); Sarah Claire Dunstan, "A Tale of Two Republics: Race, Rights, and Revolution, 1919–1962" (PhD diss., University of Sydney, 2019); Todd Shepard, *The Invention of Decolonization: The Algerian War and the Remaking of France* (Ithaca, NY: Cornell University Press, 2006); Elizabeth Thompson, *Colonial Citizens: Republican Rights, Paternal Privilege, and Gender in French Syria and Lebanon* (New York: Columbia University Press, 2000). For an alternative account that stresses the impact of Christianity over secular republicanism, see J. P. Daughton, *An Empire Divided: Religion, Republicanism, and the Making of French Colonialism, 1880–1914* (New York: Oxford University Press, 2006).

other, private allegations of abuses committed by the French state in its colonial territories. The latter were sent to the United Nations by individuals and NGOs from around the world, including colonial subjects themselves. The vast majority of private petitioners did not refer explicitly to UN documents and international norms. Rather, they typically employed a vocabulary of rights common to both international organizations and longstanding national idioms.[5] The focus here, reflecting that of the source material, is on controversies involving anti-colonialism and human rights in France's African colonies, particularly those of the Maghreb: Algeria, Morocco, and Tunisia.[6]

Evaluating whether anti-colonialism was a human rights movement requires accounting for not only the attributes of anti-colonialism itself but also those of the rights discourses employed by colonizer and colonized alike. The drafting of human rights accords at the United Nations placed French governments in the unenviable position of having to take a public stance on whether all French colonial subjects should be afforded the same civil, political, economic, social, and cultural rights as individuals in the metropole. French delegates involved in the intergovernmental negotiations over these texts regarded them as constitutive of a single coherent body of international norms derivative of French declarations of rights and constitutional texts since the French Revolution. Meanwhile, back in Paris, French officials were deeply divided as to the compatibility of these norms with the rights language of the French constitution, the pluralism of colonial law, the potential repercussions on French colonial

---

[5] For analyses of transnational anti-colonial rights claims in relation to France's African empire, see the work of Meredith Terretta, especially: "Anti-Colonial Lawyering, Postwar Human Rights, and Decolonization across Imperial Boundaries in Africa," *Canadian Journal of History* 52, no. 3 (2017): 448–78; *Petitioning for Our Rights, Fighting for Our Nation: The History of the Democratic Union of Cameroonian Women, 1949–1960* (Oxford: Langaa RPCIG, 2013); "'We Had Been Fooled into Thinking that the UN Watches over the Entire World': Human Rights, UN Trust Territories, and Africa's Decolonization," *Human Rights Quarterly* 34, no. 2 (2012): 329–60. On the debates over the right of petition at the UN General Assembly from the 1940s through 1970s, see Burke, *Decolonization and the Evolution of International Human Rights*, 59–91.

[6] On the international history of decolonization in francophone Africa, see Matthew Connelly, *A Diplomatic Revolution: Algeria's Fight for Independence and the Origins of the Post-Cold War Era* (Oxford: Oxford University Press, 2002); Jennifer Johnson, *The Battle for Algeria: Sovereignty, Health Care, and Humanitarianism* (Philadelphia: University of Pennsylvania Press, 2016); Fabian Klose, *Human Rights in the Shadow of Colonial Violence: The Wars of Independence in Kenya and Algeria*, trans. Dona Geyer (Philadelphia: University of Pennsylvania Press, 2013); Jessica Pearson, *The Colonial Politics of Global Health: France and the United Nations in Postwar Africa* (Cambridge, MA: Harvard University Press, 2018).

rule, and the inclusion of exceptions clauses that would limit their application in colonial territories.[7]

By the time the codification of new international human rights standards was underway at the United Nations, republican governments had for more than half a century promised the progressive realization of the universal rights of man across the French empire. According to the assimilationist school of colonial theory, colonized peoples were to be integrated into the legal and constitutional framework of the French metropole. At the same time, in line with the doctrine of associationism that emerged in opposition to that of assimilationism, the empire was conceived as a pluralistic constellation of heterogeneous cultures, each coexisting with the other according to their own local laws and constitutional relationship to the metropole.[8] In the parlance of these colonial theorists, it was the category of "civilization" rather than "race" that determined the constitutional and legal regimes that governed the colonized.[9]

During the life of the Fourth Republic (1946–58), the freedoms and protections accorded to colonial subjects were marked by ambiguities and inconsistencies left unresolved in France's new postwar constitution. Building on the federalist doctrine that emerged from the Brazzaville conference of 1944, the constitutional text adopted in October 1946 recast colonialism as an experiment in democratic federalism, erasing the old nomenclature of empire – the Ministry of Colonies, for example, was renamed the Ministry of Overseas France – while in practice preserving imperial hierarchies. As debates over various constitutional drafts dragged on, representatives of the colonized such as Léopold Senghor shifted from advocating an assimilationist model to a federal one that permitted a greater degree of self-determination for colonized peoples.[10] The egalitarian language establishing the new "French Union," the name now given to the French empire, appeared to signify a repudiation of the subordination of the colonies to the metropole. The constitutional

---

[7] On the relationship between colonialism and international law, see Antony Anghie, *Imperialism, Sovereignty, and the Making of International Law* (Cambridge: Cambridge University Press, 2007); Lauren A. Benton and Lisa Ford, *Rage for Order: The British Empire and the Origins of International Law* (Cambridge, MA: Harvard University Press, 2016); Andrew Fitzmaurice, *Sovereignty, Property and Empire, 1500–2000* (Cambridge: Cambridge University Press, 2014); Martti Koskenniemi, *The Gentle Civilizer of Nations: The Rise and Fall of International Law, 1870–1960* (Cambridge: Cambridge University Press, 2002); Martti Koskenniemi and Walter Rech, eds., *International Law and Empire: Historical Explorations* (Oxford: Oxford University Press, 2017).

[8] Shepard, *Invention of Decolonization*, 19–39.

[9] Guy Perville, *De l'Empire français à la décolonisation* (Paris: Hachette, 1991), 65, 74.

[10] Dunstan, "Tale of Two Republics," 182–91.

preamble declared, "France forms with its overseas peoples a Union founded on the equality of rights and duties, without distinction of race or religion." It was left ambiguous, however, whether "the equality of rights and duties" was collective, referring to relations of reciprocity between the peoples of a French overseas federation, or individual, meaning that all persons residing in the colonies and metropole enjoyed the same rights.[11]

The vast majority of the colonized peoples of the empire were not consulted on the integration of their territories into the French Union, nor were they able to vote in the popular referenda on the approval of constitutional texts. Federalist rhetoric suited those who wished to mask the reality that the rights accorded to so-called "natives" would not be commensurate with those granted to individuals of European descent. It was envisioned that these rights would not be codified uniformly in colonial legislation but rather according to the circumstances present in a given territory. According to Article 80 of the constitution, which promised universal French citizenship, "[p]articular laws" would "establish the conditions under which they will exercise their rights as citizens." In practice, settlers of French or European origins constituted a privileged caste that exercised a different set of citizenship rights and legal rights than the colonized.[12]

The standing of the French Union under international law remained uncertain.[13] After World War II, the word "colonial" disappeared from the parlance of international law, replaced by euphemisms such as "non-self-governing territories" (territoires non-autonomes). The French delegation took advantage of the proclamation of equal citizenship rights for colonial subjects, the integration of the overseas departments into metropolitan administrative structures, and the granting of the Indochinese "associated states" jurisdiction over their internal affairs, to argue at the United Nations that many of their colonies should no longer be classified as non-self-governing territories.[14] The French government was not prepared to accept that it was accountable to international organizations or courts for its conduct toward its colonial subjects, nor were most

[11] Alfred Grosser, *La IVème République et sa politique extérieure* (Paris: Armand Colin, 1972), 247–8.

[12] Shepard, *Invention of Decolonization*, 39–54; Alexis Spire, "Semblables et pourtant différents: La citoyenneté paradoxale des 'Français musulmans d'Algérie' en métropole," *Genèses*, no. 53 (2003/4): 48–68.

[13] Raymond F. Betts, *France and Decolonisation, 1900–1960* (Basingstoke, UK: Palgrave Macmillan, 1991), 24–5, 61; J. B. Duroselle, "France and the United Nations," *International Organization* 19, no. 3 (1965): 700–1.

[14] Marie-Claude Smouts, *La France à l'ONU: Premiers Rôles et Second Rang* (Paris: Fondation Nationale des Sciences Politiques, 1979), 217–18.

French international lawyers.[15] Nevertheless, over the course of the 1950s and 1960s, the actions taken by anti-colonial forces in the UN General Assembly, above all those of the Arab League of States and the "Afro-Asian bloc" had a sizeable impact on domestic and international public opinion, as well as discussions among French officials.[16]

Imperial Anxieties over the Emergence of Postwar Human Rights Norms

The French government worked furiously behind the scenes to dampen awareness of UN human rights standards across the French empire. It was particularly concerned with restricting the translation of the Universal Declaration into Arabic in light of its reception in Algeria and the North African protectorates. The solution arrived at, in coordination with the Belgian and British governments, was to promulgate the text of the Universal Declaration throughout the overseas empires, but only in their official languages, that is, French and English.[17] The three colonial powers also agreed to launch inquiries into whether independent Middle-Eastern and Asian states had published the Universal Declaration in their native languages. French diplomats took great interest in whether any governments had circulated Arabic translations of the Universal Declaration.[18]

This was an acknowledgment that the Universal Declaration had the potential to gain traction among anti-colonial movements. The foreign ministry had become aware of an editorial in the *Gazetin'ny Malagasy* arguing that the French government's continued opposition to Madagascar's independence contradicted the spirit of the French constitution, UN Charter, and Universal Declaration. The newspaper's editor, Maurice Andriamampianina, addressed a letter to the French government accusing it of violating the prohibition on discrimination set forth in the Universal Declaration's second article. Diplomatic officials proposed measures be taken to ensure that the local Malagasy press clarify that the

---

[15] See, for example, Maurice Flory, "Algérie et droit international," *Annuaire Français de Droit International* 5 (1959): 817–44.

[16] Maurice Vaïsse, "La Guerre perdue à l'ONU?," in *La Guerre d'Algérie et les Français: Colloque de l'Institute d'histoire du temps*, ed. Jean-Pierre Rioux (Paris: Fayard, 1990), 451, 462.

[17] Ministry of Overseas France memorandum no. 557/SC, June 29, 1949; correspondence no. 306/SC, NUOI Box 380, Centre des Archives Diplomatiques, La Courneuve (hereafter abbreviated as CAD).

[18] Ministry of Overseas France letter no. 1797/SC, June 10, 1949; memorandum no. 182/SC, November 2, 1949; memorandum no. 947/SC, December 8, 1949; and memorandum no. 350/SC, December 8, 1949, NUOI Box 380, CAD.

Universal Declaration was a mere expression of ideals without legal force and in no way justified the right to resist French colonial rule.[19]

The French delegation to the UN saw no dissonance between a colonial policy premised at once on universal republican ideals and cultural difference.[20] At the same time, the French government was under no illusion that French colonial rule was compatible with UN human rights standards. Officials in the Ministry of Foreign Affairs, Ministry of Justice, and Ministry of Overseas France noted in their internal correspondence that French colonial legislation and administrative practices were incompatible with many of the articles of the Universal Declaration. There were glaring discrepancies between the legal systems of the colonies and the metropole, including the existence of dual electoral colleges, in which different classes of citizens enjoyed divergent political rights, and colonial decrees limiting civil liberties, such as the restrictions on freedom of assembly and the press decreed in response to the ongoing Malagasy Uprising. The right to a nationality was said to be inapplicable to the populations of Cameroon and Togoland, as these trustee territories operated under the terms of the UN Charter rather than the French constitution. Guarantees of mutual consent in marriage allegedly ran contrary to the "Muslim statute" operative in Algeria. Another source of consternation was the dearth of social legislation overseas that appeared to conflict with the economic, social, and cultural rights provisions of the Universal Declaration.[21]

According to René Cassin, the French delegate to the UN Human Rights Commission, it would be impossible to immediately and effectively guarantee these rights in the "less advanced territories" of member states. The constitutional preamble guaranteed rights such as "the equality of men and women" and "the right to work" that in Cassin's view could only be realized progressively in the French Union. "There are vast sections under French rule where implementation of these principles clashes with strong traditions that cannot be transformed but in stages,"

---

[19] Ministry of Overseas France memorandum, February 28, 1949, Fonds Ministériels, Affaires Politiques Box 219, Centre des Archives d'Outre-Mer, Aix-en-Provence (hereafter abbreviated as CAOM).

[20] Burke, *Decolonization and the Evolution of International Human Rights*, 114.

[21] Robert Delavignette, Ministry of Overseas France memorandum no. 1547, February 22, 1949, Fonds Ministériels, Affaires Politiques Box 219, CAOM; Henri Damey to Robert Delavignette, Ministry of Overseas France correspondence, February 26, 1949, Fonds Ministériels, Affaires Politiques Box 219, CAOM; Robert Lecourt to Robert Schuman, Ministry of Justice memorandum, August 20, 1948, NUOI Box 380, CAD; Ministry of Overseas France memorandum, February 28, 1949, Fonds Ministériels, Affaires Politiques Box 219, CAOM.

he noted in a July 1949 memorandum.[22] Cassin was a prominent liberal internationalist who had acted as chief legal adviser of the Free French during the war and now served as head of France's highest administrative court. He played a leading role in the drafting and adoption of the Universal Declaration of Human Rights.[23] He was also a liberal imperialist who, like most of the French legal establishment, saw no contradiction between championing universal rights and the differential application of these rights to various categories of colonial subjects.[24]

For Cassin, it was incumbent on France, as birthplace of the rights of man, to continue its historic vocation of diffusing its republican ideals abroad by taking the lead in constructing an ambitious new global system of human rights guarantees. The Universal Declaration was said to be a successor to the declarations of the rights of man of the French Revolution and the constitution of the Fourth Republic. In Cassin's view, the next step toward regenerating France as a beacon of civilized norms was to translate the rights of man enshrined in the Universal Declaration into a binding UN treaty with effective supranational mechanisms of implementation – without, however, interfering with French colonial affairs.

The right of petition was paramount to realizing Cassin's vision. Rather than render the governments of UN member states the sole subjects of international human rights law, he favored granting UN bodies powers to receive, examine, investigate, and adjudicate petitions from private individuals and groups.[25]

Whether a human rights treaty would include the right of petition was one of the most controversial questions confronting the Human Rights Commission. The UN Secretariat, along with the majority of

---

[22] René Cassin, Ministry of Foreign Affairs memorandum, July 4, 1949, NUOI Box 382, CAD.

[23] On the multifarious influences on Cassin's internationalism and activities in the international human rights field across his lifetime, see Marc Agi, *René Cassin: prix Nobel de la paix, 1887–1976; père de la Déclaration universelle des droits de l'homme* (Paris: Perrin, 1998); Jay Winter and Antoine Prost, *René Cassin and Human Rights: From the Great War to the Universal Declaration* (New York: Cambridge University Press, 2013). On the role of Cassin and the Ministry of Foreign Affairs in the drafting of the Universal Declaration, see Georges-Henri Soutou, *La France et la Déclaration des droits de l'homme* (Paris: Les Éditions du Diplomate, 2008).

[24] On the relationship between Cassin's views on human rights and empire, see Chapters 6 and 13 in this volume, as well as Emma Stone Mackinnon, "Declaration as Disavowal: The Politics of Race and Empire in the Universal Declaration of Human Rights," *Political Theory* 47, no. 1 (2019): 68–74; Glenda Sluga, "René Cassin: Les droits de l'homme and the Universality of Human Rights, 1945–1966," in *Human Rights in the Twentieth Century*, ed. Stefan-Ludwig Hoffmann and Samuel Moyn (New York: Cambridge University Press, 2010), 107–24.

[25] René Cassin, Ministry of Foreign Affairs memorandum, February 2, 1948, NUOI Box 382, CAD.

delegations, preferred that the Secretariat be responsible for filtering petitions and distributing a confidential list to members of the Commission, who would simply take note without having the power to discuss or investigate them.[26] In August 1947, the Economic and Social Council of the UN General Assembly adopted ECOSOC Resolution 75(V) stipulating that the Commission have "no power to take any action in regard to any complaint concerning human rights." Notwithstanding numerous attempts to revise this principle, it was to remain in effect for another two decades.[27] The question of petitions caused a deep rift between Cassin and legal experts advising the French government on account of their colonial implications. The French colonial state had created an elaborate administrative regime whereby claims submitted by colonial subjects could be heard in courts without fundamentally challenging the restrictions imposed on the rights of the colonized. Granting all residents of colonial territories the ability to appeal or bypass these local mechanisms of redress was most unsettling.[28] Many French officials, frustrated with the broad leeway that Cassin enjoyed in the fledging years of the UN, suspected that allowing the Commission to engage in an even a highly delimited discussion of petitions might turn that body into a de facto international court where grievances against colonial powers would be aired.[29]

A staple of the assimilationist strain of French colonial ideology since the late nineteenth century had been a belief in France's exceptional status as an empire founded on the diffusion of universal republican ideals overseas, as opposed to what French liberal imperialists described as the arbitrary rule of other European colonial powers, such as the Belgians and British, who unabashedly organized the administrative governance of their empires on the basis of rigid ethnic and racial categories. This exceptionalism, while more rhetoric than reality, complicated cooperation between the French, Belgian, and British governments when colonial matters arose before the UN General Assembly.[30]

---

[26] Ministry of Foreign Affairs memorandum, March 5, 1947, NUOI Box 382, CAD.

[27] Jakob Möller, "Petitioning the United Nations," *Universal Human Rights* 1, no. 4 (1979): 57–61.

[28] Charles Chaumont, Ministry of Foreign Affairs memoranda, April 5 and 21, 1947, NUOI Box 382, CAD. On the internal discussions between the Ministry of Foreign Affairs and Cassin on the colonial dimensions of human rights at the UN, see Soutou, *La France et la Déclaration des droits de l'homme*, 24, 38–41, 44, 54, 58, 70, 72, 76, 80, 82.

[29] Ministry of Foreign Affairs memorandum, May 26, 1947, NUOI Box 380, CAD.

[30] On the imperial anxieties that weighed on the United Kingdom's participation in the UN Human Rights Commission, see Simpson, *Human Rights and the End of Empire*, chs. 6–10.

Less than a month following the adoption of the Universal Declaration, functionaries from the foreign ministry's Africa Division met with Belgian and British officials to coordinate their efforts to obstruct any moves by the Human Rights Commission that might impact on their overseas empires. Yet there was no consensus in the French government as to whether to support the United Kingdom's more transparent efforts to impede the full application of a UN human rights treaty to colonial territories. A number of French officials, particularly those in the Ministry of Overseas France, believed that the National Assembly would never ratify a treaty that made explicit exceptions for the rights of colonized peoples, because many French deputies, including parliamentarians representing overseas territories, would argue that this ran counter to the constitution of the Fourth Republic.[31]

When the UN General Assembly debated that December the insertion of a provision that would apply a human rights pact to all territories of contracting states, the French government was divided on whether to join the British and Belgian delegations in opposition. The Ministry of Overseas France insisted that France must defend "the fundamental principle of specialized overseas legislation."[32] The Ministry of Foreign Affairs responded that France could not always align its policies with Britain and Belgium, citing "the contradictory positions that we are forced to adopt, which consist of posing at once as the defenders of the colonial clause and, if the debates lead us to undertake an exegesis of our Constitution in front of foreign auditors, the promoters of a policy of assimilation."[33]

Whereas the British delegation dispensed with subtleties in favor of open confrontation with critics of its colonial practices, the French strategy was to avoid public contestations over colonial questions.[34] French diplomats, ever more obstructionist, took advantage of the constitutional jigsaw puzzle of the French empire. With the reorganization of the French empire into the French Union, the majority of colonies were classified as overseas territories under the purview of the Ministry of Overseas France. Others fell under the ambit of the Ministry of Foreign Affairs, governed according to separate treaty arrangements, such as the

---

[31] Ministry of Foreign Affairs memorandum no. 398/SC, May 14, 1949, and correspondence no. 5259, June 23, 1948, NUOI Box 385, CAD.

[32] Michel Leroy-Beaulieu, Ministry of Foreign Affairs memorandum, March 19, 1951, NUOI Box 385, CAD.

[33] Vincent Broustra, Ministry of Foreign Affairs memorandum no. 28/SC, December 8, 1950, NUOI Box 384, CAD.

[34] Martin Thomas, "France Accused: French North Africa before the United Nations, 1952–1962," *Contemporary European History* 10, no. 1 (2001): 105.

associated states of Indochina, the protectorates of Morocco and Tunisia, and the UN trust territories of French Cameroon and Togoland. Several colonies, including Algeria, were administered as overseas departments of the French Republic under the supervision of the Ministry of the Interior.[35] Both colonies and the metropole were represented in the Assembly of the French Union, a parallel consultative body to the National Assembly of the French Republic. The Assembly of the French Union included representatives of the associated states of Indochina, which were now said to exercise jurisdiction over their internal affairs. The French delegation exploited these features of their empire to justify the impossibility of a straightforward application of a human rights accord to all French territories, citing necessity of consulting first with each colony.[36]

Though the French government prevented representatives of the colonized from expressing their views at the UN General Assembly, colonial parliamentarians did weigh in on the first binding human rights treaty of the postwar era: the European Convention on Human Rights, which the Council of Europe adopted in November 1950. In the spring of 1954, the Assembly of the French Union was the site of fierce contest over the ratification of the European Convention. This debate that brought to the fore tensions between the tropes of assimilation and difference inflecting French republican ideologies of empire. At issue were the array of limitations imposed on the exercise of the rights enumerated in the European Convention, above all those limiting the treaty's application in colonial territories. Members states of the Council of Europe, which had adopted the European Convention in November 1950, could choose at their discretion to extend human rights guarantees across their empires and, even if they did so, these guarantees would be implemented in the colonies "with due regard, however, to local requirements."[37]

In the ensuing debate, the *rapporteur* of the ratification bill, Camille Héline, an establishment liberal parliamentarian from the metropole, declared that France, "especially since the adoption of the Constitution of 1946," had respected the rights of man in its colonial territories,

---

[35] Pierre François Gonidec, *Droits d'outre-mer* (Paris: Montchrestien, 1959–1960), 13–14. For an example of a textbook on French colonial law during the Fourth Republic, see François Luchaire, *Manuel de droit d'Outre-Mer: Union française, Afrique du Nord, territoires d'Outre-Mer* (Paris: Recueil Sirey, 1949).

[36] Michael Leroy-Beaulieu, Ministry of Foreign Affairs memorandum, August 16, 1950, NUOI Box 385, CAD.

[37] On the colonial considerations that shaped the British government's role in the drafting of the European Convention, see Simpson, *Human Rights and the End of Empire*, chs. 11–15.

despite occasional "abuses" he attributed "not to the vices of our legislation but to errors or excesses in execution by authorities." Invoking the tropes of French republican exceptionalism, Héline averred that France's "civilizing mission, its conception of human dignity, and the ideal that it holds out to the populations that it guides and protects can be compared favorably to the work of other powers, colonial or no."[38] The Cameroonian politician André-Marie Mbida, a Catholic centrist, argued that the colonial exceptions in the European Convention marked a regression away from the purported universalism of the French republican rights of man tradition. These exceptions were reminiscent of the statutory regime of *l'indigénat*, whereby African colonial subjects who had not attained French nationality were subjected to discriminatory treatment, including forced labor and repressive measures. He objected that accounting for "local requirements" in each colony "offers local administrations the possibility of violating the very liberties safeguarded in the convention." Describing the conception of rights enshrined in the European Convention as a retrogression to the unjust colonial practices of earlier decades, he told representatives of the metropole, "Instead of going forward, you always go back."[39]

Mbida replicated a longstanding rhetorical strategy of black francophone elites who, rather than argue for outright independence, sought to secure the rights of the colonized by shaming French governments into following their own professed republican principles.[40] His colleagues on the left held that the European Convention enshrined a "reactionary" capitalist conception of rights incompatible with local African traditions. Monique Lafon, a communist, pointed out that the protection of property in the European Convention's Protocol did not account for African tribal conceptions of collective ownership and could be used to further strip Africans of their land and resources in the service of European business interests.[41] African parliamentarians, joined by left-wing members from the metropole, described the derogations and limitations on the exercise of rights in the European Convention as subverting the more ample freedoms proclaimed in the French constitution and the

---

[38] *Journal officiel de la République française*, débats de l'Assemblée de l'Union Français, March 9, 1954 session, 218.

[39] Ibid., 219, 332.

[40] On the republicanism of assimilated African *évolué* elites, see James E. Genova, *Colonial Ambivalence, Cultural Authenticity, and the Limitations of Mimicry in French-Ruled West Africa* (New York: Peter Lang, 2004); Saliha Belmessous, *Assimilation and Empire: Uniformity in French and British Colonies, 1541–1954* (Oxford: Oxford University Press, 2013), 156–200.

[41] Genova, *Colonial Ambivalence*, 352.

Universal Declaration. As the debate progressed, speakers referred to examples of ongoing abuses in the colonies in which colonial officials imposed restrictions on rights similar to what were found in the European Convention. Rather than arguing for France to recognize the right of petition, they cast doubt on whether commissioners and judges appointed by Western European governments would ever rule against the interests of colonial powers. In the end, notwithstanding pleas from a number of parliamentarians from the metropole, the Assembly of the French Union voted overwhelmingly to reject the ratification of the European Convention.[42]

Anti-colonial Petitioning and Decolonization in France's North African Empire

The most contentious human rights issue facing France in the UN General Assembly throughout the 1950s concerned its actions in its North African colonies. Delegates from Arab League member states accused France in October 1951 of violating the principles enshrined in the UN Charter and Universal Declaration. A year later, they succeeded in placing the question of Moroccan and Tunisian self-determination on the agenda, resulting in the adoption of resolutions in December 1952 exhorting France to enter into negotiations for the establishment of free democratic institutions in its protectorates, though stopping short of demanding independence. Following the deposition and exile of Mohammed Ben Youssef, Sultan of Morocco, in August 1953, the Afro-Asian Group attempted, without success, to have the UN Security Council intervene and subsequently failed to obtain a UN General Assembly resolution condemning the French government.[43] Throughout these debates, the Afro-Asian Group argued that French colonial authorities had violated international law, as the treaties signed between France and its North African protectorates were between sovereign states; that violations of individual civil and political rights in Morocco and Tunisia constituted a breach of the principle of self-determination enshrined in the UN Charter; and that French actions constituted a threat to international peace under the Charter and hence warranted intervention.[44]

The late 1950s was marked by a wave of memoranda to the UN Secretary General by the governments of Arab League states on the

---

[42] Ibid., 220, 331–3, 350–6, 396–7.
[43] Charles-Robert Ageron, *La décolonisation française* (Paris: Armand Colin, 1994), 83–4.
[44] Thomas, "France Accused," 99.

subject of Algeria. Most African and Asian delegations were slow to champion Algerian independence. In 1954, with the exception of Saudi Arabia, their governments were reluctant to support the claims of the Algerian National Liberation Front (FLN) at the United Nations, but reversed course the following year, emerging victorious in a UN General Assembly vote to condemn French repression in Algeria, prompting a French boycott. The year 1955 witnessed the granting of independence to Morocco and Tunisia, as well as the addition to the United Nations of seventeen African, Asian, and Eastern bloc member states. That September the UN General Assembly voted to begin discussion of the Algerian question. In the ensuing debate, France was accused of breaching the Universal Declaration in its actions in Algeria. Although France fended off efforts in 1956–8 to have the United Nations endorse outright independence, the UN General Assembly voted to affirm Algerians' right to self-determination in accordance with the Charter.[45]

After the fall of the Fourth Republic in May 1958 as a direct consequence of developments in Algeria, Charles de Gaulle assumed leadership of the nascent Fifth Republic, which reconstituted the French Union as the French Community. In September 1959, de Gaulle publicly embraced the principle of self-determination enshrined in the UN Charter and offered French colonies the possibilities of self-government under French auspices, outright integration with France, or independence, though in the case of Algeria this was accompanied by the threat of partition.[46] Finally, in December 1960, at the end of a year marked a wave of decolonization in Africa, the UN General Assembly adopted Resolution 1514(XV), known as the Declaration on the Granting of Independence to Colonial Countries and Peoples. Citing the UN Charter on three occasions and the Universal Declaration once, Resolution 1514(XV) described colonialism as a breach of range of fundamental UN principles, including "human rights," "self-determination," "universal peace," and "the social, cultural, and economic development of dependent peoples," as well as endorsing "non-interference in the internal affairs of States." While the resolution was not binding under international law, it did provide for the creation of a committee on decolonization and left no doubt that anti-colonialism, self-determination, and human rights were indivisible principles.[47]

[45] Connelly, *Diplomatic Revolution*, 75, 93, 130; Klose, *Human Rights in the Shadow of Colonial Violence*, 209–13.
[46] Connelly, *Diplomatic Revolution*, 209.
[47] Burke, *Decolonization and the Evolution of International Human Rights*, 55; Klose, *Human Rights in the Shadow of Colonial Violence*, 225–7; Steven L. B. Jensen, *The Making of*

Were the anti-colonial declarations agreed upon at intergovernmental forums representative of anti-colonial human rights discourse more generally? Delegations to the UN General Assembly not only included current and former members of the UN Human Rights Commission but were advised by diplomatic officials much better versed in the panoply of UN resolutions and treaties than the average anti-colonial activist. Petitions sent to the UN by private individuals and non-governmental organizations provide an alternate snapshot of the relationship between anti-colonialism and postwar human rights norms. The following is an analysis of those petitions that the UN Secretariat transmitted in full text form to the French delegation and eventually deposited in the foreign ministry archives at the Quai d'Orsay in Paris. These do not constitute the totality of communications received by the United Nations on French colonial matters, some of which were under the purview of the Trusteeship Council and others which were noted in statistics kept by the UN Secretariat without finding their way into French diplomatic archives. Nevertheless, the first human rights complaints sent to the United Nations during the 1950s offer a valuable, though partial, perspective on the languages of rights deployed by anti-colonial actors.[48]

Between 1950 and 1962, almost two hundred of these petitions referred to violations of rights in French colonial territories. Approximately six out of ten referred to Algeria, two out of ten to Morocco, one out of ten to Tunisia, and one out of ten to other French colonies. Only a handful named territories outside of Africa. Anti-colonial petitioning occurred in two phases. The first phase (1950–3) was above all in response to the repression of independence movements in Morocco and, to a lesser degree, those in Algeria and Tunisia.[49] The frequency of these complaints peaked in 1952, coinciding with the inscription of the Moroccan and Tunisian questions on the agenda of the UN General Assembly. This phase was marked by a relatively large number of references to UN texts as well as a high proportion of petitions from trade unions and communist-affiliated organizations concerned with abuses committed against pro-independence workers' organizations. This first phase was followed by a lull in 1954–5, when Morocco and Tunisia

---

International Human Rights: The 1960s, Decolonization and the Reconstruction of Global Values (Cambridge: Cambridge University Press, 2016), 54–6.

[48] The petitions transmitted from the UN Secretariat to the French Ministry of Foreign Affairs are found in the French diplomatic archives housed in Corneuve. See NUOI Boxes 389, 390, and 926, CAD.

[49] For a survey of colonialism and decolonization in Algeria, Morocco, and Tunisia, see Yvette Katan Bensamoun and Raman Chalak, *Le Maghreb: De l'empire ottoman à la fin de la colonisation française* (Paris: Belin, 2007).

gained their independence. The second phase of anti-colonial petitioning emerged in response to the intensification of the Algerian War of Independence, also known as the Algerian Revolution (1954–62). The frequency of complaints transmitted to the foreign ministry peaked in 1958 following the French army's brutal victory over the FLN in the Battle of Algiers. Many of these human rights complaints were directed at persuading the United Nations to intervene against the imprisonment, torture, and execution of Algerian nationalists. There was a greater diversity of petitioners during this second phase and UN documents were rarely cited in the petitions themselves.[50]

These anti-colonial complaints were typically lodged by NGOs rather than by individuals. Of the petitioners whose names the UN Secretariat listed, a majority were trade union federations, many of them communist or communist-leaning, and most of the remaining NGOs had communist connections as well. Communist petitioners, while frequently foregrounding infringements on trade union rights, also highlighted violations of civil and political rights. The latter included press censorship, torture, arbitrary arrests, and restrictions on freedoms of association, assembly, expression, and movement. A large proportion of transmitted petitions remained anonymous. The UN Secretariat did, however, list the nationalities of almost all petitioners. During the first phase of anti-colonial petitioning in the early 1950s, about four in ten were from one of the North African colonies, one in ten from Egypt, one in ten from communist Central and Eastern Europe, one in ten from Western Europe, and one in ten from other regions. The second phase of anti-colonial petitioning, coinciding with the Algerian War, witnessed a much greater proportion of petitions being sent from outside the French empire along with a broader geographic dispersion of petitioners from Europe and the Middle East, with Egyptians and Germans being the nationalities most prominently represented. Across both phases, hardly any anti-colonial petitions were sent from the metropole.[51]

Many petitioners who supported colonial independence movements invoked the right to self-determination, often coupled with a denunciation

---

[50] The authorization of torture and abuse of civil liberties by French authorities in Algeria has been the subject of much recent scholarship. See, in particular, the seminal work of Raphaëlle Branch and Sylvie Thénault: Raphaëlle Branche, *La torture et l'armée pendant la guerre d'Algérie, 1954–1962* (Paris: Gallinard, 2001); Sylvie Thénault, *Une drôle de justice: Les magistrats dans la guerre d'Algérie* (Paris: La Découverte, 2001).

[51] On the transnational anti-colonial politics of communists and the far left, see Young-Sun Hong, *Cold War Germany, the Third World, and the Global Humanitarian Regime* (New York: Cambridge University Press, 2015); Eleanor Davey, *Idealism beyond Borders: The French Revolutionary Left and the Rise of Humanitarianism, 1954–1988* (Cambridge: Cambridge University Press, 2015).

of violations of the "rights of man," meaning civil and political rights.[52] Most anti-colonial petitions referred to individual freedoms from state coercion, including prohibitions on forced labor and torture, freedom from arbitrary arrest, and the right to a fair trial, in addition the freedom of assembly and association of individuals into political organizations and trade unions. Petitions clustered around high-profile cases of a single individual denied their civil and political rights, such as protests in the early 1950s against the treatment of Tunisian nationalist Habib Bourguiba, head of the pro-independence Neo Destour party, and Moroccan trade union leader Mahjoub Ben Seddik, or appeals in the late 1950s for the United Nations to intervene to stop the execution of Algerian nationalist Djamila Bouhired, an FLN activist. Discrimination against women was rarely mentioned, though the abuse of female anti-colonial activists was a subject of a number of complaints and the Women's International Democratic Federation was a petitioner.[53]

Often petitioners sent short communications that eschewed specifics in favor of more abstract and elastic signifiers such as "freedoms," "liberties," and "rights." In French and other Romance languages, "the rights of man" (*droits de l'homme*) was commonly used instead "human rights" (*droits humains*), as was the case in official versions of UN documents, or in some cases, "the rights of the human person" (*droits de la personne humaine*). Both phrases had deeper historical origins in Enlightenment and Christian thought. Whereas among English speakers the usage of "human rights" had a contemporary internationalist resonance, the term being rarely used in the anglophone world before the adoption of the UN Charter, this was not necessarily true of the "rights of man," nor was it the case for the phrase "human rights" in other linguistic contexts. In German, for example, "human rights" (*Menschenrechte*) was not a phrase of recent vintage.

Some petitioners were not averse to pointing out French hypocrisy, highlighting the contradictions between the republican rhetoric of the rights of man and the realities of colonial rule. As an anonymous individual petitioner from the United Kingdom wrote in November 1953 when noting that "a native is liable to be executed for arguing or if he shows any dissension with the French authorities": "Surely it is in accordance with the UN Charter, any man and woman, regardless of race and creed, has

---

[52] Communications dated November 2, 1950, February 11, 1951, and February 25, 1952, CAD, NUOI 389.

[53] Communications dated February 22 and March 26, 1952. On the WIDF's use of the UN Charter, see Katherine McGregor, "Opposing Colonialism: The Women's International Democratic Federation and decolonization struggles in Vietnam and Algeria 1945–1965," *Women's History Review* 25, no. 6 (2016): 935–8.

the right of expressing his or her opinion and the right of freedom of speech. Why, the French themselves uttered the slogan 'Liberty, Equality, Fraternity.'"[54] In 1959, twenty-five African and Asian delegations would choose Bastille Day as the moment to petition for the inscription of the Algerian question on the UN General Assembly agenda.[55]

Petitioners often cast rights as both legal and moral claims, combining the language of citizenship rights with that of universal rights. In November 1950, for example, a Moroccan NGO accused France of "the suppression of all freedom of opinion and the press in our oppressed country . . . in the name of the sacred rights inscribed in the French constitution and the Charter of the United Nations."[56] The expulsion of the Moroccan trade union leader André Leroy in May 1951 was denounced by two Moroccan trade unions, the Fédération nationale des Travailleurs des PTT and Union locale des syndicates de Fès, as a violation of specific provisions of the October 1946 constitution and the Universal Declaration.[57] That November, an NGO based in Luxembourg defended Ben Seddik's right to speak out against French colonial authorities, observing, "He has simply made usage of a democratic right, a natural right, a right of man, of which nobody can deprive him."[58] Another from Italy wrote, "Our organization ventures to appeal to the Commission on Human Rights [which] in the exercise of its functions is bound to take steps for the prevention of these unfortunate episodes and for the restoration to those citizens of the freedom which is their right."[59] In February 1952, government censorship in Algeria of the newspaper *Algérie Libre* as part of a crackdown on the MTLD (Mouvement pour le triomphe des libertés démocratiques) provoked three petitions from anonymous Algerian NGOs. One petitioner described the incident as an "attack on the freedom of expression recognized by the French Constitution itself and by the Universal declaration of the rights of man," another as a "violation of the liberty of press and expression" and "an attack on the Rights of Man," and the third as simply "attacks on fundamental liberties and the rights of man."[60]

The 1950s witnessed a dramatic decline in the proportion of anti-colonial complaints that invoked the UN Charter or the Universal Declaration of Human Rights, from a slight majority at the start of the

[54] Communication dated November 11, 1953, NUOI Box 389, CAD.
[55] Connelly, *Diplomatic Revolution*, 205.
[56] Communication dated October 7, 1950, NUOI Box 389, CAD.
[57] Communications dated May 5 and 10, 1951, NUOI Box 389, CAD.
[58] Communication dated November 30, 1951, NUOI Box 389, CAD.
[59] Communication dated December 10, 1951, NUOI Box 389, CAD.
[60] Communications dated February 2, 4, and 11, 1952, NUOI Box 389, CAD.

decade to only about one in twenty by the end. The UN Charter was twice as likely to be named as the Universal Declaration. For the average petitioner, the UN Charter was a more widely known text than the Universal Declaration. Unlike the Universal Declaration, the UN Charter was legally binding and affirmed the right to self-determination. The provisions of the Universal Declaration named in anti-colonial complaints were limited to civil liberties. Only a few transmitted petitions explicitly cited articles from the Universal Declaration, all of these clustered in the early 1950s. These comprised Article 2(2) (freedom from discrimination based on colonial status), Article 3 ("right to life"), Article 6 ("recognition everywhere before the law"), Article 13 ("freedom of movement"), Article 19 ("freedom of opinion and expression"), and Article 23(4) ("right to form and join trade unions").[61] Many of the articles of the Universal Declaration that French officials had deemed incompatible with French colonial administration were not invoked these petitions, including those concerning marriage, nationality, democratic representation, education, and social security. The defense of trade union rights, while frequent, was usually cast as the freedom to associate, protest, and strike rather than as an economic right.[62]

The overwhelming majority of references to the UN Charter and Universal Declaration were concentrated in the first phase of anti-colonial petitioning. This could have been due to a number of factors, such as the campaign in the early 1950s to place the Moroccan and Tunisian questions on the UN agenda and the half-life of the Universal Declaration, which outside of international forums appears to have faded from memory in the years following its adoption. In the first phase of anti-colonial petitioning, there appears to have been a degree of coordination among NGO petitioners in cases involving high-profile incidents of rights abuses in the French North African colonies. This is suggested by the prevalence of petitions from trade union federations and other NGOs with communist affiliations, as well as the concentration of references to UN human rights bodies and UN human rights texts. When, for example, Habib Bourguiba was denied permission to visit southern Tunisia in late March 1950, one Tunisian and two Egyptian NGOs sent petitions to the UN within a span of four days, each of them citing a violation of the freedom of movement provision of the Universal Declaration.[63] More complaints were lodged when French authorities

---

[61] Communications dated March 31, April 2, April 3, 1950; May 5 and 10, 1951; March 26, 1952, NUOI Box 389, CAD.

[62] An exception is communication dated December 24, 1951, NUOI Box 389, CAD.

[63] Communications dated March 31, April 2, and April 3, 1950, NUOI Box 389, CAD.

arrested Bourguiba, other Neo Destour leaders, and trade union leaders in January 1952 following an attempt by the Tunisian cabinet to petition the UN Security Council in support of Tunisian sovereignty in coordination with a general strike organized by Neo Destour.[64] A hunger strike by Algerian prisoners was the subject of three petitions sent between December 6 and 8, 1951, all of which explicitly named the UN Human Rights Commission, which was uncommon.[65] The sentencing of Seddik in Morocco around that time elicited five petitions from NGOs likewise addressed to the UN Human Rights Commission.[66]

References to UN texts plummeted while the diversity of petitioners increased toward the end of the decade. In early 1958, the pending execution of Bouhired catalyzed an unprecedented flood of petitions, with thirty-four communications concerning Bouhired transmitted by the UN Secretariat to the Ministry of Foreign Affairs. Whereas the petitions regarding Bourguiba and Seddik emanated from North Africa alone, the Bouhired case attracted petitions from twenty-four nations spanning the so-called First, Second, and Third Worlds, ending only when de Gaulle commuted her sentence in March.[67]

Contestations over the Human Rights Complaint Process

During the late 1950s, the French government became more active in following up on the transmitted petitions, undertaking its own internal investigations on the allegations contained therein and attempting to persuade the UN Secretariat that a petition did not qualify for circulation to the Human Rights Commission. In February 1950, the Economic and Social Council had resolved to formalize the Secretariat's procedures for processing human rights petitions, termed "communications" in official UN parlance, presumably to highlight that these were not actionable requests. The Secretariat was to sort these "communications" into two lists. One was for petitions concerning "the principles involved in the promotion of universal respect for, and observance of, human rights." The second list was for the residual category of "other communications," which in practice meant specific allegations of human rights abuses against a state with the aim of prompting the UN to take remedial action. While the Secretariat published a public summary of texts dealing with

---

[64] Communications dated January 22 and 31, 1952, NUOI Box 389, CAD; Connelly, *Diplomatic Revolution*, 55, 57.
[65] Communications dated December 6, 7, 8, and 12, NUOI Box 389, CAD.
[66] Communications dated November 30, and December 3, 6, 10, and 21, 1951, NUOI Box 389, CAD.
[67] Communications dated February 12 and March 5 to 18, 1958, NUOI Box 390, CAD.

general "principles," it rendered confidential the list of human rights complaints. The terms of ECOSOC Resolution 275(X) mandated that:

each Member State be furnished with a copy of any communication concerning human rights which referred explicitly to that State or the territories under its jurisdiction, without divulging the identity of the author, except where the authors stated that they had already divulged or intended to divulge their names and that they had no objections to their names being divulged.[68]

To the delight of French officials, it turned out that, notwithstanding sporadic, limited efforts to reform UN procedures, even many of the delegations supportive of colonial independence movements had little desire to permit the UN to investigate private complaints.[69]

According to French diplomatic officials, petitions that championed the independence of a colony, even if on the basis of the UN Charter, should not in themselves be considered communications subject to this procedure. On one occasion, Cissé Zakaria ibn Kainou, leader of an organization called the Army for the Liberation of Mauritania, sent a letter to the UN from Egypt asking the United Nations to "save the Mauritanian Fatherland from colonial subjugation" by organizing and supervising a popular referendum on Mauritanian independence. He provided detailed allegations of French atrocities against civilians on the Algerian border and the rigging of elections against Mauritanian nationalists such as Horma Babana, a socialist politician who had "asked the French government to apply in full the rights granted to Mauritanians by the 1946 Constitution" and "insisted on the abolition of forced labor and all other forms of the exploitation of man." Kainou quoted passages from the preamble of the UN Charter on the promotion of "social progress and better standards of life in larger freedom" and "international peace and security," but omitted explicit references to human rights.[70] In response, Guillaume Georges-Picot, the French ambassador to the United Nations, wrote to Foreign Minister Maurice Couve de Murville requesting that the UN Secretariat refrain from publicizing this letter on the grounds that "it cannot in effect be considered a 'petition' since it contains no formal reference to a violation of the rights of man by France in Mauritania.'"[71] The practice of rejecting the standing of petitioners appealing for independence was not new, for in the interwar

---

[68] Jeroen Gutter, *Thematic Procedures of the United Nations Commission on Human Rights and International Law: In Search of a Sense of Community* (Antwerp: Intersentia, 2006), 43.
[69] René Cassin, Foreign Office memorandum, July 1, 1952, NUOI Box 382, CAD.
[70] Communication dated September 1, 1958, NUOI Box 390, CAD.
[71] Guillaume Georges-Picot to Maurice Couve de Murville, Ministry of Foreign Affairs correspondence, September 18, 1958, NUOI Box 390, CAD.

period the League of Nations Permanent Mandates Commission refused to consider petitions that challenged the political authority of colonial powers.[72]

Faced with the growing ranks of anti-colonial delegations in the UN General Assembly, French lawyers advising the foreign ministry on matters of human rights began sharpening their arguments against codifying the right to self-determination in international law. Their hope lay in persuading other member states, above newly independent states, that the right to self-determination endangered their territorial integrity by allowing minority groups to secede. For Cassin, the right to self-determination was the successor to the minority rights protections of the League of Nations. Both in his view had no place in a human rights accord designed to safeguard individuals abstracted from their ethnicity and nationality, though he failed to see that this logic contradicted the administrative practices of the French empire.[73] According to Georges Scelle, a legal adviser to the foreign ministry and noted legal scholar at the time, "the rights of peoples to govern themselves is equivalent to the right to secession."[74] Their colleague Guy de Lacharrière drew a sharp distinction between "the rights of man" and "the right of peoples to govern themselves" (*le droit des peuples à disposer d'eux-mêmes*), as the right to self-determination was translated in French versions of UN texts. The former was a proper object of "positive law" and the latter a "political principle" not suited to codification. In his view, "individual rights" could be extrapolated to "collective liberties, exercised notably by associations, trade unions, and religious groups," but "the people" as a whole could not be a bearer of the rights of man.[75]

Though the Secretariat's Human Rights Division was sympathetic to French efforts to restrict the types of petitions circulated among

---

[72] On petitioning under the League of Nations Mandates, see the work of Susan Pedersen and Natasha Wheatley: Pedersen, *The Guardians: The League of Nations and the Crisis of Empire* (Oxford: Oxford University Press, 2015), ch. 3; Pedersen, "Samoa on the World Stage: Petitions and Peoples before the Mandates Commission of the League of Nations," *Journal of Imperial and Commonwealth History* 40, no. 2 (2012): 231–62; Wheatley, "The Mandate System as a Style of Reasoning: International Jurisdiction and the Parceling of Imperial Sovereignty in Petitions from Palestine," in *The Routledge Handbook of the History of the Middle East Mandates*, ed. Cyrus Shayegh and Andrew Arsan (London: Routledge, 2015), 106–22; Wheatley, "Mandatory Interpretation: Legal Hermeneutics and the New International Order in Arab and Jewish Petitions to the League of Nations," *Past and Present*, no. 227 (2015): 205–48.

[73] René Cassin to Robert Schuman, Ministry of Foreign Affairs correspondence, April 17, 1952, NUOI Box 382, CAD. See also Mackinnon, "Declaration as Disavowal," 70–4.

[74] De la Lacharrière, Ministry of Foreign Affairs memorandum, May 28, 1952, NUOI Box 384, CAD.

[75] Ibid.

members of the Human Rights Commission, the vague language of the procedures in place for handling petitions caused difficulties for the foreign ministry. On one occasion, French diplomats met with UN Secretariat officials to prevent the circulation of a petition from twenty-four Dutch individuals who asked, in general terms without referring to human rights or international norms, for the pardon of Algerian nationalist Moulai Ali Ben Mohamed, sentenced to death. John Humphrey, head of the Human Rights Division, agreed that the petition was not under the purview of the UN Human Rights Commission as it did not refer explicitly violations of particular human rights. But Humphrey was overruled by UN Secretary General Dag Hammarskjöld on the grounds that the petition implicitly concerned infringements of articles of a draft human rights covenant under consideration. The issue was rendered mute once de Gaulle issued a pardon before the matter could be taken up by the Human Rights Commission.[76]

Conclusion

These exchanges suggest that the criteria for admissibility of human rights complaints in the postwar era were far more elastic and less well defined than those operative today.[77] Breaking from the precedent of the postwar period, the Human Rights Committee has ruled admissibility is not to be granted to petitions from third parties "belonging to the general public" on the basis of the general interest, what is known as an *actio populars* ("action of the people").[78] Those submitting complaints are expected to have first exhausted all domestic legal remedies and be familiar with the texts of the full range of UN human rights treaties. In contrast to the 1950s, when there existed no template for petitioners and little knowledge of the logics at work in the processing of petitions, the Office of the UN High Commissioner for Human Rights today provides model complaints forms that ask complainants to "quote the relevant treaty articles which correspond to your case" and "explain how the facts of your case disclose a violation of those articles."[79]

---

[76] Communication dated December 7, 1958; Dag Hammarskjöld letters of March 5 and April 3, 1959; Ministry of Foreign Affairs memoranda dated January 28, February 11, and March 23, NUOI Box 390, CAD.

[77] On the informal logics adopted by humanitarian actors in processing petitions for assistance, see Didier Fassin, *Humanitarian Logic: A Moral History of Present Times* (Berkeley: University of California Press, 2012).

[78] UN Doc. CCPR/C/119/3, para. 13.

[79] Klaus Hüfner, *How to File Complaints on Human Rights Violations: A Manual for Individuals and* NGOs, ed. German Commission for UNESCO and United Nations Association of Germany, 5th ed. (Berlin: United Nations Association of Germany,

Not all articles, however, are created equal. The Human Rights Committee does not consider the right to self-determination to be "justiciable" on the grounds that victim status is only granted to persons as individuals. In its view, the rights to non-discrimination and culture are sufficient to safeguard self-determination, which is not understood to be a collective right but a general principle that can inform decisions concerning individual rights, such as cultural rights.[80] The cleaving of self-determination claims from human rights claims and the expectation of a petitioner's literacy in the minutiae of UN human rights documents in a narrow band of languages: these practices are strikingly reminiscent of those demanded by colonial powers.

The answer to the question of whether anti-colonialism was a human rights movement, as usual, depends on whose voices are foregrounded. Certainly, it was not regarded as such by many Western elites working in the international diplomatic and legal fields, individuals who left behind copious documentation in Western archives and libraries. Such sources, while indispensable for understanding how colonialism responded to and structured the postwar human rights system, cannot offer definitive grounds for concluding that anti-colonialism as a whole had a tenuous relationship with human rights. To view the past through their eyes alone risks being beholden to a rights dualism that all too neatly segregates the individual from the collective, the international from the national, reflecting an essentialist rather than historicized definition of human rights.[81]

After World War II, at a time when international human rights norms were embryonic and fluid, the French colonial state worked to ensure that the world would not equate anti-colonialism and human rights. Those who appealed to the United Nations in support of national independence movements in the French empire did not, for the most part, cite UN texts. Nor did they readily distinguish between natural and legal rights, or national and international normative frameworks. Nevertheless, they did consistently link the defense of individual freedoms proclaimed in the Universal Declaration with the realization of the principle of self-determination enshrined in the UN Charter, even if these documents for the most part remained unnamed.

2010), 63–4; Office of the High Commissioner for Human Rights (OHCHR), "23 Frequently Asked Questions about Treaty Body Complaints Procedures," www.ohchr .org/Documents/HRBodies/TB/23FAQ.pdf

[80] Andrew Pullar, "Rethinking Self-Determination," *Canterbury Law Review* 20 (2014): 107–8.

[81] For a critique of scholarship that relies on Western sources to draw conclusions about human rights and decolonization in the African context, see Chapter 1 in this volume.

In the waning years of French colonial rule, hundreds of private petitioners from North Africa and around the world appealed to the UN to right colonial wrongs. Theirs was a capacious vision of fundamental freedoms and universal values, one that cast the promotion of civil liberties, self-determination, social justice, and peace as indivisible. For colonial subjects themselves, France was guilty of violating not only the foundational principles of the United Nations but the constitutional principles upon which successive French governments had anchored their broken promises of reform. The emergence of the United Nations as a forum for anti-colonial claim making was made possible by the moral bankruptcy of the colonial ideologies of assimilation and federation, premised on contradictory assumptions about cultural difference. These proved irreconcilable in the face of demands for the indiscriminate application of UN human rights standards in overseas empires. The resistance of the French colonial state to a truly universal enjoyment of "Liberty, Equality, Fraternity" meant that the defense of human rights led inexorably to revolutionary struggle.

3 The Limits of Humanitarianism: Decolonization, the French Red Cross, and the Algerian War

Jennifer Johnson

In June 1958, at the height of the Algerian War (1954–62), the French Red Cross's monthly magazine *Vie et Bonté* affirmed that "despite the inherent difficulties of the ongoing events," the humanitarian organization in Algeria remained committed to carrying out "its humanitarian action, regardless of origin, race or religion."[1] These spirited words in the preface of the special issue harkened back to the founding principles of humanitarianism, namely impartiality and neutrality, and reiterated their ongoing power and aspirational relevance to conflicts and the people in their wake. Moreover, the preface reminded its readers of the humanitarian organization's continued efforts to apply these core values even in a colonial context.

Despite the bold claims in the opening pages of *Vie et Bonté*, the French Red Cross's leadership and its staff members struggled to provide balanced care to the varied set of actors consumed in the violence in Algeria. Its personnel regularly encountered French soldiers, Algerian nationalists, pied noirs, and Algerian civilians. According to the aforementioned statement, the French Red Cross would have and should have been able to service equally all of these constituencies. However, the war for colonial liberation exposed the deep cleavages and limitations of humanitarianism during decolonization and revealed a deeply interconnected and contradictory relationship between imperialism, militarism, and humanitarianism.

[1] Archives de la Croix-Rouge Française (hereafter CRF), *Vie et Bonté*, no. 92, June 1958, 1.
[2] Osama W. Abi-Mershed, *Apostles of Modernity: Saint-Simonians and the Civilizing Mission in Algeria* (Stanford: Stanford University Press, 2010); Benjamin Claude Brower, *A Desert Named Peace: The Violence of France's Empire in the Algerian Sahara, 1844–1902* (New York: Columbia University Press, 2009); Alice Conklin, *A Mission to Civilize: The Republican Idea of Empire in France and West Africa, 1895–1930* (Stanford: Stanford University Press, 1997); Patricia Lorcin, *Imperial Identities: Stereotyping, Prejudice, and Race in Colonial Algeria* (Lincoln: University of Nebraska Press, 2014); Jennifer E.

To be sure, this complex nexus had been well established for over one century.[2] However, what makes the 1950s and 1960s moment different from earlier periods, is that, similar to human rights in the post–World War II era, they both underwent massive revisions after 1945, resulting in a renewed global commitment to their core tenets and a common universalist vocabulary.[3] This vocabulary, in essence, expanded the terms and terrain of humanitarianism. It became accessible and applicable to everyone, colonizer and colonized alike. Human rights and humanitarianism also share a stated fundamental goal – universal protection – and they are both beholden to state sovereignty and national interests. Thus, while some scholars have posited that human rights and humanitarianism are historically distinct, this chapter suggests that their analogous aims and struggles make humanitarianism a productive counterpart alongside which to analyze the politics of empire, human rights, and decolonization.[4]

This chapter focuses on one of the most violent and contested struggles of decolonization, the Algerian War, and places at its center one particular humanitarian organization, the French Red Cross. It examines how this national Red Cross society operated during the eight-year conflict and investigates the extent to which it carried out its mission of neutrality and impartiality. Through an analysis of annual reports, committee reports, and correspondence between Algiers, Geneva, and Paris, I argue that the French Red Cross failed to meet its stated objectives because it was caught between conflicting national and humanitarian missions embedded in the organization's history. Its inability to adapt and provide equal and even care to both sides of the conflict created a real and perceived gap in humanitarian aid, paving the way for the Algerian nationalists to create their own national society, the Algerian Red Crescent.[5]

The French Red Cross's public and private actions during the war shed new light on the tripartite relationship between imperialism, militarism, and humanitarianism and demonstrate how decolonization expanded who could be a humanitarian. Throughout most of the war, the organization and its leaders exhibited preferential treatment for French soldiers, expressed derogatory views of Algerians, and repeatedly

---

Sessions, *By Sword and Plow: France and the Conquest of Algeria* (Ithaca, NY: Cornell University Press, 2011).

[3] See the Introduction to this volume.

[4] Samuel Moyn, *The Last Utopia: Human Rights in History* (Cambridge, MA: Belknap Press of Harvard University Press, 2010), 33.

[5] Jennifer Johnson, *The Battle for Algeria: Sovereignty, Health Care, and Humanitarianism* (Philadelphia: University of Pennsylvania Press, 2016), ch. 4.

ignored inquiries and requests from the Red Cross leadership in Geneva to improve services for the local population, revealing the French Red Cross's delicate and ultimately unsuccessful task of separating itself from colonial politics. The Algerian nationalists used these shortcomings to their advantage. They lobbied International Committee of the Red Cross (ICRC) representatives in Geneva to encourage French Red Cross staff to improve its aid distribution in Algeria. They also campaigned for Geneva to recognize their national society and routinely asked for and received material and financial assistance.

The French Red Cross's political allegiance to the French state is not all together surprising given the historical origins of the Red Cross movement.[6] However, the lengths to which it went during decolonization to appear balanced and impartial suggests that its leaders felt compelled to respond to unprecedented pressure from a variety of groups, including ICRC representatives, Algerian nationalists, and concerned French citizens. In an effort to refute claims of discrimination and political hierarchies, French Red Cross staff occasionally published articles in the organization's monthly magazine *Vie et Bonté*, showing its personnel treating the Algerian people with kindness and compassion. French Red Cross president André François-Poncet frequently asserted publicly and privately that the national society was steadfast in its commitment to alleviating *all* human suffering. As Lynn Festa has shown, humanitarian sentiment is frequently engineered through the process of rendering the suffering and humanity of the people in question visible.[7] Thus, one possible reason that the French Red Cross wanted to showcase their work with the Algerian people was to demonstrate to various audiences that France was committed to alleviating their ailments and, in the process, solicit additional support for the French imperial project. Therefore, it is not difficult to understand why neither the Red Cross delegates in Geneva nor the Algerian nationalists were convinced that the French Red Cross was an impartial partner during decolonization.

This study of the French Red Cross highlights the limitations and possibilities of humanitarianism and neutral universalism at the end of empire. Despite their universal pretensions, national Red Cross societies were oriented toward assisting soldiers and restoring the national army. This underlying premise greatly complicated humanitarian provisions in

---

[6] John Hutchinson, *Champions of Charity: War and the Rise of the Red Cross* (Boulder, CO: Westview Press, 1996); Caroline Moorehead, *Dunant's Dream: War, Switzerland and the History of the Red Cross* (London: HarperCollins, 1998).

[7] Lynn Festa, "Humanity without Feathers," *Humanity* 1, no. 1 (2010): 6; Festa, *Sentimental Figures of Empire in Eighteenth-Century Britain and France* (Baltimore: Johns Hopkins University Press, 2006).

a colonial context, often yielding uneven treatment. Moreover, this chapter illustrates that Red Cross officials were similarly constrained as their human rights counterparts by an inability to enforce the neutral and impartial goals of humanitarianism. By illuminating the tension inherent in the French state's arrogation of a universal civilizing mission constituted in part by humanitarian and human rights agendas, decolonization exposed how the particularities of French imperial power trumped the vaunted neutrality of humanitarianism, prompting further revisions and expanding protections for more people.[8] Furthermore, similar to the universal language of human rights, the discourse of humanitarianism offered non-state actors and anti-colonial nationalists an additional rhetorical weapon to use against their colonial oppressor, thus expanding the war's battlefield terrain beyond that of traditional military operations and forcing imperial governments and international organizations to reconsider humanitarianism's essential meaning.

France, Algeria, and the Rise of Humanitarianism

In order to better understand the stakes of the Algerian War in the 1950s and 1960s, first, it is important to contextualize Algeria in France's colonial and metropolitan imagination and to situate this unique imperial relationship alongside the origins of contemporary humanitarianism. When the French invaded Algiers in the summer of 1830, the outgoing French Bourbon Restoration government (1815–30) and the incoming Orleanist July Monarchy (1830–48) were struggling to establish political legitimacy at home. Both pursued overseas expansion, often coupled with aggressive warfare. Algeria quickly became the site where French settlers and military commanders experimented with a new form of imperialism. As Jennifer Sessions has shown, the conquest of Algeria took place at time when the French were still reeling from the effects of the Haitian Revolution (1791–1803), Napoleon's ill-fated Egypt expedition (1798–9), and his defeat at Waterloo (1815).[9] Algeria offered France the opportunity to reinvent its imperial project and to test out the civilizing mission.

The phrase the "civilizing mission" was first regularly used in the 1840s in connection with Algeria.[10] The logic of exporting French civilization to less "civilized" people was inspired by the ideals of French

---

[8] Fabian Klose, "The Colonial Testing Ground: The International Committee of the Red Cross and the Violent End of Empire," *Humanity* 2, no. 1 (2011): 107–26.
[9] Sessions, *By Sword and Plow*, 1–9.   [10] Ibid., 6.

republicanism, which revolved around a number of core principles, including universality, self-help and mutualism, anticlericalism, patriotism, morality, and respect for the individual and private property.[11] Despite the obvious contradictions between the civilizing mission and republicanism, French imperialists did not have to contend with the inherent tension underlying the colonial project for decades.

While France established its empire in Algeria in the mid-nineteenth century, the contemporary humanitarianism movement took root. Its origins were inspired by conflict in Europe, and like empire, from its inception humanitarianism was intimately linked with military action. In 1859, Henri Dunant witnessed the devastating consequences of the Battle for Solferino and he committed to trying to improve care during times of war. Dunant reflected on this issue in his 1862 book *A Memory of Solferino*, which also served as a call to arms to states and governments to humanize war.[12]

Dunant's work ignited an animated discussion among members of Europe's elite political and diplomatic circles and led to the creation of the ICRC. Its founders stressed the principles of neutrality, impartiality, and nondiscrimination and emphasized the need for national committees that would carry out the work at the local level.[13] Encouraging national Red Cross societies made practical sense for the ICRC, which was based in Geneva, for it could not adequately respond to every conflict across the world. However, in doing so, the humanitarianism movement and the subsequent national Red Cross societies became linked to the national interests of individual governments and their militaries.

From their inception in the 1860s, 1870s, and 1880s, participants in these various aid societies understood that their mission was to provide assistance to all people and avoid personal, religious, or national bias. However, given that providing aid to soldiers and the military was also a priority from the beginning of the Red Cross movement, many of the

---

[11] Conklin, *Mission to Civilize*, 7–8.
[12] Henri Dunant was not the only person struggling to render war more humane in this period. In the wake of the Crimean War (1853–6), Florence Nightingale worked tirelessly to improve the British army medical services, and over the course of the American Civil War (1861–5) Clara Barton devoted countless hours to assisting wounded soldiers. Even though Nightingale and Barton were Dunant's contemporaries, he claimed he was unaware of their efforts to improve care to soldiers. However, it is important to note that their collective efforts to render war more humane did not mean eliminating war altogether. Moorehead, *Dunant's Dream*, 28–37; David Forsythe, *The Humanitarians: The International Committee of the Red Cross* (Cambridge, UK: Cambridge University Press, 2005), 16; Hutchinson, *Champions of Charity.*
[13] Moorehead, *Dunant's Dream*, 44–6.
[14] Forsythe and Rieffer-Flanagan, *International Committee of the Red Cross*, 7.

national societies exhibited blatant "self-interest alongside humanitarian goals."[14] One explanation for this contradictory position is that from the beginning of the Red Cross movement, the goal was to provide aid to soldiers and the military. They were the intended beneficiaries and remained the central focus of national Red Cross efforts. State officials quickly realized they had incentives to militarize charity. Doing so served their interests because this special relationship came with certain privileges, chief among them, exemptions from taxes.[15] The tangible financial benefits that states enjoyed as a result of establishing national societies infused the early humanitarian efforts with political motives and set the stage for conflicts between national political agendas and transcendent universal principles.

The politicization of charity continued into the early twentieth century and by World War I, nationalism and patriotism replaced Dunant's original vision of universal and neutral protection.[16] National societies were never fully independent entities, argues David Forsythe, because individual states approved the first ones and established a precedent for a deferential relationship with states and their governments.[17] The strong bond between the state and the national society had a significant impact on how volunteers understood their role, leading some to think of themselves as an extension of the military serving the interests of the state, rather than a volunteer corps that served everyone, despite his or her national affiliation.[18] The early humanitarians' confusion illustrates the deeply embedded and problematic preeminence of the military, a problem that persisted during the world wars and colonial wars for national liberation.

This historical context sheds light on the intimate relationship between humanitarianism and the military, which was woven into the fabric of the

---

[15] Hutchinson, *Champions of Charity*, 177.

[16] Forsythe and Rieffer-Flanagan, *International Committee of the Red Cross*, 8. In peacetimes, royal families and high-ranking officials appointed delegates to national societies they anticipated would protect their interests. For example, in tsarist Russia, the empress personally selected the president of the Red Cross society. Hutchinson, *Champions of Charity*, 176.

[17] Forsythe, *Humanitarians*, 21.

[18] Hutchinson, *Champions of Charity*, 179. The most blatant example of this was the German Red Cross, which continually betrayed the ethos and spirit of universal care while laying claim to ICRC principles. In November 1933, new decrees were passed in Germany that inextricably linked the German Red Cross with the recently formed Third Reich, and, overnight, the national society became responsible to the German government. These statutes transformed the German Red Cross into "just another part of the German state machinery" with disastrous consequences for Jews, prisoners, and any other category of people deemed undesirable by the Nazi regime through 1945. Moorehead, *Dunant's Dream*, 345.

Red Cross by its founders from the start. The French Red Cross was by no means the first national society to navigate the complexities of nationalism, war, and humanitarianism. However, its activities and allegiance to the French military in Algeria throughout the Algerian War laid bare the flagrant contradictions between empire, humanitarianism, and the French universalist claims articulated in the civilizing mission and French republicanism that had motivated France's acquisition of Algeria in the nineteenth century. The French Red Cross's devotion to the French colonial project violated the fundamental principles upon which the Red Cross movement was founded and exposed the elastic meanings of humanitarianism at the end of empire in unprecedented ways.

French Red Cross Action during the Colonial Period

According to ICRC regulations, each country is only permitted one national society. This posed a challenge and moral conundrum for large empires. On the one hand, a national society signaled that that state adhered to humanitarian principles. On the other hand, the very logic and nature of empire frequently contradicted the universalist claims of humanitarianism. The French government was among the earliest supporters of Henri Dunant's Red Cross efforts; in 1864, it founded the French Red Cross, joining national societies in Germany, Belgium, and Spain.[19]

Unsurprisingly, the French Red Cross located its headquarters in Paris. In practical terms, the Paris office was meant to oversee service in all French colonial outposts, including to colonial armies and colonial subjects. If the personnel had adhered to the humanitarian ideals of the Red Cross, notably neutrality, impartiality, universality, and unity, working in contested lands would not have been a problem. However, the Red Cross's dual mission of protecting the military and local people proved especially difficult during wars for national liberation.

The French Red Cross routinely encountered racial, religious, and ethnic difference throughout the French empire. Nowhere did these differences cause the national committee to struggle to adhere to the original universal goals as outlined by Henri Dunant as much as they did in Algeria. For over 130 years, Algeria remained integral to French

---

[19] www.croix-rouge.fr, accessed April 29, 2019. For a history of the French Red Cross, see Frédéric Pineau, *La Croix-Rouge Française, 150 Ans d'histoire* (Paris: Autrement, 2014).
[20] Charles-Robert Ageron, *Histoire de l'Algérie contemporaine*. Vol. 2, *De l'insurrection de 1871 au déclenchement de la guerre de libération (1954)* (Paris: Presses Universitaires de France, 1979); Mahfoud Bennoune, *The Making of Contemporary Algeria, 1830–1987: Colonial Upheavals and Post-independence Development* (Cambridge, UK: Cambridge

politics, shaped its national identity, and played a vital role in its economy.[20] Algeria had the largest settler population within the French empire (roughly 10 percent of the total population by the 1950s), which further complicated French colonial policy and amplified the unrealized universalist claims of republicanism. From the end of World War II until 1962, tension mounted between settlers, Algerians, and French officials as they articulated wildly different visions for Algeria's future. Despite the structural inequalities of France's imperial project, as part of France, the French Red Cross was responsible for providing services in Algeria and performing humanitarian tasks until independence.

Throughout the colonial period, the French Red Cross in Algeria maintained an active agenda, which tended to reinforce the colonial enterprise, but not necessarily in an overtly political manner. It organized national health days, contributed aid to tubercular North African patients in France, assisted veterans of World War II and Indochina, and matched Algerian host families with young French missionaries for Christmas and the New Year holiday.[21] Annual reports suggest that the national society performed services for the European and Algerian populations in Algeria and neither group condemned the aid agency. In other words, the French Red Cross operated in a relatively stable and calm environment throughout most of its time in Algeria, which was largely attributable to peacetime conditions. Its staff did not yet have to make difficult decisions about care and resources amid violent military action that threatened millions of civilians, and hundreds of thousands French and Algerians fighters.

In the 1940s, however, the French Red Cross began to shift its activities as political tensions and anti-colonial sentiment grew in the wake of the killings at Sétif and Guelma, both in northeastern Algeria. On V-E Day, May 8, 1945, Algerian demonstrators wanted to capitalize on the celebratory spirit of Europe's liberation, and they gathered in Sétif to demand their own liberation from France. The encounter turned violent and by mid-morning, forty Algerians and Europeans were dead. Word of the violence circulated quickly, and open insurrection spread in the area,

University Press, 1988); Jacques Berque, *Le Maghreb entre deux guerres* (Paris: Seuil, 1979); David, Prochaska, *Making Algeria French: Colonialism in Bône, 1870–1920* (Cambridge, UK: Cambridge University Press, 1990); James McDougall, *A History of Algeria* (Cambridge, UK: Cambridge University Press, 2017); John Ruedy, *Modern Algeria: The Origins and Development of a Nation* (Bloomington: Indiana University Press, 2005); Benjamin Stora, *Algeria, 1830–2000: A Short History* (Ithaca, NY: Cornell University Press, 2001).

[21] Archives Nationales d'Outre-Mer (hereafter ANOM), GGA 1K/678, French Red Cross reports, 1942–57; ICRC Library SN/FR/13, Report on French Red Cross Activities in Algeria, 1951–3.

lasting nearly two weeks. In that time, roughly 100 Europeans were killed compared to anywhere from 1,500 to 45,000 Algerian deaths, depending on the source.[22] These were defining moments for settlers and Algerian nationalists and established a further chasm between the two.

During this time, French Red Cross action in Algeria became more visible and more scrutinized and by the early 1950s, International Red Cross staff members in Geneva noted an imbalance in the French Red Cross staff and trained personnel in Algeria. French individuals held the leadership and skilled positions such as president, secretary general, regional committee director and medical assistants, whereas a small number of Algerians primarily acted in lower-level positions, working as nurses and midwives.[23] Internal ICRC reports noticed that the French Red Cross replicated this trend in its other colonies as well.[24] A report from December 1953, which evaluated the British, French, and Belgian Red Cross in Africa, criticized the French Red Cross for its failure to integrate locals into the organizational structure or to collaborate with Algerians, exposing the fallacies in the French's initial assimilationist model, which by World War I, had given way to an association model.[25] By contrast, the report praised the British and Belgian Red Crosses for making an effort to incorporate locals and contribute to "blacks'

---

[22] Alistair Horne, *A Savage War of Peace: Algeria, 1954–1962* (New York: New York Review of Book, 1977), 23–8; Jim House and Neil MacMaster, *Paris 1961: Algerians, State Terror and Memory* (Oxford: Oxford University Press, 2006), 35–8; Jean-Pierre Peyroulou, *Guelma, 1945: Une subversion française dans l'Algérie colonial* (Paris: La Découverte, 2009); John Ruedy, *Modern Algeria: The Origins and Development of a Nation* (Bloomington: Indiana University Press, 1992), 148–50.

[23] Archives of the International Committee of the Red Cross (hereafter ACICR), B AG 121 078–006, Participation des indigènes à l'action Croix-Rouge en Afrique, Croix-Rouge Français, 1949–53, February 1954.

[24] Ibid. Madagascar was the one exception. Of all the French territories under discussion (Morocco, Algeria, Tunisia, Senegal, Togo, Soudan (Bamako), Dohomey, Madagascar, and Reunion), the French Red Cross in Madagascar had the most active engagement with locals.

[25] Raymond F. Betts, *Assimilation and Association in French Colonial Theory, 1890–1914* (New York: Columbia University Press, 1961); Alice Conklin, "Democracy Rediscovered: Civilization through Association in French West Africa, 1914–1930," *Cahiers d'études africaines* 37, no. 1 (1997): 59–84; Conklin, *Mission to Civilize*, 6, 74–5; Martin D. Lewis, "One Hundred Million Frenchmen: The Assimilationist Theory in French Colonial Policy," *Comparative Studies in Society and History* 4, no. 2 (1962): 129–52; Lorcin, *Imperial Identities*.

[26] This position is understandable for the British whose vision for imperial rule was centered around the principles of indirect rule and association. However, the position is more curious for the Belgians given that their style of rule, especially in the Congo, could neither be characterized as advocating for assimilation nor association and relied heavily on coercion. Michael Crowder, "Indirect Rule, French and British Style," *Africa* 34, no. 2 (1964): 197–205; Adam Hochschild, *King Leopold's Ghost: A Story of Greed, Terror, and Heroism in Colonial Africa* (New York: Houghton Mifflin, 1998).

evolution."[26] The Belgian Red Cross had even gained respect from the local population and had begun working with a few of the "evolved" Africans to improve sanitary and social conditions in their colonies. This collaboration was in the early stages but, the ICRC reflections note, could serve as a useful model for improving conditions for other Red Cross's throughout the continent.[27] Yet, even though the ICRC observed different patterns in Red Cross relations with local populations throughout Africa, the language the report used to describe Africans working within the British and Belgian Red Cross ranks pointed to an ongoing colonial civilizing project.

The French Red Cross did not follow the Belgian and British examples and incorporate significant numbers of Algerians into its organizational ranks. Even though the national society had been active for decades across Africa, day-to-day operations remained segregated. Settlers' oversized political power in Algeria might offer one explanation for why the French Red Cross did not integrate its staff. Given that Algerians were not visible in leadership positions or most ground operations, it is no surprise that the Algerian people perceived the French Red Cross as favoring French settlers and military personnel or that they considered the national society as biased, partial, and prejudiced.

Many French Red Cross staff members did not go out of their way to assuage Algerians' concerns. In fact, before the war for national liberation, they routinely expressed trepidation and hesitation about working with Algerians. For example, Ms. Odier, a French member of the national society, cautioned that ideally only "responsible Muslims" would carry out Red Cross duties.[28] Even though she did not specify what constituted a "responsible Muslim," her choice of words indicate that, in her view, not all Muslims were suitable to serve alongside her. She was not the only person who openly shared these opinions. In a 1953 memo about North Africa, other staff members commented on the Muslim population's "indolence" with respect to hygiene and health.[29]

This pernicious attitude about Muslim people pervaded the French Red Cross organization and extended across the Mediterranean. On occasion, the Red Cross headquarters in Geneva recognized certain French Red Cross staff members in Algeria for their continued efforts in what might have been considered a less desirable post than its

---

[27] ACICR, B AG 121 078–006, Impression d'ensemble sur les Croix-Rouges en Afrique, December 1953.

[28] ACICR, B AG 121 078–006, Short report on Mlle Odier, no date, likely written between 1949 and 1953.

[29] ACICR, B AG 121 078–006, Remarques (hors-texte) sur l'Afrique du Nord, December 1953.

metropolitan equivalent. On May 30, 1953, ICRC representative Marguerite van Berchem wrote a letter to ICRC president Paul Reugger alerting him that the president of the French Red Cross Algiers committee, Henriette Lung, would be staying in Chamonix in August. Van Berchem recommended that the ICRC invite her to its offices in order to learn more about her work amid the "difficulties and problems" she faced in a Muslim country."[30] Van Berchem applauded Lung's efforts to teach "evolved Muslims" about the "responsibilities of the Red Cross."[31] Even though the letter may at first glance appear as a simple social invitation, it reveals a subtle institutional bias about the capabilities of Muslim people and suggests that some within the ICRC shared unfavorable views of Algerians. It also underscores the paternalist attitude embedded in the French colonial project.

Certainly, the French Red Cross provided aid and assistance throughout Algeria. In 1951, the national society worked with a FF35,000 budget and focused its activities on youth outreach, the elderly, help for Muslim veterans, and assistance to soldiers fighting in Indochina.[32] In 1952, the budget remained static, but the organization shifted more resources to the aforementioned categories and expanded committees into the Sahara. In addition, staff members oversaw 172 cases of missing persons, mostly soldiers fighting in Indochina and those still unaccounted for from 1939 to 1940.[33] In 1953, the group continued its expansion into the Sahara and increased its budget by FF10,000 to carry out this work. Personnel concentrated on seeing Algerian patients in this region and they recorded 43,000 medical visits, over half of whom were children.[34] The number of Algerian patients who came in for a consultation steadily increased, which Red Cross workers interpreted as a sign of success in helping Algerians "understand and like France," a subtle gesture toward the ongoing objectives of empire.[35]

However, not all French Red Cross reports touted its successes and several acknowledged Red Cross shortcomings. A 1953 report discussed

---

[30] ACICR, B AG 121 078–007, Letter from Marguerite van Berchem to ICRC president Paul Reugger, May 30, 1953.

[31] Ibid.

[32] ICRC Library, Geneva, SN/FR/13, Report on French Red Cross Activities in Algeria throughout 1951.

[33] ICRC Library, Geneva, SN/FR/13, Report on French Red Cross Activities in Algeria throughout 1952.

[34] ICRC Library, Geneva, SN/FR/13, Report on French Red Cross Activities in Algeria throughout 1953.

[35] Ibid.

[36] ACICR, B AG 121 078–006, Note sur les Rapports annuels des Délégations Générales de l'Algérie et du Maroc, December 16, 1953.

insufficient financial means and an absence of collaboration with "cultivated Muslim classes."[36] As the report makes clear, the Red Cross's failure to integrate "cultivated" Algerians stemmed from the settlers' severe opposition. While their aggressive campaign to limit Algerians' social and political mobility likely impacted how and where the French Red Cross carried out its work, this explanation masks a different and uncomfortable truth: prior to the Algerian War, the organization struggled to distinguish between a French colonial agenda and a universal humanitarian one.[37]

The limits of universalism were also apparent in reports that point to Islam as a barrier to local recruitment and integration. On March 27, 1954, ICRC representatives Jean-Georges Lossier and Madame Zarrins met to discuss Red Cross action in Africa. They noted that the French Red Cross in particular struggled to recruit Muslim men and women into its ranks. They explained that Muslim women's evolution was still "embryonic," and by way of example, they mentioned how little contact women had with the outside world and when they did leave the private sphere, they remained veiled.[38] Despite these observations, Lossier maintained that the French Red Cross operated with the "spirit of impartiality." In order to illustrate his point, Lossier cited numerous hospital visits during which he claimed all patients – Berbers, Arabs, and Europeans – were treated in the same way. He even estimated that Muslims comprised 80–90 percent of those who benefited from French Red Cross services.[39] While the documents do not corroborate such high estimates, it is telling that Red Cross representatives were attuned to the perception of their operations in a colonial setting. They understood they were supposed to uphold humanitarian ideals, as established by Henry Dunant, yet they continually struggled to do so.

At times French Red Cross personnel cautiously corrected misperceptions about their relationship with local populations. They emphasized

---

[37] ACICR, B AG 121 078–006, Remarques (hors-texte) sur l'Afrique du Nord, December 1953.

[38] ACICR, B AG 121 078–007, Report of meeting between M. Lossier and Mme Zarrins regarding Red Cross action in Africa, March 27, 1954. For further discussion of the role of the veil, see Neil MacMaster, *Burning the Veil: The Algerian War and the 'emancipation' of Muslim women, 1954–1962* (Manchester: Manchester University Press, 2012).

[39] Ibid. This statistic is repeated (and unsubstantiated) elsewhere. ACICR, B AG 121 078–008, the French Red Cross in North Africa, December 1953.

[40] ACICR, B AG 121 078–007, Letter from Léonce Imbert to ICRC President Paul Ruegger, June 10, 1953. For an overview of the historical legacy of the Dar El-Askri, see Thomas DeGeorges, "Still Behind Enemy Lines? Algerian and Tunisian Veterans after the World Wars," in *The World in World Wars: Experiences, Perceptions, and Perspectives from Africa and Asia*, ed. Heike Liebau et al. (Leiden: Brill, 2010).

their consistent aid to Algerian veterans of World War II and offered the Dar El-Askri (Military Residence) regular support.[40] In December 1953, one report stated that it would be an error to think that the French Red Cross in North Africa did nothing for Muslim populations.[41] Yet despite this assertion, the same report admitted that the national society helped the French population before others and had difficulty remaining above colonial politics that favored maintaining Algérie française and preserving empire.[42] The Red Cross could not escape the highly politicized context and when the war for national liberation began in November 1954, it faced an even harder task of impartiality.

Debating Red Cross Responsibilities in a Colonial Context

On November 1, 1954, Algerian anti-colonial nationalists surprised the French colonial administration and the Red Cross by initiating war.[43] The National Liberation Front (Front de Libération Nationale, FLN) coordinated attacks across the country, escalating the conflict quickly. Their actions in the final months of 1954 and into 1955, as well as the international support from Third World allies helped the FLN garner global attention and prompted the ICRC to confront the inadequacies of the organization's universal mandate when operating in a colonial context.

Just prior to the beginning of the Algerian War, the ICRC had first struggled to articulate a clear set of policies for Red Cross actions and responsibilities in French Indochina and British Kenya. The Presidential Council at the time did not know how to react or what role the ICRC should take on in what it called "internal troubles,"[44] although members recognized that they posed "a serious humanitarian problem."[45] A general report on ICRC intervention in internal conflicts stated that "it could not provide a precise definition of these situations, but that did

---

[41] ACICR, B AG 121 078–006, Remarques (hors-texte) sur l'Afrique du Nord, December 1953.

[42] Ibid.

[43] For Algerian accounts of the war, see Mabrouk Belhocine, *Le courrier Alger – le Caire, 1954–1956* (Algiers: Casbah, 2000); Mohammed Harbi, *Le FLN: Mirage et réalité* (Paris: Éditions Jeune Afrique, 1980); Harbi, ed., *Les Archives de la revolution algérienne* (Paris: Éditions Jeune Afrique, 1981; Harbi and Gilbert Meynier, eds., *Le FLN documents et histoire: 1954–1962* (Paris: Fayard, 2004).

[44] ACICR, Presidential Council Reports, verbal proceedings, December 16, 1954.

[45] ACICR B AG 012 004, Red Cross principles and rules for action, report by Henri Coursier on the question of internal troubles, January 18, 1955.

[46] ACICR B AG 012 004, Red Cross principles and rules for action, internal report on ICRC intervention in civil wars and internal conflicts, n.d.

not matter ... what is important is to know when the ICRC can and should intervene."[46] It listed the following conditions for intervention:

1. The conflict must have a certain seriousness and consist of violent acts.
2. The events must be a certain length of time.
3. There must be a struggle between two or more groups that each possess an organization.
4. There must be victims.
5. Even if all four conditions are met, the ICRC is not obligated to intervene if the national Red Cross can act effectively and is willing to do so.[47]

Only in situations where conditions 1–4 occurred simultaneously would the ICRC consider taking action, and representatives would first collect information on the particular case before offering the organization's services.

The wars of decolonization easily met these criteria. However, the ICRC did not have any legal jurisdiction in Indochina and Kenya, and if it sent assistance or suggested conducting missions, it had to make requests through the European governments, not the nationalist organizations, for the countries were not yet sovereign. The Swiss delegations would neither question nor interfere in the politics on the ground and were only prepared to intervene on "moral grounds."[48] The ICRC aim of abstaining from politics proved impossible in this new form of internal conflict.

In January 1955, ICRC delegates clashed over what the organization's official position should be on internal conflicts. They were perplexed by the unique challenges Britain and France posed for the ICRC. Both imperial powers had signed the United Nations Charter and the Universal Declaration of Human Rights less than a decade prior but were now engaged in practices in their colonies that blatantly violated them. Henri Coursier, ICRC representative and member of the ICRC legal department, noted in his observations about unrest in Kenya that "Great Britain did not solicit ICRC intervention" for help in respecting "the principles of civilization. We can imagine that such an intervention, in contrast, desired by the insurgents, could in diverse situations ... render the conflict less savage."[49] He remarked that Britain signed the European Convention on Human Rights "undoubtedly with the best

---

[47] Ibid.   [48] Ibid.
[49] ACICR B AG 012 004, report by Henri Coursier on the question of internal troubles, January 18, 1955.

intentions to apply them in the countries [it] administered." Yet Coursier noticed colonial officials went to great lengths to cut off rebels from internationalizing the conflict and suppressing their ability to receive international protection. Coursier fell short of openly criticizing British action in Kenya, a common refrain throughout the wars of decolonization, but his word choice indicated he believed its colonial administration had forgotten the principles of civilization and needed a reminder. This is a strong indictment of British behavior and an implicit way of suggesting its officials openly violated accepted principles of humanitarianism.

In June 1955, six months after Coursier's internal report and three years into the violence in Kenya, ICRC representative Pierre Gaillard received a letter explaining how the British Red Cross might handle the consequences of conflict in Kenya.[50] It explained that

In the case of Kenya and the British Red Cross, I think it quite feasible that for reason of expediency and prudence it has been decided to do nothing, as to avoid any possible objection and criticism. Chairman and Vice-Chairman of the British Red Cross are not of that social strata which has practical experience and knowledge of the position of the Colonies' indigenous people. They may even feel obliged – and justified from their own point of view – to decline any activity in order to avoid being reproached for intervening in colonial political affairs.[51]

His reply encapsulates all of the potential problems with a national Red Cross society in a colonial situation and the ICRC's inability to mandate changes. In this case, British Red Cross senior staff did not know enough about the local population to make meaningful contributions, and they were compelled to abstain from providing any assistance, fearing a negative reaction for intervening in politics. What, then, was the British Red Cross there for if not to alleviate suffering to all people?

In the weeks leading up to the first ICRC mission in Kenya, after five years of trying to schedule one, Pierre Gaillard vented his stress over being repeatedly denied entrance into the East African country during a

---

[50] For histories of the Emergency (1952–60) and Mau Mau in Kenya, see David Anderson, *Histories of the Hanged: The Dirty War in Kenya and the End of Empire* (New York: Norton, 2005); Huw Bennett, *Fighting the Mau Mau: The British Army and Counterinsurgency in the Kenya Emergency* (Cambridge, UK: Cambridge University Press, 2013); Daniel Branch, *Defeating Mau Mau, Creating Kenya: Counterinsurgency, Civil War, and Decolonization* (Cambridge, UK: Cambridge University Press, 2009); Caroline Elkins, *Imperial Reckoning: The Untold Story of Britain's Gulag in Kenya* (New York: Henry Holt, 2005); Fabian Klose, *Human Rights in the Shadow of Colonial Violence* (Philadelphia: University of Pennsylvania Press, 2013).

[51] ACICR B AG 013 008, Political, religious, and cultural questions relating to the Red Cross concept; action in favor of peace: letter to Pierre Gaillard concerning the British Red Cross in Kenya, June 29, 1955.

Presidential Council meeting. He said, if the British deny the ICRC access once again, "a perfectly plausible hypothetical" situation, "we can at least have a piece [of paper] attesting that we tried to do something."[52] The British government and British Red Cross positions during the Kenyan conflict set the stage for what ICRC representatives would encounter in Algeria and foreshadowed the limits of the organization's universal principles when confronted with the actions of a national society that aligned more with the colonial power.[53]

Anti-politics and the French Red Cross's "Double Mission" during the Algerian War

The scattered nature of the ICRC position on internal conflicts and colonial wars trickled down to the French Red Cross, reflected in the dual messaging of its leaders and staff members. From the outbreak of war through to its conclusion, the official French position was that the conflict in Algeria was not a war.[54] Instead, it insisted on euphemistically referring to the violent struggle as "the events," thus undermining the possibility of outside intervention. French Red Cross correspondence and its magazine, Vie et Bonté, adopted this same terminology and devoted much of its late 1954 and early 1955 coverage to the aftermath of a sizeable September 1954 earthquake in Orléansville, Algeria.[55] Doing otherwise would have been a political statement in and of itself and left the French Red Cross open to criticism by the French government of supporting the Algerian nationalist cause. In addition to suggesting a pro-French line, the French Red Cross position also points toward the anti-politics of humanitarianism.

---

[52] ACICR, Presidential Council Reports, verbal proceedings, Pierre Gaillard, "Note for the Committee," June 7, 1955.

[53] For a discussion of the relationship between the ICRC and the different French administrations during the war, see Françoise Perret and François Bugnion, "Between Insurgents and Government: The International Committee of the Red Cross's action in the Algerian War (1954–1962)," *International Review of the Red Cross*, vol. 93, 883 (September 2011), 707–42; Perret, "L'action du Comité international de la Croix-Rouge pendant la guerre d'Algérie (1954–1962)," *International Review of the Red Cross* 86, no. 856 (December 2004): 917–51; Magali Herrmann, "*Le CICR et la guerre d'Algérie: Une guerre sans nom, des prisonniers sans statut, 1954–1958*," Mémoire de license, Université de Genève, 2006; Johnson, *Battle for Algeria*, ch. 5; Klose, "Colonial Testing Ground"; Klose, *Human Rights in the Shadow of Colonial Violence*, 128–37.

[54] The French government did not publicly recognize the war as such until 1999.

[55] ACICR, B AG 121 078–007, Letter from ICRC president Paul Ruegger to French Red Cross president Georges Brouardel (1947–55), September 10, 1954; Letter from Pierre Gaillard to William Michel, November 9, 1954.

During the early years of the war the French Red Cross maintained a relatively low profile in Algeria, which mirrored the initial metropolitan response to the conflict. In the days and weeks immediately following the FLN attacks, French leaders did not think they had reason for concern. They noticed disturbances throughout Algerian cities, but they did not consider them the opening offensive of a large-scale and long-term conflict that would end with Algerian sovereignty. For example, a November 2 article entitled "Terrorism in North Africa" in the leading French newspaper *Le Monde* reported four deaths from "deliberate action" officials believed "were part of an organized plot by the nationalists."[56] The following day, the front-page headline of the same newspaper declared "Calm Restored in Algiers and Oran."[57] A little over one week later, the French Minister of the Interior and future president François Mitterrand delivered impassioned remarks to the National Assembly, also underscoring that he did not consider the FLN a serious threat. He labeled its attacks a "hastily launched outburst, which has forced them in a difficult situation, one that will end badly for them."[58]

The nonchalant French response, however, changed quickly in 1955 as the FLN continued its military assaults in Algeria and its Third World allies began lobbying on its behalf at the United Nations.[59] In April 1955, the French National Assembly passed a bill to implement a state of emergency in Algeria, all but suspending civil liberties there.[60] In March the following year, under the Guy Mollet government, the French parliament passed the "special powers" law, which authorized the

---

[56] "Terrorisme en Afrique du Nord: Plusieurs tués en Algérie au cours d'attaques simultanées de postes de police," *Le Monde*, November 2, 1954, p. 1. The *New York Times* ran a headline with comparable language, "Terrorist Bands Kill 7 in Algeria; French Send Aid," November 2, 1954, p. 1.

[57] "Après la série d'attentats commis dimanche en algérie, le calme est revenue dans l'algérois et en oranie," *Le Monde*, November 3, 1954, p. 1. In contrast, the French communist newspaper *L'Humanité* covered the story under the headlines "Stop Repression in Algeria, Massive Arrests" (November 2, 1954, p. 1) and "Armored Vehicles in Action Against Algerians in the Aurès Mountains" (November 3, 1954, p. 1).

[58] Quoted in Todd Shepard, *Voices of Decolonization: A Brief History with Documents* (New York: St. Martin's, 2015), 102.

[59] Jeffrey James Byrne, *Mecca of Revolution: Algeria, Decolonization, and the Third World Order* (New York: Oxford University Press, 2016); Matthew Connelly, *A Diplomatic Revolution: Algeria's Fight for Independence and the Origins of the Post-Cold War Era* (Oxford: Oxford University Press, 2002); Johnson, *Battle for Algeria*, ch. 6; I. M. Wall, *France, the United States, and the Algerian War* (Berkeley: University of California Press, 2001).

[60] Sylvie Thénault, *Une drôle de justice: Les magistrats dans la guerre d'Algérie* (Paris: La Découverte, 2001).

[61] Klose, *Human Rights in the Shadow of Colonial Violence*, 103–6.

government to take extraordinary measures to maintain and restore order in Algeria.[61] In order to do so, Mollet called on French reservists to cross the Mediterranean. Protests erupted across France that spring; soldiers and civilians demonstrated, not because they identified with Algerian nationalist demands, but rather because the time away would disrupt their lives and they were not devoted to the cause of preserving Algérie française.[62] By spring 1956, French leaders had shifted their approach to the conflict and escalated their judicial and military response in accordance with war and the issue had become a focal point in French public discourse.

Despite the aggressive French military response, French Red Cross staff members and their monthly magazine *Vie et Bonté* did not mention the war for several months. Instead it continued publishing human interest stories about physicians who fought in Indochina and debated, in general terms, the decay of medical infrastructure in times of war.[63] When *Vie et Bonté* did publish articles about Algeria, such as the September–October 1956 article summarizing French Red Cross president André François-Poncet's visit there, it detailed his numerous stops throughout the country to local chapters. But it failed to report specifics about the conflict. The piece emphasized "that everywhere [François-Poncet] went he saw Red Cross achievements, personnel that honor the national society, committee presidents who often face difficult tasks supporting one another, some assisting the military and others the Muslim [population]."[64] This kind of reporting, which showcases positive attributes of French Red Cross activities is not necessarily surprising. Yet its complete omission for the reasons behind François-Poncet's visit raises questions about why the French Red Cross avoided addressing the conflict. His trip was not routine. Violence and military action had increased dramatically in the year since he became the national society's president and his trip provided the opportunity check on regional capacity and distribution in light of military and political developments in Algeria.[65] The article is significant for a second reason. It stressed Red Cross services for French and Algerians suggesting that the staff and *Vie*

[62] Martin Evans, *Algeria: France's Undeclared War* (Oxford: Oxford University Press, 2012), 163–6.

[63] CRF, "Le médecin, un combatant?" *Vie et Bonté*, no. 69, September–October 1955, 16–17.

[64] CRF, "Visite de M. André François-Poncet, president de la C.R.F., en Algérie," *Vie et Bonté*, no. 78, September–October 1956, 1.

[65] The November 1955 *Vie et Bonté* issue published a profile of François-Poncet that detailed his many years of Red Cross involvement.

et Bonté editors aimed to present an image of balanced care in the early years of the war, even if they did not refer to it as such.

French Red Cross annual reports for 1955 and 1956 maintain similar elisions about the war. Both devote considerable attention to the September 1954 Orléansville earthquake and ensuing efforts to provide relief to communities in the area. Assisting the French army was the second focus of these reports, with one-tenth of the FF21m operating budget spent in this domain.[66] Brief mention in official correspondence alluded to the current "situation." For example, cabinet director Jacques Pernet wrote a short letter to the Algiers Prefecture explaining the French Red Cross intended to collect funds for "those hit by the events" but did not elaborate further.[67] The 1955 report referenced "the insurrectional state" and "distressing events that paralyzed some regional activity" in its opening lines but, like Pernet's letter, it also fell short of clarifying what those terms meant.[68] In a June 1956 letter to ICRC president Léopold Boissier, the general director of the French Red Cross in Algiers, Léonce Imbert, boasted of the French Red Cross's "humanitarian and social action toward those who suffer ... during the difficult times at hand."[69] Imbert did not specify what or why Algeria was experiencing "difficult times." Despite chaos and repression erupting throughout Algeria, the French Red Cross did not officially acknowledge that a transformative war was taking place, pointing toward the anti-politics of humanitarianism.

In an April 1957 report, written three months into the infamous Battle of Algiers during which General Jacques Massu launched an aggressive offensive against the FLN in Algiers, the French Red Cross indirectly acknowledged the conflict. It specified that the national society had "intensified its efforts ... despite difficulties from the insurrectional state" and pacification campaigns.[70] The report focused on the society's "social and humanitarian spirit" that dispensed "charitable aid, without racial or religious distinction, to people in need, victims of natural disasters, and calamitous events, specifically floods." But it only described victims in

---

[66] CRF, "Rapport sur les activités de la Croix-Rouge Française en Algérie au cours de l'année 1955," May 1956, 2.

[67] ANOM GGA 1K/678, French Red Cross reports, 1942–57. Memo on the French Red Cross by Jacques Pernet, Office of the Prefect, Algiers, April 21, 1956.

[68] CRF, "Rapport sur les activités de la Croix-Rouge Française en Algérie au cours de l'année 1955," May 1956, 1.

[69] ACICR B AG 121 078 001–007, Léonce Imbert to ICRC president Léopold Boissier, June 11, 1956.

[70] CRF, "Rapport sur les activités de la Croix-Rouge Française en Algérie au cours de l'année 1957," April 1957, 1.

general terms. It did not profile aid distributed to destitute Algerian civilians or ALN (Armée de Libération Nationale [National Liberation Army]) soldiers affected by the war.[71] Financial and material consideration for the French army received sustained attention and French Red Cross personnel opened 170 files on behalf of French military families, a number that grew steadily for the duration of the war.[72] The national society's strong relationship with the army was also reflected in numerous articles in the French newspapers *Le Monde* and *L'Echo d'Alger* that described French Red Cross staff visiting French soldiers in hospitals and distributing cigarettes, candy, and games to raise morale.[73]

The imbalanced provision of care and allocation of resources in the first years of the war led some Algerian nationalists to question the French Red Cross's ability to carry out its universal mission and they accused it of being an extension of the French colonial state.[74] In 1957 members of the Comité de Coordination et d'Exécution, the FLN chief executive body at the time, wrote a thirty-seven-page internal memo explaining current developments in the war. One of them, they explained, was the French Red Cross's "failure" to remain neutral as the conflict progressed.[75] The memo questioned the utility of the national society if it merely replicated the colonial state's political leanings. Furthermore, it accused the humanitarian organization of disproportionately servicing French soldiers at the expense of Algerian civilians and wounded National Liberation Army (Armée de Libération Nationale) fighters.[76] In a war for decolonization, one might expect nationalists to denounce any person, institution, or organization they perceived to be affiliated with the colonial state. But the Algerian anti-colonial leaders

---

[71] Ibid.   [72] Ibid., 2.

[73] These news sources repeatedly published articles about CRF visits to French military and civilian hospitals. Often, CRF nurses would pose alongside injured French soldiers and the caption would describe the rejuvenating nature of their visits. Around Christmas, the CRF made an extra effort to visit hospitals around the country and hand out gifts to the French soldiers.

[74] Based on numerous articles published in *Vie and Bonté* in 1956, it is understandable how one might perceive bias within the national society. For example, the September–October edition presents a summary of François-Poncet's visit to the three major cities in Algeria and concludes that French Red Cross activity is "satisfactory" given the current "events." Even if the magazine does not provide statistics to add weight to French Red Cross claims, it suggests that the staff was, at the very least, committed to projecting the image of carrying out its humanitarian mission amid the war. CRF, *Vie et Bonté*, September–October 1956.

[75] Algerian National Archives, GPRA 78(i), "Plan du travail du CRA établi à l'intérieur de CCE," internal Algerian Red Crescent Work Plan, signed by Hadj Omar Boukli-Hacène, Algerian Red Crescent, Tunis, September 26, 1957.

[76] Ibid.

were not the only ones who expressed concern about the French Red Cross's ability to uphold its humanitarian mission in Algeria.

The FLN's accusations rapidly gained traction among its allies in the Arab world. In the summer of 1957 as the Battle of Algiers raged on and amid the construction of the Morice Line, an electrified fence the French built along the border with Tunisia to restrict the movement of people and arms, Syrian and Jordanian Red Crescent officials complained to the International Red Cross. They claimed the French Red Cross failed to provide assistance to Algerian nationalists or Algerian victims of war, which, in their opinion, amounted to racial discrimination. They were outraged that during a time of extreme need the national society marginalized innocent people and soldiers who were no longer in combat.[77]

ICRC president Léopold Boisser took these allegations seriously and immediately contacted French Red Cross president, André François-Poncet, to let him know about the criticisms launched against the organization.[78] With hardly any delay, François-Poncet summoned Léonce Imbert, head of the French Red Cross in Algeria, to Paris to discuss the allegations. Based on their conversation, François-Poncet wrote to Boissier "vigorously reject[ing]" the Syrian and Jordanian claims. In fact, he insisted that Algerian nationalists "were treated like any person in hospitals," with the minor exception that guards stood outside their doors as a precautionary security measure.[79] François-Poncet proudly reported that of the forty local CRF committees in Algeria, none of them had stopped or slowed down service to the local population. While his rhetoric was passionate and his assertions presumed that most Algerians had access to French Red Cross facilities and staff, he neglected to provide supporting evidence for these substantial claims.[80]

---

[77] ACICR B AG 121 078–007, Letter from Syrian Red Crescent secretary general Dr. Ch Chatti and vice president Dr. M. Chaouky to Léopold Boissier, July 22, 1957; Letter from Jordanian Red Crescent president Dr. Moustafa Khalifeh to the Secretary General of the League of Red Cross Societies, August 14, 1957.

[78] ACICR B AG 121 078–007, Letter from ICRC president Léopold Boissier to French Red Cross president André François-Poncet, August 22, 1957.

[79] ACICR B AG 121 078–007, Letter from André François-Poncet to Léopold Boissier, September 6, 1957.

[80] François-Poncet had at least one corroborating source. In June 1957, Charles Richet, a member of the Academy of Medicine, visited a civilian hospital in Algiers. During his time there he examined and compared the rooms and facilities that wounded "Muslims" and "Christians" were treated in. According to his assessment, there was "no difference" in the food patients received nor in the staff's behavior toward the two groups. The only difference he could point to, like François-Poncet, was that a guard stood watch outside the Muslim patients' rooms. ACICR B AG 121 078–007, Letter from Charles Richet to André François-Poncet, September 8, 1957.

Throughout the fall of 1957, as Algerian nationalists Abdelkader Chanderli and M'hamed Yazid campaigned on the FLN's behalf at the UN in New York, François-Poncet continued to hear murmurs that the French Red Cross devoted all of its efforts to caring for French soldiers "and neglected to [provide any care] to Muslim populations."[81] He rebuked that characterization, calling it "superficial and unfair" and emphasized the French Red Cross's robust efforts for people on both sides of the conflict that he witnessed in Algeria during his visit there one year prior.[82] French Red Cross printed materials attempted to support François-Poncet's claims. In 1957, a *Vie et Bonté* issue reported, the French Red Cross spent FF4,501,085 on civilian activities and FF8,533,114 on aid to the military in the Algiers region.[83] While the expenditures for the military were twice that of the civilian ones, these kinds of statistics might have been useful for François-Poncet to gesture toward when responding to critics and corresponding with ICRC leaders to prove to them that the French Red Cross was in fact devoting resources to the Algerian population. Yet it would have been difficult to say that the care was equally distributed.

In November of that year François-Poncet wrote ICRC president, Léopold Boissier, and told him about all of the important work the various CRF committees were carrying out in Algeria. He was said to have included a Red Cross report from the Souk-Ahras committee in the Constantine region that highlighted the staff's notable work and which he asserted was representative of French Red Cross efforts "everywhere."[84] Boissier received his letter with interest, and noted how "very gratifying" it was "to see with what care the sections of the French Red Cross in Algeria are concerned with the Muslim populations."[85] Perhaps Boissier was not fully convinced by François-Poncet's descriptions about the organization's work in Algeria because in that same letter, Boissier ended with a pressing reminder, "It is obvious that this is an area in which strict objectivity is required."[86] The ICRC had struggled to determine how to handle conflict in colonial settings and half way through the Algerian

---

[81] ACICR B AG 121 078–007, Letter from François-Poncet to Léopold Boissier, November 26, 1957.

[82] Ibid. For an overview of François-Poncet's visit to Algeria in the fall of 1956, see French Red Cross Archives, *Vie et Bonté*, July–August 1956 and September–October 1956.

[83] CRF, *Vie et Bonté*, June 1958.

[84] ACICR B AG 121 078–007, Letter from François-Poncet to Léopold Boissier, November 26, 1957.

[85] ACICR B AG 121 078–007, Letter from Léopold Boissier to André François-Poncet, December 6, 1957.

[86] Ibid.

War, its president remained acutely aware of the difficult but worthy task of pursuing a balanced and universal approach.

Even while denouncing the accusations of inequality, François-Poncet's own writings reveal that he absorbed and reproduced the French government position about the conflict. For example, when discussing a short 1957 report about the French Red Cross near Constantine he referred to it as the "troubles" rather than a war.[87] It is possible that his use of "troubles" was meant to avoid articulating a political position, for had he used a different word or term that implied war, he might have been perceived as legitimizing the Algerian nationalists' claims. This ambiguity gets at the very nature of the anti-politics of humanitarianism.

As the war progressed, the French army implemented increasingly repressive measures including the routine use of torture and extreme counterinsurgency tactics, all of which caused an uproar in the metropole and had significant implications for humanitarian activity in Algeria.[88] François-Poncet could hardly claim ignorance to the degree of conflict and serious suffering it engendered. In June 1957, he met with ICRC delegate William Michel to discuss the growing refugee crisis that had developed in Algeria and that was spilling over into neighboring Morocco and Tunisia. Tens of thousands of civilians had fled their homes amid the escalation of violence between French military forces and the FLN. When Michel explained an ICRC plan to assist refugees in Morocco, François-Poncet replied that the individuals in question "had not been driven out" of Algeria "by the French." Rather, he said, they must have left "voluntarily" and therefore he was hesitant to initiate an appeal on their behalf.[89]

In the same meeting François-Poncet described the national society's priorities and concluded that "the French Red Cross [was] not neutral" in the same way as the ICRC; above all, he claimed, its

---

[87] Ibid.

[88] On torture, see Henri Alleg, *La Question* (Paris: Minuit, 1958); Raphaëlle Branche, *La torture et l'armée pendant la guerre d'Algérie* (Paris: Gallimard, 2001); Marnia Lazreg, *Torture and the Twilight of Empire: From Algiers to Baghdad* (Princeton, NJ: Princeton University Press, 2008) Pierre Vidal-Naquet, *La raison d'état* (Paris: Éditions de Minuit, 1962); Vidal-Naquet, *La torture dans la République: Essai d'histoire et de politique contemporaines, 1954–1962* (Paris: Éditions de Minuit, 1972); Vidal-Naquet, *Les crimes de l'armée française: Algérie, 1954–1962* (Paris: La Découverte & Syros, 2001). On the French domestic response, see James D. LeSueur, *Uncivil War: Intellectuals and Identity Politics during the Decolonization of Algeria* (Nebraska: University of Nebraska Press, 2005).

[89] ACICR, B AG 280 008 006.02, Report of meeting between François-Poncet and William Michel, June 26, 1957.

[90] Ibid.

allegiance was to French soldiers.[90] His honest admission illustrates a significant difference between the ICRC and national societies and a tension between what he might have perceived as the pressure to appear and present the French Red Cross as neutral. The former was established as a vehicle for universal and apolitical humanitarian assistance. The latter was established with similar goals, but it had always been intimately tied to the nation's military and this continued to be the case during the Algerian War. François Poncet's words provide further evidence of the French Red Cross's double message. In certain settings he was willing to acknowledge that the organization prioritized French soldiers but in others he presented the image of its staff administering balanced care. ICRC representatives were disappointed in François-Poncet's wavering position and concluded that he "was not prepared to modify . . . the orientation of French Red Cross activities in Algeria."[91]

By 1958 Léopold Boissier had reason to be skeptical of François-Poncet's assurances that the French Red Cross in Algeria could rise above politics and equally serve all people in need during the war. He asked for specific information regarding the national society's outreach to displaced Algerians and especially those living in regroupment camps.[92] The regroupment policy had originated in 1955 in the Aurès mountains in northeastern Algeria as a small and disjointed French military initiative. By 1957, they had become a dominant army tactic to deny rebels of local support.[93] French military officials uprooted the Algerian population from their land and livestock, depriving them of their traditional agricultural economy and relocated them to designated areas under their control. They believed these centers would cut off Algerian combatants

---

[91] ACICR, B AG 280 008 006.02, Letter from Pierre Gaillard to William Michel, July 2, 1957; ACICR, B AG 280 008 006.02, Report of meeting between François-Poncet and William Michel, June 26, 1957.

[92] For a comprehensive study on the regroupment centers, see Michel Cornaton, *Les regroupements de la décolonisation en Algérie* (Paris: Éditions Ouvrières, 1967). Cornaton's work on regroupment centers used Inspection Générale des Regroupements de la Population (IGRP) reports and fieldwork in Algeria to substantiate his analysis. French archives on this subject remained closed for nearly thirty years after the book's publication. When the documents were released, Cornaton's claims were corroborated. Also, Keith Sutton, "Algeria's Socialist Villages – A Reassessment," *Journal of Modern African Studies* 22, no. 2 (1984): 223–48; Sutton, "Army Administration Tensions over Algeria's Centres de Regroupement, 1954–1962," *British Journal of Middle Eastern Studies* 26, no. 2 (1999): 243–70; Sutton, "Population Resettlement – Traumatic Upheavals and the Algerian Experience, *Journal of Modern African Studies* 15, no. 2 (1977): 279–300.

[93] Cornaton, *Les regroupements*, 63; Harbi, *Le FLN*, 208.

[94] Cornaton, *Les regroupements*, 62–3.

from supplies and land used to launch attacks against the colonial regime.[94] In 1957, the military created two categories of centers, temporary and permanent ones. Temporary centers were destroyed after they fulfilled their initial relocation function. Permanent centers were geared toward more long-term goals.[95] The number of regroupment centers increased dramatically from this point on. In 1957, approximately 240,000 Algerians lived in 382 temporary and permanent centers. By early 1960, 1.5 million Algerians lived in over 1,700 regroupment centers.[96] And later that year, the centers were so pervasive that nearly one-fourth of the Algerian population had been forcibly resettled into them.[97] These centers were home to some of the neediest Algerian people who had been displaced by war. They would have been an ideal setting for the French Red Cross to carry out humanitarian work but as correspondence between Geneva, Paris, and Algiers showed, the national society fell short of meeting that demand.

ICRC President Léopold Boissier had received reports suggesting that the French Red Cross was not taking the lead in humanitarian relief in the camps and that it had made "very modest progress" in assisting the local population.[98] French Red Cross officials told ICRC delegate William Michel that other medical relief initiatives such as the Special Administrative Sections (Sections Administratives Spécialisées), a comprehensive French wartime program intended to foster political and social rapprochement between Algerians and the colonial state, were more visible and active in the camps.[99] They claimed that such a division of labor was necessary in areas that were geographically isolated, since their personnel would need helicopters to access them. But they

---

[95] Sutton, "Army Administration Tensions," 256; Archives de la Service Historique de l'Armée de Terre (SHAT) 1H 2030, Centres de Regroupements, Général de Corps d'Armée Crepin to Général Commandant la Région Territoriale et le Corps d'Armée d'Oran, d'Alger, de Constantine (n.d.)

[96] Sutton, "Army Administration Tensions," 257. Sylvie Thénault estimates that nearly 400,000 Algerians lived in regroupment centers by early 1958. Sylvie Thénault, *Histoire de la guerre d'indépendance algérienne* (Paris: Flammarion, 2005), 99.

[97] Pierre Bourdieu and Abdelmalek Sayad, *Le déracinement: La crise de l'argriculture traditionelle en Algérie* (Paris, Éditions de Minuit, 1964), 13.

[98] ACICR B AG 121 078–007, Summary report of a meeting with M. Merillon of the French Red Cross written by ICRC delegate William Michel, January 7, 1958.

[99] ACICR B AG 121 078–007, Note from ICRC delegate William Michel to ICRC delegate Pierre Gaillard, January 15, 1958. On the role of the Special Administrative Sections, see Jacques Frémeaux, "Les SAS (sections administratives spécialisées)," *Guerres mondiales et conflits contemporains* 208, no. 4 (2002): 55–68; Johnson, *Battle for Algeria*, ch. 2; Grégor Mathias, *Les Sections Administratives Spécialisées en Algérie: Entre ideal et réalité, 1955–1962* (Paris: L'Harmattan, 1998).

[100] ACICR B AG 121 078–007, Note from ICRC delegate William Michel to ICRC delegate Pierre Gaillard, January 15, 1958.

reassured the ICRC that once they had this equipment, the French Red Cross would expand its outreach to include these regions.[100]

Despite his earlier admission, François-Poncet went to great lengths to try to show the national society's commitment to the Algerian people and dispel any lingering doubts the Red Cross in Geneva might have about its dedication to the honorable humanitarian ideals.[101] In June 1958, one month after Charles de Gaulle returned to power and helped change the course of the war with his rousing speeches, an overhaul of the French constitution, and a willingness to enter talks with Algerian nationalists, *Vie et Bonté*, the French Red Cross magazine, ran a cover story and twenty-four-page spread about its activities in Algeria between 1954 and 1958.[102] This issue was rare in that it focused so heavily and explicitly on Algeria and while the reporting did not use the word war, it used a plethora of other euphemisms – "pacification," "undeniable difficulties," "victims of terrorism," and "the events" – that convey to the reader the nature of those extraordinary times.

The June issue provided an overview of the four major areas where the French Red Cross was active – Algiers, Constantine, Oran, and the Sahara – and included select reports from individual committees throughout Algeria.[103] It highlighted a range of services, including medical outreach in the Sahara, events at which French Red Cross personnel distributed milk, clothing, and gifts, and efforts to establish temporary workrooms that provided local men and women with employment opportunities.[104] In addition to trying to showcase what the national society had accomplished in the first years of the conflict with ample data, the issue also promoted a similar narrative with pictures. For example, the cover photo featured seven veiled Algerian women, two Algerian men, and three Algerian children standing together next to a smiling French Red Cross nurse inside of a building. This image sought to offer an alternative interpretation of French Red Cross priorities during the war; here their emphasis was on assisting Algerian civilians, not French soldiers, and rapprochement efforts. It tried to render the hardships of Algerian civilians visible, perhaps stoking humanitarian

---

[101] ACICR B AG 121 078–007, Letter from François-Poncet to ICRC president Léopold Boissier, June 3, 1958.

[102] Charles de Gaulle, *Discours et messages* (Paris: Plon, 1970); De Gaulle, *Major Addresses, Statements and Press Conferences of General Charles de Gaulle* (New York: Embassy of France, Press and Information Service, 1964); Michael Kettle, *De Gaulle and Algeria, 1940–1960: From Mers El-Kébir to the Algiers Barracades* (London: Quartet, 1993).

[103] There were twenty-two committees in Algiers, eleven in Oran, fifteen in Constantine, and twenty in the Sahara. CRF, *Vie et Bonté*, June 1958.

[104] Ibid.   [105] Ibid.

sentiment from *Vie et Bonté* readers or making a case to the ICRC that it was fulfilling part of its mandate to provide care "without racial discrimination."[105] The June issue also reprinted pictures of French doctors, nurses, and volunteers interacting with the local population in waiting rooms, public buildings, and town squares. These powerful images, which appeared on nearly every page of the Algeria feature, sought to provide visual confirmation of the degree to which the French Red Cross was engaged with victims of the war and working to alleviate their suffering.

In that same *Vie et Bonté* issue, an equal number of articles were devoted to the services its staff provided to the French military. Alongside harrowing tales of compassion for the Algerian people were stories of hospital visits to wounded French soldiers, holiday deliveries, and care packages with cigarettes and delicacies from home.[106] Perhaps the editors of *Vie et Bonté* would have said they were fulfilling the national society's "double mission" or "double vocation" of assisting the French army and the Algerian people.[107] However, equal print coverage masked disproportionate assistance to the French: at the height of the war, there were 500,000 French soldiers deployed to Algeria compared to nine million Algerians. Given the vast demographic discrepancy and considerable resources of the military, the symmetry of coverage was almost certainly out of step with the needs of each group. Moreover, it implied parity in services and treatment during a moment of heightened ICRC scrutiny of French Red Cross activity.

The June *Vie et Bonté* issue did not succeed in quieting some ICRC critics. ICRC delegate Pierre Gaillard had a less charitable assessment of the national society at this time. He emphatically proclaimed that the French Red Cross "had hardly done anything for the civilian population" living in regroupment camps.[108] Other ICRC officials acknowledged nominal French Red Cross efforts toward the Algerians but also maintained that much work remained to be done to relieve Algerian suffering.[109] They pressed François-Poncet to provide more aid to regroupment camps with stern letters and he replied that he would direct his staff to pay more attention to regroupment camps and promised to allocate more resources toward the people in them.[110] But he failed to

---

[106] Ibid.   [107] CRF, *Vie et Bonté*, June 1956; December 1956.
[108] ACICR B AG 121 078–007, Letter from ICRC delegate Pierre Gaillard to ICRC delegate Roger Gallopin, June 9, 1958.
[109] ACICR B AG 121 078–007, ICRC vice-president Martin Bodmer to François-Poncet, June 13, 1958.
[110] ACICR B AG 121 078–007, Memo by Pierre Gaillard, November 19, 1959.
[111] ACICR B AG 121 078–007, Letter from Pierre Gaillard to Roger Vust, June 23, 1960.

follow through. In June 1960, the ICRC could only confirm nine teams in the field, while François-Poncet claimed there were fourteen.[111] Léopold Boissier and ICRC representatives used a variety of methods ranging from encouragement to criticism to try to incentivize François-Poncet specifically and the French Red Cross more broadly to uphold its humanitarian commitments in Algeria. Yet year after year until the conclusion of the war, the ICRC received letters and reports about the French Red Cross's uneven distribution of care suggesting the national society either could not or would not overcome the constraints of its self-defined double mission.[112]

Conclusion

The actions of the French Red Cross during the Algerian War provide a powerful example of the complex intersection of humanitarianism, politics, and universal discourse. As defined by the ICRC, each country is permitted one national society to carry out humanitarian work, but it had not accounted for the difficulties national society personnel would encounter in a colonial context. In the aftermath of Solferino, one hundred years prior, ICRC founders conceived of Red Cross societies helping to support the structures of national boundaries. They have not anticipated an internal competition over the boundaries of that nation or national community. But the wars of decolonization centered on that very battle and the ICRC and the national societies struggled to adapt to the new conditions.

In internal correspondence and in its own magazine *Vie et Bonté*, the French Red Cross repeatedly emphasized its "double mission" in Algeria, treating the French military as well as civilians. The self-described dual nature of the organization's priorities resulted in scattered

---

[112] The ICRC also faced a number of challenges throughout the war, which demonstrated the limits of its power and compromised its reputation as a neutral arbiter in the eyes of some of the organization's interlocutors. The most notable example of this is when the report of the seventh ICRC mission to Algeria was published in the January 5, 1960 edition of leading French newspaper *Le Monde*, violating a confidentiality agreement between the ICRC and the French government. For studies on the ICRC in Algeria and the newspaper leak, see Raphaëlle Branche, "Entre droit humanitaire et intérêts politiques: Les missions algériennes du CICR," *Revue Historique* 301, no. 1 (1999): 101–25; Johnson, *Battle for Algeria*, ch. 5; Klose, *In the Shadow of Colonial Violence*; Klose, "Colonial Testing Ground"; Françoise Perret and François Bugnion, "Between Insurgents and Government: The International Committee of the Red Cross's Action in the Algerian War (1954–1962)," *International Review of the Red Cross*, vol. 93, 883 (September 2011), 707–42; Perret, "L'action du Comité international de la Croix-Rouge pendant la guerre d'Algérie (1954–1962)," *International Review of the Red Cross* 86, no. 856 (December 2004): 917–51.

and uneven care throughout the war and even when the French Red Cross faced criticism or stern reprimands from the ICRC president and representatives in Geneva, its staff in Paris and Algeria had difficulty making meaningful changes in the ways they cared for the divided groups in Algeria. The French Red Cross leadership, helmed by François-Poncet, often fell short of delivering his promises for increased assistance to the Algerian people, but remarkably, he and the national society's staff went to great lengths to project the image of neutrality and parity. What might account for this position?

The Algerian War played out in the wake of sweeping changes to international law and a renewed commitment to the universal discourse and principles of humanitarianism that occurred in the 1940s. These important renovations revived an interest in rethinking global governance. They also expanded notions of universality and opened political possibilities for nonstate actors who mobilized the rhetoric against their colonial oppressors. In this process, the principles and discourse of humanitarianism became accessible to a larger number of people and offered them the opportunity to engage with political opponents on a more level playing field despite persistent power and military asymmetries.

The French Red Cross was caught in this shifting landscape during the Algerian War and tacked back and forth between assisting the French military and the Algerian population. Even though the national society had been tending to both constituents during the colonial period, the escalating war climate and increasing levels of violence and displacement might have appeared to necessitate a different response, or at least a different message. The French Red Cross faced significant scrutiny from ICRC president Léopold Boissier, numerous representatives of the Geneva office, Algerian nationalists, and Arab allies who all accused it of prioritizing French soldiers and failing to provide comparable aid and assistance to Algerian civilians and fighters. It is possible that French Red Cross personnel felt compelled to respond to this criticism by projecting the image of dedicated humanitarians who upheld universal principles and applied them to all people. This may appear as a minor shift, but it highlights the resonance and power of universal discourse at the end of empire. Anti-colonial nationalists and everyday people could engage with these ideas and mobilize them in the public arena in unprecedented ways, forcing French officials like François-Poncet to pay much closer attention to the perception of the French Red Cross than it previously had.

The decolonization of Algeria tested universal humanitarianism discourse. On the one hand, the rhetoric opened new pathways for engaging in the global arena. On the other hand, it exposed colonial regimes to harsh critiques for failing to uphold and practice the tenets of universality which they purported to support. Moments of intense friction and contradiction such as this one highlighted the need for the continued expansion of humanitarian law and new humanitarian organizations that better responded to contemporary political and social conditions. The Algerian War served as a critical linchpin between the rise of the postwar humanitarian regime and the explosion of humanitarian organizations in the 1970s. Without testing the boundaries and limitations of existing humanitarian structures during decolonization, we would not have seen the productive expansion of organizations and mandates that occurred at the end of formal colonial rule.[113]

[113] Klose, "Colonial Testing Ground."

4   Connecting Indigenous Rights to Human Rights in the Anglo Settler States
Another 1970s Story

Miranda Johnson

"To remain Indians and yet Americans, we believe to be a democratic principle and a human right in a free world."[1] So declared the Santa Clara Pueblo anthropologist Edward Dozier in his keynote address to hundreds of native people from across the United States gathered for the American Indian Chicago Conference in June 1961. Like other indigenous leaders and intellectuals in the postwar Anglo settler states (including Canada, Australia, and New Zealand as well as the United States), Dozier deployed the "language of the wider world," as Vine Deloria (Standing Rock Sioux) put it, in order to push forward particular claims to identity, citizenship, and land.[2]

Dozier's statement, however, raised the question of how indigenous rights claims that at that time prioritized collective identity – the preservation of Indian-ness – in the context of American citizenship was a more fundamental human right. Why, according to Dozier, were apparently parochial claims a matter that should demand the recognition of a universal human right? The answer lies in the history of dispossession and more recent experiences of assimilation that Dozier and other indigenous actors resisted. The nature of this resistance was particular, but the stakes of survival involved – that is, the right to exist as a people – they argued lay at the heart of what it meant to be human.

I would like to thank Tim Rowse and Michael Goodman for their astute comments on drafts of this chapter. Research was supported by the Australian Research Council DP150102810.
[1] "A Human Right in a Free World (1961)," in *Say We Are Nations: Documents of Politics and Protest in Indigenous America since 1887*, ed. Daniel M. Cobb (Chapel Hill: University of North Carolina Press, 2015), 115–19.
[2] Quoted in Daniel M. Cobb, "Talking the Language of the Larger World: Politics in Cold War (Native) America," in *Beyond Red Power: American Indian Politics and Activism Since 1900*, ed. Daniel M. Cobb and Loretta Fowler (Santa Fe, NM: School for Advanced Research, 2007), 162.

Dozier's reference to human rights did not refer to the protection of individuals *from* state or mass violence in this case. His claim about the right to be able to remain Indian depended on the vexed achievement of rights of American citizenship. Campaigns for equal citizenship rights were a central focus of native activism in the mid-twentieth century. Yet the security that civil rights afforded also threatened indigenous distinctiveness. Did being an American (or Australian, or Canadian) citizen mean giving up indigenous identity and sovereignty? Settler governments' postwar assimilation policies were specifically aimed at this goal. Resisting this trade-off, indigenous activists in the 1960s began to argue for additional rights to their collective indigenous identity and as a matter of survival. Dozier's invocation of a "human right" to capture these ideas was a significant moment in the evolution of native activism.

Taking a transnational and comparative approach, this chapter examines how a distinctive discourse of indigenous rights threaded claims at the level of the state – about collective identity, treaty promises, land rights, and sovereign peoplehood – together with an international language of human rights. This genealogy is distinct from the anti-colonial claims of Third World leaders for statehood, ones that also appealed to the discourse of human rights at the time as Bonny Ibhawoh argues (see Chapter 1, this volume).[3] It is also different from the revisionist account advanced by Samuel Moyn and others who argue that a modern human rights discourse came into its own in the West in the 1970s, as advocates critiqued failing postcolonial governments and aimed to protect individual citizens from state violence. The emergence of this advocacy, Moyn proposes, was both a sign and effect of the retreat of the social democratic state, distracting from the "politics of citizenship at home."[4] While revising Moyn's periodization of the full flowering of modern human rights discourse forward into the post-Cold War 1990s, Stefan-Ludwig Hoffmann similarly observes that Western human rights discourse is focused on "individual, pre-state [rights]" and is "concerned primarily with distant suffering."[5]

---

[3] See also Bonny Ibhawoh, "Colonialism," in *Encyclopedia of Human Rights*, 5 vols., ed. David P. Forsythe (Oxford: Oxford University Press, 2009), 1: 361–71. Roland Burke argues that Third World leaders were themselves crucial to the development of human rights discourse. See Burke, *Decolonization and the Evolution of International Human Rights* (Philadelphia: University of Pennsylvania Press, 2010).

[4] Samuel Moyn, *The Last Utopia: Human Rights in History* (Cambridge, MA: Belknap Press of Harvard University Press, 2010), 12. More generally see Jan Eckel and Samuel Moyn, eds., *The Breakthrough: Human Rights in the 1970s* (Philadelphia: University of Pennsylvania Press, 2013).

[5] Stefan-Ludwig Hoffmann, "Viewpoint: Human Rights and History," *Past and Present*, no. 232 (2016): 279–310, here at 282; see also the reply by Samuel Moyn, "The End of Human Rights History," *Past and Present*, no. 233 (2016): 307–22.

In the alternative genealogy traced in this chapter, indigenous peoples in the heart of "the West" claimed collective, quasi-sovereign, and sub-state rights in part by deploying, and expanding, the language of human rights. In some cases, they were remarkably successful. Indigenous peoples carved open a new space for recognition of their distinct rights and even shifted state policy away from assimilation and toward internal self-determination. By publicizing the effects of broken promises made in historical treaties and pursuing land rights claims in court, indigenous actors won wider support for their claims and they argued persuasively that the recognition of their peoplehood was a human right.

Yet the transformative possibility of recognition was dependent on the political will of settler governments. In the late 1970s, some transnational indigenous actors and activists turned their attention to the United Nations seeking international standing for their collective claims. These activists saw potential in expanding the international human rights framework to encompass their indigenous rights. As a matter of political strategy, these activists hoped that international recognition could serve to shame individual states in regard to their treatment of indigenous peoples and provide a footing for indigenous claims outside the contingency of national politics. As a matter of philosophy, the expansion of human rights to incorporate the recognition of indigenous peoplehood would realize Dozier's claim, that the right to be and remain Indian was also a core human right.

Settler Colonialism, Dispossession, and Law

The Native American activists addressed by Dozier had gathered together to oppose what they perceived as an attack on the legal and political bases of their collective rights and identities in the modern settler state. They were not alone. Mounting a surprisingly effective moral argument about their rights to exist as indigenous in the 1960s and 1970s, leaders and activists across the predominantly anglophone settler states of Australia, Canada, New Zealand, and the United States forced settler states to respond to their claims, drawing on the "language of the wider world," including that of human rights, and idioms of justice specific to their entangled colonial histories with settler societies and states.

Indeed, many of the claims that leaders brought to the law in new terms in the 1970s were decades old, in some instances stretching back into the eighteenth and nineteenth centuries. Shaped by histories of loss and struggle, such claims were themselves intergenerational and defined indigenous peoples' histories and identities. Before I turn to how and why these activist discourses became so prominent in the 1970s, I briefly describe the longer and shorter-term historical dynamics of settler colonialism in which the rising indigenous activism of the 1960s and 1970s intervened and sought to transform. This is a story of the formation of settler nations, and the dispossession of indigenous ones, in countries regarded as part of the West.

Notably, the history of settler colonialism informed neither the making of the Declaration of Human Rights in 1948 nor the design of major instruments of international law regarding rights of self-determination in subsequent decades. For most of the twentieth century, indigenous peoples were not regarded as having standing as nations within international law. At least two delegations of indigenous peoples, one from the Six Nations in Canada and another from a religious and pan-tribal movement in New Zealand, had approached the League of Nations in the interwar period asserting their nationhood, but they were turned away before they could win a formal hearing for their claims.[6] The situation did not change following the creation of the United Nations and the passage of key international declarations and conventions, which largely ignored the rights of indigenous peoples.[7] Within settler states in the immediate postwar period, few scholars referred to the history of the dispossession of indigenous peoples as a colonial one in terms comparable to those of overseas colonization. The terminology of "settler colonialism" had yet to be invented.

Today, scholars use the rubric of settler colonialism to refer to the ways in which "new world" lands were colonized, especially during periods of what historian James Belich has called "explosive colonization" of the later nineteenth century.[8] White settlers, mainly from the British Isles,

[6] On appeals to the League of Nations, see Ronald Niezen, *The Origins of Indigenism: Human Rights and the Politics of Identity* (Berkeley, University of California Press, 2003), 31–6; Ravi de Costa, "Identity, Authority, and the Moral Worlds of Indigenous Petitions," *Comparative Studies in Society and History* 48, no. 3 (2006): 669–98.

[7] Indigenous "populations" were referenced in the Convention concerning the Protection and Integration of Indigenous and Other Tribal and Semi-Tribal Populations in Independent Countries, 1957 (ILO No. 157). Indigenous activists later successfully pushed for the revision of the convention which they argued was assimilatory. See Douglas Sanders, "The UN Working Group on Indigenous Populations," *Human Rights Quarterly* 11, no. 3 (1989): 406–33; Niezen, *Origins of Indigenism*, 37. However, Tim Rowse points out that the 1957 convention did provide for the recognition of Indigenous peoples' reserve lands, and also introduced notions of cultural difference, and so was not only assimilatory. See Rowse, "Global Indigenism: A Genealogy of a Non-Racial Category," in *Rethinking the Racial Moment: Essays on the Colonial Encounter*, ed. Alison Holland and Barbara Brookes (Newcastle: Cambridge Scholars Publishing, 2011), 229–53.

[8] Belich differentiates this later and more destructive form of colonialism from earlier "incremental colonization" that did not necessarily threaten indigenous lands and economies. James Belich, *Replenishing the Earth: The Settler Revolution and the Rise of the*

flooded into North America, southern Africa, and the Pacific, intending to create more egalitarian societies than those they had left, on what they saw as vacant or under-utilized lands. In the process, settler colonizers dispossessed the original inhabitants through wars and sporadic frontier violence, squatting on unceded lands, and by using specially designed legal instruments for the seizure of land, such as land courts that redistributed titles and made it easier for individuals to sell their holdings.[9] Indigenous people were decimated by introduced diseases and the impoverishing consequences of dispossession. By the end of the century, burgeoning settler states had pushed survivors to the edges of colonial territories, forcing them onto reservations and mission stations.

Settler colonial conditions in Anglo settler states took particular forms and produced different effects compared to other sites of colonialism (and imperial metropoles) – and even in other, non-Anglo settler colonies such as French Algeria and Japanese Korea.[10] Nineteenth-century settler colonization in North America and Australasia proceeded through dispossessing indigenous peoples. The settler societies that formed on indigenous lands became majority populations who stayed. Settler colonialism was also a project of the imagination, particularly as European settlers invoked the vanishing of indigenous peoples, sometimes as a justification for their dispossession or in disavowal of what they had inflicted.[11] Patrick Wolfe argues that settler colonialism is an ongoing structure of dispossession driven by a "logic of elimination," either physical or cultural, of indigenous peoples who found themselves in the way of settler expansion, although not all indigenous peoples were destroyed nor were they completely assimilated to settler society.[12]

Wolfe's Marxist-inflected argument takes little notice of the ambiguous role of law in settler states – critical to later rights histories – as an

---

Angloworld, 1783–1939 (Oxford: Oxford University Press, 2009); see also Donald Denoon, *Settler Capitalism: The Dynamics of Dependent Development in the Southern Hemisphere* (Oxford: Oxford University Press, 1983).

[9] On the legal and extralegal instruments that setters used to take new lands, see John C. Weaver, *The Great Land Rush and the Making of the Modern World, 1650–1900* (Montreal: McGill-Queen's University Press, 2003).

[10] For example, see Caroline Elkins and Susan Pedersen, eds., *Settler Colonialism in the Twentieth Century: Projects, Practices, Legacies* (New York: Routledge, 2005).

[11] See Steven Conn, *History's Shadow: Native Americans and Historical Consciousness in the Nineteenth Century* (Chicago: University of Chicago Press, 2004); Bain Attwood, "Denial in Settler Society: the Australian Case," *History Workshop Journal* 84, no. 1 (2017): 24–43.

[12] Patrick Wolfe, "Land, Labor and Difference: Elementary Structures of Race," *American Historical Review* 106, no. 3 (2001): 865–905; Wolfe, "Settler Colonialism and the Elimination of the Native," *Journal of Genocide Research* 8, no. 4 (2006): 387–409; Wolfe, *Traces of History: Elementary Structures of Race* (London: Verso, 2016).

instrument of dispossession (a version of what John Comaroff has called "lawfare") and as a space for creative, if not emancipatory, recourse.[13] The settler states that are the focus of this chapter became liberal democracies and shared British traditions including a basis in the common law. In many cases, imperial and settler authorities had recognized some rights of indigenous peoples in the nineteenth century. (Indeed, another genealogy of recent indigenous rights claims could extend back into early modern European debates about whether native people bore inalienable natural rights or not, and dovetail with Lynn Hunt's account of and the production of "imagined empathy" in nineteenth-century European evangelical and humanitarian discourse.)[14] However, Lisa Ford argues that the imposition of settler sovereignty in territorial terms in nineteenth-century colonial Georgia and New South Wales was "uniquely destructive of indigenous rights," meaning that settler colonizers did not, on the whole, try to establish terms of indirect rule in colonized lands as they did elsewhere. Rather, they usurped the legal systems and political societies of indigenous peoples. Here, Ford uses the term "indigenous rights" to connote that precolonial plurality; my use of the term refers to a late-twentieth (re)construction of such rights in arguably "post" colonial conditions.[15]

Yet the story of colonial legal imposition was, as Ian Hunter and Shaunnagh Dorsett have argued, a creative as well as a destructive act. Understood as a story of "political improvisations and innovations,"[16] settler colonialism was a dispossessory and even at times eliminatory

---

[13] See John Comaroff, "Colonialism, Culture, and the Law: A Foreword." *Law and Social Inquiry* 26, no. 2 (2001): 305–14. "Law was central to the colonizing process but in a curiously ambiguous way," as Sally Merry argued in her classic essay. Merry, "Law and Colonialism," *Law and Society Review*, 25, no. 4 (1991): 889–922.

[14] Lynn Hunt, *Inventing Human Rights: A History* (New York: Norton, 2007), ch. 1. For legal and philosophical genealogies of native rights and justifications for empire, see Anthony Pagden, *Lords of All the World: Ideologies of Empire in Spain, Britain and France, c. 1500–1800* (New Haven, CT: Yale University Press, 1995); Andrew Fitzmaurice, *Sovereignty, Property, and Empire, 1500–2000* (Cambridge, UK: Cambridge University Press, 2014).

[15] Lisa Ford, *Settler Sovereignty: Jurisdiction and Indigenous People in America and Australia, 1788–1836* (Cambridge, MA: Harvard University Press, 2010). For critiques of use of the term "postcolonial" in settler states which the following scholars argue are sites of ongoing colonialism, see for example Linda Tuhiwai Smith, *Decolonizing Methodologies: Research and Indigenous Peoples* (London: Zed Books, 1999); Aileen Moreton-Robinson, *The White Possessive: Property, Power, and Indigenous Sovereignty* (Minneapolis: University of Minnesota Press, 2015). See also Miranda Johnson, "Reconciliation, Indigeneity and Postcolonial Nationhood in Settler States," *Postcolonial Studies* 14, no. 2 (2011): 187–201.

[16] Shaunnagh Dorsett and Ian Hunter, "Introduction," in *Law and Politics in British Colonial Thought: Transpositions of Empire* (New York: Palgrave Macmillan, 2010), 2.

form of domination that also created new institutions, including new notions of customary law itself. Imperial authorities established traditions such as treaty-making with indigenous polities, which some settler authorities continued particularly when they sought to avoid costly warfare and negotiated land and sovereignty cessions instead. Even in places where treaties were not made, settler authorities entered into less formal agreements with indigenous peoples, or established reserve lands for what they perceived as remnant populations. Arrangements such as these continued to be made well into the twentieth century, particularly in remote areas where there was little white settlement.

Treaties, land deeds, informal agreements, and even the establishment of reserves on "Crown land" were understood and reinterpreted by the different parties in very different ways over time. While settler officials may have seen treaties as expedient instruments of empire, for instance, some indigenous peoples regarded them as a vitally important recognition of their political status and standing.[17] Moreover, treaties, in written and oral form, were not negotiated in consistent terms across time and space. Early trade or alliance treaties on the North American frontier when different European empires vied for land and authority, for instance, gave way to asymmetrically designed instruments in the later nineteenth century on the United States and Canadian frontiers. These treaties were often written ahead of negotiations on the ground, reproducing many of the same clauses in vastly different regions. They required signatories to cede their rights to extensive tracts of land, in return for which Indians received small payments in kind, treaty annuities, and reservations.[18] The Treaty of Waitangi signed in New Zealand

---

[17] Robert A. Williams argues that European law, including treaty-making, was "the West's most vital and effective instrument of empire during its genocidal conquest and colonization of the non-Western peoples of the New World, the American Indians." See Williams, *The American Indian in Western Legal Thought: The Discourses of Conquest* (New York: Oxford University Press, 1990), 6; Stuart Banner, *How the Indians Lost Their Land: Law and Power on the Frontier* (Cambridge, MA: Belknap Press of Harvard University Press, 2005).

[18] On the history of treaty-making in Canada, see J. R. Miller, *Compact, Contract, Covenant: Aboriginal Treaty-Making in Canada* (Toronto: University of Toronto Press, 2009). For indigenous accounts of "Treaty" elsewhere in Canada see, for example, references to "Treaty 7 Tribal Council" in *The True Spirit and Original Intent of Treaty 7*, ed. Walter Hildebrandt, Sarah Carter, and Dorothy First Rider (Montreal: McGill-Queen's University Press, 1996), esp. 67–82; Sharon Venne, "Understanding Treaty 6: An Indigenous Perspective," in *Aboriginal and Treaty Rights in Canada: Essays on Law, Equality, and Respect for Difference*, ed. Michael Asch (Vancouver: University of British Columbia Press, 1997), 173–207. In the American context, the seminal text on treaties made with Native Americans is Francis Paul Prucha, *American Indian Treaties: The History of a Political Anomaly* (Berkeley: University of California Press, 1994). See also Stuart Banner, *How the Indians Lost Their Land: Law and Power on the Frontier*

in 1840 which purported to annex the North and South Islands for Britain, was ambiguously translated into the Maori language. It was much briefer and yet at the same time more expansive in its promises to indigenous signatories than some North American treaties.[19] Reserves, established in Australia's north without formalized treaty in the twentieth century, were granted on the premise that such land was in the Crown domain; yet indigenous peoples understood reserves as *their* land, a recognition of their ongoing sovereignty.

In many instances, land was taken without treaty, land deed, or other agreement. Even in places where indigenous peoples' lands were recognized as belonging to them, according to developing notions of customary land tenure or "native title," settler legal institutions developed mechanisms by which such lands could be easily disposed of, such as land courts and allotment policies.[20] The sharp practices of land assessors and purchasers provoked further conflict with the state and between indigenous peoples. Indigenous peoples also protested the fact that promises made to them in treaties, such as the provision of schooling or medical resources, were not forthcoming. In Australia, parts of Canada, and California where no treaties had been made with native people, or if they had been were not officially ratified, native leaders petitioned governments, the president, and, in the Commonwealth states, even the British monarch for their rights. While some claims were successful, on the whole, they were largely ignored or relegated to legal insignificance by lawyers in the settler states during the later nineteenth and early twentieth centuries.[21] However, as we shall see, resurgent appeals to settler law for native or customary land title rights began to win legal recognition after World War II, with complex and unexpected consequences.

(Cambridge, MA: Belknap Press of Harvard University Press, 2005); Robert A. Williams, *Linking Arms Together: American Indian Treaty Visions of Law and Peace, 1600–1800* (New York: Oxford University Press, 1997).

[19] The Treaty of Waitangi, particularly since its revivification in the 1970s, has become the subject of an extensive literature in New Zealand. Some key works include Claudia Orange, *The Treaty of Waitangi* (Wellington: Allen & Unwin, 1987); William Renwick, ed., *Sovereignty and Indigenous Rights: The Treaty of Waitangi in International Contexts*, (Wellington: Victoria University Press, 1991); Michael Belgrave, *Historical Frictions: Maori Claims and Reinvented Histories* (Auckland: Auckland University Press, 2005). For a comprehensive treatment of the English text, see Ned Fletcher, "A Praiseworthy Device for Amusing and Pacifying Savages? What the Framers Meant by the English Text of the Treaty of Waitangi" (PhD diss., University of Auckland, 2014).

[20] David Williams, *Te Kooti Tango Whenua: The Native Land Court, 1864–1909* (Wellington: Huia Publishers, 1999).

[21] See for example Sidney L. Harring, *White Man's Law: Native People in Nineteenth-Century Canadian Jurisprudence* (Toronto: Osgoode Society for Canadian Legal History, 1998).

Postwar Settlements: Assimilation and Equal Rights

Demographic shifts drove some of the new conflicts around indigenous rights in the 1960s and 1970s. By the mid-twentieth century, indigenous populations had significantly increased and were experiencing booming birth rates, putting paid to late nineteenth-century ideas of vanishing Indians. Moreover, the fact that settler governments continued to distinguish indigenous populations, often revising definitions of who counted as indigenous, was itself a political artefact that had ongoing effects on the distribution of resources and the grounds of identification.[22] Young indigenous men and women were leaving rural and remote homelands and searching out new economic and educational opportunities in cities as well as encountering more direct forms of racism. Indigenous servicemen, returning from fighting in the war, found their expectations of equal treatment on their return to the countries they had fought for frustrated.[23]

These experiences provoked claims for equality that were at times explicitly connected to human rights issues. In the 1950s, with support from the labor movement, for instance, Aboriginal people in Australia's north protested unequal wages seeking, as the North Australian Workers' Union put it, their "place in the community as workers and citizens." Union activists, white and Aboriginal, pushed forward the argument that they were being denied their "fundamental rights and liberties," and made appeal to the United Nations on the basis of human rights claims, intending to shame the Australian government into action.[24] Later, in 1968, the labor activist Tom (Tama) Poata created the Maori Organization on Human Rights, more commonly known as MOOHR, following his association with anti-racist and anti-apartheid organizations. MOOHR protested racism domestically, and opposed sporting ties with South Africa – a matter of considerable political dispute in a country whose national image was inextricable from its sporting prowess in rugby, and whose major rugby rival was

---

[22] On the imaginary of indigenous "populations," see Tim Rowse, *Rethinking Social Justice: From "Peoples" to "Populations"* (Canberra: Aboriginal Studies Press, 2012), esp. ch. 1.

[23] General histories of twentieth-century indigenous peoples that cover some of these issues include Charles Wilkinson, *Blood Struggle: The Rise of Modern Indian Nations* (New York: Norton, 2005); J. R. Miller, *Skyscrapers Hide the Heavens: A History of Indian–White Relations in Canada*, 3rd ed. (Toronto: University of Toronto Press, 2000); Tim Rowse, *Indigenous and Other Australians Since 1901* (Sydney: University of New South Wales Press, 2017); Richard S. Hill, *Maori and the State: Crown–Maori Relations in New Zealand/Aotearoa, 1950–2000* (Wellington: Victoria University Press, 2009).

[24] Bain Attwood, *Rights for Aborigines* (Sydney: Allen & Unwin, 2003), 132–6.

South Africa. At the same time, Poata understood the oppression of Maori in New Zealand as akin to class oppression.[25]

In response to social and civic pressures, national governments searched for ways to incorporate young and growing populations into the domestic workforce and meet intensifying demands for equality. They did so primarily by outlining new policies of assimilation, by which they envisaged indigenous peoples could become full citizens who aspired to the same things that other settlers did. Policymakers were focused on the assimilation of indigenous populations into the settler body politic. In the United States, this included discharging any remaining obligations on the part of the federal government to the tribes through the United States Indian Claims Commission, established in 1946.[26] In the 1950s, congress tried to "terminate" the special recognition of Native American tribes, first by extending criminal jurisdiction over tribal reservations.[27] Governments in Canada, Australia, and New Zealand likewise advanced policies of assimilation in respect of indigenous populations in the 1950s and early 1960s.

These policies in turn spurred a new wave of young indigenous activists, often urban-based and university educated, to protest policies of assimilation. They argued that these policies entailed the erasure of their indigeneity.[28] Young activists linked the failure of settler authorities to meet the specific agreements or promises made to their communities in the past and the contemporary language of human rights and genocide. Resisting an attempt by the federal government in Canada to terminate Indians' treaty rights there, akin to the policy of the federal government in the United States, the young Cree activist Harold Cardinal accused the Canadian government of "cultural genocide," asserting that, "If our [treaty] rights are meaningless . . . then we as a people are meaningless."[29] Activists like Cardinal who protested policies of assimilation and termination were thinking about what they had already lost in terms of

---

[25] Ranginui Walker, *Ka Whawhai Tonu Matou: Struggle without End* (Auckland: Penguin, 1990); Hill, *Maori and the State*, ch. 7.

[26] See Harvey D. Rosenthal, *Their Day in Court: A History of the Indian Claims Commission* (New York: Garland, 1990); Arthur Ray, *Aboriginal Rights Claims and the Making and Remaking of History* (Kingston: McGill-Queen's University Press, 2016).

[27] See Wilkinson, *Blood Struggle*, pt. 1.

[28] For a comparative discussion of assimilation policy in the Commonwealth settler states, see Andrew Armitage, *Comparing the Policy of Aboriginal Assimilation: Australia, Canada and New Zealand* (Vancouver: UBC Press, 1995).

[29] Harold Cardinal, *The Unjust Society: The Tragedy of Canada's Indians* (Edmonton: M.G. Hurtig, 1969), 30. On the use of the genocide concept in Australia, see A. Dirk Moses, ed. *Genocide and Settler Society: Frontier Violence and Stolen Indigenous Children in Australian History* (New York: Berghahn Books, 2004).

their own indigenous cultures and languages, particularly as a consequence of residential schooling, and they wanted to ensure that no further harm was inflicted on generations to come.

The new generation of activists also drew on the actions and ideas of anti-colonial, anti-apartheid, and American Black Power movements in confronting settler states and settler publics with their demands. As Aboriginal activists explained when they erected the "Tent Embassy" on Australia's federal parliament grounds in Canberra in 1972, "like black men in Africa, who fought so hard for the right to decide their own destiny," Aboriginal people, too, were entitled to a much greater degree of political power.[30] The language of human rights was not in this instance drawn on extensively; instead activists found common cause with anti-colonialism, and used the language of sovereignty to imagine an "Aboriginal state," apart from but still a part of the federation; or more broadly advocated a kind of cultural nationalism, as espoused by black activists such as poet Kath Walker who published a list of "Black Commandments" in 1969 that included, "Thou shalt resist assimilation with all thy might," and "Thou shall think black and act black."[31]

While these forceful critiques of assimilationist policy were gaining traction in the cities, new resource projects in remote areas provoked renewed conflicts over land. Remote areas in the geographically larger settler states that had not been of much interest to settler governments now became of increasing value to mining and energy companies, powered by post-World War II wealth and feeding the need for resources in growing Asian economies. A bauxite mine in Australia's north, and hydroelectric schemes and the building of oil and gas pipelines in Canada's north, became the focus of local then nationwide indigenous struggles. The attention that these struggles won caught settler governments in each country by surprise, since it had not occurred to them that they should consult with local indigenous peoples whose lands were affected about mining and development projects, and they assumed they were under no legal obligation to do so since governments assumed this was "Crown land."

These assumptions were about to be radically undone, as traditional leaders, lawyers, missionaries, anthropologists, and others joined forces in demanding that the settler state recognize indigenous peoples' collective land and treaty rights. Indigenous people began taking their claims to

---

[30] John Newfong, "The Aboriginal Embassy: Its Purpose and Aims," *Identity* (July 1972): 5. See also Heather Goodall, *Invasion to Embassy: Land in Aboriginal Politics in New South Wales, 1770–1972* (Sydney: Allen & Unwin, 1996), 339–51.

[31] Quoted in Russell McGregor, "Another Nation: Aboriginal Activism in the Late 1960s and Early 1970s," *Australian Historical Studies* 40, no. 3 (2009): 347–8.

the courtroom with the intention of forcing governments to respond. At times drawing on human rights ideals, these leaders pressed for distinct forms of customary land rights, thereby revivifying older colonial legal languages for the purposes of making new collective identity claims.

As indigenous peoples took their collective claims to municipal courts in the 1970s seeking recognition of land and treaty rights, many emphasized that they needed rights that went far beyond the protection of individual property interests. Their lands, waters, sacred sites, hunting grounds, and so on were so important to them because these places constituted *who they were* as a people: "the land is our history," was a commonly used phrase in activism and legal claims, doubly referencing land loss as well as the existential importance of place to identity.[32]

This broad-brushstrokes account of nineteenth-century conditions and twentieth-century pressures points to some of the historical differences that indigenous leaders and activists faced compared to other anti-colonial and civil rights movements in the post–World War II era of decolonization. Indigenous leaders' political aspirations were different from those fighting for self-determination in the form of separate statehood as in the Third World – a political claim that "turned the world into the stage of history," as historian Prasenjit Duara puts it[33] – or to end racial violence, as in the South African and African American contexts. The political and economic structures from which indigenous claims emerged, and the political futures to which indigenous peoples aspired, were unlike these situations. In the settler states of Canada, the United States, Australia and New Zealand the settlers would not go home as they had in Algeria, for example. There would be no (repeat) anti-colonial revolution. Indigenous peoples formed small minorities, unlikely to use violence or armed resistance to achieve their aims as some had done in the past. In the 1960s, most indigenous communities were poor and unevenly enfranchised, with limited electoral power and little representation at any levels of settler government.

A New Social Contract

Indigenous activists had to develop a distinct political and conceptual language to advance their claims, often in relation to the state's legal

---

[32] See for instance Galarrwuy Yunupingu quoted in Johnson, *Land Is Our History*, 54.

[33] Prasenjit Duara, *Decolonization: Perspectives from Now and Then* (London: Routledge, 2003), 1. Duara's textbook, like most on decolonization, does not include examples from the "Fourth World." On this point, see also, Tracey Banivanua Mar, *Decolonisation and the Pacific: Indigenous Globalisation and the Ends of Empire* (Cambridge, UK: Cambridge University Press, 2016), esp. the introduction.

traditions as well as their own and by appealing to histories shared and contested with settler societies. A central argument emerged from claims about historical treaty promises made but not kept. Indigenous actors used the idea of treaty to hold settler states to account in a contractual sense, as a fiduciary duty, specifically referring to what they had lost and the redress and restitution they demanded in the present. In so doing, activists further argued that the contracts that treaties represented were actually of fundamental importance to the settler states in a postcolonial age: they represented broader social contracts according to which settler states had established legal authority. If states were to maintain that authority, then they had to recognize that they were in an ongoing relationship or even partnership with indigenous treaty signatories. Claimants insisted that settling treaty grievances was a matter of moral urgency and for rethinking national belonging.[34]

At the culmination of the 1961 Chicago conference at which Edward Dozier gave his inspiring keynote, delegates released the "Declaration of Indian Purpose." Explicitly invoking the 1948 Universal Declaration of Human Rights, the declaration began thus: "We believe in the inherent right of all people to retain spiritual and cultural values."[35] By far the largest section of this declaration, however, addressed the issue of upholding the "eternal word" of American Indians' treaties, a kind of claim that was referred to neither in the Universal Declaration, nor in other versions of decolonization discourse.[36] Promises that indigenous peoples associated with treaties continued to be abrogated. The most recent example, as many attendees at the conference discussed, was the federal government's policy of "termination" which referred to the ending of distinct recognition of tribes, established in treaties, in an effort to integrate Indians into the majority population.[37]

By the late 1960s, debate about and appeal to treaties was heating up around the United States, bringing together a range of activists from different campaigns. In the Pacific Northwest, local Native Americans who were frequently being arrested for fishing in rivers without a license, protested their right to fish on and off their reservations, as promised in historical treaties. They drew the attention of national organizations, including the National Association for the Advancement of Colored

---

[34] See the discussion in Alexandra Harmon ed., *The Power of Promises: Rethinking Indian Treaties in the Pacific Northwest* (Seattle: Center for the Study of the Pacific Northwest and University of Washington Press, 2008), introduction.

[35] "This Is Not Special Pleading," in *Say We Are Nations*, 120–3.

[36] "This Is Not Special Pleading," 122.

[37] See Lurie "The Voice of the American Indian: Report on the American Indian Chicago Conference," *Current Anthropology* 2, no. 5 (1961): 478–500.

People, which provided some material support for their protests. Out-of-state activists helped local protestors to design a new campaign they called a series of "fish-ins" along the Nisqually and Puyallup rivers, explicitly recalling the "sit-in" tactics of earlier African-American civil rights campaigns. This group of "maverick fishers and pan-Indian activists" won extensive media attention, and, eventually, a remarkable court case that upheld their treaty rights.[38] One of the activists involved in this campaign, Hank Adams, become central to later nationwide Indian protests in the 1970s – sometimes referred to as "Red Power" – that included the "Trail of Broken Treaties" march of 1972 that traveled across the United States.

Often depicted as radical, these activists nonetheless often used rhetorical strategies that appealed to settler audiences by resonating with their historical identities at the same time as the movement asserted indigenous goals. As the "preamble" to the American Indian Movement's "20 Point Position Paper," issued in 1972 explained, "We seek a new American majority – a majority that is not content merely to confirm itself by superiority in numbers, but which by conscience is committed toward prevailing on public will in ceasing wrongs and doing right."[39] The wrongs that the American Indian Movement (AIM) were concerned about in particular, in common with the concerns of many Indians across the country, were violations of treaties and the failure of the federal government to uphold treaty promises. The position paper, aimed directly at Richard Nixon, who looked most likely to win the upcoming presidential election, proposed the creation of a new commission tasked with contracting a new treaty relationship with tribes around the country, and ratifying historic treaties (particularly in California) that were not officially recognized. In the fracas that followed AIM's presentation of the paper at the Bureau of Indian Affairs in Washington DC on November 3, 1972, the organization telegrammed the United Nations asking for a team to be sent to investigate the protestor's treatment and hoping that the "whole matter of Indian rights could be considered" by that body. It was not.[40]

In Canada and New Zealand, treaty claims levered open a moral space in the state as indigenous claimants and lawyers protested the "breach of

---

[38] See Alexandra Harmon, *Indians in the Making: Ethnic Relations and Indian Identities Around Puget Sound* (Berkeley: University of California Press, 1998), 233; Charles Wilkinson, *Messages from Frank's Landing: A Story of Salmon, Treaties and the Indian Way* (Seattle: University of Washington Press, 2000).

[39] American Indian Movement, "The Trail of Broken Treaties: An Indian Manifesto," October 1972, www.aimovement.org/archives

[40] See Vine Deloria, *Behind the Trail of Broken Treaties: An Indian Declaration of Independence* (Austin: University of Texas Press, 1985 [1974]), 57–8.

faith" on the part of federal or central government action (or inaction). This was perhaps clearest in the New Zealand case, where Maori activists demanded justice and politicians and jurists began to rethink the state in "bicultural" terms, focused on the Treaty of Waitangi. In the 1960s, the Treaty – signed in 1840 by Maori leaders from different polities – was officially commemorated by the settler state as the founding of a unified nation and a symbol of much-vaunted racial harmony. In the 1970s, this belief was challenged by Maori activists. In 1971, at fiery protests of the official celebrations on the grounds where the treaty had been signed, a young activist group, Ngā Tamatoa (the Young Warriors) challenged the myth of racial harmony that the Treaty of Waitangi symbolized and the idea of nationhood that it evoked. They repudiated a settler nationalist story of racial harmony and instead drew attention to the effects of dispossession, language loss, poverty, and crime on New Zealand's indigenous population.

This was a particularly critical national moment, due to fact that the country's economic ties to Britain were dissolving. New Zealand's primary agricultural export market was threatened by Britain's decision to join the European Economic Community, and the loss of the British market also provoked a rethinking of cultural ties.[41] In a moment of national uncertainty, settler leaders sought to assert an independent identity by reenacting a mythical founding moment; and Maori activists demanded a rethinking of the social contract. Some even referred to the Treaty as a "fraud."[42]

In 1975, older leaders and young activists joined forces on a nationwide "land march" to parliament, along the lines of "Trail of Broken Treaties" undertaken by Native American activists in the United States in 1972. Their cause was the retention of the last remaining lands in Maori hands and redress for dispossession. According to historian Aroha Harris "Setting up Te Matakite [the vision or prophesy] was practically as great a feat as the march itself. It was a synergy of old and new ideologies and methods, which unified a range of groups and interests: kuia, kaumātua [female and male elders] and rangatahi [youth], young

---

[41] For this reason, historian Anthony Hopkins argues that the Commonwealth settler states should be included in the postwar history of decolonization, see A. G. Hopkins, "Rethinking Decolonization," *Past & Present*, no. 200 (2008): 211–47. See also James Curran and Stuart Ward, *The Unknown Nation: Australia after Empire* (Melbourne: Melbourne University Press, 2010). None of these authors, however, draw on indigenous rights activism, its powerful critique of colonialism, and the challenge that surviving indigenous identities posed to the state, to explain or complicate their late-twentieth-century stories.

[42] See the "Treaty Is a FRAUD" poster from the late 1970s, *Te Ara: Encyclopedia of New Zealand*, www.teara.govt.nz

urban activists and older conservative traditionalists."[43] This "synergy" of old and new included the way the march drew on and reembodied the protest marches of earlier Maori leaders; that the memorial of right that the leaders took with them emphasized land rights; and that leaflets that some marchers handed out linked land loss with loss of identity and matters of class: "We want a just society allowing Maoris to preserve our own social and cultural identity in the last remnants of our tribal estate . . . the alternative is the creation of a landless brown proletariat with no dignity, no mana [authority] and no stake in society."[44]

The march added pressure on the government at the time, and the Minister of Maori Affairs Matiu Rata in particular, to establish a specially designed commission of inquiry to examine treaty breaches, which it did in 1975 in the form of the Waitangi Tribunal. The Tribunal, which did not really gain teeth until a further amendment in 1985 provided it with the power to examine breaches of the Treaty going back to 1840, was tasked not only with examining specific claims but also with defining broader "principles" of the Treaty by which the state and Iwi (tribes) could be held to account for their actions in the past and into the future.[45] Two key principles were that of "partnership," which acknowledged the ongoing political authority of Maori people, mainly as they were represented by tribal leaders; and that of "protection" which meant that the Crown was obliged to protect Maori interests and rights.[46] This modern interpretation of the treaty became the basis for its consideration in quasi-constitutional terms in what has become known as Aotearoa New Zealand.

Going to Court for Land Rights

As well as advancing the idea that indigenous peoples and settler states had to make a new social contract, premised on historical treaties, or forged through new agreements, indigenous leaders and their lawyers forced unwilling governments to recognize customary land rights in the form of aboriginal or native title. This form of title recognized the

---

[43] Aroha Harris, *Hikoi: Forty Years of Māori Protest* (Wellington: Huia Publishers, 2004), 70.

[44] As quoted in Hill, *Maori and the State*, 168.   [45] Treaty of Waitangi Act, 1975.

[46] For a discussion of Treaty principles emerging from early Tribunal reports and seminal court cases, see Janine Hayward, "Appendix: The Principles of the Treaty of Waitangi," in *National Overview: Waitangi Tribunal Rangahaua Whanui Series*, ed. Alan Ward, 2 vols. (Wellington: Waitangi Tribunal, 1997), 2: 475–94. The idea of protection itself has a long, complex history in empire. See for a discussion, Lauren Benton, Adam Clulow, and Bain Atwood, eds. *Protection and Empire: A Global History* (Cambridge, UK: Cambridge University Press, 2018).

collective property right of indigenous peoples to their lands based on their historic and ongoing attachment to them, if it had not been extinguished by settler governments in the past through treaties or other instruments.[47] Native title rights gave indigenous owners stronger rights than those of use and access that had been awarded to them on an ad hoc basis prior to the 1970s. Unlike other property rights, claimants to native title did not necessarily have to show that they exercised exclusive ownership of the lands under claim; though, considered to be "inalienable rights," neither could they sell lands awarded such title on an open market.[48]

Foregrounding their ongoing presence on and attachment to the land, native title conveyed great symbolic as well as economic value. It promised to give tangible legal form to the expression of indigenous peoples' historical claims as "first peoples" who were the prior occupiers of the land. It overturned popular historical representations of vast areas of unoccupied land, purportedly "free" of prior owners and available for the taking.[49] Implicitly, the revitalization of native title recognized a kind of sovereignty held by indigenous peoples as autonomous groups with their own laws and forms of government prior to the arrival of white settlers who had maintained a degree of autonomy despite colonization.[50] Claimants argued for the distinctiveness of their entitlements in terms of continuities with the past. These "new" rights were, they proposed, in fact very old; "indigenous rights" somehow preexisted the creation of settler states, both challenging their founding and potentially offering a new grounding for their constitution. In economic and symbolic terms, the advent of native title claims was a potentially radical historical moment within settler states, given that it was based in the possibility for rewriting both the common law in these countries and an account of history that buttressed common law doctrines.

---

[47] See McHugh, *Aboriginal Title*, ch. 1.

[48] In the nineteenth century, the inalienability of such title effectively excluded indigenous peoples from participating in the property market since they could only sell their lands to the Crown or federal state. In this sense, the doctrine portrayed indigenous peoples as living out of time with settler capitalism. See Stuart Banner, *How the Indians Lost Their Land*, esp. ch. 3.

[49] The classic statement on "free land" and the frontier was made by Frederick Jackson Turner, in "The Significance of the Frontier in American History."

[50] As Jeremy Webber explains, the recognition of a collective land title held by indigenous peoples does not mean that, within those societies, all land is held communally. Rather, native title implicitly recognizes the "political and legal autonomy of indigenous societies" and therefore their capacity to determine landholding internally. Jeremy Webber, "Beyond Regret: Mabo's Implications for Australian Constitutionalism," in *Political Theory and the Rights of Indigenous Peoples*, ed. Duncan Ivison, Paul Patton, and Will Sanders (Cambridge, UK: Cambridge University Press, 2000), 60–88.

In the United States, the revival of native title got underway before World War II, notably in the southwest Hualapai's long-running land rights battle, a story that had huge import not only for Hualapai themselves but also for the writing of American Indian history in the postwar period.[51] In Canada, a notion of "aboriginal title" was reinvented in the landmark case *Calder* v. *Attorney-General of British Columbia* (1973).[52] The most dramatic story of the resurgence of customary land title, however, occurred in Australia, where claims to distinct land rights were quite novel in the 1960s, and Aboriginal people and Torres Strait Islanders had very little recourse to the courts in protesting their retention.

British colonists in the nineteenth century did not explicitly recognize territorial rights of native people nor did they make formal treaties with landholders across the Australian continent, as was common practice in North America and New Zealand.[53] Since there was no formal recognition of land rights, campaigners in the 1960s thought it unlikely that indigenous peoples would win recognition for their land in the courts.[54] This was about to change. In 1969, Yolngu people in northeastern Arnhem Land, the far north of the country, launched a legal case for their land rights arguing that their hunting grounds and sites of cultural and spiritual significance were threatened by a bauxite mine being built on their lands without their permission. Yolngu peoples' native title claim was based on their prior and ongoing use and occupation of lands on the Gove peninsula, which had been declared an "inviolable reserve" in 1931. The government assumed that since the reserve was "Crown land" it could excise parts of it at will. But this was not the understanding of Yolngu residents; they saw the reserve as recognizing *their* land.

Their claim for native title, the first ever made in an Australian court, failed in court because while the judge recognized Yolngu customary law over the area as fact, he was not able to frame their legal system as a

---

[51] On the revival of native title by Hualapai leaders in the United States, see Christian McMillen, *Making Indian Law: The Hualapai Land Case and the Birth of Ethnohistory* (New Haven, CT: Yale University Press, 2007). For a comparative account of the revival of this legal doctrine across Anglo settler states after World War II, see Paul McHugh, *Aboriginal Title: The Modern Jurisprudence of Tribal Land Rights* (Oxford: Oxford University Press, 2011).

[52] On the importance of the case and its antecedents, see Hamar Foster, Heather Raven, and Jeremy Webber, eds. *Let Right Be Done: Aboriginal Title, the Calder Case, and the Future of Indigenous Rights* (Vancouver: UBC Press, 2007).

[53] Bain Attwood, *Possession: Batman's Treaty and the Matter of History* (Melbourne: Miegunyah Press, 2009).

[54] Johnson, *Land Is Our History*, 24–5.

source of Australian law.[55] However, the case brought unprecedented attention to indigenous peoples' land claims and the sympathetic publicity generated by the case became a key election issue in 1972. In his capstone campaign speech, the leader of the Labor opposition, Gough Whitlam promised land rights legislation "for Aborigines," arguing in high-minded terms that this was necessary "not just because their case is beyond argument but because all of us as Australians are diminished while the aborigines [*sic*] are denied their rightful place in this nation."[56]

The following year, Whitlam's Labor government delivered on the promise, at least in part, by establishing a commission to inquire into Aboriginal land rights and shifting the focus of government policy away from assimilation and toward self-determination. This would be the cornerstone of Aboriginal policy for the next three decades.[57] The commission recommended new legislation, passed in 1976 by another government as the Aboriginal Land Rights (Northern Territory) Act. It established criteria for Aboriginal communities in the Northern Territory to apply for recognition of distinct land title, and created new land councils to mediate between local communities and state authorities. It was a transformative moment that held huge promise for Aboriginal people within the Northern Territory and beyond.

In the years to come, state governments around Australia passed their own land rights legislation.[58] Finally, in 1992, the High Court of Australia found that Meriam Islanders in the Torres Strait had native title rights.[59] This decision drew explicitly on the international law of human rights in defending indigenous peoples' property interests. Justice Gerard Brennan argued that indigenous peoples' ownership of land had not been recognized previously because of how they were positioned in a racial hierarchy.

---

[55] W. E. H. Stanner, "The Yirrkala Land Case: Dress-Rehearsal (1970)," in *White Man Got No Dreaming: Essays 1938–1973* (Canberra: Australian National University Press, 1979); Nancy M. Williams, *The Yolngu and Their Land: A System of Land Tenure and the Fight for Its Recognition* (Stanford: Stanford University Press, 1986).

[56] Gough Whitlam, "It's Time for Leadership," election speech delivered at Blacktown Civic Centre, New South Wales, 13 November 1972. Online at Whitlam Institute, University of Western Sydney, www.whitlam.org/collection

[57] Nicolas Peterson, "Common Law, Statutory Law, and the Political Economy of the Recognition of Indigenous Australian Rights in Land," in *Aboriginal Title and Indigenous Peoples*, ed. Louis Knafla and Haijo Westra (Vancouver: UBC Press, 2010), 171–84.

[58] See for example Heidi Norman, *What Do We Want? A Political History of Aboriginal Land Rights in NSW* (Canberra: Aboriginal Studies Press, 2015).

[59] On the *Mabo* case, its making, and its impact, see, among many other works, Peter Russell, *Recognising Aboriginal Title: The Mabo Case and Indigenous Resistance to English-Settler Colonialism* (Sydney: University of New South Wales Press, 2005); Nonie Sharp, *No Ordinary Judgment: Mabo, the Murray Islanders' Land Case* (Canberra: Aboriginal Studies Press, 1996).

Such an "unjust and discriminatory doctrine . . . can no longer be accepted." He found that Australian common law had to be brought into line with international law declaring the "existence of universal human rights," particularly in terms of racial equality.[60] Distinctively, the human right and racial equality that Brennan invoked was not that only of the individual but also of the collective owner of land. The following year, the federal parliament passed the Native Title Act (1993) which created a process by which Aboriginal people and Torres Strait Islanders anywhere in Australia could go to a specially designed tribunal, or to court, in order to have their native title claim assessed.[61]

Internationalizing Indigenous Rights

In the 1970s in Anglo settler states, young activists and older leaders pushed forward the idea that the settler state needed to make a new social contract with indigenous peoples. Demonstrating the effects of dispossession on their communities as well as emphasizing their persistence as peoples, these actors opened up debate on their collective political futures. They were *nations* within the settler state whose collective rights to land needed to be urgently recognized particularly in the context of new mining and development ventures in remote areas. If many in the West were becoming more concerned with individual human rights in the 1970s, critiquing the excesses and failures of new postcolonial states in the Third World, in the world of indigenous rights activism notions of collective rights and internal self-determination were coming into their own. In the 1980s and 1990s, these claims began to be addressed by settler law and state bureaucracies on a nationwide scale (that is, beyond local and often ad hoc arrangements) in Canada, Australia, and New Zealand in particular. In these three Commonwealth countries, indigenous activists and leaders were able to tie their struggles for recognition of their sovereign rights to matters of national identity and the rethinking of state constitutions.

For some activists, however, working at the level of the state was not enough. In the mid-to-late 1970s, some indigenous activists primarily from the Anglo settler states created transnational rights organizations to lobby the United Nations for recognition of their right to self-determination. Their goals were political, inspired by Third World anti-colonialism, and also philosophical. According to historian Jonathan Crossen, the World Council of Indigenous Peoples, formed in

---

[60] *Mabo and Others* v. *Queensland (No. 2)* [1992] HCA 23; 175 CLR 1, 42.
[61] Richard H. Bartlett, *Native Title in Australia* (Sydney: LexisNexis Butterworths, 2014).

1974, aspired "to fundamentally change the basis of international law by incorporating a vision of Indigenous rights."[62] The World Council's founder, Secwepemc (British Columbia) man George Manuel, was strongly influenced by African socialism largely due to his executive assistant Mary Smallface Marule. A Blood Tribe (Alberta) activist and academic who had spent time in Zambia where she encountered African socialists and members of the African National Congress, Marule and her husband – an ANC activist – helped Manuel forge links with Zambian and Tanzanian leaders. Manuel credited his coinage of the term the "Fourth World" to describe the struggles of indigenous peoples in countries where the colonizers did not leave, to conversations he had when visiting with Tanzanian leaders.[63] The term was the title of a 1974 book that Manuel cowrote with a settler political scientist and that capture the imaginations of activists, artists, and intellectuals across the Anglo settler world. According to Vine Deloria, who wrote a foreword to the book, the philosophy behind the concept of the Fourth World was a universal one. The authors offered, he argued, nothing less than a "vision of human existence beyond that of expediency and the balancing of powers that speaks to the identity crisis that has gripped every land and its peoples."[64]

Another transnational organization, the International Indian Treaty Council, was also directly inspired by Third World anti-colonialism although, unlike the World Council, it did not initially aspire to represent global indigenous politics. As Crossen points out, the Treaty Council was conceived of as the "international wing" of the militant AIM in the United States and its first meeting was held on the Standing Rock Sioux reservation in 1974 following the armed stand-off at Wounded Knee. The Treaty Council prided itself on its grassroots representation and rejected state recognition; the World Council, by contrast, brought together leaders from state-recognized organizations such as the National Indian Brotherhood, the New Zealand Maori Council, and the National Aboriginal Action Committee, all of which relied on state funding. Furthermore, the Treaty Council initially aimed at winning recognition at the UN for the nationhood of particular tribes rather than indigenous peoples more broadly. Nonetheless, the Treaty Council announced a broader vision in a 1977 meeting at Geneva. According to its Declaration of Principles for the

---

[62] Jonathan Crossen, "Another Wave of Anti-colonialism: The Origins of Indigenous Internationalism," *Canadian Journal of History* 52, no. 3 (2017): 557.

[63] George Manuel and Michael Posluns, *The Fourth World: An Indian Reality* (New York: Free Press, 1974).

[64] Vine Deloria, "Foreword," ibid., xii.

Defense of the Indigenous Nations and Peoples of the Western Hemisphere, "Indigenous peoples shall be accorded recognition as nations, and proper subjects of international law." The declaration defined such peoples as those with a permanent population, defined territory, government, and the ability to enter into international relations.[65]

These organizations spearheaded a new campaign at the United Nations in the 1980s, seeking international recognition of indigenous rights within the human rights framework. Debate on what constituted indigenous human rights was fraught and lengthy, demanding considerable concessions from indigenous actors particularly around the definition of self-determination (which many states wanted to ensure did not trigger a right of secession) and a limitation of the right of self-government to internal matters. However, in 2007 the General Assembly did finally pass the Declaration on the Rights of Indigenous Peoples (UNDRIP).[66] Beginning with affirmations of equality and emphasizing principles of nondiscrimination, while also recognizing the value of diversity and rights to cultural difference, the declaration insists that indigenous peoples are full human rights subjects (Article 1) who are "free and equal" (Article 2) and who bear rights to self-determination (Article 3) and self-government (Article 4). The making of UNDRIP attests to how indigenous rights became, unexpectedly, a global issue as activists successfully connected distinctive indigenous rights claims to the broad discourse of human rights and self-determination.[67] In turn, the declaration offers hope to some indigenous leaders for a renewed understanding of indigenous rights as human rights. Thus, Pawnee attorney and legal scholar Walter Echo-Hawk claims that UNDRIP

invites us to view federal Indian law in a new way. It is possible to go beyond that amoral body of law to conceive of Native American rights as "human rights" . . . This vista sees fundamental freedoms that transcend our shores to inure to the benefit of every person worldwide.[68]

[65] See the text reproduced in Sheryl Lightfoot, *Global Indigenous Politics: A Subtle Revolution* (Routledge: New York, 2016), 213–15.

[66] On the making of UNDRIP, see, for example, *Making the Declaration Work: The United Nations Declaration on the Rights of Indigenous Peoples*, ed. Claire Charters and Rodolfo Stavenhagen (Copenhagen: IWGIA, 2009); Erica-Irene A. Daes, "An Overview of the History of Indigenous Peoples: Self-Determination and the United Nations," *Cambridge Review of International Affairs* 21, no. 1 (2008): 7–26; Lightfoot, *Global Indigenous Politics*.

[67] As I discuss elsewhere. See Miranda Johnson, "Indigenizing Self-Determination at the United Nations: Reparative Progress in the Declaration on the Rights of Indigenous Peoples," forthcoming in Journal of the History of International Law.

[68] Walter R. Echo-Hawk, *In the Light of Justice: The Rise of Human Rights in Native America and the UN Declaration on the Rights of Indigenous Peoples* (Golden, CO: Fulcrum Press, 2013), xiii.

Conclusion

The claims of indigenous activists to rights of identity and sovereignty were not considered human rights in the way that international institutions and civil society was employing the concept in the 1970s. That is, to protect individuals from violence and suffering at the hands of the state. Yet indigenous peoples in the Anglo settler states argued that their claims to collective rights were matters of concern to humanity. If many in "the West" did not (yet) appreciate the severity of threats to indigenous communities, activists themselves began to argue that their particular struggles constituted a fundamental human right. As Yolngu land rights claimants put it, who would they be without their land? Was not the cultural genocide spelled by assimilation policy and the denial of treaty rights that recognized the collective peoplehood of Canadian Indians something that a universal notion of humanity should be concerned to protect, as Harold Cardinal argued? Giving new meaning to the universal protection offered by the concept of human rights, indigenous rights activists did open up new legal and political space in the 1970s for redress and recognition within settler states and even at the United Nations. By asserting rights to land and demanding compensation for what had been lost, in terms that drew on and critiqued state policy and settler colonial history, activists challenged notions of cultural homogeneity and assimilation and invited new political futures. At the international level, indigenous activists had considerable success in expanding definitions of human rights and self-determination to encompass their collective rights. This story of indigenous activism in the 1970s demonstrates the power of the discourse of human rights for integrating discrete rights struggles. Significantly, this chapter provides an alternative story of 1970s activism in which indigenous actors in settler states stretched the discourse of human rights beyond individualist claims.

5   Privileging the Cold War over Decolonization
The US Emphasis on Political Rights

Mary Ann Heiss

The Universal Declaration of Human Rights (UDHR), approved by the UN General Assembly in December 1948, advanced the revolutionary idea that all human beings were entitled to the same basic rights regardless of "the political, jurisdictional or international status of the country or territory" in which they dwelled. This meant that it extended to the 700 million people – almost a third of the world's population – who in 1948 called the dozens of dependent territories home and injected human rights into the larger issue of decolonization of the Western colonial empires.[1] The UDHR won approval without a dissenting vote, though eight nations, including the six members of the Soviet bloc at the United Nations – the Soviet Union, Byelorussia, Czechoslovakia, Poland, Ukraine, and Yugoslavia – abstained.[2]

Although the Declaration was not a treaty and carried no force of law, it nevertheless assumed a prized place in international circles. Lebanon's Charles Malik, who served as a member of the UN Human Rights Commission and in 1948 chaired the Assembly's Third Committee, responsible for social, cultural, and humanitarian matters, called the Declaration "a document of the first order of importance." Eleanor Roosevelt, who headed up the commission, postulated that "it might well become the Magna Carta of all mankind." And Carlos P. Romulo of the Philippines asserted – at the height of profound Cold War tensions over the Soviet blockade of West Berlin and subsequent US-led airlift – that by drafting the UDHR, "the United Nations had justified its

---

[1] Article 2, Resolution 217 A (III), "Universal Declaration of Human Rights," December 10, 1948. The United Nations documents cited here, including Resolutions of the UN General Assembly, can be located via the Official Document System Search: www.un .org/en/documents/index.htm. For discussion of the inclusion of non-self-governing territories in the UDHR, see Johannes Morsink, *The Universal Declaration of Human Rights: Origins, Drafting, and Intent* (Philadelphia: University of Pennsylvania Press, 1999), 96–101.

[2] For discussion of the Soviet bloc dissent, which hinged on the relationship of individual rights to the state, see Morsink, *Universal Declaration of Human Rights*, 21–4.

existence before an anxious world" at a time when the organization was "on trial for its life."[3]

This chapter explores how US application of the UDHR over its first fifteen years became caught up in both decolonization and the Cold War. International interest in dependent territories, affirmed by the inclusion of those territories in the UDHR, had in fact been legitimized in the UN Charter, which established two different approaches to such territories: a clear and activist UN role in territories once controlled by the recently defeated Axis Powers, as well as the colonies of World War I's Central Powers that were still held as League of Nations mandates, and a vague and limited role in the territories controlled by the victors themselves. The sole obligation placed on the administering states in Article 73(e) of the Charter was regular transmission to the secretary-general of information about economic, social, and educational conditions in the territories they controlled.[4] In arguing that the universal rights it propounded applied to dependent peoples no less than their colonial rulers, the UDHR thus became part of the larger UN discussion of the disposition of the Western colonial empires. It also became caught up in the Cold War, as each side in the East–West confrontation sought to score points by scouring the other for human rights failings. Although US officials worked to present the free world coalition they led as the first line of defense against human rights abuses, it became clear as time went on that the United States privileged what Mary Ann Glendon has termed "the spiritual, public, and political rights" over others.[5] Specifically, they were more concerned with such rights as freedom of speech and assembly and free and open elections, areas where US practice set the standard – or at least US officials believed that it did, than with many of the economic or social rights that the Soviet bloc championed, where the US record was less laudatory.[6]

---

[3] Charles Malik, "Speech of Thursday, December 9, 1948," in *The Challenge of Human Rights: Charles Malik and the Universal Declaration*, ed. Habib C. Malik (Oxford: Center for Lebanese Studies, 2000), 117; Eleanor Roosevelt and Carlos Romulo remarks to 180th plenary meeting of the General Assembly, December 9, 1948, A/PV.180, 862, 867.

[4] See United Nations Charter, "Chapter XI: Declaration Regarding Non-Self-Governing Peoples," Article 73e; "Chapter XII: International Trusteeship System," and "Chapter XIII: The Trusteeship Council." This chapter uses the terms non-self-governing territory and non-trust dependent territory interchangeably to refer to the territories covered by Chapter XI of the Charter.

[5] Glendon, *A World Made New: Eleanor Roosevelt and the Universal Declaration of Human Rights* (New York: Random House, 2001), 174. For this point, see also Roger Normand and Sarah Zaidi, *Human Rights at the UN: The Political History of Universal Justice* (Bloomington: Indiana University Press, 2008), 188–96; Carol Devine et al., *Human Rights: The Essential Reference* (Phoenix, AZ: Oryx Press, 1999), 103–5.

[6] Articles 19, 20, 21, Resolution 217A (III), "Universal Declaration of Human Rights," December 10, 1948.

134   Mary Ann Heiss

Debate on the UDHR in the General Assembly, leading up to the Soviet bloc abstention, illuminated many of these differences; harsh rhetoric from both sides drove them home in the years that followed.[7] The depth of the US commitment to economic and social rights has generated a lively debate in the literature on human rights. Although the intricacies of that debate lie beyond the particular scope of this chapter, its findings lend credence to the position of those, such as Alex Kirkup and Tony Evans, who argue for the subordination of economic and social rights to civil and political ones in US policy.[8]

In bringing the two strands of the story of the US application of the UDHR together, this chapter lays bare the overriding importance of the superpower confrontation as a determining factor for US policy and the concomitant US reluctance to stand four square behind the idea of self-determination. US Cold War propaganda touted the nation's accomplishments in protecting basic political freedoms and regularly called out the Soviet Union and its satellites for failing to do so. At the same time, however, US officials were less vocal when it came to pushing their Western European allies to apply that principle to the non-trust dependent territories they administered. Despite the best efforts of the United States and its Western allies, however, the UDHR came to assume an important position for anti-colonialists at the United Nations who were waging a determined campaign to effect a broader international role in supporting decolonization and shepherding former colonies toward independent nationhood – and the membership in the United Nations that went along with that independence.

Self-Determination as a Human Right at the United Nations

The historiographical debate about whether the post–World War II drive for self-determination constituted a true human rights campaign is a long and deep one, as the contribution to this volume by Bonny Ibhawoh attests.[9] This chapter does not purport to address that debate directly but

---

[7] See, for example, Glendon, "The Deep Freeze: The Declaration in the Cold War Years," in *World Made New*, 193–219.

[8] See Daniel J. Whelan and Jack Donnelly, "The West, Economic and Social Rights, and the Global Human Rights Regime: Setting the Record Straight," *Human Rights Quarterly* 29, no. 4 (2007): 908–49; Alex Kirkup and Tony Evans, "The Myth of Western Opposition to Economic, Social, and Cultural Rights? A Reply to Whelan and Donnelly," *Human Rights Quarterly* 31, no. 1 (2009): 221–38; Daniel J. Whelan and Jack Donnelly, "Yes, a Myth: A Reply to Kirkup and Evans," *Human Rights Quarterly* 31, no. 1 (2009): 239–55.

[9] See Chapter 1.

rather draws on a succession of UN General Assembly resolutions to demonstrate that by early 1952, the organization did indeed consider self-determination to be a human right and encouraged universal extension of that principle to all territories that still lacked it. That position accompanied UN efforts to hold the administering states accountable for implementing human rights principles in general and the UDHR specifically in the non-trust dependent territories under their supervision. These efforts, which gathered momentum during the first years after the UDHR's approval, were in turn part of a larger campaign to erase the Charter-mandated distinction between the trust and non-trust dependent territories and allow for universal colonial accountability.

In 1947, as the UN Human Rights Commission was hard at work on what would become the UDHR, the General Assembly acted on that interest by making clear its intention to monitor both political development and human rights conditions in the non-trust dependent territories. Resolution 144 (II) affirmed that the voluntary transmission of political information was "entirely in conformity with the spirit of Article 73 of the Charter" and "should be . . . encouraged."[10] At the same time, in Resolution 142 (II), it approved what became known as the Standard Form for organizing, categorizing, and standardizing the information called for under Article 73(e). In addition to mandatory information about economic, social, and educational conditions, the form also provided for the optional transmission of information on a territory's "geography," "history," "people," "government" (which was another way of saying political development), and "human rights."[11]

A series of General Assembly resolutions in the coming years made the growing importance of both political information and human rights patently obvious. Assembly support for the transmission of political information deepened as the anti-colonial element gained strength, progressing from "encourag[ing]" such a move in 1947 to "recommend[ing]" it in 1952 to ultimately "urg[ing]" it in 1959.[12] In 1949, Resolution 327 (IV)

---

[10] Resolution 144 (II), "Voluntary Transmission of Information Regarding the Development of Self-Governing Institutions in the Non-Self-Governing Territories," November 3, 1947.

[11] Resolution 142 (II), "Standard Form for the Guidance of Members in the Preparation of Information to be Transmitted under Article 73e of the Charter," November 3, 1947.

[12] Resolution 144 (II), "Voluntary Transmission of Information Regarding the Development of Self-Governing Institutions in the Non-Self-Governing Territories," November 3, 1947; Resolution 637(B), "The Right of Peoples and Nations to Self-Determination," December 16, 1952; Resolution 1468 (XIV), "Voluntary Transmission of Information on Political Developments in Non-Self-Governing Territories," December 12, 1959. See also Resolution 327 (IV), "Voluntary Transmission of

made transmission of information on human rights mandatory.[13] But securing administering state acquiescence to basing that information on the UDHR proved difficult.[14] The best that reformers could do was the call in Resolution 551 (VI) for the administering states to report on their efforts to protect the principles enshrined in the UDHR, a move that received widespread support.[15] Pakistan's Mian Ziaud-Din, for example, labeled information on "the observance of human rights" even more important than "that relating to . . . political practice." Mexico's Emilio Calderón Puig went even further, plaintively declaring that "failure to [protect human rights principles] would indicate that the inhabitants of the metropolitan countries considered themselves human while feeling those of the Non-Self-Governing Territories to be sub-human."[16]

The General Assembly also devoted attention over the years to the question of whether self-determination was a universal human right. Although the rights enumerated in the UDHR applied equally to all peoples regardless of the political status of the country or territory in which they dwelled, the peoples of the non-self-governing territories by definition lacked the sort of widespread political rights outlined in the Declaration, such as participation in government and full suffrage.[17] Resolution 421 (V), which provided guidance for the continuing effort to follow the UDHR with enforceable human rights covenants, made a start toward remedying this incongruity by asking the Commission on Human Rights to study how to achieve universal colonial self-determination.[18] A little more than a year later, Resolution 545 (VI)

Information under Part I of the Standard Form Concerning Non-Self-Governing Territories," December 2, 1949; Resolution 848 (IX), "Voluntary Transmission of Information on Political Development in Non-Self-Governing Territories," November 22, 1954; Resolution 1535 (XV), "Progress Achieved in Non-Self-Governing Territories," December 15, 1960.

[13] Resolution 327 (IV), "Voluntary Transmission of Information under Part I of the Standard Form Concerning Non-Self-Governing Territories," December 2, 1949.

[14] See "Document A/1638: Report of the Fourth Committee," in "Agenda Item 34: Information from Non-Self-Governing Territories," Annexes (V) 34, 8–10; general debates of 183rd and 185th-188th meetings of Fourth Committee, November 20, 22, 24, 28, 1950, A/C.4/SR.183, /SR.185, /SR.186, /SR.187, and /SR.188; Resolution 446 (V), "Information on Human Rights in Non-Self-Governing Territories," December 12, 1950.

[15] "Standard Form" annex to Resolution 551 (VI), "Information from Non-Self-Governing Territories: Revision of the Standard Form," December 7, 1951.

[16] Mian Ziaud-Din (Pakistan) and Emilio Calderón Puig (Mexico) remarks to 39th meeting of the Special Committee on Information, October 15, 1951, A/AC.35/SR.39, 11, 10.

[17] Articles 2, 21, Resolution 217 A (III), "Universal Declaration of Human Rights."

[18] Resolution 421 (V), "Draft International Covenant on Human Rights and Measures of Implementation: Future Work of the Commission on Human Rights," December 4, 1950.

went even further, declaring that those planned for covenants should state categorically that "all peoples shall have the right of self-determination." In a move that Samuel Moyn has correctly described as "in effect, if unofficially, revis[ing] Chapter XI of] the Charter," it also called upon the administering states to promote self-determination in the territories under their supervision.[19] What that meant, of course, was that self-determination per se thereby became an international goal.

The General Assembly's December 1960 Declaration on the Granting of Independence to Colonial Countries and Peoples marked the culmination of efforts to link decolonization and human rights. Although the Soviet Union had initially introduced an inveterately anti-Western draft declaration, the final version was balanced and moderate.[20] "The subjection of peoples to alien subjugation, domination and exploitation," it affirmed, was "a denial of fundamental human rights" and "contrary to the Charter of the United Nations." "All peoples," it proclaimed, "have the right to self-determination," and "immediate steps" should be taken to bring "complete independence and freedom" to all remaining dependent territories.[21] Like the UDHR, the Colonialism Declaration, which proclaimed that self-determination was a human right, was approved without a dissenting vote, though nine states, including the United States, abstained.[22]

The Evolving US Stance on Administering State Accountability at the United Nations

As an administering power, the United States had consistently adopted an expansive policy when it came to transmitting information on the

---

[19] Resolution 545 (VI), "Inclusion in the International Covenant or Covenants on Human Rights of an Article Relating to the Right of Peoples to Self-Determination," February 5, 1952; Samuel Moyn, "Imperialism, Self-Determination, and the Rise of Human Rights," in *The Human Rights Revolution: An International History*, ed. Akira Iriye, Petra Goedde, and William I. Hitchcock (New York: Oxford University Press, 2012), 177.

[20] "Soviet Declaration on the Granting of Independence to Colonial Countries and Peoples, Submitted by the Chairman of the Council of Ministers of the Union of Soviet Socialist Republics at the 869th Plenary Meeting of the General Assembly," September 23, 1960, in "Agenda Item 87: Declaration on the Granting of Independence to Colonial Countries and Peoples," Annexes (XV) 87, 2–7.

[21] Resolution 1514 (XV), "Declaration on the Granting of Independence to Colonial Countries and Peoples," December 14, 1960.

[22] For discussion and approval see, for example, David W. Wainhouse, *Remnants of Empire: The United Nations and the End of Colonialism* (New York: Harper & Row, 1964), 9–29; David A. Kay, *The New Nations in the United Nations, 1960–1967* (New York: Columbia University Press, 1970), 150–72.

territories under its supervision. That approach dated back to the Truman administration, which trumpeted the US colonial record as "a credit to this Government" and from the start "fulfill[ed] expeditiously and in an exemplary manner" the nation's Article 73(e) responsibilities as a means of enhancing US "international prestige."[23] Administration officials, in fact, tried without success to convince their British counterparts to follow suit, with Assistant Secretary John D. Hickerson noting in 1950 "that the United States transmitted political information with no embarrassment while the British did not submit political information and were embarrassed."[24] It was not until 1961, however, as the General Assembly was poised to consider a Soviet proposal for active UN implementation of the Declaration on the Granting of Independence to Colonial Countries and Peoples, that the British consented to transmit political information. What Sir Hugh Foot of the British delegation to the United Nations dubbed "Information Yes. Intervention No" was painted as a voluntary move rather than "an act of compliance with the U.N. Charter." That move, though, was too little, too late, and the General Assembly voted in that year to create the Decolonization Committee on effective par with the Trusteeship Council, giving life to the Colonialism Declaration's goal of "bringing to a speedy and unconditional end colonialism in all its forms and manifestations" and demonstrating its conviction "that all peoples have an inalienable right to complete freedom, the exercise of their sovereignty and the integrity of their national territory." Put another way, the Decolonization Committee would fulfill the assertion, expressed now in a variety of UN resolutions, that self-determination was a human right.[25]

---

[23] Dean Acheson (acting secretary of state) memorandum for the president, April 29, 1946, Harry S. Truman Papers, White House Central Files – Official File, 85-H, Harry S. Truman Presidential Library, Independence, Missouri.

[24] John M. Martin (CO) and John D. Hickerson in "US Summary Record of Colonial Policy Talks with the United Kingdom: 3:00–5:00 p.m.," July 5, 1950, General Records of the Department of State, Record Group 59, Records of Assistant Secretary and Under Secretary of State Dean Acheson, 1941–48, 1950, box 13, folder: Colonial Talks (British), National Archives II, College Park, Maryland; FO tel. 2686 to U.K. Embassy, Washington, June 10, 1950, Colonial Office and Predecessors: Confidential General and Confidential Original Correspondence, Record Class CO 537/6568, National Archives, Kew, England.

[25] Hugh Foot untitled confidential memorandum, July 17, 1961, Commonwealth Relations Office and Commonwealth Office: United Nations Department and Successors: Registered Files (UND Series), Record Class DO 181/43, National Archives, Kew; memorandum of conversation, "U.K. Policy in the United Nations on Target Dates and Colonialism," July 26, 1961, Foreign Office: General Correspondence: Political Department, Record Class FO 371/160906, National Archives, Kew; Resolution 1514 (XV), "Declaration on the Granting of Independence to Colonial Countries and Peoples," December 14, 1960.

Notwithstanding its willingness to exceed UN requirements for the transmission of information on its own territories and its efforts to convince Britain and the other administering states to follow suit, the United States initially rejected efforts to make the transmission of political information compulsory. In 1947, when the Fourth Committee was debating a proposal to recommend the transmission of such information, US delegate Francis B. Sayre fell back on the Charter in arguing that the "precise" language of Article 73(e) made it "incontestably clear" that transmitting political information was not included among that article's responsibilities. "In legal language," he told the committee, "*expressio unius est exclusio alterius* – the express listing of certain things excluded everything else." By listing economic, social, and educational information, the drafters of the Charter had, he declared, expressly meant to exclude all other kinds of information. Although the United States had voluntarily transmitted political information, it could not countenance an effort to force – or shame through moral suasion – other states to do the same, which it viewed as deviations from the Charter all member states had approved at San Francisco.[26]

All that changed in 1960, however, when seventeen formerly dependent states, mostly from Africa, gained admission to the United Nations and provided the final tipping point in the General Assembly when it came to the issue of self-determination. Unlike most previous years, when new states had been admitted at the end of the General Assembly's session too late to take part in that session's work, those admissions took place in September 1960, which meant that new members would be full participants in all standing committee and General Assembly discussions, including debate over the Soviet proposal for a declaration on ending colonialism.[27]

US officials' appreciation of what the changing composition of the Assembly meant for questions involving self-determination occasioned a reconsideration of the long-standing US policy on encouraging the transmission of political information. This shift did not come easily, as the European Affairs Division of the State Department feared that a concession on that score might be merely the first step down a slippery slope that could culminate in extending to the Chapter XI territories the same sorts of UN supervisory rights that applied to the trust territories. Officials with broader perspective on the US role in the world, however,

---

[26] Francis B. Sayre remarks to 37th meeting of the Fourth Committee, October 3, 1947, A/C.4/SR.37, 43; Resolution 1468 (XIV), "Voluntary Transmission of Information on Political Developments in Non-Self-Governing Territories," December 12, 1959.
[27] For UN membership, see www.un.org/en/member-states.

worried that continued "ambivalent inaction" would sow the seeds of discontent among the anti-colonial majority at the United Nations.[28]

If the United States eventually came around to the idea of urging transmission of political information, it did not get on board with the effort to eliminate colonialism as embodied in Resolution 1514 (XV), which contained the Colonialism Declaration. US officials deemed the draft resolution problematic for a variety of reasons, but the initial inclination was to vote in the affirmative, in no small measure to curry favor with the almost four dozen sponsoring states and the dozens of other supporting delegations. Direct pressure from British Prime Minister Harold Macmillan convinced President Dwight D. Eisenhower to order an abstention instead, setting the United States up for considerable criticism in the General Assembly and making clear that the administration prioritized harmonious relations with key allies, and particularly Great Britain, over the explicit endorsement of the call to end colonialism and affirmation of what the General Assembly overwhelmingly agreed was the universal right to self-determination.[29]

The US Focus on Political Rights in the Soviet Bloc

US officials consistently sought to deflect UN attention from issues such as administering state reporting on political conditions and progress toward implementation of the UDHR in the non-trust dependent territories by calling attention to the lack of political freedom in the Soviet

[28] John M. Steeves (FE) memorandum to Wallner (IO), "EUR Position Regarding UN Role with Respect to Non-Self-Governing Territories," October 7, 1960, RG 59, decimal file 321.4/7–760 (hereafter RG 59, with decimal number). See also US del UN tel. 1132 to State Department, October 26, 1960, RG 59, 321.4/10–2660; US embassy (London) tel. 1979 to State Department, October 26, 1960, RG 59, 321.4/10–2560; Foy D. Kohler (EUR) memorandum to Wallner (IO), "UN Role with Respect to Non-Self-Governing Territories," September 27, 1960, RG 59, 321.4/9–2760; US del UN tel. 1180 to State Department, October 28, 1960, RG 59, 321.4/10–2860; Resolution 1535 (XV), "Progress Achieved in Non-Self-Governing Territories," December 15, 1960.

[29] For the decision to abstain see record of telephone calls, Thursday, December 8, 1960, Christian A. Herter Papers, Series I. Chronological File, 1957–1961, box 10, folder: Pres Tel Calls, 7/1959–1/20/1961, Dwight D. Eisenhower Library, Abilene, Kansas (hereafter Herter Papers, with filing information); Secretary of State Herter, memorandum for A. J. Goodpaster, December 8, 1960, Eisenhower Papers, Whitman File, Dulles-Herter Series, box 13, folder: CH December 1960 (2), Eisenhower Library; record of telephone calls, Friday, December 9, 1960, Herter Papers, box 10, folder: Pres Tel Calls, 7/1959–1/20/1961. For criticism of the US abstention, see James A. Wadsworth (US mission to UN) tel. 1775 to State Department, December 15, 1960, RG 59, 321.4/12–1560; Wadsworth (US mission to UN) tel. 1744 to State Department, December 14, 1960, RG 59, 321.4/12–1460.

Union and its satellites. The groundwork for this approach was laid in the March 1947 Truman Doctrine, which was delivered while the UN Human Rights Commission was drafting the UDHR. In stark, clear language, Truman contrasted the free, open, and hopeful non-communist world led by the United States with the controlled, repressive, and fearful societies of the Soviet Union and its satellites.[30] Although the Truman Doctrine predated the UDHR by twenty-two months, it anticipated the political rights listed in that document in the way it described the US-led free world. It also signaled the US intention to cast the East–West dichotomy in political terms, showcasing what the administration saw as the most positive features of US society – coincidentally areas where Soviet society was particularly lacking. That sort of emphasis formed the backbone of US propaganda efforts at the United Nations when it came to colonial questions, which consistently sought not only to contrast the political defects of the Soviet bloc with the purported strengths of the US-led free world but also to castigate that system for violating fundamental human rights as outlined in the UDHR.

Although the Truman administration was initially reluctant to use the United Nations as a platform for national policy, by 1951 officials in the State Department were coming to recognize the need to counter Soviet propaganda across UN forums.[31] On the issue of the UN role in decolonization, the Soviet Union pushed for UN discussion of political conditions in the non-self-governing territories and the right to offer up judgments about administering state policy. It also earned US opprobrium for what policymakers in Washington dismissed as "inaccurate" statements about Western colonial policy.[32]

The vehemence with which the members of the Soviet bloc attacked colonialism was undeniable. The inaccuracy of the Soviet critique, however, is less clear, as much of what bloc representatives said about the exploitative nature of colonialism was in fact true, even if officials in

---

[30] "President Harry S. Truman's Address before a Joint Session of Congress, March 12, 1947," http://avalon.law.yale.edu/20th_century/trudoc.asp. For an interesting analysis of the language of the Truman Doctrine, see Denise M. Bostdorff, *Proclaiming the Truman Doctrine: The Cold War Call to Arms* (College Station: Texas A&M University Press, 2008).

[31] For the Truman administration's overall approach to the United Nations, see Gary B. Ostrower, *The United States and United Nations* (New York: Twayne, 1998), 39–65.

[32] State Department paper, "Soviet Participation in United Nations Specialized and Other Multilateral Agencies, in Connection with United Nations Discussions of Dependent Area Questions," enclosure to Gerig memorandum for Sander and Taylor, January 10, 1951, RG 59, 350/1–1051; State Department paper, "Soviet Allegations of United States Violations of the Charter of the United Nations, in Connection with United Nations Discussions of Dependent Area Questions," enclosure to Gerig memorandum for Sander and Taylor, January 10, 1951, RG 59, 350/1–1051.

Washington and elsewhere preferred to think otherwise. To deflect Soviet criticism, officials in the Truman administration embarked on a campaign to expose Soviet violations of human rights, or what US officials had taken to dubbing the "conspiracy of Soviet imperialism."[33] In this way, they sought to link political repression in the Soviet bloc with the larger human rights project as reflected in the UDHR.[34]

The Eisenhower administration continued to highlight the East–West dichotomy and took the idea of Soviet imperialism to new levels, especially at the United Nations.[35] US ambassador Henry Cabot Lodge II missed no opportunity to condemn the hypocrisy embodied in the Soviet Union's purported concern for self-determination in the Western-controlled dependent territories while engaging in out-and-out repression throughout Eastern Europe, the Baltic states, and Central Asia. All of those areas, Lodge's propaganda line went, were victims of Soviet political domination in violation of the UDHR. Although US officials wanted the entire world to see the cant in Soviet pretensions to champion self-determination for the non-trust dependent territories, they were especially interested in getting that message out to the states of the developing world. In remarks before the General Assembly in March 1953, Lodge specifically warned those states that Moscow sought "world domination" despite its anti-imperialist rhetoric. Whatever the Soviets said, Lodge suggested, they were not champions of human rights.[36]

As time went on, US officials undertook an active campaign to instruct the anti-colonial faction at the United Nations about what they saw as the

[33] Porter McKelver (director of information, USUN), "Memorandum on Public Information Staff Needed for Paris Session of the General Assembly," August 3, 1951, enclosure to McKelver to Gordon Gray (director, National Psychological Strategy Board), August 3, 1951, Harry S. Truman Papers, Staff Member and Office Files: Psychological Strategy Board Files, box 26, folder: 334 United Nations, Truman Library; unsigned discussion brief for colonial talks, "Item IV (b) 8 – More Effective Measures to Counter Soviet-Inspired Propaganda Activities in Colonial Areas and Soviet Exploitation of the Theme of 'Western Imperialism' in Their Propaganda," September 4, 1951, US Department of State, *Foreign Relations of the United States, 1951*, vol. 2, *The United Nations; Western Hemisphere* (Washington, DC: Government Printing Office, 1951), 643.

[34] This theme, particularly as reflected in Eisenhower and Kennedy administration policy, is explored more fully in Mary Ann Heiss, "Exposing 'Red Colonialism': U.S. Propaganda at the United Nations, 1953–1963," *Journal of Cold War Studies* 17, no. 3 (2015): 82–115.

[35] For the Eisenhower administration's overall approach to the United Nations, see Ostrower, *United States and United Nations*, 66–97.

[36] Henry Cabot Lodge II (US delegate to the United Nations), "Soviet Imperialism: Motivated by Fear of Own People" (speech before the UN General Assembly, March 11, 1953), reprinted in *Vital Speeches of the Day*, April 1, 1953, in Dwight D. Eisenhower Papers, Administration Series, box 24, Folder: Lodge 52–3 (4), Eisenhower Library.

falsity behind the Soviet Union's anti-colonial crusade.[37] It was imperative, those officials believed, that the Soviets be prevented from "exploit-
ing colonial issues in the United Nations in order to deepen . . .
cleavages" between "colonial and anti-colonial free world states," "gain
the sympathies of dependent peoples and newly independent states, and
create difficulties for the colonial powers." They therefore advocated a
campaign to contrast progress toward independence in Western-
controlled territories with the expansion of communism throughout
Eastern Europe, the Baltic states, and Central Asia.[38]

The Eisenhower administration also worked outside the United
Nations to publicize Soviet violations of political rights. In July 1959, just
a week before Vice President Richard M. Nixon's famous Kitchen Debate
with Soviet Premier Nikita Khrushchev, it won congressional approval of
a joint resolution condemning Soviet imperialism in Eastern Europe and
Central Asia and designating the third week of July as "Captive Nations
Week" to draw attention to Soviet oppression. Although the resolution
meant little in practice, administration officials believed that taking a
public stand against Soviet suppression of freedom was a solid propaganda move.[39] They felt the same way about the various campaigns being
undertaken by the United States Information Agency (USIA) to highlight
what Washington considered the imperialist nature of Soviet policies in
Eastern Europe and the Baltic states, despite the generally lackluster
returns from those campaigns.[40] For their part, Soviet officials denied
emphatically that "there [was] any such thing as a 'captive nation' in [the]
Soviet bloc," a position that US officials disputed and one they worked to
counter by contrasting the process of decolonization, which created new
nations out of territories that were previously non-self-governing, with the

---

[37] See unsigned memorandum, "Salient Points," February 9, 1956, RG 59, lot 60 D 113,
box 44, folder: Studies; IO memorandum, "Program to Strengthen US Participation in
UN General Assembly," May 7, 1956, RG 59, lot 60 D 113, box 44, folder:
Strengthening U.S. Participation.

[38] State Department memorandum, "Review of United States Policy in the United
Nations," January 31, 1956, enclosure to Wilcox memorandum to Hartley, February
15, 1956, RG 59, lot 60 D 113, box 44, folder: Studies. See also State Department
Colonialism Working Group, "Appendix," May 15, 1956, RG 59, 700.022/5–1156;
Wainhouse memorandum to Bowie, "S/F paper on communist colonialism," August
2, 1956, RG 59, Subject Files of the Office of United Nations Political and Security
Affairs, 1945–1957, lot 58 D 742 and 59 D 237, box 11.

[39] Dwight D. Eisenhower, "Proclamation 3303 – Captive Nations Week, 1959," July 17,
1959, www.presidency.ucsb.edu/ws/?pid=107400.

[40] See, for example, Laura A. Belmonte, *Selling the American Way: U.S. Propaganda and the
Cold War* (Philadelphia: University of Pennsylvania Press, 2008), 100–2; Kenneth
Osgood, *Total Cold War: Eisenhower's Secret Propaganda Battle at Home and Abroad*
(Lawrence: University Press of Kansas, 2006), 113–50.

disappearance of self-government in Eastern Europe, the Baltic states, and Central Asia.[41]

Administration efforts to neutralize Soviet anti-colonial pretensions reached their apogee after Premier Nikita Khrushchev introduced his colonialism resolution in September 1960. In addition to backing moderate Asian and African states as they drafted a more balanced resolution, US officials undertook an all-out drive to "condemn Communist colonialism to [the] fullest" by "pointing out [that the] Soviet Union is not only [the] largest existing colonial power, but [the] only colonial regime that is still expanding and [that] has never granted independence or self-government to any subject people." Convinced that information on Soviet actions would speak louder than mere denunciations, US officials prepared a variety of printed materials about Moscow's domination of the Baltic states and Central Asia and made them available to other UN delegations. They also enlisted like-minded delegations to attack Soviet perfidy on the floor of the General Assembly. Despite the fervor of the anti-Soviet campaign, the US abstention on Resolution 1514 (XV) overshadowed it, calling into question the US commitment to self-determination, which the resolution affirmed as a human right, and handing the Soviets a significant propaganda victory.[42]

Faced with the necessity of moving on after the abstention on Resolution 1514 (XV), the new Kennedy administration shifted gears slightly by downplaying the argument that Soviet control over Eastern Europe, the Baltic states, and Central Asia was a form of colonialism and instead harkening back to the East–West dichotomy drawn in the Truman Doctrine speech. Specifically, the Kennedy administration's "World of Free Choice" campaign sought to deflate Moscow's pretensions to support self-determination and human rights in the developing world by demonstrating its impingement of basic rights and freedoms behind the Iron Curtain. As Secretary of State Dean Rusk succinctly explained the new approach in testimony before the Senate Foreign Relations Committee on May 31, 1961, "Against the world of coercion, we affirm the world of choice."[43]

[41] Henry Cabot Lodge (US ambassador, UN) tel. 123 to State Department, August 4, 1959, RG 59, 320/8–459.

[42] US embassy, Moscow tel. 617 to US del. to UN, October 6, 1960, RG 59, 321.4/10–660; State Department tel. 804 to US del to UN, November 1, 1960, RG 59, 321.4/10–2560.

[43] Rusk statement to Senate Foreign Relations Committee, "Building the Frontiers of Freedom," *Department of State Bulletin* 44 (June 19, 1961), 948. See also Arthur M. Schlesinger, Jr., memorandum to the President's Special Assistant for National Security Affairs McGeorge Bundy, "The Rusk–Morrow Memorandum on 'An Effective Countertheme to Peaceful Coexistence,'" June 19, 1961, *FRUS, 1961-3,*

At the United Nations, the administration utilized the "World of Free Choice" theme most directly to counter the Soviet Union's effort to control the implementation of the Colonialism Declaration.[44] As had been the case during debate of what became that declaration, Moscow again sought to use the issue as a way to attack the United States and the West in general, denouncing those states that persisted in suppressing independence movements across the non-self-governing world and tracing that resistance directly to the United States, which it termed "the chief gendarme and oppressor of the colonial peoples" and "an accomplice in all the bloody atrocities perpetrated by the colonial Powers in their colonies." To remedy the situation, the Soviets called for a formal UN campaign to eradicate colonialism in the year 1962, sanctions against colonial powers that refused to cede control of their territories, and the creation of what became the Special Committee on the Situation with Regard to the Implementation of the Declaration of the Granting of Independence to Colonial Countries and Peoples with broad powers on par with the Trusteeship Council.[45] US officials watched largely from the sidelines as moderate Asian and African delegations drafted the more even-handed resolution that ultimately created the Decolonization Committee.[46] They played an active role, however, in attacking the Soviet Union's "dark record of imperialist oppression and exploitation" directly, accusing it of "serious deprivations of human rights" throughout Eastern Europe, the Baltic states, and Central Asia. Proof of the

---

vol. 25, *Organization of Foreign Policy; Information Policy; United Nations; Scientific Matters* (Washington, DC: Government Printing Office, 2001), no. 124, http://history.state.gov/historicaldocuments/frus1961-63v25/d124; National Security Council Action Memorandum No. 61, "An Effective Countertheme to 'Peaceful Coexistence,'" 14 July 1961, *FRUS, 1961–3*, vol. 25, no. 126, http://history.state.gov/historicaldocuments/frus1961-63v25/d126.

[44] For the Kennedy administration's overall approach to the United Nations, see Ostrower, *United States and United Nations*, 98–115.

[45] "Letter Dated 26 September 1961 from the Minister for Foreign Affairs of the Union of Soviet Socialist Republics Addressed to the President of the General Assembly, Transmitting a Memorandum from the Government of the USSR on the Situation with Regard to the Implementation of the Declaration on the Granting of Independence to Colonial Countries and Peoples," September 27, 1961, in "Agenda Item 88: The Situation with Regard to the Implementation of the Declaration on the Granting of Independence to Colonial Countries and Peoples and Agenda Item 22: Aid to Africa," Annexes (XVI) 88 and 22, para. 29, 31.

[46] See US del to UN tel. 1423 to State Department, October 31, 1961, RG 59, 321.4/10–3161; US del to UN tel. 1438 to State Department, November 1, 1961, RG 59, 321.4/11–161; US del to UN tel. 1534 to State Department, November 7, 1961, RG 59, 321.4/11–761; US del to UN tel. 1556 to State Department, November 8, 1961, RG 59, 321.4/11–861; US del to UN tel. 1666 to State Department, November 16, 1961, RG 59, 321.4/11–1661; US del to UN tel. 1739 to State Department, November 21, 1961, RG 59, 321.4/11–2161.

undesirability of the Soviet system was as close as the fact that since World War II, some twelve million people had fled communist-controlled areas, voting with their feet, as it were, and escaping to the greater freedoms and opportunities of the West. Moving beyond its criticisms of Soviet policy, the Kennedy administration now called on the United Nations to "focus its attention as carefully on the 'colonialism' of the Soviet Union as it [did] on that of . . . any other nation." In other words, the administration wanted the United Nations to demonstrate that the political rights of the people behind the Iron Curtain were no less important than those of the people of the non-self-governing territories.[47]

President Kennedy himself highlighted the importance his administration placed on the idea of freedom in speeches to all manner of groups and organizations. Before the General Assembly in September 1961, he denounced the lack of "free institutions" in what he termed "the Communist empire" and condemned the recently constructed Berlin Wall as Moscow's attempt "to keep truth a stranger and its own citizens prisoners."[48] Kennedy's 1963 State of the Union address made many of these same points, arguing that "new nations asked to choose between two competing systems need only compare conditions in East and West Germany, Eastern and Western Europe, North and South Viet-Nam."[49] Kennedy's famous speech near the Berlin Wall in June of that year, just two weeks after he had called for sweeping civil rights reform at home, explicitly contrasted the two world systems. "Freedom has many difficulties and democracy is not perfect," the president maintained. But the United States "never had to put a wall up to keep our people in, to prevent them from leaving us," in the way the Soviet Union had been forced to do in Berlin.[50] Many of these points, including ongoing administration initiatives on civil rights, made their way into Kennedy's September 1963 speech to the General Assembly, but he also used that occasion to note the fifteenth anniversary of the UDHR that year. If that

[47] "Comments by the United States Delegation on the Memorandum of the Government of the USSR (A/4889)," enclosure to "Letter Dated 25 November 1961 from the Representative of the United States of America Addressed to the President of the General Assembly," November 25, 1961, in "Agenda Item 88: The Situation with Regard to the Implementation of the Declaration on the Granting of Independence to Colonial Countries and Peoples and Agenda Item 22: Aid to Africa," Annexes (XVI) 88 and 22, 19, 18.

[48] "Address by President John F. Kennedy to the UN General Assembly," September 25, 1961, www.state.gov/p/io/potusunga/207241.htm.

[49] John F. Kennedy, "Annual Message to the Congress on the State of the Union," January 14, 1963, www.presidency.ucsb.edu/ws/?pid=9138.

[50] John F. Kennedy, "'Ich bin ein Berliner' Speech," June 26, 1963, http://millercenter.org/president/speeches/speech-3376.

document was "to have full meaning," he proclaimed, "new means should be found for promoting free expression and trade of ideas, through travel and communication and through increased exchanges of people, books and broadcasts."[51]

More than merely a reflection of the nation's changing internal landscape, Kennedy's mention of US efforts to address domestic racial issues in his address to the Eighteenth General Assembly should also be seen within the context of the Assembly's expected consideration in 1963 of a draft declaration on the elimination of all forms of racial discrimination. Conceived as a broad condemnation of "discrimination on the grounds of race, color, or ethnic origin as a denial of the principles of the UN Charter," it called for "all states to revise government practices and to rescind laws and regulations which have the effect of creating and perpetuating racial discrimination." US officials "expect[ed] to be able to support the Declaration" when it came up for a vote in the General Assembly, despite the difficulties posed by the nation's "domestic situation," coded shorthand for the Jim Crow segregation that still divided southern US society along strict racial lines and that Kennedy's sweeping civil rights proposals were designed to address. Because the US media had "already focused the world's attention on race problems in the United States," making human rights a more prominent issue in the United Nations "might have the advantage of spotlighting human rights problems in closed societies as well, and thus shift attention beyond racial issues" to the political failings of the Soviet bloc. Officials hoped to use the debate over the draft declaration to juxtapose the prospects of progressive change in a democratic society like the United States against the immutable nature of life behind the Iron Curtain – the very point Kennedy had made in various speeches during 1963.[52]

Despite the hopes of officials in the State Department that UN consideration of the draft declaration on racial quality might shed some light on the failings of the communist bloc, it was just as likely to do the same for US society, and have potentially deleterious effects at home as well. A series of confrontations across the Jim Crow south were pushing the administration toward federal action on civil rights. So was concern about the potential fallout from incidents of racial discrimination against African diplomats, a fact that Kennedy acknowledged in his speech to the

---

[51] John F. Kennedy, "Address to the UN General Assembly," September 20, 1963, http://millercenter.org/president/kennedy/speeches/speech-5764.

[52] State Department paper, "United States Strategy at the 18th General Assembly," August 30, 1963, enclosure to Dean Rusk memorandum for the president, "Strategy for the Eighteenth General Assembly," August 30, 1963, Kennedy Papers, NSF, Series 5, box 311a, folder: Subjects UN (United Nations) General 9/1/63–9/8/63.

General Assembly in 1963. As a growing host of scholars have demonstrated, foreign policy considerations were at least partly responsible for the president's decision in June to call for sweeping federal civil rights protections.[53]

Those same considerations pushed the administration toward supporting the draft declaration on eliminating racial discrimination. This was particularly the case as apartheid became "the real gut issue" of the Eighteenth General Assembly for what US representative to the United Nations William Attwood described as "the dark-skinned delegations." "We have tended to treat the apartheid issue in the U.N. as an exercise in parliamentary tactics," he averred. "But it is more than ever an emotional issue that can no longer be sidetracked or dispelled by maneuvers, no matter how skillful."[54] Ultimately, the US delegation did support the United Nations Declaration on the Elimination of All Forms of Racial Discrimination, adopted without a vote two days before Kennedy's assassination.[55] It made clear in the process, however, that the United States intended "to carry out its terms in accordance with [US] constitutional processes."[56] In other words, support for the general principle of racial equality would not mean the wholesale implementation of that principle at home. Shielded behind the domestic jurisdiction clause of the UN Charter, the United States would continue to insist that what happened within its own borders was not a legitimate concern of the United Nations, a stance that flew in the face of US efforts to subject Soviet policy to that very sort of scrutiny and one that revealed the narrow confines of the US commitment to universal human rights.

---

[53] For some of the literature linking racial concerns to foreign policy, see Mary L. Dudziak, *Cold War Civil Rights: Race and the Image of American Democracy* (Princeton, NJ: Princeton University Press, 2002); Carol Anderson, *Eyes off the Prize: The United Nations and the African American Struggle for Human Rights, 1944–1955* (New York: Cambridge University Press, 2003); Thomas Borstelmann, *The Cold War and the Color Line: American Race Relations in the Global Arena* (Cambridge: Harvard University Press, 2003); Jonathan Rosenberg, *How Far the Promised Land? World Affairs and the American Civil Rights Movement from the First World War to Vietnam* (Princeton, NJ: Princeton University Press, 2006). For Kennedy, see John F. Kennedy, "Address to the UN General Assembly," September 20, 1963, http://millercenter.org/president/kennedy/speeches/speech-5764.

[54] William Attwood (US representative, United Nations), "Memorandum on Apartheid," November 7, 1963, enclosure to Attwood memorandum to McGeorge Bundy, "Memorandum on Apartheid," November 8, 1963, Kennedy Papers, NSF Series 5, box 311a, folder: UN (United Nations) General 10/63–11/63.

[55] Resolution 1904 (XVIII), "United Nations Declaration on the Elimination of All Forms of Racial Discrimination," November 20, 1963, www.un-documents.net/a18r1904.htm

[56] George Ball (acting secretary of state) memorandum to the president, "The Current Session of the United Nations General Assembly," December 13, 1963, *FRUS, 1961–3*, vol. 25, doc. 289, http://history.state.gov/historicaldocuments/frus1961-63v25/d289.

Conclusion: Washington's Blinkered Human Rights Vision

Although the United States joined forty-seven other nations in 1948 in signing the UDHR and considered itself a leader in the promotion of traditional political rights thereafter, the nation exhibited a halfhearted commitment to other sorts of rights, particularly UN support after 1952 for the universality of the right to self-determination. Worried about the consequences of wholesale independence across the colonial world, US leaders were often parsimonious with their support for national independence movements and resisted the campaign to expand the UN role in non-self-governing territories until that position became untenable. To offset the unpopularity of that policy as well as deflect attention from their inability to offer outright support for Western colonialism, they sought to discredit Soviet support for self-determination by painting the Soviet Union as a colonial power far worse than the Western Europeans. While traditional colonialism receded with the emergence of new nations and their entry into the United Nations, the bonds of Soviet control were tightening, as evidenced not only by rigid political controls in Eastern Europe, the Baltic states, and Central Asia, but also, after 1961, by the most visible symbol of suppression, the Berlin Wall.

If generating international ire about Soviet policy proved generally difficult, so did dealing with growing UN concern with issues such as racial discrimination and broadly conceived human rights, which signaled an important and not entirely welcome shift in the Organization's orientation and makeup, largely as a result of the admission between 1960 and 1963 of thirty formerly dependent territories. Reflecting by 1963 the concerns of the "underdeveloped 'south,'" debate in the General Assembly was coming increasingly to revolve around the differences between the haves and have nots and to present new challenges for the United States when it came to protecting its core interests.[57] Jason Parker, Matthew Connelly, and other scholars have made abundantly clear how important the racial, social, and economic issues that

---

[57] Harlan M. Cleveland (assistant secretary of state for international organization affairs) memorandum for the secretary of state, "Current Issues before the United Nations," November 27, 1963, *FRUS, 1961–3*, vol. 25, doc. 282, http://history.state.gov/historicaldocuments/frus1961-63v25/d282. See also Department of State paper, "United States Strategy at the 19th General Assembly," enclosure to Dean Rusk memorandum for the President, "Strategy for the Eighteenth General Assembly, August 30, 1963, Kennedy Papers, NSF Series 5, box 311a, folder: Subjects UN (United Nations) General 9/1/63–9/8/63; Evan Luard, *A History of the United Nations*, vol. 2, *The Age of Decolonization, 1955–1965* (New York: St. Martin's Press, 1989), 5–11.

motivated the Non-Aligned Movement became for the nations of the developing world.[58] But US propaganda, as well as actual policy decisions, consistently took on an overwhelmingly Cold War cast that downplayed such issues as racial equality and economic development and sought instead to extend the US antipathy toward communism to the developing world writ large. The US preoccupation with the Cold War placed the nation at odds with the majority of states at the United Nations, which simply did not share the US belief that the suppression of political rights that inhered in the communist system was the most important problem facing the international community. Without a true commitment to addressing the real problems facing the newly independent nations, US policy often drove them away, if not directly to the arms of the Soviet Union then toward the Cold War neutralism that US policymakers universally condemned but that became increasingly popular in the developing world after 1961.

---

[58] The importance of North–South issues for the developing world is chronicled in Jason Parker, "Cold War II: The Eisenhower Administration, the Bandung Conference, and the Reperiodization of the Postwar Era," *Diplomatic History* 30, no. 5 (2006): 867–92; Matthew Connelly, "Taking off the Cold War Lens: Visions of North–South Conflict during the Algerian War for Independence," *American Historical Review* 105, no. 3 (2000): 739–69.

Part II

Postcolonial Statehood and Global
Human Rights Norms

6 Cutting Out the Ulcer and Washing Away the Incubus of the Past

Genocide Prevention through Population Transfer

A. Dirk Moses

Introduction

The substantial literatures on decolonization, the partitions of Germany, British India, and Palestine in the 1940s, and the so-called human rights revolution, have not intersected in the manner that their simultaneity suggests they should.[1] For instance, Roger Normand and Sarah Zaidi's contribution to the UN Intellectual History Project, *Human Rights at the United Nations*, does not mention the partitions and the millions of refugees they occasioned despite devoting many pages to the formulation of the various UN human rights instruments of the later 1940s.[2] Like so many others written by lawyers and social scientists, the volume also tends to ahistoricism, presuming that the term "human rights" possessed a stable meaning or served uniform purposes from the interwar years to the present day. Thus the Czechoslovak statesman Eduard Beneš and Zionist leader Chaim Weizmann are cited as supporters of human rights already in the 1920s with the implication that they advocated the contemporary international human rights regime, an anachronism repeated by the legal historian A. W. Brian Simpson when he perceived a tension

Thanks to Volker Berghahn, Roland Burke, Giuliana Chamedes, Alon Confino, Donna-Lee Frieze, Mark Levene, Elisa Novic, Volker Prott, Gil Rubin, Philipp Ther, Lorenzo Veracini, and Patrick Wolfe for helpful comments on previous drafts dating back to 2012.

[1] Recent works that considers one aspect are Panikos Panayi and Pippa Virdee, eds., *Refugees and the End of Empire: Imperial Collapse and Forced Migration in the Twentieth Century* (Basingstoke, UK: Palgrave MacMillan, 2011); Jessica Reinisch and Elizabeth White, eds., *The Disentanglement of Populations: Migration, Expulsion and Displacement in Postwar Europe, 1944–49* (Basingstoke, UK: Palgrave Macmillan, 2011); Peter Gatrell and Nick Baron, eds., *Warlands: Population Resettlement and State Reconstruction in the Soviet–East European Borderlands, 1945–50* (Basingstoke, UK: Palgrave Macmillan, 2009); Pertti Ahonen, et al., *People on the Move Forced Population Movements in Europe in the Second World War and Its Aftermath* (Oxford: Berg, 2008).

[2] Roger Normand and Sarah Zaidi, *Human Rights at the United Nations: The Political History of Universal Justice* (Bloomington: Indiana University Press, 2008).

between advocating mass population "transfer" on the one hand and human rights on the other. Regarding Beneš, for instance, he observed that "his involvement, after the war, in the brutal expulsion of ethnic Germans and Hungarians from Czechoslovakia casts doubt upon his fundamental sincerity [about human rights], or perhaps illustrates the fact that enthusiasm for human rights and hypocrisy not uncommonly go hand in hand."[3] This chapter challenges such views in light of contemporary understandings of human rights. In doing so, I focus on the interwar years and 1940s with the temporal coincidence of the debates around the partitions of Germany, British India, and Palestine on the one hand, and the construction of the postwar international order and its human rights regime on the other.[4]

It is possible to push the argument further than the viewpoint in which the Great Powers cynically replaced the League of Nations' minority rights system with an unenforceable human rights regime so they could more easily deport destabilizing minorities. While many voices making this argument could indeed be heard in the 1940s, the concern for minority rights in Palestine and India continued to exercise British policymakers as before.[5] This policy continuity outside Europe highlights the relevance of atrocity prevention, and suggests that the new human rights discourse functioned as more than a "smokescreen" (Mark Mazower) for expulsion.[6] Accordingly, the relationship between partition, transfer, and

---

[3] A. W. Brian Simpson, *Human Rights and the End of Empire: Britain and the Genesis of the European Convention* (Oxford: Oxford University Press, 2004), 161, 325; Alfred de Zayas, *Nemesis at Potsdam: The Anglo-Americans and the Expulsion of the Germans: Background, Execution, Consequences* (London: Routledge and Kegan Paul, 1977). Most recently R. M. Douglas, *Orderly and Humane: The Expulsion of the Germans after the Second World War* (New Haven, CT: Yale University Press, 2012) complains about the human rights violations endured by Volksdeutsche in their expulsion. Latest scholarship includes Hugo Service, "Reinterpreting the Expulsion of Germans from Poland, 1945–9," *Journal of Contemporary History* 47, no. 3 (2012): 528–50.

[4] Arie Dubnov and Laura Robson, eds., *Partitions: A Transnational History of 20th Century Territorial Separatism* (Stanford: Stanford University Press, 2018), and my chapter "Partitions, Hostages, Transfer: Retributive Violence and National Security," 257–95, 344–55. A defense of the human rights revolution teleology is Akira Iriye et al., eds., *The Human Rights Revolution: An International History* (New York: Oxford University Press, 2012).

[5] For example, the work of Reginald Coupland, *Britain and India* (London: Longman, 1941, rev. eds. 1946 and 1948).

[6] Inis L. Claude, *National Minorities: An International Problem* (Cambridge, MA: Harvard University Press, 1955); Mark Mazower, "Strange Triumph of Human Rights, 1933–1950," *Historical Journal* 47, no. 2 (2004): 379–98; Mazower, *No Enchanted Palace: The End of Empire and the Ideological Origins of the United Nations* (Princeton, NJ: Princeton University Press, 2009); Eric D. Weitz, "From the Vienna to the Paris System: International Politics and the Entangled Histories of Human Rights, Forced Deportations, and Civilizing Missions," *American Historical Review* 113, no. 4. (2004): 1313–43.

human rights is only partially captured by Sam Moyn's suggestive "false start" thesis in his much-discussed book, *The Last Utopia: Human Rights in History*, in which national self-determination obtained as the predominant norm until the 1970s when it was replaced by international human rights.[7] Human rights rhetoric, I argue here, was not a mere puff or only an enabling context for expulsion in the 1940s; it performed important work in inspiring and justifying the foundational violence of the postwar order.

To answer our question about the relationship between partition, expulsion, and the "human rights revolution," it is necessary to study the interwar discussion on population transfers, as they were called, and a slightly earlier partition debate, namely the partition of Palestine recommended by a British commission in 1937. This discussion was characterized by a Janus-faced reference system: on the one hand, the commission defended its population transfer recommendation in terms of the Greek–Turkish population exchange of 1923 and, on the other, important commentators thereafter linked the partitions of Germany, British India, and Palestine with population transfer and humanitarian ideals.[8] Transfer was to be carried out not in contravention of human rights but in the name of establishing a new order based on the "rights of man" and what now is called genocide prevention; to use the contemporary terminology, they were to be expedited in the name of humanity and in a humane manner.

Significantly in this period, human rights were not yet always, or only, thought of as *international* human rights, as they are today. As Glenda Sluga has noted, continental figures like René Cassin understood the concept as translating the French *les droits de l'homme* – "the rights of man" – thereby linking it to the venerable revolutionary tradition of the national self-determination of qualified people rather than the new and abstract notion of international human rights *against* the state.[9] Accordingly, contemporaries nestled the concept in an ensemble of the Western civilizational attributes that qualified a people for independence: fundamental freedoms and democracy, the rule of law, economic progress, and

---

[7] Samuel Moyn, *The Last Utopia: Human Rights in History* (Cambridge, MA: Belknap Press of Harvard University Press, 2010).

[8] Article 143 of the earlier (1920) but superseded Treaty of Sèvres also stipulated population exchanges but on a voluntary basis. Thanks to Roland Burke for alerting me to this point.

[9] Glenda Sluga, "René Cassin, *Les droits de l'homme* and the Universality of Human Rights, 1945–1966," in *Human Rights in the Twentieth Century*, ed. Stefan-Ludwig Hoffmann (New York: Cambridge University Press, 2011), 108. This distinction is a core analytical point in Moyn, *Human Rights in History*.

modernity, often linked to successful settler projects. The relationship was cast in terms of a starkly drawn binary: human rights characterized modern, democratic, ethnically homogeneous societies; they did not obtain in feudal/premodern, undemocratic ones whose mixed populations demanded colonial supervision and/or minority protection.[10]

Self-determination and human rights entailed one another at this time, because human rights were a function of the state. Accordingly, self-determination crowned the Allied ideals declared in the Atlantic Charter of 1941. The Allied ideals required the total defeat of the Nazi occupier and the elimination of the causes of its temporary victory. Those obstacles to the progressive new order included German minorities in eastern and central Europe; and, as we will see for Zionists observing the Czechoslovak plans to expel Germans, Palestinian Arabs represented such an obstacle, although they were of course no minority but a large majority in Mandate Palestine: that they would become a minority was the avowed Zionist goal.[11]

Because human rights became synonymous with civilization and modernity, namely the project of democratic self-governance of occupied nations after the defeat of Nazi barbarism, postwar stability was elemental for their institutionalization.[12] And the key to nation-state stability was thought to be ethnic homogeneity, yet another attribute of modern societies. As already noted, the interwar discourse on population "transfers" proposed them as a "humane" solution to seemingly intractable nationality conflicts and as a precondition for social and economic development. Far from somehow in tension with partition and transfer, as supposed today, human rights and the repertoire of civilization norms for which the concept stood, actually justified them. The euphoric rhetoric about the supposed human rights revolution obscures the intrinsic role of human rights in the foundational violence of the new order.[13]

---

[10] The evidence from the interwar period suggests that the link between civilization, modernity, and human rights can be located then rather than after World War II, as suggested by Mark Mazower, "The End of Civilization and the Rise of Human Rights: The Mid-Twentieth-Century Disjuncture," in Hoffmann, *Human Rights in the Twentieth Century*, 29–44.

[11] A. Dirk Moses, "Empire, Resistance, and Security: International Law and the Transformative Occupation of Palestine," *Humanity: An International Journal of Human Rights, Humanitarianism, and Development* 8, no. 2 (2017): 379–409.

[12] Jay Winter, "From War Talk to Rights Talk: Exile Politics, Human Rights and the Two World Wars," in *European Identity and the Second World War*, ed. Menno Spiering and Michael Wintle (Basingstoke, UK: Palgrave Macmillan, 2011), 55–74.

[13] Cf. Mark Levene, *Genocide in the Age of the Nation-State*, vol. 3, *The Crisis of Genocide* (Oxford: Oxford University Press, forthcoming, 2013), ch. 4, which discusses the sacrifice of minorities and diversity for the postwar order of nation-states.

I unfold the argument in two stages. In the first, I analyze the discussion about the morality and efficacy of population "transfer" in the 1930s, because at the time it became ineluctably associated with partition, and was justified in terms of modernity and preventing ethnic civil wars. Then I show how it became related to the question of human rights in the early 1940s. In the main, my subjects are academic or quasi-academic policy analysts and advocates who advised major organizations and/or states rather than the familiar actors like Churchill, Stalin, Roosevelt, and other political elites whose support for transferring German civilians is well known. Anything but isolated academic scribblers, these half-forgotten figures not only delivered the justifications employed by governments as they negotiated a distinctive phase of decolonization and its relationship to evolving human rights norms: the end of Nazi empire in Europe and dissolution of British imperial control in the Middle East and South Asia. They also made the case for the foundational violence of the new order in which we live today. As we will see, the consensus linking partition, population transfer, and human rights emerged in a highly Eurocentric and historically specific context: that of debate around the fate of German minorities in Central and Eastern Europe, and Zionist aspirations in Palestine.

The Interwar Debate on the Humanity of Transfer

It has become a commonplace in the recent literature to highlight the 1923 population exchange convention between Turkey and Greece, blessed and supported by the League of Nations, as a precedent for later commentators, policymakers, and politicians, and so it was. It also bears recalling that it was highly controversial at the time, with leading British figures expressing their unease with its compulsory dimension and the suffering of the over one million Greek Orthodox civilians who were driven from western Turkey and the roughly 350,000 Muslims who were then compelled to leave Greece for Turkey.[14] For the post–World War I norm was not population exchange but minority protection, which entailed leaving minorities *in situ* and guaranteeing them legally articulated rights. The Treaty of Sèvres signed between the Entente

---

[14] Mark Mazower, "Minorities and the League of Nations in Interwar Europe," *Daedalus* 126, no. 2 (1997): 49; Christa Meindersma, "Population Exchanges: International Law and State Practice – Part 1," *International Journal of Refugee Law* 9, no. 3 (1997): 341; Weitz, "From Vienna to the Paris System," 1136. Despite evidence to the contrary, Howard Adelman and Elazar Barkan come to the opposite conclusion: Adelman and Barkan, *No Return, No Refuge: Rites and Rights in Minority Repatriation* (New York: Columbia University Press, 2011), ch. 2.

Powers and the defeated Ottoman government in 1920 foresaw minority protection within the rump Turkish state (the Ottoman Arab and Armenian lands having passed into Europe and American mandates respectively), indeed the return of Armenian refugees and restitution of their property, though expressing concerns about the lack of "civilized opinion" there that might restrain the state.[15] The defeat of the invading Greek forces and destruction of Smyrna by Turkish nationalist forces, led by Mustafa Kemal ("Atatürk"), in 1922 overturned the Sèvres order. Now the new Turkish government declared that Greeks would have to leave, leading to the Greek prime minister's suggestion of a formal population exchange administered by the League of Nations. The fighting had caused a major refugee problem in any event, and the exchange convention signed in Lausanne in 1923 bestowed largely retrospective blessing and logistical support for the rehabilitation of refugees, at least concerning the Greeks.[16]

Ever since Lausanne, commentators who were partial to population transfers and exchanges have pointed to the peace and stability the convention brought to the eastern Mediterranean. Its compulsory nature was a small price to pay, it was reasoned, in what was ultimately a "humane" policy because future genocidal warfare had effectively been abolished: population transfer as a form of preventing "wars of extermination." Commentators who argued in these terms were on the margins in the 1920s but found their arguments in the mainstream of even liberal internationalism a decade later, echoing earlier discourses about the removal of indigenous peoples to protect them from frontier violence.[17]

These points are well covered in the scholarly literature. What has not been registered sufficiently about Lausanne and population transfers, nor connected with the Palestine problematic, is how the commentary on these phenomena embedded them in a discourse about modernity, human rights, and the role of settler projects in its development. Eduard Beneš, the Czechoslovak leader who urged the expulsion of the Sudeten Germans, for example, complained that they were settlers or colonists in Slavic territory, of a lower cultural level to the Slavs, whereas

---

[15] Sarah Shields, "Forced Migration as Nation-Building: The League of Nations, Minority Protection, and the Greek–Turkish Population Exchange," *Journal of the History of International Law* 18 (2016): 120–45.

[16] Yeşim Bayar, "In Pursuit of Homogeneity: The Lausanne Conference, Minorities and the Turkish Nation," *Nationalities Papers* 42 (2013): 108–25.

[17] On the European context, see Matthew Frank, "Fantasies of Ethnic Unmixing: Population 'Transfer' and the End of Empire in Europe," in Panayi and Virdee, *Refugees and the End of Empire*, 81–101. Thanks to Lorenzo Veracini for pointing out the indigenous parallel.

the western European states had sent settlers around the world and "opened up new regions, and played a civilizing role."[18] While he was expressing the perspective of indigenous people, the Czechs and Slovaks, his frame of reference was the benefits that settlers brought to extra-European countries. He was merely reflecting the contemporary norm.[19]

The advantages conveyed to Greece by the refugees it received from Turkey are a case in point about the connection between population transfers, humane policies, and modernization. Zionist commentary in the 1930s in particular was fascinated by the agricultural development that the refugees brought to Macedonia, coupled with land reform, modern farming techniques, and general economic progress. What is more, the country's ethnic homogeneity made it more peaceful and modern. Norman Bentwich, the first Attorney-General of Mandate Palestine, ardent Zionist and later professor of international relations at the Hebrew University, wrote already in 1926 about "Macedonia, which was formerly the most desperate welter of nationalities and the traditional breeding ground of feuds and wars, has now obtained an almost homogeneous Greek population. The productivity of the land has been doubled, and in some cases, trebled by the settlers." He concluded by extolling the virtues of the population change's effects on Greece: "This enormous enterprise of settlement has been executed by a sustained national effort which is a lesson for the whole of Europe."[20] In this discourse, the refugee becomes the settler colonist: the bearer of modernity and its democratic social system.

This was also the view of the English colonial civil servant and politician John Hope Simpson, who three years later reported on the Refugee Settlement Commission that oversaw the integration into Greece of the Christians from Turkey. He referred to it as "the colonisation work of the Greek Government in the Province of Macedonia," which entailed cultivating uncultivated land and replacing the Muslims who had left for Turkey. Thanks to a large League of Nations loan, the administrative infrastructure was impressive: fourteen colonization bureaux each with

---

[18] Eduard Beneš, "The Organization of Postwar Europe," *Foreign Affairs* 20, nos. 1–4 (1941/2): 235.

[19] On settler colonialism, see Lorenzo Veracini, *Settler Colonialism: A Theoretical Overview* (Basingstoke, UK: Palgrave Macmillan, 2010) and the journal he has co-established, *Settler Colonial Studies*.

[20] Norman Bentwitch, "The New Ionian Migration," *Contemporary Review*, no. 130 (July/December 1926): 323, 325. The modernization theme is central to Umut Özsu, "Fabricating Fidelity: Nation-Building, International Law, and the Greek–Turkish Population Exchange," *Leiden Journal of International Law* 24 (2011): 823–47; Elisabeth Kontogiorgi, *Population Exchange in Greek Macedonia: The Rural Settlement of Refugees 1922–1930* (Oxford: Clarendon Press, 2006).

twenty-five staff, all told between 400 and 500 officials at first and increasing to 1,800. To increase crop yields to sell on the international market and diminish food imports, the Commission founded an Agricultural Colonization Service, which led to borrowing from the classic settler colony of Australia in the form of a drought-resistant and more productive strain of wheat. Massive public works improved the infrastructure of economic development while drainage increased the amount of cultivatable land. Simpson was impressed with the colonists, who on "the average is a better cultivator than the native Greek." Not only did they bring prosperity to the country, they brought stability.

> Before the transfer of populations . . . the Greek population of Greece amounted to only 80 per cent. of the total, 20 per cent. being Turks, Bulgarians and people of other races. After the transfer, of the total population 93.75 per cent. are Greeks and only 6.25 per cent. persons of other nationalities. As a result, the frequent political difficulties which used to arise owing to the presence of considerable foreign elements in the population have disappeared.[21]

This concentrated investment of resources in resettlement and agriculture demonstrated to Zionists that large-scale population transfers were viable when underwritten by states.

They were less enamored of Simpson's simultaneous deliberations on Palestine, where he was sent in 1929 to investigate the causes of the violent riots that year. Although Zionists were displeased with his report's findings, because it recommended limiting Jewish immigration and criticized Mandate economic policy that favored Jews, it was entirely in keeping with the racist developmentalism of the time. As in the Greek case, he regarded the settlers as the economically dynamic element, more so given that they were European. The pressing problem of increasing number of landless Arab peasants was a consequence of too rapid change to what he regarded as the backward Arab rural economy, in particular the widespread existence of commons at the expense of privately owned holdings. They should be privatized to increase production, he thought. Besides extensive tax reform to alleviate peasant indebtedness and sale of their lands, he recommended the Greek solution: a new department of economic development for the rural sector to repopulate the countryside more densely with landless peasants on newly privatized and irrigated land, thereby reconciling Arab and Jewish agendas. Although Simpson's modernization recommendations were controversial because they

---

[21] John Hope Simpson, "The Work of the Greek Refugee Settlement Commission," *Journal of the Royal Institute of International Affairs* 8, no. 6 (1929): 585, 586, 588, 589, 601.

dispelled the illusion that all was well in the Mandate, they were taken up in large measure by his successors.[22]

Yet another commission of inquiry was assembled the wake of the Arab rebellion that broke out in 1936. Famously or infamously, depending on your viewpoint, the Peel Commission, as it was unofficially called, recommended the partition of the mandate after determining the irreconcilable nature of the Jewish settlers' European civilization and that of the Palestinian Arabs. What is more, because it was impossible to draw borders for a viable Jewish state, it recommended the transfer of Arabs eastward into less fertile territory, allocating the more fertile coastal areas to the minority Jewish population which it regarded as the better agriculturalists. The interior was to be made habitable for the Palestinian Arabs by irrigation projects and other forms of capital investment.[23]

For the Zionist leaders making representations to the commission, the success of Greek settler-refugees after 1923 was evidence that population transfers were progressive acts that benefited all sides. The problem of landless Arab peasants could be solved this way, while bringing prosperity to the underpopulated regions of Transjordan, Syria, and Iraq. Zionist leader David Ben Gurion himself declared at a Zionist congress in 1937 that it was a "humane and Zionist ideal, to shift part of a people [Arabs] to their own country and to settle empty lands," by which he meant transferring Palestinian Arabs eastward to other countries.[24]

The Commission agreed. Its report was largely written by the Oxford historian Reginald Coupland, who sympathized with the Zionists' modernizing project.[25] The report tackled the thorny moral question of compulsion in the following way:

so vigorously and effectively was the task accomplished that within about eighteen months from the spring of 1923 the whole exchange was completed. Dr. Nansen was sharply criticized at the time for the inhumanity of his proposal, and the operation manifestly imposed the gravest hardships on multitudes of people.

---

[22] John Hope Simpson, *Report on Immigration, Land Settlement and Development* (London: HMSO, 1930); Charles Anderson, "The British Mandate and the Crisis of Palestinian Landlessness, 1929–1936," *Middle Eastern Studies* 54, no. 2 (2018): 171–215.

[23] *Palestine Royal Commission Report 1937* (London: HMSO, 1937).

[24] Quoted in Benny Morris, "Refabricating 1948," *Journal of Palestine Studies* 27, no. 2 (1998): 86. Generally, see Patrick Wolfe, "Purchase by Other Means: The Palestine *Nakba* and Zionism's Conquest of Economics," *Settler Colonial Studies* 2, no. 1 (2012): 133–71.

[25] Penny Sinanoglou, "The Peel Commission and Partition, 1936–1938," in Rory Miller, ed., *Britain, Palestine and the Empire: The Mandate Years* (Aldershot: Ashgate, 2010), 119–40; Arie M. Dubnov, "The Architect of Two Partitions or a Federalist Daydreamer? The Curious Case of Reginald Coupland," in Dubnov and Robson, *Partitions*.

But the courage of the Greek and Turkish statesmen concerned has been justified by the result. Before the operation the Greek and Turkish minorities had been a constant irritant. Now the ulcer has been clean cut out, and Greco-Turkish relations, we understand, are friendlier than they have ever been before.[26]

Again, population transfer was seen as an anti-genocidal measure (although the word genocide did not yet exist, being coined in 1944), or a "question of humanity," as the report put it. Reasoning analogically, and in view of the massacres of Assyrians by Iraqi Arabs in 1933, the Commission applied these lessons to the Palestine, concluding that it could not entrust the Jewish minority to the sovereign authority of the Arab majority.[27] In doing so, the British continued their belief, shared by scholars today like the Israeli historian Benny Morris, that non-European majorities could not be trusted to protect the rights of minorities, especially a European one. The report's reference to post-colonial Iraq conveniently omitted the fact that the British preordained the retribution against Assyrians by enlisting them to police the majority Arab population during its mandate. What is more, the British demanded the inclusion of the Ottoman vilayet of Mosul in the British-dominated Iraqi state in 1924–5 on minority protection grounds, although its oil reserves were the draw card.[28] Protection, partitions, and transfer participated in the same logic as minority protection: the prevention of ethnic warfare by imperial design or supervision.

The Commission had also been influenced by minority issues elsewhere, determining that "If . . . the settlement is to be clean and final, this question of the minorities must be boldly faced and firmly dealt with. It calls for the highest statesmanship on the part of all concerned" – like the leaders of the Lausanne settlement, the report implied.[29] Modernization also played a key role in the option for partition: the Jews had developed a modern capitalist economy that was unmanageable for an Arab government "not fully acquainted with financial and commercial problems on a worldwide scale."[30]

---

[26] *Palestine Royal Commission Report 1937*, 390.   [27] Ibid., 141.

[28] Thanks to Laura Robson for discussions on this point. Laura Robson, *States of Separation: Transfer, Partition, and the Making of the Modern Middle East* (Berkeley: University of California Press, 2017), 36; Sarah Shields, "Mosul, the Ottoman Legacy and the League of Nations," *International Journal of Contemporary Iraqi Studies* 3, no. 2 (2009): 217–30; cf. Benny Morris, "Explaining Transfer: Zionist Thinking and the Creation of the Palestinian Refugee Problem," in *Removing People: Forced Removal in the Modern World*, ed. Richard Bessel and Claudia Haake (Oxford University Press, Oxford, 2009), 349–60. The murderous attack on Jews in Hebron in 1929 shocked the Zionist leadership in Palestine, which commenced self-defense measures and pressed the Mandate authorities for greater protection.

[29] *Palestine Royal Commission Report 1937*, 390.   [30] Ibid., 141.

As might be expected, many Zionists were excited by the transfer aspect of the report, as was the Polish government, which saw it as an opportunity for Jews to migrate from Poland.[31] Typical was the Jewish Agency's Kurt Mendelsohn, who traveled to Greece to inspect the results of the exchange so as to urge its analogous benefits for the Palestine case. Writing in 1938 in a pamphlet called *The Balance of Resettlements: A Precedent for Palestine,* he took pains to counter the moral scruples about compulsory transfer. "The circumstances accompanying their realization or execution may indeed tend to obliterate the idea, or may even bear the stamp of inhumanity," he wrote, "but this is by no means an inherent element." However strong the "impression of injustice, suffering and cruelty" associated with what he euphemistically called "the withdrawal of the Greeks from Anatolia," Mendelsohn stressed the "constructive and progressive features even in these difficult circumstances."[32] They were the familiar trinity of economic development, social reform, and international peace. Population transfer was linked to the end of reactionary social relations and onset of modernity. Of Lausanne, Mendelsohn wrote "Not until the unmixing of population and the creation of homogeneous States and territories, was the way cleared for the economic development of these countries, for the victory over feudalism, and for the social liberation of the peasants. Only with the exchange of population, and under the pressure of the exigencies of resettlement was this incubus of the past washed away."[33] He continued that the situation resembled the British settler colonies a century earlier, namely the combination of unused population reserves and empty land – all to the benefit of the indigenous Arab population of course.

Mendelsohn dealt with the compulsion question in the following manner: "Even if a resettling process is carried out as humanely as possible, with the greatest consideration for the individual and the group, the separation from what had hitherto been home will always be very painful to many and there are undoubtedly indications that a part of the old generation are not yet reconciled to their forced transfer," he conceded. Then comes the inevitable qualification: "But it is as certain that the growing generation have taken firm root in their new country and

---

[31] Yossi Katz, "Transfer of Population as a Solution to International Disputes," *Political Geography* 11, no. 1 (1992): 55–72. On the Polish government's position, see Susan Pedersen, "The Impact of League Oversight on British Policy in Palestine," in Miller, *Britain, Palestine and Empire,* 57.

[32] Kurt Mendelsohn, *The Balance of Resettlements: A Precedent for Palestine* (Leiden: A.W. Sijthoff's Uitgeversmaatschappij, N.V., 1939), 3.

[33] Ibid., 19.

have completely adapted themselves to the new conditions of life."[34] These Zionists thinkers were hardly alone in making such arguments. They only were echoing Lord Curzon's statement in 1923 that "the suffering entailed, great as it must be, would be repaid by the advantages which would ultimately accrue to both countries from a great homogeneity of population and from the removal of old and deep-rooted causes of quarrel."[35]

Now, for all that, few statesmen at the time were willing to publicly endorse the thorny issue of *compulsory* transfer; indeed Curzon himself famously had huge misgivings about the Lausanne Convention. After all, the Greek–Turkish case had been a fait accompli thanks to Turkish expulsions. *Initiating* transfers to affect a partition was quite another matter, one that bore on the question of what we today call human rights. While Reginald Coupland and Jewish Agency operatives were prepared to entertain this proposition because of the perceived long-term benefits to both parties, others like Yosef Weitz, head of the Jewish National Fund's Land Department, preferred to devise incentives for Arabs to abandon their land because he could not envisage any power to forcibly transfer the Arabs.[36] And, sure enough, the Foreign Office and Anthony Eden rejected Coupland's plan as unfeasible, as they could not foresee imposing it upon the majority Arab population whose leaders made it clear that they were not to be enticed to abandon their villages and fertile land for arid areas in the east on the promise of irrigation and development.[37]

The question of compulsion and repatriation as great power policy was placed on the table by Hitler and Nazi Germany's agreements with the Soviet Union and other European states to bring Germans "home into the Empire" (*heim ins Reich*). Hitler's logic was the following:

the whole of East and South-east Europe is interspersed with untenable splinters of the German nation. In this lies the reason for the continued disturbances between States. In this age of the nationality principle and the racial idea it is utopian to believe that members of superior race can simply be assimilated. It is

---

[34] Ibid., 28.

[35] Lord Curzon, January 27, 1923, Lausanne Conference on Near Eastern Affairs, quoted in Michael Barutciski, "Lausanne Revisited: Population Exchanges in International Law and Policy," in *Crossing the Aegean: An Appraisal of the 1923 Compulsory Population Exchange between Greece and Turkey*, ed. Renée Hirschon (New York: Berghahn, 2003), 29. A more balanced assessment can be found in J. R., "The Exchange of Minorities and Transfers of Population in Europe since 1919–I," *Bulletin of International News* 21, no. 15 (June 22, 1944): 579–88.

[36] Katz, "Transfer of Population," 64–5.

[37] Roza I. M. El-Eini, *Mandated Landscapes: British Imperial Rule in Palestine, 1929–1948* (New York: Routledge, 2006), 367–8.

therefore one of the tasks of a far-seeing regulation of European life to carry out resettlements in order thus to remove at least part the causes of conflict in Europe.[38]

The revisionist Zionist leader, Ze'ev Jabotinsky, who had opposed the partition and transfer recommendation of the Peel Commission because it entailed relinquishing significant parts of Palestine to the Arabs, softened his opposition to population exchanges in light of Germany and Italy's agreement about populations in South Tirol in 1939.[39] As we will see, Hitler's reasoning was taken up by Beneš and the British Labour Party international relations expert and politician, Hugh Dalton, in the 1940s. It is no accident that Beneš and Dalton knew one another in London, as Dalton moved in exile circles.[40] A closer inspection of Beneš's views shows that he provided the template for reasoning about forced population expulsions, democracy, and human rights.

Human Rights and Transfer

What, then, was the relationship between human rights language, population transfer, and self-determination? In the early 1940s, Beneš was publishing in English-language journals to advocate "the transfer of populations" in view of the failed minority protection regime and the success of the Greek–Turkish exchange nearly twenty years before; it had prevented "a systematic mass murder of millions of people." Not only was it an exercise in genocide prevention, and therefore humane, the praxis could also be humanized: "If the problem is carefully considered and wide measures are adopted in good time, the transfer can be made amicably under decent human conditions, under international control and with international support."[41] He elaborated his case in a well-known essay, "The Organization of Postwar Europe," published in that venerable journal, *Foreign Affairs*, whose editor was sympathetic to

---

[38] Quotation in Wenzel Jaksch, "Mass Transfer of Minorities," *Socialist Commentary*, October 1944. A different translation appears in J. R., "The Exchange of Minorities and Transfer of Population in Europe since 1919-II," *Bulletin of International News* 21, no. 17 (August 19, 1944): 658, and in Matthew Frank, *Expelling the Germans: British Opinion and Post-1945 Population Transfer in Context* (Oxford: Oxford University Press, 2007), 40.

[39] Joseph B. Schechtman's biography of Jabotinsky, *Fighter and Prophet: The Vladimir Jabotinsky Story, the Last Years* (New York: Barnes, 1961), 325–6. Discussions of the vigorous Zionist debate on partition include Aaron S. Kleiman, "The Resolution of Conflicts through Territorial Partition: The Palestine Experience," *Comparative Studies in Society and History* 22, no. 2 (1980): 281–300; Itzhak Galnoor, "The Zionist Debate on Partition (1919–1947)," *Israel Studies* 14, no. 2 (2009): 74–87.

[40] Frank, *Expelling the Germans*, 63–4.

[41] Eduard Beneš, "The New Order in Europe," *Nineteenth Century*, no. 130 (September 1941): 154.

Beneš's views. A future European federation of democratic states enjoying self-determination could no longer allow Germany to use its minorities in other countries as a fifth column to tyrannize their democratic majorities. What is more, Nazi crimes deserved punishment, and the German people as a whole were responsible for them as any people were responsible for its state's actions. Indeed, German minorities had become what he called an "international menace," and they should be transferred, though he disavowed "any method which involves brutality or violence." Presumably, this scruple was consistent with his reference to Hitler's precedent: "Hitler himself has transferred German minorities from the Baltic and from Bessarabia. Germany, therefore, cannot *a priori* regard it as an injury to her if other states adopt the same methods with regard to German minorities."[42] All these measures also entailed the modernization of the country, he added.

Dalton proposed Beneš's ideas as Labour Party policy, also invoking Hitler. "The German 'national minorities' were one of the plagues of Europe in the inter-war period," he wrote in a draft party report in 1943. "This time, the frontiers having been drawn, having regard to geographical and economic convenience, all minorities should be encouraged to join the national States to which they belong. In particular, all Germans left outside the post-war frontiers of Germany should be encouraged to 'go home to the Reich'": here he consciously invoked Hitler's terminology, turning the Nazi logic against the Germans.[43] Again, Lausanne was referred to as a successful precedent. Rather than adjust borders to people, one should adjust populations to borders. Consistently, the Labour Party and Dalton also supported transfer in Palestine, although that did not become British government policy after the war.[44]

How could these arguments be justified in terms of human rights? The question is relevant because Beneš was a member of the Institut du Droit International that in 1929 issued a declaration on the "international rights of man," and in 1942 he himself wrote an article called "The Rights of Man and International Law" that made a case for an international regime to promote democracy as the postwar norm.[45] Democratic rights were

---

[42] Beneš, "Organization of Postwar Europe," 227–8.

[43] Frank, *Expelling the Germans*, 66.

[44] On British policy, see Wm. Roger Louis, *Ends of British Imperialism: The Scramble for Empire, Suez and Decolonization* (London: I.B. Tauris, 2007).

[45] It is translated with a commentary by George A. Finch as "Declaration of the International Rights of Man," *American Journal International Law* 35, no. 4 (1944): 662–5; Edward Beneš, "The Rights of Man and International Law," *Czechoslovak Yearbook of International Law* (1942): 1–6. Background to the 1929 declaration can be found in Jan Herman Burgers, "The Road to San Francisco: The Revival of the Human Rights Idea in the Twentieth Century," *Human Rights Quarterly* 14 (1992): 447–77.

human rights for Beneš: "The protection of minorities in the future should consist primarily in the defense of human democratic rights and not of national rights." The resulting stability, he was arguing, was the precondition to federal blocs of democratic countries with progressive social policy dedicated to development. While "Human Rights must be constitutionally established throughout the world," they should not become an excuse to intervene capriciously or opportunistically in the affairs of other countries.[46]

There was no perceived contradiction between human rights and population expulsion, as commonly supposed, because at this point human rights were to be guaranteed primarily by the state and only as a last resort by an international organization like the UN. The first priority was to establish the modern, democratic, and homogeneous nation-state dedicated to human rights. The expelled minorities' temporary suffering was for the greater good and, besides, they were collectively guilty in this case. The United Nations could then host a human rights regime that applied to all countries, rather than selectively like the interwar minorities treaties; it could condemn the persecution of individuals as necessary, but minorities as such would enjoy no collective rights. Beneš assured the international public that the "protection of the democratic and human rights of every citizen are guaranteed in Czechoslovakia forever," but retained a loophole for his expulsion program. Only those citizens could stay who had "remained faithful to the Republic, kept its laws and helped defend its independence" during the Nazi occupation, meaning that only those few Germans who joined the anti-Nazi resistance were safe. What is more, those who threatened what he called "Czechoslovak national tradition of humanitarian democracy" with the prospect of "a most serious civil war," namely the Germans and Hungarian minorities, could not be allowed to remain.[47] Individual human rights were selectively applied for the greater good of a new human rights order.

This was not isolated reasoning. Beneš's colleague, the Czechoslovak foreign minister in exile, Jan Masaryk, also saw no place for the German minority in the state when Nazi tyranny ended. The majority of ethnic Germans had welcomed the annexation of the "Sudetenland" and took on German citizenship. There would be a reckoning with them, he implied in 1943, when comparing the "liberation" of the country from

---

[46] Beneš, "Organization of Postwar Europe," 237; Beneš, "Czechoslovakia's Struggle for Freedom," *Dalhousie Review* 21 (October 1941): 259–72, esp. 269.
[47] Eduard Beneš, "Czechoslovakia Plans for Peace," *Foreign Affairs* 23, nos. 1–4 (1944/5): 33, 35–6; cf. Bruce R. Berglund, "'All Germans Are the Same': Czech and Sudeten German Exiles in Britain and the Transfer Plans," *National Identities* 2, no. 3 (2000): 225–44.

Austro-Hungarian rule in 1918 with the coming liberation: whereas there was no "retribution" against the German oppressors, who had come as "settlers" hundreds of years earlier and taken over, after World War I, there would be after the second one. The "minority problem shall be settled radically and with finality," he declared to his Jewish audience in London, for interests of economic, political, and religious "security."[48]

It was also no accident that other celebrated members of the Institut du Droit International advanced such arguments: Nicolas Politis, the Greek-French jurist and politician, and René Cassin, the French lawyer instrumental in the formulation of the UN's Universal Declaration of Human Rights. Politis also incarnated the easy reconciliation of liberalism, internationalism, and population transfers. A highly regarded proponent of "international morality," the "juridical conscience," collective security and arbitration, Politis was at the vanguard of the League's mission to convert diplomacy from force to law. Reform, whether at home or abroad, required stability, and because minorities led to instability, he shared the policy of liberal Greek governments to homogenize the non-Greek populations gained with northern territory won in the Balkan Wars of 1912–13. He drafted the treaty with Bulgaria after World War I to voluntarily exchange populations and the compulsory population exchange with Turkey soon thereafter, which he regarded as a raging success for reducing the minority population, increasing the overall population and cereal production. Writing in 1940 soon after Nazi German had commenced extensive population exchanges with neighboring states to import ethnic Germans, he commended the policy with striking candor to his French audience. Minority agitation had destabilized Europe, he declared, agreeing with Hitler. He was equally candid that compulsory exchange was inconsistent with "humanity" but, like other transfer proponents, stressed on the long-term benefits. Significant for our purposes is his invocation of human rights in this regard. "International human rights," he assured, "will one day be a valid rule for all States, without any exception." But not yet. First national and international "health" had to obtain, by which he meant national homogeneity to guarantee stability. "Surgery" was required to effect continental recovery. "It is a painful operation, but it

---

[48] Jan Masaryk, "Minorities and the Democratic State," Lucien Wolf memorial lecture (Jewish Historical Society of England, 1943), 19–20. On the Jewish question in Czechoslovakia, see Jan Lánícek, *Czechs, Slovaks and the Jews, 1938–48: Beyond Idealisation and Condemnation* (Basingstoke, UK: Palgrave Macmillan, 2012); Livia Rothkirchen, *The Jews of Bohemia and Moravia: Facing the Holocaust* (Lincoln: University of Nebraska Press, 2012).

is true of all operations," he conceded, the gain, however, should not be "arrested by false feelings," a distorted sentimentalism.[49]

Cassin argued in similar terms in relation to Zionism and Palestine. At the same time as he advocated human rights at the UN in 1947, he led the French Alliance Israélite Universelle campaign for the UN's partition of Palestine in 1947, a marked change from its French republican prewar hostility to a Jewish state or nation. Jewish national rights trumped Palestinian ones – Arabs were not mentioned by name in the memo he wrote, "On the Palestine Problem." Again there was no contradiction in his mind between his agendas because the benefits of the new order would justify the means of its establishment, in this case Jewish settlers acting as the vehicle of democracy in the darkness of the orient: "the democratic hope in the Near East can only progress under the influence of the Jewish ambition in Palestine," he wrote. The establishment of Israel, Cassin was suggesting, would at once alleviate the Jewish refugee crisis in Europe and inaugurate a human rights order in a part of the world run by what he called the "thieving and bloody indigenous masters" of Jewish minorities in the Middle East, namely the Arabs whom he saw as oppressors of Jewish minorities on North Africa.[50]

Arab human rights were entirely consistent with their denationalization. As Chaim Weizmann had argued a few years before, although Jews "will control their own immigration" in their future state, all citizens will enjoy "complete civil and political equality of rights . . . without distinction of race or religion, and, in addition, the Arabs will enjoy full autonomy of their own internal affairs."[51] In this mode, human rights did not trump minority rights; here they trumped Arab *majority* rights. In the worldview making human rights a marker of democracy, dangerous and/ or backward peoples like German minorities and Arab majorities had to make way for the progressive and modern nation-state led by civilized titular minorities or majorities. The right to self-determination did not

[49] Nicolas Politis, "Le transfert des populations," *Politique étrangère* 5, no. 2 (1940): 93–4; Robert Kolb, "Politis and Sociological Jurisprudence of Inter-War International Law," *European Journal of International Law* 23 no. 1 (2012): 239; Marilena Papadaki, "The 'Government Intellectuals': Nicolas Politis – An Intellectual Portrait," ibid., 221–31; Umut Özsu, "Politis and the Limits of Legal Form," ibid., 243–53.

[50] René Cassin, "Mémorandum de l'AIU sur le problème palestinien," June 9, 1947, p. 3, Alliance Israélite Universelle Archive, Paris, AM Présidence 030. The second quotation is taken from Jay Winter, "René Cassin and the Alliance Israélite Universelle," *Modern Judaism* 32, no. 1 (2012): 16.

[51] Chaim Weizmann, "Palestine's Role in the Solution of the Jewish Problem," *Foreign Affairs* 20, nos. 1–4 (1941/2): 337. He immediately added that "if any Arabs do not wish to remain in a Jewish state, every facility will be given to them to transfer to one of the many and vast Arab countries."

belong to defeated Axis powers and their supporters. The Palestinians, Weizmann, said, were after all supporters of the Axis powers. And as the Peel Commission had determined, they were most definitely not modern. These assumptions also underlay the Programme for Peace produced by the Committee on Peace Aims of the New Zealand League of Nations Union in 1942. Chaired by Professor Julius Stone of the University of Sydney, it advocated "large-scale settlement" of the persecuted "Jewish people in central and eastern Europe" to Palestine and elsewhere "in conformity with the dictates of humanity," although Stone opposed Beneš's transfer notions because it implied a mono-national state. His main target was Britain's 1939 White Paper that restricted Jewish migration to Palestine.[52]

The discursive link between Europe, Palestine, and India was also provided by the Lithuanian Jewish jurist Jacob Robinson. Born in 1891 in (what is now) Lithuania, he worked for Zionist causes before the war, fleeing to New York in 1940, where he established the Institute of Jewish Affairs, sponsored by the American and the World Jewish Congresses.[53] That he was a major Jewish thinker of global order and the place of Jews in it was evident in his various positions. Until 1948, a special consultant for Jewish affairs to the US chief of counsel at the Nuremberg trials, and a consultant to the UN Secretariat in the establishment of the Human Rights Commission, the Jewish Agency appointed him a legal advisor when the Palestine question came before the UN, and in 1948 he entered the service of the new State of Israel.

Like many European Jewish lawyers of his generation, he was a proponent of the minority protection treaty regime that sought to safeguard Jewish and other minorities after World War I. I only have space here to outline his views very briefly. By 1943, he had largely abandoned his faith in the minority protection regime and saw the future of the surviving

---

[52] Julius Stone, *The Atlantic Charter: New Worlds for Old* (Sydney: Angus & Robertson, 1943), 134, 78–9. Like many of his generation, Stone was a proponent of the minorities treaties before becoming a partisan of Israel: Stone, *International Guarantees of Minority Rights: Procedure of the Council of the League of Nations in Theory and Practice* (London: Oxford University Press, 1932); Stone, "Behind the Cease-Fire Lines: Israel's Administration in Gaza and the West Bank," in Shlomo Shoham, ed., *Of Law and Men: Essays in Honor of Haim M. Cohn* (New York: Sabra Books, 1971), 79–110; Stone, *Israel and Palestine: Assault on the Law of Nations* (Baltimore: Johns Hopkins University Press, 1981).

[53] Omry K. Feuerstein, "Geschichterfahrung und Völkerrecht: Jacob Robinson und die Gründung des Institute of Jewish Affairs," *Leipziger Beiträge* 2 (2004): 307–30; Mark A. Lewis, "The World Jewish Congress and the Institute for International Affairs at Nuremberg: Ideas, Strategies, and Political Goals, 1942–1946," *Yad Vashem Studies* 36, no. 1 (2008): 181–210.

European Jews in the mass colonization of Palestine.[54] Debates within the World Jewish Congress show that most Jewish leaders disagreed with his Palestine exclusivism and advocated continuing protection for Jewish rights in the diaspora. There was some alarm at Beneš's transfer and anti-minority position at a time when German authorities were deporting Jewish minorities to "the east," so assurances were sought from him that he did not mean to expel Jews from Czechoslovakia.[55] Robinson therefore modified Beneš's approach in an ingenious argument. In an article called "Minorities in a New World" in 1943, he criticized the tendency to condemn all minorities as "vicious fifth columns who contributed to the downfall and ruin of their states." Adopting the tone of moderation, he argued that distinctions needed to be made between irredentist minorities and those that reconciled themselves to their minority status, as he did not think the League of Nations minorities rights system had abjectly failed. Any weaknesses were attributable to *"Those groups which permitted themselves to be used as tools for the disruptive plans of their powerful co-nationals."*[56] German minorities were the worst of irredentist minorities, while Jewish minorities were a model minority that did not cause problems for their host state.

The urgent need, he continued, was to consider what he called "specific danger zones where this problem is of special importance, regions like Central-Eastern Europe, India, and others." The post–World War I period offered two solutions to the problem, namely transfer and minority protection. And now some new special provisions included "guarantees of human rights."[57] He doubted the efficacy of any human and minority rights; after all, the minority protection treaties had not saved the Jews from genocide, and nor likely would human rights declarations. "Realistically," he concluded, "we must envisage . . . the transfer of populations" in these danger zones.

Regarding the coercion question, he admitted that "Of course, the humanitarian aspect cannot be neglected, and hardship must certainly be avoided, or at least reduced. Moreover, it is certainly undemocratic to force a person to emigrate against his will." Like commentators since Lausanne twenty years earlier, he immediately qualified this humanitarian

---

[54] Jacob Robinson, "Uprooted Jews in the Immediate Postwar World," *International Conciliation* 21 (1942–3): 291–310.

[55] Gil Rubin, "The End of Minority Rights: Jacob Robinson and the Minority Question in World War II," *Jahrbuch des Simon-Dubnow-Instituts* 11 (2012): 55–72.

[56] Jacob Robinson, et al., *Were the Minorities Treaties a Failure?* (New York: Institute of Jewish Affairs, 1943), 260. Emphasis in original.

[57] Jacob Robinson, "Minorities in a Free World," *Free World* 5, no. 5 (May 1943): 450–4.

sensibility and theodicy of the future pay-off with a sentence beginning with "but":

> But after all, the peace of Europe and the world is of greater importance than adherence to certain procedures for the protection of minorities . . . If it is well established that both the state and the minority will otherwise remain dissatisfied, why not – with all necessary safeguards against hardships and with guarantees for the property of transferred – remove the reasons for the perpetuation of hatred and dissension?[58]

By 1947, Robinson had embraced the coming human rights regime because it meant that what he called "militant Fascist minorities" could not appeal as collectives to an international body against the democratic majority, an argument made by Beneš before him.[59] Indeed, he cited Beneš as the "prophet" of population homogeneity and progress, noting that population transfer enabled the "liberated peoples to destroy the last vestiges of Nazism and Fascism and to create democratic institutions of their own choice. This is the principle of the Atlantic Charter," he wrote, "the right of all peoples to choose the form of government under which they live – the restoration of sovereign right and self-government to those people who had been forcibly deprived of them by the aggressor nations." Henceforth, they could "form interim governmental authorities broadly representative of all democratic elements in the population." Human rights, then, depended on the ability to create "conditions of stability and well-being which are necessary for peaceful and friendly relations among nations." And such conditions entailed mobilizing what he called, in a notably Soviet-sounding statement, "all democratic elements in the population" against the irredentist, fascist ones.[60] That is why Churchill had said the Atlantic Charter norms did not apply to the Axis powers, and why the Allies were able to ignore the minorities protection treaties when agreeing to expel the Germans at their Potsdam meeting in August 1945.[61] For all his modifications, Robinson followed Beneš in making human rights a license to expel. Writing that year, Hans Morgenthau declared the stabilizing formula to be "partition and repatriation."[62]

---

[58] Robinson, "Minorities in a Free World," 453.

[59] Cf. Joseph B. Schechtman, "Decline of International Minority Protection," *Western Political Quarterly* 4, no. 1 (1951): 2.

[60] Jacob Robinson, "From Protection of Minorities to Promotion of Human Rights," *Jewish Yearbook of International Law* 1 (1949): 137–41. This article was likely written in 1947.

[61] E/CN.4/367, Commission on Human Rights, sixth session, April 7, 1950, "Study of the Legal Validity of the Undertaking Concerning Minorities Treaties," 60.

[62] Hans Morgenthau, *Germany Our Problem* (New York: Harper, 1945), 160.

Robinson apparently did not write much about Palestine until he was appointed by the Jewish Agency to represent its case in the UN in 1947. The figure who connected the dots between partition, transfer, and human rights in the Middle East was Joseph Schechtman, long cited as the authority on population exchanges. Recent scholarship has reminded us that he was a Russian-born revisionist Zionist, indeed a biographer of Jabotinsky, with a personal investment in the subject.[63] Early in the 1940s, he was employed by Robinson at the Institute for Jewish Affairs to write about the German expulsions and colonization in Europe.[64] Subsequently, in 1949, he was engaged by the State of Israel to justify the expulsion of Palestinian Arabs and the refusal to allow their return.[65]

Impressively industrious, he published his book *Population Transfers in Asia* in 1949, covering South Asia and the Middle East. Of the former, he wrote that "Both Pakistan and Indian leaders . . . stubbornly refused to accept the exchange of population as a bitter but inevitable necessity and to conduct it in a constructive way" and, in the last section of the book, he made a case for an exchange of Jewish and Arab populations in the Middle East: Jews in Arab countries going to Israel and Arabs in Palestine replacing them in other parts of the Middle East. Partition by itself was insufficient there, he argued. For "The minority problem, which is a question of life and death for the success of any constructive scheme for Palestine," wrote Schechtman, "cannot be solved without resorting to what the last President Eduard Beneš of Czechoslovakia called 'the grim necessity of transfer.'"[66] Using the same arguments as Robinson, Schechtman was effectively saying that the Arabs were an irredentist minority – or rather majority – for their inexplicably stubborn refusal to be reduced to minority status in a majority Jewish Palestine.[67]

---

[63] Nur Masalha, "From Propaganda to Scholarship: Dr. Joseph Schechtman and the Origins of the Israeli Polemics on the Palestinian Refugees," *Holy Land Studies* 2 (2002): 188–97; Mazower, *No Enchanted Palace*, 117–23; Antonio Ferrara, "Eugene Kulischer, Joseph Schechtman and the Historiography of European Forced Migrations," *Journal of Contemporary History* 46, no. 4 (2011): 715–40.

[64] Ferrara, "Eugene Kulischer, Joseph Schechtman."

[65] Rafael Medoff, *Militant Zionism in America: The Rise and Impact of the Jabotinsky Movement in the United States, 1926-1948* (Tuscaloosa: University of Alabama Press, 2002), 214–15.

[66] Joseph B. Schechtman, *Population Transfers in Asia* (New York: Hallsby Press, 1949), 86. There is no footnote for this quotation, but we know he was quoting Beneš, "Speech at the Foreign Press Association, London, 28 April 1942," in Holborn, *War and Peace Aims of the United Nations*, 427–8; cf. Masalha, "From Propaganda to Scholarship"; Ferrara, "Eugene Kulischer, Joseph Schechtman."

[67] Morris makes the point that in the 1930s Zionist leaders had adjudged a future Palestinian minority to be irredentist: Morris, "Explaining Transfer," 353.

Norman Bentwich, now at the Hebrew University, agreed. Also writing in 1949 in the wake of the Palestine refugee crisis, he regarded the massive population transfers in India's partition as a success and, referring to the Palestinian refugees, wrote that "Some large transfer of population was inevitable, and it offered the most humane as well as the most realistic solution," as well as ending what he termed "stagnation in that part of the world" by enabling the foundation of Israel in terms reminiscent of Cassin's memo two years before. They should be resettled, he concluded, like the refugees of Indian partition, and thereby halt the "enmities in what has been for thirty years one of the danger spots of the world." In a few sentences, he repeated the well-worn arguments for transfer since Lausanne: the prevention of ethnic warfare and stimulation of material progress. And, like Cassin and Weizmann, he asserted that the self-determination of Jews in their ancestral homeland would benefit all. The Arabs could not return, he added, now that their houses had been occupied by Jewish refugees from Europe; again resorting to analogy, he observed that their position resembled those of the Orthodox Greeks driven from Turkey into Macedonia in 1922.[68]

The 1948 conflict between Zionist and Arab forces provided the opportunity for forced transfer that was missing after the Peel Commission a decade earlier. Presciently, a year before, in 1947, in an unpublished memo, Robinson had warned Zionists that India's planned partition offered no model for Palestine because South Asia was what he called "static" whereas Palestine was still a "dynamic" situation.[69] The message of his guarded prose is not difficult to decipher. "Dynamic" was the term that Zionists like Mendelsohn used to depict Palestine's malleable demography: "not only to consider mechanically the present relative strength in the number of the two populations but the differences in their economic quality and in their potentialities," by which he meant "not only the actual but probable number of immigrants, the country's absorptive capacity and the scarcity of settlers in the neighbouring countries."[70] The problem with the Indian case – Robinson was writing before the population expulsions in the second half of 1947 – was that it left large minorities in India and Pakistan; population exchanges were not seriously envisaged by the Muslim League and Congress leaders, and nor were provisions made for their protection: that is why it was a static situation. In view of his earlier advocacy of transfer in "danger zones,"

[68] Norman Bentwich, "The Arab Refugees," *Contemporary Review*, no. 176 (1949): 81–2.
[69] Jacob Robinson, "Partition of India: Implications for Palestine," Confidential Memo #24, 1947, Central Zionist Archive, S25/9029.
[70] Mendelsohn, *Balance of Resettlements*, 30.

it is fair to suppose that he was implying that transfer was still on the cards in Palestine, and he was right.

Conclusion

What then of the relationship between these partitions, transfer, minorities, and the question of refugees? A common misunderstanding is that the British imposed partition on India and Palestine with a perfidious imperial policy of "divide and quit." In fact, they referred the Palestine Mandate to the UN in part because they were unwilling to impose partition on the Arabs, and because the Zionists had commenced a violent uprising against its plan to hand over the state to the majority Arab population as set out in the White Paper of 1939. The British only reluctantly resorted to partition in India when they could not convince the contending parties to sign off on the Cabinet Mission's federal solution in 1946. Leo Amery, the Secretary of State for India, asked Reginald Coupland, the English architect of the abandoned 1937 Palestine partition proposal, in late 1940 to write a study of the problem. This time he opposed partition because he did not think population exchanges were viable in the Indian case; the numbers were far too large for the "clean cut" envisaged by such a policy.[71] In the end, the British only supported the partition of Germany's 1937 borders and population transfers, and even then they were taken aback by the extent and vehemence of the expulsions. Given the wild cleansings and Soviet annexation of eastern Poland, the British and Americans were presented with a fait accompli, as were the Greeks and League of Nations in 1922 and 1923 when the Turks expelled its Orthodox population. It was far from the "orderly and humane" procedure that the Potsdam Agreement had licensed.

In effect, the UN Palestine partition plan and the partition of India were closer to the League of Nations model of statehood: new states with large minorities and no population exchanges, and with domestic minority protection guarantees. While the British favored national homogeneity in eastern and central Europe, they entreated heterogeneous federations in South Asia and the Middle East that would allow

[71] Reginald Coupland, *India: A Re-Statement* (London: Oxford University Press, 1945), 263; T. G. Fraser, "Sir Reginald Coupland, the Round Table and the Problem of Divided Societies," in *The Round Table, the Empire/Commonwealth, and British Foreign Policy*, ed. Andrew Bosco and Alex May (London: Lothian Foundation Press, 1997), 413–14. Dalit leader B. R. Ambedkar admired the Lausanne solution and thought it a model for India. See my discussion in A. Dirk Moses, "Partitions, Hostages, Transfer: Retributive Violence and National Security," in Dubnov and Robson, *Partitions*.

them to retain the residual imperial presence they deemed essential to their global security strategy. This time, though, in India and Palestine, nationalists on each side prevailed on the ground, or rather the civil war broke out that the British had feared all along, and in which they did not wish to become embroiled. The 1923-style refugee exchange fait accompli occurred in India as well, sanctioned after the fact by the two new states in 1950. That it has not been so sanctioned in Palestine – that is, that the Palestinian refugee issue remains on the international table – vexes Zionists today who, like Schechtman and Bentwich in 1949, assert that a Lausanne-style retrospective blessing of transfer should occur.[72]

Why it has not occurred is part of the later story of human rights as well as of self-determination and its roots in the assumption of the new world order that all peoples should be housed in their national homeland. The logic of homeland belonging and self-determination claimed by Zionists can be easily utilized by Palestinians as well, after all. As time passed, Palestinians and their supporters could dislodge human rights from its nesting in the nation-state and claim it as an abstract norm to protest their treatment – or to make self-determination a human right. Thus in 1961, in his debate with the Israeli foreign minister, the historian Arnold Toynbee said "I submit that the human rights of the native inhabitants of a country have an absolute priority over all other claims upon that country, and that these overriding rights are not forfeited if the native inhabitants are dispossessed of their homes and property." By paying the price for Germany's genocide of the Jews – that is, expulsion from their country – he concluded, "The Palestinian Arabs have, in fact, been treated as if they did not have human rights."[73]

The "human rights revolution" of the 1940s and early 1950s was ultimately disastrous for Palestinians. For while Arab governments

---

[72] Adelman and Barkan, *No Return, No Refuge.* They ignore the minimum requirements for consensus identified by Dimitri Pentzopoulos, *The Balkan Exchange of Minorities and its Impact upon Greece* (The Hague: Mouton, 1962), 248–52. First, the affected countries should both accept the exchange; second, the exchange must be carried out under international supervision; third, economic compensation must be provided for the refugees; and fourth, there must be an effective management to accommodate, feed, and integrate the refugees into the new society. Thanks to Volker Prott for this reference.

[73] Arnold Toynbee, "Jewish Rights in Palestine," *Jewish Quarterly Review,* n.s., 52, no. 1 (1961): 1–11. Although human rights is the subject of his chapter that ends with European Jewish refugees possibly replacing Palestinian refugees, as Bentwich urged, G. Daniel Cohen does not thematize the question. The "human rights revolution" was nevertheless "at work" with the displaced persons in Europe, he argues: Cohen, "The 'Human Rights Revolution' at Work: Displaced Persons in Occupied Europe," in Hoffmann, *Human Rights in the Twentieth Century,* 59–60.

successfully insisted that the right to "return to his country" be included in Article 13 during of the UN Declaration of Human Rights,[74] and the Fourth Geneva Convention prohibited "individual or mass forcible transfer . . . regardless of their motive,"[75] it came a year too late for Palestinians. Moreover, the Refugee Convention of 1951 gestured primarily to the plight of European refugees whose imperative was the granting of asylum elsewhere rather than right of return, although Arab governments were able to water down Cassin's attempt to enshrine the right to asylum with a lesser right to "seek and enjoy" it.[76] German advocates of those expelled from Central and Eastern Europe argued in similar terms, invoking a right of return and of homeland, again without legal effect.[77] Likewise, the UN General Assembly's resolution 194 of December 11, 1948 for the return of Palestinian refugees has no standing in international law and has proven impotent even though it was hardly an unqualified approval of mass repatriation: it made any return contingent upon the refugees' acceptance of the new State of Israel (i.e., no longer constitute an irredentist entity).[78]

Arab commentators, like the Secretary of the Arab League, Edward Atiyah, had conceded that Jewish displaced persons (DPs) possessed "a human and moral right against the whole civilised world," but not a right to asylum in Palestine where they would come as settlers to overwhelm or displace the Indigenous Arabs – as Weizman, Bentwich, Robinson, and Cassin always intended; the DPs should be granted asylum "on an international basis, by all the countries of the United Nations opening their doors to them in proportion to their resources and absorptive capacities."[79] Atiyah's main point, however, was to contest the UN's decision to partition Palestine, a decision in which the plight of the DPs had played a large role. The right of indigenous people to resist the settler would not prevail for the reasons Coupland had set out in his shelved report of 1937. Zionist advocates had supplied it to the UN delegates, but it is difficult to say whether Coupland's arguments swayed them; certainly Coupland thought that the UN

---

[74] Mary Ann Glendon, *A World Made New: Eleanor Roosevelt and the Universal Declaration of Human Rights* (New York: Random House, 2001), 153.
[75] www.icrc.org/ihl.nsf/WebART/380-600056
[76] G. Daniel Cohen, *In War's Wake: Europe's Displaced Persons in the Postwar Order* (Oxford: Oxford University Press, 2012), 21.
[77] Lora Wildenthal, "Rudolf Laun and the Human Rights of Germans in Occupied and Early West Germany," in Hoffmann, *Human Rights in the Twentieth Century*, 125–44.
[78] UNGA Resolution 194 (III), December 11, 1948.
[79] Edward Atiyah, "Palestine," *Contemporary Review*, no. 174 (1948): 7.

partition recommendation endorsed his ideas.[80] We do know that in June 1948 Moshe Sharett, Israel's future foreign minister and prime minister, told an interim government meeting that the flight of Palestinian Arabs resembled the expulsion of Germans from Czechoslovakia as well as the earlier, omnipresent Lausanne precedent. He concluded with a statement that summarized the basis of the postwar order: "they are not coming back . . . they need to get used to the idea that this [a possible return] is a lost cause and this is a change that cannot be undone."[81]

---

[80] Fraser, "Sir Reginald Coupland," 417. Abba Eban reports thus on his meeting with Coupland whom he visited in Oxford; Eban, *An Autobiography* (London: Weidenfeld & Nicolson, 1978), 85.

[81] Eban cited in Alon Confino, "Miracles and Snow in Palestine and Israel: Tantura, a History of 1948," *Israel Studies* 17, no. 2 (2012): 42–3; cf. Abba Eban, *How to Solve the Arab Refugee Problem* (New York: Israel Office of Information, 1957).

7 Codifying Minority Rights
Postcolonial Constitutionalism in Burma, Ceylon, and India

Cindy Ewing

Introduction

The decolonization of Asia after 1945 catalyzed a radical transformation of the region's legal orders. In Burma, Ceylon, and India, a key feature of the massive, uneven transfer of power that marked the end of British rule was the drafting of constitutions – the written expression and embodiment of statehood. As these new nations set out to frame their constitutions, they grappled with the meaning of their postcolonial sovereignty and the scope of rights entitled to their citizens, especially the rights of minorities. At the same time, so too was the United Nations (UN) in the process of creating a new world order through an array of instruments such as the Universal Declaration of Human Rights (UDHR). During the late 1940s, the drafting of UN human rights instruments and postcolonial constitutions, though distinct in their aims, contributed to a burgeoning global discourse of rights on a number of intersecting planes, national and international.

Questions about how to define which rights and whose rights anchored the debates on the meaning and purpose of these documents. The shape of these rights emerged concurrently in two spaces: the indigenous assemblies drafting national constitutions and the international bodies establishing universal standards. They shared important characteristics, namely a deliberative process and the production of a written text. Yet the new rights declarations also signaled departures from earlier systems of law. For the postcolonial nations in Asia, a codified constitution marked a shift away from Britain's colonial rule and uncodified constitutional doctrines. For the UN Human Rights Commission, the declaration concretized the aspiration – however illusory – for the new world body to improve upon its predecessor, the League of Nations and set new international standards.[1] Whereas the UDHR did not establish rights for

---

[1] Mark Mazower, *No Enchanted Palace: The End of Empire and the Ideological Origins of the United Nations* (Princeton, NJ: Princeton University Press, 2009).

minorities and subnational groups, the pressing questions of how to provide individual and collective rights were dealt with in excruciating detail as part of the constitutional debates of the decolonizing states in South Asia and Southeast Asia. Constitution-making, I argue, offered a site for the materialization of a unifying rights discourse in Asia that first paralleled, and then intersected with human rights projects at the UN.

This chapter proceeds by integrating the histories of national constitution-making in Burma, Ceylon, and India, in particular the protection of individual and group rights in their national legal frameworks at the moment of decolonization in the aftermath of World War II. Building on recent histories of international law, this chapter adopts a transnational rather than comparative approach to the study of how rights-making occurred across boundaries as part of an emergent postcolonial constitutionalism.[2] Political elites spread these new rights ideas across realms, though many of them are not immediately visible in contemporary histories of human rights. Their travels crisscrossed deliberative bodies from the local to the international, bringing decolonization to the UN and paving the way for national self-determination to be enshrined in international human rights law.

The independence constitutions of India and Burma provided a similar set of inalienable entitlements to their citizens, codified as "fundamental rights," as a result of their common constitutional adviser, the Indian civil servant and lawyer, B. N. Rau. Though most histories of the Indian constitution understandably focus on its drafting committee chairman B. R. Ambedkar, it was B. N. Rau who gave shape to the fundamental rights enshrined by the Indian and Burmese postcolonial constitutions. Rau was a champion of what Harshan Kumarasingham has called "Eastminster" or the "common constitutional heritage" that the Asian postcolonial nations shared through their adoption of the Westminster parliamentary model.[3] As Charles Parkinson has shown, how the British negotiated constitutions with its dependencies evolved gradually throughout the 1950s, but the Colonial Office firmly opposed such

---

[2] For examples of a global turn in the history of international law, see Antony Anghie, *Imperialism, Sovereignty and the Making of International Law* (Cambridge, UK: Cambridge University Press, 2005); Martti Koskenniemi, *The Gentle Civilizer of Nations: the Rise and Fall of International Law, 1870–1960* (Cambridge, UK: Cambridge University Press, 2010); José-Manuel Barreto, "Imperialism and Decolonization as Scenarios of Human Rights History," in *Human Rights from a Third World Perspective: Critique, History and International Law*, ed. José-Manuel Barreto (Newcastle upon Tyne: Cambridge Scholars Publishing, 2013), 140–71.

[3] Harshan Kumarasingham, "Eastminster – Decolonisation and State-Building in British Asia," in *Constitution-Making in Asia: Decolonisation and State-Building in the Aftermath of the British Empire*, ed. Harshan Kumarasingham (Abingdon, UK: Routledge, 2016), 27.

constitutional bills of rights before 1962.[4] Rau importantly departed from the conventions of the British common law by pursuing explicit provisions enumerating individual rights. Only Ceylon, working the most closely with Whitehall on its constitutional reform of the Asian postcolonies, decided against a bill of rights, though there was popular agitation for one. Here, the recovery of paths not taken alters the picture of postcolonial constitutional rights by more sharply defining the colonial continuities that suppressed popular demand for rights. This opens a perspective departing slightly from the existing literature on Asian constitutionalism that tends to highlight the perspective of British lawyers and colonial officials in the transfer of power. From the viewpoint of postcolonial elites, securing independence entailed building transnational networks, advocating for rights internationally, and using existing legal systems to reach for other constitutional models; through formal drafting and informal advocacy, they drew up new rights previously unavailable to them under colonial rule. And as emissaries of their states, postcolonial elites extended those ideas from their local deliberations in Delhi, Colombo, and Rangoon outwards to global settings.

Recognizing the importance of decolonization to the history of the Cold War, this chapter foregrounds the intersection of local and international politics with foundational texts.[5] While scholars have delved into the connections between human rights and decolonization, independence constitutions remain absent in the literature even though such documents signified postcolonial sovereignties and demarcated the aspirations and intentions of the new nations.[6] Similarly, studies on the so-called Third World tend to ignore the role of rights in the political

---

[4] Charles O. H. Parkinson, *Bills of Rights and Decolonization: The Emergence of Domestic Human Rights Instruments in Britain's Overseas Territories* (Oxford: Oxford University Press, 2007).

[5] See Odd Arne Westad, *The Global Cold War: Third World Interventions and the Making of Our Times* (Cambridge, UK: Cambridge University Press, 2005); Ryan M. Irwin, *Gordian Knot: Apartheid and the Unmaking of the Liberal World Order* (Oxford: Oxford University Press, 2012); Robert J. McMahon, ed. *The Cold War in the Third World* (New York: Oxford University Press, 2013); Sandra Bott et al. eds., *Neutrality and Neutralism in the Global Cold War: Between or within the Blocs?* (Abingdon, UK: Routledge, 2015).

[6] See Roland Burke, *Decolonization and the Evolution of International Human Rights* (Pennsylvania: University of Pennsylvania Press, 2013); Fabian Klose, *Human Rights in the Shadow of Colonial Violence: The Wars of Independence in Kenya and Algeria* (Philadelphia: University of Pennsylvania Press, 2013); Jan Eckel and Samuel Moyn, eds., *Breakthrough: Human Rights in the 1970s* (Philadelphia: University of Pennsylvania Press, 2015); Steven L. B. Jensen, *The Making of International Human Rights: The 1960s, Decolonization, and the Reconstruction of Global Values* (Cambridge, UK: Cambridge University Press, 2017).

discourse of postcolonial elites, even though rights were central to post-colonial state-building and postwar international institutions.

By turning away from procedural histories of the UDHR, this chapter considers alternative contexts in which individual and collective rights were debated, contested, and configured. The UDHR did not inspire the codification of rights in Asia, a process that had other roots and was already in motion. Nonetheless, postcolonial nations gained their independence in a highly conscious moment of self-creation when international institutions and international law were themselves undergoing change. This simultaneity allowed postcolonial elites to draw on the rights-making experiences of other nations while shaping the international development of human rights. In later years, postcolonial nations would lead the way in deploying human rights for political and anticolonial ends, leveraging those processes to reinforce their own post-colonial sovereignty. While some historians focus on whether anticolonialism was – or was not – a human rights movement, this chapter recasts the causal question with an eye toward those entangled state-building processes at the end of empire to deepen our understanding of the diverse strands of transnational rights discourses that intersected around the time of the adoption of the UDHR in 1948.[7] Through constitution-makers who also served diplomatic functions for new states, a postcolonial rights imaginary spread to the UN just as powerful states were beginning to turn away from human rights.

Limits to Rights-Making at the End of Empire

In an atmosphere mixed with optimism and apprehension, the creation of the UDHR began in 1946 when the UN Economic and Social Council established the Commission on Human Rights and a small committee to organize its activities. At its helm was Eleanor Roosevelt, the former US First Lady who brought celebrity to the UN through her daily newspaper column. Away from the commotion of the main assembly, the committee reached immediate consensus that the future Human Rights Commission should prepare an international bill of human rights "as soon as possible."[8] Roosevelt wrote, "many of us thought that the lack of

---

[7] A. W. Brian Simpson, *Human Rights and the End of Empire: Britain and the Genesis of the European Convention* (Oxford: Oxford University Press, 2004), 301; Samuel Moyn, *The Last Utopia: Human Rights in History* (Cambridge, MA: Belknap Press of Harvard University Press, 2010); Leela Gandhi and Deborah L. Nelson, "Editor's Introduction," *Critical Inquiry* 40, no. 4 (2014): 285–97.

[8] John Humphrey, *Human Rights and the United Nations: A Great Adventure* (Dobbs Ferry, NY: Transnational Publishers, 1984), 17.

standards for human rights the world over was one of the greatest causes of friction among the nations."[9] Even so, the committee showed reluctance to contemplate human rights in light of the other major transformation in the international system in the late 1940s: the tidal wave of decolonization in Asia and Africa. Resistance to linking the problem of colonialism with the new rights project came from all corners of the UN. Colonialism and the future of trust territories were not included in the deliberations of the commission's early meetings, with critics accusing the United States of "helping to bolster up crumbling European empires."[10] Denying avenues to decolonization, it would be another year and a half before the status of colonies would arise at the Human Rights Commission.[11]

When the Economic and Social Council session concluded in June 1946, the Council's rapporteur K. C. Neogy made the journey back to India. All summer, public debate in India raged over the Cabinet Mission plan. Frederick Pethick-Lawrence, the Secretary of State for India and Burma, broadcast the announcement that the future Union of India would comprise three tiers of government with autonomy for the provinces. The proposal aimed to break the deadlock between the Indian National Congress and the Muslim League by laying a path toward an inclusive constituent assembly. The plan also rejected Muhammad Ali Jinnah's call for the creation of a separate Pakistan. As part of this quasi-federal constitutional vision, the Cabinet Mission instead recommended that an advisory committee arrange "the list of Fundamental Rights, the clauses for the protection of minorities, and a scheme for the administration of the tribal and excluded areas, and to advise whether these rights should be incorporated in the Provincial, Group, or Union constitution."[12] This brief reference to minorities demonstrated British resignation to continued discord between Hindus and Muslims, as the Cabinet Mission was unable to resolve the communal minority problem or respond to exigent minority demands.[13] The plan also forced into conflict the aspiration to create rights-bearing citizens with the imperative of the state to become an integrated unit. Even though the British Colonial Office stressed "that no attempt should be made to impose a

---

[9] Eleanor Roosevelt, *Courage in a Dangerous World* (New York: Columbia University Press, 1999), 157.

[10] "Colonial Empires Assailed in Rally," *New York Times*, June 7, 1946.

[11] Johannes Morsink, *The Universal Declaration of Human Rights: Origins, Drafting and Intent* (Philadelphia: University of Pennsylvania Press, 2009), 97.

[12] Para. 20, Cabinet Mission Plan, May 16, 1946, IOR/L/PJ/10/56, British Library (BL).

[13] "A Policy for Withdrawal from India by the Viceroy Field-Marshal Viscount Wavell," September 5, 1946, India Office Records and Private Papers, L/PO/6/118, BL.

unitary constitution on British India" to reflect the Cabinet Mission plan's quasi-federal vision, a unitary state was the expected outcome of any Congress-led constitutional process.[14]

Gandhi called the plan "the best document the British Government could have produced," which built support for provincial elections to determine the make-up of the constituent assembly.[15] In September 1946, Jawaharlal Nehru took the reins of government and attempted to guide a fractious state through the transition. But Nehru admitted his failure to "put an end to communal friction" or persuade the Muslim League to join the new government. Gyan Prakash notes that while Nehru and the other Congress leaders did not imagine "India as a Hindu state," their "category Indian [w]as indivisible" and fixed an uncompromising conviction that the future Indian state would be "unitary and assimilative."[16] Thus it was no surprise that when the constituent assembly opened in December 1946, the Muslim League boycotted the first session and reiterated its commitment to "a complete sovereign Pakistan."[17] Shortly thereafter, the League called for the constituent assembly to dissolve altogether.[18] This difficult start irreparably divided the Congress and the League, resulting in the bitter partition of the subcontinent and the formation of a separate constituent assembly for Pakistan.

India's approaching independence sent ripples throughout Asia. Acknowledging the cascade, new British Prime Minister Clement Attlee invited the leaders of neighboring Burma to discuss a path to self-government, destined after having acceded to India's independence and approved Ceylon's Order in Council.[19] The decolonization of all three nations, though markedly different in their politics and mobilizations, were enjoined by Whitehall's negotiation timeline as well as by the effort of its leaders to cooperate with one another in the name

---

[14] P. J. Griffiths, "Memorandum for Cabinet Mission," April 1946, IOR/L/PJ/10/56, BL.

[15] Mohandas Gandhi, May 20, 1946, *Harijan*, IOR/L/I/1/338, BL. The Congress and the Muslim League initially accepted the Cabinet Mission Plan but in July 1946 the Congress announced that it would no longer abide by the scheme and the League withdrew its acceptance of the plan.

[16] Gyan Prakash, "Anxious Constitution-Making," in *The Postcolonial Moment in South and Southeast Asia*, eds. Gyan Prakash, Nikhil Menon, and Michael Laffan (London: Bloomsbury Academic, 2018), 145.

[17] Jawaharlal Nehru to Archibald Wavell, October 23, 1946, in *Selected Works of Jawaharlal Nehru: Second Series*, vol. 1 (New Delhi: Jawaharlal Nehru Memorial Fund, 1984), 195 (hereafter *SWJN*).

[18] B. N. Pandey, *The Indian Nationalist Movement 1885–1947: Select Documents* (London: Macmillan, 1979), 207.

[19] Maung Maung, *Burma's Constitution* (The Hague: Martinus Nijhoff, 1961), 179.

of an emerging internationalist ideology of Asian unity. Charles Parkinson has written that "it is not meaningful to speak of an Asian tradition of bills of rights" because the conception of rights in their constitutions was universal and did not depart from existing international charters.[20] At the same time, the drafting of Asian postcolonial constitutions demonstrated a specific understanding of sovereignty shared by nationalist leaders across former British India as they sought to develop legal institutions specific to their needs and in clear distinction to colonial practice.

Burma's Quest for National Unity

Burma, historically a secondary strategic priority for Britain, was the first postcolonial nation in Asia to produce an indigenously written independence constitution. The leader of Burma's nationalist front, the Anti-Fascist People's Freedom League (AFPFL), was the charismatic young general Aung San. Having demanded complete independence from Britain by the end of January 1947, Aung San was an immensely popular figure in Burma and forcefully articulated Burma's case for independence. Whitehall responded to the fast-moving events in Burma by agreeing to negotiations, which empowered Aung San and the AFPFL to pursue "the task of organising and mobilising our entire people in the country for our common national objective . . . national unity."[21] The AFPFL ended a massive general strike and expelled the Communist Party of Burma (CPB) from its ruling coalition.[22] However, the CPB was unwilling to concede to Aung San and continued staging uprisings in the countryside. Undeterred, Aung San sought to build support for national unity by reaching out of tribal groups beyond ministerial Burma, professing that, "We cannot confine the definition of a nationality to the narrow bounds of race, religion, etc. Nations are extending the rights of their respective communities even to others who may not belong to them."[23] The future independent Burma would thus provide "freedoms

---

[20] Charles O. H. Parkinson, "British Constitutional Thought and the Emergence of Bills of Rights in Britain's Overseas Territories in Asia at Decolonisation," in Kumarasingham, *Constitution-Making in Asia*, 46.

[21] Aung San, Inaugural Address at AFPFL Convention, January 1946, in *The Political Legacy of Aung San*, ed. Josef Silverstein (Ithaca, NY: Southeast Asia Program, Cornell University, 1993), 65.

[22] U Tin Tut, "The Burmese Constitution," *Pakistan Horizon* 1, no. 1 (March 1948): 43.

[23] Aung San, Address Delivered to Anglo-Burman Council, December 8, 1946, in *Political Legacy of Aung San*, 92.

of equality" through a new conception of national union to be devised by the constitution.[24]

Aung San also appealed to nationalist leaders beyond Burma and stressed the need for unity not only at home, but all across Asia through "the development of inter-Asian relations."[25] Nehru shared this vision of regional solidarity, and when the Burmese delegation stopped in Delhi on its way to London, Aung San delivered an address on All-India Radio in which he proclaimed, "Asia is one in spite of diversity on the surface and the colour of the people."[26] Under this banner of Asian unity, Indian and Burmese nationalists adopted a common approach to their negotiations with Whitehall. While nationalist leaders recognized the importance of cooperation with the British, it was even more crucial for "the neighbouring countries in Asia [to] become closer" to bring internal stability to their countries.[27] When Aung San arrived in New Delhi, Nehru arranged for winter clothes for Aung San to wear in London over his typical khaki military uniform. During his brief visit, Aung San and Nehru discussed the key questions surrounding Burma's independence, the most urgent of which was the minority question, critically important to India's own experience as well.[28] The commonalities between the future postcolonial states extended beyond the rhetoric of its leaders; they were forged in the decolonization process at multiple scales of planning, not only at the highest levels of politics but also in the development of its foundational texts as well. The links that tethered the Indian and Burmese constitutions reflected this common vision of Asian unity promoted by its leaders and the goodwill they enjoyed in this foundational period.

In London, Aung San pressed for a constitutional path toward Burma's immediate independence.[29] The British Governor in Rangoon, Hubert Rance, had alerted Whitehall that the AFPFL was "determined to have their freedom . . . if they do not get it by constitutional means they are quite prepared to take it by force."[30] As a sign of the AFPFL's readiness to formalize its devolution, the Burmese constitutional

---

[24] *Burma's Fight for Freedom: Independence Commemoration* (Rangoon: Ministry of Information, 1948), 92–3.

[25] Jawaharlal Nehru, "Burma and Indo-China," January 7, 1947, *SWJN* 2, vol. 1, 559.

[26] Aung San, Speech on All-India Radio, New Delhi, January 5, 1947, www.aungsan.com/Asiatic_Unity.htm

[27] Jawaharlal Nehru, "Interview to the Press," September 26, 1946, *SWJN* 2, vol. 1, 493.

[28] Indian and Burmese nationalist leaders already enjoyed diplomatic relations and exchanged representatives to one another's capitals. In October 1946, M. A. Rauf became India's representative in Burma. See footnote 14, *SWJN* 2, vol. 1, 495.

[29] Clement Attlee, *As It Happened* (New York: Viking Press, 1954), 217–20.

[30] Hubert Rance to Lord Pethick-Lawrence, December 17, 1946, IOR: M/4/2621, BL.

adviser Chan Htoon joined the delegation and worked on a draft constitution during Aung San and Clement Attlee's negotiations. In late January 1947, Aung San and Attlee agreed to terms for the transfer of power, including national elections, a pledge of £7.5 million in loans, and support for Burma's membership at the UN. Chan Htoon meanwhile discussed parameters for the future Burmese constitution with the Foreign Office, ensuring that executive power would be passed into the hands of the AFPFL in exchange for a British-appointed High Commissioner in Rangoon. Concerned for the integrity of the union, the discussions also included the pressing question of Burma's ethnic minorities, some of whom had realized Britain's worst fears and begun aligning with the communists.[31] The status of the minorities would depend on Aung San's personal persuasion.

Aung San's vision entailed a federated union for Burma that would be democratic and constitutional, by which the provision of aid to the frontier areas would be accompanied by clearly delineated political and cultural rights. Upon returning from London, Aung San trekked to Panglong in the Shan hills to meet with the tribal leaders. There, he charismatically delivered speeches about the devastation of the war and the importance of working toward national solidarity. The leaders of the Shan and Kachin hills wanted pledges of autonomy and noninterference in their tribal customs.[32] Other minority groups, such as the Karens, developed good relations with the British officers of the Frontier Service and wanted Burma to remain in the British Commonwealth. At the opposite end, Muslim leaders in northern Arakan discussed joining the new Pakistan state. Aung San promised that constitutional deliberations would include their concerns on cultural autonomy, rehabilitation of infrastructure, and economic development. Though the leaders of the Karens boycotted the talks, Aung San secured the commitments of many of these leaders to join the planned constituent assembly.[33] The participation of indigenous groups in the constitutional process was a significant victory for Aung San and the AFPFL. The Panglong Agreement designated forty-five seats of the future assembly to the frontiers. When elections for the constituent assembly took place that spring, a Shan chief was elected president.[34] However, the continued communist

---

[31] Constitutional Files, Post-Independence Records, Acc. No. 63, National Archives of Myanmar (NAM).

[32] Maung Maung, *Burma's Constitution*, 80.

[33] Kyo'Vaṅ, *The 1947 Constitution and the Nationalities*, vol. 1 (Yangon: Universities Research Centre, 1999), 130.

[34] Virginia Thompson, "The New Nation of Burma," *Far Eastern Survey* 17, no. 7 (1948): 82.

insurgency fractured the assembly and, in a dramatic defeat to national unity, the conservative leaders U Saw and Thakin Ba Sein resigned their ministerial positions.

Although the British tried to remain abreast of these fast-moving events in Burma, they were foremost absorbed by India. On February 20, 1947, Attlee announced that Britain would withdraw from India by the end of June in the following year. The interim government promptly began arrangements for a constituent assembly to frame a national constitution. At the start of its proceedings, Nehru introduced the Objectives Resolution to serve as the guiding light of the assembly's work.[35] Articulating need and aspiration, Nehru declared, "The first task of this Assembly is to free India through a new constitution to feed the starving people and the clothe the naked masses."[36] Even as he emphasized the needs of the Indian nation, he drew a direct connection between the constituent assembly and the UN as the "only way to remove the doubts and dangers of the world," though "the United Nations is not free from big gaps and fissures."[37] Nehru's conjoining of these two emerging institutions – the Indian legislature and the UN – reflected the international dimension of his nationalism and congruity between its respective texts.

Relating Individual Rights to Minority Rights

Nehru long rooted his aspirations for India in a global context. Just before the start of the constituent assembly, Nehru proclaimed that India should "work in complete cooperation with other countries."[38] Even before India gained its independence, preparations were underway for an international conference of leaders to discuss "the problems which are common to all Asian countries."[39] At the Asian Relations Conference of March 1947, Nehru laid out his vision for the "new Asia" and called for Asian nationalists to work together to survive the "mighty transition" of the postwar.[40] The conference offered a testing ground for ideas that Asian leaders later brought to the UN, especially the ideology of "complete Asian solidarity" that India, Burma, and other Asian states invoked

---

[35] India, *Constituent Assembly Debates: Official Report*, vol. 1, December 13, 1946 (New Delhi: Lok Sabha Secretariat, 1966–7), 58 (hereafter CAD).

[36] CAD, vol. 2, January 22, 1947, 317.   [37] Ibid.

[38] Jawaharlal Nehru, "Resolution on Congress Objectives," November 22, 1946, *SWJN 2*, vol. 1, 22.

[39] Jawaharlal Nehru, "Invitation to the Inter-Asian Relations Conference," September 7, 1946, *SWJN 2*, vol. 1, 483.

[40] Telegram B.256, Press Information Bureau, New Delhi, March 23, 1947, IOR/L/I/1/152, BL.

while fighting for Indonesia's sovereign rights in its dispute with the Netherlands and the rights of the Indian minority in South Africa.[41] Asian leaders drew on this common language of rights to coordinate their international activities and regional cooperation.

This global dimension of Nehru's nationalist rhetoric linked the task of constitution-making with the broader effort to secure the rights of national self-determination elsewhere in Asia. As the Asian Relations Conference took place, the subcommittees of the Indian constituent assembly held private sessions to debate the prospective bill of rights. Nehru reminded the assembly that they not only shouldered the cause of India's independence but also "the responsibility of the leadership of a large part of Asia."[42] In Nehru's internationalist worldview, the drafting of India's constitution mattered for all of Asia, since India was "the meeting point of western and northern and eastern and southeast Asia."[43] While this revived Asian ideology featured prominently in Nehru's foreign policy, it also applied to local matters, particularly with regard to minorities. "The one thing that should be obvious to all," Nehru told the constituent assembly, was "that there is no group in India, no party, no religious community which can prosper if India does not prosper."[44] To Nehru and others in the assembly, unity in India required the creation of a secular state that protected religions but did not privilege any religious group over any other. However, the status and rights of minorities proved to be among the most difficult issues facing the assembly.

At the center of this entanglement was the Advisory Committee on Fundamental Rights, Minorities and Tribal and Excluded Areas, which was formed in January 1947. Its chair, Sardar Vallabh Bhai Patel saw this committee as responsible, above all else, for ensuring a smooth constitutional process. One of its core tasks was to appoint subcommittees on the most difficult issues facing the assembly, not least of all minorities and fundamental rights. Patel argued that the best path forward for the assembly was to provide explicit safeguards for minorities to ensure the protection of their fundamental rights. This understanding of the special classification of minority rights gained popularity in the constituent assembly in light of the presence of many minority groups, including religious, ethnic, and caste populations that sought formal representation in the national government.

---

[41] Nehru to V. K. Krishna Menon, October 6, 1946, *SWJN* 2, vol. 1, 171.

[42] CAD, vol. 2, January 22, 1947.

[43] Jawaharlal Nehru, "Inaugural Address," March 23, 1947, in *Asian Relations: Being Report of the Proceedings and Documentation of the First Asian Relations Conference, New Delhi, March-April 1947* (New Delhi: Asian Relations Organization, 1948), 23.

[44] CAD, vol. 2, January 22, 1947.

Against a background of communal tension, the minority question loomed large and tested the constituent assembly's stated commitment to explicitly defining individual and group rights for India. One of the committee members, Govind Ballabh Pant, flatly stated that "many a constitution has foundered on this rock . . . unless the minorities are fully satisfied we cannot make any progress."[45] Some of the minority groups wished to maintain their personal laws while others demanded a reserved number of parliamentary seats. Patel warned against conceding such rights up front, but acrimonious debate threatened to unravel the assembly. In order to protect both individual and group rights, India's constitutional adviser B. N. Rau prepared a key brief that changed how rights were expressed and enumerated in the constitution. His September 1946 note on fundamental rights expounded on justiciability and the need to identify which rights would be enforceable in court. Justiciability thus became a way to bridge the gap between committee members who wanted to write in as many rights as possible and those who wanted a more narrow set of rights. Rau laid out a scheme to divide fundamental rights into two categories: legally enforceable and not enforceable, pointing to the Irish constitution as a model for framing "a distinction between two broad classes of rights," referring to "certain rights which require positive action by the State and which can be guaranteed only so far as such action is practicable, while others merely require that the State shall abstain from prejudicial action."[46] The fundamental rights subcommittee debated Rau's proposal in February 1947, with committee members K. M. Munshi and B. R. Ambedkar initially opposing splitting these rights. Munshi invoked the 1928 Nehru Report, 1931 Karachi Resolution, and the 1945 Sapru Committee report as major precedents of Congress's commitment to a complete bill of rights. Rau maintained that a single list of individual rights would invalidate any enforcement mechanism that could be put into the constitution.

The question of minority representation relatedly emerged in the Fundamental Rights subcommittee. A separate draft constitution prepared by the prominent Hindu nationalist K. M. Munshi contained a more vague expression of equality than that of Ambedkar's draft.[47] His equality provision stated, "All persons irrespective of religion, race, colour, caste, language, or sex are equal before the law and are entitled

---

[45] Quoted in B. Shiva Rao, *The Framing of India's Constitution*, vol. 5 (New Delhi: Indian Institute of Public Administration, 1968), 746.

[46] B. N. Rau, "Notes on Fundamental Rights," September 2, 1946, in Rao, *The Framing of India's Constitution*, vol. 2, 33.

[47] K. M. Munshi, "Note and Draft Articles on Fundamental Rights," ibid., 47.

to the same rights."[48] However, this version did not explicitly call universal franchise a fundamental right, which concerned Ambedkar, himself a Dalit from the depressed classes in India.[49] Dalits were considered a minority group according to the Cabinet Mission Plan, and Ambedkar worried that any ambiguity over the nature of universal franchise would ensure the caste system's longevity. Ambedkar insisted on revising the provision and was supported by fellow committee member Hansa Mehta and others.[50]

Mehta's moral support for Rau's fundamental rights proposal and Ambedkar's equality provisions became a crucial ballast in the debate. As one of the few women participating in the Constituent Assembly and as a member of the fundamental rights subcommittee, Mehta was foremost concerned with expanding rights through concrete mechanisms of enforcement. She connected both processes in her advocacy for enforceable rights in all the arenas in which she worked. At the Indian constituent assembly, Mehta consistently favored the elucidation of individual and group rights, which also meant defining their justiciability. At the UN, Mehta served as India's representative at the Human Rights Commission and the Sub-Commission on the Status of Women. In a 1965 article, she later recalled how "the sub-committee had before it the Declaration of Human Rights" and compared its articles to those of the fundamental rights section of the draft constitution.[51]

In the wake of partition, the thirty-five million Muslims who stayed in India feared for their future; they now represented the largest religious minority in India. They sought the establishment of a separate electorate and the right to use the Shariat as personal law. Munshi and Rajendra Prasad, the president of the constituent assembly, strongly opposed these ideas and favored a uniform civil code for all of India. Questions of national language revealed similar divisions. Nehru sided with the minority groups against the Congress line; the secular state ideal necessitated religious tolerance. In March 1947, after the subcommittee concluded debate, the assembly agreed to the expansive bill of rights and divided fundamental rights into two sections based on Rau's original proposal. The minority question also came to a head at the full assembly. Some members such as Munshi wanted negative rights

---

[48] Ibid., 182–3.
[49] Wenzhen Zhang, *Constitutionalism in Asia: Cases and Materials* (Oxford: Hart, 2014), 552.
[50] Universal franchise was eventually adopted by the assembly in 1949 as Article 326. Rao, *Framing of India's Constitution*, vol. 2, 460–2.
[51] Hansa Mehta, "Woman in the Indian Republic," *India Weekly*, 1965, in Hansa Mehta, *Indian Woman* (Delhi: Butala & Company, 1981), 91.

protecting individuals from the state whereas others wanted the constitution to include positive social and economic rights as well. To settle the disagreement, Patel motioned for the assembly to adopt Rau's proposal to separate justiciable and nonjusticiable rights. One section of the constitution would deal with the fundamental rights of the individual and be enforceable in court, while the directive principles would lay out the nonjusticiable duties of the state toward the improvement of social and economic life. Supporting the motion, assembly member N. G. Ranga said this would "give to our masses in this country more democratic, more liberal, more comprehensive, and more fundamental rights than are being enjoyed in any other country, not even excluding Soviet Russia."[52]

Protections for minorities had a long but checkered history in India's constitutional development. During the independence struggle, Nehru's father, Motilal Nehru, led the effort to define which rights a future Indian government ought to guarantee to its people. The All-Parties Conference Nehru organized released a report in August 1928 stating the demands of the Indian National Congress, including its plan for a new dominion constitution. The report contained a declaration of fundamental rights, which delineated nineteen inherent and inalienable rights of Indian citizens that were necessary for self-government and the resolution of communal strife including personal liberty, equality before the law, and the freedoms of speech, association, conscience, and economic and social rights. In March 1931, the Indian National Congress adopted a resolution with even stronger language, stating that fundamental rights were part of the *swaraj*. Nationalists pointed to these resolutions as evidence that the Congress was ready to lead India and govern the nation. The 1935 Government of India Act further developed some of the same ideas on minorities but excised any mention of fundamental rights. This connection between rights and minorities became part of the 1945 Wavell Plan to restructure the Governor-General's Executive Council and the 1946 Cabinet Mission Plan.

In early April 1947, Rau completed the fundamental rights report. The constituent assembly convened for its third session later that month and each subcommittee presented its findings over a series of raucous debates. In these sessions, Patel presented the new draft bill of rights, which was adopted by the assembly on August 28, 1947. Observing these sessions at Constitution House was Chan Htoon, the Burmese constitutional adviser. Aung San tasked Chan Htoon with studying the

---

[52] CAD, vol. 3, April 29, 1947.

constitutions of different countries and developing relationships with members of the Indian legal academy.[53] Having developed a friendship with Rau, Chan Htoon discussed the draft constitution with Rau in the setting of the constituent assembly.[54] The cross-border consultations between India and Burma led to the intertwining of their constitutional ideas, best exemplified by their provisions on individual rights and state duties. Rau reviewed Chan Htoon's draft constitution and assisted in collecting materials for the Burmese constituent assembly. Rau ensured significant areas of commonality between the two constitutions. For example, the preamble to the Burmese constitution drew directly on Nehru's Objectives Resolution.[55] The rights provisions of the Burmese constitution closely followed the "form and content" of the articles proposed by the Advisory Committee of the Indian constituent assembly, in particular "rights relating to religion, cultural and educational rights, economic rights, and rights to constitutional remedies."[56] The Burmese draft also contained a chapter with directive principles to guide the government in its creation of a socialist welfare state in accordance with the AFPFL slogan of *pyidawtha* (the happy land).

Ceylon's Bill of Rights Denied

This special relationship between India and Burma's constitutional advisers differed significantly from Ceylon's experience. Unlike the subcontinent, elite opinion on the island favored supervised devolution into dominionhood. D. S. Senanayake, the leader of the independence movement and a minister in the State Council of Ceylon, formed a constitutionalist party that worked toward independence through the existing colonial administration. By cooperating with the British on reforming Ceylon's colonial legal system, this conservative rationale presumed that such reforms could guide Ceylon into becoming a dominion within the British Commonwealth. However, this line of thought drew out intense political contestation in Ceylon. Other political groups, namely the Ceylon National Congress, the All Ceylon Tamil Congress, the Youth League, and local labor organizations, wanted more radical methods of change toward independence, but they were outpaced by D. S. Senanayake and his constitutionalist faction. From Senanayake's perspective,

---

[53] Burma Independence Bill, 1947, Acc. No. 78 12/1, NAM.
[54] Constitution of Burma, Acc. No. 4043, Cab 134/346, National Archives of India.
[55] B. N. Rau, *India's Constitution in the Making* (Bombay: Alled Publishers, 1963), 473.
[56] B. N. Rau, "The Constitution of the Union of Burma," *Washington Law Review & State Bar Journal* 23, no. 288 (1948): 288.

this strategy of cooperation with the British colonial government had always been the nationalist approach by the Ceylon National Congress since the early twentieth century and would produce the best outcome for assuring dominionhood.

By 1943, disagreements over the nature of constitutional reform resulted in Senanayake dramatically resigning from the Ceylon National Congress at the end of the year. He was unwilling to embrace the anticolonial and charged rhetoric of the Congress and resolved to pursue negotiations on his own. In May, the British government issued its highly anticipated Declaration of Policy on its plans for Ceylon's transition to independence. The declaration announced the preparation of a new constitution by the cabinet in Ceylon, the Board of Ministers, but stopped short of what Senanayake most hoped for: dominion status. Sir Ivor Jennings, the British constitutional lawyer and vice chancellor of the newly created University of Ceylon, was appointed to aid Senanayake and the cabinet on the new constitution. Along with another constitutionalist leader, Oliver Goonetilleke, the three men together developed a new draft. Jennings later recalled that they formulated a "grand strategy" for Ceylon to unfold over the subsequent five years.[57]

Working with Senanayake and Goonetilleke, Jennings drafted provisions on a wide range of contentious issues, such as granting rights and status to the Tamil ethnic minority clustered in the northern tip of the island. Jennings tried to persuade Senanayake of the merits of explicit representation of minorities in parliament and helped author an anti-discrimination clause to put into the constitution. Jennings insisted that these protections would do more to establish national unity on the island than a bill of rights. The draft developed by Jennings became the basis of Senanayake's negotiations for independence.[58] At the same time, the Ceylon National Congress planned its response to Senanayake's constitutional bill and began developing an alternative text. It also called on the Board of Ministers to open proceedings to consider their more inclusive "Free Lanka" constitution. Its early drafts drew on the 1928 Nehru Report and the 1931 Indian National Congress resolution, amounting to an act of direct opposition not only to the British government but also D. S. Senanayake and the more conservative constitutionalists.

[57] Jennings quoted in A. W. Bradley, "Sir William Ivor Jennings: A Centennial Paper," in Kumarasingham, *Constitution-Making in Asia*, 192.

[58] Ivor Jennings, *The Dominion of Ceylon: The Development of Its Laws and Constitution* (London: Stevens & Sons, 1952), 36–47.

In December 1945, the Governor-General Lord Soulbury undertook a mission to Ceylon "to consult with various interests, including minority communities."[59] Soulbury conceded some value to the concept of fundamental rights and even thought that they might alleviate tensions between the Sinhalese and Tamil ethnic communities.[60] Yet, Soulbury relied on the expert government-sanctioned view of scholars like Jennings and Kenneth Wheare that recognizing rights did not necessitate writing them into an explicit bill of rights. British legal thought at the time opposed the inclusion of such bills, making the Indian and Burmese departures more significant for its turn to foreign sources of law. Thus, Soulbury's recommendations for the constitution omitted both fundamental rights and explicit minority protections. His report drew the condemnation of the Ceylon National Congress, which voted to boycott his mission a year earlier and refused to meet with him when he attempted to contact them. Senanayake also pledged to boycott the Soulbury Commission, though he nonetheless arranged for informal ways for them to interact throughout Soulbury's tour of the provinces. In January 1945, the Congress presented a "Declaration of Fundamental Rights" with eight articles at its annual session. During the commission's visit, the State Council also reviewed the Free Lanka bill, which Soulbury noted "became well known to us through the Press and other channels."[61] The text posed a clear challenge to the Senanayake–Jennings draft, which conceded to Britain's Colonial Office policy against bills of rights.

The alternative construction of a constitutional framework proposed by the Congress was meant to provoke the British by holding up its flagrant disregard for its commitments under the 1941 Atlantic Charter. Sri Lankan historian K. M. de Silva shared Lord Soulbury's attitude toward the Free Lanka text and dismissed the constitution as "a piece of political play-acting . . . not to be taken too seriously."[62] In advancing a constitution containing a chapter on rights, the Ceylonese National Congress molded the Free Lanka constitution in the image of the Indian National Congress and wrote to its counterparts in New Delhi and elsewhere to publicize their text. Schonthal recounts their essential claim that "the British, as participants in the newly formed allied United

---

[59] "The Soulbury Report," *The Roundtable: The Commonwealth Journal of International Affairs* 36, no. 141 (1945): 56.

[60] B. H. Farmer, *Ceylon: A Divided Nation* (Oxford: Oxford University Press, 1963), viii.

[61] United Kingdom, Colonial Office, "The Ceylon Constitution: Report of the Commission on Constitutional Reform," August 31, 1945, C.P.(45)138, 4.

[62] K. M. de Silva and Howard Wriggins, *J. R. Jayewardene of Sri Lanka: 1906–1956*, vol. 1 (London: Anthony Blond/Quartet, 1988), 179.

Nations, were bound by the 'human rights' expressed in the Declaration" and therefore were required to grant these human rights to Ceylon.[63]

Nonetheless, the declaration remained only an act of protest. By May 1946, the Ceylon Constitutional Order in Council completed the official devolution of power to the Senanayake government with the final text of the constitution with the recommendations from the Soulbury mission and the Senanayake–Jennings draft. With Senanayake in London finalizing the constitutional text, Ceylon's steps to independence were secured, though only after Senanayake signed a defense agreement with the British government and the Indian National Congress accepted the Cabinet Mission Plan.[64] As a last symbolic gesture, Senanayake refused the opportunity to be knighted. The constitution adopted at independence in 1948 did not contain fundamental rights, though it prohibited discrimination of minorities. While Ceylon's decolonization is upheld as an example of harmonious devolution, its constitutional process was exclusionary, suppressing anticolonial remonstrations and the fundamental rights proposed by the Ceylon National Congress in the Free Lanka constitution.

In spite of Ceylon's distinct decolonization process, all three postcolonial states retained significant features of British law, as some of the legal infrastructure, such as law reports, were intact and easy to revive, but also because of the pressure imposed by government-appointed advisers like Ivor Jennings in shaping the constitutions. Additionally, the leading legal minds in all three countries were trained in Britain and predisposed to the Westminster model, securing the inheritance of English common law. These individuals populated the new national cabinets, courts, government agencies, and civil service. That colonial continuity defined Ceylon's independence constitution, stripped of any minority protections that might undo the Sinhalese Buddhist majority in power or any explicit fundamental rights as proposed by the Ceylon National Congress. The rejection of a bill of rights for Ceylon echoed Britain's decision to deny India a similar set of rights in the 1935 Government of India Act. Such anticolonial struggles waged in the name of rights found little success early on, but they laid the groundwork for an emancipatory and indigenous rights discourse to emerge in India and

---

[63] Benjamin Schonthal reads greater depth in Congress's campaign and details its transnational dimensions ("Ceylon/Sri Lanka: The Politics of Religious Freedom and the End of Empire," in *Politics of Religious Freedom*, ed. Winnifred Fallers Sullivan et al. (Chicago: University of Chicago Press, 2015), 153).

[64] Krishna P. Mukerji, "Indo-Ceylon Relations," *Indian Journal of Political Science* 18, no. 1 (1957): 41–54.

Burma's constituent assemblies and much later when Ceylon formed its first constituent assembly in 1970.

Seeking Constitutional Advice across Borders

Facing similar challenges, Burma elected to provide a bill of rights in its constitution on Rau's recommendation. With a new draft in hand, Chan Htoon returned to Rangoon in time for the start of the national AFPFL convention in May 1947. Elections the previous month produced an AFPFL landslide with Thakin Nu as its new president.[65] At the conference, Aung San laid out his constitutional vision: "True democracy alone must be our basis if we want to draw up our constitution with the people as the real sovereign and the people's interest as the primary consideration."[66] Htoon presented his draft to a special subcommittee and set about revising the document with the assistance of a small staff. The urgent question facing the assembly was whether Burma should remain in the British Commonwealth. The British had worked for months to convince party leadership that Commonwealth membership would benefit the future state. Privately, Aung San agreed that it "would be best for Burma to stay."[67] But he had spoken boldly about Burma's independence and insisted that the new nation would be fully autonomous. On the second day of its deliberations, the constituent assembly decided it would seek complete independence as a sovereign republic.[68] In response, Aung San declared that the AFPFL "will not break any promises . . . as imperialists used to do."[69] The draft constitution reflected this anticolonial sentiment; it read, the "republic of Burma will be a State founded on the principle of a new war-born democracy, not the old time-worn democracy of the Anglo-Saxons."[70]

The constitution did not produce unity as Aung San hoped, however. As the constituent assembly deliberated, communist rebellions broke out in Arakan and sent Rangoon into panic. Hostility and resentment toward

---

[65] "Burma Election," *The Straits Times*, April 17, 1947.

[66] Aung San, Speech before AFPFL Convention, May 23, 1947, in *The Speeches of Bogyoke Aung San* (Rangoon: Sarpay Beikman, 1971), 300–1.

[67] Aung San quoted in C. A. Bayly and Timothy Harper, *Forgotten Wars: Freedom and Revolution in Southeast Asia* (Cambridge, MA: Belknap Press of Harvard University Press, 2010), 307.

[68] Bogyoke Aung San to Clement Attlee, May 13, 1947, PRO: CAB 127/95, The National Archives of the United Kingdom-Kew (TNA).

[69] "Building a Lasting Federal Union of Myanmar," in *Prisms on the Golden Pagoda: Perspectives on National Reconciliation in Myanmar*, ed. Kyaw Yin Hlaing (Singapore: NUS Press, 2014), 91.

[70] "The Burma Constitution," *Australian Outlook* 2, no. 2 (1948): 98–101.

the hill areas only dampened support for minority rights and the idea of a Union of Burma. These high tensions erupted into a full-blown crisis when news spread that on July 19, an assassin shot Aung San and six other members of the Executive Council. The premiership then fell to Thakin Nu, a shy and unpopular member of the AFPFL who even called himself the least qualified person in the party to lead.[71] In this atmosphere of crisis and defeatism, the constituent assembly met for its second session. Nehru sent a message of condolence, maintaining close communication between the two assemblies. At the end of the summer, the drafting committee completed the final text and sent it to B. N. Rau in New Delhi. In the preface of the printed constitution, Chan Htoon specified, "human rights and cultural autonomy are secured by the provisions in the Chapter containing fundamental rights."[72] The new Burmese constitution was adopted on September 24, 1947, a month after India and Pakistan's independence and well before either country completed its own constitution. As the first indigenously drafted Asian postcolonial constitution, Burma's national law exemplified the transnational rights discourse emerging in the region.

The fall of 1947 ushered in difficult transformations in the legal order. Decolonization in South and Southeast Asia was inconsistently and unevenly achieved. One Burmese journalist said the new constitutions of Asia had been "written in sand" and worried about the durability of the documents and the rights they granted given unyielding crisis.[73] In all three countries, it was unclear whether any of the independence constitutions would hold. Only Ceylon became a republic in a bloodless process, a feat in which its leaders took great pride. But Ceylonese leaders also decided against a democratic constituent assembly and prepared its own constitution in secret. Moreover, India and Pakistan were faced with violent conflict in the wake of partition.[74] The unresolved status of Jammu and Kashmir remained a perennial problem; the line of control was redrawn by assembly members with every successive accusation.[75]

[71] U Nu, *Saturday's Son* (New Haven, CT: Yale University Press, 1975), 136.

[72] Burma, Office of the Constituent Assembly, *The Union of Burma: Constitution* (Rangoon: Government Printing and Stationery, Burma, 1947), 1.

[73] *The Nation*, September 13, 1947; *New Times of Burma*, September 13, 1947, IOR: Mss Eur D1080/9, BL.

[74] One British staff officer deemed the event "human misery on a colossal scale." Stanley Ismay quoted in Sankar Ghose, *Jawaharlal Nehru: A Biography* (New Delhi: Allied Publishers, 1993), 159.

[75] Vijaya Lakshmi Pandit to Jawaharlal Nehru, Vijaya Lakshmi Pandit Papers, 1st installment, S.No.47, 1946–8, Nehru Memorial Museum and Library (hereafter NMML).

Indian leaders reached beyond their borders to work through its political challenges. In October 1947, B. N. Rau embarked on a tour to the United States, Canada, Ireland, and the United Kingdom to discuss the draft constitution with the top legal minds in those countries.[76] In the United States, Rau met with several supreme court justices and wrote in glowing praise of his conversations, even crediting associate justice Felix Frankfurter with the idea of removing the due process clause from the draft text as a way to constrain the power of judges.[77] In his conversations with justice Learned Hand, Rau concluded that amendments would be necessary to protect the national project for social welfare from individual rights. Rau conveyed these new views to Rajendra Prasad, stating that "the general welfare should prevail over the individual right."[78] He said he was made aware of "the dangers of attempting to find in the Supreme Court – instead of in the lessons of experience – a safeguard against the mistakes of the representatives of the people."[79] The intellectual freedom with which Rau sought academic advice reflected the assembly's conscientious decision to diverge from English legal traditions. In another key departure, the assembly borrowed from the US constitution the idea that the constitution itself would be supreme, and not the parliament. While India retained the Westminster model of parliamentary democracy, it strove to design a system of government that would address its specific needs. This commitment to federalism, modified from the US model, distinguished India from its former colonial ruler, while setting a trend that several Asian nations would adopt in the coming years, including its immediate neighbors.

On the basis of Rau's recommendations, the assembly revised the draft article on due process. As a fundamental right, this article granted more power to the legislature to interpret law, eliciting some protest that the constitution was expanding the state at the expense of individual liberty. To preserve the egalitarian vision of the fundamental rights section, the assembly also decided to separate the fundamental rights and directive principles sections, ensuring that fundamental rights would be justiciable and therefore, impose obligations on the state to protect individual liberty. The fundamental rights chapter provided seven core negative

---

[76] Rau, *India's Constitution in the Making*, xiii.

[77] Frankfurter criticized substantive due process and opposed its use as a legal doctrine because of its aggrandizement of the judiciary. "Letters, A Legacy from Justice Frankfurter," *Harvard Law School Bulletin* 18–20 (1966): 34.

[78] B. N. Rau to Rajendra Prasad, November 19, 1947, in Rajendra Prasad, *Correspondence and Select Documents* (Ahmedabad: Allied Publishers, 1987), vol. 7, 395–6.

[79] Rau, *India's Constitution in the Making*, 328–41; Felix Frankfurter, *Felix Frankfurter Reminisces* (New York: Reynal, 1960), 299–301.

rights preventing state encroachment on individual liberty: the right to equality, the right to freedom, the right against exploitation, the right to freedom of religion, cultural and education rights, right to property, and the right to constitutional remedies. In contrast, the directive principles conferred positive rights that framed the obligations of the state to the individual. Together, these two sections constituted an expansive bill of rights marking India's departure from the English legal tradition.

Providing Justiciable Rights in India

The spirit of consensus by which India provided fundamental rights came to the UN through its delegation. The second session of the Human Rights Commission, opening in December 1947, was the first since India's independence. Commission members noticed a renewed determination in the Indian delegation, especially in Hansa Mehta's call for implementation through enforcement mechanisms.[80] Throughout the session, hundreds of communications reached the commission by mail, many of them written by hand alleging human rights violations and detailing personal stories of forced detentions and property seizures. At the plenary, the commission admitted that its powers were limited and agreed to circulate the letters privately to member states. Without a specific mechanism, the commission was unable to act in any meaningful way to address the petitions. However, by deciding it would return to the subject after the measures for implementation had been established, the commission implicitly acknowledged the existence of a right to petition but resolved not to act.[81] This question of the right to petition arose repeatedly throughout the drafting. The Director of the UN Human Rights Division, John Humphrey, prepared a first draft declaration, which was integrated into the recommendations of the French representative, René Cassin, who provided his own documentary resources and extensively reworked the draft.[82] The full draft was then submitted to all member states for their comment.[83] However, the commission ultimately determined that the declaration would have to be developed alongside, but separately, from a legally binding covenant and that implementation would have to wait.

---

[80] Mehta held the chairmanship of the Working Group on the Question of Implementation at the Human Rights Commission. In the first session of the Commission on Human Rights, she submitted a draft resolution on implementation. See E/CN.4/53; Doc. E/CN.4/AC.4/1; E/CN.4/21, Annex H, 92.

[81] Simpson, *Human Rights and the End of Empire*, 453.

[82] "The Commission on Human Rights," *World Affairs* 110, no. 4 (Winter 1947): 252–7.

[83] Annex A, December 16, 1947, E/CN.4/77.

The commission then established three working groups, naming Mehta to lead the group on the measures of implementation.[84] As both the US and British representatives shifted away from supporting enforceable provisions in the human rights covenant, Mehta criticized Eleanor Roosevelt's sudden reluctance to write legally binding rules to protect human rights.[85] In her speeches at the UN, Mehta invoked her country's pending constitution to illustrate the importance of enforcing rights. Mehta's lone quest for implementation mechanism in these meetings signaled a shift in India's role in the drafting. Without having to frame India's independence in explicit human rights terms, Mehta brought the experience of India's constitution-writing to bear on the human rights process.

Hansa Mehta had long been active in India as an advocate for women's rights. In 1945, Mehta presented a Charter of Indian Women's Rights in her presidential address to the All-India Women's Conference. She argued that gender equality should be a core part of citizenship and worked to challenge traditional views on marriage and property rights in Hindu law. This campaign to reform personal law was a central feature of Mehta's political activism. Mehta and fellow AIWC member Amrit Kaur comprised the two female members of the Fundamental Rights subcommittee, where they agitated for the same reforms.

In the constituent assembly, they proposed a uniform civil code to contain a list of justiciable rights such as mutual consent in marriage. They found some success for their efforts in committee, but they did not win mass support for the reason of conflicting with cultural traditions. At the Human Rights Commission, Mehta likewise fought to ensure that the first article of the declaration would be gender inclusive. When Mehta argued that there needed to be a charter that established "the freedom of woman and her equality with man," she pointed to examples from the Indian independence movement, such as the Karachi Resolution and the Sapru Committee report.[86] Mehta brought into the UN debate the long-standing demand in India for fundamental rights by linking India's prewar constitutional reform with contemporary efforts to establish bills of rights. More specifically, Mehta called for the commission to work on creating implementation measures

---

[84] Report of the Commission on Human Rights, Second Session, December 17, 1947, E/600, 157; Report of the Working Group on the Declaration of Human Rights, Commission on Human Rights, December 10, 1947, E/CN.4/51/ADD.1.

[85] Commission on Human Rights, December 5–9, 1947, E/CN.4/AC.4/SR/2.

[86] "Presidential Address before the 18th Session of the All India Women's Conference at Hyderabad (Sind) by Mrs. Hansa Mehta," *Roshni*, February 1946, Hansa Mehta Papers, Subject File No. 21, NMML.

alongside the declaration drafting, even in the form of an international court or tribunal. The debate in the fundamental rights subcommittee on justiciability foreshadowed the deliberations of the Human Rights Commission at the international level, thus joined together by Hansa Mehta's participation in both forums.

These developments were set back by the shocking assassination of Mohandas Gandhi on January 30, 1948, which brought the turmoil of the partition to a crescendo. The constituent assembly temporarily suspended its sessions for several days. Home Minister Patel, who was with Gandhi when the bullet struck, solemnly reopened the assembly a week later. When it reconvened, the tenor of the assembly had changed. Some of the members demanded swift action to bring stability to India, such as new restrictions on citizenship and discretion to limit fundamental rights by legislation. The assembly also excised the long-debated provision on due process in order to make preventive detention constitutional. The new language of Article 15 read, "no person shall be deprived of his life or personal liberty except according to procedure established by law."[87] This attenuated conception of individual liberty, intended to be temporary, nonetheless appeared in the final text of the Indian constitution.

In the same month, Burma declared its independence and its constitution went into effect on January 4, 1948.[88] Nu signed a treaty with Clement Attlee that previous October after the British Parliament passed the Independence Bill the previous year, in November 1947. In his announcement, Attlee called Burmese independence a "departure from the British family of nations" and more poignantly, "an occasion for deep regret."[89] Nu officially became prime minister, taking the reins of a fragile country with sobriety and hesitation as the shadow of the July assassination still hung over Burma. Gandhi's assassination later that month worsened the sense of chaos further still while the new year renewed tensions between India and Pakistan over the status of Jammu and Kashmir. Moreover, Pakistan was in the process of its own constitutional transformation, with its constituent assembly staggered by the death of Muhammad Ali Jinnah in September just thirteen months after the proceedings opened. For its part, the Indian constituent assembly published its full draft constitution by January 1948, turning it to the

---

[87] This became Article 21.

[88] Robert Ely McGuire, "Reflections," IOR: MSS EUR E 362/6, BL; Hubert Rance, Report, IOR MSS EUR E 362/15, BL.

[89] Great Britain, Parliament, House of Commons, November 5, 1947, vol. 443, Coll. 1836–7.

public for their suggestions and comments. The following month, D. S. Senanayake completed the official transfer of power from Britain and declared Ceylon's new dominion status on February 4, 1948.

As Ceylon celebrated its independence, the Indian constituent assembly reconvened for its most challenging round of discussions. The assembly published notices that it would accept comments and suggested amendments from the public; thousands of letters poured into Parliament Hall from across the subcontinent. The assembly agreed to review over two thousand amendments and transmitted a selection of these letters to the drafting committee. Following their review, the drafting committee returned a revised draft to the constituent assembly. In late October 1948, the assembly began debating the second draft in painstaking detail. The fundamental rights section was the "most criticized part" of the draft and Ambedkar was brought before the assembly to justify its formulation.[90] Critics decried Ambedkar's draft for imposing limits on fundamental rights by not making them absolute. Because these rights were not absolute in the sense that the state could not amend them in any way, such rights were accused of being a "deception" that were not truly fundamental. Given the opportunity, Ambedkar launched into professorial explanations in defense of his discretionary use of constitutional precedents in some areas and his license to innovate in others. He was "sorry to say" that the criticisms of the fundamental rights chapter were mainly based on a simple "misconception" of how rights work in constitutions.[91] Ambedkar insisted that the fundamental rights in the Indian constitution were a "gift of the State" and not an agreement reached between private parties. Therefore, the state could "qualify them" by its own discretion. Ambedkar's legal theory, developed over decades of practice and activism on behalf of the depressed classes, upheld centralized authority though he later came to accept the role of federalism in India's union. He observed that while the same principle appeared in the US constitution through the institution of the Supreme Court, the Indian constitution would be even less constrained in its dependence on legal institutions while still recognizing individual rights.[92]

With regard to the directive principles, Ambedkar also explained that the section was a "novel feature" of the constitution drawn from the Irish constitution.[93] The directive principles established a Gandhian welfare

---

[90] CAD, vol. 7, November 4, 1948.   [91] Ibid.
[92] Sudhir Krishnaswamy, "Constitutional Federalism in the Indian Supreme Court," in *Unstable Constitutionalism: Law and Politics in South Asia*, ed. Mark Tushnet and Madhav Khosla (New York: Cambridge University Press, 2015), 356.
[93] At the time, the Irish constitution was the "only other constitution framed for Parliamentary Democracy." CAD, vol. 7, November 4, 1948.

state at the heart of independent India, premised on "a social order in which justice–social–economic and political shall inform all the institutions of national life," as stipulated by Article 38. However, other assembly members nonetheless still pressed for removing the directive principles. Naziruddin Ahmad called them "pious declarations." Ambedkar defended them by stating that even though the directive principles would have "no binding force in law," they served the important function of being "instruments of instruction" that the state "cannot ignore."[94]

India's rights bill reflected a liberal and secular theory of rights, one that distinguished the negative and positive rights of the individual. Importantly, Ambedkar moved the draft provisions on the village (*panchayats*) into the nonjusticiable Part IV, thus formalizing his critique of villages as an ideal type no longer central to India's rights-based framework. He applauded the assembly for having "discarded the village and adopted the individual as its unit," which would best provide "safeguards for minorities."[95] This argument for minority rights complemented Ambedkar's theory of individual rights and its later turn to federalism.[96] India's constituent assembly strove to reconcile several concurrent problems: the relationship between state authority and individual rights, the distribution of power between the provinces and the center, and upholding a socialist identity against the imperatives of state-building. After three years of deliberation, the constituent assembly adopted its constitution, an enormous document with its remarkably long bill of rights.

Conclusion

Asia moved into its postcolonial legal order, with Burma, Ceylon, and India achieving independence within a year of one another. The formal expression of their sovereignty was the written constitution, developed in distinct processes but all sharing several elements in their legal framework. Postcolonial constitutions displayed a hybrid form of federalism, empowering strong executives while conferring rights to individuals and autonomy to its provinces. This quasi-federal arrangement disclosed the fragility of the postcolonial condition, which depended on the cohesion of millions of people from varying cultural, religious, and linguistic traditions. To build their nations, postcolonial elites invented political geographies that folded minorities into federal unions, even involving, in

---

[94] Ibid.   [95] Ibid.
[96] Durga Das Basu, *Introduction to the Constitution of India* (Calcutta: Sarkar, 1960), 63; M. V. Pylee, *Constitutional Government in India* (London: Asian Publishing House, 1960), 190–5.

Burma's case, explicit provisions permitting eventual secession. The individual person also gained new status in the national self-understanding. Individuals became rights-bearing citizens possessing explicit capabilities in these constitutionally reinforced democracies. Their rights were written clearly for them to see, worked out in detail alongside tenacious confrontations with groups previously invisible in the colonial era. This tension between individual and group rights manifested the paradox of the postcolonial nation-state, a boundary that left unspecified in Ceylon's constitution.

The other major self-constituting act in 1948 was the adoption of the UDHR. Like postcolonial constitutions, the declaration outlined a vision for the future through the enumeration of individual rights. The Human Rights Commission completed the draft declaration in the summer of 1948 and transmitted it to the Economic and Social Council. Preoccupied with other agenda items, the Council quickly approved the text and passed it to the General Assembly in Paris. There, the declaration underwent its final review, article by article over eighty meetings from September to December 1948 just days before the assembly vote.[97] When the declaration came before the General Assembly, two rights provisions had been removed. Draft provisions on the rights of minorities and the right to petition were cut from the final text. The General Assembly included notes on both rights in addenda, recommending that the Human Rights Commission and the Minorities Sub-Commission pursue studies "to take effective measures for the protection of racial, national, religious or linguistic minorities."[98] Though the initial terms of reference in the UN Charter mentioned minority protection, by 1948, it proved to be a fault line. Neither the UN Charter nor the UDHR mentioned minority rights. Just past midnight on December 10, 1948, the General Assembly adopted the UDHR, giving credence to the importance of the individual in international law.[99] In 1948, implementation remained one of the outstanding issues of the new human rights system. With the presence of the Indian delegation, the postcolonial nations had already begun to register their dissatisfaction with the new documents, not for its content but for the work yet to be done.

Postcolonial constitutions aligned with the foundational premises of the UN, which in turn provided institutional legitimacy to entrants from

---

[97] General Assembly, Third Committee, Summary Records of Meetings, September 21–December 8, 1948, A/C.3/SR.797.

[98] Report of the First Session of the Sub-Commission on Prevention of Discrimination and Protection of Minorities, E/CN.4/52; Charles Malik to Theodore Spalek, August 25, 1948, Charles H. Malik Papers, Library of Congress.

[99] General Assembly Resolution 217A (III), December 10, 1948, A/810.

the Global South. The new rights bills, whether local or international, reinforced the primacy of the nation-state as the locus of sovereign power. The important distinction, however, was the enduring attention to minorities in the postcolonial constitutions of Asia. Even though Ceylon did not include a formal bill of rights in its constitution, the status of ethnic minorities was central to the passage of the national constitution. Similarly, Aung San's project to unify Burma depended on his overtures to minorities in the frontier areas. In the decolonization of Asia, the question of minorities became a site through which discourses of nationhood, sovereignty, and rights flowed and intersected. As decolonization expanded the ranks of new nations in the international system, it also carried with it a priority on the implementation of rights and the need to provide protections to minorities, both key lessons from the postcolonial constitutions. Taken together, the drafting of new legal orders at the local and international levels supply a fuller picture of how a global rights discourse emerged at the midcentury, entangling its promises as well as its predicaments.

8 Between Ambitions and Caution
India, Human Rights, and Self-Determination at the United Nations

Raphaëlle Khan

Introduction: Bringing India into the Human Rights Debate

The recognition of the historically contingent and contested nature of human rights by a new human rights history has brought into focus the role of decolonized states in shaping the global human rights regime.[1] Yet, although India was a major actor in the early days of the United Nations (UN) where that regime emerged, we know relatively little about its understanding of human rights there, particularly within the context of larger debates on sovereignty.[2] This chapter investigates India's participation in the emergence of the UN human rights system as a lens through which to revisit the historical relation between the human rights discourse, anti-colonialism, and decolonization.

A major bone of contention in recent scholarship on human rights has been whether anti-colonialism in the 1940s was a human rights movement.[3] Critics refuting this idea do not deny that human rights were present in anti-colonial discourses, but stress that anti-colonial leaders

---

[1] For a reassessment of the initial role of human rights at the UN, see Mark Mazower, "The Strange Triumph of Human Rights, 1933–1950," *Historical Journal* 47, no. 2 (2004): 379–98. For different interpretations of the role and attitude of decolonized states vis-à-vis human rights, see below.

[2] More generally, our understanding of India's role at the UN is greatly incomplete, as it is still mostly based on former diplomats' narratives lacking archival evidence. A new wave of historians has started to offer more rigorous accounts of India's involvement internationally. See for instance the works of Rakesh Ankit, Rudra Chaudhuri, Srinath Raghavan, and Vineet Thakur.

[3] Samuel Moyn's seminal book, *The Last Utopia*, crystallized these debates by arguing that human rights as individual rights against the state only date back from the 1970s with the development of nongovernmental organizations. In opposition, Burke argued that a "first variant of a global human rights enterprise" emerged at the UN in the 1940s with Third World activism. See Samuel Moyn, *The Last Utopia: Human Rights in History* (Cambridge, MA: Harvard University Press, 2010); Roland Burke, "The Internationalism of Human Rights," in *Internationalisms: A Twentieth-Century History*, ed. Glenda Sluga and Patricia Clavin (Cambridge, UK: Cambridge University Press, 2017). On the larger debate about the genealogy of human rights, see the Introduction to this volume.

saw their use as instrumental to the larger cause of collective liberation.[4] Other historians have countered these claims by arguing that Third World states strongly promoted universal human rights in the face of often reluctant and ambivalent Western powers. They have documented the role of Asian, African, and Arab states in shaping the UN human rights program in the 1940s and 1950s, though without focusing specifically on India.[5]

In the context of this debate, this chapter advances three main arguments. First, in the case of India, human rights were not a means to promote the principle of self-determination. A newly independent India sought to distance itself from its colonial predecessor by using the language of human rights, believing that the nascent nationalist regime could transform itself into a postcolonial (and anti-colonial) actor that rejected an older international order in which state sovereignty reigned supreme. From the first session of the UN General Assembly (UNGA) in 1946, the Indian delegation made it clear that the existence of human rights limited the scope of Westphalian sovereignty, understood as a strict compliance with the principle of domestic jurisdiction codified in Article 2(7) of the UN Charter. These interventions, coming as they were after India's own independence from colonial domination was already achieved, could not be understood merely as aimed at ending British rule. Rather, they were central to India's leadership in shaping a post-imperial global normative order in the initial years of decolonization.

Second, Indians subsequently saw human rights as a framework through which to protect Indians living outside India as a result of years of organized migration during the colonial period. This concern for

---

[4] Reza Afshari, "On Historiography of Human Rights: Reflections on Paul Gordon Lauren's *The Evolution of International Human Rights: Visions Seen,*" *Human Rights Quarterly* 29, no. 1 (2007): 1–67; A. W. Brian Simpson, *Human Rights and the End of Empire: Britain and the Genesis of European Convention* (Oxford: Oxford University Press, 2001); Jan Eckel, "Human Rights and Decolonization: New Perspectives and Open Questions," *Humanity* 1, no. 1 (2010): 111–35; Moyn, *Last Utopia*.

[5] See notably Roland Burke's work; Susan Waltz, "Universalizing Human Rights: The Role of Small States in the Construction of the Universal Declaration of Human Rights," *Human Rights Quarterly* 12, no. 1 (2001): 44–72; Meredith Terretta, "'We Had Been Fooled into Thinking that the UN Watches over the Entire World': Human Rights, UN Trust Territories and Africa's Decolonization," *Human Rights Quarterly* 34, no. 2 (2012): 329–60; Bonny Ibhawoh, "Testing the Atlantic Charter: Linking Anticolonialism, Self-Determination and Universal Human Rights," *International Journal of Human Rights* 18, no. 7–8 (2014): 1–19. On the role of the Global South vis-à-vis human rights in the 1960s, see Steven L. B. Jensen, *The Making of International Human Rights: The 1960s, Decolonization, and the Reconstruction of Global Values* (New York: Cambridge University Press, 2016).

"Indians overseas," as these Indians were often referred to in contemporary debates, led the nationalist government of India to become a proponent of a strong mechanism of implementation for the protection of individuals against state violations of human rights. Put differently, the leaders of a soon-to-be independent India did not envision "human rights" only as an ideal that would help usher in a new world order, for these were also a set of norms formulated through an engagement with the more pragmatic question of the condition of the Indian diaspora. That diaspora had come into being as the result of an empire now in decline; how to deal with this long-standing issue was one of the central questions for a post-imperial world to come. India's conceptualization of "human rights" was fundamentally shaped through its attempts to answer that question. This explains, in large part, why Indian delegates advocated a strong human rights regime at the UN Commission on Human Rights between 1947 and 1948, the period coinciding with the drafting of the Universal Declaration of Human Rights (UDHR), and, in the 1950s, during the preparation of the International Covenant on Civil and Political Rights (ICCPR).

Third, India's quest for "normative leadership" at the UN and the concern for diasporic Indians did not lead, however, to an unqualified advocacy for human rights. Rather, India's position on human rights was characterized by both determination and restraint. This chapter offers a counterpoint to an emergent scholarly narrative in which the initial enthusiasm for universal human rights among the countries of the newly decolonized world waned in the 1960s as many of them came under authoritarian rule. The latter account posits a shift reflected in the rise of a relativist position regarding human rights, as well as a stark binary between human rights and national sovereignty.[6] I argue that India's positions on human rights do not fit easily within this suggested trajectory for Third World countries. Rather, India was from the very beginning simultaneously ambitious and cautious in its promotion of human rights at the UN. This ambivalence had nothing to do with any authoritarian turn, as India remained a postcolonial democracy.

A similar ambivalence could also be witnessed with regard to India's position on the other major conceptual framework through which the terms of decolonization were contested at the UN: self-determination. India strongly promoted the principle of self-determination in 1946,

---

[6] See Roland Burke, "From Individual Rights to National Development: The First UN International Conference on Human Rights, Tehran, 1968," *Journal of World History* 19, no. 3 (2008): 275–96; Roland Burke, *Decolonization and the Evolution of International Human Rights* (Philadelphia: University of Pennsylvania Press, 2010).

while striving to limit its scope during the preparation of the international covenants. In this case, the contingencies of postcolonial state formation were in tension with the normative leadership it aspired to at the UN. More generally, India's particular trajectory vis-à-vis human rights and self-determination in the early years of the UN was informed by its efforts to reimagine the global order, while at the same time emerge as a nation-state within this order and address political questions left unresolved at the end of the British empire.

By investigating India's ambivalence over human rights and self-determination, this chapter aims to provide a more qualified and historicized image of India as a global actor at the vanguard of the decolonization project at the UN, one not captured through neat binaries of sovereignty versus human rights or authoritarianism versus human rights. The following account will develop these arguments by revisiting the role of India at the UN during its first decade. The first part considers India's case against South Africa at the UN in 1946. The second part then focuses on India's position in subsequent years in the related fields of human rights and self-determination, examining the Indian delegation's contributions at the Commission on Human Rights and the preparation of the ICCPR, as well as the debates on South West Africa and the status of the princely state of Hyderabad.

A Postcolonial Transition through the Case against South Africa: 1945–1946

The Fusing of Two Indias

Both Indian struggles for self-determination and the evolution of the British Empire in the preceding decades prompted an internationalization of Indian politics. On the one hand, Indian nationalists reached international fora such as the League of Nations to lobby for self-rule. On the other hand, colonial India became increasingly integrated into the international politics of the British Empire, obtaining its own, though subordinated, delegation at the League of Nations in 1919 and at the UN Conference on International Organization (UNCIO), the so-called San Francisco Conference, in 1945. This double evolution led to the formation of a two-track diplomacy. Indian nationalists lobbied at the international level in the name of a nationalist India, while representatives of the Government of India participated in international debates in the name of a colonial India. This dualism survived and intensified during World War II, as this period witnessed a deadlock in the negotiations between the British government and nationalist parties – the Indian

National Congress and the Muslim League. It is during the case against South Africa that the two strands of India's internationalized identity fused into one.

As in 1919, India in 1945 became a founding member of the main international organization of its time, the UN, which replaced the defunct League of Nations. Hardly visible in the apparent continuity of its international persona after World War II are the changing political realities subsumed under the word "India." In 1945, internationally "India" was an old diplomatic player, as such an automatic UN member,[7] whereas domestically it was an entity undergoing transformation. By succeeding the government of India, the new nationalist interim government formed in early September 1946 appropriated the international persona of colonial India for the Indian Republic. The new Indian diplomatic service could also count on a corps of seasoned diplomats trained during colonial times. From that perspective, independent India emerged at the UN partly through the persona of the government of India that nationalist leaders had opposed in the past. There was less of a break with the war, and later independence, than often assumed.

At the same time, nationalist rhetoric, which the Congress carried into the interim government, endowed the new India with an anti-colonial legitimacy. Jawaharlal Nehru, who was both a vice-president of the interim government and Minister of External Affairs and Commonwealth Relations, could draw upon legacies of anti-colonial discourse and legitimacy garnered through the nationalist movement in positing a "new" India. The first delegation that Nehru selected to attend the second part of the first session of the General Assembly in October 1946 could look like India's "first venture on a somewhat different plane from those previously"[8] although, earlier that year, the colonial government of India had sent a delegation to the first part of the first session of the Assembly. From then on, the Indian delegation had the additional advantage of representing one of the first decolonized states. Both India's experience gained at the League of Nations, and its special position of being a decolonized state in a world still dominated by colonialism, provided it with a "comparative diplomatic advantage in the postwar world."[9]

---

[7] Because of its specific status within the British Empire and its anomalous position as an international person, India became a founding member of the League of Nations and, following this precedent, an original member of the UN.

[8] "To K. P. S. Menon," London, December 5, 1946, in *Selected Works of Jawaharlal Nehru* [*SWJN*], 2nd series, vol. 1, general ed. Sarvepalli Gopal (New Delhi: Jawaharlal Nehru Memorial Fund, 1984), 551.

[9] Karl J. Schmidt, "India's Role in the League of Nations, 1919–1939" (PhD diss., Florida State University, 1994), 258.

Ironically, both the legacy of older colonial structures and its new anti-colonial legitimacy helped create a basis for India's emergence as a key UN actor.

India's Postcolonial Transition

India's first tour de force at the UN, its case against South Africa, bears the marks of this dual colonial and nationalist legacy and illustrated their transformation. The interim government challenged the global status quo by transforming its case against South Africa previously referred to the UN by the former colonial government of India earlier in 1946. Several studies already exist on this case.[10] Mark Mazower argues that it effectively transformed the former imperialism-friendly UN "into a key forum for anti-colonialism," while it allowed Nehru to "push his wider agenda" and "put India in the vanguard of the movement to challenge colonial domination."[11] What has been overlooked is how, by opening up the field for normative contestations regarding the shape of the international system, this case was constitutive of India's own transformation from a colonial to a postcolonial actor on the global stage.

India's case against South Africa had roots in long-running disputes between the government of India and the Union of South Africa, which until then had only resulted in a series of unsuccessful negotiations. The government of India, and beyond it "the British polity,"[12] had in fact fostered the conditions at the origin of this dispute. In the nineteenth century, imperial policies of indentured labor had encouraged and organized Indian emigration throughout the empire. At the end of the century, when Mohandas Gandhi arrived in South Africa, the Indian community numbered around 50,000 individuals.[13] Their situation deteriorated when South Africa began to pass new discriminatory measures against the Indian population: the Trading and Occupation of Land

---

[10] On this case, see Lorna Lloyd, "'A Family Quarrel': The Development of the Dispute over Indians in South Africa," *Historical Journal* 34, no. 3 (1991): 703–25; Lorna Lloyd, "'A Most Auspicious Beginning': The 1946 United Nations General Assembly and the Question of the Treatment of Indians in South Africa," *Review of International Studies* 16, no. 2 (1990): 131–53; Mark Mazower, *No Enchanted Palace: The End of Empire and the Ideological Origins of the United Nations* (Princeton, NJ: Princeton University Press, 2013), 149–89; Manu Bhagavan, *The Peacemakers: India and the Quest for One World* (New Delhi: HarperCollins India, 2012); Vineet Thakur, "The 'Hardy Annual': A History of India's First Resolution," *India Review* 16, no. 4 (2017): 401–29.

[11] Mazower, *No Enchanted Palace*, 152 and 171–2.

[12] Lanka Sundaram, *India in World Politics: A Historical Analysis and Appraisal* (Delhi: Sultan Chand, 1944), 180.

[13] Ramachandra Guha, *Gandhi before India* (London: Allen Lane, 2013), 18.

(Transvaal and Natal) Restriction Act, 1943 (the "Pegging Act") and the Asiatic Land Tenure and Indian Representation Act (the "Ghetto Act") in June 1946. The latter involved racial segregation. Other dominions followed such discriminatory policies, but the situation in South Africa was the worst.[14] Restrictions on immigration, residence, land occupation, and property rights were extended through legislation from the 1910s to the 1930s. Generally speaking, the situation worsened as dominions gained autonomy and the Colonial Office, formerly the traditional mediator for Indian grievances, receded into the background.[15] The situation of the Indian community abroad (which totaled around four million in 1944) became a subject of concern in India and a major bone of contention with the rest of the British Empire.

The idea of raising the issue at the UN, and the actual referral, preceded the interim government. The status of Indians within the empire, in South Africa in particular, was first discussed at Imperial War Conferences. Following unsuccessful measures and attempts at negotiations over the subsequent decades, the idea of a UN referral finally emerged. It is unclear whether the Natal Indian Congress made such a suggestion first,[16] or whether Narayan B. Khare, who headed the Department of Indians Overseas from 1943, got the idea after reading the "constitution of [the] U.N.O."[17] After the Central Legislative Assembly passed an adjournment motion against the government of India, the Viceroy's Council decided in April 1946 to refer the issue to the UNGA, "if it was found practicable to do so" and to examine "the form and manner in which this should be done." Quickly afterwards, the government of India decided to refer the question to the UN.[18]

It was therefore the colonial government that first faced the question of domestic jurisdiction, central to subsequent UN debates on human rights. At the External Affairs Department, in March 1946,[19] civil servants began to grapple with the crux of the problem: With the treatment of Indians in South Africa, India was concerned with Indian nonnationals and therefore South Africa was likely to make an objection under Article 2(7) of the UN Charter. However, the exact meaning of this

---

[14] And this, even though the emigration scheme stopped in 1911.
[15] On this, see Sundaram, *India in World Politics*, 182; Subimal Dutt, *With Nehru in the Foreign Office* (Columbia: South Asia Books, 1977), 7–8.
[16] Mazower, *No Enchanted Palace*, 173.
[17] N. B. Khare, *My Political Memoirs or Autobiography* (Nagpur: J. R. Joshi, 1959), 171.
[18] B. N. Banerjee, "Subject: Reference of the Indian Question in South Africa to U.N.O," June 15, 1946, Commonwealth Relations (CR) Department, File "United Nations – Question of Raising the South African Indian question in the United Nations Assembly," 14 (25) PWR/46, National Archives of India (NAI), 69.
[19] This is only when the file begins. In 14(25) PWR/46, NAI.

article on domestic jurisdiction, representing the principle of nonintervention, remained undecided and thus controversial.[20] Internal debates around the identification of the UN organ to appeal to and the implications of a referral are a testimony of the relative autonomy that India had acquired in the field of foreign policy by the mid-1940s. The Commonwealth Relations Department was aware that "[o]ur proposal to UNO [would] once raise one of the most contentious and difficult points of interpretation of the Charter,"[21] and accordingly drafted a presentation of the case where it considered the procedure, validity and admissibility of a reference to the UN.[22] "[W]e should be armed with sufficient ammunition to refute the South Africa stand."[23] Ultimately, it advanced arguments based on Articles 10 and 14, which could potentially "only require a simple majority for decision,"[24] therefore ensuring that "the South African question falls within the scope of the functions of the General Assembly."[25] Rejecting the claim that the treatment of Indians was a domestic issue, the presentation argued that it was an international question involving two nations.[26]

Three important aspects of this position should be noted. First, it did not include any mention of human rights. Second, as India's move would be a new type of action, Hugh Weightman, Secretary to the Government of India in the External Affairs Department, was wary of a possible "dangerous precedent" if the General Assembly was involved, "from the point of view of India herself" – an issue he raised during internal discussions.[27] Lastly, Weightman also suggested to "eschew any argument based on the wording of the preamble to the Charter" and "to avoid raising the colour question" as "there will be less danger of forfeiting American sympathy and of the case degenerating, as a result of Russian manoeuvres, into one of these Soviet vs. Western democracy issues."[28] Along these lines, Khare's secretary drafted a complaint for the consideration of the Viceroy's Council around two arguments: "(1) The Government of South Africa is acting against the U.N.O. Charter which

---

[20] Kawser Ahmed, "The Domestic Jurisdiction Clause in the United Nations Charter: A Historical View," *Singapore Year Book of International Law* 10: 183. For different interpretations, see Abdulrahim P. Vijapur, "The Question of Domestic Jurisdiction and the Evolution of United Nations Law of Human Rights," *International Studies* 47, no. 2–4 (2010): 247–65.

[21] Note, CR Department, May 15, 1946, 14(25) PWR/46, NAI, 10–11.

[22] "Presentation of the case of Indians in South Africa before the United Nations," CR Department, 14(25) PWR/46, NAI.

[23] Note, CR Department, May 15, 1946, 14(25) PWR/46, NAI, 10–11.

[24] Ibid., NAI, 14(25) PWR/46, 54.   [25] Ibid., 58.   [26] Ibid., 59.

[27] Copy of a note, CR Department, 14 (25) PWR/46, NAI, 5.

[28] Note, Hugh Weightman, CR Department, May 24, 1946, 14(25) PWR/46, NAI, 16.

provides that there shall be no racial discrimination in any country which is a member of the U.N.O. (2) The South African Government has broken all treaties and agreements made with the Government of India in the matter of treatment of Indians domiciled there."[29]

On June 22, 1946, Sir Ramaswami Mudaliar, India's UN representative, requested that the issue of treatment of Indians in South Africa be included in the provisional agenda of the first session of the General Assembly.[30] His letter stressed that "[a] situation has thus arisen which is likely to impair friendly relations between India and South Africa and, under Articles 10 and 14 of the Charter."[31] His letter described Indians' worsening situation in terms of "discrimination and deprivation of elementary rights," and stressed the "continuing responsibility" that the Government of India felt as "a party to the arrangements which resulted in Indian emigration to South Africa." Additionally, South Africa's new legislation of discriminatory measures repudiated older agreements made with India in the 1920s and 1930s.[32] India also submitted a factual memorandum on the history of discriminatory measures against Indians. The colonial government of India thus not only referred the case to the UN, but also decided its framing as an issue regarding domestic jurisdiction and to be addressed by the General Assembly.

By August, the Indians were aware that the main South African argument against their case would indeed be the domestic jurisdiction clause, Article 2(7) of the Charter.[33] By September, Nehru was officially in charge of foreign affairs.[34] He attached high importance to the case of South Africa, which took a new dimension under his government.[35] He asked a prominent lawyer, Tej Bahadur Sapru,[36] for his views on how best to present the case, notably for arguments against South Africa's objection that "the General Assembly has no jurisdiction to deal with this matter as the issue is essentially within the domestic jurisdiction of the

[29] Khare, *My Political Memoirs*, 181–2; see "Indian question in South Africa: Appeal to the United Nations Organisation," Summary, R. N. Banerjee, CR Department, April 2, 1946, 14(25) PWR/46, NAI.

[30] Letter, Ramaswami Mudaliar to UN Secretary-General, June 22, 1946, 6(22)-CC/46, NAI, 48.

[31] Ibid., NAI, 6(22)-CC/46, 48–50.   [32] Ibid.

[33] As mentioned in Telegram, UN Secretary-General to Hugh Weightman, August 26, 1946, 6(22)-CC/46, NAI, 69.

[34] The interim government of India, led by Nehru, was formed on September 2, 1946.

[35] Mazower notes that "South Africa was the first issue Nehru raised with Wavell," in *No Enchanted Palace*, 175.

[36] Sapru was also a statesman and a former member of the Imperial Legislative Council (1916–20) as well as law member of the Viceroy's Council (1920–3).

Union of South Africa."[37] Sapru underlined the importance of taking a nonlegal angle and noted that "more stress should be laid on facts as stated in the draft letter or the Memorandum than on pure questions of law."[38] Considering the absence of an "Empire nationality," Indians in South Africa "must be treated as bound by the laws of South Africa," however,

those laws affect the *fundamental human rights* of Indian subjects there and as the home of origin of their ancestors and of many of those Indians is India, the Indian Government are under an obligation, moral and political, to see to it that they are treated properly, fairly, justly and consistently with the Charter of the United Nations.[39]

Sapru's framing transformed the nature of the case. His invocation of human rights implied a reference to the Preamble of the Charter because it "was conceived and expressed not in terms of race, colour or creed, but in terms of social justice and fundamental human rights."[40] Moreover, he reckoned that because of its international character "the Preamble [was] even more binding than . . . Parliamentary statutes."[41] The concept of human rights became an important moral argument to justify bypassing domestic jurisdiction – and a radical departure from Weightman's argumentation. Following Sapru's advice, in September, Nehru rejected claims that the matter was purely one of domestic jurisdiction, and emphasized that:

the treatment of Indians in South Africa is fundamentally a moral and human issue which, in view of the "Purposes" and "Principles" so clearly stated in the Charter of the United Nations, the General Assembly cannot disregard.[42]

With that, India's frame of reference shifted: it was no longer only about Indians in the empire and its goal was no longer solely India's equal status. Khare had situated the issue of Indians abroad within India's relation to the empire and the Commonwealth, and formulated it as a right to equal treatment for Indians. As such, he advocated for "[doing] something in defence of the self-respect of the Indians in South Africa."[43] Now, India's fight was for the struggle against racialism in general on the basis of universalist principles. Indeed, the interim

---

[37] Confidential memorandum, part I, October 3, 1946, Pandit Papers, II Inst., Subject File I, Sno. 2, 91–118, Nehru Memorial Museum & Library (NMML).

[38] Ibid., 102–3.   [39] Emphasis mine (ibid., 105).   [40] Ibid., 111.

[41] Ibid., 113. This contrasted with the view of prominent lawyers such as Hans Kelsen who thought that the Preamble was without effect. See Mazower, "Strange Triumph of Human Rights," 394.

[42] "An independent foreign policy," September 26, 1946, *SWJN*, 2nd series, vol. 1, 496–7.

[43] Khare, *My Political Memoirs*, 155.

government's argumentation for its case expanded the definition of the victims concerned – from Indians to Asians to a larger Third World population. Two days after the interim government started functioning, Nehru reassured the Vice-President of the Transvaal Indian Congress that the new government "[would] not give in till we secure full recognition of Indians' rights and India's honour."[44] The rhetoric was not new, but what followed revealed the broader perspective in which Nehru viewed the status of Indians in South Africa. "The struggle in South Africa," Nehru added, was "not merely an Indian issue":

It concerns all Asians whose honour and rights are threatened, and all the people of Asia should, therefore, support it . . . It is a struggle for equality of opportunity for all races and against the Nazi doctrine of racialism . . . Our cause thus becomes a world cause in which all people who believe in freedom are interested.[45]

Nehru was explicitly defining a free India's emergence not only in relation to an equalization of status within the empire, but to the broader movement of freedom for colonies worldwide.[46] Such rhetoric was not new for Nehru but, in this context, his interpretation contributed to qualitatively transform the terms of the case. For Khare, the case concerned Indians and represented a "radical blow on the very conception of the Empire."[47] For the new government, it concerned the world and represented a blow to an unequal and racial conception of the international order.[48] In this context, the idea of human rights opposed that order not only through its moral symbolism, but also through its implications for the norm of sovereignty.

Accordingly, at the General Assembly convened for the second part of the first session, on October 23, 1946, the new Indian delegation infused the old dispute with a fresh meaning – and important implications. On the one hand, it kept the initial overall strategy of invoking Articles 10 and 14, although Article 10 was not meant to allow the General Assembly to deal with matters seen as within a state's domestic jurisdiction.[49] On the other hand, its intervention sanctioned appeals to human

---

[44] "Indian Struggle in South Africa a World Issue," Message given to Ismail A. Cahalia, September 4, 1946, *SWJN*, 2nd series, vol. 1, 437.
[45] Ibid.
[46] See for instance "India and Africa," September 27, 1946, *SWJN*, 2nd series, vol. 1, 425.
[47] Khare, *My Political Memoirs*, 183. Traditionally, intra-Commonwealth disputes were solved informally within the empire. However, from 1927, relations between India and South Africa were no longer mediated by Britain but were direct.
[48] See Mazower, *No Enchanted Palace*.
[49] Kawser Ahmed, "The Domestic Jurisdiction Clause in the United Nations Charter: A Historical View," *Singapore Year Book of International Law* 10 (2006): 186–7.

rights by arguing for the primacy of morality over law and technicality and for increasing the role of the General Assembly. Vijaya Lakshmi Pandit, Nehru's sister and the leader of the Indian delegation, argued that the issue was moral and political rather than legal. Moreover, "fundamental questions concerning human rights were not essentially domestic matters of member states."[50] Lastly, the new terms in which the case was presented challenged nothing less than the normative foundations of "Western civilisation."[51] Pandit viewed "the future of a large section of the human race" as being at stake.[52] This language, which differentiated the framing of the postcolonial government from that of the colonial government, further marked a shift in independent India's identity within the international system.

Such a shift, for the Indian delegation, implied more generally arguing that the UN Charter restricted the principle of domestic jurisdiction. This view appeared clearly when, unsurprisingly, Jan Smuts disapproved of India's interpretation of the UN Charter,[53] and argued that the dispute was *ultra vires*. Smuts, representing South Africa at the UN,[54] stressed that there was neither an internationally recognized formulation nor a definition of human rights in the Charter – therefore, member states had no obligations.[55] In response, the Indian delegation made explicit the restrictive notion of state sovereignty that their interpretations of the Charter implied. Justice M. C. Chagla argued that signing the Charter committed sovereign member states to a "contraction of the domain of essentially domestic matters." Indeed, "[t]he Charter would become merely a scrap of paper if it was suggested that any signatory could, with impunity, violate its terms without the United Nations having any right to take action."[56] Furthermore:

[50] Indian Council of World Affairs (ICWA), *India and the United Nations: Report of a Study Group* (Westport, CT: Greenwood Press, 1974), 113.

[51] "The issue, in her opinion, was whether western civilization was to be based on the theory of racial supremacy or whether the barriers imposed between man and man on grounds of colour were to be broken down and justice and equality were to be considered the due of all." General Assembly Official Records (GAOR), 2nd part of the 1st session, Joint Committee of the First and Sixth Committees, 3rd meeting, November 26, 1946, 24.

[52] Vijaya Lakhsmi Pandit, Address to Chairman, November 26, 1946, Pandit Papers, II Inst., Subject File I, Sno. 2, NMML, 85–6.

[53] GAOR, 2nd part of the 1st session, Joint Committee of the First and Sixth Committees, 1st meeting, November 21, 1946, 3.

[54] Formerly in the Imperial Cabinet during World War I and South Africa's representative at the Peace Conference. He became Prime Minister of South Africa between 1919 and 1924 and between 1939 and 1948.

[55] Lloyd, "Auspicious Beginning," 140.

[56] GAOR, 2nd part of the 1st session, Joint Committee of the First and Sixth Committees, 2nd meeting, November 25, 1946, 10.

Could there be any doubt concerning the meaning of "human rights and fundamental freedoms for all without distinction as to race, sex, language or religion" and similar provisions in the Charter?[57]

Chagla went on to suggest that the UN should have the right to take action in case of a violation of the binding terms set out in the UN Preamble.[58] As a study group of an Indian think tank phrased it in 1974, "[i]n India's view it was for the Organisation to decide whether any matter was so essentially domestic in its nature that the United Nations would refrain from interfering with the exercise of discretion by a sovereign state."[59]

For the Indian delegation, this subversive view about the principle of domestic jurisdiction went hand in hand with its position on the jurisdiction of the UNGA. This was significant because a jurisdiction determined the possible scope and nature of the case, and hence could lead to different conceptions of sovereignty.[60] Chagla argued that the International Court of Justice was not "qualified to express an opinion on this question."[61] At the fourth meeting of the UNGA Joint Committee on Indians in South Africa, Britain along with the United States and Sweden co-proposed a resolution that asked the Court of Justice for its advisory opinion on the question of domestic jurisdiction.[62] US delegates feared that the case against South Africa could create a problematic precedent for their own country by enabling the UN to investigate racially discriminatory practices. Pushing to use the Court of Justice was part of their attempt to "move the Indians' complaint out of the UN's jurisdiction altogether" and to "focus only on the nature of the treaties and completely ignore the issues of human rights and domestic jurisdiction."[63] However, France moved an alternative resolution amended by Mexico, which declared that the General Assembly should

---

[57] To which the South African representative replied that "Political rights were not fundamental." In GAOR, 2nd part of the 1st session, Joint Committee of the First and Sixth Committees, 2nd meeting, November 25, 1946, 10 and 21.

[58] Human rights are mentioned in the Preamble. See M. C. Chagla, *Roses in December: An Autobiography with Epilogue* (Bombay: Bharatya Vidya Bhavan, 1978), 237.

[59] ICWA, *India and the United Nations*, 113.

[60] See Martti Koskenniemi, "The Politics of International Law: 20 Years Later," *European Journal of International Law* 20, no. 1 (2009): 7–19.

[61] GAOR, 2nd part of the 1st session, Joint Committee of the First and Sixth Committees, 2nd meeting, November 25, 1946, 11.

[62] GAOR, 2nd part of the 1st session, Joint Committee of the First and Sixth Committees, 5th meeting, November 28, 1946, A/C.1&6/20, 43.

[63] Carol Anderson, *Eyes off the Prize: The United Nations and the African American Struggle for Human Rights, 1944–1955* (Cambridge, UK: Cambridge University Press, 2009), 87–8.

judge the present dispute and contested that the issue was domestic – a resolution that India ultimately supported. That resolution was adopted without the other one being put to a vote.[64] Accordingly, on December 8, 1946, the General Assembly adopted the Resolution 44(I) "Treatment of Indians in the Union of South Africa," which dismissed South Africa's argument of domestic jurisdiction and maintained that its "actions should conform to the Charter's human rights provisions."[65] This Indian victory against South Africa opened a way for a human rights discourse at the UN and, as argued by Mazower, opened a breach for a fundamental reorientation of the UN toward anti-colonialism.

The French–Mexican resolution included the argument of impaired friendly relations but did not mention human rights and fundamental freedoms. Yet Nehru interpreted the passage of this resolution as a victory for human rights, arguing that "the General Assembly [had] not only vindicated India's honour but [had] shown itself a guardian of human rights."[66] Similarly, the Indian delegation interpreted this outcome as "a victory not merely for the cause of Indians in South Africa or for the weaker races all over the world but for those high principles so clearly enunciated in the Charter of the United Nations."[67] A former UN officer observed that "[c]autiously, and without fanfare," the UNGA "had slipped into the human rights field."[68] Domestic jurisdiction, in a turnaround, came to be seen as a "hindrance to maintaining international peace" rather than one of its conditions.[69] From a legal perspective, although the wording of the Resolution 44(I) was not strong, Chagla interpreted the meaning of the case in radical terms – fundamentally impacting state sovereignty in relation to the UN:

[I]n becoming a member of the United Nations a sovereign country voluntarily puts a restriction and limitation upon its own sovereignty by agreeing to the principles and purposes of the Charter. Further, it was established that no country can with impunity treat its own nationals in violation of the principles of human rights enshrined in the Charter. And thirdly, that the United Nations had the right to call a delinquent country to account.[70]

---

[64] GAOR, 2nd part of the 1st session, Joint Committee of the First and Sixth Committees, 30 November 1946, A/C.1&6/12, 51.

[65] Richard Schifter, "Human Rights at the United Nations: The South Africa Precedent," *American University Journal of International Law and Policy* 8 (1993): 363.

[66] "UN Resolution on South Africa," Message to Pandit, New Delhi, December 9, 1946, *SWJN*, 2nd series, vol. 1, 469.

[67] "Extract from the Report of the India Delegation to the second part of the first session of the General Assembly," 2(19)-UNO(I)/47, NAI, 8.

[68] Schifter, "Human Rights at the United Nations," 364.

[69] Ahmed, "Domestic Jurisdiction Clause," 176.   [70] Chagla, *Roses in December*, 240.

Thus, a question initially framed in a colonial context crystallized a problem of domestic jurisdiction, which the nationalist interim government broadened into something new. India's case against South Africa at the UN differed from its first colonial articulation in at least three respects: first, although it kept to the path of India's fight for the honor of overseas Indians, its frame of reference was no longer the empire in which India sought an equal status, but the world stage on which it defended its arguments on a universalist basis. Second, the case illustrated India's desire for normative change in the international system and, by breaking the lock of international law, opened possibilities for further normative struggles. The handling of the case provided a basis both for India's leadership and for new normative dynamics at the UN through an appeal to human rights. Third, Justice Chagla's remarks on the case against South Africa prove that there was a streak of radical thinking on domestic jurisdiction among the Indian elite.

From 1946 onwards, the terms of decolonization were debated at the UN through two main conceptual frameworks: human rights and self-determination. Yet, while India was an early voice for anti-colonial movements in this world forum,[71] to what extent did it promote human rights and self-determination after 1946? The next section examines India's ambitions and tensions in this respect.

Human Rights and Self-Determination at the UN: 1947–1950s

Human Rights: A Framework to Protect Overseas Indians

The case against South Africa illustrates how the language of human rights served India's global anti-colonial ambitions at a pivotal moment. At another level, though, the case was simultaneously about arguing for Indians in South Africa. As such, it also represented nationalist India's struggle with the problematic legacy of British imperial politics. Even after the case against South Africa ended, the concern for overseas Indians continued to shape India's interest in human rights at subsequent UN debates. Indians envisioned a human rights regime as a potential framework through which to protect overseas Indians against state violations of rights. A protection that the Indian state could not provide them.

---

[71] See for instance L. P. Singh, *India and Afro-Asian Independence* (New Delhi: National Book Organisation, 1993).

In January 1947, India's delegate to the Human Rights Commission, Hansa Mehta, received a message from Nehru anticipating the first meeting of the Commission. His first point precisely mentioned that Indians "recently had to face discrimination in South Africa" and had "difficulties" in Ceylon and East Africa.[72] Significantly, Mehta's subsequent brief was prepared by the Commonwealth Relations Department, which focused on the situation of overseas Indians and was therefore "vitally interested in the discussions of [the] Commission [on Human Right]."[73] At the request of that Department, Lanka Sundaram, who had represented Indian Overseas Associations in India, accompanied Mehta as legal adviser.[74] On the very first day of the Commission, Mehta described how the indentured labor system had left four million Indians outside India and created "numerous cases of denial of rights both in law and equality due to administrative practices."[75] From then on, India strived to solve this specific colonial issue by shaping a human rights regime at the UN.

After the case against South Africa, it became difficult to distinguish between the government's wish to protect Indian minorities abroad and its desire to project India's normative leadership internationally. Both India's global aspirations and a long-standing concern for an issue born from imperial politics drove its participation in the Human Rights Commission – and Mehta's attempts to limit the principle of domestic jurisdiction. Yet, situating India's position on human rights as a new global order was being shaped reveals simultaneous strains of ambition and caution, ideals and qualifications, not to mention success and failures in institutionalizing a regime of global norms. It is incorrect to view India, much less Third World countries in general, as indifferent to human rights or interested in human rights primarily in instrumental terms. At the same time, while India propounded some of the most expansive ideals of human rights, it nevertheless treaded cautiously at important junctures.

---

[72] Letter, G. S. Bajpai to Hansa Mehta, January 22, 1947, Washington, Mehta Papers, I Inst., Subject File, Sno. 12, "Corr. of External Affairs Ministry with Hansa Mehta regarding her nomination as India's representative on the Human Rights Commission, UNO, 1947," NMML.

[73] Letter, H. Trevelyan to Hansa Mehta, January 10, 1947, New Delhi, Mehta Papers, I Inst., Subject File, Sno. 12, NMML.

[74] Mentioned in CR Department, "Brief for the Indian delegation to the Human Rights Commission," in "Commission on Human Rights of the Economic and Social Council. Provision of Briefs to India's representative on –," External Affairs (EA) Department, 15 (3)-CC vol. II, 66, NAI.

[75] Hansa Mehta, speech before the Commission on Human Rights, January 27, 1947, Mehta Papers, I Inst., Subject File, Sno. 15(i), NMML.

India's stand on human rights at the UN is not well documented.[76] Samuel Moyn has noted that "no serious record" shows Gandhi referring to human rights "in the era after the Atlantic Charter," while Nehru, with the exception of UN petitions for Indians in South Africa, "did not invoke international rights."[77] This description of India's contribution on the topic of human rights is insufficient. For a start, India's official delegation intervened quite forcefully on this question at the UNCIO in 1945.[78] Arguably, human rights were not legally formed yet; their meaning was undefined.[79] Defining them was precisely a stake of UN politics.

In 1947, in keeping with Justice Chagla's earlier interpretation that the emergence of the UN substantially altered the domain of domestic matters, Mehta actively promoted a strong human rights regime at the Human Rights Commission, where she represented India until 1952. Being a women's rights campaigner, she contributed to drafting women's rights in the UN Sub-Commission on the Status of Women,[80] before participating in the preparation of the 1948 UDHR at the Human Rights Commission.[81] There, she advocated an internationalist agenda similar to the one advocated by the French representative, René Cassin.[82] She promoted a strong version of human rights along three lines: by advocating a UN mechanism of implementation and enforcement for these rights, their binding character, and a right of petition by individuals and organizations. By their very nature, all these proposals sought to limit state sovereignty. As seen in the following section, the way Mehta promoted them illustrates both India's ambitions and restraint.

At the Commission, India supported the idea of an international bill of rights taking both the form of a declaration and a convention – which

---

[76] One important exception being Manu Bhagavan's *Peacemakers*.

[77] Moyn, *Last Utopia*, 90.

[78] See Paul Gordon Lauren, *The Evolution of International Human Rights: Visions Seen* (Philadelphia: University of Pennsylvania Press, 2003), 167 and 176–80.

[79] This allowed Jan Smuts to use this expression while believing in white supremacy and following openly racist policies in South Africa. On Smuts's ideas, see Saul Dubow, "Smuts, the United Nations and the Rhetoric of Race and Rights," *Journal of Contemporary History* 43, no. 1 (2008): 43–71.

[80] *Times of India (ToI)*, "Women's Charter of Rights: Mrs. Hansa Mehta on UNO's Task," June 12, 1946; Bhagavan, *Peacemakers*, 83–4; Waltz, "Universalizing Human Rights," 63–4.

[81] Burke, *Decolonization*, 21. On Mehta's contribution to the principle of nondiscrimination, see Mary Ann Glendon, *The Forum and the Tower: How Scholars Have Imagined the World from Plato to Eleanor Roosevelt* (Oxford: Oxford University Press, 2011), 216.

[82] Glenda Sluga, "'Spectacular Feminism': The International History of Women, World Citizenship and Human Rights," in *Women's Activism: Global Perspectives from the 1890s to the Present*, ed. Francisca de Haan, Margaret Allen, June Purvis, and Krassimira Daskalova (Abingdon, UK: Routledge, 2013), 50.

included implementation.[83] As early as January 1947,[84] Mehta advocated to enforce a bill of human rights, "whenever human rights are violated" in UN member states "through the establishment of a world court of human rights, reference to the International Court, or action by the Security Council."[85] The draft resolution she submitted for the General Assembly clarified that the Security Council "shall be seized of all alleged violations of human rights, investigate them and enforce redress within the framework of the United Nations."[86] She could deal with questions as they arose in the Commission;[87] the draft resolution was her own initiative. As Manu Bhagavan has noted, Mehta was advancing "a radical redefinition of 'security' and the Council meant to defend it," even more so as the General Act would be an "obligation" for member states.[88] Furthermore, Mehta suggested that the Human Rights Commission lists for every country the "legal and administrative measures tending to decrease human rights within the meaning of the principles of the Charter."[89] These drastic proposals contrasted with the other suggestions available. While Australia also promoted strong implementation measures, the United States, supported by Britain and the USSR, favoured more minimalist measures, i.e. just incorporating a bill of rights in a resolution to the General Assembly.

Mehta, however, did not push her resolution further. On February 1, 1947, a telegram from Nehru reminded her of India's more cautious brief: India did not intend to submit any formal resolution to the Human Rights Commission "at this stage and before consideration by Sub-Commissions." Moreover, Nehru feared that referring to the Security Council in the resolution might involve amending the Charter, and

---

[83] Manu Bhagavan has provided a valuable account of Mehta's role at the Human Rights Commission in *Peacemakers*, chs. 4 and 5, and in "A New Hope: India, the United Nations and the Making of the Universal Declaration of Human Rights," *Modern Asian Studies* 44, no. 2 (2010): 311–47. While he argues that India's contribution to the Commission illustrates a Nehruvian vision of a new (post-sovereign-nation-states) world order, this chapter rather examines India's relation to sovereignty within the specific debate on human rights.

[84] At the second meeting of the first session.

[85] Hansa Mehta, speech before the Commission on Human Rights, January 27, 1947, Mehta Papers, I Inst., Subject File, Sno. 15(i), NMML.

[86] Draft of a resolution for the UNGA submitted by India, Commission on Human rights, January 31, 1947, E/CN.4/11, 1.

[87] Letter, Bajpai to Mehta, January 22, 1947, Washington, Mehta Papers, I Inst., Subject File, Sno. 12, NMML.

[88] Bhagavan, *Peacemakers*, 88.

[89] Summary records of the Commission on Human Rights, 1st session, 2nd meeting, January 27, 1947, E/CN.4/SR.2, 4.

favored "[relying] on [the] General Assembly rather than on [the] Security Council which was dominated by a few powers."[90]

Henceforth, Mehta was placed in a seemingly awkward position. On the one hand, she kept advocating enforceable principles of human rights by the UN and a legally binding convention. Her position was markedly different from other delegates, since the "general consensus" favored a declaration adopted through a General Assembly resolution.[91] On the other hand, the Director of the UN Division of Human Rights, John Humphrey, noted that Mehta did not explain the "exact juridical character" of the General Act that she had invoked and how the latter could be adopted by the General Assembly and "constitute 'an obligation undertaken by member states.'"[92] Moreover, while she now advocated that the General Assembly enforce the Act, she did not try to respond to the argument that the Assembly could not adopt binding instruments or implement resolutions. Humphrey concluded: "Had the Indian government been serious about its proposal, it could have been redrafted to take [these objections] into account; but it was never heard of after the first session of the commission."[93] Instead, Mehta emphasized that her delegation would not press for a vote on the matter and would "fight for its ideas" on implementation after a bill was drawn.[94]

At the second session,[95] where she chaired the Working Group on Implementation, Mehta kept promoting ambitious plans, such as "a special UN committee ... that would work in conjunction with an international court to hear cases by and against individuals, groups and states."[96] That proposal was passed by the Working Group, which agreed on the principle of a right of appeal by an individual or organization to an international court. Significantly, in her report of December 1947, Mehta noted that "[i]mplementation at the international level would mean some encroachment on the National Sovereignty."[97] Subsequently, in the Commission, the Soviet delegate opposed her suggestion precisely on the ground that it attempted to interfere in the state's

---

[90] "Telegram to Hansa Mehta," February 1, 1947, *SWJN*, 2nd series, vol. 2, 485.
[91] John P. Humphrey, *Human Rights and the United Nations: A Great Adventure* (New York: Transnational Publishers, 1984), 26.
[92] Ibid.   [93] Ibid.
[94] *ToI*, "Bill of Human Rights: Drafting Committee Appointed," February 7, 1947.
[95] Between December 2–10, 1947.
[96] Bhagavan, *Peacemakers*, 90. His footnote 69 details internal discussions on this.
[97] Hansa Mehta, "Report of the Human Rights Commission, Session: from 2nd December 1947 to 17th December 1947," in "Second Session of the Human Rights Commission of the Economic & Social Council," EA and CR Department, 5(68)-UNO I, 1947 (secret), NAI, 73.

domestic affairs.[98] In June 1949, she told the delegate that the UN system had indeed altered the meaning of sovereignty: "the Protection of Human Rights had been envisaged by the Charter," which "implied a certain degree of interference with national sovereignty . . . the question of national sovereignty could have been raised at the time of the signing of the United Nations Charter, but not at this stage."[99]

Along with Lebanese delegate Charles Malik and Filipino delegate Carlos Romulo, Mehta also pushed for a right of petitions for individuals and organizations and for empowering the Human Rights Commission to study them.[100] The draft resolution she submitted in January 1947 proposed that a General Act incorporate a universal, individual "right to access to the United Nations, without risk of reprisal, whenever there is an actual, or threatened infringement of human rights."[101] This Act would automatically be valid for non-self-governing areas and areas under UN trusteeship.[102] Interestingly, while this proposal had a universal dimension, the problem of overseas Indians once again partly motivated India's advocacy. Mehta highlighted that their "cases of denials of rights in law" "[must] be solved within the meaning of the terms of reference of the Commission on Human Rights and the principles of the Charter." From this perspective, a right of petition aimed at protecting minorities against discrimination.[103]

In contrast, through fear of dissent, embarrassment, and outside interference, representatives had been told by their governments to reject claims that the Human Rights Commission had powers to act with respect to individual complaints of human rights violations.[104] When the Commission started to discuss implementation in May 1949, only the French and Australian delegates and Mehta were "really interested in doing any[thing]." Humphrey foresaw that the UK–US proposal to limit the right of petition to states would prevail – turning petitions into "an instrument of high policy and an occasion for international conflict or ..."

---

[98] Cited ibid., 91.

[99] *ToI*, "'Human Rights Pact an Interference': Soviet Delegate's View," June 2, 1949. The debate was on freedom of movement of individuals.

[100] For an account of debates in the Commission and the role of other states, see Burke, *Decolonization*, ch. 3, 61–9.

[101] Draft of a resolution for the UNGA submitted by India, Commission on Human Rights, January 31, 1947, E/CN.4/11, 1.

[102] Ibid.

[103] January 28, 1947, E/CN.4/SR.2. Cited in Robert Normand and Sarah Zaidi, *Human Rights at the UN: The Political History of Universal Justice* (Bloomington: Indiana University Press, 2008), 159–60.

[104] Lauren, *Evolution of International Human Rights*, 212.

the machinery [would] never be used."[105] In the debates of June 1949, the Lebanese, French, and Indian representatives fought for a right to petition against US opposition.[106]

In this case, however, India's ideas were defeated. In May 1950, India's proposal to establish a "UN Committee which would act as a 'watchdog' over human rights throughout the world" was rejected in the Human Rights Commission; the delegates prefered a Committee with no supervision powers but only a right of mediation between states.[107] Ultimately, it was decided that the rights enshrined in the UDHR "would only have suggestive, moral force."[108] The proposal of an individual right of petition was also defeated: the draft of a Human Rights Covenant was finalized along the lines of US and British wishes, i.e., only states would have a right of petition.

Years later, in 1954, India's Permanent Representative at the UN, Rajeshwar Dayal, again proved "the most forceful champion" of individual petitions. During debates at the Human Rights Commission to prepare the international covenants, he maintained that "a human rights programme without a petitions procedure was a pointless farce" and pushed to agree on an individual right of petition.[109] At the next meeting, another Indian delegate defended the right of petition against criticisms raised by other delegates.[110] Nevertheless, at a subsequent meeting, he declared that the sponsors of a joint proposal on a right of petition (which included India) prefered not to press for a vote "to avoid the rejection of the joint proposal by the Commission being interpreted as a rejection of the principle of the right of petition."[111] Ultimately, the Commission did not recognize this right.

What these episodes reveal is India's complex trajectory vis-à-vis human rights in the early years of the UN. Indian delegates at the Human Rights Commission championed proposals that were more ambitious

---

[105] John P. Humphrey, *On the Edge of Greatness: The Diaries of John Humphrey, First Director of the United Nations Division of Human Rights*, vol. 1, 1948–9 (Montreal: McGill University Libraries, 1994), 170.

[106] Ibid., 174.

[107] *ToI*, "Supervision of Human Rights: India's Proposal in U.N. Rejected," May 15, 1950.

[108] Bhagavan, *Peacemakers*, 93.

[109] Burke, *Decolonization*, 66; Summary Record of Commission on Human Rights, 435th meeting, March 16, 1954, E/CN.4/SR.435/, 16.

[110] Summary Record of the Commission on Human Rights, 436th meeting, April 2, 1954, E/CN.4/SR.436, 8–9.

[111] "Draft International Covenants on Human Rights and Measures of Implementation. Draft Covenant on Civil and Political Rights. Chile, Egypt, India, Philippines and Uruguay: Revised Article on Right of Petition," March 16, 1954, E/CN.4/L.341/Rev.1; Summary Record of the Commission on Human Rights, 437th meeting, April 16, 1954, E/CN.4/SR.437.

than what most delegates were ready to accept because they modified the balance between the UN and member states on the question of domestic jurisdiction. However, beyond the fact that their ideas seemed too radical to create a consensus, they themselves watered down, abandoned, or withdrew several of their proposals over the course of the debates – even while maintaining an avant-garde discourse. Consequently, these ideas have been mostly forgotten. As the following section shows, one can also discern simultaneous strains of ambition and caution in India's attitude towards the principle of self-determination.

India's Ambivalence on Self-Determination

For Nehru, India, and its freedom, had been "the crux of the colonial question."[112] The right to self-determination was at the basis of its freedom and, as such, was both an essential element of India's nationalist struggle and part of a Nehruvian vision for a new world order. "[S]overeignty resides in the people of [dependent] territories concerned and ... they must ultimately decide their constitution and way of living, subject to the general principles of the United Nations." Nehru urged India's UN delegation to demand the principle of self-determination along these lines.[113] At the General Assembly of October 1946, Mrs. Pandit therefore presented the independence of colonial people as "the vital concern of freedom-loving peoples everywhere."[114] This approach made explicit India's active support for the independence of non-self-governing territories. In this respect, Indians could congratulate themselves for their "magnificent and prolific record of a sustained and spirited crusade against colonialism and racialism."[115] Yet, the case of South West Africa and India's stand on self-determination during the drafting of Covenants provide a more complicated view of India's relation to self-determination and its relation to state sovereignty in the early years of the UN.

The question of the status of South West Africa arose around the same time as the question of the treatment of Indians in South Africa. South West Africa had been a German colony since the nineteenth century when, in 1920, it fell under the administration of South Africa. The mandate system under the newly constructed League of Nations allowed the latter to become a mandatory power of a Class C territory, i.e., South

---

[112] "Policy on dependent territories," September 15, 1946, *SWJN*, 2nd series, vol. 1, 446.
[113] Ibid., 448.   [114] Pandit, UNGA, 37th plenary meeting, October 25, 1946.
[115] R. R. Parihar, "India's Crusade against Colonialism and Racialism: An Appraisal," *Indian Journal of Political Science* 25, no. 2 (1964): 65.

West Africa could be "administered under the laws of the Mandatory as integral portions of its territory."[116] Simultaneously, this system hindered Jan Smuts's vision of a "Greater South Africa" by preventing his country from annexing South West Africa.[117] In 1934, South Africa began to press for incorporating that former colony; it renewed its demands for annexation at the San Francisco Conference and at the final session of the Assembly of the League of Nations in April 1946. By that time, the UN Charter had replaced the mandate system by an international trusteeship system, which now operated over former mandated territories.[118] South Africa refused to bring South West Africa under this new system on the ground that the mandate had lapsed after the demise of the League. Following a contested referendum/consultation in May–June 1946, it reiterated its demand of incorporation in November.

The case of South West Africa represents a founding moment of India's commitment to the principle of self-determination at the UN. In September 1946, the Indian cabinet decided that India's delegation should oppose South Africa's claims, although without taking a "leading part" and by being "careful to state their argument … as dispassionately as possible."[119] It conceded, however, that "[i]f necessity arises, India can take a leading part."[120] Before the case was brought before the UN, the Government of India had noted that, from India's perspective, South West Africa was not significant due to the presence of Indian residents there (only fourteen nationals in 1936, unknown in 1946) but rather in relation to her "objection to South African Government's treatment of Asiatic (and African) populations."[121] For Nehru, opposition to South Africa's plans became a "point of principle."[122] More generally, he wrote to India's Foreign Secretary (K. P. S. Menon) that "[o]n principle we must oppose any such annexation of mandated or any other territory anywhere and ask for U.N.O. trusteeship, recognizing that sovereignty

---

[116] Article 22 of the League Covenant spelled out the terms of a mandate system organized around three tutelage configurations, depending on development-related, geographic, and economic criteria. Mandated territories were not annexed per se but brought under the administration of 'advanced nations' that had to guarantee 'a sacred trust of civilization.'

[117] Michael Crowder, "Tshekedi Khama, Smuts, and South West Africa," *Journal of Modern African Studies* 25, no. 1 (1987): 25.

[118] Chapters XI, XII, and XIII were the core basis of this new arrangement.

[119] "Meeting of the Cabinet," September 16, 1946, 6(12)-CC/46, NAI, 14.

[120] Extract, brief for the India Delegation to the UNGA, October 23, 1946, 6(12)-CC/46, NAI, 15.

[121] Secret Telegram, Governor General (EA Dept.) to Secretary of State for India, New Delhi, April 6, 1946, 6(12)-CC/46, NAI, 7.

[122] "An independent foreign policy," September 26, 1946, *SWJN*, 2nd series, vol. 1, 496–7.

ultimately resides in the people concerned and their wishes and interests are paramount."[123] The Indian delegation was instructed to urge that South Africa put South West Africa under trusteeship.

Thus, when Smuts explained to the Trusteeship Committee in November 1946 that South Africa was "legitimately concerned in securing [its] annexation" because of its "physical contiguity" and its "ethnological kinship" and stressed that a consultation had favored incorporation, the leader of the Indian delegation, Mrs. Pandit, reacted.[124] She interpreted his plea as a "strong but specious plea for annexation."[125] Maharaj Singh, another Indian representative, affirmed that the people of non-self-governing territories could be reassured that India understood their case and was in favor of "autonomous and independent governments installed as quickly as possible in every part of the world." Accordingly, sovereignty lay with the people and not with the authority that administered their territory. Transfering sovereignty to this authority would be a "breach of the principle" of non-annexation recognized by the Versailles Peace Conference.[126] Singh also declared that while India assented to the principle of trusteeship, its final object, i.e. the autonomy of trust territories, and opposition to racial discrimination, should be clearly stated.[127] Singh advocated that South West Africa be put immediately under the trusteeship system.[128] Finally, in a subcommittee of the UNGA, V. K. Krishna Menon introduced a draft resolution with a "stronger wording" than a US resolution.[129] His resolution asserted that the UN "could not entertain any proposal which would sanction annexation,"[130] in opposition to Smuts's claim that South Africa "had acted in the interest of the people and could not disregard the wishes expressed by the majority."[131] The Indian resolution was adopted. The following resolution adopted by the General Assembly on December 14, 1946 rejected accordingly South Africa's demand for the incorporation of South West Africa and

[123] "On South Africa's Proposal to annex South-West Africa," Note to Foreign Secretary, September 5, 1946, *SWJN*, 2nd series, vol. 1, 438.
[124] GAOR, 2nd part of the 1st session, 4th Committee, 14th meeting, November 4, 1946, 63.
[125] Secret Telegram, Leader of the Indian Delegation in New York to Foreign, New Delhi, November 6, 1946, 6(12)-CC/46, NAI, 15.
[126] GAOR, 2nd part of the 1st session, 4th Committee, 15th meeting, November 5, 1946, 69.
[127] Ibid., 70.
[128] GAOR, 2nd part of the 1st session, 4th Committee, 20th meeting, November 14, 1946, 111.
[129] GAOR, 2nd part of the 1st session, 4th Committee, 21st meeting, December 8, 1946, 122.
[130] Ibid.   [131] Ibid., 123.

recommended that the territory be placed under the trusteeship system.[132] In this case, self-determination was construed as "decolonisation through internationally accountable institutions" as opposed to a "merger between metropole and mandate."[133] This outcome was a victory for the views of India, whose intervention strenghtened the anticolonial ethos of the UN.[134]

Ironically, however, India's handling of the question of South West Africa revealed some ambiguities of its own anti-colonial identity. US UN delegate Philip Jessup highlighted this tension when stressing that "a large number of states, chiefly located in the Middle East and Asia . . . are the vocal and active champions of the dependent people," but that for some of them "their situation as they gain in power is somewhat akin to that of the colonial powers."[135] Jessup specifically cited India's position regarding the former princely state of Hyderabad. In 1947, the Government of India interpreted the principle of self-determination in the case of Hyderabad in quite a different way – contradictory to the position it took on South West Africa. Under British rule, Hyderabad, one of the two largest princely states in India, had enjoyed sovereignty as a "minor state," i.e. subordinate to the empire but sovereign.[136] In June 1947, the ruler of Hyderabad (the Nizam) therefore announced that his state would not accede to either India or Pakistan for the time being and strived to defend the idea of Hyderabad's independence. While the Nizam mainly argued on legal grounds, the Government of India refused the idea of a popular plebiscite to decide on the question of the state's accession to India. Instead, Hyderabad was integrated by force into the Indian Union in 1948.[137] India's actions regarding Hyderabad turned out to be striking in their similarity to South Africa's. If "the title to South West Africa [rested] on the right of military victory" and the government of the Union "made policy as though South Africa was sovereign there,"[138] India's

---

[132] Resolution 65(I) on the "Future Status of South West Africa."

[133] Richard Dale, "The Political Futures of South West Africa and Namibia," *World Affairs* 134, no. 4 (1972): 328.

[134] Although South West Africa was further incorporated by South Africa in the 1950s.

[135] Secret Memorandum, Philip Jessup to George Perkins, Washington, April 30, 1952, *Foreign Relations of the United States* (*FRUS*), Foreign relations, 1952–4, vol. III, 1108–9.

[136] Eric Beverley, *Hyderabad, British India, and the World: Muslim Networks and Minor Sovereignty, c.1850–1950* (Cambridge, UK: Cambridge University Press, 2015).

[137] On the negotiations leading to the integration of Hyderabad by police action, see Lucien Benichou, *From Autocracy to Integration: Political Developments in Hyderabad State (1938–1948)* (London: Sangam Books, 2000); Clyde Eagleton, "The Case of Hyderabad before the Security Council," *American Journal of International Law* 44, no. 2 (1950): 277–302.

[138] Dale, "Political Futures of South West Africa," 325–43 and 327.

actions in Hyderabad were analogous. Both states used arguments of contiguity and kinship against a principle of self-determination. That India used double standards or inconsistencies is not remarkable in itself. Of interest here is that, with the case of South West Africa, the Indian delegation condemned the same tactics that the Government of India used in Hyderabad.

During the *travaux préparatoires* of the ICCPR, India's relation to the principle of self-determination was further complicated, since it actively sought to circumscribe the scope of this principle. First, in 1952, Indian delegates proposed to clarify in Article 1 that the notion of "people" who possessed a right to self-determination should be understood as "large compact groups." Moreover, self-determination would ensue from "a conscious demand on the part of a large section of people who are under the sovereignty of an alien rule" and "their demand shall be granted by the power concerned and the transfer of power shall be made within the period agreed upon by the parties concerned."[139] These proposals were not voted upon and, finally, no definition of "the people" was agreed. However, these suggestions indicate that India hoped to define "people" and a right to self-determination as narrowly as possible, uncomfortable with the potential of claims of secession it could trigger within its own borders. Indeed, India was among the states which asserted that there was no right of secession.[140] The Indian government, via its delegates, came out in favor of a strengthened state sovereignty against the principle of self-determination.[141]

These instances, while not exhaustive of the record, show that India was both at the forefront of a discourse on human rights and self-determination at the UN, and cautious on both accounts. It might not seem surprising that India, as a state in the making, supported state sovereignty. Newly decolonized Third World states tended to clearly oppose a right of self-determination to subnational claimants, who could

---

[139] India, Commission on Human Rights, 8th session (1952), in Marc J. Bossuyt, *Guide to the "Travaux Préparatoires" of the International Covenant on Civil and Political Rights* (Dordrecht: Martinus Nijhoff, 1987), 32.

[140] Secession can be seen as the negative expression of a right to self-determination, "understood as the illegitimate dismemberment of a state entity, above all in countries that have a clearly anti-secessionist tradition." In Jörg Fisch, *The Right of Self-Determination of Peoples: The Domestication of an Illusion* (New York: Cambridge University Press, 2015), 272.

[141] As Quane noted, "the blanket denial of a right to secession suggests that groups within States or colonial territories cannot be regarded as peoples for the purposes of Article 1." Helen Quane, "The United Nations and the Evolving Right to Self-Determination," *International and Comparative Law Quarterly* 47, no. 3 (1998): 559–60.

fragment and destabilize them.[142] Yet, what is striking about India is the amplitude of its views on sovereignty at each end of the spectrum. Initially, Indian delegates pushed for a strong UN role on human rights and therefore a reinterpretation of state sovereignty, and rose to defend an anti-colonial position in the case of South West Africa. At the same time, India also proved restrained on human rights, more defensive than other states on a right to self-determination, and sometimes stricter in its interpretation of the UN Charter.

Conclusion

This chapter has examined how India's attitude in the initial years of the UN can lead us to reassess the historical relation between the concept of human rights and the process of decolonization. India's early use of the notion of human rights at the UN illustrates the country's efforts and difficulties with moving from an imperial to a postcolonial state and system in the 1940s and 1950s. Introducing the concept of human rights in its case against South Africa at the UN in 1946 enabled independent India to make its postcolonial transition and become a new kind of international actor. More broadly, by undermining the principle of domestic jurisdiction through its use of a human rights language, India pursued a change in the international normative order as part of the development of a wider anti-colonial discourse. Subsequently, Indian delegates kept promoting a radical interpretation of how the UN altered the domain of domestic jurisdiction for member states. From 1947 to 1948, at the Human Rights Commission where an international bill of rights was to be prepared, India's delegate defended a strong human rights regime. For India, which supported the UDHR adopted on December 10, 1948, human rights were integrated to its long-standing fight against an imperial global order – unlike, for instance, the People's Republic of China.

However, there was another reason for India's ambitious plans for human rights at the UN: through a nascent international framework, the newly independent country attempted to solve a specific colonial issue inherited from the functioning of the British Empire. In a system of states, the Indian state could no longer claim to protect directly the rights of the Indian diaspora that was not on its soil and, furthermore, had not yet another citizenship (the basis of rights in a state) except, ironically, in South Africa. In a sense, then, international law was

---

[142] The General Assembly championed this view through the 1960 Declaration on the Granting of Independence to Colonial Countries and Peoples.

supposed to replace intra-empire negotiations with the dominions. Human rights were a potential non-Westphalian tool to preserve, to a certain extent, a non-territorial and diasporic understanding of India.

India proved at once ambitious and cautious with the promotion of human rights at the UN. It pushed to protect individuals against the state as well as to have state sovereignty recognized. In that sense, as for other Third World newly decolonized states at the UN, the terminology "human rights" was not just a pretext to promote self-determination, as these states did not see a contradiction between human rights and the respect for state sovereignty as well as state-building.[143] However, India had its own complex trajectory vis-à-vis human rights and self-determination and, therefore, vis-à-vis the norm of sovereignty and decolonization more generally. Its trajectory does not conform to the general narrative of Third World states' passage from embracing human rights to dismissing them in favor of an intransigent view on state sovereignty two decades later. India rather proved variously flexible and inflexible about aspects of sovereignty from the early days of the UN. This observation enables a reassessment of its place in the historiography of human rights.

India's case illustrates the need to have a more granular approach to the history of human rights, one that considers the domestic and external factors that explain a newly decolonized country's attitude towards human rights and the principle of domestic jurisdiction. India's approach to human rights and the principle of self-determination points to the complex interplay of domestic concerns and international ambitions in 1946–1947. India was negotiating international norms and constructing itself as an international actor while still emerging as a state and dealing with issues created by imperial politics. It sought an ambitious role in shaping a new global order while facing more immediate problems with its diaspora and undertaking an extraordinarily complex project of building a unified national space out of a diverse and fractured polity. India found itself at the crossroads of the creation of a nation-state, the end of the British empire, and its desire for normative leadership and a post-imperial order. Its attitude in the early years of the UN was shaped by this period of political transformations and tensions.

One such tension appears in its relation to two kinds of minorities. The postcolonial government defined its ambivalent relation to sovereignty partly through its awareness of, and distinction between, its minority diaspora and a potentially secessionist internal minority. On the one

---

[143] Burke, *Decolonization*. Burke makes this argument with regard to the Third World in general rather than India in particular.

hand, the situation of the Indian diaspora, scattered throughout the British empire, was one of the critical motivating factors for India's promotion of a human rights regime at the UN. A right for individual petitions was meant to help Indians fight against the denial of their human rights in South Africa. On the other hand, the risk of secession by a princely state or minorities within India seems to have pushed the government to try to limit the scope of the principle of self-determination. Thus, India reacted differently to external and internal claims to self-determination. Such paradoxes reflect both the ambitions and constraints with which India emerged and developed as an independent state. They refer to India's dual postcolonial task during debates at the UN – as a former colony tackling issues created during colonial times by the functioning of the British Empire and as a new actor striving to transform international relations.

More broadly, the Indian story raises critical questions about the meaning of sovereignty during decolonization and the political dynamics at the UN. It suggests a more nuanced understanding of sovereignty during the process of decolonization and of decolonization as a quest for sovereignty, illustrating how independent India's emergence as a normative actor was mediated through a challenge to the principle of domestic jurisdiction. While decolonization was a demand for sovereignty, it was not simply a demand for its Westphalian version. Attaining sovereignty required far more than being legally recognized as a state. Rather, sovereignty also required a change in the normative structure of the international system so that the newly decolonized states could be viewed, not just in law, as equal actors. Sovereignty was therefore embodied in the capacity to initiate this international normative change, one in which the principle of human rights was instrumental. Such acknowledgment compels a reconsideration of historical narratives that assume a simple binary opposition between promoting state sovereignty and human rights.

9 "From This Era of Passionate Self-Discovery": Norman Manley, Human Rights, and the End of Colonial Rule in Jamaica

Steven L. B. Jensen

Introduction

The Caribbean region is not unknown to human rights historiography. The Haitian slave revolution led by Toussaint L'Ouverture in the 1790s has been featured occasionally and rightly belongs among the three Atlantic revolutions of the era – the American, the French, and the Haitian – with the latter more firmly making anti-slavery, anti-racism, and anti-colonialism a significant companion to this story.[1] In the context of twentieth-century human rights, the Caribbean has been consigned to the periphery in this as well as other transnational histories until recently. The realities of the global economy and the distribution of political power and influence have helped determine this fate. For all that, Jamaica emerged as a global leader in international human rights diplomacy after the island's independence in 1962, with its government immediately moving to energize the international human rights project.[2] By 1964, the country was recognized at the United Nations as a leader in the

---

[1] Laurent Dubois, *Avengers of the New World: The Story of the Haitian Revolution* (Cambridge, MA: Harvard University Press, 2004). See also Laurent Dubois, "Why Haiti Should Be at the Center of the Age of Revolutions," *Aeon Magazine* (2016), https://aeon.co/essays/why-haiti-should-be-at-the-centre-of-the-age-of-revolution

[2] Steven L. B. Jensen, *The Making of International Human Rights: The 1960s, Decolonization and the Reconstruction of Global Values* (Cambridge, UK: Cambridge University Press, 2016). This chapter expands on my book but is based on new archival research conducted at the National Archives of Jamaica in Spanish Town, the National Library of Jamaica and the Library of the University of the West Indies (MONA Campus) in Kingston, the British National Archives in Kew, and the Bodleian Library, University of Oxford. I would like to thank former Cabinet Secretary and Head of the Jamaican Civil Service the Hon. Carlton E. Davis for providing me with valuable insights into the background history of Jamaica's Central Planning Unit and Michelle Neita for invaluable assistance during my research visits to Jamaica. Senior Lecturer in Law Tracy Robinson and Professor of History Matthew Smith both from the University of West Indies gave particular valuable advice and suggestions in connection with a seminar organized at UWI on a draft version of this chapter in November 2017. I would also like to give special thanks to Heidi Betts for her extensive and insightful comments on several draft versions of this chapter.

field – a role it maintained until the end of the decade.[3] The same year, Jamaica launched its first foreign policy strategy – most likely the first such strategy to integrate human rights as a key priority herein.

This role and dedicated emphasis, which by the end of 1968 had achieved a string of noteworthy results, did not emerge out of nowhere. It may appear obvious to look at international developments – such as apartheid in South Africa or racial discrimination more broadly – to explain Jamaica's focus on human rights. This however is too narrow a lens to provide a comprehensive understanding of what guided their efforts. What was thought to be one of many countries on the periphery of human rights appears, in fact, to be at its center. So what happens when the periphery proves to be the center?

This chapter explores the domestic political history behind the ambitious legal and political agenda that Jamaica laid out at the United Nations during the 1960s.[4] Its focus is mainly on the final years of colonialism in Jamaica from 1955 to 1962 and on the leading politician Norman Manley, his vision and the intellectual networks he nurtured. The following account traces how domestic political developments during this period shaped Jamaica's international human rights diplomacy immediately after independence, exploring the policy space between colonialism and independence that gradual self-governing entailed. Jamaican public policymaking at this time must be situated in the history of Jamaican constitutionalism, development planning and the tradition of domestic social and economic research that emerged in Jamaica from the 1950s and associated with the renowned Caribbean economist Arthur W. Lewis. A policy synthesis emerged in 1960–1961 as a result of a convergence of three different policy strands characterizing Jamaican decolonization, namely development planning, human rights, and nation-building. The chapter is structured to illustrate this convergence. Though the story concludes with the human rights policy synthesis at the twilight of empire in Jamaica, the language of human rights is not always the main protagonist but instead appears as a supporting act – or a component part of a larger historical process.

In January 1961, the Manley government announced that human rights should become guiding principles in the country's national development planning. The intention was to produce "a Ministry Paper containing a declaration of Government policy in respect of Human Rights" and place it before the Jamaican parliament for debate and adoption. In the preceding months, human rights had been a topic in

---

[3] Ibid., 85–7.   [4] Ibid.

cabinet discussions and had featured in a review of "Government Policies for Long Term Development."[5] The policy represented both a vision for Jamaican statehood and a form of economic crisis management, illustrating how an emphasis on human rights was nurtured with increasing depth by domestic political actors in response to local political realities. In tracing the mid-twentieth-century Caribbean roots of what would become a prominent feature of global politics, I argue that the emergence of international human rights was more closely entangled with nation- and state-building processes, with national development planning and debates over inequality and the standard of living than previously understood. The end of empire in the Caribbean was to have a formative influence on universal human rights.

The significant challenge in assessing decolonization in Jamaica and the wider Caribbean has been accurately captured by Spencer Mawby:

> At the end of empire, democratically elected politicians were expected to rectify problems which had been left wholly unaddressed by generations of imperial policymakers; they took on the remedial task of diversifying economic activity and achieving a measure of social progress in an international environment over which they had almost no influence. Any attempt to tell the story of the transition to political independence in the Anglophone Caribbean which does not take account of these factors is incomplete.[6]

Mawby's critique of the historiography is that it is biased in that, to a considerable extent, it blames the shortcomings of effective self-government on the politicians in the region while downplaying or even ignoring the responsibility of the British colonial government in producing political failures. Mawby has emphasized the colonial power's stalling tactics, condescension, failure to commit to solutions, and unwillingness to fully put political and economic weight behind the West Indies Federation – as undermining the support and legitimacy of the Federation itself.

Three temporal dimensions have defined the historiography of decolonization in Jamaica – one that is often interwoven with the wider British Caribbean. However, viewing it through Mawby's lens should inspire us to take a fresh look at the historical record.

The first temporal dimension bridges the full decolonization story from the 1930s to the 1960s. It could be labeled, "The Making of

---

[5] "Cabinet Submission: Declaration on Human Rights," Note by N. W. Manley, Premier, January 6, 1961, Box 1B/31/27, Norman Manley Papers, National Archives of Jamaica, Spanish Town.

[6] See Spencer Mawby, *Ordering Independence: The End of Empire in the British Caribbean, 1947–1969* (Basingstoke, UK: Palgrave Macmillan, 2012).

Modern Jamaica/the Modern West Indies." Labor protests across the islands in the late 1930s changed the political dynamics in the region and started the long process toward independence which came in the 1960s. This timeframe is well acknowledged in the historiography.[7] The interests of Great Britain as the colonial ruler and the United States as the new superpower added a larger geopolitical context for Caribbean politics during this period.

The second temporal dimension operates with a shorter timeframe and focuses on the ill-fated West Indies Federation that existed from 1958 to 1962. Federation was for a long period seen as the viable option for independence despite constant tensions between the political entities. These tensions would decide the fate of the West Indies Federation. The process, however, provides the explanatory framework for the final outcome of decolonization in the region. The Federation is well studied but remains so central that it still stimulates new insightful works.[8]

The third temporal dimension focuses on Jamaica's independence in 1962. This covers the short, intense political process from the autumn of 1961 until August 1962 when independence was finally achieved. The drafting of the independence constitution was a vital part of this process. Jamaica decided to include a "Bill of Rights" in the independence constitution after a significant debate on human rights.[9]

---

[7] The classical work is Gordon K. Lewis, *The Growth of the Modern West Indies* (London: MacGibbon & Kee, 1968). See also Jessie Harris Proctor, Jr., "British West Indian Society and Government in Transition 1920–1960," in *The Aftermath of Sovereignty: West Indian Perspectives*, ed. David Lowenthal and Lambros Comitas (Garden City, NY: Anchor Books, 1973), 31–65. See also Jason Parker, *Brother's Keeper. The United States, Race and Empire in the British Caribbean, 1937–1962* (Oxford: Oxford University Press, 2008). Recent contributions focusing specifically on Jamaica include Colin A. Palmer, *Freedom's Children: The 1938 Labor Rebellion and the Birth of Modern Jamaica* (Chapel Hill: University of North Carolina Press, 2014); Birte Timm, *Nationalists Abroad: The Jamaica Progressive League and the Foundations of Jamaican Independence* (Kingston: Ian Randle, 2016). The novelty of Timm's book is the centrality of the diaspora element which provides a revision to the traditional focus on actors representing the two-party political system that emerged in Jamaica after 1938.

[8] See Mawby, *Ordering Independence*; Eric D. Duke, *Building a Nation: Caribbean Federation in the Black Diaspora* (Gainesville, FA: University of Florida Press, 2015); Adom Getachew, *Worldmaking after Empire: The Rise and Fall of Self-Determination* (Princeton, NJ: Princeton University Press, 2019).

[9] Classical works are James B. Kelly, "The Jamaican Independence Constitution of 1962," *Caribbean Studies* 3, no. 1 (1963): 18–83; Trevor Munroe, *The Politics of Constitutional Decolonization: Jamaica 1944–62* (Kingston: Institute of Economic and Social Research, University of West Indies, 1972); Lloyd G. Barnett, *The Constitutional Law of Jamaica* (Oxford: Oxford University Press, 1977). For more recent studies, see Simeon McIntosh, *Caribbean Constitutional Reform: Rethinking the West Indian Polity* (Kingston: Ian Randle, 2002); Tracy Robinson, "Gender, Nation and the Common Law Constitution," *Oxford Journal of Legal Studies* 28, no. 4 (2008): 735–62.

Norman Manley and the Birth of Modern Jamaica: 1938

In 1963, the Jamaican government launched its *Five Year Independence Plan 1963–1968*. In the introduction, Edward Seaga, the recently appointed Minister for Development and Welfare, reflected on the country's journey since 1938 toward its newfound independence:

An urgent need for new definitions seemed to seize Jamaicans of every sort after 1938. In every aspect of life, from social relationships to artistic expression, new voyages of discovery were made. It was as if Jamaica realized, for the first time, that it did not know its own face nor the sound of its own voice. From *this era of passionate self-discovery* the Jamaica of today has emerged.[10]

Decolonization in Jamaica had been a process of becoming, a process of assertion and of facing "a profound cultural crisis"[11] related to both the development of a national political identity and the prospects of ensuring functioning governance. Jamaica had faced these questions with increasing intensity over a period of twenty-five years. On the cusp of independence, this was the self-image that was articulated:

Present-day Jamaica is a microcosm of the world, mixing many of its peoples, having many of its problems, some of its misfortunes, and endeavoring to answer the question that must concern every country today, large or small, namely, can a small country achieve and maintain at once, parliamentary democracy, economic viability and social justice.[12]

This was not merely political rhetoric, but a reflection of deeper ingrained experiences linked to ending colonialism in Jamaica – experiences in which human rights played an interesting role.

What was set in motion following widespread labor riots in 1938 was a process of nation- and state-building. The historical trajectories were never that straightforward, however, despite what often appears to be the evolutionary nature of the transition toward greater self-rule, constitutional reform, and eventual independence. Understanding what shaped the road to 1962 requires understanding both the political visions and the specific political priorities advocated by the main Jamaican actors.

In domestic political discourse, 1938 became a constant reference as *the* turning point for the ensuing developments and subject of continued contestations over who best represented its meaning and its legacies.

---

[10] *Five-Year Independence Plan 1963–1968: A Long Term Development Programme for Jamaica* (Kingston, July 1963), 4 (emphasis added). The national development plan launched in 1963 was presented by the JLP government but in reality it was a plan developed by the Manley government while still in office.

[11] Ibid., 4.   [12] Ibid., 6.

A century after emancipation, with poverty, squalor, and the remnants of a plantation economy still too dominant, something needed to change. Out of the 1938 labor riots, where fourteen people were killed and many more injured, two political parties emerged both with strong trade union and social movement affiliations. Norman Manley's People's National Party (PNP) would compete for political influence with the Jamaican Labour Party led by Alexander Bustamente.

While the Jamaican Labour Party would perform well and win the first national elections after their introduction in 1944, there can be little doubt that the most influential person in this story is Norman Manley. A lawyer by profession and a World War I veteran, he emerged in 1938 as an important voice in the national movement, defending the rights of protesters and issuing refined critiques of the failures of the British colonial administration.[13] He would be at the vanguard of political developments for the next three decades due to his vision for Jamaican society, its governance and its engagement with the wider world, as well as because of his remarkable ability to snatch principled victories – enhancing the democratic functioning of Jamaican politics – from the jaws of his own and his party's political defeats. Known as "the Man with the Plan," Manley led Jamaica during the years that saw the end of empire from 1955 to 1962, a period in which he ensured vital constitutional and institutional reforms and in which his emphasis on advancing societal planning and a strong legislative record laid the groundwork for post-independence Jamaica.

The 1938 riots led to calls for widespread political change. In their immediate aftermath, Manley was a key player in the creation of the PNP that called for full adult suffrage and self-government. This was an ambitious agenda compared to the usual staleness of Jamaican politics and the conservatism of British colonial rule. Manley advocated discreetly for it in a series of confidential conversations with the British governor of Jamaica. He focused on the need for constitutional reform because the existing constitution ensured that "no training for future Self-Government is possible," and he called for a "positive policy for the advancement of a people as distinct from the casual administration that has no bigger aim than preserving the fictitious equilibrium of the status quo."[14] The analysis was echoed by Governor Arthur Richards who provided his own even harsher analysis of the situation. The Governor

---

[13] Arnold Bertram, *N. W. Manley and the Making of Modern Jamaica* (Kingston: Arawak Publications, 2016), 149–62.
[14] "Memorandum on Constitutional Change for Jamaica," N. W. Manley, February 8, 1939. British National Archives, CO 137/834/7.

wrote that "there is no administrative service" and that "the administration of Jamaica is, and always had been, a sham."[15] Self-reflection or even self-criticism appeared to have little currency in the Colonial Office in London so the finger was never pointed at the British colonial administration itself when it came to assigning responsibility for the dire situation. The Colonial Office was more focused on identifying political risks and this may have spurred an initial willingness to consider Manley's proposals for reform as they did resonate with those of Governor Richards.

Norman Manley had emerged as the "ablest" and most insightful conversation partner when it came to the constitutional reforms needed in Jamaica but hopes for a constructive relationship soon turned sour as Governor Richards began to arrest critics of the regime.[16] World War II could have stalled developments but political change had been set in motion, local political actors were positioning themselves and by the early 1940s what would become the future party system had begun to emerge. The demands for reform had not disappeared. The debates over constitutional reform would turn increasingly bitter and the negative approach of the governor and the Colonial Office back in the UK was indisputably a contributing factor.

The debates on a new constitution involved a range of issues connected to the project of increased self-government in Jamaica. The debates brought forward an issue that Norman Manley and his party had been promoting with increasing conviction, namely the introduction of universal suffrage in forthcoming elections once the new constitution was in place. This proposal prevailed in the Jamaican constitution that was pronounced in November 1944. With the December 1944 elections, Jamaica became only the third member of the British Commonwealth – after New Zealand and the United Kingdom – to introduce universal adult suffrage that included women's right to vote. This was a marked change from the old model where voting rights for the small Legislative Council had only been granted to men with a certain level of property and wealth. The number of eligible voters increased by 1,000 percent with the introduction of universal adult suffrage in 1944.[17] Norman Manley had by no means been the only political actor pushing for these changes but he was the most prominent and influential advocate who

---

[15] Memo from Governor Arthur Richards, Kingston to Malcolm MacDonald, Secretary of State for the Colonies, London, April 22, 1939, 3. British National Archives, CO 137/834/7.

[16] Palmer, *Freedom's Children*, 281.

[17] Tracy Robinson, Arif Bulkan, and Adrian Saunders, *Fundamentals of Caribbean Constitutional Law* (London: Sweet & Maxwell, 2015), 32.

emerged from the process – a reality that was apparent when the crowds cheered him on the occasion of the public announcement of the constitution in Kingston on November 20, 1944.

From 1938 to 1944, the decisive role of the PNP in brokering these political changes in Jamaica did not bring them a majority in the House of Representatives. The Jamaican Labour Party led by Alexander Bustamente was able to directly mobilize a large part of the electorate through their very strong trade union affiliation. The PNP served as the opposition from 1944 to 1955, a period when there was only a slow movement toward more self-government. Its various political programs were informed by human rights thinking such as their Plan for Progress from 1949 that declared as the party's political goal "to afford to every man, women and child in Jamaica the human dignity, the rights of freedom, knowledge and opportunity which should repose in every human being."[18] The inspiration for this could have had several sources. There was the Universal Declaration on Human Rights adopted at the UN in 1948 but equally likely is the fact that Norman Manley and key PNP persons were part of a transnational political debate that from the 1940s included human rights. There had been suggestions in 1946 and 1948 as part of the West Indies Conference of the Caribbean Commission to develop a "Bill of Human Rights and Obligations" for the Caribbean. This could have influenced the PNP program. During these years Norman Manley played a significant role as the leader of the opposition and as a political thinker, planner, and practical hands-on politician he would wield significant political influence.[19] The PNP, however, could not fully realize the potential of their more carefully considered and planned approach to the project of self-government until they obtained full political power. By the time they achieved this theirs would soon become a project of ending empire in Jamaica.

The PNP Government and Democratic Planning as "Self-Discovery": 1955–1960

The PNP led by Norman Manley were finally able to form a government after the parliamentary elections of January 1955. The party had been preparing for this moment for many years and came to power with a

[18] Peoples National Party: Plan for Progress, 1949, National Library of Jamaica, Richard Hart Collection, MST 126a–b, Pamphlets Jamaica, vol. 2, 1945–9.
[19] For an insightful elaboration on this, see Stuart Hall, "Norman Manley Memorial Lecture 1984," *Norman Manley Memorial Lectures 1984 & 1986* (London: Norman Manley Memorial Lecture Committee, 1986), 7–20.

strong political platform which also included references to human rights.[20] The PNP embarked on an ambitious agenda aimed at modernizing the economy, combining a broad range of industrial and social reform policies, institution building as well as ambitious arts and culture policies producing a remarkable legislative record in the process. The core of the modernization project was a new and more ambitious approach to the whole question of societal planning. Manley identified poor planning as the cause of the poor performance of the previous Jamaica Labour Party (JLP) administration. Two days after his election victory in a national broadcast he announced the creation of a Central Planning Unit.[21] By April 1955, the Unit was established and became vital to the work of the government. The Unit became a separate entity situated between Manley's office and the Ministry of Finance and represented a revolution in the development of government planning capacity in Jamaica.[22]

Two important developments came about as a result of the Central Planning Unit. The first related to the intellectual, scholarly, and political networks that provided a fertile community of discussion partners that in various ways could support the aims of the Unit and the journey of "self-discovery" that Jamaica had embarked upon. The creation of the Jamaica-based Caribbean scholarly journal *Social and Economic Studies* in 1953 was one significant illustration of the "domestication" of quality social science expertise from the 1950s. The Central Planning Unit brought new forms of expertise into play and further professionalized what public administration entailed. The second feature was a convergence of policy thinking and approaches that were applied in an innovative and experimental manner and made this small island in the Caribbean an intellectual force in development practice worldwide.[23]

---

[20] See Peoples National Party: Plan for Progress, 1954, National Library of Jamaica, Richard Hart Collection, MST 126a–b, Pamphlets Jamaica, vol. 3, 1950–6.

[21] Bertram, *Manley and the Making of Modern Jamaica*, 252. Norman Manley was also Minister for Development. From 1957 his main title was that of Premier Minister.

[22] As late as the 1940s, literature researching or investigating economic questions was dominated by official reports prepared for or by the UK government. See Adlith Brown and Havelock Brewster, "A Review of the Study of Economics in the English-Speaking Caribbean," *Social and Economic Studies* 23, no. 1 (1974): 48.

[23] This fertile environment would lead to international recognition for a number of the persons involved. The Head of the Central Planning Unit was G. Arthur Brown who became UNDP Deputy Administrator in the 1970s. The Permanent Secretary of the Ministry of Finance Egerton Richardson who was closely involved with the Central Planning Unit became Jamaica's UN ambassador in 1962 and was the mastermind behind Jamaica's remarkable human rights diplomacy. Arthur W. Lewis, Vice-Chancellor of the University of West Indies (1958–62), won the Nobel Prize in

It was out of this convergence of policy thinking that the government's 1961 human rights policy grew.

However, with large-scale unemployment and an ever-expanding population base, the economic situation was challenging. There was private sector-led growth in the 1950s mainly because of bauxite mining that became an important source of export earnings. Demographic trends showed that large youth generations would continue to rapidly expand the population size, but it was clear that the economy could not absorb new generations into the workforce as employment was in severe shortage. With the lack of land reform to expand access to farming combined with high levels of unemployment, the workforce migration out of Jamaica to the UK, Canada, and the United States became a desperately needed lever to alleviate the situation. The task was how to manage an impoverished, underdeveloped country with the colonial legacies still ever present.

The PNP government framed a significant part of its response to this dilemma by trying to link an advanced philosophy of societal planning with a practical adaptation of the theoretical lessons from the emerging field of development economics – the latter represented especially by the Caribbean economist Arthur W. Lewis. It was this response that was nested in the Central Planning Unit. Norman Manley wanted the most advanced expertise to inform the functioning of the Unit. He traveled to New York to meet with UN experts to identify an international adviser on planning. The person identified was George Cadbury who had strong experience from British wartime planning before he joined the UN in the 1950s. Cadbury and Manley became close during the former's period in Jamaica which lasted from 1955 to 1959.

The Soviet Union was at this point seen by many – especially in the developing world – as being the vanguard of state planning and an example to follow. However, Manley and Cadbury represented a distinct anti-Soviet philosophy of democratic planning. They found Soviet planning too mechanical, too dogmatic, and lacking the reflective qualities that a more dialogue-oriented approach offered. Their anti-Soviet philosophy was coherent with a refined anti-colonial philosophy of enhancing scientific planning and this defined their government's approach. During his time as adviser to the Central Planning Unit,

Economics in 1979. Another Jamaica-based university academic, and occasional adviser to the Manley government from 1960, the development economist Alister MacIntyre became a senior director at UNCTAD – the UN Conference on Trade and Development in the 1970s. Interview with Sir Alister McIntyre, Kingston, Jamaica, June 27, 2013.

George Cadbury elaborated on the planning philosophy and practice that was being applied in Jamaica. In a paper prepared for a conference of the Inter-American Society of Planners in Lima, Peru in November 1958 he laid out the following vision:

There is, I believe, a need to recognize that no one approach to planning whether by an economist, a sociologist, an architect, a doctor or an educationist is enough; they must all rely on one another. Each of them will probably find themselves in competition for the limited revenues of a government so that they must in the end conform to some wider discipline. It is this concept of planning on as wide a basis as the physical and the political jurisdiction of the government concerned, and as sensitive to democratic demands by recognizing the politician as an essential fellow craftsman, that is emerging under the title of comprehensive planning.[24]

This was a remarkably precise articulation of the planning vision that informed Manley's government. It represented a broad-ranging approach to societal planning well beyond the traditional focus on physical planning that was mainly concerned with infrastructure. It also suggested a unique role for the responsible politician to tie different forms of expertise into a larger whole in decision-making processes. In the colonial setting of late-1950s Jamaica, the elected politician was assigned an important role in bringing democratic accountability and scientific endeavor together. It made a subtle but clear argument; namely that government could not rule from London but needed a solid foundation and authority based in Jamaica itself. The implication was that colonial rule was an archaic and outdated form of governance. The thinking was rather eloquent in the way it positioned itself both in the context of the East–West Cold War dynamics and North–South colonial dynamics. It also illustrated how planning was a nation- and state-building project in itself.

The second part of the PNP response was the engagement with the newest thinking in the field of economics relevant to poor and under-developed settings. In 1954, the St. Lucian-born economist Arthur W. Lewis published an article still regarded as a seminal piece in the

---

[24] "Comprehensive Democratic Planning in Practice," Draft Paper by George Cadbury sent to Norman Manley September 23, 1958, Box 4/60/2A/24, Norman Manley Papers, National Archives of Jamaica, Spanish Town. Cadbury's job title in Jamaica was UN Economic and Social Advisor. The draft paper was later published in a revised version, see George Cadbury, "How to Plan in a Democracy," Democratic Planning – a Symposium. Ontario Woodsworth Memorial Foundation, Toronto, 1962, 3, 4–5. For more on the planning debate in the West Indies context, see Rudolph Knight, "Progress and Democracy – A Concept of Modern Planning," West Indian Economist 2, no. 1 (July 1959): 26–8.

founding of development economics.[25] The article entitled "Economic Development with Unlimited Supply of Labour" presented a two-sector model – focusing on the agricultural and industrial sectors in the under-developed world – and argued that the unlimited supply of laborers in the traditional agricultural sector would be absorbed in the urban industrial sector as this sector expanded. The theory was highly influential in development thinking during the 1950s and the 1960s and was part of the reason that Lewis was awarded the Nobel Prize in Economics in 1979.[26] Lewis's influence on the Central Planning Unit as well as the wider political debate in Jamaica in the late 1950s was due both to his intellectual influence and his physical presence in Jamaica as he served as Principal for the University of the West Indies from 1958 to 1962 and on the board of the influential magazine the *West Indian Economist*.

In the debates on national development planning in Jamaica the relationship between agriculture and industry was a central topic but the transfer model that Lewis had outlined was not straightforward as large parts of both sectors were inefficient and the necessary investment capital was in too short a supply.[27] The 1957 National Development Plan for Jamaica, prepared by the Central Planning Unit and launched by the Manley government, identified education as a major priority to help ensure social and economic development and to serve as an inter-mediary between agriculture and industrialization to secure growth. This policy innovation was an interesting and strategic adaptation of Lewis's model that also challenged its basic premise.[28] The Manley government's version of the two-sector model consisted then of agri-culture and education. Agriculture and education were Jamaica's two main national development priorities in the national development plan launched in 1957.

The government had realized that it could not force industrialization in a way that would solve the many economic challenges that Jamaica faced. Improvement in the educational level across the island was regarded as a prerequisite for development and for eventually achieving a diversifica-tion of the economy. The 1957 National Development Plan also applied rights language as it talked about ending discrimination in access to education, that the educational opportunities "provided by Government

---

[25] Hamid Hosseini, "Arthur Lewis' Dualism, the Literature of Development Economics, and the Less Developed Economies," *Review of European Studies* 4, no. 4 (2012): 132.

[26] For a recent study illustrating this political significance, see Getachew, *Worldmaking after Empire*, 146.

[27] For a perspective on Jamaica's agricultural sector, see editorial, "Is Jamaica the Model?," *West Indian Economist* 1, no. 5 (November 1958), 7–10.

[28] *A National Plan for Jamaica, 1957–1967.*

should be open and available to allow a basis of genuine equality" and in a section on health for the rural population it was stated that the government would aspire to ensure that Jamaicans would have "equal opportunity to enjoy good health regardless of where he or she lives."[29]

The creative application of a philosophy and practice of planning, the remarkable intellectual work that went into a much more refined national development plan than had ever existed before in Jamaica[30] and the short distance from plan to legislative program served as an excellent base for taking the project of self-government forward but it was not sufficient to overcome the realities of social and economic distress in Jamaica. This became a widely debated topic in the newspapers as well as influential magazines such as *Public Opinion*. It also featured prominently in another media outlet – the monthly magazine the *West Indian Economist*, a Caribbean affiliate to the London-based *The Economist*. From 1958 onwards the *West Indian Economist* served as a seismograph for some of the most important social and economic debates in the Caribbean. In particular, its discussion of the rule of law and social conditions in the region reflected in a series of editorials throughout 1960 seem to have influenced the Jamaican cabinet to initiate the debate on a human rights policy in the late autumn of 1960 which in turn led to the PNP government's human rights policy announcement in January 1961.

The starting point for the magazine's discussion was an observation that the West Indies had never operated as a society governed by the rule of law.[31] This reflected a colonial legacy but now in its retreat the editors asked: what did people want in its stead?[32] The point argued was that the economic advancement the region had witnessed especially since the mid-1950s was insufficient to build viable and independent societies. The question the editors felt needed to be asked was: "Does the West Indies as a growing nation really value its citizens?"[33]

---

[29] Ibid., 5, 40, 45.

[30] This is clear when comparing the 1957 development plan with its predecessor, see *Report on the Revision of the Ten-Year Plan of Development for Jamaica as Approved by the House of Representatives on 28 November 1951*.

[31] It is worth noting that at exactly this time the International Commission of Jurists embarked on work worldwide to elaborate conceptually and practically the linkages between human rights and the rule of law. This was done through a series of country reports and international conferences. See International Commission of Jurists, *The Rule of Law in a Free Society: A Report on the International Congress of Jurists, New Delhi, India, January 5–10, 1959* (Geneva: ICJ, 1959). The West Indies Bar Association had sent a representative to the New Delhi meeting.

[32] Editorial, "The Case for Law Reform (1): Return to the Rule of Law," *West Indian Economist* 2, no. 9 (March 1960): 7.

[33] Editorial, "The Case for Law Reform (2), The Conditions Affecting Demand," *West Indian Economist* 2, no. 10 (April 1960): 7.

This went to the heart of the *West Indian Economist*'s concern that the region's governments were overly concerned with economic and political development and did not pay sufficient attention to the social well-being of citizens and societies at large. The governments were "preoccupied with measures that act as mere palliatives to the pressures for social change that are building up in the community" but were doing too little to change "the status quo of social structure."[34] The editors of the magazine accused the governments in the West Indies of ducking their political responsibilities since they always focused on providing economic opportunities as avenues of social mobility and made no real attempts "to install into the society at large objective values of social justice."[35] The *West Indian Economist* was arguing that there was a fundamental balance between the social, the economic, and the political that needed to be struck but which was actually being ignored. This failing would have a profound effect on the region's future. The social fabric in the West Indies needed particular attention for the larger project of independence to succeed.

It appears that the PNP heeded this call because it was exactly at this juncture that Manley's cabinet started their debate on making human rights a government response to this well-articulated critique of the West Indies' situation and challenge to its record while in office. Around this time, human rights were making their presence felt in Jamaican political life also in other ways. In 1958, British colonial officials were struck by the vibrancy by which Jamaicans had celebrated the tenth anniversary of the Universal Declaration on Human Rights.[36] Furthermore, from 1958 and over the next years the US sociologist Wendell Bell conducted a series of surveys and interviews with Jamaican politicians and civil servants to study their values and attitudes. Bell was struck by their focus on equality and on human rights which he argued seemed to "reflect some underlying principle of change."[37]

The Human Rights Policy and Its Trajectory: 1961

In 1961, Jamaica was a British colony and one of ten island states that formed the West Indies Federation established in 1958. Throughout the year, Jamaican politics balanced on a knife's edge on issues that went to the core of its future governance and what it meant to be a political entity

---

[34] Ibid., 7–8.   [35] Ibid., 8.

[36] See correspondence on Jamaica in the file "Celebrations in colonies on tenth anniversary of adoption of Declaration of Human Rights," British National Archives, FO 371/145426.

[37] Wendell Bell, *Jamaican Leaders: Political Attitudes in a New Nation* (Berkeley: University of California Press, 1964), 49.

in a rapidly changing world. The political contestations were over colonial status versus independence; over the choice of regional federation versus national sovereignty; and over who would be in power and what type of politics would dominate. This balancing was also highly visible due to the existing social and economic tensions that found expression in the public debates on inequality and on living standards.

Beneath these contestations lay competing visions for national development linked to disagreements over Jamaica's and the West Indies' place in a decolonized world. These contestations would shape a controversial political year and change Jamaica's political trajectory with enduring legacies that influence Caribbean politics to this day. The year started with the announcement of the Manley government's human rights policy on January 6, 1961. It was based on several rounds of cabinet discussions in the final months of 1960 and early January 1961. The background documents for the cabinet debate on human rights had been prepared by the Central Planning Unit and in a policy paper the Unit had laid out the basis for the discussions. The first problem identified was that neither the constitution of the West Indies Federation nor any of the constitutions of its member units included a statement on the ideals and objectives of the West Indies populations or of the principles on which their multiracial societies should be founded. The urgency for such an articulation was felt strongly to help propel the political projects toward independence in the Caribbean:

The necessity for a clear statement on our national goals is more pressing than ever at this time, when, in the absence of any declared social ends (other than the maximization of national production), materialism as a national creed, has undoubtedly captured the popular imagination – thus awakening aspirations which are obviously incapable of solution in the present circumstances. This gives rise to unhealthy feelings of frustration among the "have nots" and manifests itself in class and race antagonisms.[38]

This was an accurate reflection of the debates that had taken place and the tensions that had shaped recent political developments. The situation, it was argued, required that the state acknowledge a set of obligations to its citizens:

It is the duty of the Government first to make it clear to the people of this country that they enjoy intangible rights and privileges of far greater value than material things – and secondly, to make those rights and privileges as real as possible to the average man.[39]

---

[38] "Human Rights," Memorandum by Central Planning Unit, November 15, 1960, Box 1B/31/27, Norman Manley Papers, National Archives of Jamaica, Spanish Town.
[39] Ibid.

It was recommended that the government not wait for action at the federal level but "take immediate action by local legislation" and make official declarations of its human rights policies. The starting point proposed by the Central Planning Unit was an anti-discrimination law that would make it "an offence for any person to be discriminated against in a public place or in employment on the grounds of his race, colour, political belief or religion."[40] Also on their radar was discrimination against women in the workplace and the Central Planning Unit made "equal pay for equal work" one of the guiding rights principles. The Central Planning Unit had drafted "a prototype" for a local bill of rights that laid out these principles combining civil, political, economic, social, and cultural rights with inspiration from the 1948 Universal Declaration on Human Rights and the Bill of Rights from the 1960 Nigerian constitution.[41]

Anti-discrimination measures featured prominently in the policy paper as the government realized it was up against pervasive values and structures in Jamaican society that continued to have a negative influence on people's lives. This led the Planning Unit to place an increased emphasis on employment practices and on investments in education – the latter an issue that was already a central priority in the country's national development plan. Education was part of an economic policy but also a component of the nation-building project that had so occupied Norman Manley's work as leader of the PNP. "The right to education and cultural development" was defined as one of the rights that deserved either constitutional or other formal policy status because education was one of the main priorities around which the government was balancing public demands for social improvements with the political realization that such improvements could only be realistically achieved at a much slower pace than demanded – a dilemma well known to developing countries. The Central Planning Unit explained it as: "Complete social integration is a process which cannot be rushed, but improved economic and educational opportunities will work insidiously towards this end."[42]

The Manley government had made a commitment with the National Plan for Jamaica, 1957–1967 to ensure universal primary education for children between 7 and 11 years of age and had as part of these reforms

---

[40] Ibid.   [41] Ibid.

[42] Ibid. There does not appear to exist any intellectual histories of the Central Planning Unit's work. There are some more general accounts, including Roderick Rainford, *Central Planning Unit to Planning Institute of Jamaica: Anchoring 50 Years of Development Planning in Jamaica* (Kingston: Planning Institute of Jamaica, 2006); Gladstone Mills, "Planning in Jamaica – The Early Years," *Planning Institute of Jamaica 50th Anniversary* (Kingston: Planning Institute of Jamaica, 2005), 32–44.

also invested in securing 2,000 free places annually to secondary schools to help children of poor parents to secure the opportunity of a good grammar school education.[43] In this context, the human rights policy was an attempt to underpin an existing policy framework with the acknowledgment of individual rights as state obligations and thereby add a stronger human rights dimension to the government's national plan for development. This was intended to be a work in progress in the relationship between government and citizens or as it was explained:

Having set itself and the country at large, these worthy social objectives, the government in co-operation with the general public could then set about the task of making these rights a more tangible reality than at the present moment.[44]

Put differently, the interface between the "Government policy in respect of Human Rights,"[45] as Norman Manley described it, and national development planning was part of the nation- and state-building project of the PNP government. The question was: how would this play out?

It was clear that 1961 would be a decisive and complicated political year because the Jamaican referendum on continued participation in the West Indies Federation was on the calendar later in the year. The British Caribbean was on the verge of independence but exactly which political structures would gain independence was uncertain as long as Jamaica was rethinking the decision of whether or not to stay in the Federation. Without Jamaica – one of the larger territories in the Federation alongside Trinidad and Tobago – it was unlikely that the federation had any future and the different islands would have to achieve independence as separate island states causing regional integration to be severely weakened.[46]

Jamaica was holding the future of the British Caribbean in the balance. Norman Manley was a strong proponent of the Federation. He viewed it as being in both Jamaica and the West Indies' interest because of the benefits for the internal development of the Federation's different Units but also to ensure a stronger voice to promote and protect the interests of the West Indies globally. The leader of the opposition Alexander

[43] Bertram, *Manley and the Making of Modern Jamaica*, 260. This was a significant expansion of education that would benefit generations of young Jamaicans in the decades that ensued.

[44] "Human Rights," Memorandum by Central Planning Unit, November 15, 1960, Box 1B/31/27, Norman Manley Papers, National Archives of Jamaica, Spanish Town.

[45] Ibid.

[46] For a helpful account of the importance of Federation during this period of the process toward decolonization, see Michael Collins, "Decolonization and the 'Federal Moment,'" *Diplomacy and Statecraft* 24, no. 1 (2013): 21–40. See also Getachew, *Worldmaking after Empire*, 125–31.

Bustamente had decided to turn against the federation, partly as a populist means to try and undermine the Manley government after its second election victory in 1959 that had left the JLP weakened. Because of the divisive stance, Bustamente and the Jamaican Labour Party had taken, Manley decided to call a referendum to bring clarity to the political situation. He would have to face the populist brand of Bustamente later in the year in order to secure the federation project, a foreboding sign given their history and the dynamics of Jamaican politics in the previous two decades. It would lead to a major clash later in 1961 and force a clarification of Jamaica's postcolonial status.

In the meantime, the Manley government had the human rights agenda to take forward. The cabinet discussions had highlighted a major gap with the constitutional developments taking place in the Caribbean since the 1940s. The constitutional reforms toward greater self-government had neither for the Federation nor for Jamaica included the adoption of a bill of rights. This was now placed more firmly on the political agenda and would become an important part of the negotiations building up to the 1962 Independence Conference in London.

In April 1961, Manley spoke before a gathering of some of the most important figures in the local communities across Jamaica, namely the Union of Teachers. In this major speech, he talked about the same issues that had influenced the government's decision to adopt a human rights policy a few months earlier. Manley acknowledged the "tension and stresses and strains" that had been disclosed recently while defending the government's record of trying to increase the speed of development. As he often did, Manley placed current issues in historical context.

The more you progress in an underdeveloped country the sharper the demands grow for betterment. Because when nothing is happening people stagnate. For decades in this country – literally for decades – nobody agitated about anything. Nobody clamoured about anything. People were taught to believe that what happened to them in life was some whim of Providence who had called them to belong to the station where they found themselves. But when you start moving, movement becomes visible to everybody, and people are no longer prepared to stand still or to wait forever.[47]

Manley defended the government's record when it came to securing increases in the real incomes of workers despite the claims of increasing inequality being part of the criticisms leveled against his government's management of the economy. He believed that they had moved "a large

---

[47] Norman Manley, "Address by the Premier Hon. Norman Manley, Q.C. to the Jamaica Union of Teachers Conference," April 12, 1961, Kingston, Jamaica, 2–3.

number of the have-nots" into the category of "haves" and expanded the tax base in the process. Manley called for calm, reason, and a recognition of efforts taking place in Jamaica to try and improve living conditions. While not a surprising statement from a politician holding power it was noteworthy that he employed rights language to elaborate his argument. The economic tensions in Jamaica had ignited the risk of racial tensions[48] and here Manley tried to place the Caribbean experience in both a global and an American context with which his audience was familiar. Seeing the US civil rights movement's mobilization as an interesting model from which to draw inspiration, Manley idealistically explained that the "great Negro leaders":

> have denounced with the utmost vigour, discrimination and intolerance wherever it is to be found . . . And I who have constantly gone there, and I daresay, many of you have constantly gone there and talked to their leaders, must have been astonished to find how they fight for their rights. Many of them would die for their rights for equal citizenship, but do not denounce the white majority nor create a state of hatred, race against race. They denounced the thinking that will allow people to rebel against being asked to share a school with a coloured child. They will denounce the thinking, they will fight against it, but the one thing they are working for is the day when equality before the law, and equality in society shall come in the land.[49]

Manley was echoing the emphasis on anti-discrimination measures reflected in the government's human rights policy proposals. He used the comparison to make an argument about the lessons for domestic politics once again using Jamaica's journey since 1938 as a baseline. In doing this he articulated the national project, as he saw it, drawing on history by contrasting the centuries-long history of colonialism and slavery with the short, intense period in which steps toward ending empire had had the chance to be nurtured:

> I don't pretend we have put an end to all forms of colour discrimination in Jamaica. You don't wipe out three hundred years in twenty years. But I know that from 1938 those of us who saw what was ahead, bent ourselves to the task of putting power in the hands of the ordinary men and women of this country, knowing that the only way to end discrimination is on two fields – the field of power where your own people control your institutions, political and otherwise; and the field of education where their growth in skill and quality fits them to take charge of everything for themselves.[50]

---

[48] This became a theme in contemporary Jamaican fiction of the 1950s; see for example John Hearne's 1955 novel *Voices under the Window*.

[49] Manley, *Address*, 5–6.

[50] Ibid., 7. See also Kingsley Martin, "The Jamaican Volcano," *New Statesman*, 61, no. 1566 (March 17, 1961), 416–18.

His statement illustrates why education had achieved such prominence both as a key priority in national development planning and as a specific right in the bill of rights proposed by the Central Planning Unit and submitted to the cabinet. Manley paraphrased this recent document by returning to the theme of social integration. Education's primary task, Manley believed, was to remedy the damning legacies of the past and ensure "the integration of the people of the country" and help develop "an integrated society that believes in itself." Once again, development policy, rights, and nation-building were closely interwoven in Manley's vision. His statement also revealed the less than solid ground that existed for a politician building a new polity in the midst of brokering the end of empire. The PNP government had been criticized for its record on the economy, especially over questions on standards of living, but Manley's main policy response to economic criticism appeared to be the long-term prospects offered by educational policies where the benefits often only become tangible with time (at the least a generation's perspective) and not the short-term gains that parts of the Jamaican electorate were now demanding. The politics of decolonization proved again to be the politics of balancing on a knife's edge. The social divisions and the lack of cohesion in the country were ever pervasive and forced the technical exercise of development planning toward a much larger ambition of deliberate nation-building. Manley talked about the need for laying down "a national tradition" for everybody in the country. In grappling with the very real legacy of societal incohesion the political system was forced to lay down the tracks while the train toward decolonization was moving ever faster toward an uncertain future. As Manley explained to the Union of Teachers, a group that was placed at the forefront of his national project, tradition was important to broker social and political cohesion and to shore up resilience to face the challenges ahead:

Tradition in the sense in which I talk means that there is a set of values equally shared, by and large, by everybody, and that those values are understood in the same sense and interpreted in the same way . . . It is all those shared values, those shared beliefs, those shared responsibilities that bind a society together so that in the months of crisis and difficulty the voice of cohesion is stronger than the voice of division. It is tradition in that sense of which I speak.[51]

This was a fair reflection of the political vision that Manley had promoted ever since his intervention in 1939 when he had laid out the need for constitutional change in Jamaica. However, it would not be long before the PNP government's whole project – and its hold on

---

[51] Manley, *Address*, 10.

power – would be seriously challenged. In the process the trajectory for the human rights policy endorsed by the PNP government in January 1961 would change.

The West Indies Federation had come into existence in 1958. It was still in the nascent stages of efforts to develop closer regional cooperation and integration. There was a federal parliament based in Trinidad that had come into operation. There were challenges with the large geographical distance between the federal units – a fact that did not help instill a sense of cohesion. However, the federation did look like the vehicle to secure independence for the islands of the British Caribbean and the quickly approaching date for independence in the West Indies was expected to be May 31, 1962. The problem was that Jamaica was holding up the process due to the referendum. As it was explained in the Jamaican House of Representatives during a major debate on the Federation, no law to secure independence for the West Indies could be enacted in the British parliament until the Jamaican referendum had taken place.[52]

This debate crystallized more than ever the question of the future of Jamaica's self-governing project. Was federation or national sovereignty to Jamaica's best advantage? The debate was partly a heated exchange on the political journey since 1938, partly about the social conditions of the people in Jamaica and the West Indies and partly about the nature of independence in a decolonizing world. Manley argued strongly for the economic and political advantages that federation provided. The West Indies needed a strong voice in the midst of changing international trading patterns. With the United Kingdom hoping to join the European Common Market, this left the Caribbean at risk of being left behind and further isolated. The Jamaican Labour Party argued for the benefits of the Jamaican people going it alone claiming that they would otherwise end up subsidizing the smaller islands of the Federation. It was a house divided.

The referendum on September 19, 1961 was a defeat for Norman Manley. He had invested all his energy and a significant amount of political capital in securing a vote in favor of Federation. The country had gone with Bustamente and the JLP. It would mean the collapse of the West Indies Federation and that Jamaica would have to secure independence on its own. The end of colonial rule in Jamaica was fast approaching and the post-referendum debate in the House of

---

[52] Norman Manley, July 10, 1961, Jamaica Hansard, Proceedings of the House of Representatives, Session 1961–2 (April 12–July 26, 1961), National Library of Jamaica, Kingston, 359.

Representatives naturally had to address the changed situation. A large part of the debate, however, went back to the years of 1938 to 1944 and onwards from there. It was a historical contestation over the legitimacy of who should lead the process toward national independence: a defeated Norman Manley who was head of government and still had the parliamentary majority or a victorious Alexander Bustamente who nevertheless only had a minority in the House of Representatives. The post-referendum debate also focused on the specific task of preparing a Jamaican constitution which would be one of the most important tasks in the months ahead. To a significant extent the debate focused on the freedoms, civil liberties, and individual rights to be included in the new founding document. Norman Manley would get the final word in this debate. He reflected both on the work on human rights carried out by his own government and drew up the larger global context that Jamaica would have to navigate:

There is a lot of talk about the problem of preserving certain principles, constitutionally by enshrining in the Constitution basic human rights. Mr. Speaker that is a matter that has been studied intensively in the last few years all over the world. The Declaration on Human Rights made by the United Nations, as followed not long afterwards by a European Declaration [*sic*] of Fundamental Rights. And since then a number of Constitutions have tried one way or another, write into their Constitutions the fundamental human rights and entrench them in the Constitution in such a way as to ensure that they may last for all time even against the most evil intentions of rulers . . . We have here in Jamaica quite extensive literature on the subject because it has been under intense study for over a year and it is not only a number of Constitutions on it [*sic*] but we have elaborate analyses and reports by distinguished legal persons on the difficulties and problems involved.[53]

During the last months of colonial rule it was this foundation Manley believed was necessary to consolidate in the independence constitution because the fate of Jamaica was being decided exactly in these processes that now lay before the politicians of the two parties. The divisions created by the Federation referendum needed – as the election result had become clear – to be substituted with a sense of common purpose:

I think it is so vital and important to restore that sense of inner unity in the life of this country because the first few years of Independence, as have been proved all over the world, and more proved with every passing year as new nations come into the world, the first few years of Independence create special problems,

---

[53] Norman Manley, October 17, 1961, Jamaica Hansard, Proceedings of the House of Representatives, Session 1961–2 (October 12–December 13, 1961), National Library of Jamaica, Kingston, 528. This is quoted correctly from the source despite the awkward language.

special strains, special stresses, special difficulties of their own. And it is in those years that one must strive to create once and for all the pattern of life on which your future will rest.[54]

Despite the bitter referendum campaign the two parties were able to quickly close ranks and work together on a new constitution.[55] It was agreed that a bill of rights would form part of this foundational docu-ment. This followed the precedent – as Manley had indicated in his speech to the House of Representatives quoted above – of a number of other newly independent states that had made such a bill part of their constitutions.[56] The proposal also had public backing judging from the newspaper debate.[57] However, there was a caveat.

The bill of rights was an important step forward for constitutional designs in the Caribbean but also represented one significant shortcom-ing: the Jamaican constitution focused only on civil and political rights. It did not feature the right to education which had otherwise been part of the draft bill of rights that the Central Planning Unit had presented to the government in late 1960 and which furthermore was recognized as one of the two main priorities in the national development plan that had empha-sized enhancing equality in educational opportunities and which Manley had promoted as a key sector for the "national project." Instead, there was significant pressure to entrench the right to property in the consti-tution. This was pushed especially from members of the business com-munity, including the wealthy JLP politician Neville Ashenheim.[58] The proposed formula had the potential to seriously curtail the government's decision-making authority when it came to large-scale projects to strengthen social and economic development. It posed a significant dilemma for the politicians both regarding its inclusion but especially on the question of the status of the "bill of rights" in the constitution. Were the politicians about to grant decision-making authority over vital parts of socioeconomic development planning to the judiciary where property owners would have a much stronger legal hand? These types of questions shifted the nature of the human rights debate from the discussions that had emerged from the cabinet and the Central Planning

---

[54] Ibid.   [55] Kelly, "Jamaican Independence Constitution," 36.
[56] Charles O. H. Parkinson, *Bills of Rights and Decolonization: The Emergence of Domestic Human Rights Instruments in Britain's Overseas Territories* (Oxford: Oxford University Press, 2017); S. A. de Smith, *The New Commonwealth and Its Constitutions* (London: Stevens & Sons, 1964).
[57] See e.g. Patrick Leach, "A Bill of Rights a Necessity," *Sunday Gleaner*, October 22, 1961, 6; editorial, "The People's Rights," *Daily Gleaner*, January 10, 1962, 10; Douglas Judah, "Human Rights – Now or Then," *Daily Gleaner*, January 10, 1962, 10.
[58] N. N. Ashenheim, "Bill of Rights Is a Must," *Daily Gleaner*, September 28, 1961.

Unit one year earlier. Parallel to this process, the right to protection against slavery, a sensitive issue in Jamaica, was dropped from the constitution.[59] "Freedom from slavery and forced labour" was one of the issues that the Central Planning Unit had suggested the government give serious consideration to, but protection from it was not to be part of the Jamaican constitution.[60]

There seems to be a valid lesson in contrasting the two processes – that is the Central Planning Unit memo to the cabinet and the constitution – that produced a human rights framework. From a human rights perspective, constitutionalization, while embedding a range of highly important protections, was too conservative an approach to state-building to fully address the needs of this developing country. Leaving out education was a serious omission compared to the political vision and national development planning that had nurtured a highly advanced level of human rights thinking in Jamaica during that "era of passionate self-discovery" that preceded Jamaican independence in August 1962. Nevertheless, the human rights principles in the Jamaican constitution were not imposed. It was rather that they chose to follow the "Westminster model" for the constitution. This meant a focus on fundamental rights provisions that did not consider social and economic rights. Lloyd Barnett, a leading Jamaican constitutional scholar, made a special point out of this when arguing that the human rights provisions in the constitution, "protects the individual against arbitrary government but does nothing to protect him from many insidious forms of oppression, or to stimulate and encourage his material or moral advancement."[61]

It was a combination of the two approaches that informed Jamaica's human rights diplomacy at the United Nations led by their first ambassador there, Egerton Richardson, who came from the post of Permanent Secretary in the Ministry of Finance and in this capacity had been closely connected to both the cabinet and the Central Planning Unit. As an independent country Jamaica would immediately raise the importance of human rights during its first participation in a United Nations General Assembly Session in the autumn of 1962. They immediately suggested making 1968 a UN international year for human rights which would include a five-year process by which the international community could get its house in order on human rights and plan accordingly for the occasion. This would require finalizing the floundering project of turning

[59] Kelly, "Jamaican Independence Constitution," 48.
[60] "Human Rights," Memorandum by Central Planning Unit, November 15, 1960, Box 1B/31/27, Norman Manley Papers, National Archives of Jamaica, Spanish Town.
[61] Barnett, *Constitutional Law of Jamaica*, 434.

human rights into international binding law and agreeing on implementation mechanisms. This process received renewed momentum at least in part due to Jamaica's human rights year project. Jamaica subsequently proposed and fought to secure backing for the organization of the First World Conference on Human Rights that would take place in 1968. Throughout the 1960s, the impact of their initiative was profound as they worked to enhance international human rights diplomacy by e.g. expanding NGO involvement in UN human rights processes, brokering international acceptance that international humanitarian law and international human rights law were linked, inspiring Soviet dissidents in the way they adopted the international language of human rights from 1968 alongside a number of other achievements.[62]

Conclusion

A significant body of human rights research focuses on the normative dimensions of human rights while studies of anti-colonialism have often focused on the ideological contents of these movements. Both approaches are too narrow when it comes to analyzing the historical roles played by human rights in the post-1945 world. Anti-colonial movements had many iterations and deserve a nuanced historical treatment. The Jamaica case illustrates that the experiential and experimental dimensions of human rights politics are also historical factors that we need to contend with, analyze, and understand. Human rights was a meaningful set of principles for the Jamaican actors who were challenging the shortcomings – and increasingly the outdated nature – of British colonial rule and who were looking toward developing self-government that was more responsive to the needs of the population on the island. Social and political experiences made human rights appear as a meaningful political language to manage the challenges of building a nation and a viable state from the weak foundations of empire.

The experimental nature of the political responses stands out as the most striking feature of postcolonial politics. The Manley government operated with the broad human rights framework but placed special emphasis on some of its component parts, such as the right to education, nondiscrimination measures and in the early stages of the story the right to vote. These responses were attempts to solve major social, economic, and political challenges. They were not necessarily perfect or highly effective responses in and of themselves; the challenges for securing

---

[62] See Jensen, *Making of International Human Rights*, 69–101, 174–208.

socioeconomic development for Jamaica proved massive. To attempt to quantify "success" by a standard means of measurement is not only inappropriate but unfairly simplistic. However, their considered responses to their country's formation had significant influence on shaping the complex nature of Jamaican political culture that developed from "the process of self-discovery" en route to independence – and on the global trajectories for international human rights after the 1960s.

The initial question then remains: what happens when the periphery proves to be the center? Ultimately, and inevitably, our historical accounts must change. First, the traditional mold of narrating human rights history requires a rethink. This rethinking must welcome a revisiting and a reinterpretation of previously overlooked historical processes in order to capture and explain how central roles and contributions came into existence. Second, it must also accommodate an expansion of a source base beyond what has typically been part of human rights scholarship. Here, in this context, all evidence begins to point toward the nexus between human rights and decolonization – and more specifically with the end of empire in Jamaica and the wider Caribbean.

The Caribbean came into existence as part of the crossroads of empire. Independent Jamaica emerged during the twilight of empire as part of a different crossroads, namely one consisting of a nation- and state-building project, a remarkable political vision, constitutional advancements, the economics of poverty (also known as development economics), a refined articulated philosophy of planning and the evolving notion of human rights principles and laws. Norman Manley wryly observed, "History is history." His vision and outlook on the world – both local and global in its scope – became an important part of Jamaican history. And that history – through its remarkable emphasis and promotion of human rights – became part of our global history.[63]

---

[63] See the chapter "From Jamaica with Law: The Rekindling of International Human Rights, 1962–1967," ibid., 69–101.

10 Reentering Histories of Past Imperial Violence

Kenya, Indonesia, and the Reach of Transitional Justice

Michael Humphrey

Introduction

Human rights accountability for crimes against humanity did not figure prominently in decolonization.[1] From the transitional justice perspective, decolonization was an instance of transition where there was invariably no accountability, in other words, where impunity of the former colonial power for past political crimes prevailed. Recent legal cases in London and The Hague brought by former colonial subjects seeking compensation for atrocities committed during decolonization are challenging this impunity. The Hague Civil Court and the High Court in London have agreed to hear the claims of victims/survivors of past colonial crimes committed more than fifty years ago at the end of empire. The first case relates to a massacre in the village of Rawagede by Dutch colonial troops in December 1947, and the second to the illegal torture and detention of Mau Mau veterans during the struggle for independence (1952–60). The recent decision to hear these cases, blocked for years by the Dutch and British courts respectively on the basis of the statute of limitations, has been seen internationally as a sign of further progress and consolidation of human rights/international law and accountability to challenge the long-standing impunity for past

---

[1] This absence is notable in historical accounts of human rights and decolonization, such as Roland Burke, *Decolonization and the Evolution of International Human Rights* (Philadelphia: University of Pennsylvania Press, 2010); Bonny Ibhawoh, *Human Rights in Africa* (Cambridge, UK: Cambridge University Press, 2018); Charles Parkinson, *Bills of Rights and Decolonization* (Oxford: Oxford University Press, 2007); Steven Jensen *The Making of International Human Rights: The 1960s, Decolonization, and the Reconstruction of Global Values* (Cambridge, UK: Cambridge University Press, 2016); Fabian Klose, *Human Rights in the Shadow of Colonial Violence: The Wars of Independence in Kenya and Algeria* (Philadelphia: University of Pennsylvania Press, 2013); Meredith Terretta, *Petitioning for Our Rights, Fighting for Our Nation: The History of the Democratic Union of Cameroonian Women* (Oxford: Langaa, 2013); Jan Eckel, *The Ambivalence of Good Human Rights in International Politics Since the 1940s* (Oxford: Oxford University Press, 2019).

colonial crimes. These cases reveal the severity of political repression used by the counterinsurgency colonial state to try to prevent decolonization. However, they also reveal how these victims of colonial counterinsurgency were marginalized to realize independence and how the independence agreements between the colonial administration and the successor postcolonial political elite were often made at the cost of the victims of the struggle for national independence.

These high-profile legal cases about colonial crimes have revisited the national cultural trauma of decolonization and prompted survivors/victims, now mostly in their eighties and nineties, to bring forward claims at a time when the window of opportunity for these victims and other potential claimants is rapidly closing. They have also led to greater historical scrutiny of decolonization through a human rights lens in both the former colonial and postcolonial states. Even more significant has been the impact of these hearings in London and The Hague as analogical devices for victims of human rights violations committed by the post-independence state with impunity. In Indonesia, The Hague Civil Court judgments led to widespread demands for justice by victims and families of the postcolonial massacres of the Soeharto New Order regime. In Kenya, the High Court hearings in London on the Mau Mau reinforced contemporary demands by human rights organizations and victims for an end to political impunity – as in the forty-nine mock coffins protest in front of parliament house demanding the burial of political impunity.[2] The Kenyan parliament's failure to establish a special tribunal to investigate responsibility for post-election violence in 2008, as required by a national accord brokered by the international community, resulted in the International Criminal Court (ICC) initiating prosecutions against key political leaders to challenge impunity.[3]

This chapter examines the consequences of the expansion of human rights accountability to address past colonial crimes. Rather than seeing the prosecution of colonial crimes as merely evidence of the strengthening of global human rights standards and human rights consciousness, it explores the ambivalent relationship of the role of human rights in different political transitions: during the age of decolonization and the post–Cold War democratization. When decolonization is viewed as mitigated or incomplete, the underlying processes of elite political

---

[2] Kimani Nyoike, "Demonstrating Kenyans Leave 49 Coffins at Parliament," *UPI Next*, June 29, 2012.
[3] Geoffrey Lugano, "Counter-Shaming the International Criminal Court's Intervention as Neocolonial: Lessons from Kenya," *International Journal of Transitional Justice* 11, no. 1 (2017): 9.

consensus and impunity so apparent in recent authoritarian transitions comes into focus. What is new about the reach of human rights accountability to address colonial crimes is how it has allowed invisible victims/-survivors to reenter history, but only if constructed as suffering victims of human rights abuse. In his book *Europe and the People without History*, the anthropologist Eric Wolf argued that nonliterate cultures were rendered invisible and largely excluded from Western historical narratives. Here, I argue that the victims of the colonial counterinsurgency state have also long been invisible in the historical narrative of decolonization, in both the former colonial states and postcolonial states. The invisibility of the victims of decolonization first helped conceal the terms of the historical pact between the colonial state and nationalist elites which produced impunity; second, preserved the myth of consensual decolonization in the former colonial states; and, third, avoided human rights scrutiny of subsequent internal repression in the postcolonial states.

This chapter explores why these cases entered the UK and Netherlands courts so long after the crimes had been committed, what impact these court decisions/hearings have had on the victims, and what meaning these hearings and judgments have had for the former colonial and postcolonial states and societies more widely.

Human Rights Revisionism of Colonial History

The UK High Court and the Hague Civil Court cases have become part of a human rights historical revisionism of colonial history that allow victims to reenter the history of decolonization as individuals rather than subordinated as bodies sacrificed in the name of a national collective memory of either progressive colonialism or national unity and liberation.[4] In the Netherlands, counterinsurgency violence of decolonization suffered from a problem of memorability "the degree to which a past is memorable, recallable within certain frames of remembrance."[5] The Dutch national narrative of benign or ethical colonialism excluded it. The UK had long been held up as an example of "consensual decolonization," a successful negotiated transition with the emergent nationalist elites.[6] In this historical narrative, the Mau Mau were excluded as rebellious outlaws by both the British and President Kenyatta.

---

[4] Paul Bijl, "Colonial Memory and Forgetting in the Netherlands and Indonesia," *Journal of Genocide Research* 14, nos. 3–4 (2012): 441–61.

[5] Bart Luttikhuis and A. Dirk Moses, "Mass Violence and the End of the Dutch Colonial Empire in Indonesia," *Journal of Genocide Research* 14, nos. 3–4 (2012): 27.

[6] Gary Wasserman, *Politics of Decolonization: Kenya Europeans and the Land Issue 1960–1965* (Cambridge, UK: Cambridge University Press, 1976), 4.

Why have these legal campaigns acquired momentum and resonance now, so many decades after the events? In a recent book on amnesty and human rights accountability, Francesca Lessa and Leigh Payne declare that "we now live in an age of accountability in which governments and international institutions are expected to hold perpetrators of atrocities legally responsible."[7] In a similarly progressive vein, Kathryn Sikkink refers to the spread of human rights as "the justice cascade" in which a new international norm of accountability has been established.[8] These optimistic visions of global accountability extend aspects of the "transitional justice" movement that gained momentum in the 1980s. They all point to a rising effort to challenge historical impunity by applying human rights law and accountability in political transitions. It was concerned with bringing an end to political agreements that denied the human rights of victims and the legal responsibility of perpetrators. Reaching back now to encompass past colonial crimes represents an expansion of human rights law and accountability to earlier political transitions, in this case decolonization.[9]

A key focus of the analysis of political transition and human rights is the concept of "transitional amnesty," the asymmetrical relations determining the balance between justice and impunity in political transitions. This term was coined to differentiate amnesty as a political agreement between parties affirmed in amnesty laws from the use of amnesty as a precursor to bring about "liberalizing political change."[10] Traditionally, amnesty laws were the product of agreements between parties to a conflict that offered amnesty to all combatants irrespective of the crimes committed or level of responsibility of the offender.[11] They are the outcome and legacy of the way authoritarian power can be projected into emergent democratic institutions. Law, or what Jean and John Comaroff term "lawfare," is used to underwrite a political agreement dictated by the inequality between parties that exempts the powerful from

---

[7] Francesca Lessa and Leigh A. Payne, "Introduction," in *Amnesty in the Age of Human Rights Accountability: Comparative and International Perspectives*, ed. Francesca Lessa and Leigh A. Payne (Cambridge, UK: Cambridge University Press, 2012), 2.

[8] Kathryn Sikkink, *The Justice Cascade: How Human Rights Trials Are Changing the World* (New York: Norton, 2011), 5.

[9] Paige Arthur, "Introduction: Societies in Transition," in *Identities in Transition: Challenges for Transitional Justice in Divided*, ed. Paige Arthur (Cambridge, UK: Cambridge University Press, 2010), 1.

[10] Ruti G. Teitel, *Transitional Justice* (Oxford: Oxford University Press, 2000), 53.

[11] Louise Mallinder, "The Role of Amnesties in Conflict Transformation," School of Law, Queen's University, Belfast, 2009, accessed June 29, 2012, http://ssrn.com/abstract=1275048

accountability and denies justice to those marginalized by the deal.[12] These asymmetrical amnesties traded off present justice for the hope of longer-term political benefits and peace.[13] In practice, "transitional amnesty" was the product of a consensus between political elites based on reciprocal amnesty for crimes/violations committed and the marginalization of victims, especially those who continued to demand accountability, as the basis for political reconciliation.[14] Decolonization, I suggest, was until recent years, characterized by the features typical of "transitional amnesty."

The chapter is framed as a comparative study of "transitional amnesty" during decolonization and the transition from postcolonial authoritarian to democratic regimes, and the role of cultural trauma in competing national narratives of unity and justice. These hearings in the Dutch and British courts highlight the different role human rights played during these transitions. In the former, the human rights priority emphasized self-determination while in the latter the priority became accountability for individual crimes and recognition of the victims. Both transitions were characterized by political compromise that included either quarantining or limiting justice, ensuring it was bounded by both time and a single, collective remedy – independence. These "transitional amnesties" have been based on political consensus and legal constraint shaped by asymmetrical power and a desire to limit scrutiny of the past and any possibility of accountability. In both Kenya and Indonesia, decolonization produced an official narrative that combined the colonizer's silence on colonial repression and the colonized's celebration of national liberation as a unifying force. Transitional amnesty was gradually eroded during post–Cold War democratization with the globalization of human rights and the effective mobilization of victims as claimants and human rights advocates as moral entrepreneurs seeking to reveal past wrongs. The ascendancy of the accountability agenda in international politics occurred in the immediate post–Cold War era in response to war in the former Yugoslavia. First, the war became constructed as a "human rights" crisis rather than a "humanitarian" crisis and, second, the Dayton Agreement helped expand the legal reach of human rights with the

---

[12] Jean Comaroff and John L. Comaroff, *Law and Disorder in the Postcolony* (Chicago: University of Chicago, 2006).

[13] Antje Du Bois-Pedain, *Transitional Amnesty in South Africa* (Cambridge, UK: Cambridge University Press, 2007).

[14] Michael Humphrey, "Marginalizing 'Victims' and 'Terrorists': Modes of Exclusion in the Reconciliation Process," in *Reconciliation after Terrorism: Strategy, Possibility, or Absurdity?*, ed. Judith Renner and Alexander Spencer (London: Routledge, 2012), 48–68.

establishment of the International Criminal Tribunal for the former Yugoslavia (ICTY). The creation of the ICTY, and then the International Criminal Tribunal for Rwanda (ICTR), changed the political and legal significance of human rights movements and their transnationalized profiles and networks.

Through their legal focus on the victims of decolonization, these cases reveal the invisible costs of the "silence" and "unity" narratives of independence and the implications of human rights revisionism for examining decolonization and the political and legal legacies for these postcolonial states. Reframed as human rights violations, the "cultural trauma" of the survivors of colonial repression presents a major challenge to the "collective memory" of national societies. "Cultural trauma" refers to the memory of a group evoked by an event or situation that is laden with negative affect and lived as indelible. Collective memory "refers to knowledge about the past that is shared, mutually acknowledged, and reinforced by a collectivity."[15] Transitional justice has allowed cultural trauma to be articulated through the language of human rights. Victim/survivor testimonies destabilize amnesia and the dominant historical narratives about the past.

However, the extent to which their testimonies have been able to produce unifying collective memory is another matter. The victim-centered transitional justice process, particularly the truth commissions, has "sequestered" individual violence stories of victims and subordinated them to new national narrative about the past – i.e. one based on victimhood rather than victory. As a consequence, while human rights has provided an emancipatory discourse for unrecognized victims of political violence it has done so only selectively. A moral lens judging who deserves to be recognized as a victim usually produces a hierarchy of victims, e.g., innocent victims are seen as the most deserving.[16] What is more, amnesty is not merely a problem of accepting illegality or legal exceptionalism. Repealing amnesty laws by itself does not usually dismantle the underlying political basis for impunity.

The key factor in the expansion of transitional justice has been the entrance of victims into history through their construction as victims of human rights abuse. Transitional justice has been victim-centered in two ways; first, through its focus on suffering victims as a source of truth

[15] Joachim J. Savelsberg and Ryan D. King, "Law and Collective Memory," *Annual Review of Law and Social Science* 3 (2007): 191.
[16] Michael Humphrey, "The Politics of Trauma," *Arts: The Journal of the Sydney University Arts Association* 32 (2010): 37; Kieran McEvoy and Kirsten McConnachie, "Victimology in Transitional Justice: Victimhood, Innocence and Hierarchy," *European Journal of Criminology* 9, no. 5 (2012): 527.

about human rights violations and, second, through the construction of victims/survivors as embodying the cultural trauma of the nation. These legal hearings into the victims of colonial crimes have also highlighted their role as essential "carrier groups" of the memory of historical injustice and trauma made visible through the courts. In transitional justice, victims have been constructed as embodying large cultural traumas: the Holocaust under the Nazis, racialized repression under apartheid in South Africa, "ethnic cleansing" in Bosnia, disappearance under the Argentine junta, and dispossession under white settler colonization in Australia. Individual victims can quickly become instrumentalized as symbolic vectors to shape national collective memory.

Cultural trauma is more than a question of human rights and accountability. It becomes the core of a moral metanarrative about past wrongs and a source of renewal of national unity and identity. In decolonization, the founding violence of the post-colonial nation included the stories of the victims of colonial repression and the heroes of the national liberation struggle. However, national inclusion during decolonization was not guaranteed simply on the basis of suffering or victimhood; it is nearly always selective. Decolonization may have nation-building and national unity as political goals, but it usually conceals a fragmented polity, yet to be fully integrated. Forging national unity almost always involves overcoming regionalism, competition between elites and subduing resistance to decolonization itself. Individual victims may now be used to symbolize the legitimacy of the struggle for independence, but the process of decolonization was less concerned with individual justice than their collective subordination to the story of national sacrifice.

This chapter analyzes the changing role of cultural trauma in relation to the project of national unity and human rights in colonial and post-colonial periods. The construction of cultural trauma, Alexander argues, is a process

that involves (a) claims-making by agents; (b) carrier groups of the trauma process (with material and ideal interests); (c) speech acts by carrier groups, who address an audience in a specific situation, seeking to project the trauma claim to the audience; and (d) cultural classifications regarding the nature of the pain, the nature of the victim, the relation of the trauma victim to the wider audience, and the attribution of responsibility.[17]

The legal recognition of human rights violations in London and The Hague reaffirms the moral wrongs of colonization and binds these citizens to a founding cultural trauma and revised collective memory of the

[17] Savelsberg and King, "Law and Collective Memory," 191–2.

nation, but it has also served as an analogical device by opening the space for other victims to highlight impunity and social exclusion in the post-colonial state. Ironically, these legal decisions in The Hague and London to recognize and compensate victims of colonial political crimes are today being upheld by human rights activists in both Kenya and Indonesia as exemplary justice, even if delayed by more than sixty years, unavailable in their own national courts.

Rawagede Widows in The Hague Civil Court

On September 14, 2011, The Hague Civil Court awarded compensation of €20,000 to each of eight widows and a survivor of a massacre of around 400 men committed by Dutch colonial troops in Rawagede (now Balongsari) West Java in December 1947.[18] The widows claimed compensation for the suffering caused by the execution of their husbands when the Dutch military resorted to brutal counterinsurgency methods against nationalist guerrilla warfare tactics. The estimated casualties of the independence struggle were around 5,000 on the Dutch side and 150,000 on the Indonesian side. The Dutch government publicly apologized through the Dutch ambassador Tjeerd de Zwaan at the local commemoration day at the victims' monument in Rawagede.[19] However, none of the soldiers involved were ever prosecuted.

For a long time, Dutch governments had avoided acknowledging responsibility or apologizing for the Rawagede massacre even though evidence for the massacre was well known. At the time the massacre was condemned by the UN Committee of Good Offices on Indonesia and the Dutch military looked into the incident but decided not to prosecute because of the context of the counterinsurgency and guerilla tactics of the opposition.[20] In 1969, a Dutch military report reviewing the excesses committed by Dutch troops between 1945 and 1950 denounced the killings but alleged that Rawagede was suspected of being a major center of insurgency in West Java.[21] In 2008, nine surviving relatives

---

[18] *Wisah Binti Silan et al.* v. *The State of The Netherlands (Ministry of Foreign Affairs)*, District Court of The Hague, Case No. 354119/HA ZA 09–4171, September 14, 2011, accessed July, 12, 2012, www.internationalcrimesdatabase.org/Case/1006/Silan-et-al-v-The-Netherlands

[19] Nicole L. Immler, "Narrating (In)justice in the Form of a Reparation Claim," in *Understanding the Age of Transitional Justice: Crimes, Courts, Commissions, and Chronicling*, ed. Nanci Adler (New Brunswick, NJ: State University of New Jersey, 2018) 151.

[20] Larissa van den Herik, "Addressing 'Colonial Crimes' through Reparations? Adjudicating Dutch Atrocities Committed in Indonesia," *Journal of International Criminal Justice* 10 (2012): 695.

[21] Ibid., 696.

launched a civil case in Dutch courts on the basis that the killings were wrongful acts and that Dutch failure to investigate and prosecute the military officers responsible was also wrongful in law. On both counts the Dutch government invoked the statute of limitations but did acknowledge that the summary executions were wrongful and allocated €850,000 in development aid to the village of Rawagede.[22] In its defense before the court the Dutch state also held that the Dutch–Indonesian financial agreement reached in 1966 was understood as a definitive settlement for compensation to cover the whole colonial period.[23] In practice, the Dutch state ignored the victims of the colonial wars, including Dutch ones. Nevertheless the Dutch government did conduct war crimes trials in 1946 in the Dutch East Indies against the former Japanese occupiers and also against Indonesian nationalists who they prosecuted as wartime collaborators. By prosecuting Japanese crimes against Europeans and non-Europeans alike these war crimes trials were designed to show that all sides had suffered under the Japanese thereby contrasting the purportedly benign colonial rule of the Dutch with a distinctively criminal colonial rule of the Japanese. It was an exercise that reaffirmed the legitimacy of the return of Dutch colonial rule.[24]

In granting the Rawagede widows the right to a hearing, The Hague Civil Court overturned earlier Dutch court decisions that had held the statute of limitations on accountability had expired. The plaintiffs' lawyer, Liesbeth Zegveld, argued that the decision was important because it meant "that the state can't just sit in silence for 60 years waiting for the case to go away or the plaintiffs to die and then appeal to the statute of limitations."[25] "Dutch silence" about the colonial past and the "Indonesian myth" of the heroic unifying national independence war had shaped the history of decolonization.[26] In reality, decolonization was divisive and militarily asymmetrical. The very nature of the guerrilla insurgency militated against the emergence of a unifying experience or narrative of national liberation. Divisions had emerged between regions, Dutch loyalists and nationalists, and rural and urban society. The victims of Rawagede were remembered locally but within the context of the

---

[22] Ibid.   [23] Ibid., 699.

[24] Lisette Schouten, "Netherlands East Indies' Crimes Trials in the Face of Decolonisation," in *War Crimes Trials in the Wake of Decolonization and Cold War in Asia, 1945–1956: Justice in Time of Turmoil*, ed. Kerstin von Lingen (London: Palgrave Macmillan, 2016), 219.

[25] Event sheet Rawagede, "Stop Impunity! Information and Documentation on Impunity in Indonesia," accessed July 3, 2012, www.stopimpunity.org/page51.php

[26] Stef Scagliola, "The Silences and Myths of a 'Dirty War': Coming to Terms with the Dutch–Indonesian Decolonization War (1945–1949)," *European Review of History* 14 (2007): 237.

Indonesian myth of national unity in a heroes' cemetery, a diorama depicting Dutch troops conducting the massacre and an annual village commemoration on December 9. Even though the massacre is referred to in a well-known poem by Chairil Anwar still recited by children, the Rawagede massacre was not widely known in Indonesia.[27]

The Hague Civil Court decision transformed the Rawagede massacre from a local collective memory framed by the "Indonesian myth of unity" to the broader issue of the legal recognition of suffering of victims through the official Dutch apology and compensation. Significantly, the Dutch court's decision opened the way for other victims of human rights violations to seek legal recognition and compensation including other surviving relatives of instances of Dutch colonial repression as well as the victims of the postcolonial Indonesian state's repression.[28] As a result of the Rawagede widows judgment, the Dutch government established the Civil Settlement Scheme giving access for widows of victims of mass killings committed by Dutch troops between 1945 and 1949 to make reparations claims.[29] The court's requirement that the Dutch government apologize for wrongful acts and compensate the survivors of victims of colonial crimes at Rawagede added to the existing momentum for accountability in Indonesia that had emerged with the democratic transition from Soeharto's New Order authoritarianism in 1998. By 2000, growing demands for accountability saw Law No. 26 passed creating the legal framework to address mass human rights violations which included the 1965 transition to the Soeharto regime, events in May 1998 in Jakarta and other mass crimes in Maluku, Poso, Timor Leste, Acheh, and Papua.[30] However, the outcome has amounted to de facto amnesty for those responsible for repression under Soeharto: in the operation of the human rights courts created in the post-Soeharto era there has been an almost 100 percent acquittal rate for security forces.[31] A 2004 law creating the Truth and Reconciliation Commission working alongside the

---

[27] Niniek Karmini, "Massacred Village in Indonesia Awaits Dutch Amends," *U-T San Diego News*, September 23, 2011.

[28] Haris Azhar, the Coordinator of the Human Rights group KontraS, commented at the time: "They don't want to talk about human rights no matter who did that violence or abuses in the past." "Because if they mention about the Dutch failure in the past they, the Indonesian government will have to also admit what they did in the past." See Kate Lamb, "Dutch Apologize for Indonesian Massacre," *Voice of America*, December 8, 2011.

[29] The Netherlands State, 'STAATSCOURANT Nr. 25383' (Koninkrijk der Nederlanden, September 10, 2013), accessed May 3, 2019, https://zoek.officielebekendmakingen.nl/stcrt-2013-25383.html

[30] Patrick Burgess, "De Facto Amnesty? The Example of Post-Soeharto Indonesia," in Lessa and Payne, *Amnesty in the Age of Human Rights Accountability*, Kindle Edition, 264.

[31] Ibid., 288.

courts has also been a failure.[32] It never had effect because a court decision overturned the law as unconstitutional for the reason that it negated legal protection and justice. The law was criticized on a variety of bases – its mandate was too narrow, it promoted amnesty, it failed to investigate the systematic nature of the violations, and it was not required to produce a report or circulate its findings.

In Indonesia, the Dutch court's decision prompted the Commission for Disappearances and Victims of Violence (KontraS),[33] a national NGO focused on repression under Soeharto, to comment that "[The Hague decision] will send a message to our government that they should take responsibility for their own abuses in Indonesia."[34] They pointed to the responsibility of the Soeharto regime for a series of massacres including the 1965 Communist massacre, the 1984 Tanjung Priok massacre in Jakarta, and the 1991 Dili massacre. Their main focus has been the Indonesian state's failure to address responsibility for the 1965 massacres of alleged Communists in which between 500,000 and one million died in the transition to the army-backed New Order regime of President Soeharto. The 1965 repression classified the population into groups – A, B, C. Group A were subjected to execution or life imprisonment and Groups B and C were imprisoned or exiled on Buru Island between 1966 and 1979. When released in the 1970s, these ex-detainees lost political and other rights, including the right to travel, and their children and relatives have been excluded from government employment as teachers, civil servants, and military. Survivors of the 1965 massacres still suffer institutionalized discrimination and school-children are still taught about the heroic military defeat of the corrupt Communists. Only recently the government of President Joko Widodo organized a forum to discuss the events of 1965, but the president ruled out any criminal investigation opting instead for a statement of "remorse for past events."[35]

In Indonesia, the key to challenging impunity has been the victims/survivors as carrier groups of cultural trauma and justice impetus created by their "human right to know the fate of family members" under the International Convention for the Protection of All Persons from

[32] Louise Mallinder, "Global Comparison of Amnesty Laws," in *The Pursuit of International Criminal Justice: A World Study on Conflicts, Victimization, and Post-Conflict Justice*, ed. M. Cherif Bassiouni (Antwerp: Intersentia, 2010).

[33] KontraS was established in 1998 to investigation disappearances that had occurred at the end of the Soeharto New Order regime. See www.kontras.org (accessed December 12, 2016).

[34] "Indonesian Rights Activists Applaud Rawagede," *Jakarta Globe*, September 15, 2011.

[35] "Truth and Reconciliation in Indonesia," *New York Times*, April 21, 2016.

Enforced Disappearance. Decolonization based on Dutch silence and the Indonesian myth of the unifying struggle excluded victims from the national narrative except as sacrificed martyrs, not as individual bearers of human rights. Until the recent Rawagede widows judgments, the survivors were denied international recognition because of the Dutch state's denial of legal responsibility. Their cultural trauma existed in the conditions of "cultural aphasia," historically absent "because of a lack of vocabulary or a lack of possibilities for expression."[36] They have been politically marginalized in Indonesia because of the problem of state impunity for post-independence repression. Under the Soeharto New Order (1967–98) historical debates about decolonization were avoided in the context of an "enormous fog" about state suppression of ethnic conflicts, religious insurrection, and internal warfare.[37] Even in the post-Soeharto era impunity has persisted. It seems everyone has been able to avoid the juridification of the past by banking on the passage of time extinguishing the possibility of victims making claims because they would no longer be alive to make any claims.[38]

Unfortunately the widows who benefited from Dutch court decision on historical injustice in Rawagede did not emerge as national symbols of a new justice or a focus for community solidarity. When their fellow villagers, many of whom had shared the same predicament and suffering but were not part of the lawsuit, learned about the amount of compensation they were envious and demanded a share.[39] They tried to force widows to hand over their compensation and in one case a widow who fled the village in fear was sought out in Jakarta by other massacre survivors demanding she return to the village and sign over her court-awarded compensation (€20,000) to all the families.[40] Even the development aid granted by the Dutch government in 2008 as a form of collective reparation in acknowledgment that the killings at Rawagede were unlawful has yet to be distributed because of disputes over village representation. Rather than evidence of the expansion of historical justice, albeit very delayed, the Rawagede widows' experience highlights international law's highly symbolic and limited impact on redressing the injustices of colonial rule.

[36] Bijl, "Colonial Memory and Forgetting," 456.
[37] Remco Raben, "On Genocide and Mass Violence in Colonial Indonesia," *Journal of Genocide Research* 14, nos. 3–4 (2012): 494.
[38] van den Herik, "Addressing Colonial Crimes," 704.
[39] Niniek Ka, "Indonesian Village Riven by Dutch Massacre Compensation," *Jakarta Globe*, July 16, 2012.
[40] "The Netherlands Apologies for Rawagede Massacre, Pays Compensation" Dutch News.nl, December 11, 2011.

Mau Mau Veterans in the High Court London

The Mau Mau movement emerged from the dominant Kikuyu tribe in Kenya as an armed guerrilla campaign against continued British colonial rule in 1950. In response the British declared the "Mau Mau Emergency" (1952–60) and mounted an armed guerrilla campaign during which they detained 160,000–320,000 Mau Mau partisans and forced the large-scale relocation of Kikuyu communities to transit camps and reserves.[41] Suspected Mau Mau members were detained, tortured, and some subjected to capital punishment. Between 1952 and 1958 around 3,000 Mau Mau were put on trial for capital crimes and 1,090 were executed.[42] Suspected Mau Mau sympathizers were subjected to collective punishment through enforced villagization which concentrated 1,050,899 Kikuyu into 804 villages enclosed with barbed wire and through seizures of Kikuyu land.[43]

In June 2009, five Mau Mau veterans who were members of the Mau Mau War Veterans Association filed "claims for damages for personal injuries brought against the Foreign and Commonwealth Office ("the FCO") (representing the British government) in respect of the 'torts' (actionable wrongs) of assault and battery, and negligence" to the High Court.[44] The Mau Mau claimants, represented by the London law firm Leigh Day with the support of the Kenya Human Rights Commission, sought an apology and damages for torture they suffered while in detention between 1954 and 1959. A further 5,228 individuals were joined to the case after Leigh Day interviewed a further 15,000 Kenyans.[45] The case was opposed by the UK government on the grounds the government could not be held responsible and that "the claims are time barred and should be thrown out of the High Court."[46] However, as occurred in The Hague Civil Court which initially refused to hear the Rawagede widows' claims on the grounds of the statute of limitations, the UK High Court

---

[41] Caroline Elkins, *Imperial Reckoning: The Untold Story of Britain's Gulag in Kenya* (New York: Henry Holt, 2005), 430.

[42] David M. Anderson, *Histories of the Hanged: Britain's Dirty War and the End of Empire* (London: Weidenfeld & Nicholson, 2005), 7.

[43] Caroline Elkins, *Imperial Reckoning: The Untold Story of Britain's Gulag in Kenya* (New York: Henry Holt, 2005), 235.

[44] Caroline Elkins, "Alchemy of Evidence: Mau Mau, the British Empire, and the High Court of Justice," *Journal of Imperial and Commonwealth History* 39 (2011): 732.

[45] Jennifer L. Balint, "The 'Mau Mau' Legal Hearings and Recognizing the Crimes of the British Colonial State: A Limited Constitutive Moment," *Critical Analysis of Law* 3 (2016): 272

[46] "Veterans of 1950s Mau Mau Uprising in Kenya Seek UK Damages," *BBC News*, July 15, 2012.

determined (July 21, 2012) that the claimants could sue the British Foreign Office for their alleged torture fifty years ago. The High Court found they had an "arguable" case and it would be "dishonourable" to block the action.[47] The four Kenyans, Ndiku Mutwiwa Mutua, Paulo Muoka Nzili, Wambugu Wa Nyingi, and Jane Muthoni Mara, all in their seventies and eighties, suffered systematic abuse in special concentration camps. A fifth claimant had died since the action began. The claims were set to go for full trial when in 2013 the UK government reached a reparations agreement in settlement of the claims but refused to accept responsibility for the harms which contradicted the widely publicly accepted "colonial narrative of Britain as saviour."[48] A key shift in legal reasoning in determining the case should go to trial was that Justice McCombe found that there existed a "duty of care" for these historical harms in former colonies.[49] The UK government had come under significant pressure from international and national human rights NGOs who pointed out that Britain's obstructive stance toward allegations of torture sent out the wrong message to African governments who act with impunity.[50]

The Mau Mau veterans' claims in the UK High Court were framed by a human rights construction of decolonization as struggle between perpetrators and victims. While in one sense this version is accurate in another it ignores the Mau Mau veterans' experience as marginalized and criminalized victims in the independence negotiations and the politics of post-independence Kenya. The cultural trauma of decolonization did not put the Mau Mau at the center of a unifying national narrative of *Uruhu* (independence) even though today the ruling party, Kenya Alliance for National Unity (KANU, originally Kenya African National Union), dominated by the Kikuyu elite, present themselves as the legatees of the Mau Mau as anti-colonial heroes.[51] Historically, the Mau Mau war was divisive and they were feared and suspected by Kikuyu loyalists and the minority tribes.

Unlike the Dutch East Indies decolonization in Kenya was a managed process in which the British set out to determine to whom they would hand over power to best safeguard their own post-independence interests. The 1954 Lyttleton constitution essentially laid the ground for the fundamental divisions of post-independence Kenyan politics between

---

[47] Dominic Casciani, "Mau Mau Kenyans Allowed to Sue UK government," *BBC News*, July 21, 2012.
[48] Balint, "'Mau Mau' Legal Hearings," 268.   [49] Ibid.   [50] Ibid., 275.
[51] Daniel Branch, *Defeating Mau Mau, Creating Kenya: Counterinsurgency, Civil War, and Decolonisation* (Cambridge, UK: Cambridge University Press, 2009).

nationalist (centralist) and *majimboist* (federalist based on tribal and ethnic identities) politics. The competition between Kenya African National Union (KANU) as nationalist and the Kenyan African Democratic Union (KADU) as federalist was along these lines. The Mau Mau war produced a political landscape divided between "loyalists" and "liberationists" which framed the conditions for the transition from settler colonialism to independent majority rule. Colonial propaganda demonized the Kikuyu as Mau Mau extremists and sowed distrust in Kikuyu politicians among other Kenyan ethnic groups that was reinforced by a historical fear of the extension of Kikuyu colonization of Kenya's Rift Valley and Western Highlands that had occurred during more than fifty years of colonial rule.[52]

Decolonization in Kenya fits the "transitional amnesty" model – transition based on elite political consensus and mutual amnesty and the marginalization of those who oppose the deal or want justice. The British forged a political consensus between regional tribal identities as a counter to centralized power and the "loyalists," those willing to implement British decolonization policy. While the Mau Mau and many of their families were held in detention the "loyalists" were able to take advantage of the bureaucratic process of decolonization.[53] The detainees lost their land to Kikuyu loyalists through colonial land consolidation programs and were excluded from new civil service jobs that loyalists monopolized. From the perspective of the Mau Mau detainees the "loyalists" extended the privilege they held under the British into the postcolonial state and continued their war against the Mau Mau by rejecting their claims for restitution and rehabilitation.[54]

As in Indonesia, the post-independence narrative of decolonization was based on the colonizer's silence and the colonized's myth of the heroic unifying national struggle. Official British silence on the colonial past was epitomized in the recent the Hanslope Disclosures.[55] Vast numbers of sensitive and incriminating files had been repatriated from

[52] David M. Anderson, "'Yours in Struggle for *Majimbo.*' Nationalism and the Party Politics of Decolonization in Kenya, 1955–64," *Journal of Contemporary History* 40 (2005): 552.

[53] Derek R. Peterson, Review of *Defeating Mau Mau, Creating Kenya: Counterinsurgency, Civil War, and Decolonization* in *Journal of Imperial and Commonwealth History* 38 (2010): 337; David M. Anderson, "Making the Loyalist Bargain: Surrender, Amnesty and Impunity in Kenya's Decolonization, 1952–63," *International History Review* 39, no. 1 (2017): 48–70.

[54] Branch, *Defeating Mau Mau.*

[55] Elkins, "Alchemy of Evidence," 742; David M. Anderson, "Mau Mau in the High Court and the 'Lost' British Empire Archives: Colonial Conspiracy or Bureaucratic Bungle?," *Journal of Imperial and Commonwealth History* 39 (2011): 699.

British colonies in order to quarantine the colonial past from scrutiny. Interestingly, the significance of the still unknown Hanslope Disclosures had become apparent to historians of the colonial period (Caroline Elkins, David Anderson, Huw Bennett) working in support of the Mau Mau veterans' claims.[56] Their own research interviews with the veterans revealed that their experiences were missing from the existing Kenya colonial archives.

The myth of national unity became the independence platform adopted by President Kenyatta in 1961 to distance himself and KANU from the stigmatized Mau Mau partisans so as to be able to represent KANU as an inclusive national party. The national unity narrative was also juxtaposed to the platform of KADU and the anti-Mau Mau loyalists who favored ethnic/tribal pluralism and federalism (*majimboism*).[57] Still today when KANU emphasizes its nationalist credentials by claiming the Mau Mau as nationalist heroes they at the same time "position the Luo, the Kalenjin and other ethnic groups at the margins of Kenya's political theatre."[58]

The Mau Mau claims before the UK High Court emerge from broader transitional justice initiatives in Kenya to address the chronic political violence around elections and the problem of impunity.[59] The Kenyan Human Rights Commission report *Justice Delayed: Historical Injustices in Kenya* lists unaddressed human rights violations dating back to the colonial period. Using human rights as an objective lens with which to condemn historical impunity, and avoid political fallout in the present, the report lists the following massacres committed with impunity: "Kisumu town massacres (1969), Bulla Kartasi (1980 – Garissa); Malka Mari (1981 – Mandera); Wagalla (Wajir – 1984); Bagalla (1998 – Garissa); Elwak (2008 – Mandera); Turbi (2005–2009 – Marsabit); Mathira (2009 – Nyeri); Isiolo (2009), among others."[60] The report identifies systemic patterns of massacre, political assassination, population displacement, ethnic/tribal targeting of violence, and land grabs which extended from the colonial to the postcolonial era, as in Indonesia.

The electoral violence that followed the December 2007 election resulting in 1,300 dead and the displacement of 300,000 saw a variety of transitional justice measures introduced to investigate responsibility

---

[56] Elkins, "Alchemy of Evidence," 743.
[57] Anderson, "Yours in Struggle for *Majimbo*," 547.
[58] Peterson, Review of *Defeating Mau Mau*, 337.
[59] Kituo Cha Katiba, *Revisiting Transitional Justice: A Non-Partisan and Non-Governmental Engagement* (Nairobi: Ford Foundation, December 7, 2007).
[60] Davis Malombe, *Justice Delayed: A Status Report on Historical Injustices in Kenya* (Nairobi: Kenya Human Rights Commission, 2011), 9.

for the post-election violence and to promote national reconciliation. One measure was the establishment of the Truth, Justice and Reconciliation Commission of Kenya that President Kibaki (KANU) launched in 2009. However the TJRC has been accused of bias and neglect from its inception until the recent release of its findings.[61] The lack of effective official investigation saw the ICC indict four senior politicians for a trial beginning in September 2012.[62] This decision to prosecute senior political leaders put the ICC process right in the middle of the electoral contest for the 2013 presidential elections.[63] Two of the co-accused who had been electoral opponents in 2007, Uhuru Kenyatta and William Ruto formed the Jubilee Alliance in an anti-Western anti-ICC campaign and were elected president and deputy president.

The Mau Mau High Court hearing in London is the result of the persistence of a survivor "carrier group," the Mau Mau veterans, in making rights claims and the expansion of transitional justice mechanisms in the context of chronic political violence in post-independence Kenya. The claimants were galvanized by the emergence of a revisionist history of decolonization,[64] the transitional justice initiatives post-2008 electoral violence and most recently by the ICC indictment of six senior Kenyan politicians. Yet the cultural trauma of decolonization as experienced by the Mau Mau partisans and the Kikuyu population was not easily integrated into the myth of unifying national struggle. Even today KANU's embrace of the Mau Mau as anti-colonial heroes is inextricable from the long-standing political competition between centralists and federalists. The juridification of the past and the challenge to impunity it signifies remains overshadowed by the neocolonial legacies of Kenya's decolonization which include strong tribal identities.

The Mau Mau High Court case has broken the British official silence on decolonization, especially the discovery of the Hanslope colonial archive unearthed by British historians working on the Mau Mau claims. By framing the Mau Mau's human rights as an instance of historical injustice violations the Kenyan Human Rights Commission has placed impunity for political violence and repression in the postcolonial state on the public agenda – this is what the '49 Coffins Protest' highlighted.

[61] Peter Orengo, "Civil Society Wants Kenyans to Reject TJRC Report," *Standard Digital,* March 22, 2012.

[62] Laban Wanambisi and Afp, "Kenya: Cases against Kenya 4 to Kick off in April 2013," allAfrica.com, July 9, 2012. "The ICC and Kenya: Understanding the Confirmation of Charges Hearings," *Kenyans for Peace, Truth and Justice Bulletin,* September 2011.

[63] International Crisis Group, "Kenya: Impact of the ICC Proceedings," Africa Briefings, No. 84, January 9, 2012.

[64] Elkins, "Alchemy of Evidence," 736.

However the limitations of human rights accountability in challenging impunity have recently become very apparent first in the UK High Court's rejection of the second Mau Mau claim in 2018 and second in the Kenyan political elite's denunciation of the ICC intervention as a neocolonial institution after they had been indicted by it for post-election violence in 2008. The political protagonists and indictees, Uhuru Kenyatta and William Ruto, joined forces in the Jubilee Alliance and won the 2013 election in a campaign focused on delegitimization of the ICC prosecutions.[65] In the end the ICC prosecutions failed because of the obstacles it faced in gathering information and securing witnesses.

Conclusion

The hearing of the Rawagede widows' and the Mau Mau veterans' claims for compensation for past colonial crimes in the Netherlands and the UK respectively extend the reach of the restorative justice project into the colonial past. Individuals denied justice for more than fifty years have reentered history recognized as survivors of human rights violations. Their experience highlights the contemporary role of this cohort as a carrier group whose personal memory and cultural trauma embodies injustices and provides the legal means to initiate investigations and prosecutions for past crimes long after the actual events. Through these judicial hearings, their stories have articulated the cultural trauma of colonization as a metanarrative of the historical wrongs of colonizers. The human rights construction of the subject positions of perpetrator/ victim simplifies decolonization into the crimes of the colonizer committed against the colonized.

The reason why the Rawagede widows and Mau Mau veterans have only just become visible as victims of past human rights violations relates to the distinct role human rights has played during the age of decolonization and post–Cold War democratization. Human rights informed the global movement for decolonization by legitimating the right to self-determination, but it did not shape political transition as a moment requiring accountability and restorative justice at that time. Decolonization was a managed transition shaped by transitional amnesty – the asymmetrical power of the colonizer to determine the terms under which they handed over power. Independence was constructed as a moment of complete rupture with the past reinforced by Dutch and British silence about the repression during decolonization and by Indonesian and

---

[65] Sara Kendall, "'UhuRuto' and Other Leviathans: The International Criminal Court and the Kenyan Political Order," *African Journal of Legal Studies* 7 (2014): 417.

Kenyan myths of the unifying national struggle for independence. Negotiated decolonization involved transitional amnesty that managed victims of human rights violations by either subordinating their trauma as collective sacrifice for national independence or by excluding them as disruptive of the official narrative of national unity.

The Rawagede widows and Mau Mau veterans emerged as claimants in the context of expanding international law and the human rights advocacy of international moral entrepreneurs creating new opportunities for the juridification of the past. More specifically their claims were the result of the introduction of transitional justice initiatives in Indonesia after the fall of Soeharto's New Order regime in 1998 and in Kenya after the large-scale post-election violence in 2007. A variety of measures promoting accountability and reconciliation were adopted including human rights courts and truth commissions. These transitional justice initiatives were directed at the problem of authoritarianism and internal political repression and chronic impunity of political elites in these postcolonial states.

The UK and Dutch court hearings have opened the way for other claimants, but it is unlikely there will be many more because the survivors of colonial repression are near the end of their lives and because the legal obstacles and costs are high. Hence in 2013 the UK government in settlement of the original case brought by five torture victims paid out more than £19.9 million in costs and compensation to 5,228 Kenyans who suffered torture and abuse during the Mau Mau uprising a second much larger case was dismissed in December 2018.[66] The second claim involving 40,000 Kenyans against the British Foreign Office for abuse suffered during the Mau Mau Emergency (1952–60), after a massive litigation that spanned 232 hearing days, failed when the judge decided not to extend the statute of limitations on their claims.[67] Because the litigation proceeded on the basis of "no win, no fee" the lawyers who had worked on the second claim received no remuneration for six years' work. Children of victims of Dutch counterinsurgency repression in Sulawesi in 1947 have also made claims for compensation in The Hague.[68] Of greater significance may be its analogical effect with the mobilization of claimants from across the spectrum of victims of postcolonial repression to challenge impunity in the postcolonial state.

---

[66] "UK to Compensate Kenya's Mau Mau Torture Victims," *The Guardian*, June 6, 2013.

[67] Simon Murray, "The Kenya Emergency Group Litigation Concludes," *Lexology*, December 21, 2018.

[68] "Dutch Apology for Indonesian Colonial Atrocities Opens Old Wounds," *The Straits Times*, May 1, 2014.

The historical revisionism of decolonization as a chronicle of human rights violations in need of restorative justice is being extended to include a critique of the post-colonial narrative of sacrifice and national unity as exclusionary and unjust. Citizens already view national political leadership as compromised, not heroic, and the claims of the victims of human rights violations against the postcolonial state have become a barometer of the degradation of citizenship. While the recent trials in the UK and Dutch courts involving victims of colonial repression may have served to evoke a feeling of national unity anchored in the historical anti-colonial struggle human rights claims about repression under the postcolonial state seem to do the opposite. Claims of victimhood against the postcolonial state are more likely to divide and fragment society along ethnic, religious, and regional lines rather than unify society through human rights solidarity. In Kenya one impact of the ICC prosecutions was to intensify the ethnicization of politics, reinforce elite pactism, and perpetuate elite impunity.

Part III

Colonial and Neocolonial Responses

11 The Inventors of Human Rights in Africa
Portugal, Late Colonialism, and the UN Human Rights Regime

Miguel Bandeira Jerónimo and José Pedro Monteiro

Introduction

In 1966, eleven years after the admission of Portugal to the United Nations, Franco Nogueira, the Portuguese Minister of Foreign Affairs and one of the leading advocates of the multiple doctrines of exceptionality that governed the Portuguese postwar imperial ideology, stated that "we, and only we, [the Portuguese] brought the notion of human rights and racial equality to Africa, before anyone else." Echoing a particular set of ideas subsumed under the name of lusotropicalism, proposed by the Brazilian sociologist Gilberto Freyre and used instrumentally by the authorities, Nogueira added that the Portuguese were the only ones who practiced "multiracialism," the "most perfect and daring expression of human fraternity and sociological progress."[1] These statements, whose meaning and purpose were shared by many not only within the imperial and diplomatic administrative chain, were made in Lourenço Marques, five years after the beginning of conflicts in Angola and almost three years after the extension of colonial war to Guinea-Bissau and Mozambique itself. Despite the fact that the *indigenato* regime – the legal framework that assigned distinct legal and penal statues and social and cultural rights to "citizens" (white Portuguese and "assimilated" Africans) and "natives" – was only abolished *de jure* in 1961, more than a decade after the Universal Declaration of Human

This research was cofinanced by FEDER (Fundo Europeu de Desenvolvimento Regional) through COMPETE 2020 – Programa Operacional Competitividade e Internacionalização (POCI) and by national funds through FCT (Fundação para a Ciência e a Tecnologia), in association with the research project "The Worlds of (Under)development: Processes and Legacies of the Portuguese Colonial Empire in a Comparative Perspective (1945–1975)" (PTDC/HAR-HIS/31906/2017 | POCI-01–0145-FEDER-031906) and also by the individual research project CEECIND/01714/2017/CP1042/CT0004, funded by the Portuguese Foundation for Science and Technology. The authors of this chapter want to thank the editors of this volume – Roland Burke, Marco Duranti, and Dirk Moses – for their critical remarks and suggestions. The same appreciation goes to Eva-Maria Muschik and Steven Jensen.

[1] Franco Nogueira, *O Terceiro Mundo* (Lisbon: Ática, 1967), 197.

Rights, and despite the continuation of widespread forms of social and racial discrimination in the "overseas provinces," the languages of citizenship and human and social rights were appropriated in a particular way by the Portuguese authorities.

The convoluted and historically dense relationship between the affirmation and universalization of idioms and repertoires of human rights and the process of global decolonization has been the subject of growing attention from numerous scholars in the last few years. A sophisticated literature about such interaction has emerged – some supporting, some contradicting – assessing multiple chronologies and geographies, though so far omitting the case of Portuguese colonialism.[2] The absence of Portugal is, in important ways, a crucial ellipsis in the scholarship because it is one of the very few that endured into the apparent "breakthrough" moment of the 1970s, a decisive point in the evolution of contemporary rights discourse.[3] It is still more so given the centrality of human rights as one of the prime languages through which international condemnation of the Salazar regime was expressed. Like the case of apartheid South Africa, a country much more prominent in human rights literature, Portugal was a late "de-colonizer."[4] Its incorporation in the literature enables, or reinforces, the introduction of a distinct temporality in the debates about the connections between human rights and the end of empire. It further historicizes, in a more nuanced way, the affirmation and development of a lingua franca of human rights. As the ongoing

[2] For some major contributions, see Bonny Ibhawoh, *Imperialism and Human Rights: Colonial Discourses of Rights and Liberties in African History* (New York: SUNY, 2007); Roland Burke, *Decolonization and the Evolution of International Human Rights* (Philadelphia: University of Pennsylvania Press, 2010); Jan Eckel, "Human Rights and Decolonization: New Perspectives and Open Questions," *Humanity* 1, no. 1 (2010): 111–35; Andreas Eckert, "African Nationalists and Human Rights, 1940s–1970s," in *Human Rights in the Twentieth Century*, ed. Stefan-Ludwig Hoffmann (Cambridge, UK: Cambridge University Press, 2011), 283–300; Meredith Terretta, "From Below and to the Left? Human Rights and Liberation Politics in Africa's Postcolonial Age," *Journal of World History* 24, no. 2 (2013): 389–416; Fabian Klose, *Human Rights in the Shadow of Colonial Violence* (Philadelphia: University of Pennsylvania Press, 2013); Steven Jensen, *The Making of International Human Rights: The 1960s, Decolonization and the Reconstruction of Global Values* (New York: Cambridge University Press, 2016).

[3] The relationship between human rights and decolonization is patently understudied in the literature about Portuguese late colonialism and decolonization. A first systematic approach is underway. Miguel Bandeira Jerónimo and José Pedro Monteiro, *Os inventores dos direitos humanos: Portugal, o colonialismo tardio e o regime dos direitos humanos (1948-1975)* (forthcoming).

[4] See Saul Dubow, *South Africa's Struggle for Human Rights: The History of Rights in South Africa* (Athens: Ohio University Press, 2012); Saul Dubow, *Apartheid, 1948-1994* (Oxford: Oxford University Press, 2014); Ryan Irwin, *Gordian Knot: Apartheid and the Unmaking of the Liberal World Order* (Oxford: Oxford University Press, 2012).

arguments about the genealogies of human rights reveal, and the Portuguese case demonstrates – timing matters.[5]

Another fact that makes the Portuguese case an important contribution to the overall debate on the tensions between imperialist, nationalist, and internationalist visions on human rights is the authoritarian nature of the regime and, also, the fact that a predominantly racialized juridical order survived the disintegration of the majority of European colonial empires. The study of the chronologies and of the modalities of intersections between human rights and nondiscrimination, on one hand, and self-determination and decolonization, on the other, gains a new crucial observatory. This chapter reveals why and how, historically questioning the strict boundaries commonly established between technical and political domains, between individual and collective rights. It interrogates how the historical dynamics of Portuguese late colonialism were affected by human rights politics. It examines the uses of the latter as a political instrument against the modus operandi of the Portuguese colonial empire, but also as a crucial device that an imperial formation used to tentatively demonstrate its international legitimacy and its *progressive* ability to govern subject peoples. The focus on the period 1955–65 enables an understanding of such impact before and after the eruption of the colonial wars. It will also address, less extensively, developments during the late 1960s and early 1970s to illustrate the continuities and the ruptures entailed by the intensification of the colonial conflicts within and international pressures over the Portuguese empire.

The first part deals with the Portuguese initial engagement with the United Nations (1955–60). It explores the impact of the growing internationalization and politicization of the Portuguese colonial question. The latter prompted new efforts of imperial self-scrutiny, compelling the Portuguese authorities to dialogue with the emerging idioms and repertoires of human rights, adjusting their own discourses and arguments of imperial justification, with a view to counteract criticism from abroad. Such criticism was, increasingly, defined by the invocation of human rights as the basis for challenging imperial legitimacy. These dynamics, moreover, fostered a reformist imagination within the bureaucratic chain.

The second part focuses on a period (1961–5) marked by the persistence of transformative nexuses between international scrutiny and denunciation, imperial self-scrutiny, administrative rationalization and

---

[5] See, for instance, Jan Eckel and Samuel Moyn, eds., *The Breakthrough: Human Rights in the 1970s* (Philadelphia: University of Pennsylvania Press, 2014).

adaptation, and eventual reform. Due to several critical developments – in the colonies, at the metropole and at international forums – this period was characterized by far-reaching political and ideological transformations.

Although the latter were characterized by numerous ambiguities regarding their presiding motivations and their intended direction and scope, they surely aimed to counterbalance criticism targeting the prevailing politics of *difference*. These were seen as ostensible violations of the evolving human rights regime, which condemned political and juridical orders based on the distinction and discrimination of groups on grounds of race or "cultural advancement."

Thus, this chapter illuminates the fundamental implications of Portuguese engagement with international human rights repertoires, namely in what relates to its impact on imperial politics and on the strategies of the Portuguese empire-state. It then focuses on a series of episodes that took place after the outbreak of the colonial wars, stressing the incorporation of human rights languages in anti-colonial initiatives and, also, highlighting the efforts of their appropriation by the Portuguese authorities, with a view to sustain their strategies to cope with pressures toward decolonization.

Finding a Modus Operandi: The Challenges of International Integration (1955–1960)

On the Political Usefulness of Statistics

In October 1956, the Overseas Ministry sent a letter to the Director of the Institute of Overseas Studies, Adriano Moreira, asking for a list of works published in Portugal about human rights. Moreira, future minister and well-known imperial ideologue, stated that no single study existed. Resulting from a request by the UN, it was also a symptom of a growing concern in Portugal with developments on the topic. The international integration of Portugal was expanding, and faced fresh challenges. Human rights needed to be studied, its novel idioms mastered, its precise scope determined, and its political implications evaluated.[6] Since the admission to the UN, Portugal focused its imperial diplomatic strategy on the Fourth Committee of the General Assembly, which was responsible for trusteeship over the nonautonomous territories and decolonization-related affairs. The main concern related to the

---

[6] Overseas Ministry to Adriano Moreira, 18–10–1956; Adriano Moreira to Overseas Ministry, 9–11–1956, Archive of the Ministry of Foreign Affairs [hereafter AMFA]/ MU-GM-GNP-RRI-00562.

contested debate about Article 73, which determined the provision of information on economic, educational, social progress, and political development by colonial administrations. It deeply conditioned the relationship with the UN given the Portuguese government's refusal to provide the requested information, arguing that it had no self-governing territories.[7] Gradually, however, this selective approach to UN activities became untenable. The engagement with the Third Committee, its debates and consequences, direct and indirect, was the most revealing example of a gradual strategic redefinition. Dealing with social, humanitarian, and cultural matters and human rights, it was a privileged observatory of the challenges and the opportunities posed by postwar international momentum.[8]

In November 1956, the Portuguese representative Henrique Martins de Carvalho, colonial affairs expert at the Foreign Affairs Ministry, provided a "factual verification" of a major problem: the Portuguese stand was ideologically, legally, and in practice distinct from the great majority of the UN members.[9] The detrimental impact of this fact was immediately emphasized by Portuguese officials in New York. The delegation needed to be prepared to deal with the vast set of issues being gradually addressed at the Third Committee and, perhaps more importantly, to be able to foresee its political consequences. The list of fundamental issues to be reviewed was revealing: the national legal expression of concepts of self-determination and religious freedom; the (in)equality of rights between men and women; the right and duty to work (associated with "forced labour"); freedom of association; the role of the "political police"; the uses of penal labour; or the existing rights of ethnic minorities (a "delicate" problem given the "overseas native populations"). The likely contradictions between the related imperial legal framework and respective social practices and the new principles being fiercely debated in New York should be solved immediately.[10]

The "inconvenient recommendations" that derived from the proposal made by the Greek Constantin Eustathiades increased the urgency of

---

[7] Aurora Santos, "A Organização das Nações Unidas e a Questão Colonial Portuguesa, 1961–1970" (PhD diss., Lisbon: FCSH/UNL, 2014); Fernando Martins, "Portugal e a Organização das Nações Unidas" (MA diss., FCSH/UNL, 1995).

[8] Miguel Bandeira Jerónimo and António Costa Pinto, special issue "International Dimensions of Portuguese late colonialism and decolonization," *Portuguese Studies* 29, no. 2 (2013): 137–276.

[9] Note by Carvalho, 16–11–1956, AMFA/POI-135.

[10] Note by Carvalho and J. M. Fragoso, "confidential – urgent," 30–11–1956, AMFA/POI-135.

this process of information gathering, self-scrutiny, renewed strategic orientation and decision-making, and, conceivably, reform. The Portuguese believed that the "unity thesis" promoted at the Fourth Committee should be advocated at the Third Committee. Coherence was fundamental. But if no "colonial pact," no colonial clause, was recognized by the latter, the "situation of the population overseas" would surely come under critical evaluation.[11] Moreover, it was expected that a proposal for a high commissioner on human rights, with executive powers, would be advanced by the Uruguayan delegation, a historically protracted "contested project."[12] That would likely enhance international scrutiny and "interventionism." "Pessimism" pervaded the delegation, a state of mind surely enhanced by the fact that the questions of "colonialism, racial segregation and religious persecution" would be discussed soon. In such discussions, Portugal was bound to fare poorly. More legal and statistical information was needed about the topics highlighted above but also, crucially, about overseas realities.[13]

In a confidential report, in early 1957, the Greek and the Uruguayan proposals were described as an "offensive to administration powers." Despite being both defeated at the end, they continued to be feared. Supervision was considered a form of interventionism, and should be rebuffed. Several delaying strategies had been so far effective. Bureaucratic procrastination was used, and abused. So far, the results were "favourable" to all that countries that "feared" the transformation of the covenants into "an instrument of intervention." But the move from a "humanitarian problem" to a "political problem" was seen as hardly stoppable, not least because the debates about human rights were carried on in "contexts always inflamed by demagogy." The intensification of the politicization of human rights debates was foreseen.[14]

A specific example of topics being debated with serious political implications – one that exemplified the assessment of the commission as a forum of expected difficulties – was education. The repercussions of the norms on "fundamental education" and "religious education" could

---

[11] Ibid.
[12] See Theo Van Boven, "The United Nations High Commissioner for Human Rights: The History of a Contested Project," *Leiden Journal of International Law* 20 (2007): 767–84; Roger S. Clark, *A United Nations High Commissioner for Human Rights* (The Hague: Martinus Nijhoff, 1972); Andrew Clapham, "Mainstreaming Human Rights at the United Nations: The Task of the First High Commissioner for Human Rights," *Collected Courses of the Academy of European Law*, vol. II, Book 2 (1999), 159–234.
[13] Vasco Garin to Ministry of Foreign Affairs, 7 and 15–12–1956, AMFA/POI-135.
[14] Henrique Martins de Carvalho, *Relatório da Terceira Comissão* (Lisbon: February/March 1957). Confidential, AMFA-Library, 8, 10, 58–9, 70, 72.

jeopardize Portuguese advocacy of the unity thesis.[15] The comparative statistical assessment of educational realities would surely reveal unpleasant facts. Recent publications highlighted Portuguese Guinea as one of the regions of the world with lower literacy rates. As a consequence, the officials argued, other "useful" statistics were needed, in order to "demonstrate" two points: that the percentage of illiteracy in the overseas provinces was sometimes "identical (if not smaller)" to certain metropolitan areas and that the percentage of illiteracy in the overseas provinces was "not worse than those of certain independent countries." The comparison with postcolonial territories was always an attractive strategy, one shared by other colonial powers.[16] As Nogueira proclaimed, "our provinces of Africa are more developed, more progressive, more advanced in all domains than any territory recently independent in Africa South of Sahara."[17]

Self-determination, of course, was always a dominant concern. The idea to create an ad hoc commission to study of the "concept of self-determination" was particularly feared. This solution would necessarily be "anti-colonial": it would include a member of the Soviet bloc, probably India, and another "neutralist." To impede its presumed negative effects, the approval of the "Portuguese unity" thesis within the Fourth Committee was crucial. That way the overseas provinces would be outside of the commission's scope. Otherwise, enquiries and requests for *in situ* missions were to be expected. Refusal was an option, but one with significant political costs. The overall impression was that the "existing or upcoming attacks" against Portugal in the Fourth Committee would occur as well in the Third. The latter debates about economic, social, and cultural rights, on one hand, and on political and civil rights, on the other, would have consequences. The "problem of self-determination" would certainly be addressed "with greater acuteness." To reinforce the strategy being carried out was crucial. The argument should be repeated: "the problem is not with us, as all Portuguese territories are self-governed." Given such a proposition, Portugal could "behave as many countries of the UN" and even "accuse colonial countries." But the Third Committee's workings widened the challenges, multiplied its potential implications, and increased the costs of particular policies to the Portuguese government. The ways to critically address the colonial question diversified. Again, a "more careful preparation of the Portuguese representation" was

---

[15] Phillip W. Jones, *International Policies for Third World Education: Unesco, Literacy and Development* (London: Routledge, 1988); Chloé Maurel, *Histoire de l'Unesco: Les trente premières années, 1945–1974* (Paris: L'Harmattan, 2010).
[16] Garin to Ministry of Foreign Affairs, 17–12–1956, AMFA/POI-135.
[17] Nogueira, *O Terceiro Mundo*, 198.

considered mandatory. Technical counseling was desperately needed. In 1956–7, no expert on labor issues was present. For the years 1957–8, experts on labor and education were regarded as fundamental. These considerations perhaps explain, to a certain degree, the scarce Portuguese participation at the debates of the Third Committee, which was determined by instructions coming from Lisbon.[18]

The appearance of proposals that could hamper the overall Portuguese strategy and the diversification of potential topics of criticism about the metropolitan and colonial realities were duly noted. These facts triggered alerts within the Portuguese government and imperial administration. The assumed process of politicization of human rights and the acknowledgment of the need to increase and improve the expertise to deal with the growing engagement within the UN continued to capture the imperial 'official mind' in the coming years. In 1958, ten years after the Universal Declaration of the Human Rights, the two main challenges to be faced at the Thirteenth General Assembly were singled out by one official. The first was the "problem of the non-autonomous territories." The second, closely related, was the creation, by the UN Economic and Social Council (ECOSOC), of the Economic Commission for Africa, which mandate was focused on the production and diffusion of economic expertise that could bolster development in the continent. The need to create a permanent body that could prepare an effective participation at the UN meetings, based on a knowledgeable and strategic engagement with their agendas, was seen as imperative by the 'official mind.' Given the abovementioned challenges, an interministerial committee was suggested. The committee should be the forum in which the gathering of information, self-scrutiny and policy assessment, diplomatic and political decision-making should occur.[19] As Nogueira stated, the recommendations regarding technical matters formulated by the committee should always take into account "aspects of political nature." The "technical" issues were intrinsically political.[20]

On How to Fit into "International Classifications," and Not Offend the "Sensibilities" of the "International Arena"

According to those at the Ministry of Foreign Affairs, the Portuguese "justifications to the international community" should be governed by a

---

[18] Carvalho, *Relatório da Terceira Comissão*, 12, 71, 78, 80, 128.
[19] Report by Fragoso, 4–1–1958; Letter by Paulo Cunha, MNE, 22–1–1958, AMFA/POI-33.
[20] Inter-ministerial Committee for the United Nations [hereafter IMCUN], First session, 29–4–1958, AMFA/MU/GM/GNP/171/1/ONU.

fundamental principle: they could not contradict, in any way, the imperial unity thesis. The submission of information came to be seen as fundamental in order to strengthen the country's position internationally. A new overarching rationale and strategy might be possible, perhaps desirable. It was becoming clear that "the difficulty to find new arguments to advocate our thesis" increased by the day.[21] Moreover, the thesis created problems at the International Labour Organization (ILO), where colonies were "non-metropolitan territories."[22] The modalities of ratification of its conventions mirrored the separation between metropole and overseas territories. This was a tacit acknowledgment of an "incompatible differentiation" that undermined the proclaimed imperial unity. According to the Overseas Minister, the solution was to turn Portugal into an "independent country with aborigine populations." Nogueira argued that the "sui generis character" of the Portuguese nation – given exceptional "historical, political and moral" reasons – was so "specific and almost unique" that did not fit "existing international classifications." The solution proposed would entail that the "aborigines were considered citizens with full rights." This did not happen with the "natives" in Portuguese overseas territories, as J. M. Fragoso aptly noted. And this was not the only inconsistency that the unity thesis involved. So far, the "adversaries" failed to fully grasp them, but that situation would not last long. It was clear that "legislation did not match the principles." The duality of legal procedures and requirements that reigned would soon face severe criticism.[23]

The most obvious contradiction related to the *indigenato* regime itself. The very possibility of promoting the country internationally as an "independent country with aborigine populations" recommended its reassessment, starting with its congruence with international norms. A major problem was identified: a "special reference to black race" existed in the legal text. The statute was a legal instrument exclusively based on racial grounds, targeted at particular communities. This would surely offend the "sensibilities" of the "international arena," which was "declaredly anti-racist." The suppression of the racial profiling was advocated. Another issue was that the Portuguese "designation of natives" entailed the "admission of a certain degree of discrimination." It was possible to argue that the natives were not "part of the nation." They should start to

---

[21] IMCUN, Third session, 30–5–1958; Fourth session, 11–6–1958, AMFA/MU/GM/GNP/171/1/ONU.

[22] Daniel Maul, *Human Rights, Development and Decolonization: The International Labour Organization, 1940–1970* (New York: Palgrave, 2012).

[23] IMCUN, Fourth session, 11–6–1958, AMFA/MU/GM/GNP/171/1/ONU.

be addressed as "citizens." The situation enabled the "criticism of discrimination." "Non-evolved" or "non-assimilated" were the preferred designations. For some, it was more important to identify the "particularity of socio-economic areas" than to make "abstract references to factual racial situations." It was fundamental to "eliminate any possibility" that the definition of "native" could be "interpreted as an indication of racism." The point was to find a way to keep "existing human differentiations through administration without damaging a common juridical order." The "semantic decolonization" promoted by the constitutional revision of 1951, which merely turned colonies into "overseas provinces," and the limited revisions of the *indigenato* regime in 1954, needed to move further. Reform, even one with significant cosmetic intents, was necessary, in order to cope with the circumstances, some directly connected with the emergence of human rights idioms and repertoires. Accordingly, a recommendation was issued: the replacement of the *indigenato* by a juridical regime built around the notion of Aboriginals should be strongly considered, the "racial content" of the statute should be eliminated, and nationality should be given to all of the population "as a stage before citizenship."[24]

Another example of the imagination of conceivable reforms was the question of "native" labor. The existing regime was "seriously damaging the country's reputation." For instance, the possibility of imprisonment in cases of contract breaches, only applicable to native workers and legally sanctioned, contravened Article 11 of the draft covenant on civil and political rights.[25] But this was not confined to labor issues. "Maximum priority" should be given to the studies focused on the revision of "all administrative practices" that failed to reflect existing legislation. Educational policies and realities added to the reasons why the Portuguese were increasingly "vulnerable": the "implications on the international arena" were obvious, and needed to be mitigated.[26]

"Portuguese Colonialism on Trial for the First Time," Again . . .

Side by side with the dynamics of self-scrutiny promoted by the need to properly cope with growing international integration demands, the

---

[24] IMCUN, Fifth session, 26–6–1958; Eleventh session, 2–9–1958, AMFA/MU/GM/GNP/171/1/ONU.

[25] IMCUN, Eleventh session, 2–9–1958; Thirteenth session, 10–9–1958; Seventeenth session, 23–2–1959, AMFA/MU/GM/GNP/171/1/ONU. See also José Pedro Monteiro, *Portugal e a Questão do Trabalho Forçado: um império sob escrutínio (1944–1962)* (Lisboa: Edições 70, 2018).

[26] IMCUN, Nineteenth session, 6–4–1959, AMFA/MU/GM/GNP/171/1/ONU.

numerous indictments of the imperial modus operandi and the colonial modus vivendi, coming from a multitude of sources with heterogeneous motivations, fostered reformist thinking, and strategic reorganizing. Recurrent in nature, with a long and rich genealogy, the criticisms about the workings of the Portuguese colonial empire gained momentum after the admission to UN.

On April 30, 1956, at the ECOSOC, the Portuguese criticized the Anti-Slavery Society (ASS) for reporting the existence of a "system of forced labour" in the colonies. The ASS was a longstanding contrarian to the Portuguese justificatory operations regarding accusations of colonial inequities, being frequently the channel through which local grievances gained international diffusion.[27] The *Anti-Slavery Reporter*, its official organ, frequently published critical accounts of Portuguese "overseas provinces" conditions. Its senior figures regularly sent information to the British government with updates about them, namely regarding labor conditions. Such was the case of a memorandum sent to by C. W. W. Greenidge, ASS director, to Alan Lennox-Boyd, Secretary of State for the Colonies, in August 26, 1955, titled "Forced labour in Portuguese colonies," which was also sent to the Secretaries of State for Foreign Affairs and for Commonwealth Affairs. It aimed at making the government exert pressure upon the Portuguese to radically change the procedures of labor organization and administration.[28]

In a joint operation with the ILO, in August 30, 1955, the ASS sent another memorandum to the joint ECOSOC/ILO ad hoc Committee on Forced Labour about the "extensive scale" in which "native labour" was exacted. The operation was "little different from slavery," and "two international courts" already confirmed the general accusation, the ad hoc Committee itself, in its 1953 report, and the ILO's Committee on Forced Labour (1956). For instance, the situation in San Thome was considered to "be similar to that of workers under a system of forced labour for economic purposes." A good additional element to support this reasoning was the fact that Portugal's adherence to ILO normative standards regarding work freedom was weak. Even with the ratification of international conventions, and given past records, Greenidge firmly believed that "that would not make much difference to the treatment of the Africans." This information was provided in 1956 to Roger Baldwin

---

[27] For previous moments, see Miguel Bandeira Jerónimo, *The "Civilizing Mission" of Portuguese Colonialism (c.1870–1930)* (Basingstoke, UK: Palgrave Macmillan, 2015).

[28] Greenidge to Lennox-Boyd, 26–8–1955, in Papers of the Anti-Slavery Society, Bodleian Library, University of Oxford [hereafter ASSP], Mss. British Empire, S22/G638–641/ Portuguese Africa.

of the International League for Human Rights. It was also sent to the UN Division of Human Rights.[29]

In April 30, 1956, Garin addressed the ECOSOC aiming to refute the ASS's "unfounded and unwarranted accusations." According to the Portuguese government, national legislation was "in complete harmony" with the ILO 1930 Forced Labour and 1936 Recruitment ("native workers") conventions. The ASS was a "windmill which keeps working although it has no grain to grind": there was nothing new in the 1955 allegations that had not been presented before. And these had been duly responded to, according to Garin. The ASS's "traditional misguided preconceptions" and "clouded judgements" were criticized, while the prevailing Native Labour Code of 1928 was considered "more favourable to the indigenous population" than international normative instruments on the matter. Moreover, the "sociological, juridical, political and unitarian reality" of Portuguese pluricontinental nation made allegations regarding the negative treatment of Indigenous populations untenable: the persistent "brotherly relations" between communities, "under centuries old policies and traditions of non-distinction and non-discrimination of race, colour or religion," were mobilized to prove the point. Accordingly, and this was a key point, the ASS had to "produce factual evidence of the breaches of the principles of justice or humanity." So far, it had not. These ideas, and more, were present in the official rebuttal of the findings of the ad hoc Committee, dated December 15, 1955.[30] However, these proclamations were insufficient to stop the persistence of denunciations about labor and racial conditions. For instance, just one year later, in April 1957, Baldwin wrote to Garin, sending a lengthy document titled "Forced Labour in the Ancient Congo Kingdom (Angola)," which listed several "plantations" in regions of Angola where working conditions were detailed. For both organizations, the labor conditions were clear examples of a negative human rights record.[31]

Violent political repression was another topic of denunciation. On December 1, 1959, J. Bouvier, of the Arbeitskreis der Freunde Ghanas (a group based in West Germany), sent a telegram to Secretary-General Dag Hammarskjöld. The message was clear: "stop the constant

---

[29] ASS, "Memorandum on Forced Labour," 1–3–1956; Greenidge to William Cadbury, 2–10–1956, in ASSP, Mss. British Empire, S22/G638–641/Portuguese Africa; Greenidge to Baldwin, 10–7–1956, International League for Human Rights Records, New York Public Library, 207/C2/D4/Box 5; UN Documentation, E/2815, 324–9.

[30] ASSP, Mss. British Empire, S22/G638–641/Portuguese Africa; see also UN Documentation, E/2815, 329–31.

[31] Baldwin to Garin, 28–4–1957, AMFA/ONU/M24/S3.E89 P1–38179.

atrocities and savage killings against the African people of Guinea and Angola." The "liberation of political prisoners" and the suspension of "preparations for repression" should be enforced. This telegram would later be presented at a press conference of the American Committee on Africa (March 7, 1960). Bouvier also contacted the Portuguese Overseas Ministry, denouncing the imprisonment and "disappearance" of 200 Africans in the province of Cabinda, after claims for independence. Two members of the União das Populações de Angola (UPA), Libório Nefwane and Lello Figueira, had been imprisoned in 1956, in the "concentration camp" of Bié. Others "disappeared after being tortured." Since March 1959, according to the letter, the political police had made "hundreds of arrests," afterwards prosecuting the offenders for "crimes against the external security of the state." Using the framework of the Universal Declaration of Human Rights, the group claimed that they were political prisoners. They were fighting for self-determination and "the colonial situation of African countries under Portuguese domination" was obvious.[32]

In February 1960, Baldwin wrote to Garin informing him that the League had a list of "natives" recently arrested in Angola, "evidently on political charges of having asserted the right of self-determination." "Familiar" with the policies of the Portuguese regarding the growing "demands for self-determination," and also with "the concept that all overseas territories are internal parts of Portugal, not subject to self-determination," the League nonetheless stressed the ongoing "violation of basic human rights," connected to the arrest and prosecution of persons solely for "claiming a right so generally recognized."[33]

In March, Abel Djassi, *nom de guerre* of Amílcar Cabral, wrote a declaration titled "Portuguese colonialism on trial for the first time." The "tragic situations" in the "African 'zone of silence'" were highlighted: "11 million human beings" were considered to be "living like serfs in their own country." The "most basic human rights" were missing, in conditions worse than under "Nazism." "Abject misery," enforced "ignorance," and "forced labour" prevailed. The "myth of multi-racialism" and the "constitutional sham of 'national unity'" could not erase these realities. A "complete suppression of all human rights" reigned, in efforts that combined "the colonial Gestapo, the army, the administration and the settlers." Two hundred individuals had been "arrested and reported

---

[32] J. Bouvier to Dag Hammarskjöld, telegram, 1–12–1959; Bouvier to Minister of Overseas, 25–2–1960; João da Costa Freitas, Overseas Ministry, to Director of the Political Police, confidential, 14–3–1960, AMFA/MU-GM-GNP-RRI-00562.

[33] Baldwin to Garin, 17–2–1960, AMFA/ONU/M24/S3.E89 P1–38179.

as missing"; since March 1959 circa 100 persons were arrested in several colonies, some were in exile, and over 1,000 Africans were "killed in massacres" in São Tomé, and over 50 in Guinea-Bissau. The ongoing trials should be "the first public judgement of Portuguese colonialism," a "case between Portuguese colonialism and humanity." This was included in a dossier sent to the ECOSOC by the ASS, which considered the affair so grave that a UN observer should attend the trials in Loanda.[34] In Lisbon, despite the evidences, Cabral's accusation was seen as a mere manifestation of foreign "illegitimate interests," not as an expression of local grievances and claims becoming internationalized.[35]

Also in March, an unnamed organization based in Accra alerted the UN's secretary-general to the human rights situation in Angola. A cablegram was sent to draw "attention to the atrocities inflicted on Angola nationalists arbitrarily detained in Luanda Prison." Those detained had reacted against the colonial modus vivendi, "characterized by forced labour, the spoliation of territory to the benefit of the settlers, obscurantism and the absence of public liberties." These movements by African people, "demanding their human rights," were not the result of the influence of a "handful of Protestants, animists and communists," as the Portuguese alleged. It was crucial "to alert international opinion in respect of the atrocities and acts of genocide committed by the Portuguese colonialists." The international sphere was instrumental in widening and strengthening anticolonial claims and protests.[36] The role played by a transregional human rights network in this process was fundamental.[37] These denunciations provoked a ferocious reaction from Portuguese authorities, from "man-hunt" and "mass arrests" to the intimidatory increment in military presence.[38]

Colonial riots or protests were not unknown to Portuguese authorities. In Batepá, S. Tomé, in 1953, in Pidjiguiti, Guinea-Bissau, 1959, and in Mueda, Mozambique, 1960, local Africans expressed their grievances vehemently. They were fiercely repressed by Portuguese authorities. However, none of these events had the impact abroad of those that marked the year of 1961 in Angola. This was a critical year

---

[34] Amílcar Cabral, 3–3–1960; Thomas Fox-Pitt to the Secretary of ECOSOC, 1–4–1960; Ministry of Foreign Affairs to Overseas Ministry, 4–6–1960, AMFA/MU-GM-GNP-RRI-00562.
[35] Adriano Moreira, "Problemas Sociais do Ultramar," in Adriano Moreira, *Ensaios* (Lisbon: Junta de Investigações do Ultramar, 1960), 154.
[36] See Eckert, "African Nationalists," esp. 285; Burke, *Decolonization*, esp. 35–58.
[37] Terretta, "From Below and to the Left?"
[38] "Communication from an organization in Ghana, 29 March 1960," AMFA/ONU/M24/S3.E89 P1–38179.

for the Portuguese imperial project. As a combined result of several factors, between January and February local Africans of the Baixa do Cassange (Angola) revolted against the administrators of the cotton concessionaire, COTONANG, and colonial authorities. Extreme violence followed as ferocious repressive measures were adopted.[39] On February 4, 1961, a group of armed Africans attacked several government buildings, including prisons and police stations, which led to several deaths. The action was said to have been planned in order to generate international repercussions, by taking place in a moment when several foreign journalists were in Loanda, waiting for the announced arrival of the hijacked vessel *Santa Maria* by Portuguese oppositionists, which never materialized. In the following days, indiscriminate repression against Africans, by the military and by the white settlers, caused numerous deaths and left others wounded. Hundreds were arrested. These events prompted a series of international initiatives, mainly by independent African states. On March 15, diverse attacks on northern Angola, led by UPA, killed several white settlers, African residents, and workers. Again, Portuguese reaction led to indiscriminate arrests and killings, widespread torture, and air bombings, causing the mass exodus of Africans to the neighboring countries.[40]

This last problem was of special importance, being immediately noted abroad. In June 1961, the Security Council (SC) adopted a resolution "deeply deploring the large-scale killings and the severely repressive measures in Angola." Requests of information were sent to the High Commissioner for Refugees.[41] According to the estimates of the League of Red Cross Societies, the number of refugees rose from 10,000 in April to 131,000 in September.[42] One of the first *in situ* reports of the

---

[39] Alexander Keese, "Dos abusos às revoltas? Trabalho forçado, reformas portuguesas, política 'tradicional' e religião na Baixa de Cassange e no Distrito do Congo (Angola), 1957–1961," *Africana Studia* no. 7 (2004): 247–76; Diogo Ramada Curto and Bernardo Pinto Cruz, "Terror e saberes coloniais: Notas acerca dos incidentes na Baixa do Cassange, janeiro e fevereiro de 1961," in Miguel Bandeira Jerónimo, ed., *O Império Colonial em Questão* (Lisboa: Edições 70, 2012), 3–36.

[40] See, among others, John Marcum, *The Angolan Revolution: Anatomy of an Explosion (1950–1962)* (Cambridge, MA: MIT Press, 1978).

[41] Resolution S/4835, 9–6–1961; Carlos Salamanca to Félix Schnyder, 14–6–1961; Archives of the United Nations High-Commissioner for Refugees (hereafter AUNHCR)/Fonds 11/ Series 1/Box 251/"Angolan Refugees." On the HCR and decolonization, see Jérôme B. Elie and Jussi Hanhimäki, "UNHCR and Decolonization in Africa: Expansion and Emancipation, 1950s to 1970s," in Anja Kruke, ed., *Dekolonisation: Prozesse und Verflechtungen, 1945–1990* (Bonn: Dietz, 2009), 53–72.

[42] Gervais Bahizi to Secretary-General, 7–9–1961; Félix Schnyder, "Account of the situation of refugees from Angola and of the action taken to assist them as at 1 July 1961"; AUNHCR/Fonds 11/Series 1/Box 251/"Angolan Refugees."

situation, made at the border in June and resulting from interviews with refugees, confirmed 90,000 refugees, but noted that "hundreds" were crossing the border every day. According to information gathered at Thysville, channeled by Reverend Fullbrook of the Baptist Mission at Moerbecke, the refugees were not planning to return to Angola. The government was "systematically arresting all Africans of education or of powers of leadership." Many Angolans had been "shot," those arrested were "executed." "Aerial bombing" burned villages to the ground. The "causes of the uprisings" were ascribed to the "oppressive conditions" prevailing in Angola, but also to the "reported violent methods of the UPA." Many refugees were interviewed, and appeared to show "little if any bitterness towards the Portuguese." But the reasons advanced were significant: "they appear to regard shootings, killings and reprisals by both sides as a perfectly natural way of life." Moreover, "tribal warfare" was common, and many of the refugees regarded the Portuguese "rather as another tribe."[43]

In November 1961, another report of a mission to the Congo, related to the UNHCR relief program, stated that this exodus amounted to 148,000 registered refugees. A visit to two sectors of the refugee area near the border led the rapporteur to stress the fact that "the refugees appear to be more primitive than the native population. Many children apparently never went to school in Angola and those who went are said to be behind the Congolese children." According to the refugees, the return to Angola would be dependent on the end of military operations, but also on the "presence of troops and occasional hunting shots." "One thing is clear," concluded the reporter, "the problem of refugees from Angola is not finished."[44] In 1963 it was estimated that 200,000 to 300,000 refugees from Mozambique were in Tanganyika, Kenya, Uganda, and the Federation of Rhodesia and Nyasaland, and more than 150,000 from Angola were in the Congo (Léopoldville). The refugees question contributed to place, again, the colonial modus vivendi under the spotlight.[45]

---

[43] J. D. R. Kelly, "Report on Refugees from Angola" and "Interviews with Refugees" (Annex 4), 26–6–1961; J. D. R. Kelly to Félix Schnyder, 27–6–1961; AUNHCR/ Fonds 11/Series 1/Box 251/"Angolan Refugees."

[44] R. T. Schaeffer to Henrik Beer, 21–11–1961, "Report on Congo visit November 14– November 19, 1961"; V. A. Temnomeroff to High Commissioner for Refugees, 20–11– 1961; AUNHCR/Fonds 11/Series 1/Box 251/"Angolan Refugees."

[45] D. Protitch, Under-Secretary for Trusteeship and Information from Non-Self-Governing Territories, to Félix Schnyder, April 4, 1963, AUNHCR/Fonds 11/Series 1/Box 251/"Refugees from Portugal and territories under Portuguese administration – General."

Navigating the Storm: The Uses of Human Rights (1961–65)

"The World Is Mad and We Are the Ones Who Have to Suffer the Consequences"

The 1961 events increased international pressure on the empire. The ongoing trajectories of decolonization enabled regular critiques of Portuguese colonialism by newly independent states. After the incidents, anti-colonial initiatives became more internationalized and institutionalized, and deeper in scope. In February 1961, Liberia's representative at the UN asked the SC to include the situation in Angola in its agenda. Another note argued that it was crucial to "prevent further deterioration and abuse of human rights and privileges in Angola." The SC meeting coincided with the eruption of the riots in northern Angola. For the Portuguese, this was proof that the "terrorists" had external support and orientation. More than thirty African and Asian states supported Liberia's motion. A subcommittee to study the situation should be established. The motion was rejected, but a similar motion was approved later at the General Assembly.[46] The contents and the workings of the subcommittee on Angola are particularly revealing of the intersections between discourses on human rights and self-determination, and about the ways in which Portugal engaged with them.

The subcommittee activities included the gathering of existing information regarding local conditions in Angola, for instance those provided by a report of Edward Lawson, of the Division of Human Rights, or by documents of the ad hoc Committee on Forced Labour.[47] Legal and statistical information about Angola was provided to the subcommittee by the Portuguese government, although, it was stressed, not under the auspices of the Article 73. Information about the numerous reforms that took place in September 1961 was also sent, a fact to which we will return below. A meeting with Salazar and the Foreign Affairs and Overseas ministers was permitted. Critically, the Portuguese government refused an *in situ* inspection, a fact that led to efforts to interview witnesses in Leopoldville, including Angolan refugees, representatives of the nationalist movements and African political associations. One of those testimonies was provided by Holden Roberto, which made a clear connection between the colonial modus vivendi and the subsequent riots and revolts:

---

[46] United Nations, i, S/4994, 22–11–1961, 8–28.
[47] John Humphrey to Dantas de Brito, 2–10–1961, Archives of the United Nations (AUN)/PO-230/Folder-A.

Africans had "no rights, only obligations," had to work "14 hours per day," were "insulted and beaten," sometimes "deported," and had to pay heavy "taxes." Moreover, "forced labour still" reigned.[48]

The establishment of a clear nexus between the social, economic, and political conditions of the Angolans and the recent violent revolts was also patently stated in the subcommittee's report. Beside other important topics, such as the incidents in Angola and Portuguese repressive measures, and their potential impact on international security and peace, the third part of the report was entirely devoted to the "background and context of the situation." Detailed information was gathered about the political and constitutional organization of the empire, the juridical status of the *indígenas*, racial and political relations, taxation, labour, compulsory cultivation, education, health, and land policies, among others. The evaluation was severe. The *indigenato* regime was seen as the "basic distinction between Europeans and non-Europeans," one that permeated "all phases of life," "the basis of various discriminatory practices." Political rights were not granted to "indígenas" and the "assimilation rates" were residual (circa 95 percent of the Angolans were "natives"). The "native tax" was unbearable, and was frequently linked to the exaction of "compulsory labour." Labour practices and recruitment, the residual participation of "natives" in the higher echelons of administration, the lack of educational facilities, and the dual nature of the educational system were also criticized. The report also emphasized that "beatings and arrests" appeared to be an integral part of everyday life in Angola.[49]

The reforms meanwhile undertaken were addressed, but their implementation and impact were judged with reservation. This was particularly true in relation to one of the central concerns in the UN: the question of self-determination equated as anti-colonial independence. Moreover, the report dismissed the Portuguese allegations that the incidents in Angola were the action of an international coalition of communist and anti-colonial subversives. The same happened with the argument that "peace and harmony" reigned in Angola before 1961. Recent developments in Africa – namely the rise of anti-colonial nationalism and the attainment of independence by various neighboring colonies – were recognized as important aspects, but the causes for revolt were located elsewhere: the "grievances and aspirations of the Angolan people." The disenfranchisement and lower juridical status of most of the African population fostered the widespread "feeling that they were

---

[48] United Nations, *Report of the Sub-Committee*, 15–28; *News summary*, 26–5–1962, AUN/Series0805/Box 3/File 6.

[49] United Nations, *Report of the Sub-Committee*, 65–7, 69–70, 72–93.

treated as strangers in their own land and that they could not acquire fundamental rights unless they adopted an alien way of life." The nexus between the restrictions on the exercise of "fundamental freedoms and human rights" by the *indigenas* and the incidents was therefore strongly advanced. The systematic denial or violation of human rights was evident, and was not necessarily equated with, or reduced to, self-determination-inspired concerns.[50]

The subcommittee was not the only locus of activities against Portuguese colonialism. Several states regularly pressed UN authorities to take more energetic measures to obstruct the Portuguese imperial designs. Dozens of letters were sent to the UN secretary-general office addressing the causes and consequences of the rebellions. The Association Internationale des Juristes Démocrates appealed to the SC to stop the massacres of Angolans; the Associação de Naturais de Angola (Association of Angola-born people), which claimed to be composed of blacks, *mestiços*, and whites, on the contrary demanded that the SC abstain from interfering in Portuguese internal affairs, clearly in tune with government desires. Oppositionists at the metropole also participated: for instance, the Comité para a Defesa das Liberdades Democráticas denounced the "inhumanity of repression," which was close to "genocide, in blatant violation of the Rights of Man [*sic*] Declaration." The language of human rights was clearly mobilized. But criticism went beyond the more shocking events of rebellion and repression. For instance, despite condemning the "war of extermination in Angola," the South Africa Congress of Trade Unions highlighted the fact that Angolan native workers were deprived of "the most elementary human rights," being "subjected to forced labour on a scale unknown anywhere else in the world."[51]

The momentum of internationalization and institutionalization of colonial grievances was also explored by heterogeneous coalitions in specialized agencies such as the ILO.[52] Forced labor, a perennial topic of reformist or anti-colonial-inspired dissidence, was the subject chosen by Ghana to file a complaint in February against Portugal at the ILO for not

---

[50] Ibid., 45, 71, 86, 92 104, 121, 131.

[51] Letter by Association Internationale des Juristes Démocrates, 10–10–1961; Letter by Associação de Naturais de Angola, 11–10–1961; Letter by Comité para a Defesa das Liberdades em Portugal, 15–1–1961; Letter by South Africa Congress of Trade Unions, 4–7–1961, AUN/PO230/PI S/NC/1961/Folder B-6.

[52] Regarding the decades-long historical intersections between colonial labor, decolonization and international institutions in the long term, see Miguel Bandeira Jerónimo and José Pedro Monteiro, "Colonial Labour Internationalised: Portugal and the Decolonization Momentum (1945-1975)," *International History Review* (Ahead of print, 2019).

abiding to Convention 105 on the Abolition of Forced Labour, ratified in 1959. A direct link between colonialism and the prevailing inhumane practices and laws was stressed for the first time that a sovereign government filed a complaint against another government at the ILO.[53] The Portuguese reaction was (or pretended to be) one of surprise. As Ribeiro da Cunha stated, "the world is mad and we are the ones who have to suffer the consequences." Yet, it differed substantially from the one being carried out at the UN. Full cooperation with the commission of enquiry was decided, its members' visit to Angola and Mozambique allowed. The perception of a more accommodative stance vis-à-vis colonial powers by the ILO definitely contributed to this outcome.[54]

Obviously connected to (geo)political motivations, the allegations made by Ghana nonetheless illuminated the abundant inconsistencies between Portuguese legislation and administrative practices, and between these and international labor standards. The existence of a particular "native labour code" that differed from the metropolitan one and enabled several modalities of compulsory labor was a revealing example. The "moral duty to work," incumbent on all native adult males, was seen as the cornerstone of the system. It enabled the involvement of official authorities in its enforcement through "persuasion" or coercive measures, for instance in the migration of hundreds of thousands of Mozambican workers to the Rand mines, to the compulsory cultivation programs or to specific agricultural and mining companies. All these aspects were confirmed, in varying degrees, by many other sources that fed the commission of enquiry. Associated to the complaint, the United Arab Republic provided secondary bibliography that included works from authors such as Amílcar Cabral, James Duffy, or Basil Davidson.[55] The International League for Human Rights and the International Commission of Jurists channeled written testimonies provided by institutions formally unable to intervene, such as the American Committee on Africa or the Baptist Missionary Society.[56] The amount

---

[53] ILO, "Report of the Commission Appointed under Article 26 of the Constitution of the International Labour Organization to Examine the Complaint Filed by the Government of Ghana concerning the Observance by the Government of Portugal of the Abolition of Forced Labour Convention, 1957 (no. 105)," *Official Bulletin*, 45, no. 2, Supplement II (Geneva: ILO, 1962), 117–41. See also Monteiro, *Portugal e a Questão do Trabalho Forçado.*

[54] Ribeiro da Cunha to Victor Gomez, 3–1961; *Apontamento*, Ribeiro da Cunha, 29–4– 1961, AMFA/MU-GM-GNP-RRI-0790–12432.

[55] ILO, "Report of the commission," 5–7, 142.

[56] Letter by International League for Human Rights, 22–8–1961, ACD-14-1-3-2; Letter by International Commission of Jurists, 8–8–1961, ACD-14-1-3-1, both at Archives of the International Labour Organization.

of information gathered, if not always accurate or up to date, was substantial, and revealed the workings of important international and transnational networks and connections. Anti-colonial activists, post-colonial governments, philanthropic and human rights associations, and *engagé* intellectuals coalesced to put Portuguese colonial social policies on trial, assessing them also through human rights lenses. The Portuguese reacted with examples of reforms undertook during the process. This in part explains the relatively positive verdict of the commission, which was substantially exaggerated by the Portuguese authorities.[57]

The Portuguese stand was not merely defensive. In August 1961, a similar complaint against Liberia was filed by the Portuguese government at the ILO. The complaint had a clear political, and patently strategic, overtone. Two aspects were crucial. First, Liberia could not reasonably justify any proved wrongdoings on a previous colonial relationship. Second, if the complaint succeeded, the Portuguese authorities could give a factual standing to the so-called Belgian thesis, that is, the argument that postcolonial states such as Liberia, but also the USA or Canada, had their own exceptional politico-juridical regimes for "backward" populations. This argument was powerful as it de-exceptionalized the nature of a formal colonial relationship. The fact that Liberia had a dual juridical regime, which allowed for modalities of coerced labor, made it a perfect target. It was also a practical way of internationally claiming that self-determination equated as anti-colonial independence had no direct relation with each state's human rights' record.[58]

As happened in the Portuguese case, the complaint against Liberia triggered new reforms and increased the ILO's scrutiny over the country. However, the fact that Liberia's government failed to meet formal juridical obligations, allowed for a strong condemnation, unlike what happened in the Portuguese case. Portuguese authorities did not miss the chance to widely diffuse the event through diplomatic channels. The Portuguese government even constituted an interministerial committee to study further complaints, but ILO officials argued against the idea. In sum, human rights talks could also be mobilized as a diplomatic strategy of imperial resilience.

---

[57] ILO, "Report of the commission," 227–53.
[58] José Pedro Monteiro '"One of Those too Rare Examples": The International Labour Organization, the Colonial Question and Forced Labour (1961–1963)," in Miguel Bandeira Jerónimo and José Pedro Monteiro, eds., *Internationalism, Imperialism and the Formation of the Contemporary World* (Basingstoke, UK: Palgrave, 2017), 221–49.

"Revise, without Delay"

These events marked a decisive moment in the institutionalization of international scrutiny of the conformity between the Portuguese imperial policies and practices and the novel international norms, especially regarding nondiscrimination and the expansion of a myriad of rights to groups until then deemed too *backward* to wisely exercise them. This process entailed dynamics of reform. The actions of the "inventors of human rights" and the practices of multiracialism needed to be demonstrated. Change and reform, even if cosmetic, were closely associated to international developments. International pressures accelerated, and expanded, the reformist response. Of course, the timing, content, and scope of the reformist process were also clearly connected to other international, metropolitan, and colonial pressures, being also related to previous dynamics of international and transnational (and even interimperial) integration. But some changes went well beyond the prevailing imperial imaginations. The engagement with debates about human rights became crucial. The survival of the lusotropical justificatory arguments depended on it.

In May 1961, a series of decrees tackled some of the most contentious aspects of Portuguese labor legislation, just a few days after Wilfred Jenks, ILO deputy-director general, visited Lisbon, related to topics such as the creation of labor inspectorates in the colonies or the repeal of the cotton compulsory cultivation programs. Regarding the workings of the UN subcommittee, it is known that Portuguese authorities were in touch with its chairman, Carlos Salamanca, and were probably aware of the most contentious topics being studied. Therefore, it is not surprising that the repeal of *indigenato* and the sudden incorporation of all natives as full citizens in relation to political rights occurred just a few months (September 1961) after the beginning of the subcommittee activities. Already in late 1960, a Portuguese representative at the UN urged the government to "revise, without delay, some aspects of the juridical structure of our overseas provinces." The persistence of the *indigenato* weakened the Portuguese argument about imperial unity. His correspondent argued that it was fundamental to extend political rights to the "natives," since at the UN almost nobody would be satisfied with mere "apparent changes." Yet, the initiative was postponed.[59] The promulgation, in September 1961 as well, of several decrees that dealt with the local political participation of the Africans or with the land question was

---

[59] Note by Overseas Minister office to GNP, 24–11–1960; "Note on the native statute," Overseas Ministry, 1–10–1960, AMFA/MU/GM/GNP/RRI/0721/12127.

the recognition by the Portuguese authorities that a dual juridical regime was untenable. It contradicted the official discourse that stressed the idea of national unity, while fueling and justifying the grievances thereby generated. As the Portuguese indicated to the subcommittee, reforms were designed to "offset alleged misunderstanding abroad and to rationalize procedures."[60]

The close association between international initiatives and reformist drives was even more evident regarding labor policies. The study of a new labor code was first announced in the final report of the commission of enquiry, in February 1962. Its enactment would depend on the sanctioning by the ILO Committee of Experts on the Application of Conventions and Recommendations. The new Rural Labour Code, published a couple of months later, was in fact supervised by the ILO structures. The "moral duty work" was repealed, no modality of compulsory labor was allowed, administrative interference on the recruitment processes was forbidden and no ethnic, cultural, or racial discrimination in labor regimes was thereon legally permitted. The code was presented as a fundamental step in the universalization of social, and to a certain extent political, rights. The right of "native" workers to participate in collective bargaining and unionizing (still strictly limited given the nature of the political regime) was one example. A high degree of conformity with the ILO standards was pivotal to the effort made to contradict accusations of discrimination. The demonstration, even if merely from a legal point of view, of non-discrimination and of the extension of socioeconomic rights to the subject populations was imperative. As one Overseas Ministry official wrote, since forced labor was one "of the accusations more frequently made against us ... if the most responsible agency of the United Nations affirms that those practices ... are forbidden by the Portuguese government ... that statement would be extremely useful internationally and will demolish the campaign that in this important sector is directed against us."[61]

Despite the persistence of a pervasive racialized perspective over African communities, the protraction, and the shortcomings of much of the sanctioned reforms, these illustrations show how the particular historical conjuncture of 1961 and 1962 forced Portuguese authorities to devise new legislation to expand its subject populations' rights. The increasing vigor of the human rights discourse and the assertion of

---

[60] UN, *Report of the Sub-Committee*, 138.
[61] Note by ITPAS-Mozambique to ILO, 1962, AMFA/MU-GM-GNP-RRI-0721–00507; "Apontamentos," AMFA/MU-GM-GNP-RRI-0790–12529.

nondiscrimination on a racial basis at its core made it harder for the Portuguese officials and diplomats to simply dismiss the international zeitgeist, or merely promote a simulacrum of change.

Reforms became powerful diplomatic tools, despite the claim that they were a result of endogenous dynamics and gradual evolution, not of international pressures. In the projected reply to the subcommittee report, the Portuguese government insistently highlighted the reforms carried out, "far-reaching in its scope and effects." References were made to the liberalization of cotton production, for instance, but it was argued that this change was introduced "as soon as the farmers familiarized themselves with the appropriate technique." Concerning the subcommittee remarks about a dual labor regime, the delegation pointed to the extension of the application of a few ratified ILO conventions to all the overseas provinces. Reforms, equal rights irrespective of race, nondiscrimination, national (imperial) unity were the core arguments of Portuguese diplomatic rhetoric and strategy.[62]

In New York, Vasco Garin insisted that Portugal had been "progressively adapting itself to the changing world," as a result of its century-long commitment to the edification of a multiracial society. Moreover, Portugal "was the very first country in the world to defend the dignity and the equality of all men without distinction of race." Portugal was the inventor of human rights. The rejection of the application of self-determination to the overseas populations was explained with the argument that they "have been integrated in the Portuguese Nation for centuries" and were "already free and independent as full citizens of Portugal." The way new legislation was minimized was lamented. The same happened with the putative failure to recognize the suppression of the *indigenato* and the provision of "full political rights on a footing of absolute equality." Significantly, he concluded his speech saying that the delegation "indignantly" repudiated "the charge of repression and denial of human rights and fundamental freedoms." Such aspects were of fundamental importance to Portuguese authorities.[63]

Accusations regarding the violation of fundamental social, economic, civil, and political rights deeply impacted on the dynamics of juridical and political change at this particular conjuncture. But the Portuguese "official mind" truly believed that reformism and engagement with discourses about human rights would strengthen its political stance at

---

[62] "Some comments of the Portuguese delegation to the XVI General Assembly of the United Nations on the Report of the Sub-Committee on Angola," AMFA/MU-GM-GNP-171-3.

[63] "Comments of the Portuguese Delegation," 16-1-1962, AUN/PO-230-Folder A.

international forums, and assert its imperial legitimacy abroad. For instance, Archibald Ross, British ambassador in Lisbon, considered that the new Rural Labour Code should be "welcomed, for it marks the beginning of a practical and enlightened attempt to tackle the fundamental problems of the Overseas Provinces at the grassroots."[64] Of course, some of these new legislative instruments had considerable pitfalls and loopholes, and fell short of really generalizing and bring into uniformity the rights of Europeans and Africans. For instance, G. Mennem Williams, based on local sources, believed that the reforms were "designed primarily to quiet foreign criticism" and that it was "extremely unlikely" that they would significantly "improve the situation of the African in Angola."[65] Nevertheless, they represented a major juridical departure within an imperial polity characterized by an extremely slow pattern of normative and political change. In sum, Portuguese authorities engaged with and reacted to human rights-centered debates, but always with the intent of dissociating human rights and self-determination equated as anti-colonial independence. The embrace of a particular idiom of human rights was also part of a diplomatic strategy that aimed to normalize the Portuguese imperial solution. The debates on human rights, and about its universalistic rationale, were received as menaces to Portuguese international assertions of imperial legitimacy. The engagement with such debates was feared. But the costs of outright dismissal of that engagement were also perceived as being too high. Certainly before, but especially after 1961, Portuguese experts, policymakers, and diplomats gradually understood that the language and the repertoires of human rights – as an idiom of colonial progressivism and as practical justifications of social intervention in the overseas territories – could have a valuable political and diplomatic instrumental use.

Conclusion

The processes analyzed throughout this chapter had a long-lasting impact on Portuguese imperial options, right until decolonization. This was especially so as a more explicit association between human rights and nondiscrimination and, obviously, self-determination materialized, in the 1960s and early 1970s, with the multiplication of international

[64] Dispatch no. 49, Archibald Ross, 8–5–1962, National Archives UK, LAB 13/1599.
[65] Letters by Mennem Williams to the State Department, 12–9–1961 and 17–1–1962, NARA, USA, RG 59 General Records of the Department of State, Central Decimal File, 1960–3 Box 1815.

initiatives and instruments designed to expand the human rights normative regime.[66]

The creation of the United Nations Declaration on the Elimination of
All Forms of Racial Discrimination in 1963 and of the international
convention with the same name in 1965 required new efforts by the
authorities. After being asked by the UN secretary-general to provide
examples of measures that would meet the aims of the Declaration, they
stated that "racial equality" had been proclaimed by the Portuguese "five
centuries ago." Laws and interactions with other communities "were
divested of all racial prejudice."[67] To dissociate self-determination and
human rights was the strategic goal. In an aide-memoire formulated to
explain the British position regarding the draft of the Convention,
the British ambassador struck the right cord: "there is no necessary
connexion, in logic or in practice, between racial discrimination and
colonialism."[68] Of course, a pragmatic approach always guided the Portuguese engagement in and with human rights and nondiscrimination
debates. As Nogueira stated in 1963, the internationalization of the
"Portuguese overseas problem" entailed an "immediate politicization"
(and "psychological terrorism") that needed to be systematically dealt
with.[69] After a new demarche by the UN secretary-general on the 1965
convention, a list of numerous statements about the country's secular
precedence in the promotion of human rights and racial harmony was
compiled. The government would not ratify the convention because
discrimination was unknown to Portuguese society and, therefore, no
measures to tackle racial discrimination and prejudice were needed.
However, the real motivation for this refusal was that the convention
permitted several modalities of petitioning. To ratify the convention
would be to "give an additional opportunity" and also "a supplementary
weapon" for more "attacks against the Portuguese overseas policy."[70]

Despite the rhetoric regarding the centuries-old multiracial society, the
challenges of initiatives based on human rights persisted. The affirmation
of nondiscrimination as a central concern of the human rights-related
bodies continued to place the Portuguese colonial question in the international spotlight. The decision to create an ad hoc group of experts
within the UN Human Rights Commission, with the task of studying the
actual records on human rights, apartheid, and racial discrimination in

---

[66] For this period, see Burke, *Decolonization*, 59–111; Jensen, *Making of International Human Rights*, 102–37, 174–208.
[67] Note by Foreign Affairs Ministry, 4–7–1964, AMFA/POI-139.
[68] Aide-memoire, 13–11–1964, AMFA/POI-139.
[69] Franco Nogueira, *Les nations Unies et le Portugal* (Paris: Fayard, 1963), 11, 125, 128.
[70] Note, Gaspar da Silva, 26–5–1966, AMFA/POI-139.

Angola, Mozambique, Guinea-Bissau, South Africa, South West Africa, and Rhodesia, was one of the initiatives that significantly increased the scrutiny on enduring colonial situations.

Despite the centrality of self-determination demands, efforts to prove that those regimes prevented their subject populations from exercising a diverse repertoire of fundamental rights were permanent. For instance, in 1967 a resolution by the Human Rights Commission stated that "the basic dissatisfaction" of the African populations in Portuguese territories was essentially a by-product of a "colonial relationship." But the resolution also stressed that despite the abovementioned reforms those populations continued to be deprived of the "same civil and political rights" enjoyed by Europeans. Moreover, "forced labour practices" continued to be a reality, "basic aspirations" of Africans were not met, and no significant modification had occurred in respect of "political, economic, social and educational conditions." The ad hoc group of experts denounced mass political murders ordered by the authorities, unscrupulous practices of forcing the Africans to sell their products to government-defined buyers, corporal punishments, and the bombing of populations with napalm and phosphorous. In sum, human rights were pivotal in the arguments against Portuguese colonialism.[71] At the ILO, for instance, denunciations about forced labour in the Portuguese colonies persisted. In the late 1960s, the Portuguese government asked for the establishment of *direct contacts* with the ILO in order to counter allegations. This led to a new exercise of international scrutiny, led by Pierre Juvigny, a former member of the UN Sub-Commission on the Prevention of Discrimination and Protection of Minorities. His visit to Angola and Mozambique in 1970 subsequently sparked new reformist initiatives.[72]

The historiographies of Portuguese colonialism and decolonization, on the one hand, and of human rights, on the other, have been so far mostly disconnected. Given the colonial track record and the ways in which it was contested internationally, one would expect a more regular and fruitful historiographical dialogue. In the emerging and innovative literature about Portuguese colonialism in the twentieth century, the topic of international human rights fares poorly. This chapter argues that the study of the

---

[71] Telegram from the Portuguese Permanent Mission at the UN, 19–10–1970, AMFA/POI52; Telegram from the Portuguese Permanent Mission at the UN, 2–7–1970; Telegram from the Portuguese Permanent Mission at the UN, 4–7–1970; Telegram from the Portuguese Permanent Mission at the UN, 7–7–1970; Telegram from the Portuguese Permanent Mission at the UN, 14–7–1970, AMFA/PAA-178.

[72] See Miguel Bandeira Jerónimo and José Pedro Monteiro, "Internationalism and the *Labours* of the Portuguese Colonial Empire (1945–1974)," *Portuguese Studies* 29, no. 2 (2013): 142–63, esp. 160–1.

interconnections between these two historical processes can enrich both. The articulations between global decolonization and international human rights can only be properly addressed if the number of case studies is expanded, if both pro-imperial and anti-colonial actors are brought into the analytical picture, and if these and other actors are studied to assess how human rights rationales and languages were actually deployed. Human rights entanglements with colonialism were not confined to the 1950s, they have diverse chronologies. Human rights languages were not only given instrumental use as a way to condemn imperialism and get access to sovereign political power; they were also appropriated to tentatively legitimize imperial resilience. When relating to debates over colonialism, their historical appropriations were rather nuanced and malleable, being the result of diverse political and ethical motivations and outlooks. Moreover, these uses must be analyzed beyond institutionalized gatherings; they must be scrutinized in the multiple *loci* – colonial, metropolitan but also international and transnational – where the ideals and rhetoric of a universalized set of rights met the aspirations of African and Asian peoples and leaders to get rid of the European yoke.[73] However, the relevance in studying the Portuguese case is not limited to these aspects. This case poses new questions that might be useful to broader debates about human rights and decolonization.

First, as shown in the previous pages, the language, or inspired arguments, of human rights was ubiquitous in the broader history of international denunciations and condemnations of Portuguese imperialism during the protracted decolonization process. This was true for the global, institutionalized repudiations of Portuguese colonialism in places such as the UN or the ILO at a time when the imperial solution was no longer acceptable. It was also a reality for the earlier, less coordinated initiatives that denounced particular harmful aspects of its colonial policies and practices. The unwillingness or inability of the Portuguese imperial authorities to cope with a new, internationally codified set of norms that aimed to grant a minimum of rights to all human beings irrespective of race were regularly censored by reformist-minded or anti-imperial activists, metropolitan oppositionists, and international institutions. To be sure, some of these initiatives configured political expedients for the more urging quest for independence. But a crucial fact persisted: the Portuguese empire's intrinsic and fundamental negation of a universalized rights regime. As a consequence, whatever the degree of instrumental use given to the issue of human rights, these actors consistently

---

[73] Eckel, "Human Rights and Decolonization."

mobilized rights talk to challenge imperial legitimacy. The racialized juridical–political structure of the empire, with its reverberations on social and economic policies and conditions, was frequently identified as a gross violation of the international normative regime of human rights *and* as the fundamental causal explanation for anti-imperial and anti-colonial dissidence. For the diverse group of contemporary actors that criticized the Portuguese empire-state, regardless of their motivations and political purposes, the strict boundaries between the so-called individual and collective rights were far from clear.

Second, the historical emergence of human rights as a fundamental tenet of the postwar international order impacted heavily on the ruminations, corrective efforts, and reformist initiatives of Portuguese imperial authorities. Certainly, this impact was contingent on imperial and colonial circumstances. Yet, the fear of the consequences of a new internationalized language of universal rights persisted. The challenges posed by the articulation of human rights norms and precepts and the development of critical assessments of, and eventually challenge to, Portuguese colonialism accordingly shaped pro-imperial arguments, the imperial administrative organization, its political imaginations, and its propagandistic strategy. This process expanded the limits of reformist efforts within the imperial administrative chain and conditioned the Portuguese diplomatic strategies. The reforms of the early 1960s were a clear example of how the international and transnational mobilization of the idea of universal human rights required novel legal and political frameworks from Portuguese imperial rulers and advocates. For sure, this nexus could be identified in other imperial formations. But its centrality in the Portuguese case was particularly significant, as the authoritarian nature of the metropolitan political system entailed severe limits to internal, especially anti-colonial, dissidence. Moreover, the reforms represented a significant departure from long-standing, entrenched, racialized ideological and political projects. The timings and contents of legal and political transformations were closely related to international denunciations of the gap between multiracialist proclamations and actual colonial realities. But such transformations were also fundamental to the strengthening of the diplomatic strategy of imperial resilience. Supported by the myth of Portuguese alleged paternity of the "rights of man" and by the juridical and political dissociation between self-determination equated as anti-colonial independence and human rights, Portuguese imperial rulers strove to prove the existence of an equitable legal and political order across the empire. In this sense, human rights became a device to ascertain Portuguese imperial progressivism and to resist anti-colonialist pressures, internally and externally. They were also fundamental to denounce the duplicity of some of its critics, as the complaint against Liberia testifies. This double instrumentalization of human rights – as a powerful instrument of anticolonial criticism and as a crucial device for imperial resilience – contributed to the historical *vernacularization* of human rights.[74]

Finally, the study of the historical intersections between human rights politics and global decolonization can also benefit from the inclusion of the Portuguese case given its particular trajectory as an empire-state. The relative durability of Portuguese colonialism can be helpful to qualify, and enrich, the intellectual disputes in human rights historiography, for instance regarding the debates about its foundations, chronologies, or *ups* and *downs*.[75] As a late decolonizer that refused to discuss self-determination until the end, as a stern resistant to the establishment of an all-encompassing common juridical and political framework, the Portuguese empire provides a fruitful case study. The numerous *décalages* between the Portuguese case and the others pose novel challenges to the study of the historical relationship between human rights and decolonization. This *exceptional* temporality had consequences in the discourses both of pro-imperial and anti-colonial advocates; it impacted as well in the formulation of innovative institutional instances that merged human rights and anti-colonial arguments; and in the actions and tactics of human rights-inspired groups. For instance, the nature and intents of the activities of the ASS, an old-time denouncer of Portuguese colonial malpractices, was substantially different from those of the groups, more grassrooted and less institutionalized, that mobilized European and American public opinions against the violations of human rights in the Portuguese empire later on. The denunciations of the massacre of Wiriyamu, Mozambique, in 1972, or the boycott of Angolan coffee by a Dutch-based Angola committee, with significant international ties, in the early 1970s are two examples of the latter.[76] But all of them are part

---

[74] Bonny Ibhawoh, "Testing the Atlantic Charter: Linking Anticolonialism, Self-Determination and Universal Human Rights," *International Journal of Human Rights* 18, no. 7–8 (2014): 842–60, 855.

[75] See Eckel and Moyn, *Breakthrough*; Roland Burke, "'How Time Flies': Celebrating the Universal Declaration of Human Rights in the 1960s," *International History Review* 38, 3 (2016): 394–420; Ibhawoh, "Testing the Atlantic Charter"; Jensen, *Making of International Human Rights*.

[76] For the ASS's role, see Bandeira Jerónimo, "Civilizing *Mission*"; Monteiro, *Portugal e a Questão do Trabalho Forçado*. Regarding the Wiriyamu and the Dutch-based committee see, respectively, Mustafa Dhada, *The Portuguese Massacre of Wiriyamu in Colonial Mozambique, 1964–2013* (London: Bloomsbury, 2015); Miguel Bandeira Jerónimo and José Pedro Monteiro, "Internationalism and Empire: The Question of Native Labor in the Portuguese Empire (1929–1962)," in Simon Jackson and Alanna O'Malley, eds., *From the League of Nations to the United Nations: The Institution of International Order* (London: Routledge, 2018), 206–33.

of a long genealogy of mobilization of human rights issues to challenge Portuguese colonialism. And, notwithstanding the authoritarian nature of the Portuguese empire-state, or perhaps due to that, the "official mind" was no less sensitive or reactive to these international and transnational efforts, as this chapter shows.

These are just some of the reasons why the scrutiny of the intersections between Portuguese late colonialism and decolonization and the evolving international institutionalization and political and cultural mobilization of a human rights discourses can contribute to the development of both historiographies. The Portuguese case provides new challenges, qualifies rigid perspectives, and neat distinctions in the history of the relationship between human rights and the ends of European colonial empires. Moreover, the rich and vibrant literature on human rights, its diverse themes, problems, and contributions, allows for novel ways of enquiring the dynamics and trajectory of Portuguese imperial disengagement.

12 "A World Made Safe for Diversity"

Apartheid and the Language of Human Rights, Progress, and Pluralism

Roland Burke

In a coincidence often noted by historians of human rights, the formal commencement of apartheid in South Africa (SA), and the enunciation of the postwar human rights vision at the fledgling United Nations occurred almost simultaneously.[1] The year 1948 witnessed both the accession to power of the National Party (NP), led by Daniel Malan, in May, and the adoption, on December 10, of the Universal Declaration of Human Rights (UDHR) by the UN General Assembly. Both promised ruptures with the past: the NP in its rejection of the prevailing system of segregation, and a bold if ill-defined promise of a new model of a racialized polity; the UDHR in its proclamation of a wide set of individual human rights as "common standard of achievement" for all. Eleanor Roosevelt, chair of the Commission on Human Rights for key moments in the drafting process of the UDHR, spoke hopefully of "a world made new," born from the UN Charter and its new sibling, the UDHR.[2]

The NP spoke of total racial separation, full apartheid, as an "ideal" to strive toward, while cautioning that such a utopian plane would always be in the distance. Apartheid's aspiration to racialized "utopia" was most famously encapsulated in September 1948 by the principal architect of the system, Hendrik Verwoerd, who asserted in his inaugural speech to parliament that "in every field of life one has to fix one's eyes to the stars and see how close one can come to achieving the very best, to achieving perfection." Verwoerdian "perfection" was territorial separation, grand apartheid, on racial criteria.[3] The gulf between these two idealisms was

---

[1] See for instance, Saul Dubow, *Apartheid 1948–1994* (Oxford: Oxford University Press, 2014), 47; Audie Klotz, *Norms in International Relations: The Struggle against Apartheid* (Ithaca, NY: Cornell University Press, 1995), 42; Bronwyn Leebaw, *Judging State-Sponsored Violence, Imagining Political Change* (Cambridge, UK: Cambridge University Press, 2011), 9; Mary Ann Glendon, *A World Made New: Eleanor Roosevelt and the Universal Declaration of Human Rights* (New York: Random House, 2001), xvi.

[2] Glendon, *World Made New*, ix.

[3] Senate Record, September 3, 1948, quoted in Alexander Hepple, *Verwoerd* (Harmondsworth: Penguin, 1967), 235–6.

among the most profound of the postwar world. Nevertheless, for over three decades, the NP sought to position itself within Roosevelt's "world made new," even as it was insistently cast to its margins, and ultimately de facto expelled from the halls of the UN.[4] In the process, the arc of SA history intersected with a third major event of 1948, the completion of George Orwell's *1984*, a work which revealed the oppressive capabilities of a subverted language, "Newspeak."[5]

This chapter examines apartheid SA's effort to engage with the "world made new" of the postwar order, and a constellation of ideas which posed a mortal threat to the apartheid project. The embrace of international languages of human rights, self-determination, and collective identity by the multiracial, democratic opposition movement has been the subject of extensive scholarship, but the NP's deployment of these same terms to defend the legitimacy of apartheid is almost forgotten in the burgeoning new transnational history.[6] The failure of the apartheid system, even on its own problematic terms, to deliver dignity, prosperity, and rights for all South Africans, and the appalling abuses that characterized NP rule, has left it as friendless in scholarship as it was in international affairs. While its pariah status in international diplomacy was well deserved, its marginal place within histories of internationalism is not.

The relative coherence of apartheid's global rebranding reveals that even modern, post-1945 discourses of emancipation and humanitarianism were readily susceptible to abuse. Paradoxically, the lexicon of rights, self-determination, cultural identity, and social development – all of which ultimately rendered the regime unsalvageable – were sometimes the only useful terrain on which to pursue its defense of the apartheid ideology.[7] As the language of global legitimacy shifted, the NP was, from

---

[4] For detailed analysis, see Alison Duxbury, *The Participation of States in International Organisations: The Role of Human Rights* (Cambridge, UK: Cambridge University Press, 2011).

[5] George Orwell, *1984* (London: Penguin, 2004). The final manuscript was concluded in the first week of December 1948.

[6] The catalogue of these works, almost all of them highly impressive, is voluminous. For a representative sample of the scholarship, see Håkan Thörn, *Anti-Apartheid and the Emergence of a Global Civil Society* (New York: Palgrave, 2006); Roger Fieldhouse, *Anti-Apartheid: A History of the Movement in Britain* (London: Merlin, 2005); Robert Skinner, *The Foundations of Anti-Apartheid: And Transnational Activists in Britain and the United States* (London: Palgrave, 2010); Simon Stevens, "Why South Africa? The Politics of Anti-Apartheid Activism in Britain in the Long 1970s," in *The Breakthrough: Human Rights in the 1970s*, ed. Samuel Moyn and Jan Eckel (Philadelphia: University of Pennsylvania Press, 2013), 204–25.

[7] For history of human rights in South Africa, with reference to NP's abusive utilization of group rights, see Saul Dubow, *South Africa's Struggle for Human Rights* (Athens: Ohio University Press, 2012), 80–109.

the 1960s onward, reasonably adept at modulating its own rhetoric to align with the new vocabulary. After an initial period of confusion, characterized by restatements of an archaicized imperial racism, apartheid was defended using the terms of its enemies, as opposed to a singular reliance on blunt assertions of sovereign prerogative and noninterference. Within a handful of years, NP ideologues were conversant in the new internationalist phraseology, an agility which had questionable impact on global perception, but demonstrated that discourses of human welfare and emancipation had ample capacity for subversion. Apartheid, a project of essentialist, racially determined nationalism, could be, and was, translated into various internationalist dialects.

The Arrested Development of "Separate Development" History

Within the more specialized, national histories of apartheid and its intellectual foundations, there is extensive analysis of the tensions, contradictions, and evolution of the official discourse over time.[8] However, historiography from international, and more recently, transnational, perspectives has been disinclined to pursue the NP's strange relationship with these ideas in any serious manner. The majority of the literature on the NP's defensive diplomacy has instead focused upon its exploitation of realist calculation, principally the economic benefit to Western multinational corporations, and the geostrategic implications of losing a reliable anti-communist partner.[9]

Very few have pursued the international promulgation of rhetoric on "separate development," "plural relations," and "cultural rights" beyond the pejoration properly accorded to the policy. Among the handful of exceptions is the pioneering contribution from Ryan Irwin, which does address apartheid's political philosophy in an international context, primarily as it related to the United States.[10] Irwin has demonstrated the complexity with which SA's governmental elite negotiated the new world, both in its relationships with the Western powers, and

---

[8]   Adam Ashforth, *The Politics of Official Discourse in Twentieth-Century South Africa* (Oxford: Clarendon, 1990); Aletta Norval, *Deconstructing Apartheid Discourse* (New York: Verso, 1996); John Lazar, "The Role of the South African Bureau of Racial Affairs (SABRA) in the Formulation of Apartheid Ideology, 1948–1961," *Collected Seminar Papers: Societies of Southern Africa in the 19th and 20th Centuries* 14, no. 37 (1986): 96–109.

[9]   For examples, see Thomas Borstelmann, *Apartheid's Reluctant Uncle* (New York: Oxford University Press, 1993); Sue Onslow (ed.), *Cold War in Southern Africa: White Power, Black Liberation* (London: Routledge, 2009).

[10]   Ryan Irwin, *Gordian Knot: Apartheid and the Unmaking of the Liberal World Order* (Oxford: Oxford University Press, 2012).

within international institutions. Jeremy Shearar, a former diplomat for the Republic, has investigated the NP's failed efforts to arrive at a modus vivendi with the UN's human rights initiatives.[11] Most recently, Saul Dubow's outstanding survey of the apartheid era reveals with the manner with which apartheid navigated an altered and altering post-colonial world.[12]

By contrast, the scholarship on the global campaigns against apartheid, and their influence on the development of the twentieth-century human rights movement, is rich. Apartheid's place in the account of human rights progress is firmly established, and often cast as one of the few signature triumphs of an international human rights mobilization. The narrative of apartheid's defeat couples the language of rights, self-deter-mination, and internationalism to emancipation and multiracial democratic freedom, which defeated the nationalist, sovereign assertion of the NP. This chapter seeks to complicate that story of triumph by demonstrating the ways in which the NP wielded the same lexicon on the world stage. The struggle to defeat apartheid was more than recalcitrant sovereign right holding out against the tide of postwar ideals, and involved a battle to persuade the world, or portions of it, that the apartheid vision was consonant with those same ideals.[13]

This sale of apartheid as consistent with human rights principles intuitively reads as cynicism, but to some degree, this understates the pernicious sincerity of belief on the part of apartheids proponents. While the proselytization campaign by NP diplomats were a public relations exercise, their fundamental content should not be reduced to self-conscious hypocrisy. The outward-facing rhetoric of apartheid's defend-ers was the nexus between the internal philosophy of the NP and the norms which now prevailed in the wider world. Whether intended or not, it did subvert and co-opt the language of human rights. However, fully resolving intentions and the interior understanding of those who embarked on this synthesis is a different question. Whether animated by cynical expediency or myopic conviction, human rights were suffi-ciently capacious to be understood, and presented, as compatible with apartheid. The voluminous verbiage the NP apportioned to these efforts demonstrated that they viewed a campaign to interface apartheid with rights as necessary for survival.

---

[11] Jeremy Shearar, *Against the World: South Africa and Human Rights at the United Nations 1945–1961* (Cape Town: UNISA Press, 2011); Jan Christiaan Heunis, *United Nations versus South Africa* (Johannesburg: Lex Patria, 1986), 312–33.

[12] Dubow invites further scholarship on this question, *Apartheid*, ix–x.

[13] Author note: It was not.

South African Racism Adrift in a World of Universality

From its accession to power in 1948, and into the 1950s, the NP struggled with the vertiginous shifts inaugurated by the postwar settlement. That settlement was contested and ambiguous, but the obvious fragility of Western imperial structures, and the increasing unacceptability of open claims of white civilizational superiority, were certainly apparent. International concern for the plight of SA's Indian community, and other features of racial discrimination, had already soured the United Party's (UP) legations enthusiasm for the new United Nations, and they held grave reservations about the draft UDHR. The NP contingent, led by the cabinet minister, Eric Louw, was at least as reticent, and much less constrained by the need to feign cooperation. As a self-fashioned statesman, UP Prime Minister Jan Smuts was compelled to a level of engagement.[14] Malan's government had no such impulse. Its diplomatic corps was mostly somnolent in the debates. Behind the scenes, their memoranda were filled with alarm.[15]

SA's delegation to the third session of the General Assembly reported with unease on the emerging draft UDHR. An article-by-article analysis of the provisional declaration revealed the cleavage between the NP's philosophy and the notional standards that would govern "all peoples and all nations." Many of the articles were outright unacceptable; not least the bedrock Article 1, which mandated the equality of rights for all individuals. Almost all of those which remained needed substantial qualification and deflation, and in many instances, revision into near oblivion.[16] SA was, predictably, among the eight states which abstained on December 10. There was an optimistic assumption that this vote "was understood for the honesty of its purpose."[17] It was not so understood, and SA, along with Saudi Arabia, were arguably the most fundamental in their rejections, a position more honest than the Soviet bloc abstention,

[14] Saul Dubow, "Smuts, the United Nations and the Rhetoric of Race and Rights," *Journal of Contemporary History* 43, no. 1 (2008): 45–74.

[15] See, for example, Secretary of the South African Delegation, Confidential: Second Session of the Drafting Committee of the Commission on Human Rights, May 27, 1948; Political Section, Department of External Affairs, "An Account of the Activities of the United Nations Commission on Human Rights Leading up to the Adoption at the Third Regular Session of the United Nations General Assembly of a Declaration of Human Rights," *c.* May 1949; Annex II, Harry Andrews, Address to the General Assembly, on Declaration of Human Rights, Full Text, December 1948. BVV 22, Human Rights Commission – 11/4/3, 1948, SAB, Pretoria.

[16] Secretary of External Affairs (presumptive from document context), Comments on Draft International Declaration on Human Rights, *c.* July 1948. BVV 22, Human Rights Commission – 11/4/3, 1948, SAB, Pretoria.

[17] Quoted in Shearer, *Against the World*, 72.

but tactically unsound.[18] Their explanation of the dissenting vote marked out the regime as one which rejected universal human rights in principle, as opposed to merely violating them in practice.

Apartheid's diplomats reported their initial disorientation.[19] Yet they were in some ways better equipped than the preceding, notionally more liberal, UP, to handle the new principles that had been set out in the UN Charter. Although former PM Smuts had coauthored that foundational document, his party, now in opposition, was more aligned to the genealogy of conventional British imperial thought. The comparative novelty of apartheid's intellectual foundations, while not especially amenable to equal rights and self-determination, were more readily adapted than the exhausted heritage of British trusteeship and segregationist rule. While racialized imperial language, notably from France, Britain, and Belgium, lightly revised to terms of "civilization" and "advancement," persisted into the early 1950s, its power was failing. During deliberations on the draft covenant on human rights, the legally binding successor to the UDHR, the persuasive abilities of "civilization" collapsed. Proposals for a colonial application clause, which was eloquently justified on the need to proceed cautiously when dealing with "backward" territories with their own traditions, were decisively defeated.[20] Human rights treaties were held to apply to all the territory of the states which ratified them. Remixed imperialism was on the edge of full obsolescence; and none of the Western colonial powers had any candidates to replace it.

By contrast, apartheid's ideological foundations were still vibrant. Unlike the Western empires, which had few voices interested in renovating any moral basis for imperialism, SA was immersed in that project.[21] Across the universities and the parliament, a cohort of intellectuals, many who moved into government, formulated racial segregation in terms that were notionally postimperial. They spanned from the highly "idealistic" Werner Eiselen, F. R. Tomlinson, Geoffrey Cronjé, and Nicolaas Diederichs, through to the more pragmatic, such as the author of the NP's apartheid policy report, Paul Sauer, and the future prime minister,

[18] Johannes Morsink, *The Universal Declaration of Human Rights: Origins, Drafting, and Intent* (Philadelphia: University of Pennsylvania Press, 1999), 21–7.

[19] D. B. Forsyth, Secretary of External Affairs, Pretoria, to Ambassador of the Union of South Africa, Washington, DC, "Human Rights," July 24, 1950, 1. BVV 23, Human Rights Commission – 11/4/3, 1950, SAB, Pretoria.

[20] Burke, *Decolonization and the Evolution of International Human Rights* (Philadelphia: University of Pennsylvania Press, 2010), 40–1, 116–21.

[21] Hermann Giliomee, "The Making of the Apartheid Plan, 1929–1948," *Journal of Southern African Studies* 29, no. 2 (2003): 373–92; Martin Legassick, "Race, Industrialization and Social Change in South Africa: The Case of R. F. A. Hoernle," *African Affairs* 75, no. 299 (1976): 224–39.

Hendrik Verwoerd. The milieu that generated apartheid was deeply exercised by the implications of decolonization and imperialism.[22] They were also acutely aware of the tactical possibilities afforded by cultivating tradition and identity.

Faced with a domestic situation that was already mired in the contradictions of imperial administration, the circle that authored the broad outlines of apartheid perceived the end of Western imperialism perhaps more astutely than the imperial powers themselves. Founded on a distinct phylum of imperial and racial nationalism, a century diverged from the main lineage of European imperialism, their propositions, however tortured, opened future possibilities for apartheid's defense that were infeasible for doctrinaire models of liberal paternalism. This was leavened, in some instances, by a vestigial ancestry in liberal ideas.[23] With a short period of adjustment, apartheid's theorists, and the NP, arrived at a new means of defending white rule. There would be a new postimperial world, but Afrikaner nationalism would be on its vanguard, not a redoubt of the colonial past. Apartheid was now "Separate Development," a plan which promised to grant the universal right to collective identity.

As the contours of the new global moralism began to emerge, apartheid ideologues railed against "liberal universalism," the rhetorical companion of empire. Even as the UN was being formulated at Dumbarton Oaks in 1944, future NP Prime Minister Malan was protesting "the egalitarian policy of the British Empire."[24] Verwoerd was just as forthright, "the Afrikaner has learned," he boasted, "to strike a defence against the intrusion of the social philosophy which is coupled with British liberalism and imperialism."[25] In August 1948, with the UDHR taking its final shape, the incoming NP Minister for Economic Affairs, Nicolaas Diederichs thundered to the House of Assembly that "the fight" was now "between Nationalism and Liberalism," a "Liberalism that stands for equal rights for all civilized human beings."[26] There was, he argued, "nationalism, which believes in the existence, in the necessary existence, of distinct peoples distinct languages, nations, and cultures, and which regards the fact of the existence of these peoples and these cultures as the basis of its conduct." Arrayed against this virtuous creed

---

[22] Christoph Marx, "From Trusteeship to Self-Determination: L. J. du Plessis' Thinking on Apartheid and His Conflict with H. F. Verwoerd," *Historia* 55, no. 2 (2010), 50–75.

[23] Notably in the figure of N. P. van Wyk Louw, see Mark Sanders, "'Problems of Europe': N. P. van Wyk Louw, the Intellectual and Apartheid," *Journal of Southern African Studies* 25, no. 4 (1999): 607–31.

[24] Malan, September 19, 1944, *Die Transvaler*, quoted ibid., 113.

[25] Verwoerd, July 26, 1944, *Die Transvaler*, quoted ibid., 218.

[26] Diederichs, Assembly Record, August 19, 1948, quoted in Hepple, *Verwoerd*, 63.

was "liberalism," and faith in "the individual with his so-called rights and liberties."[27] While it might perhaps have been news to the UK Foreign and Colonial Office, then desperately trying to balance human rights, colonial rule, and Cold War imperatives, universal human rights were a British imperial tradition, one which had been defeated on the high veldt half a century earlier.

The first major tests of the apartheid's effort to speak the new international language of human rights and self-determination struggled for coherence. Led by the South African Bureau of Racial Affairs (SABRA), a quasi-academic body that was arguably more maximalist than the NP itself, separate development was set within the context of a rapidly changing world system. SABRA's introduction to the policy, published in 1952, emphasized the virtues of separate development as a response to the rising wind of independence movements. As a matter of urgency, "the Bantu must be given the opportunity for political development," because across "the rest of Africa constitutional developments" had proceeded "all too fast."[28] It was nevertheless obvious that SA could not cauterize the trend.[29] The new policy of territorial separation and eventual independence would respect the right of political self-determination for the white nation, and promised the same for the African population (in always plural "nations"). This early rhetoric was not entirely harmonious. Carefully crafted statements on the parity of different peoples, inherent rights to national self-determination, and protection of cultural traditions were shattered by adjacent sentences which lapsed back to unvarnished racial supremacism. An elderly Prime Minister Malan was among the most problematic, and mixed the overt racial domination of *baaskap* with its purportedly enlightened successor, separate development. His March 1953 election launch speech in Stellenbosch, intellectual birthplace of apartheid, complained that the UN was inciting "revolt among more primitive races." Malan conceded that "all men are equal before God," and thus deserved to be "treated as human beings with human rights," but found this proposition unhelpful for finding a resolution to SA's specific situation.[30]

Nevertheless, apartheid's pidgin internationalist vocabulary rapidly progressed to a more effective creole, exemplified by the various essays and lectures prepared in defense of the 1953 Bantu Education Act. Drafted by the Secretary for Native Affairs, Eiselen, an anthropologist

---

[27] Quoted ibid., 162.

[28] *Integration or Separate Development?* (Stellenbosch: SABRA, 1952), 11, 13.

[29] Ibid., 34.

[30] Albion Ross, "Malan Will Press Segregation Plan," *New York Times*, March 6, 1953, 3.

by training, Bantu education was a showcase for the logic of anti-universalism. In place of the Christian missionary system, the state would educate black South Africans, with a new "Bantu curriculum." This new educational program, Eiselen's report claimed, was more appropriate for a student "conditioned in Bantu culture," who "was imbued with values, interests and behaviour patterns learned at the knee of a Bantu mother."[31] The international sale of Bantu education was the first sustained effort to explain NP policy in terms of the emergent global standards, and it was again SABRA that led the campaign.

Coauthored by G. H. Franz, Minister for Bantu Education in Transvaal, SABRA's 1955 booklet *Bantu Education: Oppression or Opportunity* boasted that the policy marked "a New Deal in the education of the Bantu."[32] Filled with cheerful photos of diligent students, new school halls, and neatly tabulated figures on the apparent generosity of the state, the booklet responded to charges of racial discrimination with cultural self-determination arguments. Bantu education, and separate development, enabled the "full and unfettered development of the Bantu individual and the Bantu communities."[33] Although the lengthy essay dropped into the register of supremacy at points, and spoke with unhelpful disdain about so-called *human rights*, most of its exposition on Bantu education studiously avoided older-style racialism.[34] More than a narrow defense of Bantu education, its publications were the prototype for international translation of apartheid precepts in the general case, as they were extended into the bolder architecture of "self-determination" of the Bantu peoples in their "Homelands."

As the decade drew to a close, the NP had found a postimperial equilibrium. Universalism of rights for individuals was countered by another postwar slogan, the universalism of collective rights. In his epochal speech at the anniversary of Blood River in December 1958, Prime Minister Hendrik Verwoerd, custodian of grand apartheid, packaged the former universalism as synonymous with centuries-old liberal imperialist fantasy. In the years since the South African War, and the struggles over the constitutional fate of the Cape, this liberal imperialism had altered in expression, but retained a lineage to the colonial presumption of a common set of values for all humanity.

We all know how a spirit of emancipation arose among humanity during the French Revolution, a spirit of freedom and brotherhood and equality of all people. It originated from the circumstances of the Europe of that time and was

---

[31] Eiselen Report, para. 773, quoted in G. H. Franz et al., *Bantu Education: Oppression or Opportunity?* (Stellenbosch: SABRA, 1955), 45.
[32] Ibid., 10.   [33] Ibid., 47.   [34] Ibid., 9.

then wrongly applied to the outside world which was different. The application of
the idea of freedom, equality and fraternity of all people ... revealed the prevailing
misconception regarding the life of people in other countries under different
circumstances ... What is the position today? There is a remarkable similarity.
Is it not so that today a liberalistic current very similar ... is again moving across
the world? A spirit which originates from World War II?[35]

The postwar order promulgated by the West was not a vision of the
future; its genealogy was the deep past. For Verwoerd, and an Afrikanerdom that survived the corruptions of the Enlightenment nestled in their
distant sanctuary site, there were no universal answers, and no universal
humans. Each was indissolubly bound to national traditions, their visions
of freedom specific to local community values. Under the grand apartheid canopy, at that point taking legislative form, the distinctive versions
of freedom that inhered in each nation could be pursued. This was the
bedrock justification of separate development, the future foundation of
apartheid's international defense across the 1960s and 1970s.

Separate Development as Self-Determination: Apartheid Rides the "Wind of Change"

From 1950 onward, self-determination was proclaimed by the emergent
Asian and Arab group as the foremost of human rights. Collective national
liberation was, in the words of one formulation, the "essential prerequisite" for all freedom.[36] Although bitterly opposed by Britain and France,
and, more diplomatically counselled against by the United States, the
right to self-determination was inscribed into the successor documents
to the UDHR, the two human rights covenants. In both the International
Covenant on Civil and Political Rights (ICCPR) and its companion, the
International Covenant on Economic, Social, and Cultural Rights
(ICESCR), self-determination took pride of place, set as the premier
article in both texts. Alongside self-determination, there were the first
cautious expressions of collective minority rights, a concept that had been
exhaustively considered in the UDHR.[37] In the drafting of the UDHR,
minority rights had been fiercely opposed as an archaic holdover from the

---

[35] Nancy Clark and Edward Alpers (eds.) *Africa and the West: Volume 2* (New York: Oxford
University Press, 2010), 130, 132.
[36] Summary Records of the Third Committee, 311th meeting, November 10, 1950, A/C.
3/SR. 311, para. 4.
[37] Morsink, *Universal Declaration of Human Rights*, 269–80. Cf. Article 27, on minority
rights protection, in the ICCPR, in Marc Bossuyt, *Guide to the travaux préparatoires of the
International Covenant on Civil and Political Rights* (Dordrecht: Martinus Nijhoff, 1987),
493–9.

League of Nations era, rendered irrelevant by the new philosophy of universal rights inhering in all individuals.[38] That moment of enthusiasm for universality had since waned, and protections for collective identity were once again explicitly written in to international law.

By the 1950s, when the covenants were being drafted, the NP had already disengaged itself from much of the UN program, disenchanted with the scrutiny and condemnation that had met SA since the organization's inaugural session.[39] The acerbic ambassador Eric Louw assailed apartheid's critics in the General Assembly, but SA's contributions to the covenants were limited.[40] There was no obvious acknowledgment of the tactical possibilities that might be afforded by the emphatic privileging of self-determination as a human right, or its ascendant position as the preeminent norm in international relations. In an environment marked by hostility to the NP's policies, and the fact that SA's chief critics were the same Asian and Arab states which promoted the right to self-determination most forcefully, the prospect of self-determination's rise as an opportunity was difficult to perceive at first.

That such an avenue might be available was hinted at by the enthusiastic recirculation of excerpts from an article from Charles Malik, a coauthor of the UDHR, by the South African mission. A large excerpt of Malik's piece, and the "rather contentious questions" entailed by self-determination was reproduced by the South African legation for circulation to assist in navigating what would "no doubt" be a perennial agenda item.[41] It surveyed the various features of self-determination, and noted the unresolved tensions between the concept and universal human rights. Malik pondered "the great question of 'cultural self-determination'" and group rights to identity. The Lebanese Thomist, an ardent defender of universality, asked was "there such a thing?" "Are people, for instance, entitled to suppress freedom of thought, conscience, and inquiry in the name of 'cultural self-determination'?"[42] Malik posited no answer – others

---

[38] For discussion, see Mark Mazower, "The Strange Triumph of Human Rights," *Historical Journal* 47, no. 2 (2004): 379–98; Mazower, "Minorities and the League of Nations in Interwar Europe," *Daedalus* 126, no. 2 (1997): 47–64.

[39] General Assembly Resolution: Treatment of Indians in the Union of South Africa, December 8, 1946, A/RES/44 (I).

[40] Eric Louw and Hugo Biermann (eds.), *The Case for South Africa* (New York: Macfadden, 1963).

[41] Deputy Permanent Representative, New York, to Secretary of External Affairs, Pretoria, "Human Rights: The Right to Self-Determination," September 5, 1952, with enclosure: excerpt of an article from Charles Malik, "Self-determination," published in the September 1952 issue of *UN Journal*. BVV 24, Human Rights Commission – 11/4/3, 1951, SAB, Pretoria.

[42] Charles Malik, "Self-determination," *UN Journal* (September 1952), 2.

would. By the 1970s, collective cultural rights were exalted as the most privileged category of freedom by defenders of the regime. The maximalist apartheid exponent, Dr. Albert Hertzog, leader of the extreme ethnonationalist Purified NP, explained that "whereas the English lay emphasis on the rights of the individual, we believe that the rights of the community are supreme."[43] Still more explicit was the self-cultivated "reformist" Prime Minister P. W. Botha, who emphasized, "the principle of identity" and "the realization of sovereignty and own communities with the maintenance of culture and self-determination." "In other words," stated Botha in 1980, "we serve the ideal of Freedom."[44]

The swing to self-determination as an intrinsic, and prioritized, element of human rights discourse had furnished, for the first time, one shared term with the "new world." NP philosophy was fluent in cultural particularism and group sovereignty, and these variants of nationalism were now an emerging part of human rights discourse. Self-determination was already part of, and arguably central to, grand apartheid's lexicon. Separate development did not have to be justified *de novo*. It could borrow from the legitimacy already accorded to the right to self-determination. While unlikely to be convincing to most of SA's critics, the argument was shifted to the content and implementation of self-determination, a debate that allowed ample obfuscation. Material for this project of persuasion was prepared by the Department of Information with considerable skill. Unlike the tirades from ambassador Louw that characterized the 1950s, which relied on legalist obstruction and *tu quoque* lines of attack, apartheid's public diplomacy moved from opposition to subversion.

In the wake of the Sharpeville massacre in March 1960, the need for a more capable sale of the NP's vision was a serious priority. International outrage briefly shook the NP, and transformed perceptions of the regime's standing, which went from unpromising to catastrophic.[45] Confrontation between apartheid's internationalism, and that of the UN, intensified. Much of this was conducted as monologue, with the African, Asian, and Soviet-led assaults in the General Assembly, its committees, and a recently proliferated raft of purpose-built anti-apartheid forums. Persuasion here was seemingly dismissed as futile. However, the case of South West Africa, adjudicated at the International Court of Justice (ICJ), did appear to exercise a more conscientious engagement from the NP, and a

---

[43] Nicholas Ashford, "Is the Afrikaners' Choice between Change and National Suicide?" *The Times* May 23, 1977, 7.

[44] Botha quoted in Norval, *Deconstructing Apartheid*, 208.

[45] Tom Lodge, *Sharpeville: An Apartheid Massacre and Its Consequences* (Oxford: Oxford University Press, 2011), 164–279.

number of its Western supporters.[46] The legitimacy of the SA mandate over South West Africa placed the apartheid conception of self-determination on trial, and provoked an intricate juridical defense. Aside from legal formalism, SA furnished its claim to the mandate on its putative alignment with human rights, development, and humanitarianism. Armed with academic experts, such as Stanford's Stefan Possony, it began to find the benefits of a more activist posture.[47]

One of the paradoxes of the diminished security of SA's domestic jurisdiction claims was an alteration in the balance of defensive argument, which relied markedly less on tired invocations of Article 2(7). The continued need for Western support, however resentfully given, was imperative, and the NP responded with a crash program. This new strategy entailed the adoption of what ambassador Naude privately counselled were "the main constituents of the political jargon," which were, "namely, self-determination for the Bantu peoples, respect of human rights, respect for the dignity of the individual."[48] With the Kennedy administration's gestures toward a less quiescent approach to apartheid, the US was a major focus. As Irwin has demonstrated, this transliteration effort, and the creation of new lexical carapace under which to pursue separate development, was undertaken with involvement from the most senior levels of government.[49] By 1974, the regime was gleefully invoking British Prime Minister Harold Wilson's famous "Winds of Change" speech – and claiming of its superior performance on the promises Britain had failed to deliver.[50]

A long excursus on the consonance of apartheid with the UN Charter was issued in 1964.[51] SA's defenders sought to repulse the charges of the Group of Experts by engagement, as opposed to sovereign refusal of UN jurisdiction, a strategy which defined its approach to milder intrusions in the preceding decade. Separate development was not a matter of domestic jurisdiction, on which the world should be silent, it was the implementation of internationally endorsed principles. "By Separate

---

[46] Irwin, *Gordian Knot*, 117–22.

[47] Among the more striking portions of Possony's testimony, given to the ICJ in October 1965, was his assertion that "Mankind with all its diversities has never accepted a single unit to impose a single writ," and a warning that "to impose a single formula would be ideological imperialism." Possony, quoted ibid., 121–2.

[48] Quoted ibid., 65.   [49] Ibid., 64–8.

[50] *Multi-National Development in South Africa: The Reality* (Pretoria: Department of Information, 1974), 77–8. For contextualization, see Saul Dubow, 'Macmillan, Verwoerd and the 1960 'Wind of Change' Speech," *Historical Journal* 54, no. 4 (2011): 1087–114.

[51] Hilgard Muller, *South African Policy and the U.N. Charter* (Pretoria: Department of Information, 1964); Muller, "The Official Case for Apartheid," *New York Times*, June 7, 1964, SM28.

Development," SA had ensured "the attainment by the peoples concerned – as the other free nations (including those of Africa) have done – of freedom from domination and discrimination and the securing of their human rights, freedoms and equality as neighbour nations."[52]

Alongside a relentless campaign of explanation from SA's diplomats and politicians, the NP also escalated and professionalized its public relations system. A generously funded Department of Information authored dozens of dedicated booklets, and the production quality of its periodical, *South African Panorama*, which had been established in 1956, was sharply improved from the early 1960s. *Panorama* was complemented by a companion journal, *Bantu*, from 1960, which was focused on "national" life in the homelands. The *Official South African Yearbook* was also revivified with contemporary style, photo reproduction, and layout.[53] Brutal wars of secession, in Biafra, and later Bangladesh, were frequently alluded to in the various publications. Separate development entailed the peaceful preemption of such bloodshed, it was the prophylactic exercise of the right to self-determination. The widely circulated publication, *Progress through Separate Development* was a breviary of the refashioned rhetoric of apartheid, and the boldest example of the NP's attempt to annex the legitimacy that had been afforded to the right to self-determination.[54] Republished in four editions between 1963 and 1973, its central purpose was to demonstrate the ways in which self-determination was being enacted through separate development. It opened with a favored fiction of the NP, that of a simultaneous settlement of SA's territories by white and Bantu, a claim which sought to dispel comparison with white settler colonialism elsewhere.[55]

Professions of fealty to the right to self-determination, and the closely coupled concept of the rights of collective groups, now officially consecrated as the most privileged of all human rights, Article 1 of both ICCPR and ICESCR, were the mainstay of the arguments across the 1960s.[56] Their perspective was an oddly refracted Wilsonianism, insistent its belief in a state for each nation; a principle apartheid ideologues hoped to enact with rather more thoroughness than the piecemeal

[52] Matthys Botha, *South Africa's Answer to United Nations "Group of Experts"* (New York, Pretoria: Department of Information, 1964), 14.

[53] On SA and public relations agencies, see Irwin, *Gordian Knot*, 165.

[54] *Progress through Separate Development* (New York: Information Service of South Africa, 1968).

[55] See also W. J. de Kock, *History of South Africa* (Pretoria: Information Service of South Africa, 1971). Cf. Robert Weisbord, "Who Got There First?" *Africa Today* 13, no. 2 (1966): 10–12.

[56] An initial foray was made in the late 1950s, with the publication of Hendrik Verwoerd's *Separate Development: The Positive Side* (Pretoria: Department of Native Affairs, 1958).

compromises in 1919. Their enthusiasm for actually making this self-determination real, as opposed to a reconfigured organization of racial subordination, was limited to nonexistent. Nevertheless, the intellectual case for cleaving groups into states was endlessly advertised as the centerpiece of South African political, economic, and cultural life across the 1960s and into the 1970s.[57] Backed by a growing edifice of legislative instruments effecting this "self-determination," separate development represented a meaningful refurbishment to the language of 1950s apartheid.[58] It repartitioned the rhetorical center of gravity away from superiority, and toward illusory parity and particularist identity. Prime Minister John Vorster, who had once opined "rights of free speech, assembly and protest" had been "getting out of hand," had little difficulty with the group rights of separate development.[59] He confidently proclaimed in 1970 that SA had nothing to hide in its policy. "Separate development," Vorster boasted, "is not the denial of the human dignity of anybody." Rather, the policy of "Separate Development guarantees the inalienable right of everybody to be and remain himself."[60]

Welfare, Modernization, and Social Services: Social Development in "Separate Development"

Alongside the new priority right of self-determination, the 1960s produced another dislocation in the model of human rights articulated in 1948, the dramatic elevation of modernization. The UDHR had included very significant provisions for economic and social rights, such as health, housing, education, and welfare. All of the rights were presented as an organic, indivisible whole, and none was set apart as more or less fundamental. As with self-determination, separate development could parasitically draw from the prestige that was accorded to development, which was now among the most exalted items on the UN's human rights agenda. It was another sphere where the regime could work in the mode of subversion and co-option, rather than rejection, and with a degree of plausibility that was almost certainly greater than anything

---

[57] For the first public relations salvo, see *The Progress of the Bantu Peoples towards Nationhood* (Johannesburg: Department of Information, 1964).

[58] A number of major legislative measures that were threaded into the separate development narrative, Bantu Authorities Act, 1951 (in retrospect); the Promotion of Bantu Self-Government Act, 1959; the Transkei Constitution Act, 1963; the Bantu Homelands Citizenship Act, 1970; and the Homelands Constitution Act, 1971.

[59] Joseph Treaster, "John Vorster, Former South African Prime Minister, Dies at 67," *New York Times*, September 11, 1983.

[60] "South Africa Ready to Defy World," *The Guardian*, April 28, 1970, 1.

possible with civil and political rights. The imprecision of the relationship between development and human rights was another virtue. Unlike arbitrary detention, discriminatory legislation, and denied freedoms of association and assembly, respect for economic and social rights was measured in the vague, exhortatory terms of "progressive realization."[61] Accordingly the "development" dimension of separate development was increasingly invoked as a testament to apartheid's human rights credentials.[62] Indices of health, housing, education, and other social services were recited, often in proud comparison to the achievements of other African states, though rather less often with white SA.[63] As with many other authoritarian regimes which offered development as the metric of human rights realization, notably the Shah's Iran, Lee Kuan Yew's Singapore, Park's South Korea, and later, the People's Republic of China, the NP evaded questions about other freedoms. The indivisibility of the UDHR had been divided, and the component somewhat and superficially more accommodating to apartheid's case was clung to as a lifeline to legitimacy. Less obviously, the temporal aspect implicit in "development" shifted the focus away from intra-South African comparison (the central site of gross injustice), and into intracommunity or group progress over time. Cross-racial comparisons were always a losing terrain: longitudinal ones were more promising, where progress in material and social development could purchase legitimacy.

At precisely the moment that social development and economic and social rights were being elevated on the UN's agenda, in the 1969 Declaration on Social Progress, SA issued a triumphalist catalogue of the social services that had been secured by separate development.[64] Entitled *Care: Welfare Services for South Africa's Peoples*, it was partitioned into sections for each of the "different civilizations" that comprised apartheid SA. Its front cover was a tableau of children's faces, with representative portraits from each of the myriad "nations" of SA. All of the individual faces were safely cauterized from each other, contained

---

[61] International Covenant on Economic, Social and Cultural Rights, GA Resolution 2200A (XXI), December 16, 1966.

[62] On surveying the situation in Southern Africa, the *Guardian* observed that "the only justification attempted for the system in South Africa is based on that country's prosperity." See "Neighbours in Apartheid," *The Guardian*, June 24, 1969, 8.

[63] On occasion, there was serious dishonesty when these comparisons were made, see, for instance, the selections and ellipses across the 1974–8 editions of the *South Africa: Official Yearbook of the Republic of South Africa* (Pretoria: Department of Information, 1974–8).

[64] Resolution 2542 (XXIV), Declaration on Social Progress and Development, December 11, 1969; and preparatory drafting debates, Summary Records of the Third Committee, 1575th–1605th meetings, October 16–November 12, 1968, A/C.3/SR.1575–1605.

within a thick frame, with wide margins of separation. The back of the volume had the now pro-forma table of the varied populations of each "nation," with SA's black citizens disaggregated into the official ethnic groups, a now shopworn device for obscuring the minority status of the white population. Within its covers, *Care* related the impressive progress in maternal and infant health, nutrition, education, housing, recreation, pensions, and services for the disabled, in the jarring phrase of the authors, "cripples."[65] Statistical measures were tabled, often of opaque significance and context. Optically, the effect was of inexorable progress, most arced ever upward, excepting those indices, like mortality, where the progress followed the line of virtue down (presumably to eventual immortality for all Bantu nation citizens). Virtually every high-gloss page had images, many in color, of the fruits of separate development, including its hypermodern computerized system for pensions.[66] *Care* carefully balanced the suggestion of parity and autonomy alongside calibrated suggestion of white SA's beneficence in expediting each of the "nations" in their own path to development.

A close companion work was published alongside *Care*, focused on Transkei, the notional flagship for separate development. *The Transkei: A Progress Report and Multi-National Development in South Africa* reported the gains in health, welfare, education, and amenities.[67] Images of modern and traditional spaces and dress were interlaced across the text, a syncretic encounter with development, pursued by Transkei's "citizens" on their own terms.[68] A further sibling, on the success of the "pluralized" system of education, was also issued – once. Its vision of future, separate citizens brought into the twenty-first century via "multi-nation" education was emphatically disproven less than a decade later, with the Soweto uprising.[69]

A Ghetto in South Africa was perhaps the most perilously self-congratulatory effort mounted by the Department of Information.[70] It rejoiced in the fires of Watts, and the tearing asunder of the civil rights

[65] *Care: Welfare Services for South Africa's Peoples* (Pretoria: Department of Information, 1969), 3.

[66] Ibid., 35.

[67] *The Transkei: A Progress Report and Multi-National Development in South Africa* (Washington, DC–South African Embassy: Department of Information, 1968).

[68] The Indian community was given its own celebratory booklet in the 1970s, see *The Indian South African* (Pretoria: Department of Information, 1975).

[69] *Stepping into the Future: Education for South Africa's Developing Nations* (Pretoria: Department of Information, 1969).

[70] John Steyn, *A Ghetto in South Africa* (Pretoria: Department of Information, 1977); Department of Information, *The Integration Model* (Pretoria: Department of Information, 1974).

consensus in the late 1960s. As the Great Society lay in ruins, the plural "societies" of SA were rendered as peaceful and flourishing. By eschewing the illusion of integrationism and shared equal citizenship, apartheid had avoided the inevitable violence of white reaction and radical black nationalism. As America agonized over the Moynihan Report on African American families, and pondered the findings of Nathan Glazer's *Beyond the Melting Pot*, SA had already arrived at the answer to intercommunal tensions.[71] It had moved beyond the "melting pot" via the fractional distillation of its constituent nations. The results of this path were meant to be self-evidently superior, in the contrast between the urban decay of the US, and the pristine amenities provided under Bantu self-government and SA suzerainty.

The Rise of Identity Internationalism: Plural Relations and "Human Rights" to Culture

In the late 1960s, after a decade of dormancy, ideas of cultural, religious, and national–historical identity had begun to visibly fracture the superficial consensus on universal human rights. The sweeping universalism of the UDHR, a world order of self-determined states, and a shared aspiration for development, to which most swore hypocritical fealty, was supplanted by assertions of collective cultural human rights and essential difference. The renascent belief in cultural essentialism and group identity brought human rights markedly closer to apartheid's core doctrines, and was easily reconciled with the propositions that subtended separate development. As early as 1964, South African academic Charles Manning boasted in *Foreign Affairs* of the alignment between this new global mood for "pluralism" and apartheid.

Honored voices have lately proclaimed the ideal of a world made safe for diversity. What else is this but the very principle of the apartheid program? Just as in the world as a whole there are many societies, each distinctive in its peculiar culture, so also within the confines of geographical South Africa there are more than one or two societies. That very self-determination which his fathers fought for is what the Afrikaner now envisages for each of the African peoples still subject to the white man's rule.[72]

---

[71] Daniel Patrick Moynihan et al., *The Negro Family: The Case for National Action*, March 1965, available at www.dol.gov/oasam/programs/history/webid-meynihan.htm (accessed May 14, 2016); Nathan Glazer and Moynihan, *Beyond the Melting Pot* (Cambridge: MIT Press, 1963).

[72] Charles Manning, "In Defense of Apartheid," *Foreign Affairs* 43, no. 1 (1964): 148.

While the universalism of the UDHR, which presupposed equal rights inhering in each individual, was impossible to co-opt with any plausibility, vastly fewer linguistic evasions and logical acrobatics were required to render apartheid as a system of collective, cultural human rights.

Particularist critique of rights was not of itself novel, famously expressed in the American Anthropological Association's rejection of the draft Universal Declaration in 1947, and in reservations to human rights treaties from the imperial powers.[73] It had, however, mostly receded from view across the 1950s, submerged by the enthusiasm for universality among early postindependence regimes. Nevertheless, particularism was never entirely absent from debate. An early sign of the limits of human rights universalism was on the 1961 Convention on Consent and Minimum Age for Marriage, on which Nigeria dissented on the basis of differences in custom and tradition. SA was among the handful of states not to endorse the text, citing the importance of respect for "Bantu custom."[74] UNESCO, always a forum uneasy about universality, with an institutional preference that always gravitated toward plurality, provided another useful endorsement of national and historical particularism in education in 1962. The UNESCO findings were promptly seized upon by ambassador Hilgard Muller, who cited them as testament to the wisdom of Bantu education.[75] Eiselen, the father of Bantu education, was seemingly a prophet, whose insights were now being recognized by independent Africa and the learned philosophers at the Place de Fontenoy.

Universality was further weakened by the precipitous dissolution of multiparty democracies and the severe curtailment of basic civil and political rights across the postcolonial world. As these new dictatorships themselves began to assert the incompatibility of "Western" human rights norms, and on the need for standards more consistent with endogenous values, the once lone voice of SA now had its pan-Africanist and scientific socialist enemies preaching national human rights exceptionalism. The tepid reaction from much of the West, and the acceptance of statements that parliamentary forms and individual freedoms were

---

[73] Burke, *Decolonization*, 112–20.   [74] Ibid., 128–9.

[75] Hilgard Muller, address to Royal African and Royal Commonwealth Societies on November 15, 1962, reproduced in Muller, "Separate Development in South Africa," *African Affairs* 62, no. 246 (1963): 57. He neglected to mention SA had withdrawn from UNESCO in 1955, when its opinions were perceived as less useful to the NP. UNESCO's dedicated report on Bantu education, prepared in 1967, was unsparing in its denunciation of the NP's policy, see UNESCO document SHC SS.67/D.30/A, *Apartheid and Its Effects on Education, Science, Culture, and Information* (Paris: UNESCO/Imprimeries Réunies de Chambéry, 1967).

alien to Third World traditions and conditions, were rebroadcast with delight by SA's diplomatic corps.[76]

The shift in the later 1960s was in the framing of particularism, which was no longer set against human rights, or a marginal variation at its edges. Group collective identity was cast as an integral component of the human rights project. No longer the disreputable excuse of Western colonial administrators, particularism was the new universal norm, asserted across the UN General Assembly, its regional human rights seminars, and within UNESCO's academic convocations on human rights philosophy.[77] The June 1965 UN Seminar on Human Rights in a Multinational Society, held in Ljubljana was a favorite of Department of Information publications, with its recommendation quoted at length in NP defenses of separate development.[78] The bulk of proceedings had condemned apartheid as a pathological example of racial determinism, but much of substance of the resolutions at Ljubljana were superficially conformal to what "separate development" had notionally delivered.

At the first World Conference on Human Rights, held in Tehran in 1968, apartheid was again subject to severe condemnation, with effusive support for armed struggle by the ANC and PAC, and comparisons with slavery. Yet Tehran's proceedings also witnessed a widespread dissent against universality. The UDHR itself, according to the Shah, who delivered the inaugural address, was in need of revision to meet the demands of a new postcolonial world, a world marked by an immense pluralization of national circumstances.[79] The NGO Human Rights Conference, held several weeks earlier in Montreal, was also more mindful of the diversity of a postimperial globe, and appeared to qualify, if only mildly, the universalism of the UDHR at some points. There was a pragmatic moderation of the UDHR's unalloyed universality, a recognition that "the world of today is one of great differences in levels of

---

[76] Muller, "Separate Development in South Africa," 57.

[77] United Nations Educational Scientific and Cultural Organisation, "Looking at the Universal Declaration of Human Rights in 1965," Round-table meeting on human rights, Oxford, November 11–19, 1965, UNESCO/SS/HR/1–7; Meeting of Experts on Cultural Rights as Human Rights, November 1968, Place de Fontenoy, UNESCO/SHC/120/1; and the papers, proceedings, and report collected in *Cultural Rights as Human Rights* (Paris: UNESCO, 1970).

[78] Department of Information, *Multi-National Development in South Africa*, 11; for further detail, see Report of the Seminar on the Multinational Society, Ljubljana, Yugoslavia, June 8–21, 1965, UN document ST/TAO/HR23; William Mackey and Albert Verdoodt (eds.), *The Multinational Society: Papers of the Ljubljana Seminar* (Rowley, MA: Newbury, 1975).

[79] Roland Burke, "From Individual Rights to National Development: The First UN International Conference on Human Rights, Tehran 1968," *Journal of World History* 19, no. 3 (2008): 275–96.

economic development of different social systems and traditions, and of countries giving different priorities to their needs."[80] This was subsequently pursued by SA as evidence of the harmony between its principles and contemporary human rights thought. Its abstention vote on December 10, 1948 was prescient, not perverse.

By the time of the UN's Cairo Seminar a year later, in September 1969, universality was being challenged more explicitly. Intended to advance an initiative on regional human rights institutions for Africa, the Cairo meeting, which assembled jurists, diplomats, scholars, and political figures, saw blunt assertions of African difference. There was, according to the report, "a basic lack of confidence in the fundamental texts on human rights because they failed to reflect non-European civilizations and traditions," a defect that was apparent in the UDHR itself.[81] This was all the more reason for an Africanist variant, because its human rights norms would be informed by "the tenets and traditions of African peoples."[82]

Human rights were almost certainly less menacing in this context. If the UDHR's universality was changeable according to sociohistorical specifics, then its lethality to separate development was no longer obvious. What could not be endorsed in 1948 had been sufficiently compromised in the intervening decades. In August 1970, future Foreign Minister "Pik" Botha delivered a maiden speech to the parliament, in which he urged SA to endorse the text it had rejected in 1948.[83] The speech won him few friends in the NP, but in a world where universal human rights were being reauthored as less, rather than more, universal, the dissonance of the UDHR with separate development was appreciably diminished. Botha's interventions had been carefully crafted and considered, he had leaked the idea to the *Cape Times* in advance, and even the orthodox voice of Afrikanerdom, *Die Burger*, endorsed it. A less enthusiastic, and potentially more perceptive analysis was delivered by *The Star*. Its editorial speculated that Botha's exhortation to support the UHDR indicated that the NP "must have evolved some smooth and specious way of identifying human rights with their concept of separate nationhoods."[84] The increased prominence of human rights in official rhetoric across the 1970s supported this more skeptical appraisal.

---

[80] Montreal Statement of the Assembly for Human Rights, March 22–27, 1968.

[81] Report of the Seminar on the Establishment of Regional Commissions on Human Rights with Special Reference to Africa, Cairo, UAR, September 2–15, 1969, UN document ST/TAO/HR/38, para. 23.

[82] Ibid.   [83] Theresa Papenfus, *Pik Botha and His Times* (Pretoria: Litera, 2010), 104–8.

[84] Editorial, August 28, 1970, quoted ibid., 108.

By increment, the inflexion of separate development was adjusted to exploit the rise of human rights particularism. *Multi-National Development: The Reality*, published in March 1974, was among the earliest works to leverage a visibly weakened universality.[85] Alongside the conventional rationales for separate development, which was in the process of being transitioned to "Multi-National Development," SA's case now included a much sharper comment on the rise of particularism within the currents of human rights debate. The report opined that the "programme of Separate Development" was almost invariably – and always unfairly – rejected as "a denial of fundamental human rights," as it had failed to implement the "neat and tidy package" of "a Bill of Rights" and a unitary constitutional settlement.[86]

That "integrationist" critique, however, had misunderstood the cultural, social, and historical specificity of human rights.

> What are these rights? Those of the Communist bloc, Western World or Third World whose interpretation of human rights differs radically? ... It is surely a fundamental human right for a people – a nation – to be themselves and to live according to their own preferences, needs and beliefs.[87]

Separate development lent each of SA's peoples the "apparatus to attain self-determination," which meant the "the freedom, when independence has been reached, to decide on the nature of its society *that* after all, is the real meaning of self-determination."[88] Its authors returned to the proposition of a universal system, with common individual rights in a single state, and asked its readers, whether this was "not a pattern of thinking derived from the history of imperialism?"[89] Such arguments accorded with the mood of the General Assembly, where Third World dictatorships and the Soviet bloc were denouncing the human rights imperialism of the proposed High Commissioner for Human Rights.[90]

Four years later, Dawie Cornelius Van der Spuy prepared an almost book-length exposition of the cultural relativist critique of human rights.[91] At the time of its publication, March 1978, it was the most sustained assault on universality yet circulated, only overtaken in 1979 with the publication of Adamantia Pollis and Peter Schwab's landmark volume.[92] In its demolition of the "paper standards" of false universality

---

[85] Cf. Joseph Lelyveld, "South Africa's Black Homelands: Some Home; Some Lands," *New York Times*, December 21, 1980, E5.

[86] *Multi-National development in South Africa*, 75.   [87] Ibid., 88.   [88] Ibid.   [89] Ibid.

[90] Burke, *Decolonization*, 130–41.

[91] D. C. van der Spuy, *Amnesty for terrorism* (Cape Town: Department of Information, 1978).

[92] Adamantia Pollis and Peter Schwab, *Human Rights: Cultural and Ideological Perspectives* (New York: Praeger, 1979).

promulgated from London, South African Department of Information had prefigured the famous essay from Pollis and Schwab, "Human Rights: A Western Construct of Limited Applicability." Apartheid's human rights counter-offensive was state of the art, issuing its arguments to the world while the academic equivalents were still in page proof. "Diversity" and "pluralism" became the next iterations of separate development.[93]

Conclusions

For human rights advocates, and to a lesser extent, scholars, the principal obstacle to the advance of the cause has been identified as national sovereignty, manifest in demands for noninterference in domestic affairs. While assertions of sovereignty remained a crucial weapon against serious scrutiny and intervention in the South African case, this conventional defense was complemented by a dangerous degree of engagement with the new moral lingua franca of the postwar world, human rights, self-determination, development and welfare, and cultural identity. In the celebration of the emancipatory potential of human rights, and in particular, the dramatic emergence of the transnational NGO movement of the 1970s, state responses have largely been neglected. This absence risks a mischaracterization of the struggle – which was carried out not only as sovereign right versus international concern. Increasingly, the struggle extended to a battle waged within, and for, that same internationalist language.

In numerous histories of human rights, apartheid has been cited as inadvertently pivotal in the dissolution of norms against noninterference. Yet there was second irony here, born of the receding efficacy of purist sovereignty arguments: the pursuit of new means against human rights scrutiny and global public pressure. NP ideologues and politicians could speak the axioms of progressive internationalism, including its flagship propositions of human rights and self-determination, a legacy of the metamorphic quality of the original constellation of apartheid ideas. Few were listening, and fewer still believing, especially by the late 1970s, but the perils of more baroque defenses of repression were not confined to South Africa. The NP's diplomacy was a pioneer in the use of a modernized phrasebook of cultural and historical particularism to repulse the application of universal human rights, a logic that was a natural extension of apartheid propositions. A comparative novelty in

---

[93] See, for example, *A Plural Society: An Exhibition of Photographs* (London, South Africa House: Department of Information, 1977).

1978, the NP's lengthy disquisition on cultural relativism and human rights would, in some respects, define two decades of future debate, and prefigure the sorts of phrases deployed by the Islamic Republic of Iran, to the PRC, to Malaysia and Singapore in the 1980s and 1990s.[94]

Authoritarian regimes had learned, as the NP did, that restatements of sovereign privilege were insufficient; co-option and subversion were required. The notorious *Progress through Separate Development* has its contemporary counterpart in *Human Rights in China*, complete with the boasts of modernization, and unique historical conditions.[95] Whatever power human rights held resided in their moral clarity, the more turbid the contest could be made, the better for repressive states. As is evident in the assorted state submissions to the UN's Universal Periodic Review of human rights, dictatorships have migrated to greater subtlety, fighting human rights critique with human rights language, on rights to subsistence, to culture, to life, and to modern social services.[96] Fighting within "human rights" and its sibling phrases is now the tactic of preference. As human rights historiography becomes progressively richer, and reclaims with ever finer precision the place of transnational NGOs, it is also worth considering that their custodianship of rights language was bitterly contested. Apartheid was an important crucible for revivified human rights networks of the 1970s. It was also a crucible for new means for authoritarian counterattack. Apartheid is dead – but both of these legacies survive.

---

[94] On the Iranian case, and state instrumentalization of relativist arguments, see Reza Afshari, *Human Rights in Iran: The Abuse of Cultural Relativism* (Philadelphia: University of Pennsylvania Press, 2001).

[95] Information Office, State Council of the People's Republic of China, *Human Rights in China* (Beijing, 1991).

[96] See state submissions to the UPR process, available at *Office of the High Commissioner for Human Rights: Universal Periodic Review* www.ohchr.org/en/hrbodies/upr/pages/uprmain .aspx (accessed October 10, 2016).

13 Between Humanitarian Rights and Human Rights

René Cassin, Architect of Universality,
Diplomat of French Empire

Jay Winter

This chapter distinguishes between two forms of rights discourse in the writings and practice of René Cassin, evident in his capacity as vice president of the Conseil d'Etat from 1944 to 1960 and in his role as a French delegate to the United Nations from 1945 and as an international human rights advocate in a number of organizations thereafter. The first position he adopted was that of an advocate of humanitarian rights, understood as falling within the laws of war. Victims of war, in or out of uniform, had the right to demand reparation, as a right and not as charity. His work on behalf of disabled WWI veterans was the origin of this commitment.

Overlapping with humanitarian rights were human rights, as adumbrated in the Universal Declaration of Human Rights Cassin helped to draft and to persuade the UN to adopt in December 1948. In short, human rights set down a supranational standard against which all nations had to measure their actions in peacetime as well as in wartime. The problem was that when he dealt with the Jewish population of Palestine, he saw their cause in terms of human rights, the right to form their own state, whereas when he approached the question of Palestinian rights, he framed them in terms of humanitarian rights. The same was true for Muslims in Algeria. He failed to speak out on human rights violations both in Israel and in Algeria during the ongoing Arab–Israeli conflict and during the Algerian War of Independence.

The blind spot in Cassin's thinking was in treating non-Europeans – Palestinians and Muslim Algerians – differently from Europeans in terms of the nature of their rights. The contradiction in his thought was that of his generation: men and women born in the 1870s and 1880s who fought in the Great War and who did not see that having an empire was a crime. From 1940 to 1944, they fought against the Nazis from Africa. After 1945 they believed that imperialism had to come to an end, peacefully and permanently, but still adopted a double standard when dealing with rights violations. His universalism fractured when it came to violent conflicts between Europeans and non-Europeans in the process of decolonization after 1945.

The Arab–Israeli Conflict

It is easier to understand why René Cassin championed the Zionist cause than why he was tone deaf to the Palestinian cause. He was a secular Jew, twenty-six of whose family members were deported and killed during the war. Family property was either Aryanized or stolen, and even for an eminent jurist, it took decades to sort out the mess in family affairs created by Vichy's Jewish legislation. Cassin's role as a public figure took multiple forms. He was the founder of the French veterans' movement, and a key figure in the fashioning of pensions policy after the Great War. He had been a French delegate to the League of Nations from 1924 to 1938, and from 1940, he was the jurist of France Libre. In 1943 he was asked by Charles de Gaulle to take on the presidency of the Alliance Israélite Universelle (AIU), a Jewish organization running an archipelago of schools teaching in French from Morocco to Persia. He remained head of this body until his death in 1976.

The AIU, created in 1860, had been aloof from Zionism until 1940. Thereafter it moved toward Zionism, just as a substantial part of the French population did. Cassin's was diasporic Zionism, unwavering support for those who wanted to make their home in Israel, though he himself remained rooted to France. From 1945 on, the Alliance did everything it could to foster the case for partition and the creation of the state of Israel. On June 9, 1947, Cassin himself authored and sent to the UN Secretary-General, Trygve Lie, a "Memorandum of the AIU on the Palestinian problem," which put the case for Jewish statehood in unequivocal terms. After the Holocaust, expediting Jewish immigration to Palestine "is the first duty of the international community." The reason was clear: "The survivors of Israel in Central and Eastern Europe desire, by a large majority, to build a new life in Palestine." To the Alliance, "this is a right humanity cannot refuse them." "The Alliance believes," he wrote, "that today the Jewish community in Palestine aspires to a change in its status, permitting an independence merited by their work and their creative spirit. We believe that the democratic spirit of the Near East can only but prosper through the influence of Jewish accomplishments in Palestine."[1] The unstated continuation of

---

[1] AIU, AM Présidence 030, René Cassin, "Memorandum de l'AIU sur le problème palestinien," June 9, 1947.

342   Jay Winter

this argument is that Jews could prosper alongside Arabs, whose aspirations were entirely separate.

Critically, Cassin supported Zionism as a means of saving hundreds of thousands of victims of the war in Europe. Persecution forged his identification with the Jewish people. In 1948, René Cassin received many letters of congratulation on his election to the Academy of Moral and Political Sciences. One was from an admirer who rejoiced in the honor Cassin had brought to the Jewish people. Cassin protested that this "immense praise" was gratifying though unjustified. Cassin went on:

I will say only that I have been given virtues that I do not have. In particular my loyalty to Judaism is quite specific, for I do not attend synagogue frequently. Only since the persecution of 1933 have I stood in solidarity among the persecuted. But if one day they became the persecutors, I will no longer be with them.[2]

Cassin's standpoint was shared by most Jewish Republicans at this time, including the great historian Marc Bloch. Bloch was a man of Cassin's generation – he was born in 1886 and Cassin in 1887. He was a soldier of the Great War too, and in his testament of 1943 he refused any "cowardly denial" as to his Jewishness, but continued: "Remote from any religious form as well as any so-called racial solidarity, I have felt, through my whole life, above all, simply a Frenchman."[3]

Occupation, resistance, and the Shoah brought Cassin to identify with the Jewish people – his people – and the Zionist project as a matter of human rights. Both Bloch and Cassin resisted the wartime diminution of their Frenchness. Consequently, they wore their Jewish identities with defiance and even pride. As Bloch wrote, "I announce my Jewish origins only when face to face with an anti-Semite."[4] In his last will and testament, Cassin followed Bloch's lead. In 1974, he wrote: "I would lose the confidence of thousands and even millions of Jews [Israélites], as well as that of the persecuted masses with whom I stand in solidarity, if I were to refuse to be buried in the Jewish rite."[5] Here we see a new identity born out of the war, an identity which inspired a new form of social and political engagement with the Zionist project. While he never considered making *aliya*, he defended the right of those who chose to do so. This was Cassin's line throughout the 1940s and 1950s. He also defended the

[2] AIU, AM Présidence 001e, Cassin to Sam Lévy, directeur des *Cahiers Sfaradis*, in Neuilly, April 12, 1948.
[3] Marc Bloch, *L'étrange défaite* (Paris: Albin Michel, 1957 [1st ed. 1946]), 224.
[4] Ibid., 31.
[5] 382AP194, Documents testamentaires de Monsieur René Cassin, August 25, 1974 [dated by the context].

Israeli state time and again during the 1967 and 1973 wars. In the case of 1967, this meant a collision with de Gaulle.

On May 18–19, 1967, U Thant, UN Secretary-General, withdrew the peacekeeping troops separating Israel and Egypt, thereby making the outbreak of war a real possibility. On May 22, Egypt's president Gamal Abdul Nasser attempted to enforce a blockade of Israeli ships in the straits of Tiran, cutting off the port of Eilat from international traffic. Despite the illegal status of the blockade, French president Charles de Gaulle urged Israeli restraint on May 24 and again on June 2. The first to open fire would not have his support.[6]

It was at this point that René Cassin, President of the European Court of Human Rights in Strasbourg and de Gaulle's jurist throughout World War II, intervened publicly in the discussion of the war crisis. Cassin challenged the policy of the French President, Charles de Gaulle, directly. In an article published in *Le Monde* dated June 3, but which appeared the day before, Cassin asked "What is aggression?"[7] He was in a particularly strong position to pose this question, since he had studied it as a member of the French delegation to the League of Nations in 1933, in the context of the World Disarmament Conference. It was a question debated time and again in the United Nations after 1945, and in that respect, Cassin followed the Soviet position, accepted by the UN on January 6, 1952. Fifteen years later, the USSR backed Nasser, but in 1952 it had defined an aggressor state as "that state which would establish a naval blockade of the ports and coast of another state." The same Soviet argument had it that an aggressor state was "that which would provide support to armed bands, which were trained on its territory, and which invaded the territory of another state, or despite the demand of the invaded state, to refuse to take all measures in its power to deny aid and protection to such groups."

This Soviet position was restated after the 1956 war, Cassin noted, adding this time the idea that the category of "economic aggression" includes "measures of economic pressure amounting to an infringement of the sovereignty of another state and its economic independence thereby endangering the economic life of this state." Cassin pointed out how critical these principles of free navigation were for the Soviet navy's passage through the Skaggerak in the Baltic Sea or the Bosphorus in the Black Sea. The implication was clear. Calling Israel the aggressor in the confrontation of June 1967 was nonsense. The message to de Gaulle could not have been more obvious.

[6] Declaration of de Gaulle after the meeting of the Council of Ministers, June 2, 1967.
[7] René Cassin, "Qu'est-ce que c'est l'agression?," *Le Monde*, June 3, 1967, 3.

Cassin repeated his defense of Israel as the target of Egyptian aggression in an article written before the war but published in *Ici-Paris* in its issue of June 6–12, 1967. In it, Cassin scoffed at the view that Israel was an aggressor. It was as absurd as viewing Czechoslovakia as the aggressor in its conflict with Nazi Germany, which ended so ignominiously in 1938. Israel would fight to defend its existence, "But this does not make it a warmonger. It had the instinct and the desire to consolidate long-lasting roots in the Middle East to reach with the neighboring Arab peoples a fruitful agreement," including a just settlement of the refugee problem. To him the Palestinian refugees were "pitiable instruments of those who ordered them in 1948 to flee from Palestine."[8] Later scholarship would prove this assumption to be false, and in some cases, a lie, though it was commonly accepted at the time.[9] Still, their plight was real, Cassin insisted, but it did not justify siding with Egypt, the real aggressor in this conflict.

In the end, Cassin's logic was simply bypassed by de Gaulle's *raison d'état*. One well-documented account of the diplomatic exchanges leading up to the war put it this way. On May 24, de Gaulle warned Israeli Foreign Minister Abba Eban: "Don't make war. You will be considered the aggressor by the world and by me. You will cause the Soviet Union to penetrate more deeply into the Middle East, and Israel will suffer the consequences. You will create a Palestinian nationalism, and you will never get rid of it."[10] Eban duly reported the message, but the Israeli government declined de Gaulle's protection, and launched the war that transformed the Middle East on June 5, 1967.

Two days before the war broke out, France imposed an arms embargo on the Middle East. Shortly thereafter, France's support for Israel's nuclear program came to an end. Both meant little in material terms, since Israel won the war decisively. The United States stepped into the gap and became Israel's chief defender and arms supplier, while the Israeli nuclear program carried on, without a hitch. This reorientation of French foreign policy toward Israel and the Arab world is the background against which to set an even more direct confrontation between de Gaulle and Cassin. De Gaulle had warned that he would hold accountable which ever state started the war. In his press conference of November 27, 1967, he set this parting of the ways between France and

---

[8] René Cassin, "Pour éviter un nouveau Munich," *Ici-Paris Hebdo*, June 6–12, 1967, 2.

[9] Efrat Ben Ze'ev, *Remembering Palestine 1948: Beyond National Narratives* (Cambridge, UK: Cambridge University Press, 2010), ch. 1.

[10] Edward Sheehan, *The Arabs, Israelis, and Kissinger: A Secret History of American Diplomacy in the Middle East* (New York: Reader's Digest Press, 1976), 31. There are many other sources which support his account of the Eban–de Gaulle exchange.

Israel in a long-term context. He noted that the creation of "a Zionist home" and later a Jewish state in Palestine then had raised "some degree of apprehension." Would there not be inevitably "incessant, interminable friction and conflict"? "There are even those who feared that Jews, so long dispersed, but remaining what they had always been, that is, a superior people, sure of themselves and domineering, once installed in the site of their ancient grandeur, would change the very moving desire they had nourished for nineteen centuries into an ardent ambition toward conquest."

Despite this danger, the Jews had found substantial sympathy among Christians, de Gaulle went on, "by their constructive work and the courage of their soldiers," and France was prominent among those states which welcomed the creation of the Jewish state and the arrival of many new immigrants from Arab lands. Urging moderation on the state of Israel, France had been open to stronger ties with Arab lands once the war in Algeria was over. The existence of the state of Israel, de Gaulle insisted in this press conference, "was a fait accompli." That was not in question. What mattered was the transformation by Israel of the crisis of 1967 into an occasion for the expansion of Israel itself. The closure of the Gulf of Tiran, "unfortunately created by Egypt," had provided "a pretext to those who wanted to fight." Consequently, de Gaulle observed, "Now, Israel is organizing on the territories it holds an occupation which can only lead to oppression, repression, expulsions, and against which there already is a resistance, which Israel calls terrorism."[11]

There were other turbulent issues at stake; on the same day and at the same press conference, de Gaulle announced his veto of Britain's application to join the European Economic Community. He thereby reoriented French foreign policy in fundamental ways, at variance with Washington, and its Trojan horse in London. Domestically, the rejection of the British application was less controversial than his comments on Israel, the conflict in the Middle East, and on his characterizations of Jews and Jewish history. The fallout from this press conference was very heavy.

Cassin, alongside other Jewish leaders, was incensed by de Gaulle's comments. He signed denunciations of the president's language, and shared the indignation the Chief Rabbi Jacob Kaplan expressed personally to de Gaulle on January 1, 1968, during the formal exchange of New Year's greetings. De Gaulle assured the rabbi "that he had not the intention to insult Jews"; indeed, he thought "what he had said about

---

[11] For the full text of the press conference, see *Le Monde*, November 29, 1967.

the Jewish people was a eulogy." Kaplan replied that "certain terms in his declaration had been used by our enemies." Nevertheless, the rabbi urged de Gaulle to use his influence to promote a just peace in the Middle East. "As to my authority, de Gaulle said, I have none. I asked Mr. Eban not to attack and he attacked."[12]

Here the personal and the political were braided together. De Gaulle took Israel's decision to go to war as a rejection of his offer of protection; but his case against Israel was more than that it had chosen war when its survival was not, in his estimate, at stake. It was that Israel would keep what it held, and consequently peace was impossible to achieve in the Middle East. He thought, from a geopolitical point of view, that it was in the interest of France to reorient its stance away from an alliance with Washington, London, and Tel Aviv. Had he pulled off a miracle of mediation avoiding war in June 1967, his standing as a peacemaker would have been enhanced substantially. He had already settled the war in Algeria, at great risk. What stood in his way in the Near East, he believed, were those in Israel who had used as a *casus belli* Nasser's gambit of closing the straits. He had personally urged Israel to hold its hand, and he had been rejected. In a test of will between two forces, each "sure of itself and domineering," de Gaulle's advice had been ignored. The bite in his rhetoric came from this simple fact, but behind the words was a strategic choice de Gaulle had made in the interests of France.

Cassin understood the matter differently. Who was as loyal to de Gaulle as Cassin had been since the first meeting they had had in London in June 1940? Who had accepted more laconically whatever decisions de Gaulle had made to move him from one part of the political constellation of Free France to another? This time de Gaulle had gone too far. De Gaulle's position was unjustified and immoral. It confused aggression with legitimate defense, and added insult to injury by drawing from the cesspool of anti-Semitic stereotypes to characterize what was a political and diplomatic dispute. De Gaulle's remarks and the language he used to describe the "Jewishness" of the position of Israel left lasting scars.

A few weeks later, Cassin took up the matter in person, on the occasion of a lunch for the Constitutional Council at the Elysée Palace. The episode was recounted by Bernard Ducamin who was in attendance and described the General and Cassin in discussion in front of a window having coffee. We have Cassin's own account of the encounter. On January 31, 1968, he told the Central Committee of the AIU in Paris

---

[12] Ariel Danan, "De Gaulle et Jacob Kaplan. Un document d'archives inédit," *Archives juives* no. 40 (2007): 137–41, drawn from the archives of the Israeli Ministry of Foreign Affairs.

that he had "taken the opportunity of a recent lunch with the Constitutional Council in the Elysée Palace to raise the issue of relations with Israel. The general approached him at the end of the meal, and said, notably, with respect to his press conference, "But I thought I was praising the Jewish people." Cassin would have none of it. "The word 'domineering' is used by propagandists hostile to Jews and in particular by the 'Protocols of the Elders of Zion.' It was not only a discriminatory word, but a murderous word. The Russians used it in that manner in their propaganda."[13]

We have no record of further exchanges between the two men, but we do know that Cassin took up the matter discretely with the president's Secretary-General, Bernard Tricot, sending him his article in *Le Monde*, dated June 3, 1967. He enquired of Tricot whether the general's position was that Israel had to agree to evacuate the occupied territories as a precondition of peace negotiations, or whether the negotiations could consider the matter in due course. At no point then nor in subsequent years did Cassin argue that Israel had the right to annex territories acquired in the course of the 1967 war. He thought, however, that the conflict had to be solved by direct negotiation between the parties.

In the last decade of his life, between 1967 and 1976, both during de Gaulle's presidency and afterwards, Cassin followed the growing tendency among French Jews to view their government's foreign policy as hostile not only to Israel but to Jews as such. De Gaulle's choice of words made that argument plausible. He had spoken not of "the state of Israel" or "the Israelis," but of "Jews" as "a domineering people." Where could that possibly have left Jewish Republicans like René Cassin, other than outside the Republican orbit, subjects of a double identity – Jews and Frenchmen – of the very kind Vichy had concocted and de Gaulle and Free France had struggled finally to erase? Why in the world had de Gaulle, who had shown not the slightest sign of anti-Semitism in his dealings with Cassin, come to this view?

De Gaulle's presidency came to an end a year later. In 1970, he died, and Cassin was one of the mourners who attended his interment at Colombey-les-deux-Eglises. The ties of respect between the two men were too deep to be broken by what was ultimately a matter of state. But for Cassin, the principle at stake here was one of fairness and the equal application of the rule of law to all parties to a dispute. Time and again in the last decade of his life, Cassin protested against the lack of even-handedness, the blatant bias in international condemnations of Israel.[14]

---

[13] AIU archives, Paris, AM Central Committee, January 28, 1968, minutes, 10–11.
[14] AIU, AM Présidence 013a, Cassin to Général Koenig, January 19, 1970.

In 1973, before the Yom Kippur War, Cassin privately prepared a position paper for the use of the Israeli Foreign Minister, Abba Eban. The specific occasion to which Cassin responded was the international condemnation of an Israeli commando raid on Beirut, in which several leaders of the Palestine Liberation Organization were killed. Claiming that his remarks were provisional, based on a partial, and not an exhaustive, study of the matter under international law, he hoped it would be useful for Israel "to recall some principles all too often ignored since 1967."[15]

The first point Cassin made was that "When certain parties to the conflict openly violated the ceasefire order, the Security Council showed its weakness and its partiality, in reserving its condemnation for the only party which had responded to attack – at times with rough reprisals – without condemning those responsible for the initial attacks." Second, he recalled that "the violation of international law continued in another direction when the Security Council implicitly admitted by terming them 'Resisters'" that Palestinians were "belligerents," and therefore had a duty to respect the Hague Convention of 1907, but proudly declared they would not respect the laws of war." "Since then," Cassin argued, "the war took on a new aspect." The international community not only "left, without censure, the perpetrators of hostile acts and even of terrorism against a third country," but also "it has accepted that terrorist organization committing such acts" were sheltering in a third country, "Lebanon, not involved in this conflict."

Here Cassin returned to a point he had made before the outbreak of the 1967 war. The international community had lost sight of established practice on the identification of an aggressor under international law. "Since the Litvinoff doctrine, formulated in Geneva in 1933–4, applied to several treaties signed by the USSR and remains valid until the UN adopts a new definition of 'Aggression,' and of who is considered 'an aggressor,' a state may be considered an aggressor against a neighboring state when it continues to shelter bands of armed men and those commanding them." This was evidently the case with respect to Israel and Lebanon in 1973. Consequently, "Israel had the right to accuse Lebanon of aggression in these international incidents." How could the great powers view Israel as an aggressor in light of this doctrine? "If, however, there is no state of war between two states, in light of the behavior of Palestinian bands, which the Security Council tolerates and

---

[15] AIU, AM Présidence 015, "La situation respective des Etats Israël et du Liban au regard du droit international," April 13, 1973.

accepts, there is still a persistent violation of international law." Under these conditions, "it is just to set aside the law of reciprocity." It was precisely this lack of balance in the application of international law which outraged Cassin. International security and a respect for the peaceful lives of neighboring states were both contractual matters. If broken by one party, it was not possible for that party to claim a grievance, a point Cassin had made as long ago as 1914 in his thesis on contracts.

Abba Eban thanked Cassin for his position paper on May 3, 1973.[16] Not long thereafter war broke out in the Middle East. Cassin shared the relief of the Central Committee of the Alliance that Israeli forces had repelled the surprise attack of October 1973. He wrote to both the Israeli ambassador to France and to the president of the State of Israel to express "the anxiety we had all shared" when Israel was "once more a victim of evident aggression" and "the complete admiration we have for the courage of the Israeli nation, the discipline of the people, and the behavior of the army."[17]

The following year, Cassin went to Israel, accompanied by Ghislaine Mareschal, to inaugurate the new Lycée René Cassin in Jerusalem. Having always considered the question of Jerusalem a separate matter, Cassin was personally involved in the fundraising for this project, and agreed to give his name to the school, despite the fact that it had been constructed across the "Green line," that is, in a part of the city in no-man's land between Jordanian and Israeli Jerusalem. Consequently, the French government did not send any officials to the ceremony.[18] What a contrast between this moment and the time in 1958 when Cassin had had full French backing and praise for the creation of a French lycée under his name in Tel Aviv. What a contrast between the celebration in 1960 of the centenary of the Alliance in Paris and in Jerusalem, cities whose governments were now world apart.

In his last years, despite infirmity and hospitalization, Cassin continued to speak out on issues of importance to French Jewry. In June 1972 he participated in an international conference in Uppsala in Sweden, a meeting he had helped to fund. He contributed to the writing of what is known as the Uppsala Declaration, a text modeled on the Universal Declaration. Its preamble of twenty articles stressed the need for all countries to develop and enforce freedom of movement "through

---

[16] AIU, AM Présidence 015, Eban to Cassin May 3, 1973.
[17] AIU, AM Présidence 015a, Cassin to Katzir, October 29, 1973. See also Cassin to Asher Ben Natan, October 10, 1973.
[18] AIU, AM Présidence 016a, on arrangements for the inauguration of the school.

international agencies and according to the law and to international procedures."[19] In Uppsala, he drew attention to the "sad and persistent problem of Soviet Jewry," a problem which "merited the sympathetic attention of the Soviet government, in light of its power and the prestige of this great country . . . The only solution consistent with the restoration of the indestructible core of human rights, is freedom of choice, which in this case means the freedom to stay or to leave."[20] This message was published in the *New York Times* on March 23, 1973; it became the rallying cry of a growing movement to force the Soviet Union to liberalize its policy toward those of its citizens who wanted to emigrate to Israel. The very last communiqué with his signature attached to it was a protest, dated December 24, 1975, on the plight of Soviet Jews, as yet unaffected by the final act of the Helsinki conference, establishing Western surveillance of human rights as the price the Soviet Union paid for guarantees of its western borders.[21] Cassin could not have known that Helsinki was a major event in the history of the human rights movement, one with unanticipated consequences for both the Soviet Union and the world.

Cassin was a committed Zionist. His loyalty to Israel was very deep, and increasingly so, as time went on. The question remains, though, as to how to square Cassin's commitment to human rights with his record of solidarity for and advocacy on behalf of the State of Israel after the Six-Day War? The answer is mixed. On the one hand, his commitment to the AIU was for Jewish emancipation, toward which the establishment of the State of Israel was, in his view, a triumphant step. He recalled in his later years the joy he felt in the United Nations in 1948 when he heard that David Ben Gurion had announced the establishment of the Jewish state. Cassin believed firmly that it was the right of Jews to create a homeland in Palestine, especially after the Shoah, and to leave their countries of birth, such as the Soviet Union, to go to Israel, if they choose to do so. The right to emigrate is imbedded in the Universal Declaration of Human Rights.

The problem of Israel and human rights became more complex after the occupation of Jerusalem, the West Bank, and the Gaza Strip. Under these circumstances, is there any basis for the claim that Cassin was guilty of imbalance himself, in treating the rights of Israelis or Jews as somehow worthy of greater respect than the rights of Palestinians or Muslims? The

---

[19] Karel Vasak and Sidney Liskofsky, eds., *The Right to Leave and to Return: Papers and Recommendations of the International Colloquium Held in Uppsala, Sweden, 19–20 June 1972* (New York: American Jewish Committee, 1976), xi.

[20] Ibid., xxi–xxii.

[21] AIU, AM Présidence 017a, Communiqué on plight of Soviet Jews, December 24, 1975.

answer is yes and no. He did believe that there had to be a settlement of the Palestinian refugee problem as part of an overall settlement, but he tended to use the term "population exchange" in this context. On October 23, 1974, Cassin urged the president of the French senate to consider as parallel the position of immigrants from Arab countries to Israel and the position of Palestinians in exile.[22]

Such a formulation is flawed, since it does not acknowledge that such a "population exchange" would leave Palestinians with unfulfilled national aspirations, while Jews could enjoy theirs. It was not a neutral step for him to accept giving his name to a school built on land in East Jerusalem. He did not speak out for the human rights of Palestinians under Israeli occupation. But, in the end, the way Cassin treated the Palestinian problem as a refugee question was characteristic of his entire approach to politics. They were victims of war, and deserved to have their grievances met in an honorable fashion. In the same way, Cassin had championed Israel as a haven for Jewish victims of war and genocide. His position is located in the period bracketed by World War II and the Six-Day War. Then there was force in the claim that Zionism was an ideology of liberation and of the rescue of the victims of the Holocaust. Thereafter, when Arab populations were subject to occupation, and land was taken for Jewish settlement, the meaning of Zionism began to change, and the political coloration of the Israeli state changed with it.

Cassin himself had said in 1948 that his commitment to the Jewish people grew out of their suffering.[23] If they were to become oppressors, he would not be with them. The timing of his death meant that he did not have to face the difficult dilemmas following the Israeli invasion of Lebanon and the massacres of Sabra and Shatilah, but there is nothing in his life or writings to indicate that he would have stood by and supported blindly human rights violations whoever committed them and wherever they occurred.

On the level of political analysis, though, it is evident that it was de Gaulle rather than Cassin who had the more penetrating vision of the contradictions at the heart of the Middle East conflict in 1967. However crude his characterizations of Jews as "a domineering people," he was right about the cruelties imbedded in the Israeli occupation of the West Bank and Gaza. No one in 1967 imagined that the stalemate would last for fifty years. It was de Gaulle, not Cassin, who foresaw this tragic impasse, right at the outset of the new balance of power arising from

[22] AIU, AM Présidence 016a, Cassin to Alain Poher, Président du Sénat, October 23, 1974.
[23] See n. 9.

Israel's victory in the Six-Day War. It was de Gaulle who saw that a resistance movement would emerge, and that Israelis would crush it using all instruments at their disposal, including torture, assassination, administrative detention, and deportation. De Gaulle, who had no commitment to human rights himself, saw the human rights contradiction in which Cassin was trapped. Defending Israel meant distinguishing between those who had one set of rights, leading to a state, and those who had another set of rights, leading to humanitarian aid. That untenable position was widely held in the last years of René Cassin's life, and its contradictions must be recognized.

The War in Algeria

The second set of contradictions in Cassin's record as a champion of human rights emerged during the Algerian War of Independence. Like all other wars of decolonization, the Algerian War posed fundamental problems for the defense of human rights. Cassin was one of the founders to the campaign to install the right of petition as a fundamental human right, and he was well aware of the risk of the violation of human rights in a colonial setting. In the French case, as the Conseil d'Etat had to judge the appeals of victims of state powers, Cassin was in charge of assuring the respect for human rights within the sphere controlled by the French state, including Algeria. How did he emerge faced with this challenge?

It would be absurd to ignore the limitations imposed on him by the very nature of the Conseil d'Etat. It is a collective body, and we cannot assume that everything the Conseil did during his presidency reflected his views or influence alone. Its members were not a small group of political activists, as was the Comité Juridique in Algiers. They were higher civil servants, involved at times in policymaking, who understood all too well the force of compromise in the daily work of the state. They were colleagues of the key advisers of ministers and other high civil servants, and were preoccupied with not impeaching them.

At this point, we need to separate the two facets of the Conseil d'Etat, its litigation work and its advisory role vis-à-vis the government. With respect to litigation, only a few cases were introduced to the Conseil d'Etat pertaining to incidents in the Algerian uprising.[24] In general, as Jean Massot, former section president said with heavy understatement,

---

[24] Sylvie Thénault, "La guerre d'Algérie au Conseil d'État," in Jean Massot, ed., *Le Conseil d'État et l'évolution de l'outre-mer français du XVIIIe siècle à 1962* (Paris: Dalloz, 2007), 199–220. See also her book *Une drôle de justice: Les magistrats dans la guerre d'Algérie* (Paris, La Découverte, 2001).

its decisions were "lenient" and "resigned" to accepting what could not be altered.[25] Under Cassin's presidency, the Conseil d'Etat even accepted violations of fundamental principles, by giving military authorities and justice wide powers. In a notorious case, a meeting of the general assembly of the Litigation section, at which Cassin presided, endorsed the legality of "internment centers" in Algeria which had been explicitly forbidden by a law of 1955.[26] These centers were well known for being places where torture was routinely practiced.

On less fundamental subjects, the Conseil d'Etat was more vigilant, concerning matters of circumstance and dates, in order to ensure that special police powers were not used abusively against journalists or civil servants and that they would not become permanent. That said, its main concern was not to limit the freedom of action of the army and the police. And there is the nub of the problem.

The second facet of the work of the Conseil d'Etat was to oversee legislation proposed by the government. The Conseil was certainly not severe when considering matters touching on Algeria. The law of 3 April 1955 defining the state of emergency was examined by the permanent commission of the Conseil d'Etat. It considered that the provisional status of this law reduced its gravity: the state of emergency lasted only for six months, and its prolongation required a new law. The permanent commission imposed a geographically explicit limit on those zones in which the state of emergency operated, recognizing that "such measures constitute dangers of an incontestable gravity for public liberties." The bill proposed to displace cases normally heard in ordinary courts to military courts. The permanent commission said that such a shift would be only a possibility and not a rule, which did nothing to limit recourse to this form of military justice. The permanent commission did not require systematic control over administrative internments, but only gave internees the right to appeal to a consultative commission against this measure, which had the option of hearing the appellant, should it so choose.[27]

The law of March 16, 1956 on special powers was passed by the permanent commission of the Conseil as well.[28] Later on, the renewal of

---

[25] Jean Massot, "Le rôle du Conseil d'Etat," in Jean-Pierre Rioux, ed., *La guerre d'Algérie et les Français* (Paris: Fayard, 1990), 271.

[26] The Zaquin case, Assemblée générale, March 7, 1958, *Lebon*, 150. The Conseil decided that the law of 1956 on the basis of which internment was ordered did not violate the provision of the law of 1955 prohibiting camps of internment.

[27] CAC, 19990025/367, dossiers 266-502 and 503. Decree, April 23, 1955; CAC, 19990025/371, dossier 266-734. Sylvie Thénault, "L'état d'urgence (1955–2005). De l'Algérie coloniale à la France contemporaine. Destin d'une loi," *Le Mouvement social* no. 218 (January–March 2007), 63–78.

[28] CAC, 19990025/409, dossier 269-058.

these two laws on the state of emergency and on special powers were but formalities. The Conseil was somewhat more strict about the law of October 7, 1958, extending the possibility of administrative internment to metropolitan France. Such a measure would be subject to the control of a supervisory committee, as was the case in legislation of 1944, but with longer delays – one month in place of fifteen days – to render its judgment, and a purely written procedure. The general assembly of the Conseil d'Etat accepted that the supervisory committee could hear the internees and provide them with an interpreter, but such was not established as a right for the internees.[29] On this crucial issue, the contrast between the Comité Juridique of Algiers and the Conseil d'Etat is striking. We can see the great weight the Conseil gave not to substitute its thinking for that of the legislators and not to tie the hands of the government.

We are dealing here with a matter fundamental to human rights. The Conseil refrained from condemning administrative detention without review by a judge; it thus even stood back from affirming what in the Anglo-Saxon tradition is the rule of habeas corpus. Cassin's legacy as vice president of the Conseil d'Etat cannot be measured fairly or fully without recognizing this glaring contradiction in his commitment to human rights.

Why was he so restrained? One possibility is that he thought that the majority of the Conseil d'Etat was not prepared to give human rights so much importance. Another is that if he had stood his ground on this issue, and had resigned, the practice of administrative detention would not be affected at all. It was better to remain within the Conseil, as in London in 1941, or as in Algiers in 1943, than outside the institutions of state. Yet another possibility is that he shared the opinion of the majority. Cassin believed that decolonization was inevitable, but he may have opposed the uprising in Algiers as the way to achieve it.

Cassin had a strict idea of the reserve a judge had to maintain. As he said to a professor of law who wanted to keep his freedom of expression: "In so far as you exercise the function of a magistrate, you must be silent on those problems posed by this responsibility."[30] He never spoke in public about human rights in Algeria. In the executive board of ENA (the National School of Administration), which we will discuss below, the subject of students sent to Algeria was raised several times, without

---

[29] CAC, 19990025/526, dossier 275-410.
[30] Discussion about the Conseil constitutionnel, General Assembly of the Conseil d'Etat, October 28, 1958, Commission des archives constitutionnelles de la Ve République, *Volume 1, octobre 1958–30 novembre 1958* (Paris: La Documentation française, 2008), 480.

comment by Cassin. He refused an invitation to join a committee created by Guy Mollet in 1957, to investigate cases of abuse of state powers in Algeria, probably because he thought that his presence would be used to whitewash government policies.[31]

Cassin issued only one public statement about the Algerian War. On April 7, 1958, he gave a speech to a meeting held during (but not officially within) the UF annual conference.[32] He had not spoken in an annual meeting of the UF since 1946. He said nothing about the gangrene of human rights violations in Algeria, and did not raise the case of a French air force bombardment of the border town of Sakhiet sidi Youssef in Tunisia, in which many civilians were killed, despite the evident fact that this incident was a violation of international law. In his speech, Cassin spoke as the delegate of France in the Human Rights Commission of the UN, from which he had just returned. In New York, he had met many Americans:

With the honest but simplistic mind which inspires a young and passionate people, under the influence of the press and elementary feelings, many concluded: "After all, it is obvious that the transition to independence of Morocco and Tunisia did not lead to the disaster some believed would come, and so it would be the same for Algeria.[33]

Nothing that he had to say would dissuade them:

This they do not believe: the normal idea of anti-colonialism, of the emancipation of people is alive in their minds, and whatever information or propaganda you offer, you will not overcome this idea. Virtually all Americans say: "if you do not want foreign intervention, get your house in order" . . . The foreigners with the best intention toward France say, as did the last general assembly of the UN: "Let the French handle their own troubles, but let them get on with it." In this position, we have the responsibility: we have to accept any necessary sacrifice.[34]

There is much ambiguity in these words. Here he did not specify what had to be done, but something had to be done, and rapidly to change the status quo.

France could not wait too long before voting on a new status for Algeria, and whatever it would be, this time, as opposed to 1947, it would have to be applied to the letter, despite the huge forces which

---

[31] Raphaëlle Branche, "La commission de sauvegarde pendant la guerre d'Algérie, chronique d'un échec annoncé," *Vingtième Siècle, revue d'histoire* no. 61 (January–March 1999), 14–29.

[32] This "magnificent lecture" was published in *Cahiers de l'Union fédérale* no. 118 (June–August 1958). It is striking that it is not listed on the program of the Congress; the UF gave Cassin the venue, but did not engage directly in the subject of his lecture.

[33] Ibid.   [34] Ibid.

would oppose it. Cassin rejected the idea of separating the oil-rich Sahara from the rest of Algeria, and French isolation within the international community. Cassin said that France still had allies, and it would lose them should it oppose the emancipation movement of colonial peoples.

Do not be carried away by those who say: "You can live in isolation and can withdraw from the UN and NATO." The newly independent people see in the UN an ideal . . . It is impossible that newly independent nations like Togo, the Cameroons, and some states in French West Africa would abandon the creed of full equality in the international domain, which made them the equals of France.[35]

And, in conclusion, he said, "The first sacrifice is to struggle against violence by the application of force, and the second is to achieve through justice what must not be attained through violence. This is precisely what France has to do in Algeria."[36]

The sense of this compact phrase is that the violence of the parties engaged in the Algerian civil war, on both sides, must be ended through the establishment of a new legal order. Second, France had to make these new arrangements because they were just, and not because it was unable to control violence.

Here we see the multifaceted thinking of René Cassin. He took decisions in the Conseil d'Etat which effectively meant that he looked away from some of the ugliness of the conflict in Algeria. How else can we interpret his silence on the question of internment camps? But it would be unfair to ignore the way he tried to integrate his concerns about human rights into his thinking about decolonization and about France's international position during this period.

Cassin's approach was similar to de Gaulle's on international matters. In order to preserve its international standing, France had to solve the Algerian question. Cassin did not believe that full independence was the only solution. "We must underscore that it is in the world's interest that France remains in Algeria," he said, but added "in accord with the Muslim people."[37] One month later was May 13, 1958, and the insurrection of the French population of Algiers, of which General Massu took the lead. It is likely that Cassin's support for de Gaulle's return to power in 1958 was more than simply loyalty to the head of Free France. He probably thought that by solving the Algerian question, the general would restore France's place in the community of nations.

More generally, Cassin's speech to the UF shows that he supported progressive decolonization. However impossible we may think this term

[35] Ibid.   [36] Ibid.   [37] Ibid.

to be, many people at the time adopted it. Cassin's participation in UN debates had convinced him that colonization was a thing of the past. In a discussion about the School of Overseas France in 1956, during a meeting of ENA's executive board, he said:

I see from your unanimous reaction, the anguish which we all share because too many people have put blinkers on. At the end of the war, I believed that a change was possible, we promised it to the peoples who took part in the war with us, we promised it and we do not keep our word. What frightens me . . . is that I am a spectator faced by the growing closure of the Ministry of Overseas France . . . All that leads to a major explosion . . . Our responsibilities do not extend to this domain, but we cannot be silent in the face of what is coming . . . You perfectly well know that one part of the African civil service will be in African hands.[38]

Decolonization was a long and complex phenomenon, and Cassin treated it with the assumptions of his generation, born in the late nineteenth century, and fully aware of the significance of empire in the survival of France during the two world wars.

Conclusion

René Cassin was a man of his generation. He spoke with the inflections and passions of a youth growing up at the time of the Dreyfus affair. He never forgot the horrors of World War I, and dedicated his life to help those who were victims of war. Among them were millions of disabled veterans, who, like Cassin himself, never escaped for a single day the pain of their embodied memory of war. It was natural that he would see human rights as emerging out of humanitarian rights. The rights which arose from the work of the Red Cross and other bodies in the nineteenth century were generalized by him and his colleagues into a code for those who had earned their war pensions through their injuries and hardships. It is this sense of entitlement, not charity, which unifies all that he did in the veterans' movement in the interwar years.

By the 1940s, Cassin's position within the inter-Allied commission on war crimes enabled him to enter into the group of people who created UNESCO, the UN, and the Commission on Human Rights. Here he spoke with the same voice as he had done in the League of Nations in the fourteen years he served as a French delegate. There some of his earliest work was on the right of citizens to aid from natural disaster. This extension of humanitarian rights from war to peace was significant in the evolution of human rights as *les principes géneraux du droit*, as the

---

[38] 382AP88 and CAC 19900256/3, Conseil of February 17, 1956.

framework of rights which makes justice and the rule of law possible. But, as we have seen, Cassin himself lived a set of contradictions in the universality of these very principles. He was a French patriot, for whom the existence of the French empire was one of the reasons Republican France had emerged from the dark years of World War II. It was in Algiers that he personally led the legal campaign through the Comité Juridique to reestablish Republican legality and to begin the process of *épuration*, which he continued in his early years as vice president of the Conseil d'Etat.

And yet, when the Algerian War of Independence brought the French army and administration to engage in the systematic and widespread use of torture in internment camps designed precisely for this abuse, Cassin said nothing. Was his silence like that of Albert Camus, a stance implicitly critical of those who, like Sartre, wrapped themselves in virtue at the speed of light? Was it that he was in a minority in the Conseil d'Etat? We do not know. There was another form of silence he could have adopted: he could have resigned, pled his war wounds, and gone into dignified retirement. He did not do that either.

Cassin's silence on the suffering of Palestinian Arabs from 1948 on is similarly problematic. Here, Cassin probably adopted another strategy. For him Palestinians were victims of war, and the world community had to respect their humanitarian rights and help them restore a life of dignity denied to them by the horrors of war. Why he never came to see that they had human rights too, and not merely humanitarian rights is difficult to say. As I have noted, he himself moved from a position advocating humanitarian rights, arising from the laws of war, to human rights, as a pillar of the laws of peace. Perhaps the two overlapped in the case of the Palestinians. But, more likely, his clear and continuing support for the existence of the State of Israel arose from the impact of the Holocaust on his family and on his thinking. The Jews in Palestine had the right to form a state because the survivors of the Holocaust needed a homeland. Their cause, from his perspective, came first, before any consideration of the Palestinian cause. His priorities were those of his generation of French Jews.

After the 1967 war, Cassin heartily agreed to giving his name to a high school built across the old green line separating Israeli and Jordanian Jerusalem. He went to the opening ceremony and was puzzled that the French embassy did not participate in the celebration. This is another instance of his bias when it came to the question of Israel and Palestine. The older he got, the more he identified with the Jewish people, and the more he spoke out on their behalf. The very last protest he signed was one urging the Soviet Union to let his people go.

The upshot of this mixed portrait of achievement and silence is that anyone who divides the world between those worthy of humanitarian rights and those worthy of human rights is bound to fail to live up to his own *universalist* aspirations. Either everyone has human rights, or no one does: this was a phrase he himself used on occasion. René Cassin was a great jurist, but like other utopians, his vision performed the contradictions of the time in which he lived.

14 The End of the Vietnam War and the Rise of Human Rights

Barbara Keys

When US President Jimmy Carter embraced international human rights promotion in 1977, he was configuring a new framework for US engagement in the world after the Vietnam War.[1] The long, brutal, and ultimately unsuccessful war led many Americans to question the long-entrenched Cold War dogma about the need to align with repressive dictatorships as long as they were anti-communist. By undermining the Cold War consensus, the reaction to the Vietnam War opened up space for new foreign policy paradigms. Though rarely articulated explicitly, the connections between the Vietnam War and the human rights boom in the United States reinforce a causal link between empire's end and embrace of human rights. The Vietnam War, after all, is readily characterized as an imperial venture. The United States entered the Indochina conflict by taking the place of the former colonial power, France. Though it disavowed imperial motives and claimed to be fighting for South Vietnamese self-determination, the intervention bore the marks of empire-building: the support of an authoritarian client regime dependent for its survival on US aid and, beginning in 1965, the attempt to impose control on a foreign population with overwhelming military force.[2]

---

[1] This chapter is a revised and expanded version of material in Barbara Keys, *Reclaiming American Virtue: The Human Rights Revolution of the 1970s* (Cambridge, MA: Harvard University Press, 2014), chs. 4 and 6. The author would like to thank Robert K. Brigham for helpful comments on a draft of this chapter. This research was funded by the Australian Research Council (Discovery Project 110100424).

[2] On how the US war in Vietnam fits into a story of US empire, see Michael H. Hunt and Steven I. Levine, *Arc of Empire: America's Wars in Asia from the Philippines to Vietnam* (Chapel Hill: University of North Carolina Press, 2012). Hunt and Levine offer this definition of empire: "a centrally directed political enterprise in which a state employs coercion (violence or at least the threat of violence) to subjugate an alien population within a territorially delimited area governed by another state or organized political force" (ibid., 3). Some historians, noting, for example, that the resources flowed from Washington to Saigon and not the other way around, would dismiss the idea that the war was imperial, but this wartime imbalance did not reflect the longer-term goals of the US presence in Indochina.

The demoralizing defeat in Vietnam marked the temporary end of US imperial ventures backed by large-scale military intervention. Because it ended in ignominy, with the reputation of the United States in tatters abroad and crippling doubts about US foreign policy at home, it left Americans yearning to feel once again that the country was a benevolent force in the world. International human rights promotion was a means to reclaim US virtue: it was a form of domestic therapy, healing the psychic trauma of the war by repositioning the country on the side of morality.[3] The legacy of the Vietnam War explains not only the timing of the human rights surge, but also its content, for the liberal version of human rights that came to define foreign policy priorities in the late 1970s made political prisoners and torture its central causes – abuses that became prominent in part because of their connections to South Vietnam.[4]

The signing of the Paris Peace Accords in January 1973, leading to the withdrawal of US ground forces, falls within months of events that mark the origins of both conservative and liberal versions of international human rights promotion as a new, post–Vietnam War paradigm for US foreign policy. In September 1972, just a few months before the accords were signed, Senator Henry "Scoop" Jackson launched a human rights-based attack on the Soviet Union, appropriating the language of Soviet dissidents and US Jewish groups to rekindle the Cold War. In this conservative guise, human rights promotion reasserted America's fundamental morality in the wake of debilitating liberal self-flagellation for the failings the war was alleged to have revealed. Jackson's constant refrains were US pride and virtue and rejection of guilt and shame.[5]

Liberal enthusiasm for international human rights promotion emerged in full force in the year after the war ended and was entwined with efforts to learn from and to move past the Vietnam experience. Eager to wipe out the last vestiges of US involvement in Indochina – halting further bombing, slashing aid levels, and dissociating from the brutality and corruption of the Saigon regime – liberals picked up a variety of tools, including human rights talk. Though they connected America's ill-fated

---

[3] See Keys, *Reclaiming American Virtue*.

[4] On antecedents that focused liberal attention on torture, though without bringing universal human rights to the fore as the central grounds for action, see Barbara Keys, "Anti-Torture Politics: Amnesty International, the Greek Junta, and the Origins of the U.S. Human Rights Boom," in Akira Iriye, Petra Goedde, and William I. Hitchcock, eds., *The Human Rights Revolution: An International History* (New York: Oxford University Press, 2012), 201–22.

[5] See Keys, *Reclaiming American Virtue*, 103–26.

efforts to prop up a right-wing dictatorship in South Vietnam with US support for repressive right-wing dictators elsewhere, the original impetus for raising the banner of international human rights was very much a product of distaste for the South Vietnam regime and of an overwhelming desire to disentangle from Indochina.

We know a great deal about how and why a conservative strand of human rights appeared in congressional legislation in these years. Detailed studies have thoroughly charted the interplay among Senator Henry Jackson's presidential ambitions, the newly felt political clout of the US Jewish lobby, the role of Holocaust consciousness and the 1967 Arab–Israeli War in focusing US Jewish attention on the plight of Soviet Jews, the right's distrust of détente (heightened by the Soviets' manipulation of the US trade system in the "great grain robbery" of 1972), and sympathy for the plight of individual *refuseniks* – would-be Jewish emigrants denied exit visas and harassed by the Soviet state. How these elements came together over two years to effect passage of the 1974 Jackson–Vanik amendment, which tied the granting of trade privileges to the Soviet Union to more open emigration, is well established.[6]

The ground-shifting significance of the human rights initiatives launched by congressional liberals is acclaimed in a growing literature on human rights in the 1970s. In contrast to the Jackson amendment, however, the origin of the liberal human rights sensibility has often been treated as obvious or logical rather than as a development in need of rigorous explanation. The reasons why liberals on Capitol Hill seized on the language of human rights at this time and why majorities in Congress voted to pass so much of the legislation liberals put forward have thus too often been skimmed over. When scholars offer explanations (and often they do not: the earliest piece of legislation, section 32, often springs on the scene as if by immaculate conception), they point to broad structural factors, such as a surge of congressional activism in foreign policy in the post–Watergate era; the weakening of anti-communism in the wake of the Vietnam War; institutional changes in Congress that gave rank-and-

---

[6] Paula Stern, *Water's Edge: Domestic Politics and the Making of American Foreign Policy* (Westport, CT: Greenwood Press, 1979); A. D. Chernin, "Making Soviet Jews an Issue," in *A Second Exodus: The American Movement to Free Soviet Jews*, ed. Murray Friedman and Albert D. Chernin (Hanover: Brandeis University Press, 1999); Robert G. Kaufman, *Henry M. Jackson: A Life in Politics* (Seattle: University of Washington Press, 2000); Gal Beckerman, *When They Come for Us, We'll Be Gone: The Epic Struggle to Save Soviet Jewry* (Boston, MA: Houghton Mifflin Harcourt, 2010). On the larger story, see James Loeffler, *Rooted Cosmopolitans: Jews and Human Rights in the Twentieth Century* (New Haven, CT: Yale University Press, 2018).

file members new powers; and the apparent proliferation of especially objectionable human rights abuses – sometimes deemed in themselves to have provoked human rights activism as a "natural" response.[7] In this interpretation, the Vietnam War offers a context in which changing views of international relations, among other factors, pushed liberals in the direction of human rights.

But the end of the Vietnam War triggered human rights advocacy in a surprisingly direct way, as a close examination of the legislative history of the congressional human rights surge reveals. The first human rights legislation to come out of Congress was directed at South Vietnam. Its passage, and the passage of subsequent legislation that built directly on its precedent, succeeded because the end of combat activities in Vietnam opened political space for moralistic members of Congress to vent long-brewing anger at the conduct and content of US foreign policy. US human rights diplomacy was born in a cauldron of anger, frustration, guilt, and longing to be *done with Vietnam*, origins which would indelibly shape – and sharply limit – the liberal strand of human rights promotion at least through the end of the Cold War.

At the end of 1973, Congress passed the first of what would become a string of legislative initiatives tying foreign aid to human rights consider-ations: section 32 of the 1973 Foreign Assistance Act, a watered-down version of an amendment offered by a one-term senator from South Dakota, Democrat James Abourezk. The measure banned economic and military aid to regimes that held political prisoners, linking US aid policy to a cause recently brought to international prominence by Amnesty International and its campaigns on behalf of "prisoners of conscience." A year later, Abourezk described the measure as "the first time" that Congress had "expressed its concern for the human rights of people who are citizens in countries which receive U.S. foreign aid."[8] Human rights scholars often cite Abourezk's measure as the inception of a series of legislative initiatives that for the first time incorporated explicit human rights considerations into US foreign policy, but almost none

---

[7] See, for example, Congressman Robert Drinan's formulation: "Human rights provisions were adopted." Robert F. Drinan, *Cry of the Oppressed: The History and Hope of the Human Rights Revolution* (San Francisco: Harper & Row, 1987), 74. William Korey erroneously attributes section 32 to Donald Fraser: *NGOs and the Universal Declaration of Human Rights; "A Curious Grapevine"* (New York: St. Martin's Press, 1998), 184. A 1981 account by political scientist Lars Schoultz contains what is still the best account of the passage of the Harkin amendment, but he only briefly touches on section 32. Schoultz, *Human Rights and United States Policy toward Latin America* (Princeton, NJ: Princeton University Press, 1981), 195–7.

[8] 119 Cong. Rec. S12367 (July 15, 1974).

acknowledge that it targeted South Vietnam.[9] The story is central to understanding why some legislators seized on the language of human rights at this time, why majorities in Congress voted to pass so much of the legislation liberals proposed, and precisely how the end of the Vietnam War gave rise to human rights as a new organizing rubric for US foreign policy.

A major part of the explanation lies in the antiwar movement and its choice of tactics. Peace activists had sharply stepped up criticism of the brutality and corruption of Nguyễn Văn Thiệu's regime in Saigon beginning in 1971, while at the same time redoubling efforts to push Congress to set a date for an end to the war. The anti-Thiệu prong of the peace movement aimed to expose the Saigon regime as an obstacle to peace rather than an ally to fight for.[10] When the war ended and much of the antiwar movement dissipated, a group of hardcore antiwar activists remained, still focused on the same goals: ending all US involvement in Indochina and highlighting the failings of the Thiệu regime as a way to achieve this goal.[11]

Proponents of cutting off aid to Thiệu presented it as an urgent requirement of peace, needed to avoid "another Vietnam." For congressional liberals of the late 1960s and early 1970s, the lesson of the Vietnam War was that economic aid created a slippery slope. It was the commitment to prop up South Vietnam, first through economic and then military aid, that had drawn the United States into a full-fledged war. Noting that US funds to Thiệu in 1973 were being used to perpetuate a war machine, for example, longtime antiwar activist and journalist Don Luce told Congress: "We are back to 1964. Congress

[9] See, e.g., Apodaca, *Understanding U.S. Human Rights Policy*, 34–5; Weissbrodt, "Human Rights Legislation," 241; Robert A. Pastor, *Congress and the Politics of U.S. Foreign Economic Policy, 1929–1976* (Berkeley: University of California Press, 1980), 304; Schneider, "New Administration's New Policy," 7; Schoultz, *Human Rights*, 194–5. Joe Renouard cites the 1973 coup in Chile as the precipitating concern of the congressional push: *Human Rights in American Foreign Policy: From the 1960s to the Soviet Collapse* (Philadelphia: University of Pennsylvania Press, 2016), 79–80.

[10] Charles DeBenedetti, *An American Ordeal: The Antiwar Movement of the Vietnam War* (Syracuse, NY: Syracuse University Press, 1990), 312–13.

[11] On the postwar antiwar movement, see "Viet Prison Cruelty Is Debated," *Washington Post*, January 12, 1974, A15; "Militant Antiwar Movement Shifts Tactics, Not Targets," *Washington Post*, June 2, 1974, G6; "'The Movement,' with the War Ebbing, Ponders Its Role in a Nation at Peace," *New York Times*, February 18, 1973, 60; "Antiwar Groups to Oppose U.S. Aid to Saigon Prisons," *New York Times*, September 19, 1973, 17; "Senate Liberals Will Seek to End Aid to Saigon Police," *New York Times*, September 16, 1973, 1; Bill Zimmerman, *Troublemaker: A Memoir from the Front Lines of the Sixties* (New York: Doubleday, 2011), 359–64.

can fund war, masked as economic aid, and watch our military involvement grow."[12]

Critics of Thiệu's regime directed their fiercest ire at the issue of
political prisoners in the South. Activists observed that maltreatment of
political prisoners aroused strong emotions:

We recognized that this would be a tender issue for American political liberals, to
lift up the cause of people who are *just like us* – religious people, humanists,
artists – liberals. They were being imprisoned for doing the things that we do – for
signing petitions, going to rallies, for associating with other people. For having
children who do things. And they are held upside down and water is forced up
their nostrils, they are held in tiger cages.[13]

As activists anticipated, the media found the issue compelling. In November 1972, as the peace negotiations grappled with civilian prisoners
among other issues, Amnesty International reported that "probably at
least two hundred thousand civilians" were in custody in Indochina,
many in South Vietnam.[14] The (inflated) figures were widely reported,
as were (accurate) charges that political prisoners were often tortured.
Newsweek, for example, reported in December: "Many of those arrested
are tortured during their interrogation. The catalogue of their agonies
reads like the stuff of lurid pulp fiction: electric prods jabbed into the
genitals, pins stuck through hands, fingernails ripped out and a unique
mind-bending ordeal where the victim sits in an oil drum filled with water
while interrogators beat on the sides of the drum with clubs."[15] Amnesty
International's 1973 *Report on Torture* alleged that 100,000 civilians were
imprisoned by Saigon. "In revolting detail," liberal columnist Anthony
Lewis commented in the *New York Times*, the report detailed "what is
done to human beings" in South Vietnamese prisons: "the use of electri-
city, beating, water; the crippling and death that result."[16]

---

[12] 119 Cong. Rec. 30086 (September 18, 1973). California Democrat Augustus Hawkins
similarly cited Amnesty figures, tiger cages, and torture in a speech urging that Congress
"refuse to pay the bill" for such abuses. "Political Prisoners in South Vietnam," 119
Cong. Rec. 30766 (September 20, 1973).

[13] Tom Cornell quoted in Nancy Zaroulis and Gerald Sullivan, *Who Spoke Up? American
Protest against the War in Vietnam, 1963–1975* (Garden City, NY: Doubleday, 1984), 405.

[14] Amnesty International News Release, n.d. [November 1972], Folder 1184, Amnesty
International, International Secretariat Records, International Institute for Social
History, Amsterdam.

[15] "Vietnam: Political Prisoners," *Newsweek*, December 18, 1972.

[16] Anthony Lewis, "Peace with Honor," *New York Times*, July 16, 1973, 29. For a
conservative critique of Amnesty's estimates and of the political prisoner campaign as
communist inspired, see Stephen J. Morris, "Human Rights in Vietnam under Two
Regimes: A Case Study with Implications for American Foreign Policy," in *Human
Rights and American Foreign Policy*, ed. Fred E. Baumann (Gambier, OH: Public
Affairs Conference Center, Kenyon College, 1982), 137–55.

Publicity about "tiger cages" vividly brought home to Americans the suffering inflicted on Vietnamese political prisoners. In 1970 a congressional delegation had uncovered so-called tiger cages housing political prisoners on Con Son Island: shallow, overcrowded underground pits where prisoners were held, shackled to the ground, with so little room for movement that their legs often atrophied to the point that they lost the ability to walk.[17] In 1973 the evening news programs showed former tiger-cage prisoners moving themselves slowly along the ground by their arms, their legs entirely immobilized.[18] "It is not really proper to call them men any more," *Time* magazine commented in an explicitly dehumanizing description. "'Shapes' is a better word – grotesque sculptures of scarred flesh and gnarled limbs ... [forced] into a permanent pretzel-like crouch. They move like crabs, skittering across the floor on buttocks and palms."[19]

Senator Abourezk's ground-breaking human rights legislation was surely influenced by the antiwar movement, though how this influence was exercised and its extent remain unclear.[20] In 1973, the liberal Democrat had just begun his first term as a senator, having served one previous term in the House. He was already known as an outspoken maverick with, as one commentator put it, "a marvelous unwashed style and a howitzer laugh that he uses constantly to shoot down Senatorial pomposities."[21] One of Nixon's advisers judged him even more liberal than his fellow South Dakotan, George McGovern, whose presidential candidacy in 1972 had pulled the Democratic Party so far to the left that near-civil war in the party had ensued.

---

[17] "The Cages of Con Son Island," *Time*, July 20, 1970, 22; "South Vietnam: School of Hard Knocks," *Newsweek*, July 23, 1973, 11.

[18] "Vietnam/Political Prisoners," *ABC Evening News*, March 9, 1973, record number 25261, Vanderbilt University Television News Archive, at tvnews.vanderbilt.edu

[19] Quoted in Anthony Lewis, "Whom We Welcome," *New York Times*, March 31, 1973, 35.

[20] Abourezk's memoirs recount his bitter opposition to the war and his early efforts as a freshman in the House from 1971 to 1973 to cut off funding for the war, but barely mention his involvement in human rights legislation. He recounts that he was decisively moved by a 1973 visit to his Senate office from Brady Tyson and a Brazilian opponent of the Médici dictatorship. The Brazilian's tales of torture shocked him into offering an amendment to the Foreign Aid Bill to "deny U.S. foreign aid to any country that violated the human rights of its own citizens." He recalls that Hubert Humphrey shot down the amendment, but his recollections seem to be faulty: there is no evidence in the *Congressional Record* that he offered such a general amendment in 1973; rather, Humphrey refused to support a more strongly worded version of the political prisoners provision. James G. Abourezk, *Advise and Dissent: Memoirs of South Dakota and the U.S. Senate* (Chicago: Lawrence Hill Books, 1989), 131.

[21] Robert Sherrill quoted in Mark J. Green, *Who Runs Congress?*, rev. ed. (New York: Bantam Books, 1975), 206.

Like McGovern, Abourezk was a fervent opponent of the Vietnam War. He believed that US aid to South Vietnam had set in motion an escalating commitment that led to full-scale war. In his view, continuing aid created the risk that the slippery slope from aid to intervention could draw the United States into renewed combat. As a member of the House in 1971 and 1972, he had joined with liberal Democrats such as Bella Abzug, John Conyers, and Don Edwards in efforts to cut off funding for the war. He had contacts with antiwar groups and attended events they sponsored.[22] In early 1974 he described the war in these terms: "Most Americans have been repelled by our experience in Southeast Asia – a misadventure in which we allowed ourselves to be dragged into the inhuman position of destroying a community in order to save it and of conducting mass bombing attacks ... This is a horror that we would like to dismiss as a bad dream." It had been, he said, "an emotional disturbance that brought the country to the brink of chaos."[23]

In his first year in office, he, like many others, took aim at Indochina policy by targeting the foreign aid bill. Declaring that "the Cold War is over," he condemned the foreign aid program as a relic of the past that was not humanitarian in its aims.[24] Much of it, he argued, went to augment repression in authoritarian regimes. He was successful in pushing an amendment to ban aid funds from being used for police training, which, like section 32, was directed primarily at South Vietnam, even if it was worded more generally.[25]

Five months after the Paris Peace Accords were signed, Abourezk took up the cause of South Vietnam's political prisoners. Testifying to the Senate Foreign Relations Committee, Abourezk spoke movingly of US responsibility for repression in South Vietnam. "We have been deeply involved in the creation of the entire [police and prison] system, and we are still paying the bills," he said. He noted that US funds had been used to build the prisons where political prisoners were held, to train the staff at the interrogation centers where prisoners were tortured, and to prop up the repressive regime that ran them. The Paris Accords required "the end of American participation in Vietnamese

---

[22] Abourezk, *Advise and Dissent*, 94.
[23] Statement of Senator James Abourezk before the Senate Armed Services Committee, March 19, 1974, f. 51, Box 713 (0250B), Papers of James G. Abourezk, University of South Dakota, Vermillion [hereafter Abourezk Papers].
[24] Senator Jim Abourezk, Washington Report, June 24, 1974, f. 71, Box 713 (0250B), Abourezk Papers.
[25] See, e.g., 119 Cong. Rec. S2291 (February 26, 1974).

internal political affairs," he declared, and it was time to stop helping Thiệu "squash" his political opponents.[26]

The amendment that would become section 32 recommended cutting off military and economic assistance to any country that practiced "the internment or imprisonment of that country's citizens for political purposes," and, in arguing for it, Abourezk tentatively began to draw connections in human rights terms. He drew a parallel between South Vietnam's repressive policies and those in Rhodesia, Pakistan, and the communist bloc, where "we point to the cruelty of such policies as contrary to the basic rights of man and condemn the torture of these prisoners as gravely inhumane."[27] In a lengthy address to Congress in October pressing for a stronger version of his amendment, he said US support for repression in South Vietnam, Brazil, Greece, and Indonesia had detracted from "basic human rights" and "clings like a filthy stench on the American people," who "share in the guilt and horror."[28]

Why did the measure pass with ease?[29] Congress was eager to challenge President Nixon, now weakened by a growing Watergate scandal, and to extract revenge for being shut out of decision-making about the war for so long. But the specific target was Vietnam because desire to end US involvement in Indochina was running high. Congressional support for Saigon was eroded by Thiệu's blatant manipulation of the 1971 elections and reports of corruption and mismanagement of the economy – to many in Congress it looked as though US aid was siphoned off into private hands.[30] Abourezk's measure was but one element of a broader congressional assault on the executive's power to subsidize Thiệu's regime and continue limited combat operations in Indochina. When

---

[26] *Foreign Economic Assistance, 1973*, 244–50.

[27] 119 Cong. Rec. 23804–23805 (July 13, 1973).

[28] 119 Cong. Rec. 32284–32286 (October 1, 1973).

[29] It was unanimously adopted by the Senate Foreign Relations Committee; the Senate then adopted the amendment and, at the end of the year, a House–Senate conference committee wrote it into the Foreign Assistance Act of 1973. 119 Cong. Rec. 32286–7 (October 1, 1973); Conference Report, Foreign Assistance Act of 1973, November 27, 1973, 93rd Cong., 1st. Sess., House of Representatives Report no. 93-664, CIA Records Search Tool, National Archives, College Park, MD. The amendment garnered little press attention. Although several articles in major newspapers mentioned Abourezk's related effort to cut off aid for foreign police training, when the *New York Times* reported on the bill that emerged from the Senate, it did not comment on the political prisoners measure. "Senate, 54 to 42, Votes $1.2 Billion for Foreign Aid," *New York Times*, October 3, 1973, 93.

[30] For an example of American anger at the elections, see Charles W. Yost, "Growing Resentment: Vietnam Is Alive as a Political Issue," *Washington Post*, 10 October 1971, C6. On corruption and congressional cutbacks in aid, see DeBenedetti, *American Ordeal*, 318; John Prados, *Lost Crusader: The Secret Wars of CIA Director William Colby* (New York: Oxford University Press, 2003), 283.

the administration continued bombing in Cambodia, an obstreperous Congress undertook a series of headline-making votes that resulted in a compromise August 15 deadline for ending Cambodian operations. Later that year, overriding Nixon's veto, Congress tried to reclaim its constitutional prerogative to declare war by passing the War Powers Act. In the foreign aid bill, Congress set a ceiling on military assistance to South Vietnam and Laos, slashing $285 million off the figure the administration had requested. In 1974, as fighting in the region escalated, Congress cut both economic and military aid levels far below the administration's request, added further restrictions, and put specific country-by-country ceilings in place. In 1975, in the final months of the war, Congress refused Ford's urgent pleas for additional military aid that, the president said, was the only way to save Saigon from communism.[31] Throughout the period 1973–5, even as most of the rest of the country turned weary eyes away from the region, Indochina remained a central arena for the tug-of-war between Congress and the executive.

The proposal's success was also a function of rising congressional frustration with the foreign aid program. By the early 1970s foreign aid was foundering: liberals criticized it for buttressing oppressive regimes without helping their poorest citizens while conservatives condemned it as a giveaway, and both sides cited US economic woes as cause for rethinking the multibillion-dollar program.[32] Twice in the early 1970s, in unprecedented moves, the Senate had defeated foreign aid authorization bills. One reason liberal human rights initiatives were successfully attached to foreign aid bills in the mid-1970s is that arch conservatives like Jesse Helms and Strom Thurmond were willing to support any measure that might lower aid expenditure.[33]

Abourezk himself attributed his success in part to the backing of the antiwar movement, and particularly groups such as the Coalition to Stop Funding the War, which pushed his measure to help spotlight a political prisoner campaign in the fall, as the foreign aid bill came up for a vote.[34] Activists energetically lobbied an increasingly receptive Congress. Massachusetts Senator Edward Kennedy, among others, spoke out forcefully

---

[31] For details, see *Congress and the Nation: A Review of Government and Politics*, vol. 4 (Washington, DC: Congressional Quarterly Service, 1977), 890–5.

[32] A useful survey of the arguments for and against can be found in the debate in the Senate: 119 Cong. Rec. 32593–32598 (October 2, 1973). Liberal disenchantment with foreign aid can be seen in the fact that Abourezk and other liberals including Frank Church and William Fulbright voted against the 1973 bill.

[33] Patricia Weiss Fagen, "U.S. Foreign Policy and Human Rights: The Role of Congress," in *Parliamentary Control over Foreign Policy: Legal Essays*, ed. Antonio Cassese (Germantown, MD: Sijthoff and Noordhoff, 1980), 109–121.

[34] DeBenedetti, *American Ordeal*, 362–3.

against funding Saigon's police system, and the House Subcommittee on Asian and Pacific Affairs held hearings in September on Saigon's treatment of political prisoners, at which charges of brutality and torture were again aired.[35]

No one in Congress was willing to defend political imprisonment. As Amnesty International had demonstrated so well since its formation in 1961, the issue served as a kind of lowest common denominator: people across the political spectrum could oppose it as a minimal aim. Yet section 32 was also so weak as to be patently toothless. It was worded as a "sense of the Congress" statement rather than as a binding legal requirement, and its lack of a definition of political prisoner virtually guaranteed semantic stonewalling. Both Saigon and the US Embassy maintained with straight faces that according to their definition the regime held no political prisoners. Although Abourezk had undertaken his fight in the naive faith that it would work – "it would frighten those governments into stopping torture and imprisonment. I am sure they are not going to give up this sizable fortune from the US taxpayers in order to keep torturing their people," he said – section 32 had absolutely no effect on funding to South Vietnam.[36]

Despite – or more accurately, because of – its ineffectiveness, section 32 laid the ground for a wave of human rights legislation that built directly on its precedent. Six months after the passage of the 1973 act, Congressman Donald Fraser began drafting the amendment that would become section 502B of the 1974 Foreign Assistance Act, the first congressional requirement to incorporate general human rights considerations into foreign aid decisions. As a relatively junior member of the House Foreign Affairs Committee that shepherded the annual foreign aid bill through Congress, the liberal Minnesotan had been trying to limit aid to dictatorships since 1967, with no success.[37] He saw an opening when the executive branch admitted that it had ignored section 32, recognizing that he could build on congressional–executive tensions to push for an expansion of section 32 that would achieve the outcomes he had so long desired. In June 1974, Fraser elicited from the State

---

[35] "Prisons and Political Prisoners in South Vietnam," 119 Cong. Rec. 17838–41 (June 4, 1973); *Treatment of Political Prisoners in South Vietnam by the Government of the Republic of South Vietnam: Hearing before the Subcommittee on Asian and Pacific Affairs, September 13, 1973* (Washington, DC: US Government Printing Office, 1973), 1.

[36] 119 Cong. Rec. 32287 (October 1, 1973).

[37] See the note from Don Ostrom on Fraser's staff to Don Edwards, 21 July 1967: "Don is interested in the whole issue. He has been trying to amend the Foreign Aid Bill to prohibit military aid to totalitarian countries. Alas, like many of causes, he has been unsuccessful – so far." Box 41, Don Edwards Papers, San Jose State University.

Department an admission that it had taken no steps to implement section 32.[38] The flagrant obstruction was intolerable to many members of Congress who, regardless of their feelings about section 32, were steeped in intense resentment of the executive branch's perceived arrogance, deception, and lack of consultation. Fraser's amendment was, in his own characterization, an attempt to limit executive power in foreign policy.[39]

Fraser considered offering an amendment that would have required the president merely to report on implementation of section 32, but chose to put forward a measure that broadened section 32 into a more generalized human rights requirement directed at military assistance. The language of an early draft echoed the Abourezk amendment on political prisoners but expanded the target to include any government that "engages in a consistent pattern of gross and reliably attested violations of human rights." It also introduced a reporting mechanism, whereby in cases of gross abuses the president would have to present a justification for aid on security grounds.[40] The final version of the amendment deleted the reference to political prisoners, adding instead examples of "gross violations" including torture and prolonged detention without charges and, drawing on Article 3 of the United Nations Universal Declaration of Human Rights, referring to "right to life, liberty, and the security of the person."[41]

---

[38] John Salzberg, "A View from the Hill," in *The Diplomacy of Human Rights*, ed. David D. Newsom (Lanham, MD: University Press of America, 1986); Weissbrodt, "Human Rights Legislation," 241 n. 39; Robert Ingersoll, Department of State, to Thomas Morgan, Chairman, Foreign Affairs Committee, 27 June 1974, 149.G.13.8F, Fraser Papers. Ingersoll explained that in April instructions to gather information were sent to posts in countries receiving aid, but that when it came to cutting off aid, the Department believed that other methods would be more effective. Salzberg later lauded section 32 as having "caused the State Department to begin thinking in terms of human rights." John Salzberg and Donald D. Young, "The Parliamentary Role in Implementing International Human Rights: A U.S. Example," *Texas Journal of International Law* 12, nos. 2–3 (Spring–Summer 1977), 270.

[39] See, e.g., Fraser's July 1973 comment that he wished to "put the President under much more constraint than he is today in the field of foreign affairs. It is a very difficult thing to do." 119 Cong. Rec. 26167 (July 26, 1973).

[40] Memo, John Salzberg to Don Fraser and Robert Boettcher, July 3, 1974, 149.G.13.8F, Donald Fraser Papers, Minnesota Historical Society, St. Paul [hereafter Fraser Papers]. See also "Executive Branch Action on Section 32," June 13, 1974, 149.G.13.8F, Fraser Papers.

[41] On section 502B, see Barbara Keys, "Congress, Kissinger, and the Origins of Human Rights Diplomacy," *Diplomatic History* 34, no. 4 (2010): 823–51. Section 502B was passed by voice vote in the House Foreign Affairs Committee mark-ups sessions, becoming part of the bill eventually passed by the House and then agreed on in House–Senate conference. Memo, "Summary of July Foreign Assistance Act Mark-Up Sessions," August 20, 1974, 149.G.13.8F, Fraser Papers. In putting the amendment to

That section 32 was a starting point for human rights advocates is evidenced in another proposal from New York's liberal Republican Senator, Jacob Javits, who also offered a direct expansion of the Abourezk measure. It would have left Abourezk's wording as it was and added a new subsection cutting off economic and military aid to any country unless the president certified that its government did not violate human rights with respect to political or religious arrest or persecution; denial of the right to a fair and prompt trial; or torture.[42] It appears that Javits backed off his version and supported 502B instead.[43]

The ease with which the Abourezk and Fraser measures passed, after similar country-specific efforts had failed for years, has everything to do with their timing. The Vietnam peace agreement opened the door for Congress at last to exert itself on Indochina, and it took aim at Thiệu's regime, creating support for a more general distancing of the United States from right-wing dictatorships by building on years of discontent with policy toward South Vietnam. The international human rights movement was spurred by other sources – General Augusto Pinochet's brutal coup in Chile in September 1973 and the heroic stature accorded to Soviet dissidents in the wake of Aleksandr Solzhenitsyn's *Gulag Archipelago* were also important drivers – but the initial entry of human rights into US bilateral foreign policy was triggered above all by the unleashing of energy and emotion made possible by the 1973 peace accords.[44]

Why were the origins of liberal human rights legislation in a measure targeting South Vietnam forgotten?[45] The final section 32 legislation made no mention of South Vietnam; it was directed generally at political imprisonment. But the amendment's roots in concern over the South Vietnamese police system and political prisoners was unmistakable at the time. Its legislative progression was carefully tracked at the time by the State Department and the US Embassy in Saigon: they were acutely

the Committee, Fraser was able to report that the White House had posed no objections to it, presumably because it would be so easy to circumvent. "Fraser Amendment: Executive Branch Position," August 15, 1974, 149.G,13.8F, Fraser Papers.

[42] S. 3394, referred to the Senate Committee on Foreign Relations, 149.G.13.8F, Fraser Papers.

[43] This conclusion is based on the absence of any record of the amendment in the *Congressional Record.*

[44] On Solzhenitsyn's influence on human rights advocacy in the United States, see Mark Philip Bradley, *The World Reimagined: Americans and Human Rights in the Twentieth Century* (Cambridge, UK: Cambridge University Press, 2016).

[45] It was not quite universally forgotten. One of the very few post-1975 accounts I have found that mention the Vietnam origins of the legislation was in a clipping from the Liberation News Archive: Pacific News Service, "International Collision Course Nears on Human Rights," 1977, in Liberation News Archives, Temple University, Philadelphia.

aware of which country the measure targeted.[46] Section 32's subsequent extraction from the context of the war suggests that the story was not useful to the human rights movement that it helped empower. After the fall of Saigon in April 1975 to a regime that incarcerated and killed political opponents on a scale that dwarfed Thiệu's repression, congressional action against Thiệu's regime no longer looked so heroic. The familial relationship between the antiwar movement and the new human rights movement, manifested in the composition of the ranks of human rights activists, was incompatible with the apolitical ethos of human rights work at this time. It was supposed to transcend Cold War categories, not flow logically from the divide the Vietnam War had created. Moreover, for a movement that aimed at reclaiming America's rightful position at the top of a global moral hierarchy, America's connection to repression in Vietnam was too close for comfort. The human rights movement criticized abuses in other countries and shifted the locus of evil abroad, and the Vietnam War was too much a reminder that the United States itself had recently been directly involved in torture, murder, and repression. Thus the war was erased as a direct trigger for human rights efforts and recast merely as a spur for rethinking the dangers of Cold War obsessions.

If Western enthusiasm for human rights had to await the formal end of colonialism, as Samuel Moyn and others have suggested, the relationship, in the case of the United States, is demonstrably one of cause and effect. Roughly since 1968, most liberals in Congress had opposed the Vietnam War. Few did so with the anguish of George McGovern, who said he thought about Vietnam every day and told his fellow members of Congress that their chamber "reeked of blood," but most watched the war with horror, guilt, and mounting anger. Between 1965 and January 1973, they offered ninety-four measures to limit or halt US involvement in the war.[47] Not one of these efforts succeeded while the war went on, for the simple reason that a majority in Congress baulked at taking responsibility for losing a war. Only after the war was over and the stakes were vastly lowered would Congress impose limits on US involvement in Indochina.

It would not be entirely wrong to say that the Abourezk legislation aimed at ending US imperialism in Vietnam, while Nixon and Ford were

[46] See telegram, Saigon to Washington, July 1, 1974, "FAA Section 32 – Political Prisoners," Central Foreign Policy Files, US State Department, available at aad .archives.gov

[47] *Congress and the Nation: A Review of Government and Politics*, vol. 3 (Washington, DC: Congressional Quarterly Service, 2006), 853.

trying to salvage it.[48] But it would be too simple. Congress did pass measures for humanitarian relief in South Vietnam, funding a Kennedy-sponsored initiative to help Vietnamese children, for example, but on the whole it succumbed to an impulse to cut and run. Having failed to stop the war, liberals wanted to wash their hands of Vietnam. They acknowledged a measure of US responsibility for conditions in South Vietnam but hoped that by removing US funding they could create a situation in which the South Vietnamese became responsible for their own fate, almost instantly. The imprint of the impulse to withdraw as a means of reclaiming US virtue would be felt in human rights diplomacy throughout the 1970s, which almost without exception centered on punitive acts, designed to extract Americans from the taint of responsibility for abuses abroad without clear evidence of any mitigating effect on those abuses. The US human rights boom of the 1970s was born of an anti-imperial urge, but it was also very much part of an attempt to look beyond rather than to confront imperialism's painful legacies.

---

[48] The dilemmas of granting self-determination to South Vietnam are vividly apparent in this 1974 exchange between Senate Foreign Relations Committee chairman William Fulbright and AID administrator Daniel Parker:

FULBRIGHT: We deny having any aspirations to own [South Vietnam], don't we? ... We are not seeking to make a colony out of it, are we?
PARKER: No, sir.
FULBRIGHT: What is it we seek to achieve? Is it trade? Is it anticipated there is a lot of oil there? Leaving out the moral aspects for the moment, are there any tangible benefits to be achieved?
PARKER: Well, gentlemen, I consider avoidance or the reduction of war a very tangible benefit.
FULBRIGHT: We caused the war, the worst war they ever had... If we could remove our intervention, wouldn't it settle down and they could solve their problems and seek a solution on their own terms, if we would get out and allow them to?

Committee on Foreign Relations, United States Senate, *Foreign Assistance Authorization Hearing, 93rd Congress, 2nd Session, June and July 1974* (Washington, DC: US Government Printing Office, 1974), 102

15 Decolonizing the Geneva Conventions
National Liberation and the Development of Humanitarian Law

Eleanor Davey

The Protocols Additional to the Geneva Conventions, drafted over four sessions from 1974 to 1977, were the twentieth century's last major revision of international humanitarian law. Celebrated by later advocates for drawing the curtain on "a whole chapter of international humanitarian law which had ... come under attack as being too Western-oriented," for some at the time the demand to decolonize the Geneva Conventions represented an assault on the foundations and indeed the very nature of the law itself.[1] Even delegates of the International Committee of the Red Cross (ICRC), always measured in their choice of words, acknowledged that they were witnessing "a complete revision of general international law."[2]

Legal scholars have recently emphasized the place in international law of countries and thinkers from what at the time was known as the Third World.[3] The reform of international humanitarian law in the 1960s and 1970s can be placed among the events in the "unfolding of decolonization," after Sundhya Pahuja, while also reflecting the contradiction Pahuja identifies between international law's regulatory and emancipatory

I am grateful to Valérie Gorin and to the editors for their thoughtful comments as this chapter was in preparation, and to participants of the World Conference on Humanitarian Studies in Addis Ababa, March 2016, at which a version of this chapter was presented. The research and travel was funded by a British Academy Postdoctoral Fellowship.

[1] René Kosirnik, "The 1977 Protocols: A Landmark in the Development of International Humanitarian Law," *International Review of the Red Cross* 37, no. 320 (2010): 490; David E. Graham, "The 1974 Diplomatic Conference on the Law of War: A Victory for Political Causes and a Return to the 'Just War' Concept of the Eleventh Century," *Washington and Lee Law Review* 32, no. 1 (1975): 25–63.

[2] Procès-verbal de la séance de la délégation à la Conférence diplomatique, Session on April 10, 1974, 11am, 2, Archives of the International Committee of the Red Cross (ACICR) B AG 152–044.01. Translation from original French here and throughout by the author.

[3] Antony Anghie, *Imperialism, Sovereignty, and the Making of International Law* (Cambridge, UK: Cambridge University Press, 2005); Arnulf Becker Lorca, *Mestizo International Law: A Global Intellectual History 1842–1933* (Cambridge, UK: Cambridge University Press, 2015); Sundhya Pahuja, *Decolonising International Law: Development, Economic Growth and the Politics of Universality* (Cambridge, UK: Cambridge University Press, 2011).

dimensions.[4] Yet the Additional Protocols and the Diplomatic Conference on the Reaffirmation and Development of International Humanitarian Law Applicable in Armed Conflicts (henceforth Diplomatic Conference), as the official discussions are properly known, remain an example of what historian Mark Mazower called the "ghetto within a ghetto" of "the history of how law has been deployed in international politics."[5] For a long time, accounts of the consultations and official meetings were dominated by experts who participated in them,[6] with much scholarship on the Additional Protocols, like commentaries on them, primarily focused on legal issues such as their contribution to the regulation of guerrilla warfare or internal conflict.[7] However, a later wave of critical studies has drawn attention to the importance of this episode in its challenge to imperialist formulations of whose suffering mattered under international law and how anti-imperialism shaped the law.[8] Nonetheless, there remains extremely little on the implications of this process for those who were simultaneously involved in offering care in ongoing decolonization conflicts, an oversight which isolates the legal debates from one of their key contemporary contexts and reduces our understanding of their contingencies. This is partially comprehensible given the

---

[4] Sundhya Pahuja, "Decolonization and the Eventness of International Law," in *Events: The Force of International Law*, ed. Fleur Johns, Richard Joyce, and Sundhya Pahuja (Abingdon, UK: Routledge, 2011), 92.

[5] Mark Mazower, "The Strange Triumph of Human Rights, 1933–1950," *Historical Journal* 47, no. 2 (2004): 380.

[6] George H. Aldrich, "Some Reflections on the Origins of the 1977 Geneva Protocols," in *Studies and Essays on International Humanitarian Law and Red Cross Principles in Honour of Jean Pictet*, ed. Christophe Swinarski (Geneva: ICRC/Martinus Nijhoff, 1984): 129–38; Detlev F. Vagts et al., eds., *Humanizing the Laws of War: Selected Writings of Richard Baxter* (New York: Oxford University Press, 2013); Frits Kalshoven, *Reflections on the Law of War: Collected Essays* (Leiden: Martinus Nijhoff, 2007); Keith Suter, *An International Law of Guerrilla Warfare: The Global Politics of Law-Making* (London: Frances Pinter, 1984).

[7] Michael A. Meyer, ed., *Armed Conflict and the New Law: Aspects of the 1977 Geneva Protocols and the 1981 Weapons Convention* (London: British Institute of International and Comparative Law, 1989); Yves Sandoz, Christophe Swinarski and Bruno Zimmerman, eds., *Commentary on the Additional Protocols of 8 June 1977 to the Geneva Conventions of 12 August 1949* (Geneva: Martinus Nijhoff/ICRC, 1987).

[8] Helen Kinsella, *The Image before the Weapon: A Critical History of the Distinction between Combatant and Civilian* (Ithaca, NY: Cornell University Press, 2011), esp. ch. 7, "The Algerian Civil War and the 1977 Protocols Additional"; Kinsella, "Superfluous Injury and Unnecessary Suffering: National Liberation and the Laws of War," *Political Power and Social Theory* 32 (2017): 205–31; Amanda Alexander, "International Humanitarian Law, Postcolonialism and the 1977 Geneva Protocol I," *Melbourne Journal of International Law* 17, no. 1 (2016): 15–50; Jessica Whyte, "The 'Dangerous Concept of the Just War': Decolonization, Wars of National Liberation, and the Additional Protocols to the Geneva Conventions," *Humanity: An International Journal of Human Rights, Humanitarianism and Development* 9, no. 3 (2018): 313–41.

difficulty of access to certain core sources, including notably the ICRC's preparations for and records of the Diplomatic Conference – crucial materials in light of the organization's key role in the process of shaping and disseminating international humanitarian law. Nonetheless, with international humanitarian law at the nexus of human rights and humanitarianism, both of which have become popular terrain for historical research, this neglect is striking.[9]

Scholarly attention on the consequences of the Diplomatic Conference instead of its conduct reflects and reinforces the view that the rhetorical battles over decolonization can be separated from – and are less significant than – its legal achievements. This tendency derives at least in part from the drafting process: with progress made more steadily in later sessions as controversy waned, it became possible to consider the arguments of the early years as rhetorical storms destined to be displaced by more constructive attitudes. It underestimates how much rhetoric, like emotion, has shaped the way human rights proposals have been achieved (or not).[10] And it privileges the perspectives of jurists over the operational questions that also affected the aid organizations that were active at the heart of these conflicts.

This chapter helps to renew a focus on this period by showing how the views and experiences of those still fighting for decolonization became part of the conversation around remaking humanitarian law. The participation of armed opposition movements in the official discussions to reform the law was one of the flashpoints of the Diplomatic Conference. Western powers had fought against it, while supporters in the Afro-Asian and Eastern blocs, as well as some Nordic states, backed the liberation movements as legitimate representatives of their peoples – peoples, moreover, suffering the effects of war which the law was intended to mitigate. From one point of view, therefore, this period revisited the historical phenomenon of liberation and revolutionary movements as human rights movements, dating back to the French Revolution. From

---

[9] The language of human rights and humanitarianism was particularly entangled in these debates. See Keith Suter, "An Enquiry into the Meaning of the Phrase 'Human Rights in Armed Conflict,'" *Revue de droit pénal militaire et de droit de la guerre* 15, nos. 3–4 (1976): 393–430; Amanda Alexander, "A Short History of International Humanitarian Law," *European Journal of International Law* 26, no. 1 (2015): 109–38. On this phenomenon in the 1940s, see Boyd Van Dijk, "Human Rights in War: On the Entangled Foundations of the 1949 Geneva Conventions," *American Journal of International Law* 112, no. 4 (2018): 553–82.

[10] Roland Burke, "Emotional Diplomacy and Human Rights at the United Nations," *Human Rights Quarterly* 39, no. 2 (2017): 273–95; Martin Thomas and Richard Toye, eds., *Rhetorics of Empire: Languages of Colonial Conflict after 1900* (Manchester: Manchester University Press, 2017).

another, it reflected the postcolonial novelty of Third World countries' dominance of international forums for human rights, addressing their previous exclusion from "the process of defining human rights as part of international law."[11] The first section discusses the road toward the Diplomatic Conference, establishing the dynamics that enabled the anticolonial agenda to shape international humanitarian law. The second section turns to the dialogue with national liberation movements established by representatives of the ICRC in the lead-up to the Conference. The final section shows how these were intertwined with the use of multilateral forums for the promotion of national liberation.

The Road to Reform

The four sessions over four years that it took to draft the Additional Protocols are often contrasted with the four months in which the Geneva Conventions of 1949 were agreed, yet there were similarities between the two periods. Preparations in both cases were considerable, the ICRC first raising the prospect of reforming the law in 1945. In both cases, the Committee ran consultations and drafted texts, positioning itself as the impartial guardian of the law, with neutral Switzerland serving as official host and depository of the Conventions. The ICRC's position in the 1940s was, as in the late 1960s, embattled: having faced criticisms for its stance during World War II, it was confronted with suspicion from the United Kingdom, obstructionism from the Soviet Union, and competition from the League of Red Cross Societies.[12] Resistance movements and partisans did not participate but the keen interest of European countries (many of which had experienced occupation and armed resistance) in asserting their legitimacy did see them included in the convention on prisoners of war.[13] Thus World War II and the Holocaust had created, among some key governments at least, a level of familiarity with

---

[11] Andreas Eckert, "African Nationalists and Human Rights, 1940s to 1970s," in *Human Rights in the Twentieth Century*, ed. Stefan-Ludwig Hoffmann (Cambridge, UK: Cambridge University Press 2011), 294; Roger Normand and Sarah Zaidi, *Human Rights at the UN: The Political History of Universal Justice* (Bloomington: Indiana University Press, 2008), 243–88; Roland Burke, *Decolonization and the Evolution of International Human Rights* (Philadelphia: University of Pennsylvania Press, 2010); Steven L. B. Jensen, *The Making of International Human Rights: The 1960s, Decolonization, and the Reconstruction of Global Values* (Cambridge, UK: Cambridge University Press, 2016).

[12] Boyd Van Dijk, "'The Great Humanitarian': The Soviet Union, the International Committee of the Red Cross, and the Geneva Conventions of 1949," *Law and History Review* 37, no. 1 (2019): 209–35; Geoffrey Best, *War and Law since 1945* (Oxford: Clarendon Press, 1994), 80–99.

[13] Best, *War and Law since 1945*, 127–8.

the law and a willingness to broach additional limitations on the conduct of war. When pressure for reform arose barely two decades later, both the ICRC and the Swiss government, which traditionally hosted the Diplomatic Conferences, were fearful that renegotiating the rules of international humanitarian law would result in fewer protections during wartime instead of better ones.[14] For this reason, the process was not one of revision but of "reaffirmation and development" of the law.

The ICRC's preference for discretion, and with it a cautious pace, met external and internal challenges as the issue gained momentum from the late 1960s onward. The Committee certainly recognized the need for reform: it had unsuccessfully initiated moves to update the law on civil conflicts in the 1950s, an issue to which it returned at the 20th International Conference of the Red Cross in 1965. Anti-colonial and postcolonial wars, notably in Southern Africa, Vietnam, Nigeria, and the Middle East, demonstrated that the law was neither well respected on its own terms nor well adapted. Moreover, the ICRC's performance in relief work and attempts to improve respect for the law in these conflicts was not distinguished. Particularly following the Nigeria–Biafra War (1967–70), evidence of shortcomings and anachronisms in the ICRC's responses and its standing in Africa had prompted the organization to question its ways of operating.[15] As Committee members acknowledged, it had not always reflected upon its experiences or responded to well-founded criticisms.[16]

Nonetheless, with the UN's interest in "human rights in armed conflict" quickening the collective pace on reform, there was little choice but to act.[17] Former colonies and other Third World states dominated the UN's human rights agenda, with significant implications for its operational agencies.[18] In 1968, the International Conference on Human

---

[14] David Forsythe, *The Humanitarians: The International Committee of the Red Cross* (Cambridge, UK: Cambridge University Press, 2005), 261–2; Suter, *Guerrilla Warfare*, 100–1.

[15] Marie-Luce Desgrandchamps, "'Organizing the Unpredictable': The Nigeria–Biafra War and Its Impact on the ICRC," *International Review of the Red Cross* 94, no. 888 (2012): 1409–32.

[16] Max Petitpierre, *Ligne de conduite à suivre par le CICR dans la politique internationale actuelle*, speech to ICRC Assembly, July 3, 1974, 2–3, ACICR B AG 012–054.

[17] Richard Baxter, "Humanitarian Law or Humanitarian Politics? The 1974 Diplomatic Conference on Humanitarian Law," in *Humanizing the Laws of War*, ed. Vagts et al., 290–1; Sandesh Sivakumaran, *The Law of Non-International Armed Conflict* (Oxford: Oxford University Press, 2012), 44–6; Suter, *Guerrilla Warfare*, 37–82; Gerd Oberleitner, *Human Rights in Armed Conflict: Law, Practice, Policy* (Cambridge, UK: Cambridge University Press, 2015), 52–60.

[18] Burke, *Decolonization*; Jensen, *Making of International Human Rights*; Daniel Maul, *Human Rights, Development and Decolonization: The International Labour Organization, 1940–1970* (Basingstoke, UK: Palgrave Macmillan, 2012).

Rights, held in Tehran, passed Resolution XXIII on human rights in armed conflict. From that time until 1977, at least 16 General Assembly resolutions were passed on protections in conflict, sometimes intertwined with the promotion of self-determination, and driven by the same bloc of Third World countries that was propelling the anti-colonial campaign.[19] Reports from the Secretary-General (at the General Assembly's request) on human rights in armed conflict specifically considered protections in wars of national liberation.[20] These diplomatic steps sat, whether advisedly or not, on a foundation of transnational advocacy of anti-colonialism and self-determination.[21] Nongovernmental organizations (NGOs) also helped to advance this agenda in its legal form, epitomized by the role of Seán MacBride, then Secretary-General of the International Commission of Jurists. Thanks in large part to MacBride's lobbying, the Tehran resolution linked the insufficiency and lack of respect for laws of war to the abuses of "minority racist or colonial régimes."[22] Reacting to these developments, the Swiss government's legal department described the geographically expanded interest in reform to international humanitarian law as positive while sounding a note of caution about the need to "safeguard" the ICRC's role.[23]

The first session of the Diplomatic Conference came at what Geoffrey Best identified as "just about the climax" of the "sustained crescendo of liberationist agitation."[24] The Organization of African Unity (OAU, forerunner to the African Union) was a crucial broker of the national liberation agenda – an issue it prioritized over human rights.[25] UN assistance was restricted to groups recognized by the OAU, making such recognition a means of increasing profile and resources. But it was important to newly independent states that self-determination not become a conduit for all manner of secessionist movements that might

---

[19] François Bugnion, "The Geneva Conventions of 21 August 1949: From the 1949 Diplomatic Conference to the Dawn of the New Millennium," *International Affairs* 76, no. 1 (2000): 45; Oberleitner, *Human Rights in Armed Conflict*, 53–6.

[20] *Respect for Human Rights in Armed Conflict: Report of the Secretary-General*, UN Document A/8052 (1970), 62–74.

[21] Alexander, "Postcolonialism and Geneva Protocol I," 36–48; Kinsella, "Superfluous Injury and Unnecessary Suffering," 215–17.

[22] Resolution XXIII, in *Final Act of the International Conference on Human Rights, Teheran, 22 April to 13 May 1968*, UN Document A/CONF. 32/41 (1968), 18. See Suter, *Guerrilla Warfare*, 24–31.

[23] *Note pour Monsieur l'Ambassadeur Thalmann*, October 29, 1968, 6, Swiss Federal Archives (SFA), E2003A#1980/85#1397*, o.411.621, Droit humanitaire: protection des droits de l'homme en cas de conflit armé, 1968–9. MacBride's role specifically was viewed with concern by some members of the Swiss international organizations department.

[24] Best, *War and Law*, 344.   [25] Eckert, "African Nationalists and Human Rights," 297.

threaten their stability and viability. The groups privileged with the OAU's national liberation status were therefore usually limited to those fighting against imperial Portugal (in today's Angola, Guinea-Bissau and Cape Verde, and Mozambique) and white minority rule (in today's Namibia, South Africa, and Zimbabwe); the Palestinian Liberation Organization also featured as a liberation movement in the Middle East, recognized by the League of Arab States.

As in the UN, decolonization had brought numerous new participants to Red Cross gatherings. They cooperated in pushing the anti-colonial agenda, leading to more politically explicit resolutions than was customary and – particularly with regards to apartheid-era South Africa – highly unusual moves against specific offending countries. The dynamics of national liberation also marked preparations for the Diplomatic Conference in Red Cross forums. In the consultations managed by the ICRC, national liberation was a contentious and inconsistent but ultimately persistent thread, in its own right but also through the related questions of the regulation of guerrilla warfare and non-international armed conflict. Terms such as "wars of liberation" and "liberation movements" figured in official documentation, though the ICRC was careful to note that these were terms in current usage and did not denote any particular opinion on its part.[26] Whether wars of national liberation should be considered international and afforded a special status became the subject of fervent discord at the second Conference of Government Experts, in May–June 1972, with one participant asserting that "a denial of the essential nature of these just wars was a denial of human rights."[27] During the Diplomatic Conference, as Whyte has emphasized, delegates from the anti-colonial bloc proposed "a contrasting vision of justice" that refused the colonial and imperial underpinnings of international law.[28]

As an organization, the ICRC's approach was to avoid stating any position on such questions. Well into the Diplomatic Conference sessions, its delegates were consistently avoiding any specific comments on the participation of national liberation movements or the designation of wars of national liberation as international conflicts, instead merely

---

[26] ICRC, *Conference of Government Experts on the Reaffirmation and Development of International Humanitarian Law Applicable in Armed Conflicts: Geneva, 24 May–12 June 1971*, vol. V, Protection of Victims of Non-International Armed Conflicts (Geneva: ICRC, 1971), 23.

[27] ICRC, *Conference of Government Experts on the Reaffirmation and Development of International Humanitarian Law Applicable in Armed Conflicts: Second Session, 3 May–3 June 1972. Report on the Work of the Conference*, vol. I (Geneva: ICRC, 1972), 66.

[28] Whyte, "Dangerous Concept of the Just War," 323.

emphasizing the importance of "universality."[29] When national liberation movements and their supporters justified armed struggle by evoking the right to self-determination, the ICRC did not enter the debate. Nonetheless, when these same movements asserted that individual rights in wartime – the protections afforded by international humanitarian law – should be guaranteed in anti-colonial conflicts, the ICRC's commitment to minimizing suffering during conflict offered a point of convergence between these two agendas.

Engaging with National Liberation Movements

Concurrent with the official consultations of government, legal, military, and relief experts, ICRC jurists also opened dialogue with representatives of national liberation movements. This dialogue, intended to facilitate work on the draft Additional Protocols, highlighted the different attitudes held in the ICRC's legal division, based in Geneva and responsible for the development, interpretation, and dissemination of the laws of war, and its operational department, whose staff worked either in the field or at headquarters but focused on the practical work of relief and protection. Operational delegates had pragmatic reasons for engaging with liberation movements, despite their concerns that this contact could be manipulated for diplomatic or publicity gains. Ultimately, contact was necessary to continue humanitarian work in the field, above all prison visits.[30] Indeed, it was within decolonization wars that that ICRC delegates began to systematize their processes and requirements for detention visits.[31] Jurists within the ICRC likewise had pragmatic incentives to develop contacts with the movements, because of their increasingly likely presence at the Diplomatic Conference. But the legal division had additional, strategic incentives to maintain these relationships and indeed to explore the views of liberation movements, compelled by the notion that the involvement of such groups in the lawmaking process could have positive effects for international humanitarian law and its future

---

[29] *Réponse à donner aux journalistes et autres personnes qui interrogeraient le CICR au sujet de la participation à la deuxième session de la Conférence diplomatique,* January 17, 1975, ACICR B AG 152.039.01.

[30] At this time, contacts with liberation movements were managed by the regional delegations (based in Yaoundé and Addis Ababa), while contacts with the contested authorities – notably Portugal and South Africa – were handled by Geneva. See Extracts, *Procès-verbaux du Conseil exécutif concernant les relations avec les mouvements de libération en Afrique,* December 3, 1970, 2, ACICR B AG 149–008.02.

[31] Andrew Thompson, "'Restoring Hope Where All Hope Was Lost': Nelson Mandela, the ICRC and the Protection of Political Detainees in Apartheid South Africa," *International Review of the Red Cross* 98, no. 903 (2016): 810–11.

implementation. Because of their importance in contemporary wars and the international backing they received, for ICRC jurists the national liberation movements became part of the conversation about reforming the law. Their participation, politically sensitive and generally kept quiet, furthered the ICRC's publicly stated goal of "universality."

Algeria was crucial as a historical reference and a contemporary site for dialogue with national liberation movements. The Algerian War (1954–62) changed how wars of decolonization were understood, crystallizing the redefinition of civilian and combatant in the laws of war, including its vision of gender.[32] The ICRC's action during the war provided a precedent for engagement with anti-colonial movements and delegates in the 1970s suggested this model be applied in ongoing wars of national liberation.[33] Post-independence, Mouloud Belaouane, president of the Algerian Red Crescent (CRA) from 1967 to 1994, personified the connections between Algeria, humanitarian law, and late anti-colonial struggles. He was a founding member and leader of the anti-colonialist General Union of Muslim Algerian Students in the mid-1950s and a military doctor with the National Liberation Army toward the end of that decade until the end of the war.[34] When the ICRC sought individuals for expert consultations in 1969, Belaouane was nominated because of his medical experience in a war of liberation with guerrilla methods as well as his Red Crescent role.[35] He was also consulted in 1970, a year when relationships between the CRA and ICRC were strained due to a dispute about costs incurred in Nigeria. This time he additionally participated in ICRC meetings with national liberation movements based in Algiers, held there August 5–7, at which he emphasized Algeria as a precedent. The ICRC's contacts with the Algerian independence movement and the CRA, Belaouane asserted, went "considerably beyond the circumscribed rules in place and yet corresponded,

[32] Kinsella, *The Image before the Weapon*, 127–54; Alexander, "Postcolonialism and Geneva Protocol I," 40–4.

[33] Roger Santschy in untitled French-language transcript of meeting in Oslo, April 19, 1973, 80, ACICR B AG 059–397.05; *Draft Agenda for Talks with Liberation Movements on the Subject of Humanitarian Law*, March 29, 1973, 1, ACICR B AG 059.397.06. On humanitarian action and law during the war, see Fabian Klose, *Human Rights in the Shadow of Colonial Violence: The Wars of Independence in Kenya and Algeria* (Philadelphia: University of Pennsylvania Press, 2013); Jennifer Johnson, *The Battle for Algeria: Sovereignty, Health Care, and Humanitarianism* (Philadelphia: University of Pennsylvania Press, 2016).

[34] See interview with Belaouane in Clement Moore Henry, *UGEMA: Union générale des étudiants algériens (1955–1962): témoignages* (Algiers: Casbah Editions, 2010), 197–222.

[35] René-Jean Wilhelm, *Note à l'attention de Monsieur Siordet, Président du Groupe des Juristes. Concerne: Réunion d'experts sur "la restauration du droit de la guerre" – Choix d'un expert du monde arabe*, January 9, 1969, 1, ACICR B AG 149.06.

as would be the case today for ICRC contacts with these liberation movements, to undeniable humanitarian imperatives."[36] Reference to humanitarian principles, for the ICRC, enabled efforts to include different politically defined groups within action to alleviate suffering.[37]

Foremost among the issues raised in Algiers was the demand that wars of national liberation be classified as international conflicts. As articulated by José Oscar Monteiro, representative in Algeria of the Front for the Liberation of Mozambique (FRELIMO), these wars were not international because of the involvement of a foreign – that is, colonial – power, but because of the internationally recognized right of colonized peoples to self-determination. Monteiro also expressed the shared concern about implementation: "what is most important . . . is not so much to formulate pleasing legal principles as to establish an effective international check."[38] Such a wish cannot be separated from the request that the ICRC establish a presence in rebel-held zones of Guinea-Bissau, Angola, and Mozambique to deter and if need be denounce Portuguese use of indiscriminate bombing and chemical weaponry – a request that also showed how consultations on legal questions could give rise to operational discussions.[39]

While the ICRC's interlocutors in Algiers contested the simple equation of guerrilla warfare with wars of national liberation, the provisions they were keenest to discuss related to guerrilla methods. They saw the protection of civilians as the essential issue of international humanitarian law but particularly difficult in guerrilla wars. Terrorism was claimed as a necessary weapon of intimidation for independence fighters. But, as stated in the *rapport de mission*, representatives of liberation movements wished to "distinguish 'selective terrorism' which affects only those singled out as traitors or collaborators, and 'blind terrorism,' which strikes the civilian population indiscriminately."[40] Although not made explicit in the record of the meeting, their position appears to acknowledge that a broad definition of terrorism could serve moves to criminalize and marginalize opposition groups. Representatives in the UN's Sixth Committee were more explicit on this, demanding that anti-terror

---

[36] Michel Veuthey, *Consultations sur le droit humanitaire applicable dans les conflits non internationaux et la guérilla. I. Remarques et propositions de nos interlocuteurs concernant l'activité du C.I.C.R.*, August 13, 1970, 2–3, ACICR B AG 059–203.01.

[37] Andrew Thompson, "Humanitarian Principles Put to the Test: Challenges to Humanitarian Action during Decolonization," *International Review of the Red Cross* 97, nos. 897–8 (2016): 50.

[38] Michel Veuthey, *Consultations sur le droit humanitaire applicable dans les conflits non internationaux et la guérilla. II. Examen du questionnaire et du commentaire sur les conflits non internationaux et la guérilla*, August 15, 1970, 3, ACICR B AG 059–203.01.

[39] Ibid., *I*, 3.   [40] Ibid., *II*, 4–6.

regulations not offer any "excuse" to colonial powers seeking to suppress the struggle for self-determination.[41]

As consultations with independent and government experts progressed, the ICRC's legal team continued to seek the opinions of national liberation movements on the emerging draft Additional Protocols. The focal point for these dialogues on national liberation and international humanitarian law was Michel Veuthey, who joined the ICRC in 1967. He remained in the legal division throughout the preparations for the Diplomatic Conference and its four sessions, while also undertaking a doctor of law on guerrilla warfare and humanitarian law at the University of Geneva.[42] The two axes of dialogue with liberation movements as stated by Veuthey in August 1972 were "how and to what extent a guerrilla movement can respect the current humanitarian laws or those proposed by the ICRC" and "what improvements, modifications or deletions might be envisaged to concretely and legally improve the protection of victims on both sides of a guerrilla war."[43] International and non-international conflicts alike were considered.

Determining the precise practical and ideological limits of liberation movements' ability to accommodate international humanitarian law was an urgent preoccupation for the ICRC. This is seen in a questionnaire intended for liberation movements, arranged into four sections: forms of struggle; traditional laws of war; Geneva Conventions; and limits on humanitarian concessions. Some of the questions were quite straightforward and over the years of debate around the Diplomatic Conference would become familiar for governments as well as liberation movements. Others were suited only to understanding the mindset of armed opposition. Question 1, for instance, asked "Is violence in any form acceptable against an enemy considered as oppressor?" Question 16 sought reflections on the tensions of calling for respect of the law by the enemy while rejecting its constraints for their own subversive and terrorist struggle. The section on the limits of humanitarian concerns invited comments on the "importance of humanitarian considerations relative to ideological imperatives and the requirements of the struggle" (question 29) and on the "eventual desire or practical need to set in motion the 'downwards

---

[41] See for example Record of meeting of the 27th session of the UN Sixth Committee on measures to prevent international terrorism (1386th meeting), December 8, 1972.

[42] Michel Veuthey, *Guérrilla et droit humanitaire* (Geneva: Henry Dunant Institute, 1976). Veuthey continued working for the ICRC, in legal roles and other positions, until 2000.

[43] Michel Veuthey, *Réaffirmation et développement du droit international humanitaire applicable dans les conflits armés. Consultation de mouvements de libération sur le droit international humanitaire applicable dans les conflits armés,* August 2, 1972, 3, ACICR B AG 059.397.01.

spiral of terrorism–repression,' without really taking account of the bloodshed that it risks bringing" (question 32).[44] The enquiries were structured according to the logic of humanitarianism but admitted the possibility that this logic might not – indeed, in some situations would definitely not – be the primary consideration for the respondents.

Other ICRC documents on these early phase consultations reveal the existence of diverging priorities between the legal division and their colleagues in operations. This is evident in commentary by Georg Hoffmann, Delegate-General for Africa, on the same set of meetings in Algiers in August 1970 on which Michel Veuthey reported. In his operational role, Hoffmann had maintained contacts with groups fighting the Portuguese authorities, particularly regarding visits to detained soldiers; he also participated in the ICRC's work during the Algerian War and with the Biafran leadership as they fought against Nigerian rule.[45] In 1970 he warned: "We must not forget that such Movements seek above all to make use of the ICRC for political ends, as they themselves say. They are not truly interested in the issue of prisoners, unless it is for political ends."[46] Regarding assertions of the international status of self-determination, Hoffmann responded: "For ICRC's action, this question is without importance . . . The fact that civil conflicts are imperfectly covered by the Conventions does not hamper the ICRC's action."[47] This assertion is comprehensible in light of the direct contacts that Hoffmann had been cultivating with liberation movements for several years. It also reflects the problematic nature of the Algerian War as a precedent in which the risk of instrumentalization was as important a lesson as the need for engagement.

Hoffmann's commentary also recounted a meeting with FRELIMO in September 1970 which was not featured in Veuthey's *rapport de mission* (the latter having been submitted in August and the former in October). In this meeting, he indicates, FRELIMO's first claim was that "to this point FRELIMO had 'given everything' to the Red Cross without receiving anything in return." His frustration with this transactional conception of engagement between the armed group and the

---

[44] *Attitudes des mouvements de résistance à l'égard du rôle humanitaire*, May 17, 1972, 1–3, ACICR B AG 059–397.01.

[45] *International Review of the Red Cross* 9, no. 95 (1969): 88; Françoise Perret and François Bugnion, *De Budapest à Saigon: Histoire du Comité International de la Croix-Rouge, 1956–1965* (Geneva: Georg Editeur, 2009), 266; Marie-Luce Desgrandchamps, *L'Humanitaire en guerre civile: La crise du Biafra (1967–1970)* (Rennes: Presses Universitaires de Rennes, 2018), 44.

[46] Georg Hoffmann, *Notes aux deux délégations. Réf.: Mouvements de libération*, October 13, 1970, 2, ACICR B AG 219 003–002. Line break in original removed.

[47] Ibid., Appendix.

humanitarian organization is palpable. Hoffmann also defended the ICRC from FRELIMO's accusation that "the Red Cross prefers to stay quiet and keep Portugal as a 'member' than to publicly declare what is happening and risk their 'resignation.'"[48] These claims from FRELIMO were far more antagonistic than those expressed in the Algiers meetings in August 1970.

The context for these tensions was a shifting understanding in certain forums of what constituted "humanitarian" aid. The ICRC had rearticulated its principles in 1965, emphasizing that its action was to be neutral and impartial. In the 1960s and 1970s this conception of humanitarian action confronted the advocacy of "humanitarian" aid as part of the struggle against colonial rule and apartheid. The UN General Assembly issued numerous calls for assistance to the liberation movements, combining "humanitarian," educational, material, and political assistance.[49] Some supporters of national liberation went further, claiming that "direct assistance that will ensure the continuation and the extension of the armed struggle" was "also humanitarian."[50] This was a view of humanitarian assistance as being separated only by means and expertise from military assistance.[51] The erosion of boundaries between relief and support was contrary to Red Cross principles, even if history shows that other political considerations have also influenced the conduct of the ICRC, the National Societies, and the League (or Federation).

Hoffmann's frustration with FRELIMO's charges is understandable given the lack of familiarity they suggest with Red Cross goals and guiding principles, though the ICRC was aware of the responsibility it bore for its poor standing in certain parts of the world.[52] Still, the way he wrote of the Algiers meetings raises the question of how his concerns colored his analysis of liberation movement positions. Hoffmann was not part of the delegation to Algiers in August 1970; the ICRC was represented by Veuthey and Pierre Gaillard (Gaillard was a key delegate

[48] Ibid.
[49] See summary in Olav Stokke and Carl Widstrand, eds., *Southern Africa. The UN–OAU Conference, Oslo 9–14 April 1973* (Uppsala: Scandinavian Institute of African Studies, 1973), vol. 2, 259–66.
[50] Mohamed A. Foum (Tanzania), ibid., vol. 1, 86.
[51] George W. Shepherd Jr., "Humanitarian Assistance to Liberation Movements," *Africa Today* 21, no. 4 (1974): 75–87.
[52] Perret and Bugnion, *De Budapest à Saigon*, 319–26; Yolana Pringle, "Humanitarianism, Race and Denial: The International Committee of the Red Cross and Kenya's Mau Mau Rebellion, 1952–60," *History Workshop Journal*, 84, no. 1 (2017): 89–107.

during the Algerian War and Nigeria–Biafra War).[53] Hoffmann's commentary appears to have been based upon their accounts, especially Veuthey's. His reaction suggests a fundamental misunderstanding on the part of the movements; Veuthey's text creates the impression of a dialogue between interlocutors of different kinds.

If OAU and UN recognition reflected different conceptions of liberation movements, working relationships with the ICRC were not intended to "recognize" at all but only to facilitate care for victims of war.[54] That the Diplomatic Conference threatened to publicly blur this distinction was cause for concern in Red Cross circles as well as Western government ones.[55] The ICRC's engagement with nonstate movements remained secretive and on an unequal basis compared to relationships with ruling colonial or minority governments (for example, it did not submit prison visit reports to the movements as it did to governments).[56] The organization resisted moves to make the consultations known even as delegates reiterated to representatives of the national liberation movements that they would be welcome at its Geneva offices at any time.

Preparing Liberation Movements for the Diplomatic Conference

As the Diplomatic Conference drew closer, a series of more structured encounters took place between national liberation movements and Red Cross bodies. These continued in the mode of consultations but were also more explicitly oriented toward preparing the movements for future participation in larger forums. The Norwegian government played an important role and served as a link between the official consultations and behind-the-scenes work with liberation movements. The other key actor in these structured encounters was the OAU and especially its Coordinating Committee for the Liberation of Africa (or Liberation Committee). These organizations worked collaboratively with members of the ICRC as well as Red Cross societies from Africa and Norway, though not with

---

[53] Also present were Belaouane and another colleague for the CRA; and representatives of FRELIMO, the African Party for the Independence of Guinea and Cape Verde (PAIGC), and the People's Movement for the Liberation of Angola (MPLA).

[54] Yassin El-Ayouty, "Legitimisation of National Liberation: The United Nations and Southern Africa," *Issue: A Journal of Opinion* 2, no. 4 (1972): 44.

[55] See, for example, Lady Angela Limerick, Letter to Lady Priscilla Tweedsmuir, East Grinstead, February 6, 1974; and response, London, February 14, 1974, The National Archives of the UK (TNA): Foreign and Commonwealth Office (FCO) 61/1231.

[56] Département des Opérations, *Proposition concernant une politique globale du CICR dans la situation d'affrontement politique et militaire en Afrique Australe (objectives pour 1977)*, October 28, 1976, 1, ACICR B AG 149–008.01.

exactly the same aims, to strengthen the understandings and capacities of liberation movements in the lead-up to the first Diplomatic Conference session in 1974.

Norway's role as an advocate of national liberation movements and related issues in forums on international humanitarian law reflected its activist stance toward Southern Africa. Not strongly positioned in the early 1950s, the Norwegian government was brought toward a more active role on apartheid by pressure groups and solidarity organizations.[57] In this Norway was typical of its neighboring states, with the Nordic countries notable supporters of national liberation during the 1960s and 1970s, a position that developed out of their approach as the "fire brigade states" at the UN – emphasizing dialogue and commitment to international law.[58] Funding from the Nordic countries constituted a large proportion of UN assistance programs for Southern Africa and Norway's contributions during the Conferences of Government Experts in 1971 and 1972 were in keeping with this record of solidarity.

Norwegian support for national liberation continued with its hosting of the UN–OAU International Conference of Experts on Colonialism and Apartheid in Southern Africa, from April 9–14, 1973. Experts came from states (though the United States, United Kingdom, and France declined), UN bodies, the Liberation Committee, and NGOs chosen for their proximity to the question.[59] No experts from either Portugal or South Africa were invited; instead, groups from countries ruled by Lisbon and Pretoria dominated the cohort of liberation movements. The conference called for "massive assistance" to the liberation movements as "the authentic representatives of their peoples," deserving of "full international recognition" and "the complete support of the world community."[60] In the closing session, Herbert Chitepo, Chairman of the Zimbabwe African National Union (ZANU), heralded the conference's acceptance of the "inevitability of armed struggle and its support for that struggle" as its great success.[61]

The Oslo conference enabled a second, secret set of discussions that followed immediately, behind closed doors, on April 15–16. The driving

[57] Tore Linné Eriksen, "The Origins of a Special Relationship: Norway and Southern Africa 1960–1975," in *Norway and National Liberation in Southern Africa*, ed. Tore Linné Eriksen (Stockholm: Nordiska Afrikainstitutet, 2000), 12–13.

[58] Kevin O'Sullivan, *Ireland, Africa and the End of Empire: Small State Identity in the Cold War, 1955–75* (Manchester: Manchester University Press, 2012), 17; Carl Marklund, *Neutrality and Solidarity in Nordic Humanitarian Action* (London: Overseas Development Institute, 2016), 13–16.

[59] List of participants available in Stokke and Widstrand, *UN–OAU Conference*, vol. 1, 265–74.

[60] Ibid., 18.   [61] Ibid., 69.

force behind it was Hans Wilhelm Longva of the Norwegian Foreign Ministry, who had attended both of the Conferences of Government Experts, having joined the Ministry in 1966, and would go on to a distinguished diplomatic career. In response to Longva's enquiries about the conduct of the meeting and its possible outcomes, Veuthey indicated that for operational reasons the ICRC "earnestly desires to avoid giving these meetings any publicity."[62] Any attempt to use the meeting for advocacy or to demonstrate the contribution of the Norwegian Red Cross was hence quashed. The ICRC's agenda for the meeting revisited the axes of its earlier enquiries: the current practice of national liberation movements; their attitudes to existing law; their proposals for its improvement and updating.[63]

For the liberation movements the need to address a perceived colonial approach was a fundamental concern, which appeared through two linked subjects of discussion: protections for guerrilla fighters and protections for the civilian population. T. George Silundika of the Zimbabwe African People's Union (ZAPU) highlighted that "the very nature of an anti-colonial war is that you are fighting an enemy that deprives you of any possibilities of fighting in the conventional manner."[64] Much more so than in conventional war between recognized national militaries, in a "people's war for liberation," Songa Tondo of the National Liberation Front of Angola (FNLA) explained, the relationship between combatants and civilians was inherently and necessarily close and protections based on their separation could not be effective.[65] Several speakers insisted at length on that point: a clear line could not be drawn between civilians and combatants in a guerrilla struggle for popular freedom.[66] This was an assault on the most important distinction at the heart of international humanitarian law. Yet the threat that this assault would undermine the very foundation of the law never eventuated, as Helen Kinsella has argued, because it also allowed differentiation between the "civilized" and the barbarous. Anti-colonial actors sought admission to the ranks of civilization even as they

---

[62] Letter from Michel Veuthey to H. W. Konow, Geneva, March 28, 1973, 2, ACICR B AG 059–397.05.

[63] *Draft Agenda for Talks with Liberation Movements on the Subject of Humanitarian Law,* March 29, 1973, 5, ACICR B AG 059.397.06.

[64] Untitled English-language transcript of meeting in Oslo, April 30, 1973, 17, ACICR B AG 059–397.05.

[65] Untitled French-language transcript of meeting in Oslo, April 19, 1973, 48, ACICR B AG 059–397.05.

[66] In the English transcript, Gil Fernandes (PAIGC), 21. In the French transcript, José Oscar Monteiro (FRELIMO), 59; Songa Tondo (FNLA), 67.

contested the way those ranks had been constituted and defined in the past.[67] Representatives of the liberation movements challenged not only the restrictively European origins of the Geneva Conventions but the process of their redevelopment, including the questions being put to them in Oslo and elsewhere, as proceeding from a Western-centric set of assumptions. Highlighting the European bias of the law to date was not intended to justify disregarding it, speakers claimed, but to demonstrate the need for change.[68] Perhaps the most forceful critique of the process came from José Monteiro, the FRELIMO representative who had joined several meetings with ICRC members and who would later participate in the Diplomatic Conference. The consultations, he claimed, suffered from the fact that the approach used was the same as in the elaboration of the Geneva Conventions. Instead of re-imagining what law might be appropriate, or taking guerrilla warfare seriously in its own right, the process had merely considered modifications of the rules created for conventional warfare – limiting how meaningful the changes could be. The "traditional concept" of distinguishing between combatants and non-combatants had to be set aside, he argued.[69] In this logic, the mere participation of a larger number of states did not ensure the decolonization of international humanitarian law: it had also to be done differently. This understanding shaped the whole preparatory process, where delegates indicated, in Kinsella's words, that "historically, the articulation of humanity and human, which supposedly served as the foundation for the laws of war, was fully compatible with and, indeed, dependent on an imperialistic racial logic."[70]

Despite these fundamental critiques, the largely nonpolemical nature of the meeting can be seen in how participants largely sidestepped the politics of race even during lengthy discussions on different aspects of anti-colonial conflict. While most comments about Western centrism were limited to analysis of warfare, the FNLA's Tondo put his finger on the delicate issue of race when he commented that as much as the questions were being posed by friends, whether the Norwegians or the ICRC, they are "white European friends." Did this affect how they felt

[67] Kinsella, *Image before the Weapon*, 139–40; Kinsella, "Superfluous Injury"; Frédéric Mégret, "From 'Savages' to 'Unlawful Combatants': A Postcolonial Look at International Humanitarian Law's 'Other,'" in *International Law and Its Others*, ed. Anne Orford (Cambridge, UK: Cambridge University Press, 2006), 265–317.
[68] In the English transcript, Moses Garoeb (SWAPO), 16; T. George Silundika (ZAPU), 17; unidentified speaker, 21. In the French transcript, André Dominique Micheli (ICRC), 53.
[69] Monteiro in French transcript, 51–2, 59.   [70] Kinsella, *Image before the Weapon*, 138.

about white civilians in the colonies subject to attack from liberation movements, he wondered?[71] This and a passing mention of "the importance of race in the Southern African context" from Moses Garoeb of the South West Africa People's Organization (SWAPO) were the only explicit allusions to the issue recorded in the transcripts.

A second structured meeting of national liberation movements took place on January 21–25, 1974, in Dar es Salaam, just one month shy of the first Diplomatic Conference session. It brought together representatives from ten of the thirteen national liberation movements recognized by the OAU and diplomatic representatives of eleven African states. Also invited as observers were the Swiss government, the Norwegian government, and the ICRC – the latter represented by Jacques Moreillon (delegate-general for Africa), Robert Gaillard (regional delegate for West Africa), and Michel Veuthey (legal division). An OAU Council of Ministers Resolution officially requested the seminar to allow liberation movements to coordinate positions and make constructive proposals but it was privately acknowledged that it aimed to address their lack of familiarity with international humanitarian law.[72] Positive remarks throughout Veuthey's *rapport de mission* – about the quality of the chairing, the courteous, considered, and studious tone of the discussions – suggest that the week's discussions were viewed as beneficial by the legal team. For operational colleagues, too, the engagements were "positive" and their separate report declared that the goal of establishing closer contacts with the liberation movements had been achieved, at least in part because of the numerous side meetings that the seminar allowed.[73] There had always been unanimity among liberation movements on the international nature of wars of self-determination. Such was their single-mindedness on this subject that the draft of Additional Protocol II (covering non-international armed conflict) was not even discussed in Dar es Salaam, being considered irrelevant. The bulk of the five-day seminar, therefore, was devoted to discussion of the draft of

---

[71] Tondo in French transcript, 57–8. The version in the English transcript is less explicit, 24.

[72] Resolution CM/Res. 307 (XXI) of May 17–24, 1973; Churchill Ewumbue-Monono, "Respect for International Humanitarian Law by Armed Non-State Actors in Africa," *International Review of the Red Cross* 88, no. 864 (2006): 909–10; François de Rougement, *Note no. 491. Concerne: Organisation de l'Unité Africaine – Mouvements de Libération – Conférence diplomatique – Procédure de recherche de disparus*, April 28, 1973, 4, ACICR B AG 149–008.06. More generally, delegates involved in the 1970s tended to have less expertise than those who contributed to the 1949 Geneva Conventions. Kinsella, *Image before the Weapon*, 134.

[73] Département des Opérations Secteur Afrique, *Rapport de mission*, March 8, 1974, 1, ACICR B AG 252 003–046.

Additional Protocol I. Colonel Hashim Mbita, a former Tanzanian liberation military leader and then Executive Secretary of the OAU Liberation Committee, chaired the debates in which armed groups emphasized "their desire to be able to be legally bound by existing or future instruments of international humanitarian law."[74]

The remaining discussion of significance at the Dar es Salaam seminar was the issue of liberation movements' participation in the Diplomatic Conference. Members of the ICRC had been fending off enquiries on this front for months if not years, deferring to the Swiss Government as the convening authority while also indicating that the Swiss would probably refer the decision to the Diplomatic Conference itself. (Privately, the ICRC wished them to participate and Western governments acknowledged that their presence would be difficult to prevent.)[75] Jean Humbert, head of the Swiss government's Diplomatic Conference office, felt isolated at the seminar and unsupported by Longva in particular who, Humbert implied, might have taken the opportunity to help articulate the delicacies of the Swiss position.[76] The OAU, for its part, claimed to prefer not to pronounce on the form of representation that might be acceptable to the movements.[77] In Dar es Salaam, governments and liberation movements unequivocally rejected the proposal that the OAU delegation represent the movements. In Geneva a month later, the anti-colonial majority at the Diplomatic Conference ensured their participation in proceedings.

When the representatives of the liberation movements spoke in the early plenary meetings of the Diplomatic Conference, they took the opportunity both to denounce colonial oppression and to affirm their commitment to human rights. Their remaking of the law reflected a "transformative grasp of history" that identified and rejected the imperialist orientation of the law.[78] They declared, in the words of Simpson Mtambanengwe (ZANU), that "The Geneva Conventions should be amended to take into account the new situation created in the twentieth century by the struggle of peoples for their independence."

[74] Veuthey, *Consultation de mouvements de libération*, 6.
[75] *Situation Afrique*, September 14, 1973, 3, ACICR B AG 200 003–003; Confidential memorandum from British FCO UN Department to British Embassy in Berne, July 20, 1973, TNA: FCO 61/1090.
[76] Jean Humbert, *Rapport no. 9 à la Direction des organisations internationales du Département politique federal*, January 28, 1974, 2, SFA E2003A#1988/15#1140*, o.411.66, Rapports du Commissaire Général, 1973–4.
[77] Dominique Micheli, *Note no. 116: Conversation avec M. Ouattara, Secrétaire exécutif O.U.A., au sujet de la Conférence diplomatique et des contacts du CICR avec les mouvements de libération*, November 9, 1973, 1, ACICR B AG 149–008.06.
[78] Kinsella, "Superfluous Injury," 226.

Such claims about the legitimacy of anti-colonial wars were treated by Western states as a dangerous resurgence of discredited just war theory. And yet, as Mtambanengwe went on to affirm, "it was not the aim of the liberation movements to destroy society; on the contrary, they sought to promote respect for fundamental human rights."[79] His evocation of human rights served the goal of legitimizing the liberation movements as defenders of both universal rights and the particular rights of individuals suffering under colonial rule. Such statements drew power from their delivery in a forum for states, for the creation of law between states, yet they also reflected the years of dialogue through which national liberation movements had been woven into the wider lawmaking process.

Conclusion

As the sessions of the Diplomatic Conference progressed, the ICRC continued to grapple with operational and ethical questions arising from its engagement with armed groups, through them also confronting questions about what happened when its principles faced divergence or opposition. Thus a 1976 reflection by Philipp Züger took as its starting point the Marxist–Leninist orientation of the majority of national liberation movements. It described this doctrine as "diametrically and fundamentally" at odds with the Red Cross principles.[80] Züger outlined arguments the ICRC could use to establish relationships and advocate for humanitarian aid, but warned that "a potential collaboration between national liberation movements and the ICRC can only ever be opportunistic" and would meet its demise once independence had been achieved.[81] The same year, a memorandum from the operations division suggested that contacts with liberation movements be official and open, a proposal designed to strengthen the ICRC's standing in Southern Africa. However, despite all the efforts to improve liberation movements' understanding of international humanitarian law and to change the law to reflect the realities of anti-colonial conflicts, the proposed strategy expressed little hope that the Geneva Conventions would be applied by

---

[79] *Official Records of the Diplomatic Conference on the Reaffirmation and Development of International Humanitarian Law Applicable in Armed Conflict, Geneva (1974–1977)*, vol. V (Bern: Federal Political Department, 1978), 207.

[80] Philippe Züger, *Principes humanitaires et mouvements de libération en Afrique*, July 12, 1976, 2, ACICR B AG 149–008.09. Züger was responding at least in part to an earlier work advocating closer connections with liberation movements, by authors with ICRC connections: *Limites à la violence: mouvements politiques armés et principes humanitaires* (Geneva: Institut Universitaire de Hautes Etudes Internationales, 1973).

[81] Ibid., 4.

either side and fell back upon "basic principles" rather than legal frame-works.[82] This drive to find operational additions, and even alternatives, to the legalistic approach focusing on respect for the law has had a long life in the ICRC's work in conflict zones.[83]

The ICRC was not alone in confronting the challenges of national liberation. The Office of the United Nations High Commissioner for Refugees (UNHCR), for example, had first been involved in a decolon-ization conflict in 1957 when displacement from the Algerian War led the agency to offer its services outside of Europe for the first time. By 1969, roughly two-thirds of UNHCR's spending was in African countries,[84] with the large number of refugees from Portuguese colonies influencing its contacts with liberation movements. An undated document of the mid-1970s reflecting on the state of affairs acknowledged the hostility with which the refugee agency had regarded liberation movements in the previous decade and the challenges posed by the UN's aggressive pro-motion of their cause: "all happened as if, thrown off balance by the rapid evolution of events, attitudes obstinately refused to follow the current."[85] The humanitarian ethic of nonpartisan action did not grant exemption from international politics.

The development of the Additional Protocols occasioned an encounter between revolutionary, nationalist anti-colonialism and a humanitarian discourse and practice that combined universalist language and Western privilege. While some felt that this encounter represented a threat to the impartiality of international humanitarian law, others advocated it as the only way to improve the law's relevance to those in the greatest need of its protections. Different priorities within one organization at the forefront of the reform process, the ICRC, led to conflicting opinions on the most effective attitude to adopt toward national liberation movements. These tensions notwithstanding, the consultation process leading up to the Diplomatic Conference offered legal and operational delegates alike opportunities to strengthen relationships with representatives of liber-ation movements. The movements themselves, while challenging some

---

[82] Département des Opérations, *Proposition concernant une politique globale du CICR*, 8–9.
[83] See a more recent example in Jean-Daniel Tauxe, "Faire mieux accepter le Comité International de la Croix-Rouge sur le terrain," *International Review of the Red Cross* 81, no. 833 (1999): 55–61.
[84] UNHCR, *The State of the World's Refugees: Fifty Years of Humanitarian Action* (Oxford: Oxford University Press, 2000), 37.
[85] *Relations entre le HCR et les mouvements africains de libération (le point de la situation)*, undated [1975–6?], 1, Archives of the United Nations High Commissioner for Refugees (UNHCR) Fonds 11, Records of the Central Registry, Series 2, Classified subject files 1971–84, Subseries 10, Refugee Situations, General Policy on Liberation Movements 101.GEN, vol. 3.

of the fundamental tenets of international humanitarian law and the process of its construction, nonetheless had incentives to maintain their involvement in the process and access to the diplomatic advantages it promised.

The uphill campaign of human rights became steeper in the period between the Universal Declaration of Human Rights in 1948 and the Diplomatic Conference nearly thirty years later due to their politicization, relativization and increasing disregard by many newly independent states (and other older offenders) in this period. Indeed, for a while some proponents of violence also used human rights language as a weapon.[86] Nonetheless, in the 1960s and 1970s, the agenda of "human rights in armed conflict" and ultimately international humanitarian law provided an opportunity to channel the politics of self-determination into novel constructions of international law and genuine attempts to engage new actors in the process. This account suggests that the collective right of self-determination could coexist with and indeed benefit from demands for the extension of individual rights, albeit – in many discussions of international humanitarian law – through a language of protections rather than rights.[87] It was by curtailing the power of states through placing limits on their waging of war, instead of endorsing them as the defenders of rights, that these protections would be put in place. That the challenge to sovereignty was itself limited is evident in the weaker protections during civil wars and, with devastating consequences for individual rights and lives, the widespread violations of international humanitarian law after the Additional Protocols, as before them.

---

[86] Meredith Terretta, "'We Had Been Fooled into Thinking that the UN Watches over the Entire World': Human Rights, UN Trust Territories, and Africa's Decolonization," *Human Rights Quarterly* 34, no. 2 (2012): 350–3.

[87] See Samuel Moyn, *The Last Utopia: Human Rights in History* (Cambridge, MA: Harvard University Press, 2010), 84–119.

16   Liberté sans Frontières, French Humanitarianism, and the Neoliberal Critique of Third Worldism

Jessica Whyte

In January 1985, the Executive Director of the French section of Médecins sans Frontières (MSF), Claude Malhuret, invited a select group of intellectuals, humanitarians, and development specialists to an event that, he warned, would be "widely repudiated because its goal is to challenge an idea shared by nearly all our contemporaries."[1] The goal of the event was to challenge *Tiers Mondism* (Third Worldism) by contesting both its analysis of the exploitative conditions of the post-colonial economic order and its proposals for economic redistribution from the Global North to the Global South. Coined by the French demographer Alfred Sauvy in 1952, the term *"Tiers Monde"* (Third World) harked back to France's prerevolutionary Third Estate and implied a shared condition of exploitation and a revolutionary trajectory.[2] Malhuret's colloquium was the founding event of a new political foundation Liberté sans Frontières (LSF), established by MSF's French leadership in 1984 to combat the influence of Third Worldism and campaign for human rights. While Malhuret portrayed LSF's challenge to Third Worldism as an iconoclastic attempt to "challenge certain taboos," more than five years earlier, in 1979, the French philosopher

This chapter was originally presented at the workshop "Nation and Empire in the Age of Internationalism," University of Sydney, 2014. My thanks to Marco Duranti and Glenda Sluga for the invitation and to all the participants for helpful questions and provocations. I would like to thank Rony Brauman and Claude Malhuret for generously agreeing to meet with me and to share their reflections on Liberté sans Frontières. Thanks also to the editors of this volume for their incisive editorial guidance. Research for this chapter was supported by a Western Sydney University Early Career Research Award and an Australian Research Council DECRA award, DE160100473.

[1] Claude Malhuret, "Invitation de Liberté sans Frontières au Colloque des 23 et 24 Janvier 1984," January 11, 1985, accessed November 3, 2016, www.msf.org/speakingout/famine-and-forced-relocations-ethiopia-1984-1986, 24.
[2] Alfred Sauvy, "Trois mondes, une planète," *Vingtième siècle: Revue d'histoire*, no. 12 (October 1986): 81–3.

Michel Foucault had drawn attention to the "state-phobia" that had become a "kind of critical commonplace" among his contemporaries.[3] Foucault traced the development of this "great fantasy of the paranoiac and devouring state" to neoliberal thought of the 1930s and 1940s.[4] "All those who share in the great state phobia," he remarked, "should know that they are following the direction of the wind."[5]

This chapter situates LSF in the context of the development and popularization of neoliberal thinking in the second half of the twentieth century, with a focus on LSF's assimilation of the postcolonial state to the paradigm of "totalitarianism." Malhuret, a medical doctor who would soon become the Secretary of State for Human Rights in Jacques Chirac's right-wing government, explained that LSF was created "to condemn the effects that totalitarianism and the ideology of Third Worldism had on populations."[6] Its introductory materials depicted Mao's China, Ho Chi Minh's Vietnam, Julius Nyerere's Tanzania, Kwame Nkrumah's Ghana, Fidel Castro's Cuba, and the Nicaraguan Sandinistas as a succession of catastrophes that are presented as models to be emulated.[7]

A central aspect of LSF's challenge to "totalitarianism" was a campaign against structuralist accounts of global economic inequality, which its leaders argued had served to divert attention from the "disastrous strategies of local governments."[8] Its introductory material condemned attempts to explain under-development as a consequence of the "pillage of the Third World by the West," and accused those who defended such of complicity with genocidal states.[9] The invitation to its first colloquium stressed the need to challenge the "simple notions" promoted by Third Worldism: that terms of trade between rich and poor countries had deteriorated, that "multinational corporations engage in evil actions," and that a "New International Economic Order" was the only solution to underdevelopment.[10] It was necessary, the invitation stressed, to

---

[3] Malhuret, "Invitation," 24; Michel Foucault, *The Birth of Biopolitics: Lectures at the Collège de France, 1978–1979*, ed. Michel Senellart (New York: Palgrave Macmillan, 2008), 187.

[4] Foucault, *Birth of Biopolitics*, 185.   [5] Ibid., 191.

[6] Binet Laurence, *Famine and Forced Relocations in Ethiopia 1984–1986* (n.p.: Speaking Out Case Studies, MSF, 2013), accessed January 12, 2020, http://speakingout.msf.org/en/famine-and-forced-relocations-in-ethiopia, 88.

[7] Liberté sans Frontières, "Fondation Liberté sans Frontières pour l'information sur les droits de l'homme et le développement," document de présentation, Janvier 1985," in "Liberté sans Frontières – information on human rights and development," introductory materials, January 1985 (n.p.: Speaking Out Case Studies, MSF, 2013), http://speakingout.msf.org/en/node/176

[8] Ibid.   [9] Ibid., 3.

[10] Malhuret, "Invitation," 24. I consider LSF's campaign against the NIEO in more detail in Jessica Whyte, "Powerless Companions or Fellow Travellers? Human Rights and the Neoliberal Assault on Post-Colonial Economic Justice," *Radical Philosophy* 2, no. 02

reconsider the problem of economic development "unencumbered by ideological presuppositions."[11]

Existing scholarship on French humanitarianism has largely followed the actors themselves in depicting this campaign against Third Worldism as a turn away from ideology. In an astute historical account of the politics of *sans-frontièrism*, Eleanor Davey, for instance, situates the founding of LSF in the context of "a paradigm shift from political ideology to human rights" in the 1980s,[12] and depicts it as developing the themes of suffering, responsibility, and voluntarism "in a framework independent of ideological considerations."[13] Timothy Nunan portrays the MSF leadership as "skeptical of ideology," and Peter Redfield suggests their experience working with Cambodian refugees led them to "break with ideology and re-focus on human suffering."[14] Such accounts provide valuable insights into the self-image of humanitarians of the period, but, to the extent they tend to mirror the accounts of the central actors, they do not interrogate the distinctive political and ideological convictions that motivated them, in the context of what Renée Fox notes were "major ideological shifts in Paris" in the early 1980s.[15]

LSF's discourse, as the left-wing journalist Alain Gresh argued in *Le Monde Diplomatique* at the time, was deeply imbued with the "ideology" it disparaged. Gresh noted that the only countries and movements denounced in its introductory materials were those which identified as left-wing or progressive – there was no criticism of apartheid South Africa,

---

(2018), www.radicalphilosophy.com/article/powerless-companions-or-fellow-travellers. For a fuller account, see Jessica Whyte, *The Morals of the Market: Human Rights and the Rise of Neoliberalism* (London: Verso, 2019).

[11] Malhuret, "Invitation," 24.

[12] Eleanor Davey, "Famine, Aid, and Ideology: The Political Activism of *Médecins sans Frontières* in the 1980s," *French Historical Studies* 34, no. 3 (2011): 532.

[13] Eleanor Davey, "French Adventures in Solidarity: Revolutionary Tourists and Radical Humanitarians," *European Review of History: Revue européenne d'histoire* 21, no. 4 (2014): 589. In her 2015 book, Davey nuances this claim, writing that *sans frontièrisme* reformulated aspects of *tiers mondisme* "in a framework independent of *classic* ideological considerations" (my emphasis) (*Idealism Beyond Borders: The French Revolutionary Left and the Rise of Humanitarianism, 1954–1988* (Cambridge, UK: Cambridge University Press, 2015), 178).

[14] Timothy Nunan, *Humanitarian Invasion Global Development in Cold War Afghanistan* (Cambridge, UK: Cambridge University Press, 2016), 134; Peter Redfield, *Life in Crisis: The Ethical Journey of Doctors without Borders* (Berkeley: University of California Press, 2013), 59.

[15] Renee C. Fox, *Doctors without Borders: Humanitarian Quests, Impossible Dreams of Médecins sans Frontières* (Baltimore, MD: Johns Hopkins University Press, 2015), 51. Christofferson suggest that this is true of much of the scholarship on anti-totalitarianism, which tends simply to "recast into academic prose the consciousness of the anti-totalitarian moment itself" (Michael Scott Christofferson, *French Intellectuals against the Left: The Antitotalitarian Moment of the 1970s* (New York: Berghahn Books, 2004), 2).

or of Israel's occupation of Palestinian territories, and no mention of the repression carried out by US-backed regimes in Turkey or Indonesia, or of the right-wing dictatorial regimes that were then ruling over much of Latin America. Far from being pragmatically neutral, Gresh charged LSF with espousing a pro-American, Reaganite ideology.[16] A glance at the members of the LSF board suggests that the foundation was hardly as free from ideological presuppositions as its leaders claimed: LSF's Director Rony Brauman, a former member of the "ultra-Third Worldist" Maoist Gauche Prolétarienne, recalls that its members were largely "heirs of Aron" – figures of the "liberal conservative right" in the lineage of the French liberal philosopher Raymond Aron.[17]

LSF's board included several associates of the anti-communist Comité des intellectuels pour l'Europe des libertés (CIEL), whose public position was that while "all infringements of human rights are odious" the most menacing are Soviet totalitarian violations.[18] The board also included members of the Reaganite anti-communist organization Resistance International, among them François Furet, the influential historian of the French revolution who had devoted much of his career to challenging the "revolutionary catechism," Jacques Broyelle, a former Maoist who had broken dramatically with both communism and Third Worldism, and Alain Besançon, an anti-communist historian of the Soviet Union.[19] Brauman recalls that when he and Malhuret first approached the latter about joining LSF's board, Besançon outlined five conditions: the foundation must be "pro-European, pro-American, anti-communist, anti-Soviet and pro-Israeli," he stipulated.[20] "We said fine, it's perfect," Brauman recalls. "This is what we think."[21] The attacks on communism and the "ideology" of the left also piqued the interest of sections of the French far right.[22] The Catholic newspaper *Présent*, then run by former Action Française member Jean Madiran, praised LSF for enabling anti-communist themes to migrate beyond the right.[23]

---

[16] Alain Gresh, "Une fondation au-dessus de tout soupçon," May 1, 1985, accessed March 6, 2015, www.monde-diplomatique.fr/1985/05/GRESH/38576

[17] The description comes from MSF's Rony Brauman, Grelet, and Potte-Bonneville, "'qu'est-ce qu'on fait là?"

[18] Christofferson, *French Intellectuals*, 272. CIEL members on the LSF board included the liberal intellectual and editor of *Commentary* journal Jean-Claude Casanova, and the Atlanticist journalist Jean-François Revel, who is best known for his writings on totalitarianism and his extravagant praise for the United States.

[19] Gresh "Une fondation," n.p.

[20] Jessica Whyte, interview with Rony Brauman, MSF Office, Rue Saint-Sabin, Paris, October 7, 2015, transcript on file with author.

[21] Ibid. Brauman describes the last of these conditions as "the fifth, but not the last, not the least!"

[22] Davey, "Famine, Aid and Ideology," 543.   [23] Ibid.

In this chapter, I argue that, far from being free of ideology, LSF should be placed in the intellectual context of the twentieth-century development of neoliberal ideas. I show that central aspects of the LSF discourse, particularly the association of state planning with totalitarianism, had been developed by neoliberal thinkers in books stretching back to the 1940s and had become central planks of neoliberal ideology by the 1980s.[24] In contrast to LSF's leaders, the neoliberals made no pretense of being without ideology. Indeed, in 1973, Friedrich Hayek – the prominent Austrian economist who founded the neoliberal Mont Pèlerin Society (MPS) – rejected what he termed the "fashionable contempt for 'ideology'" which he depicted as a "characteristic attitude of disillusioned socialists."[25] Having abandoned their own ideologies, he argued, they have concluded that "all ideologies must be erroneous and that in order to be rational one must do without one."[26] LSF took up an ideological critique of Third Worldism and the developmental state that had been developed over the course of the previous decades by figures like Hayek and his colleague Peter Bauer, the most prominent neoliberal development theorist. Bauer, who was described by *The Economist* as being to foreign aid what Friedrich Hayek was to socialism, spoke at the inaugural LSF colloquium, where he found a sympathetic audience for his critiques of Third Worldism, the politicization of economic relations, and foreign aid.[27]

Although existing literature has noted the confluence of the rise of *sans-frontièrism* and "the promotion of neoliberal interventionism," this confluence has not been subject to any critical interrogation.[28] This chapter provides the first account of the relation between French humanitarianism and neoliberalism in the late twentieth century. I argue that LSF mobilized an account of totalitarianism developed by the Mont Pèlerin neoliberals, according to which state intervention into the market ultimately led down what Hayek infamously termed the "road to serfdom."[29] This neoliberal totalitarian theory went beyond merely criticizing the denial of political rights and the abuse of civil liberties in the Third World, to valorize liberal markets as spheres of freedom and reject all forms of collectivism, state welfarism, and social and economic

---

[24] For an early instance, see Ludwig von Mises's 1944 work, *Omnipotent Government: The Rise of the Total State & Total War* (Auburn: Ludwig von Mises Institute, 2010). [25] Friedrich A. Hayek, *Law, Legislation and Liberty: A New Statement of the Liberal Principles of Justice and Political Economy*, 3 vols. (London: Routledge, 1982), 1: 57. [26] Ibid.   [27] *The Economist*, "A Voice for the Poor," May 2, 2002. [28] See Davey, *Idealism Beyond Borders* 253. [29] Friedrich Hayek, *The Road to Serfdom*, 50th ed. (Chicago: University of Chicago Press, 1994).

rights. In this same vein, LSF's human rights discourse focused attention on abuses of civil and political rights in left-wing regimes, ignoring right-wing regimes and downgrading social and economic rights. More significantly, the humanitarians explicitly campaigned for liberal economic policies and depicted Third Worldist demands for economic redistribution as totalitarian. Foucault was right to note the popularity of neoliberal ideas in France in the late 1970s. Yet what he depicted as "state-phobia," I suggest, is better viewed as a "phobia" of the assertion of postcolonial independence, and the Third Worldist demand for an equitable postcolonial economic order.

Third Worldism in Question: Human Rights and the "End of Ideology"

The inaugural LSF colloquium, "Le tiers-mondisme en question" ("Third Worldism in Question"), was held in January of 1985 in the voluptuous surrounds of the Palais de Luxembourg.[30] The colloquium, Brauman reflects, "was an incredible success, people were flocking and we had to refuse a number of participants."[31] One of its key speeches "Tiers-monde, culpabilité, haine de soi" ("Third World, Guilt, Self-Hate") was delivered by Pascal Bruckner, the French essayist and 'new philosopher' who today is best known for his vehement attacks on multiculturalism and Islam. At the time of the LSF colloquium, Bruckner had recently published his "text-book of anti-third worldism"[32] – *Le sanglot de l'homme blanc* (*Tears of the White Man*).[33] Many of the speakers at the colloquium were themselves former Marxists and Third Worldists who had become strong critics of Marxism and Third World regimes. The Orientalist Gérard Chaliand, author of *The Palestinian Resistance* (1972) and *Revolution in the Third World* (1977), summed up the mood, in his paper "The End of Revolutionary Myths."[34] Other former gauchist participants included the historian Ilios Yannakakis, a former member of the Greek Communist Party, the former Maoist Jacques Broyelle, and Cornelius Castoriadis, whose early criticisms of the Soviet Union had

---

[30] This section draws on material in Whyte, *Morals of the Market*.

[31] Whyte, interview with Rony Brauman (October 7, 2015).

[32] Kristin Ross, *May '68 and Its Afterlives* (Chicago: University of Chicago Press, 2002), 162.

[33] The LSF introductory material describes the purpose of the major colloquium as being to "celebrate" the publication of a number of books critical of Third Worldism, including Bruckner's *The Tears of the White Man* (17).

[34] Gérard Chaliand, "La fin des mythes révolutionnaires," in *Le tiers-mondisme en question*, ed. Rony Brauman (Paris: Olivier Orban, 1986), 65–70.

ultimately led him away from Marxism altogether, and Jacques Revel, who had long ago made the transition to the French right.[35]

A central theme of the colloquium was the need for a shift from political ideology to human rights.[36] The influence of Marxism on the French left, as the anti-totalitarian political philosopher Claude Lefort had noted five years earlier, had generated a "vehement, ironic or 'scientific' condemnation of the bourgeois notion of human rights."[37] LSF's account of human rights was not ideologically neutral. The French humanitarians positioned themselves in opposition to both Marxist critiques of the formalism of rights and anti-colonial affirmations of self-determination as the foundational human right.[38] This shift of priorities was reflected in the composition of the colloquium: while Third Worldism has stressed the political agency of national liberation movements, no nationals of the countries under discussion spoke at the colloquium.[39]

In this respect, it emblematized what Kristin Ross suggests is a key legacy of French opposition to Third Worldism: the transformation of the "colonial or third-world other" from militant and articulate fighter and thinker to passive object of sympathy.[40] LSF directly rejected the position articulated most forcefully by Frantz Fanon, who argued against gratitude in the face of European aid, which he construed as reparations for colonialism: "Nor will we acquiesce in the help for underdeveloped countries being a program of 'sisters of charity,'" he warned.[41] LSF contested what Brauman criticized as the "smokescreen" that blames all the Third World's problems on colonialism and the West, and he outlined a series of "dusty myths and archaic conformisms" that LSF aimed to dispel – among them that Europe's luxury presupposes colonial pillage, that multinationals are totalitarian, and that a neocolonial world economic system makes the rich richer and the poor poorer.[42] LSF's mission, Brauman explained elsewhere, is "to challenge a perception of the problem in which their poverty is a reflection of our wealth, and our

---

[35] These papers are published in a volume of proceedings edited by Rony Brauman which also includes papers by Bauer, Brucker, Jacques Marseill, Jacques Giri, Gilbert Etienne, Michel Fouquin.

[36] Davey, "Famine, Aid, and Ideology," 543.

[37] Claude Lefort, "Politics and Human Rights," in Claude Lefort, *The Political Forms of Modern Society* (Cambridge: Polity, 1986), 900.

[38] See Roland Burke, *Decolonization and the Evolution of International Human Rights* (Philadelphia: University of Pennsylvania Press, 2010), 35; Joseph R. Slaughter, *Human Rights, Inc.: The World Novel, Narrative Form, and International Law* (New York: Fordham University Press, 2007).

[39] Davey, "Famine, Aid, and Ideology," 542.   [40] Ross, *May 1968*, 167.

[41] Frantz Fanon, *The Wretched of the Earth* (London: Penguin, 1978), 81.

[42] Rony Brauman, "Ni tiers-mondisme, ni Cartiérisme," in *Le Tiers-Mondise en Question*, Brauman, ed., 13–14.

liberties are based on the absence of theirs."[43] Through this attack on
structuralist accounts of postcolonial inequality, the Third World was
reconceived as a location for humanitarian benevolence and a screen on
which deeply hierarchical relations of sentimentality and rescue could be
performed.[44]

At the time, Brauman situated the foundation's "ideology of *droits de
l'homme*" in the context of the demise of political messianism and within
a new morality of urgency for which "man" becomes the ultimate end.[45]
This moralized human rights discourse, expressed in the claim to be
concerned with "man" and "human realities" rather than messianic,
utopian ideologies, was shared by much of the human rights movement
of the time.[46] Yet, LSF's human rights campaign differed from the moral
"anti-politics" of human rights epitomized by Amnesty International.
While the latter NGO shared both LSF's antipathy to the state and its
focus on civil and political rights, it nonetheless attempted to avoid Cold
War polarization by focusing on the "suffering simply because they are
suffering."[47] While Amnesty International adopted "prisoners of conscience" on either side of the Iron Curtain, and criticized both left and
right-wing regimes, LSF fiercely rejected such even-handedness; instead,
its leadership explicitly joined the Cold War fray, prosecuting an argument for the superiority of liberalism and campaigning against both
neutralism and pacificism, which its introductory materials depicted as
attempts to "disarm the democracies and prevent them from defending
themselves."[48]

Just as they rejected neutrality, participants at the LSF colloquium
stressed that not all human rights were created equal. Brauman turned to
the history of French political thought to distinguish LSF's liberal conception of rights from a vision that presupposed a robust account of
popular sovereignty. He rejected what he termed the "maximalist conception inherited from Rousseau," for making democracy a means to the
common good and the state the guarantor of collective welfare.[49]
Instead, he upheld a model of rights premised on the erasure of status

[43] Cited in Claude Julien, "Une bête à abattre: Le 'tiers-mondisme,'" *Le Monde
Diplomatique*, May 1, 1985, www.monde-diplomatique.fr/1985/05/JULIEN/12268
[44] For an insightful account of this shift from political agent to object of humanitarian
moralism, see Miriam Ticktin, *Casualties of Care: Immigration and the Politics of
Humanitarianism in France* (Berkeley: University of California Press, 2011), 20.
[45] Brauman, "'Ni tiers-mondisme," 12.
[46] Samuel Moyn, *The Last Utopia: Human Rights in History* (Cambridge, MA: Belknap
Press of Harvard University Press, 2010).
[47] Tom Buchanan, "'The Truth Will Set You Free': The Making of Amnesty
International," *Journal of Contemporary History* 37, no. 4 (2002): 579.
[48] Malhuret, "Invitation."   [49] Brauman, "Ni tiers-mondisme," 13.

divisions, which he attributed to the nineteenth-century liberal Alexis de Tocqueville. By contrasting Rousseau and Tocqueville, Brauman situated LSF's conception of human rights on one side of a debate that pitted the affirmation of the will of the people, which had informed national liberation movements, against a deep, aristocratic–liberal suspicion of "the masses," and support for France's colonial mission.[50] This contrast enabled Brauman to uphold a narrow, nonrevolutionary, conception of human rights, defined by civil and political rights and equality before the law, against a conception of rights as expressions of popular sovereignty, and against a role for the state in guaranteeing social welfare.

Participants at the LSF colloquium depicted civil and political rights as "categorical imperatives," while making clear that social and economic rights were "less fundamental, universal, and timelessly important."[51] This distinction was borrowed from Aron, whose influence on the men who established LSF was such that the foundation came close to being named the Fondation Raymond Aron pour le Tiers Monde.[52] Malhuret also placed the foundation in a liberal tradition stretching from Tocqueville to Aron. "We were Aronian," he reflected decades later, "which means Tocquevillian and Aronian."[53] The figure Allan Bloom called "the last of the liberals" was a distinctly French liberal, but he was also an Atlanticist who played an important role in trans-Atlantic and European liberal networks.[54] He was present at the 1938 "Walter Lippman Colloquium" when the term "neoliberalism" was coined and, just

---

[50] On Tocqueville, see Alan S. Kahan, *Aristocratic Liberalism: The Social and Political Thought of Jacob Burckhardt, John Stuart Mill, and Alexis De Tocqueville* (New Brunswick, NJ: Transaction, 1992). Tocqueville's account, in an 1840 letter, of the need for the "total domination" of Algeria was consistent with his broader support for French colonialism. See Jennifer Pitts, *A Turn to Empire: The Rise of Imperial Liberalism in Britain and France* (Princeton, NJ: Princeton University Press, 2005), 205. For incisive accounts of Rousseau and the will of the people, and Fanon's anti-colonial account of the will, see Peter Hallward, "The Will of the People," *Radical Philosophy* May–June 2009 (May 16, 2011), accessed May 16, 2016, www.radicalphilosophy.com/article/the-will-of-the-people; Peter Hallward, "Fanon and Political Will," *Cosmos and History: The Journal of Natural and Social Philosophy* 7, no. 1 (October 13, 2011), accessed May 16, 2016, http://cosmosandhistory.org/index.php/journal/article/view/244/338

[51] Fox, *Doctors without Borders*, 54.

[52] See Davey, "Famine, Aid and Ideology," 543. Aron, in turn, was drawing on Kant's account of the categorical imperative as the supreme moral principle. Immanuel Kant, *Kant: Groundwork of the Metaphysics of Morals* (Cambridge, UK: Cambridge University Press, 1998).

[53] Jessica Whyte, interview with Claude Malhuret, Sénat – Palais du Luxembourg, Paris, October 7, 2015, transcript on file with author.

[54] On Aron's relationship to Hayek and his membership of the MPS, see Nicholas Gane, "In and Out of Neoliberalism: Reconsidering the Sociology of Raymond Aron," *Journal of Classical Sociology* 16, no. 3 (2016).

under a decade later, he participated in the founding meeting of Hayek's MPS, which has famously been described as the "neoliberal thought collective."[55]

Aron and Hayek were friends, and despite their differences over the possibility of a "third way" between the free market and economic planning, which ultimately led to Aron's resignation from the MPS in 1955, the two had strikingly similar views about human rights.[56] Both men criticized the drafters of the Universal Declaration of Human Rights (UDHR) for having "confused incompatible ideas," in Aron's words, by failing to distinguish *rights*, which constrained the state in the interests of individual freedom, from social and economic objectives that relied on the extension of state power.[57] In terms that were later taken up by participants at the LSF colloquium, Aron sought to distinguish between civil and political rights, which he depicted as what Immanuel Kant had termed "categorical imperatives," or fundamental moral principles, and social objectives that may be "theoretically desirable" but do not amount to rights.[58] In his own critique of the UDHR, originally published in 1966, Hayek described the declaration as an incoherent attempt to "fuse the rights of the Western liberal tradition with the altogether different conception deriving from the Marxist Russian Revolution."[59] To speak of rights in a socioeconomic context "debases the word 'right,'" Hayek argued, and therefore threatens the fundamental basis of a free society.[60] When compared to the 1789 Declaration of the Rights of Man and Citizen, Aron argued, the UDHR reflected "the decline of all rights, of the very notion of the rights of man."[61] The eighteenth-century authors "did not entrust the state the goal of promoting what we today call 'social and economic rights,'" Aron wrote. Rather, their concern was with *limiting* state power. In contrast, the twentieth century drafters downgraded the right to private property and expanded the powers of the state to provide for the welfare of its population. In this transition, he argued, the "state is the victor," since rights no longer restrict or condemn it.[62]

---

[55] Philip Mirowski and Dieter Plehwe, eds., *The Road from Mont Pèlerin: The Making of the Neoliberal Thought Collective* (Cambridge, MA: Harvard University Press, 2009).

[56] Gane, "In and out of Neoliberalism."

[57] Raymond Aron, "Sociology and the Philosophy of Human Rights," in *Power, Modernity, and Sociology: Selected Sociological Writings*, ed. Dominique Schnapper, trans. Peter Morris (Aldershot, UK: Edward Elgar, 1988), 123.

[58] Ibid., 122.

[59] Friedrich Hayek, "Justice and Individual Rights," in *Law, Legislation and Liberty*, 103; Aron, "Sociology," 123.

[60] Hayek, "Justice and Individual Rights," 106.   [61] Aron, "Sociology," 129.

[62] Ibid., 136.

Looking back, Brauman reflected that this distinction between "the categorical imperative, like not to torture people and free speech" and "wishable social objectives," such as social security, which required a certain level of economic development, was "at the core of Liberté sans Frontières."[63] The foundation focused on violations of civil and political rights, and warned that state mobilization necessary for social and economic welfare in former colonies would threaten economic and political freedom. This position was shared by Aron and Hayek and, of the two men, it was again Hayek who put the case in the more alarmist terms: the very attempt to realize social and economic rights would only be possible, he wrote, if "the whole of society were converted into a single organization, that is, made totalitarian in the fullest sense of the word."[64] Aron did not share Hayek's contention that wealthy democracies would set forth along the "road to serfdom" if they attempted to provide for material welfare, but he worried that "under-developed countries" could not "make the passage from the formal to the material without recourse to violence."[65]

This theme played a central role in discussions at the fourth meeting of the MPS in Beauvallon, France in 1951, which Aron attended, when "Liberalism and the Underdeveloped Countries" first made it onto the society's agenda.[66] By the 1957 meeting in St. Moritz, which took place two years after the Bandung Conference, the rise of Third Worldism had elevated the topic of development up the MPS agenda.[67] The Third Worldist stress on the revolutionary aspirations of the colonized, utopian egalitarianism and a centralized developmental state significantly challenged neoliberal perspectives.[68] The neoliberal counterattack was consolidated in St. Moritz, where Edmond Giscard d'Estaing, Peter Bauer, Alexander Rüstow, Karl Brandt, and Arthur Shenfield spoke on a panel devoted to "Liberalism and Colonialism."[69] The central themes of the panelists included a rejection of Western guilt over colonialism, an argument that private property is central to freedom and human dignity,

[63] Whyte, interview with Rony Brauman (October 7, 2015). Brauman stressed that he no longer subscribed to this view.

[64] Hayek, "Justice and Individual Rights," 104.   [65] Aron, "Sociology," 136.

[66] MPS (1947–), Inventory of the General Meeting Files (1947–1998) (Ghent: Liberaal Archief, 2005), www.liberaalarchief.be/MPS2005.pdf. Aron's own paper, "Du préjugé favorable à l'égard de l'Union Soviétique" was delivered in a session devoted to "The Source of the Pro-Soviet Bias Outside Russia."

[67] Dieter Plehwe, "The Origins of the Neoliberal Economic Development Discourse," in The Road from Mont Pèlerin: The Making of the Neoliberal Thought Collective, ed. Philip Mirowski and Dieter Plehwe (Cambridge, MA: Harvard University Press, 2009), 254.

[68] Ibid., 253.   [69] Mont Pèlerin Society, Inventory, 31.

and an account of the dangers of anti-colonial violence.[70] The Stanford economist Karl Brandt told the conference that the key problem was ensuring that anti-colonial nationalism did not result in a "loss of individual liberty, society's respect for human dignity, government by law, and due process and justice."[71] Giscard d'Estaing – the father of France's President Valéry Giscard d'Estaing and the head of a company that oversaw economic transactions with the French colonies – argued that the slogan of "liberation from colonialism" was licensing an "explosion of xenophobia" and "primitive hatred" and disrupting the work of global integration.[72] Against the backdrop of the Algerian War, Shenfield warned of the aggressiveness of anti-colonialism and depicted recently decolonized societies as rife with "the crudest notions of economic nationalism and *etatisme*," which manifested in tariffs, price controls, subsidies, the fostering of trade unions, and general disrespect for the "rights of capital."[73] Increasingly, the Mont Pèlerin discourse came to focus on the dangers of totalitarianism in the Third World, and to define totalitarianism as a phenomenon of political interference in the market order.[74]

Almost three decades later, these themes had left the confines of neoliberal ideological clarification, and were mobilized in the polemics at the LSF colloquium. Speakers at the colloquium, including Peter Bauer, rejected the contention that Third World poverty was a problem of capitalist and neocolonialist exploitation, and condemned the Third Worldist support for state-led developmentalism.[75] As Brauman reflected, participants stressed that "the ravages of authoritarian planning were greater than those of capitalism" and that "liberal, free enterprise societies were the most efficacious in preventing political and economic catastrophe."[76] They did not confine themselves to defending civil and political rights. Rather, they pointed to the violence in the Third World as evidence of the bloody consequences of prioritizing social and

---

[70] Plewhe, "Origins"; Arthur Shenfield, "Liberalism and Colonialism," *Foreign Policy Perspectives* no. 4 (1986), accessed November 3, 2016, www.libertarian.co.uk/lapubs/forep/forep004.pdf, originally presented at the 1957 MPS meeting.

[71] Karl Brandt, "Liberal Alternatives in Western Policies toward Colonial Areas" (8th MPS meeting, St. Moritz: Hoover Institution Archives, 1957), 1–13 Box 11, Folder 3.

[72] Edmond Giscard d'Estaing, "Libéralisme et Colonialisme" (8th MPS meeting, St. Moritz: Hoover Institution Archives, 1957), 1, Box 12, Folder 18. D'Estaing was president of the Société Financière Française et Coloniale.

[73] Shenfield, "Liberalism and Colonialism," 3.

[74] I discuss this further in Jessica Whyte, "Powerless Companions or Fellow Travellers? Human Rights and the Neoliberal Assault on Post-Colonial Economic Justice," *Radical Philosophy* 2, no. 02 (2018), www.radicalphilosophy.com/article/powerless-companions-or-fellow-travellers

[75] Fox, *Doctors without Borders*, 53.   [76] Brauman, ibid.

economic rights over civil and political rights.[77] In terms that resembled Hayek's arguments more closely than they did Aron's more temperate criticisms, the privileging of social and economic rights was depicted as leading to genocide.[78]

Totalitarianism in Ethiopia?

It was against this background that Pascal Bruckner gave Rony Brauman a copy of Hannah Arendt's *Eichmann in Jerusalem* as the MSF chief headed to Ethiopia. "Through Arendt," Brauman reflected later, "I discovered the hard problem of totalitarianism. I identified the Ethiopian regime with Nazi totalitarianism, and myself somewhere in between the Jewish councils and Eichmann."[79] The trajectory of French *sans frontièrisme* was deeply enmeshed with the shifting politics of Holocaust memory.[80] Although the legacy of the occupation had long provided the French far left with its central motifs, Davey notes that the 1970s saw a shift from a focus on the French resistance to a newer privileging of the figure of the victim. While the former had legitimized violence, including anti-colonial violence, the latter generated a deep ambivalence about the use of political violence as a means to an end. With the rise of Holocaust memory and human rights, Nazi atrocities, became the lens through which postcolonial violence was viewed. Yet, as Moyn has astutely noted, what may have been most significant was "the coincidence of that memory with the widespread perception, spoken loudly or kept close to the vest, that decolonization had gone dreadfully wrong."[81] This was doubtless true for the French humanitarians, and leading LSF figures drew on the history of World War II in order to denounce the politics of Third Worldism. If there was a key trope that structured the LSF discourse it was neither resistance nor the victim but the collaborator: increasingly, what a previous generation had viewed as anti-imperialist solidarity with the Third World came to be viewed through the lens of Vichy.

---

[77] Fox, *Doctors without Borders*, 54.

[78] Fox notes that participants construed the genocide in Cambodia as an outcome of the "basic disregard for human rights" and the tendency to prioritize social and economic rights (ibid.).

[79] Brauman, cited in Eyal Weizman, *The Least of All Possible Evils: Humanitarian Violence from Arendt to Gaza* (London: Verso, 2012), 29.

[80] On French *sans frontièrisme* and the legacy of the Holocaust, see Davey, *Idealism beyond Borders*; Michal Givoni, "Holocaust Memories and Cosmopolitan Practices," in *Marking Evil: Holocaust Memory in the Global Age*, ed. Amos Goldberg and Haim Hazan (New York: Berghahn, 2015).

[81] Samuel Moyn, "The Intersection with Holocaust Memory," in *Human Rights and the Uses of History* (London: Verso, 2014), 95.

Nowhere was this more true than in Ethiopia. The question of LSF is deeply bound up with the politics of the Ethiopian famine, which is estimated to have killed at least 400,000 people between 1983 and 1985.[82] Ethiopia at the time was ruled by the Soviet-backed Colonel Mengistu Haile Mariam, whose Ethiopian Workers' Party was formed in August 1984, during the celebrations marking the ten year anniversary of the revolution that brought him to power. MSF soon found itself in the midst of a conflict over the Ethiopian government's resettlement and agricultural collectivization program, based on East German and Cuban designs for collective "farm-clusters," which Mengistu described as "exemplary work in which people struggled against nature and emerged victorious under the leadership of communists for the first time in Africa."[83] Although the program was presented as a way to move volunteers to more fertile lands in the south and west, it was violently enforced, and members of MSF France criticized it as motivated by a flawed ideology and the demands of counterinsurgency.[84] The transfers, they argued (accurately as we will see) were designed to weaken the support base of the secessionists in the north.

In 1985, after repeated threats to leave the country and public criticisms of the resettlement program, MSF France was expelled from Ethiopia. The expulsion came in the wake of a report by the US-based group Cultural Survival, which estimated that between 50,000 and 100,000 people had died as a direct result of the resettlement program.[85] Brauman tells of his response to reading the report: "I said to myself, 'It's quite clear.' I began to think that this was equivalent to a Stalinist power."[86] In contrast to Arendt's suggestion that the term totalitarianism be used sparingly, Brauman and other leading figures in MSF France repeatedly compared Ethiopia to Stalin's Soviet Union, Pol Pot's Cambodia, and Nazi Germany. To refuse to speak out would make MSF complicit, Brauman warned. "You've got to look beneath the surface," he said. "It reminds me of the Jewish orchestras in the Nazi concentration camps that were supposed to make it appear that everything was fine."[87] In a newsletter distributed to the press and donors, Brauman justified MSF's decision to speak out by invoking the "incredible passivity of Europeans when confronted with the deportations" during World

---

[82] Alexander De Waal and Human Rights Watch, *Evil Days: Thirty Years of War and Famine in Ethiopia* (New York: Human Rights Watch, 1991), 5.

[83] Binet, *Famine and Forced Relocation*, 27.   [84] Ibid., 18.

[85] Laurence Binet, interview with Rony Brauman, president of Médecins sans Frontières: 'MSF Will Leave Ethiopia If . . .' La Croix (France), November 1, 1985, reproduced in Binet, *Famine and Forced Relocation*, 54.

[86] Binet, interview with Rony Brauman, 53.   [87] Ibid., 55.

War II.[88] At a press conference in 1985, he had a heated confrontation with the French ambassador to Ethiopia. "I called him a Pétainist," Brauman recounts. "I said: 'you would be a Pétainist under Pétain and a Gaullist under de Gaulle.'"[89] These analogies between Ethiopia and Nazi Germany were vigorously rejected by UN figures in Ethiopia at the time; the "attempt to liken this to the holocaust is just an absolute travesty of the truth," one UN emergency operations representative told the press.[90]

MSF France's position led to conflict with other NGOs and even with other national sections of its own organization. In December of 1985, forty NGOs issued a statement to contest MSF claims that they had compromised themselves by working with the Ethiopian government. The Christian Relief and Development Association issued its own statement which described the general resettlement policy as "a defensible policy in light of the chronic drought conditions in Northern Ethiopia" and questioned MSF's allegation that the policy was responsible for thousands of deaths: "it is impossible to prove or disprove this allegation, as many of the resettlers might have died of starvation or related diseases if they had stayed either in their own villages or in the relief camps," the statement read.[91] MSF's allegation that the resettlement program had resulted in 100,000 deaths was also rejected by the UN aid coordinator in Ethiopia: "There is no way to determine how many people actually died, because there is no data on which to work," he said. "It is impossible to come up with any figure."[92] Looking back, in 2016, Brauman reflected that what took place in Ethiopia was "a huge political lie which was bought by solidarity groups, humanitarians and development organizations," and that those who sold the lie were "pure liars, pure fellow travelers, cheaters without any reservation."[93]

Among the critics of MSF France was the Belgian section of MSF, which was deeply opposed to the formation of LSF. Georges Dallemagne, MSF Belgium's Director of Operations notes that the Belgian group was not entirely convinced of MSF's accusations against the Ethiopian government, which appeared as an attempt to score political

---

[88] Givoni, "Holocaust Memories and Cosmopolitan Practices," 135.
[89] Brauman, cited in Binet, *Famine and Forced Relocation*, 74.
[90] "Ethiopia Famine Toll Unknown, Says UN Expert," *Daily Telegraph*, February 3, 1986, 93.
[91] Christian Relief and Development Association, "CRDA Member's Statement on Resettlement (draft), 18 December 1985," November 7, 2013, accessed February 16, 2016, 92. http://speakingout.msf.org/en/node/244
[92] Cited in Binet, *Famine and Forced Relocation*, 99.
[93] Whyte, interview with Rony Brauman.

points for the new foundation, LSF.[94] "We thought Claude [Malhuret] was under the influence of the neo-liberals, very close to the American foundations who wanted to settle accounts with the communist regimes," MSF Belgium's Ethiopian Programme Manager recalled.[95] Reflecting on this relation between the Ethiopian situation and the founding of LSF, Dallemagne, noted: "at a given moment the problem of Ethiopia symbolized certain things that Liberté sans Frontières intended to condemn."[96] For LSF's leading figures, Ethiopia symbolized the totalitarianism of Third Worldism and the willingness of Third Worldists to collaborate with it. "Ethiopia was a totalitarian regime hiding behind a 'Third World' façade, so it was natural to condemn it," Malhuret told an interviewer at the time.[97]

There was nothing natural, however, about the assumption that Ethiopia symbolized the totalitarianism inherent in Third Worldism, or in the decision to portray it as an analogue of the genocidal violence of Nazi Germany or Cambodia. "Far from what has been asserted in some of the literature, the Dergue was not Ethiopia's Khmer Rouge," Edward Kissi stresses in his comparative study of Cambodia and Ethiopia.[98] The resettlement policy that LSF condemned took place in the late stages of a brutal counterinsurgency campaign waged by the Mengistu regime against its Tigrayan and Eritrean separatists opponents, primarily the Marxist–Leninist Tigrayan People's Liberation Front and the Eritrean People's Liberation Front. Rather than a genocidal regime on the model of the Nazis, the violence perpetuated by the Ethiopian regime belongs in

---

[94] Dallemagne, cited in Binet, *Famine and Forced Relocation*, 87.

[95] Pierre Harzé cited ibid., 87.

[96] Georges Dallemagne cited in Binet, *Famine and Forced Relocation*, 87.

[97] Malhuret, cited ibid., 88.

[98] In his book-length comparative study of Cambodia and Ethiopia, Edward Kissi rejects this analogy between the regimes of Pol Pot and Mengistu. Kissi argues that "while genocide took place in Cambodia, it did not in Ethiopia" and he attributes the deaths in Ethiopia to "state terrorism, civil war, and famine" (xx). In an earlier book chapter, Kissi argues that the regime's resettlement program "was not a tool of genocide" but a "counter-insurgency measure" ("Genocide in Cambodia and Ethiopia," in *The Specter of Genocide: Mass Murder in Historical Perspective*, ed. Robert Gellately and Ben Kiernan (Cambridge, UK: Cambridge University Press, 2003), 321). Kissi, "Revolution and Genocide," xx. Kissi argues that the analogy between the Derg and the Khmer Rouge, became the "orthodox view" after it "was first floated by the Wall St. Journal in January 1986" (xviii). As I have shown, these analogies were utilized by the figures associated with MSF France before this time. In December of 2006, after a twelve-year legal case, the Federal High Court found Mengistu guilty of genocide under the Ethiopian Penal Code, which includes "population transfer or dispersion" and acts designed to eliminate "political groups" under the designation of genocide. Firew Kebede Tiba, "The Mengistu Genocide Trial in Ethiopia Notes and Comments," *Journal of International Criminal Justice* 5 (2007): 513–28.

a tradition of counterinsurgency warfare that was developed to respond to anti-colonial struggles and communist guerrilla movements.

MSF France's contention that the relocations were motivated by counterinsurgency not famine relief was vindicated by Mengistu himself, who told a 1985 emergency meeting of Derg officials that resettlement was a necessary measure to isolate the rebels from the population. "The people are like the sea and the guerrillas are like fish swimming in that sea," he said, mobilizing a classic counterinsurgency trope. "Without the sea, there will be no more fish."[99] Yet, in suggesting that the brutality of the Mengistu regime exposed the truth of Third Worldist ideology, the LSF figures obscured the colonial precedents of population transfer, which was used extensively against anti-colonial movements by the various colonial powers; the British in Malaya practiced what British Director of Operations Sir Harold Briggs called "the closing of all breeding areas" by forcibly relocating some 600,000 people to "New Villages," and the Americans relied on the technique extensively in the Philippines.[100] It was the French, however, who quite literally wrote the book, or the books, that informed Mengistu's strategy.[101] The Ethiopian counterinsurgency was modelled on the principles developed by French generals in the period of classical imperialism, refined by General André Beaufre in the "social laboratory" of Algeria in the 1940s, and "perfected" by another French military man, David Galula, who volunteered for Algeria in 1956 in order to "test certain theories" about counterinsurgency.[102]

Counterinsurgency, this tradition argued, should focus on the population, using both violence and "humanitarian" aid to separate the people from the insurgents and ultimately win their support. Galula was stationed in China during the communist revolution, and took seriously

---

[99] Cited in Kissi, "Genocide in Cambodia and Ethiopia," 319.

[100] Patricia Owens provides a powerful critique of the "social" impetus of such counterinsurgency strategies in *Economy of Force: Counterinsurgency and the Historical Rise of the Social* (Cambridge, UK: Cambridge University Press, 2015).

[101] On the French counterinsurgency tradition, see Owens *Economy of Force*.

[102] David Galula, *Pacification in Algeria, 1956–1958* (Santa Monica, CA: RAND Corporation, 2006), 1. That the Ethiopian counterinsurgency was informed by this tradition is the conclusion drawn by Gebru Tareke on the basis of detailed research in the Ethiopian military archives. Tareke argues that the counterinsurgency strategy used by the Derg was "modelled on the 'total strategy,' first enunciated by the French general André Beaufre." Referring to the tradition of French, anti-colonial counterinsurgency that includes Beaufre and Galula, he writes, "It can fairly be assumed that Ethiopian strategists and tacticians were, to varying degrees, influenced by the above theoreticians" ("From Lash to Red Star: The Pitfalls of Counter-Insurgency in Ethiopia, 1980–82," *Journal of Modern African Studies* 40, no. 03 (September 2002): 466).

Mao Tse Tung's contention, in his 1938 writings on guerrilla war, that the people are the water in which the guerrillas swim.[103] This formula, Galula argued, is the "key to guerrilla warfare."[104] Galula expanded on this theme in a 1962 book written for the RAND Corporation about his experience in Algeria, which was republished in 2006 to inform US strategy in the Iraq War and incorporated into the most recent US *Counterinsurgency Field Manual*.[105] There, he recounts a story he told the French troops under his command in Algeria's Kabylia region, about a bet between Hitler, Mussolini, and Churchill about who would catch the most fish in a swimming pool:

> Hitler tried first using elaborate fishing equipment, but the fish would not bite. Mussolini dived into the pool, trying to catch the fish by hand; he was lifted from the water exhausted and half-drowned. Then Churchill sat quietly by the pool, lighted a cigar, and started emptying the pool with his teacup. "It will take time but I'll get the fish!" "This is how we will proceed here," I concluded.[106]

In Algeria, the French made extensive use of *"camps de regroupement"* to isolate anti-colonial fighters and pacify the population. The French sociologist Michel Cornaton, who wrote one of the earliest studies of the camps, has suggested that 2,350,000 people were forcibly resettled during the war. Like in Ethiopia, those resettled were subjected to starvation, epidemics, and violence.[107] While Galula framed resettlement as both complex and dangerous, he advocated it as a "last resort measure" where the counterinsurgency forces are relatively weak.[108] This must have appealed to Mengistu's regime, which had just faced a dispiriting defeat in its previous attempt to pacify the Eritrean insurgency during 1981's Operation Red Star.[109] The renewed attempt, launched in 1983 just prior to the dispute with MSF France, was "the last major offensive by an ever expanding but decreasingly effectual war machine," which, despite using the latest Soviet military technology, was ultimately defeated by its adversaries.[110]

[103] "'On Guerilla Warfare,'" *Problems of War and Strategy*, 1938, accessed February 16, 2016, www.marxists.org/reference/archive/mao/selected-works/volume-2/mswv2_12 .htm

[104] David Galula, *Counter-Insurgency Warfare: Theory and Practice* (New York: Frederick A. Praeger, 1964), 37.

[105] On Galula in Iraq, see Owens, *Economy of Force*, 243.

[106] Galula, *Pacification in Algeria*, 72.

[107] Cited in Fabian Klose, "'Sources of Embarrassment': Human Rights, States of Emergency and the Wars of Decolonization," in *Human Rights in the Twentieth Century*, ed. Stefan-Ludwig Hoffmann (Cambridge, UK: Cambridge University Press, 2010), 253

[108] Galula, *Counter-insurgency Warfare*, 81.   [109] Tareke, "From Lash to Red Star," 491.

[110] Ibid., 495.

If LSF had placed Mengistu's violence in the lineage of colonial and anti-communist counterinsurgencies, rather than that of the Nazis and Pol Pot, Ethiopia may have appeared as a very different symbol – one far less suited to bolstering its campaign against Third Worldism.[111] Anxious to be free of "colonial guilt" and to combat the influence of anti-colonialism in the aid sector, the last thing LSF's leaders wanted was to highlight the French colonial precedents of the Ethiopian regime's violence. Such a focus on the continuities with colonial violence may have suggested caution about French "humanitarian intervention" as the necessary response to the plights of former colonies. If Ethiopia was what Brauman later called "the perfect image of what we wanted to refer to," the depiction of it as an image of the totalitarianism of Third Worldism was selectively constructed to bolster preexisting ideological commitments.[112] The regime's use of Stalinist language and the support it received from the Soviet Union did suggest a parallel to Stalin's domination; yet only an interpretation of the Mengistu regime's counterinsurgency that detached it from its colonial precursors was capable of turning Ethiopia into a weapon to be used in the service of a campaign to recharacterize Third Worldism as totalitarian.

While Brauman attributes his discovery of the problem of totalitarianism to Arendt's work, by the time he left for Ethiopia, anti-totalitarianism was already pervasive among French intellectuals who were breaking with communism and with their previous anti-colonial commitments. As early as 1978, Jacques Julliard had launched the media polemic against *tiers mondisme* with an article that prophesied that in Africa, "there will be no socialism except a totalitarian socialism."[113] As critics noted at the time, the terms of this *anti-tiers mondist* condemnation of the postcolonial state replicated colonialist predictions about what would eventuate in the colonies if independence were achieved, depicting them as places of barbarism and oppression.[114]

Notably absent from these critiques of totalitarianism was the central insight of Arendt's *The Origins of Totalitarianism* which depicted

---

[111] This is not to deny certain continuities between European colonialism and National Socialism, nor to reject Arendt's suggestion that there were numerous "analogies and precedents" of, what she terms, the "intermediate stages" on the way to totalitarianism. It is to suggest, however, that the violence carried out by Mengistu's regime bore far greater similarity to colonial anti-insurgency than to Nazi genocide. See Arendt, *Origins of Totalitarianism*, 440.

[112] Whyte, interview with Rony Brauman.

[113] See Kristin Ross, *May'68*, 161. On this climate, see also Christofferson, *French Intellectuals*.

[114] Sitbon, cited in Ross, *May'68*, 161.

totalitarianism as a phenomenon of imperialism.[115] Not only did Arendt stress the connection between imperialism and totalitarianism, but, as early as the preface to the 1966 republication of her magnum opus, she wrote that even the "Soviet Union can no longer be called totalitarian in the strict sense of the term."[116] Arendt's *Origins* was not published in France until 1972, and it was not taken seriously in Paris until the 1980s, when its reception was bound up with "the full explosive impact of the thought of Alexander Solzhenitsyn and the East European dissidents."[117] Given this, its reception tended to ignore nuance and assimilate her insights to a simple rejection of communism.

In a 1966 preface to the "Imperialism" section of the *Origins of Totalitarianism*, Arendt argued that foreign aid is an instrument of domination that faces those who rely on it with "the alternative of accepting some form of 'government of subject races' or sinking rapidly into anarchic decay."[118] In resisting this choice, the Ethiopian government came into conflict with its increasingly vocal critics in MSF. "I will not accept your insistence on setting conditions," an Ethiopian official told Brauman. "You will be humanitarian if you do your job. You are not competent to comment on any other aspect of our program. We have different ways of doing things in Ethiopia. We cannot be dictated to."[119] In their growing assertiveness, and belief that the role of humanitarians was not just to treat the sick but to speak out and make political judgments, MSF broke

---

[115] It was Arendt and Aron who were the explicit sources for LSF's anti-totalitarian discourse, although LSF's focus on state planning brought it closer to the anti-totalitarianism of the Mont Pèlerin neoliberals. LSF figures did not tend to refer to the history of Catholic anti-totalitarianism, which cast totalitarianism as the pathological outcome of Enlightenment liberties. James Chappel, "The Catholic Origins of Totalitarianism Theory," *Modern Intellectual History* 8, no. 3 (November 2011), accessed August 12, 2016, http://journals.cambridge.org/abstract_S1479244311000357; on Arendt's influence on Brauman, see Weizman, *Least of All Possible Evils*.

[116] Arendt, "Preface to Part Three: Totalitarianism" (1966), *Origins of Totalitarianism*, xxxvi. Arendt's preface was published the same year that the Russian satirists Andrei Sinyavsky and Yuli Daniel faced trial for publishing "anti-Soviet" stories abroad. The trial was viewed by some as the end of Khrushchev's thaw, and the beginning of re-Stalinization, while the protests against the sentences have been depicted as "the birth of the Soviet human rights movement." Roland Burke and Barbara Keys, "Human Rights," in *The Oxford Handbook of the Cold War*, ed. Richard H. Immerman and Petra Goedde (n.p.: Oxford University Press, 2013).

[117] Long before this, in 1954, Raymond Aron had published a major review of Arendt's *Origins of Totalitarianism* in *Critique*. Daniel J. Mahoney, "Introduction: Aron on Arendt and *The Origins of Totalitarianism*," in Raymond Aron, *In Defense of Political Reason: Essays*, ed. Daniel J. Mahoney (Lanham, MD: Rowman & Littlefield, 1994), 95.

[118] Arendt, "Preface to Part Two: Imperialism" (1966), *Origins of Totalitarianism*, xxi.

[119] Blaine Harden, "Ethiopia Still in Need But No Longer Starving," *Washington Post Service for International Herald Tribune* (reproduced at http://speakingout.msf.org/en/node/230), November 30, 1985, 73.

with the commitment in its charter to refrain from "any interference in state's internal affairs." In doing so, it went beyond simply challenging human rights abuses or the instrumentalization of aid, to pit itself against the entire agenda of developmentalism, collectivism, and postcolonial state formation.[120]

When asked if MSF was conducting "a crusade against Ethiopia's Marxists," Brauman noted that a tight network of counterinfluences was developing in Ethiopia. "It can't stop Ethiopia's history from being forged under the fist of a party, which wants to strengthen the nation, establish a state, and organize its farmers," he said. "But, at least we can avoid an irreversible slide into generalized collectivization and barbarity."[121] In a 1966 preface to her *Origins*, Arendt warned that the West had developed its own "official 'counter-ideology,' anti-Communism" which leads to the construction of a fiction, "so that we refuse on principle," in her words, "to distinguish the various Communist one-party dictatorships with which we are confronted in reality, from authentic totalitarian government."[122] Ethiopia was critical in reinforcing the anti-communism and opposition to Third Worldism that motivated the formation of LSF, and it confirmed the inclination of its leading figures to "view Communism and *tiers-mondisme* as antitheses of MSF's democratic, anti-totalitarian, "humanitarian spirit."[123]

In the 1980s, Ethiopia's one-party dictatorship ruled precariously over a desperately poor country that was wracked by famine, was dependent on foreign aid and foreign NGOs to feed its population, was completely unable to control its borders, and faced violent insurgencies from separatist movements in significant parts of the country.[124] For all of its unquestionable brutality, the Ethiopian state lacked the capacity to wield total domination.[125] In mapping the narrative of the Holocaust directly onto Ethiopia, and in using this construct as a weapon in a broader assault on state-directed developmentalism, Brauman had less in common with Arendt than he did with the neoliberal thinkers of the

---

[120] Fabrice Weissman, "Silence Heals: From the Cold War to the War on Terror, MSF Speaks Out: A Brief History," in *Humanitarian Negotiations Revealed: The MSF Experience*, ed. Clare Magone and Michael Neuman (London: Hurst, 2012), 178.

[121] Pierre Haski, "Doubts Over French Aid to Ethiopia," *Libération*, republished in Binet, *Famine and Forced Relocations*, 106.

[122] Arendt, "Preface to Part Three: Totalitarianism," xxvii.

[123] Fox, *Doctors without Borders*, 56.

[124] Kissi notes that, unlike the Khmer Rouge, "the Dergue faced a formidable domestic political opposition. It had no total control over Ethiopian society or monopoly over the instruments of terror" (*Revolution and Genocide*, 317).

[125] Total domination was central to Arendt's account of totalitarianism in *Origins of Totalitarianism*.

1940s and the neoliberal ideologues in the Reagan administration of the 1980s. What Moyn depicts as the disturbing fact that "the confluence of human rights and Holocaust memory came about as welfarism in its national, North Atlantic first version and in its more expansive anticolonial version were abandoned," can be better understood if we place the anti-totalitarian defense of human rights in the context of neoliberal ideas of the period.[126] In the following section, I argue that LSF's antitotalitarianism needs to be situated in the context of the neoliberal attack on postcolonial welfarism.

Neoliberal Totalitarianism Theory: Nazism as Truth

In his 1979 lecture on "state phobia," Foucault argued that it is to the neoliberals of the 1930s and 1940s that we owe "the idea of Nazism we all have in our heads"; "the negative theology of the state as the absolute evil; the possibility of sweeping up events in the Soviet Union and the USA, concentration camps and social security records, into the same critique, and so on."[127] Foucault averred that a key neoliberal coup had been the characterization of Nazism as primarily a form of *anti-capitalism*, and its correlate – the identification of capitalism with individual liberty. As far back as 1939, Hayek had already warned that if current welfarist trends were not halted, "we may find that we have defeated National Socialism merely to create a world of many national socialisms."[128] Nazism as Foucault writes, was the "epistemological and political 'road to Damascus'" which enabled the neoliberals of the 1940s to define a field of adversaries and map the necessary trajectory of Keynesianism and state planning. National Socialism, Hayek argued in the 1940s, is "the ultimate and necessary outcome of a process of development in which the other nations have for a long time been steadily following Germany."[129] Hayek reflected that he was prompted to write *The Road to Serfdom* by the belief, prominent among British intellectuals, that "National Socialism was a capitalist reaction against socialism."[130] In contrast, Hayek defined the dominant feature of Nazism as "a fierce hatred of anything capitalistic," to which there was only one alternative: liberal capitalism.[131]

By the late 1970s, Hayek's attention had shifted beyond Europe. The same year Foucault gave his lectures on "state phobia," Hayek warned that the "strongest support of the trend toward socialism comes today

---

[126] Moyn, "Intersection with Holocaust Memory," 97.
[127] Michel Foucault, *The Birth of Biopolitics: Lectures at the Collège de France 1978–1979*, ed. Michel Senellart, trans. Graham Burchell (New York: Palgrave Macmillan, 2008), 116.
[128] Hayek, *Road to Serfdom*, 224.   [129] Hayek, *Road to Serfdom*.   [130] Ibid., 5.
[131] Ibid., 246.

from those who claim they want neither capitalism nor socialism but a "middle way" or a "third world."[132] To follow them, he argued, was a sure path to socialism, and "socialism, as much as fascism or communism inevitably leads into the totalitarian state."[133] Increasingly, the Third World vision of economic redistribution was viewed not only as economically suicidal but also as totalitarian. In assimilating collectivism, economic planning, and postcolonial demands for economic redistribution, to National Socialism, the French doctors drew on an account of totalitarianism developed by the neoliberal thinkers of the MPS.

While Foucault is right to notice that, by the late 1970s, those who embraced neoliberal themes were "following the direction of the wind," there was a more direct line of transmission from the neoliberals of Mont Pèlerin to the humanitarians of LSF.[134] It was Peter Bauer who developed these themes most explicitly in relation to the Third World and problems of development, and his work was an important influence on the French humanitarians.[135] "Bauer was for me extremely important," Malhuret acknowledged later, as it was in his books that it was possible to read that everything thinkers on the left were saying about economic development and redistribution was wrong.[136] In his speech at the LSF colloquium, Bauer synthesized the key themes of his critique of Third Worldist campaigns for postcolonial wealth transfers, arguing that reducing international differentials in income would require "a quasi-totalitarian power."[137] Bauer developed an account of totalitarianism whose key mechanism was what he disparagingly termed "politicization," by which he meant state intervention into the market. In work stretching back to the 1950s, Bauer had characterized such intervention as a threat to both productivity and freedom. He criticized the attempt to set minimum wage rates in the "under-developed world," for instance, for politicizing wages and driving them "above market equilibrium levels."[138] The contrast between the market as a realm of freedom (an "outcome of voluntary transactions") and politics as inherently coercive played a central role in Bauer's totalitarianism theory.[139] Totalitarianism,

---

[132] Hayek, *Law, Legislation and Liberty*, 151.   [133] Ibid., 151.

[134] Foucault, *Birth of Biopolitics*, 191.   [135] Whyte, interview with Claude Malhuret.

[136] Ibid., 1.

[137] Peter Bauer, "L'aide au développement: pour ou contre?," in Brauman, *Tiers-mondisme en question*, 189.

[138] P. T. Bauer and B. S. Yamey, *The Economics of Under-Developed Countries* (London: Nisbet [u.a.],1972), first published 1957, 78.

[139] Peter Bauer, "Hostility to the Market in Less Developed Countries," in *The First World & the Third World: Essays on the New International Economic Order*, ed. Karl Brunner (Rochester, NY: University of Rochester Center for Research in Government Policy and Business, Graduate School of Management, 1978), 169.

according to this distinctly neoliberal vision, was less a matter of the violation of political freedoms, than it was a phenomenon of egalitarianism, which promoted coercive interference in the market. Indeed, Bauer explicitly rejected any attempt to pursue "the unholy grail of economic equality" for interfering with the voluntary transactions that produce economic inequalities.[140]

While Bauer defended the economic record of colonial rule, he nonetheless held British colonialism responsible for the politicization of life in former colonies. At the end of the British empire, he argued, limited government was replaced by economic controls and "the ready-made framework of a *dirigiste* or even totalitarian state was handed over by the British to the incoming independent governments."[141] After independence, Western aid had served to further politicize economic questions and fostered strife and conflict. The beneficiaries of such politicization, Bauer argues, are Third World governments, which extend their control over all of economic life. The recipients of Western aid, he argued, are not "the pathetic creatures pictured in the publicity campaigns of the aid lobbies," but their governments, "who are all too often directly responsible for the gruesome conditions that we wish to alleviate."[142] The conditions in aid recipient countries, he argued, are a direct result of state intervention into the economy, in the form of "coercive collectivization," suppression of private trade, restriction of the inflow of capital, limits on foreign enterprises, and massive spending on prestige projects and industrialization. In his intervention at the LSF colloquium, Bauer singled out the "catastrophic conditions" in Ethiopia as a perfect illustration of the blindness of Western aid provision.[143] This aid, he argued, has been devoted not to assisting the poorest of the population, but to enabling military advancement. By the early 1980s, Bauer's arguments were beginning to displace those of the Third Worldists of the previous decade, and his account of totalitarianism was given new life by the LSF project.

Dictatorships and Double Standards

The humanitarians who founded LSF portrayed Third Worldism as a strong and dangerous adversary, and themselves as challenging the dominant myths of their time. Much later, Brauman conceded that if LSF was

---

[140] Peter Bauer, "The Grail of Equality," in *Equality, the Third World and Economic Delusion* (London: Methuen, 1981), 8.

[141] Bauer, "Hostility," 174.

[142] Peter Bauer, "Creating the Third World: Foreign Aid and Its Offspring," *Journal of Economic Growth* 2, no. 4 (1987).

[143] Bauer, "'L'aide au développement," 186.

o timely, and so successful, this was because its adversary, *tiers mondisme*, was "already a dead body."[144] LSF was founded not in a context of insurgent anti-colonialism but against the background of the Reagan doctrine, which saw the United States provide overt and covert assistance to anti-communist guerrilla movements throughout the Third World. The Reagan administration broke with the foreign policy priorities of the Carter administration, which Jeanne Kirkpatrick had infamously criticized for failing to make critical political distinctions between "moderate autocrats friendly to American interests" and "less friendly autocrats of extremist persuasion."[145] Reagan embraced Kirkpatrick's argument that left-wing "totalitarian" regimes were a greater danger than right-wing authoritarian ones, which are generally less internally repressive, less hostile to US interests and more susceptible to democratic change. Writing in 1979 against the backdrop of the overthrow of the US-backed dictators in Iran and Nicaragua, Kirkpatrick argued that there is no evidence that "radical totalitarian regimes" would transform themselves. There is a far greater chance of liberalization in right-wing dictatorships such as Brazil, Argentina, and Chile, she argued, than in a left-wing regime like Cuba. Kirkpatrick condemned the "posture of continuous self-abasement and apology *vis-à-vis* the Third World," which she argued was neither morally necessary nor politically appropriate.[146]

Five years later, many of these arguments were taken up by the participants at the LSF colloquium. It was the reformed Maoist Jacques Broyelle who put the case most forcefully: following the contours of Kirkpatrick's argument, he told the colloquium that while no communist country had ever moved toward democracy, a large number of right-wing dictatorships had made this move.[147] Malhuret reflected much later that Kirkpatrick had been an important influence on his own understanding of human rights. The position that "Aron spent books to explain, that economic and social advances and progress are very well but they are not rights," Malhuret recalled, Kirkpatrick explained best – and most concisely.[148] The links between the Reagan administration and the LSF figures were not only intellectual but also institutional and political. Throughout the early 1980s, Malhuret made several trips to the United States, invited by Republican Senator Gordon J. Humphrey – a key supporter of the Reagan doctrine, and a promoter of the CIA's

144 Whyte, interview with Rony Brauman.
145 Jeane Kirkpatrick, *Dictatorships & Double Standards*, Commentary, November 1, 1979.
146 Ibid.
147 Jacques Broyelle, "Commentaire," in *Le tiers-mondisme en question*, Brauman, ed., 76. Broyelle was responding to a paper by Chaliand.
148 Whyte, interview with Claude Malhuret.

"Operation Cyclone" which armed the Afghan mujahideen in its struggle against the Soviet occupation.[149] In the early 1980s, MSF received several rounds of funding from the National Endowment for Democracy, a democracy-promotion initiative launched by the Reagan administration to project US power ideologically and combat communism. With the establishment of LSF, MSF's Fabrice Weissman argued recently, the "NED got what they paid for."[150]

We should be wary, however, of construing the relationship between LSF and the Reagan administration simply by attempting to discern "who paid the piper?"[151] The relation between the LSF figures and the Reagan administration is better viewed in terms of ideological commonality than as a one-way influence. Looking back, Malhuret suggested that there were important differences between the LSF figures and those in the Reagan administration (who were further to the right), and between them and Bauer (who Malhuret found "extremely important" but too conservative). Nonetheless, he suggested that all of them were part of a (Gramscian) cultural bloc that produced a shift away from communism and Third Worldism in the direction of liberalism.[152] Rather than a one-way process of transmission from the US right to the French humanitarians, the lines of influence went in both directions: the experience of the French doctors, and their seemingly impartial credentials, made them important sources of information for defenders of the Reagan doctrine. A year before the founding of LSF, in 1983, *Foreign Affairs* published Malhuret's "Report from Afghanistan" which ended with a stirring warning that the "Afghan resistance" is likely to be defeated unless there is a profound change in "the reactions of Westerners to Soviet totalitarianism."[153] In his book on the politics of intervention in Afghanistan, Nunan attributes Congress's decision to pass $60 million in humanitarian aid to that country in part to the efforts of the French doctors. "French information had opened the gates for American cash to flood the frontier," he writes.[154] Rather than

---

[149] Weissman, "Silence Heals," 181.   [150] Ibid.

[151] The quote is taken from the title of Frances Stonor Saunders's book, *Who Paid the Piper? The CIA and the Cultural Cold War* (London: Granta, 2000).

[152] Whyte, interview with Claude Malhuret.

[153] Claude Malhuret, "Report from Afghanistan," *Foreign Affairs*, n.d., Winter 1983/4 edition, www.foreignaffairs.com/articles/afghanistan/1983-12-01/report-afghanistan

[154] Nunan, *Humanitarian Invasion*, 224. Nor was the Reagan administration always to the right of the LSF figures. During his period on the LSF board, Jacques Broyelle, the former Maoist turned vehement critic of Third Worldism, was a signatory to a petition urging the Reagan administration to provide more aid to the right-wing Nicaraguan contras in their civil war against the left-wing Sandinista guerrillas. The petition, which was also signed by Bernard Henri Lévy, was published in *Le Monde* on March 21, 1985. See Ross, *Afterlives of May 1968*, 169.

Malhuret simply borrowing Washington's agenda, his account of Afghanistan and his visits to the United States – where he met with Vice President George H. W. Bush among others – helped to bolster American support for the Afghan mujahideen, and for the broader campaign against Third Worldism.

Conclusion

Several notes of caution were sounded by presenters at the LSF colloquium: Chaliand, whose own transition from Third Worldist to critic of Third World regimes had been less sensational than that of certain other participants, concluded his paper by warning against moving from "adulation of Stalin or Mao to approval of the 'hawks' of the Republican Party in the United States."[155] Moreover, he noted that for all the current concerns about human rights in Nicaragua under the Sandinistas, the human rights record of the Somoza dictatorship over the previous three decades was of little interest in the West.[156] The strongest criticisms were voiced by Castoriadis, a former Trotskyist and member of the libertarian group Socialisme ou Barbarie who had not needed Solzhenitsyn's "revelations" to open his eyes to Stalinism. Castoriadis shared the majority view at the colloquium that Third Worldism and "Fanonism" were "supremely ridiculous operations," yet he nonetheless advocated a critical focus on liberalism, given the "swing of the pendulum" that had recently seen it upheld as the sole possible political model.[157] He also sought to challenge the exclusive focus on left-wing "totalitarian" regimes, rather than right-wing authoritarian ones, and reminded his audience that "a good number of South American torturers have been 'educated' by the CIA in installations of the 'greatest democracy on earth.'"[158] Preoccupied with "the ravages of planning," LSF did little to heed Castoriadis's warning, and instead focused on attacking Third Worldism and its demands for economic redistribution.

At the colloquium, Castoriadis challenged what he depicted as the attempt to give a moral gloss to more political aims, suggesting that attempts to solve the problems of the Third World from the outside are "at best, utopian, at worst, an unconscious and involuntary cover for real

---

[155] Gérard Chaliand, "La Fin Des Mythes Révolutionnaires," in *Le tiers-mondisme en question*, Brauman, ed., 70.

[156] Chaliand, "La fin des myths révolutionnaires," 69.

[157] Cornelius Castoriadis, "Third World, Third Worldism, Democracy," in *The Rising Tide of Insignificancy* (n.p., 1959), www.costis.org/x/castoriadis/castoriadis-rising_tide .pdf, 50.

[158] Ibid., 56.

policies unrelated to the interests of the Third World."[159] Ultimately, LSF's campaign against Third Worldism and its demands for economic redistribution served the interests of the major powers and the neoliberals, who were united in their opposition to Third World demands. The actions of the humanitarians helped to sensitize populations in the West to the violence perpetuated by certain postcolonial states. But in casting such violence as the necessary correlate of any deviation from a liberal economic model, they also served to sanctify a neoliberal order that has since resulted in spiraling inequality and indebtedness. The denigration of postcolonial welfarism and demands for economic redistribution also empowered the international financial institutions, whose structural adjustment programs and debt conditionalities led to the abolition of subsidies and price controls and the privatization of public services, depriving postcolonial states of the limited capacities they once had provided for the welfare of their populations. In their war on Third Worldism and their challenge to structuralist accounts of global inequality, the humanitarians of LSF became active participants in the popularization of neoliberal ideas, and they lent their moral prestige to combating the dream of an equitable global order capable of ensuring the basic welfare of the people of the Global South. Rather than a phobia of the state, the neoliberal period has seen a redefinition of state power, which abandons the ("totalitarian") attempt to compensate for the inequalities of the market order and focuses instead on its "core" role of upholding the market order by suppressing popular demands. In the hands of the French humanitarians, the neoliberal themes of the 1930s and 1940s were given a broad public appeal, while postcolonial aspirations toward global redistribution were recast as totalitarian.

[159] Ibid.

Index

CPSIA information can be obtained
at www.ICGtesting.com
Printed in the USA
LVHW082003090820
662760LV00005B/84